Todd Webb in Africa

Outside the Frame

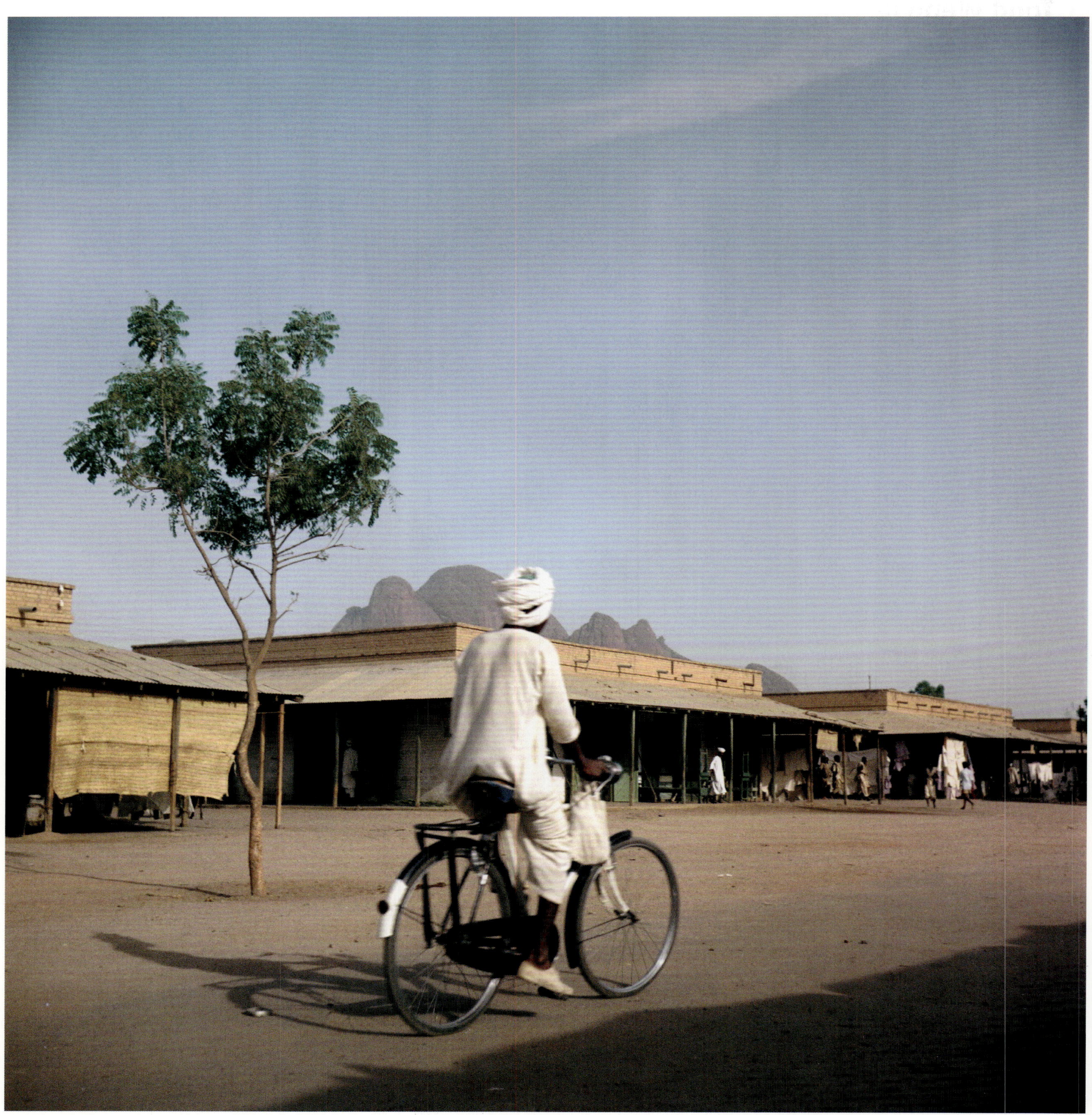

Todd Webb in Africa

Outside the Frame

Aimée Bessire and Erin Hyde Nolan

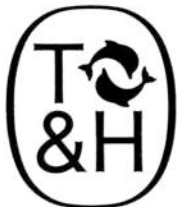

Table of Contents

Introduction

Aimée Bessire and Erin Hyde Nolan

Revealing a deep tension between comfort and discomfort, certainty and uncertainty, Todd Webb's image of a Texaco station does not fully represent the human interactions that went into its making, or the power dynamics present when the photographer focused his lens and clicked the camera shutter (see opposite). Smiling in his fresh uniform, the man in the foreground seems to exude all of the joy and optimism of the 1950s. He stands ready to fill a tank, clean a windshield, and send the customer on their journey, or so the image leads us to believe. The symmetrical arrangement of the red and white oil cans implies order, a sparkling advertisement for the corporate brand. Perhaps it's his readily returned gaze or the way he wears his uniform and green hat and holds the pump, but more than anything, the attendant appears to make the customer feel welcome in this Texaco station. Todd Webb's photograph raises deep questions about agency and power, positionality and privilege, travel and tourism, and the ways modernization is documented in the context of the African continent. The composition of the bright filling station demonstrates order and control. In Webb's framing, the rhythms of red, white, and green, and the repeated Texaco star act as emblems of progress; they suggest industriousness and the precise lines that are the hallmarks of capitalism and free enterprise. The palm trees behind the station recall the landscape of the American South, where African Americans were actively engaged in a struggle for equality in this same era, but the French words on the pump—"Prix à payer" and "Volume délivré"—reveal a different cultural context. Taken in Togoland (Togo), this image expresses both the shiny capitalism of the 1950s and the inequities of the colonial era, themes seen throughout Webb's 1958 photographs of African nations.

Todd Webb, then an established American photographer, was commissioned by the United Nations Office of Public Information to document industry and technology in what were then eight different African nations: Ghana, Kenya, the Federation of Rhodesia and Nyasaland (now Malawi, Zambia, and Zimbabwe—Webb visited the territories Northern Rhodesia, now Zambia, and Southern Rhodesia, now Zimbabwe), The Trust Territory of Somaliland Under Italian Administration (now Somalia), Sudan (now Republic of Sudan), Tanganyika and Zanzibar (now merged as Tanzania), and Togoland (now Togo).[1] Webb's photographs, like this one of the Texaco station, demonstrate processes of modernization as well as social, governmental, and industrial transformation in these disparate nations during the late 1950s. This time of global economic and technological advancement also, and not by chance, coincided with an era of colonial domination and trauma. We are reminded here, as in Webb's other photographs, of the vantage point of outsiders looking in. Webb's identities as an educated, white, American male afforded him a privilege that often distinguished him from his subjects in terms of race, socioeconomic concerns, and geographic mobility.

The image of the Texaco station illuminates the ways in which photographs can be multi-authored objects[2]—rich documents that may include the perspective of the photographer, while also embedding signs of the sometimes unequal relationship between photographer and subject, the editorial voice of the commissioning agent, and the positionality of the viewer. Understanding these photographs requires a methodological shift away from a biographical model that would privilege the artist as an autonomous maker in favor of one that seeks to encompass the image's multi-dimensionality and overlapping subjectivities, even ones where agency is implicitly denied. This includes a re-examination of the mechanics of patronage around the images Webb produced during his time on the continent. Made for the United Nations, the image of the Texaco worker is in fact inherently multi-authored. It contains clues about the intricate engineering of these photographs and their commission by the United Nations Office of Public Information. We will never know whether the Texaco attendant is posing or has been posed. If posing, he is an actor in this exchange; if posed, he is perhaps an unwilling participant. What makes this photograph multi-dimensional is the potential for hidden signs of resistance, participation, or co-creation. We know that Webb loaded the film, chose the setting, upturned his lens in what we might interpret as an admiring angle, and clicked the shutter. While we cannot know what the Togolese man intended in this depiction, the visual evidence here suggests that he performed for Webb's camera. His square shoulders and stance mirror the resolute verticality of the pump to his left and building behind him—all three of these working together, parts of a well-oiled machine.

Webb left New York City for Lomé, Togoland on April 11, by way of London. Outfitted with three cameras and charged with imaging industrial progress, he amassed approximately two thousand photographs over five months. Webb's 35mm Kodacolor and Agfa negatives from this trip present early color images of eight countries at the interstices of colonialism and independence. As the first large-scale example of color photographs in Webb's oeuvre, these images stand out from his well-known street photography of New York and Paris. In his representation of a transitional period in twentieth-century African history, Webb brought a curious mind and eager eye to this project. This process was inevitably complicated by the nature of his privilege, as an American photographer working for an international organization and "seeing Africa" (as he describes in his journal) for the first time.[3]

Webb documented mining, elections, thriving seaports, power stations, and other industrial scenes according to his assignment. His urban landscapes of Africa share a resonant aesthetic with his New York and Paris street scenes, with buildings often filling out the image frame, and clean lines of parked cars as in an image taken in Northern Rhodesia (see p. 16). Webb's photographs of the first full-suffrage election in Togoland (Togo) show the political energy, even joy expressed by some on voting day (see pp. 24–27). These are not the typical, romanticized ethnographic visuals of Africa seen in publications at the time, but express a different texture of political and social life.[4] There is also a broader interest in place, as with Webb's photographs of wall murals in Tanganyika (Tanzania) and his focus on signage, which situates many images—such as one of the photographer in Dar es Salaam, showing distances from major world cities (see p. 8). More contemplative images are also present within this photographic record. Seemingly personal images of daily life are among the most striking in the series: the fisherman standing and poling his green boat in the harbor, a soapy toddler with its mother and siblings in the midst of an outdoor bath, and the young mother with a baby on her back smiling at the viewer. Such photographs demonstrate Webb's multiple objectives in imaging the African countries: his mandate was to photograph for the UN, but as with other commissioned trips, such as his work for Standard Oil in the 1940s, he also shot images for himself, of compositions or subjects he found visually or intellectually interesting.

Despite the large number of photographs taken during Webb's trip, only twenty-two of the images were published by the United Nations Office of Public Information, in a seven-page brochure "United Nations Photos, Supplement No. 7" produced to tell the story of the "changing face of Africa" (see Appendix, pp. 244–45). The remainder of the negatives left the artist's collection in the 1970s and were only reunited with the Todd Webb Archive as part of a larger purchase in 2017 (see Betsy Evans Hunt, "Lost and Found," p. 17 for the full history).[5] The newly recovered steamer trunk

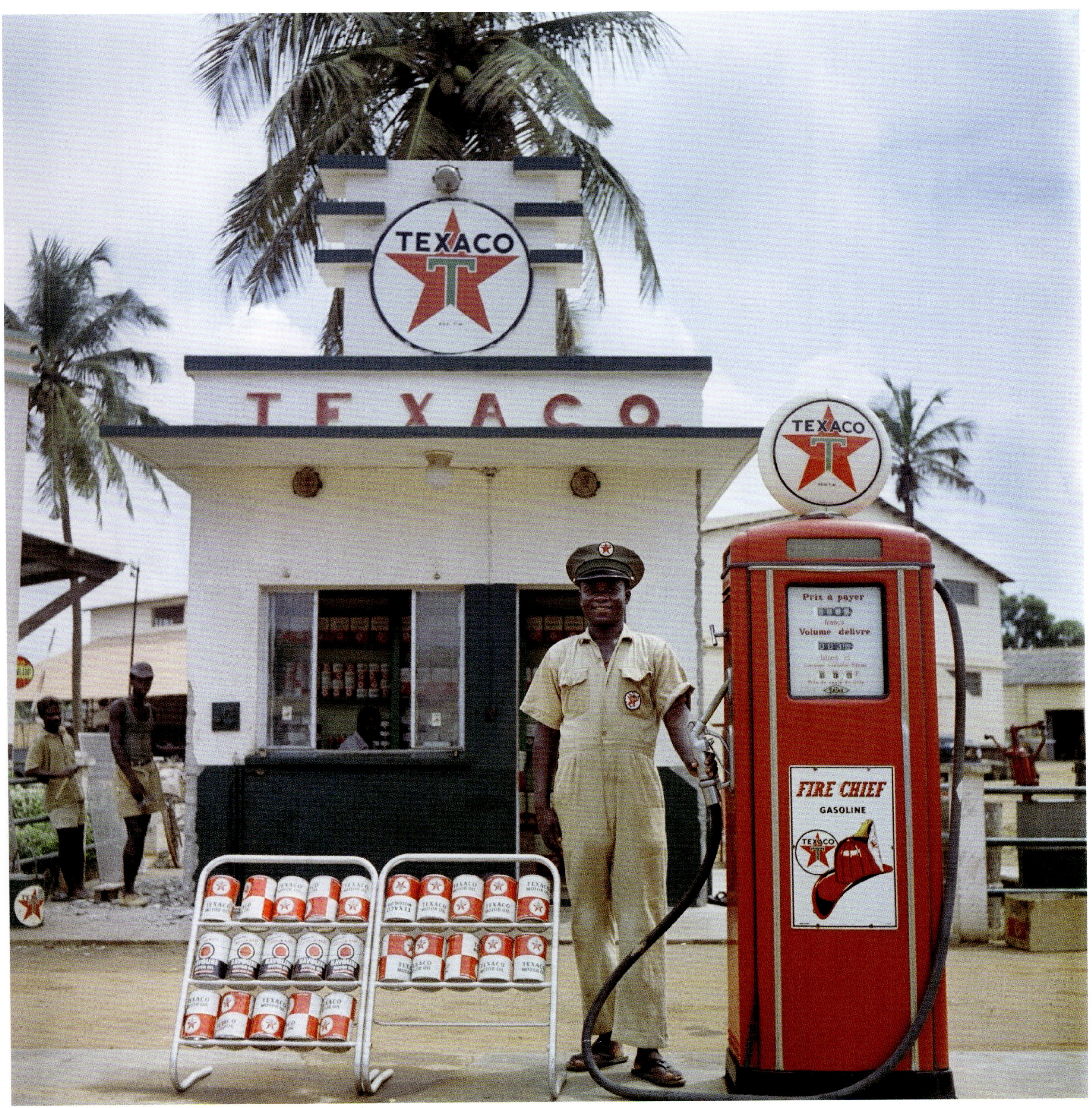

Todd Webb, *Untitled* (44UN-8002-165), Togoland (Togo), 1958
Attendant at Texaco station.

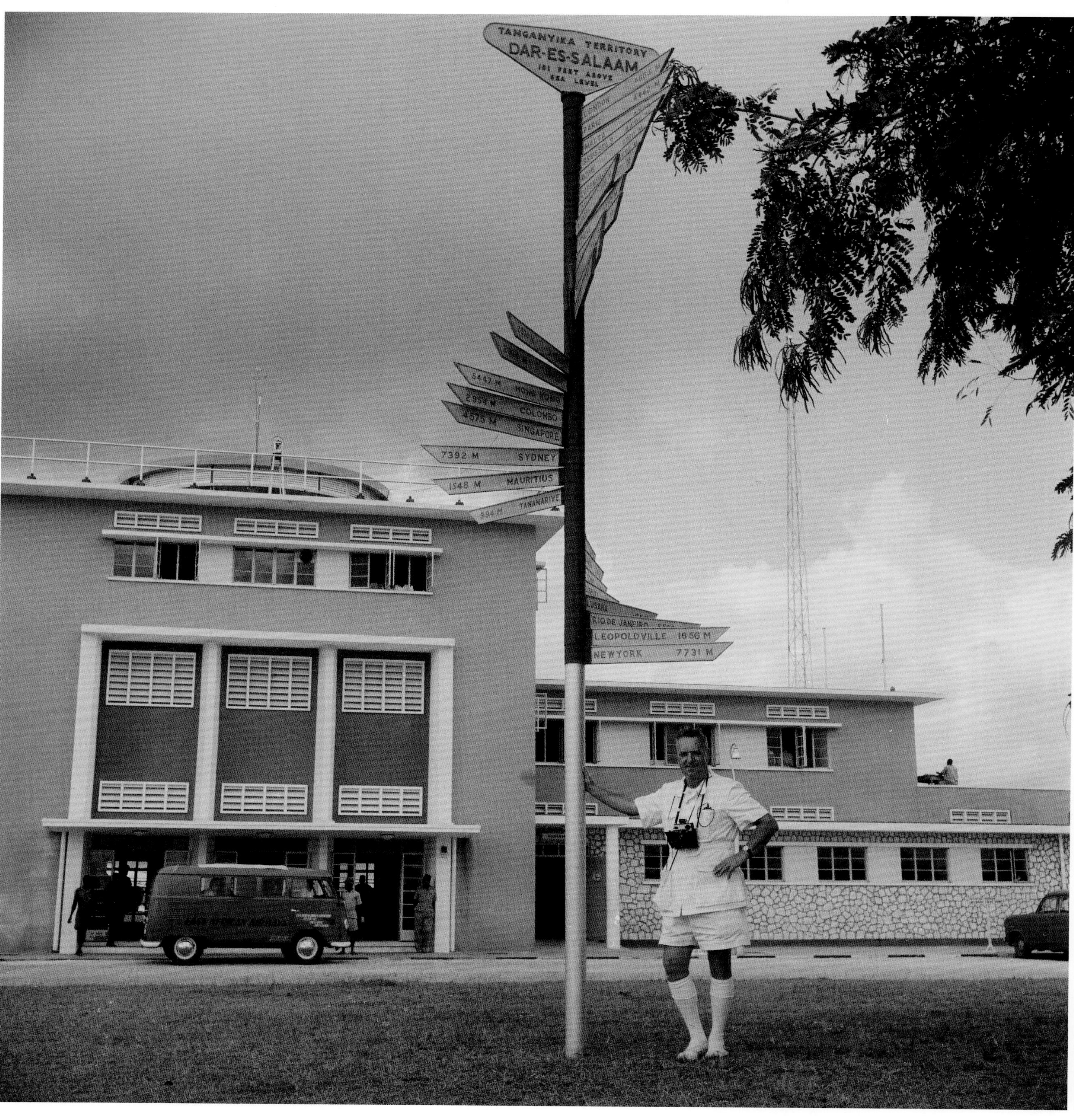
TANGANYIKA TERRITORY
DAR-ES-SALAAM
181 FEET ABOVE SEA LEVEL
LONDON
PARIS
MALTA
BRUSSELS
ROME
5447 M HONG KONG
2954 M COLOMBO
4575 M SINGAPORE
7392 M SYDNEY
1548 M MAURITIUS
994 M TANANARIVE
LUSAKA
RIO DE JANEIRO
LEOPOLDVILLE 1656 M
NEWYORK 7731 M

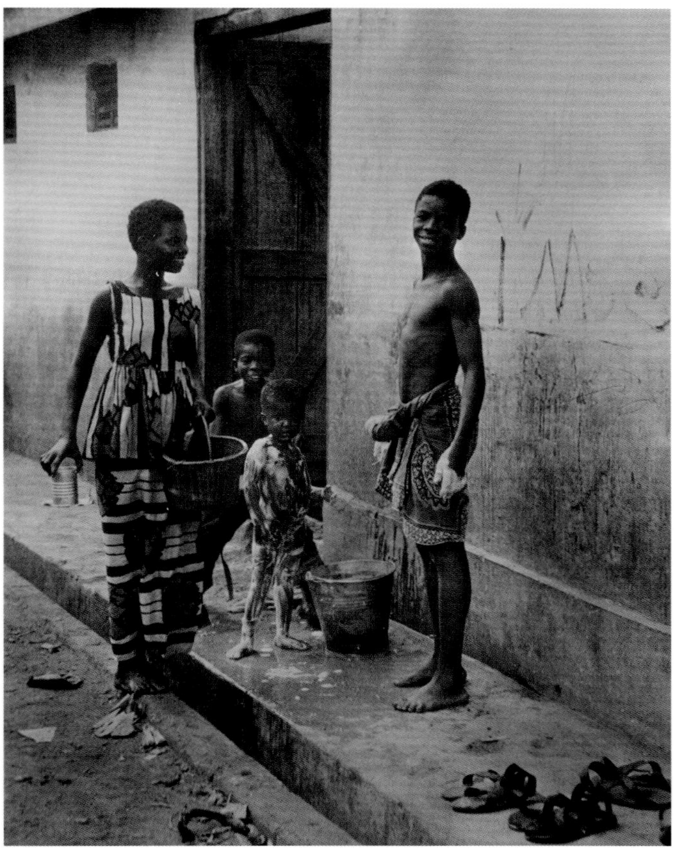

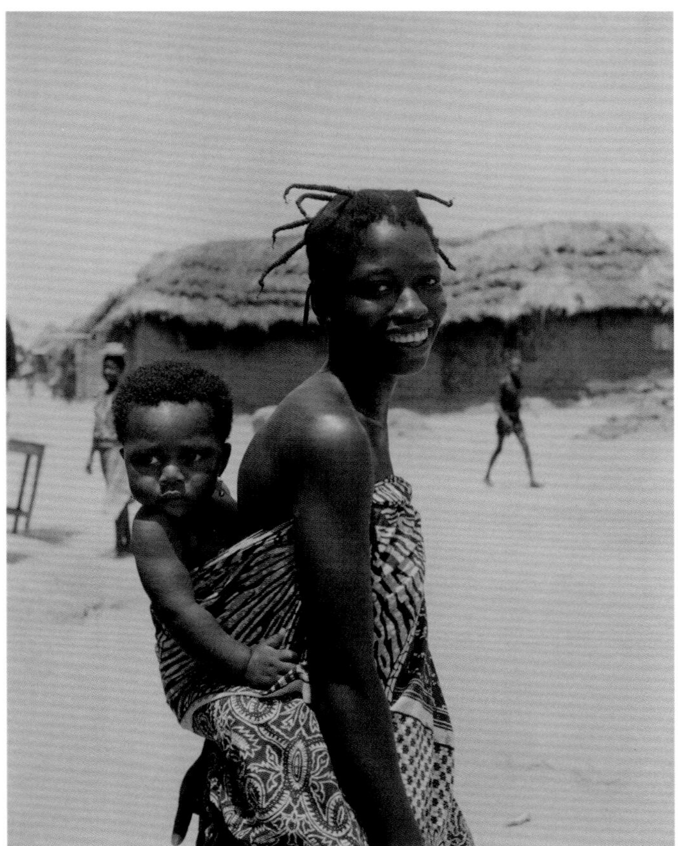

Opposite: Todd Webb, *Untitled* (44UN-T2-R1-685), Tanganyika (Tanzania), 1958
Todd Webb standing outside the Dar es Salaam airport.

Top: Todd Webb, *Untitled* (44UN-58-061), Ghana, 1958
A toddler's outdoor bath.

Above: Todd Webb, *Untitled* (44UN-58-073), Togoland (Togo), 1958
Woman with baby on her back.

contained over 170 rolls of film, black and white vintage prints, Webb's Africa journal, and souvenir ephemera such as hotel receipts and train tickets from the travels. All of this material provides a unique lens to a historic moment in the countries Webb was commissioned to visit.

Todd Webb in Africa: Outside the Frame investigates the motivations and complicated historical narratives embedded within Webb's photographs, mining a complex body of work with an intersectional mindset. Throughout the book, the authors acknowledge Webb's practices as ones that were informed by American understandings of African nations, cultures, and histories—all during a pivotal moment in race relations and civil rights in the United States. Most importantly, the essays gathered within this book acknowledge the challenges of interpreting Webb's photographic series within their colonial context and from today's temporal distance. By questioning the hegemonic role the camera plays in perpetuating different kinds of power relationships and dynamics of inequality, the scholars and artists in this book offer critical insight into visualizations of imperialism, industry, race relations, and national independence.

Todd Webb Before 1958

Photography, for Todd Webb, came later in life. After working as a stockbroker, forest ranger, and gold prospector, he was employed by the Chrysler Company in Detroit, where he joined the camera club. It was there that Webb, alongside his friend Harry Callahan, learned to make photographs under the guidance of Ansel Adams. This newfound passion did not wane during his service in the US Navy during the Second World War, and upon his return to the United States in 1945, he moved to New York to fully devote himself to making photographs.

While living with Harry and Eleanor Callahan, Webb became immersed in the social networks of the New York art world. He lunched with Beaumont Newhall at the Museum of Modern Art, visited Alfred Stieglitz at An American Place, and was introduced to the work of Eugène Atget at Berenice Abbott's studio. All the while, he walked the streets, cameras in hand (or over his shoulder), fully embedded in the topography of the urban landscape. In a journal entry from 1946, Webb described his experience of photographing on the street as a way to fully immerse himself in the fabric of the city: "I photographed around the Fulton Fish Market today—very warm and the air very moist. It was nice down there—lots there, but I can't seem to get it. I am going to borrow Helen's [Levitt] 35mm and try that."[6]

The 1950s were a formative time for Todd Webb. In 1955, he was awarded a Guggenheim Foundation Fellowship to photograph a walk across the country, the same year Robert Frank received one to drive from coast to coast. Armed with two Leicas, a Rolleiflex, and one forty-pound backpack, Webb retraced routes traveled by Euro-American colonizers west of the Mississippi in the nineteenth century. By foot, bike, boat, and Vespa, he photographed the territory stretching between New York City and San Francisco. In his application for the Guggenheim, he wrote: "I have found that my best photographs are made when I am traveling on foot. The slow speed at which one approaches new sights, the gradual changes in the aspect of the country, all contribute to a greater understanding and a deeper appreciation of what one sees."[7] Webb received a second grant to finish this project in 1956, but never completed a book with the images as originally proposed. His photographs from this trip chart a nostalgic American landscape, punctuated by the quotidian—small towns, old buildings, empty bars, and open roads. Webb's journal entries, letters, and unprinted negatives reveal a vision that is quite literally local, experienced beyond the confines of the car by photographer and viewer alike. While the images from the 1958 UN commission do not express locality in the same manner, they do illustrate Webb's connection to place, demonstrating that he truly made his best images when his feet were planted firmly on the ground. It is perhaps through his own physical engagement, even more than his

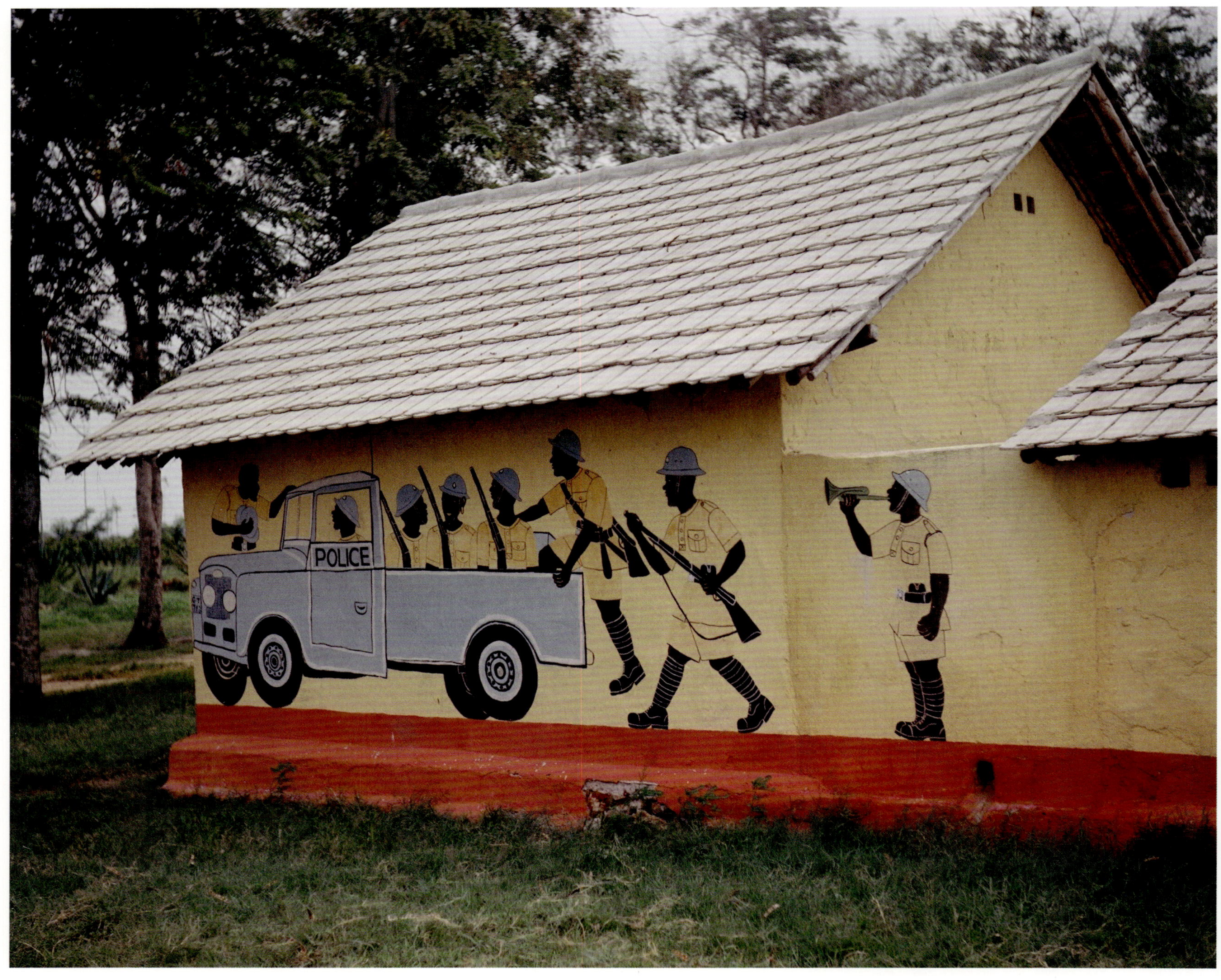

Todd Webb, *Untitled* (44UN-7803-001), Tanganyika (Tanzania), 1958
Mural of police getting in truck, Kingoni village.

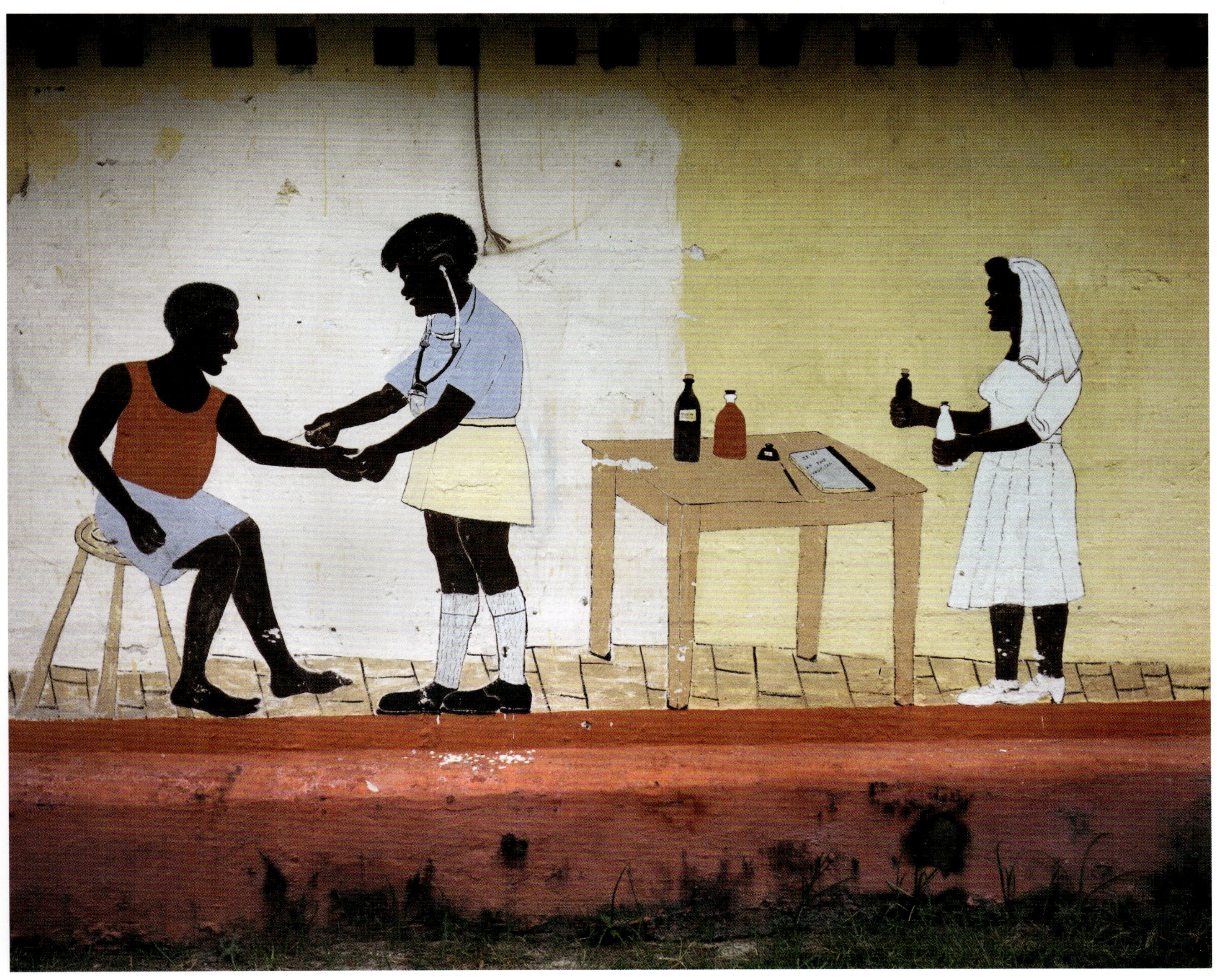

Todd Webb, *Untitled* (44UN-7803-002), Tanganyika (Tanzania), 1958
Mural of a visit to a local clinic, Kingoni village.

eye, that Webb interpreted the social, political, and cultural world around him, as he illustrated in the image looking through the car windshield at the Rhodesian road, presenting his own vantage-point (see p. 13).

John Rawson, whom Webb met while working for the Marshall Plan in Paris in the late 1940s, first connected him to the United Nations. Between September 30 and December 3, 1957, Webb photographed officials and meetings at the United Nations headquarters in New York. On January 28, 1958 he met with David Ritchie, the Chief of the Photographic and Exhibition Services at the UN, in advance of his commission to Mexico, where he was instructed to document "how the Mexican people look, work and amuse themselves."[8] It was on this same date that Webb was promised that he would "be asked to do some jobs for them overseas."[9] This was confirmed on March 11, when Ritchie asked if Webb would travel to Africa for five months. At the same time, Webb wrote in his journal that he was finishing "a small story...on some Fellows who are attending classes in the UN on Economics. They are all from African countries and one is from Somali[a], one of the countries I will visit."[10] One month later, he began his UN commission by photographing the election in Lomé, Togoland (Togo).

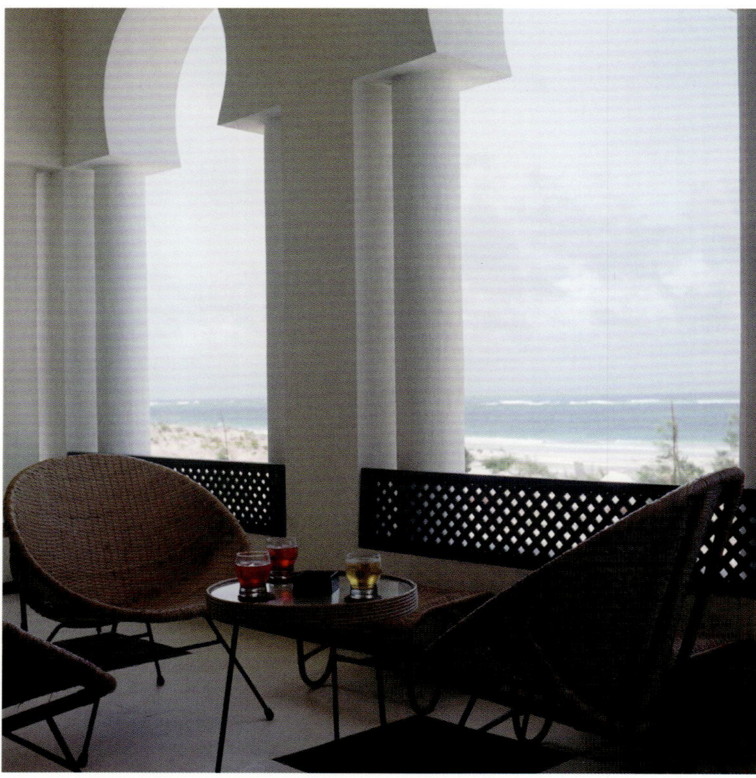

Todd Webb, *Untitled* (44UN-8006-005), Trust Territory of Somaliland (Somalia), 1958
View from hotel terrace.

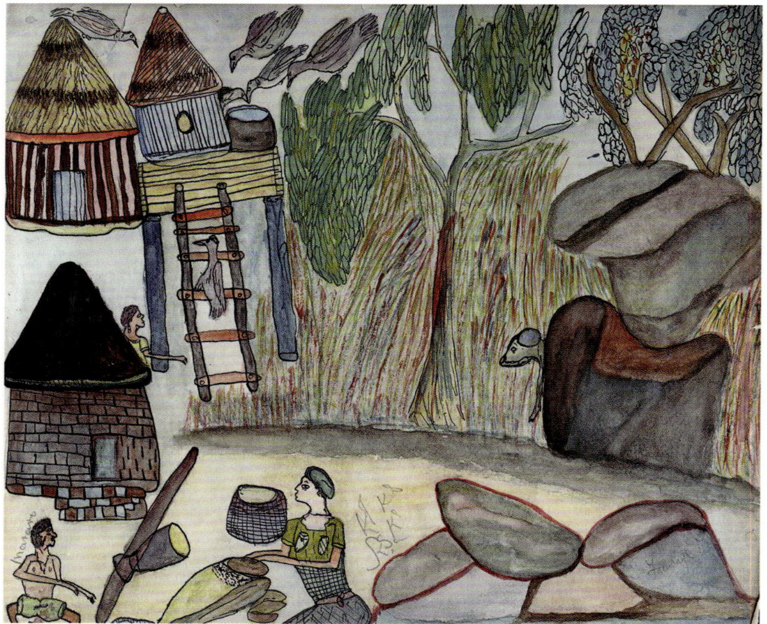

Artist unknown, drawing given to Todd Webb by a student at the Vocational School in Salisbury, Southern Rhodesia (Zimbabwe), 1958

Viewing Webb's Images Today

From a contemporary perspective, it is critical to consider the strengths, intentions, and inevitable biases that Webb brought to his photographs of these African countries. He produced images of factories, agricultural and mining landscapes, and evidence of a burgeoning urbanization. At the same time, he sought to create documents of rural life, agrarian economies, and skills that might be translated into twentieth-century commercial systems. When this photographic record is considered as a whole, what information does it provide about industry and technology in 1958? How do we interpret these images today, with a larger understanding of the history of colonialism and the depth of power imbalances that still exist on the African continent and beyond? Is it possible to reconcile the distinctions between the UN mandate to document industrial progress, the many histories of colonial violence, and Webb's more personal images—the ones he may have taken because of his own visual, intellectual, or social interest?

We view Webb's photographs with an understanding of the overt and lasting trauma of colonialism. Webb was an outsider to all of the cultures he photographed on the continent, including British and French colonial culture. As a white American male traveling through each country, his cultural mindset created complex relational perceptions of the people he met and places he visited, which were foundational to his experience on the continent. We see the results of his interactions with new situations, spaces, and individuals in the photographs, and we also see Webb bringing some of the same visual sensitivity to his images of city buildings and street scenes that he brought to the New York and Paris photographs for which he is well known.

An Outsider "Seeing Africa" for the First Time

Webb arrived in Togoland with a clear idea of what he thought Africa would be like. In his journals and letters to his wife Lucille, he wrote about his preconceived notions with such openness that it is almost disarming. He found Togoland and Tanganyika the "most African" of the countries he visited, and reading his letters, one can almost feel his disappointment and judgment when he describes parts of Rhodesia as "sort of like Omaha or some other midwestern town."[11]

Traveling to the African continent from the geographic North was an adventurous trip in 1958. In his journal Webb expressed his excitement about the five-month journey. His Airworks flight from London to Accra made many stops to refuel, first in Lisbon, then overnight in Las Palmas, the Canary Islands.[12] The next day they flew over Cape Verde and Dakar, where Webb had his first glimpse of West Africa, and refueled again in

Bathurst (present-day Banjul, The Gambia) before stopping in Freetown, Sierra Leone and ending the journey in Accra, Ghana. Romanticizing the moment before landing on the continent for the first time, Webb wrote in his journal "At last! The sight of land," and "Seeing Africa. It is hard to believe."[13]

While Webb's journal and letters chronicle a mythologized Africa, some of the photographs contradict this romantic notion of the continent. Like the image of a man mowing grass behind a chain-link enclosure at a shiny power station (see p. 198), many present the more industrial side of African life that the UN wanted Webb to capture. In this image, the metal fencing between Webb and the man creates a literal barrier between photographer and subject, and as viewers, we are positioned as voyeurs to this moment at the electrical transfer station. The progress Webb documented in such photographs demonstrates the varieties of life on the continent that were not frequently seen in publications outside of Africa. He had hoped one day to publish this material in a full-color book, but never found an interested publisher. This was due in part to the racialized assumptions of the publishing industry, which he deplored in his journal in 1960: "The Africa book is off as a picture book–too expensive and limited by its interest in economics. I think they are wrong–I have an idea that they want a picture book full of Watusi, Pigmys [sic], Ma[a]sai, lions and women with exposed breasts."[14] He was aware that his images of innovation and technology did not match the visual expectations of a publishing industry still enthralled by racially primitivizing visual paradigms and therefore preferential toward projects that objectified African nations and cultures. While the broader American public included diverse people of color, evidenced by the popularity of magazines such as *Jet* and *Ebony*, Webb marketed his project within predominantly white networks, which ultimately rejected his approach.

Webb kept two detailed diaries of his trip that enrich the understanding of his connections to the people and places he visited. He expressed another, perhaps more personal, perspective in the letters that he and his wife Lucille exchanged over his five-month journey, and also saved souvenirs of the places he visited that provide further insight into his day-to-day interactions on the continent. With everything from hotel menus to drawings by children at the Vocational School in Salisbury, Southern Rhodesia, where Webb gave a lecture about the UN, these travel souvenirs provide a lens into his lived, relational experiences throughout and between countries (see opposite, bottom). Much like the complexity of the multi-authored photograph, there is a tension and intricate interweaving between Webb's writing, the respect with which he represents his time abroad, and his efforts to pursue the United Nations' mandate.

But Webb was also economically distanced from the people he sought to portray. His travel was fully funded, and he was paid to pursue his documentary work, which included rolls upon rolls of expensive color film. He stayed in mostly comfortable hotels (see opposite, top), swam in the warm Indian Ocean waters, ate good meals, and enjoyed all the socio-economic privilege of a white tourist in Africa. In spite of such comforts, or perhaps because of them, in one letter Webb laments to Lucille that he will only break even when he balances his travel expenses with the amount he will make from the UN commission.[15]

Nonetheless, Webb was cognizant of his racial privileges during his travels. He was particularly discomfited by the conditions in Northern Rhodesia (Zambia) and Southern Rhodesia (Zimbabwe), where he witnessed the effects of systemic racism first-hand. Racial segregation shaped his experience in these territories, as he stated in a letter to Lucille: "the race thing spoils everything for me. And still it is ten times better here than in S[outh] A[frica]."[16] In many ways, his viewpoint is informed by his own understanding of race relations in the context of the Civil Rights Movement, his trips in the American South in the late 1940s, and his walk across the country in the 1950s, when he described his disgust at the racial inequalities he witnessed.[17]

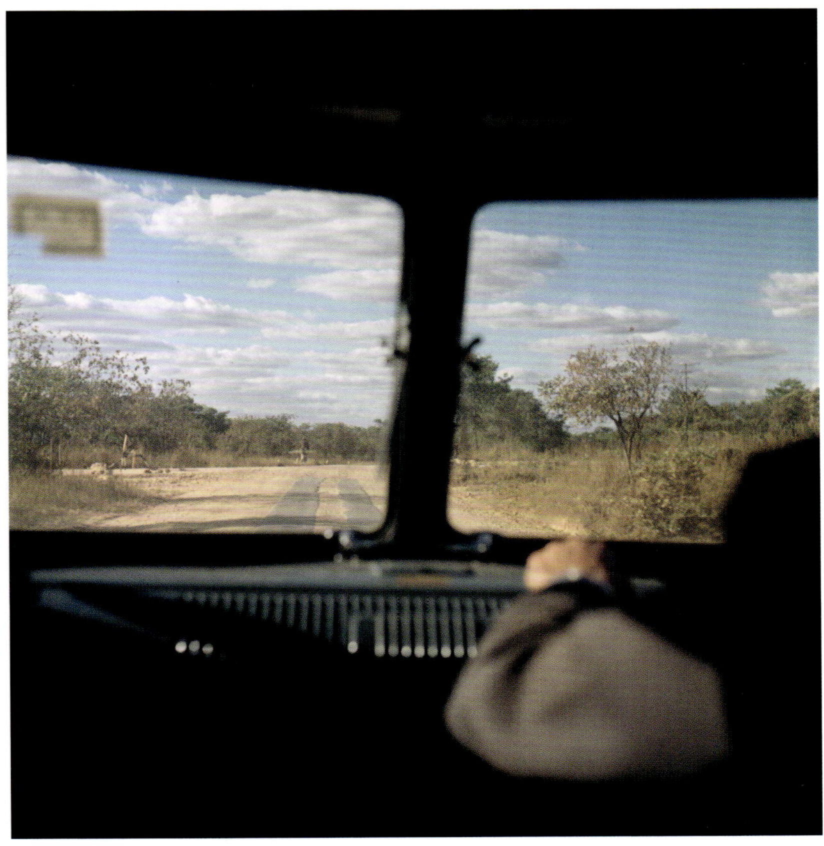

Todd Webb, *Untitled* (44UN-7994-514), Northern or Southern Rhodesia (Zambia or Zimbabwe) [exact location unknown], 1958
View through the windscreen of a moving car.

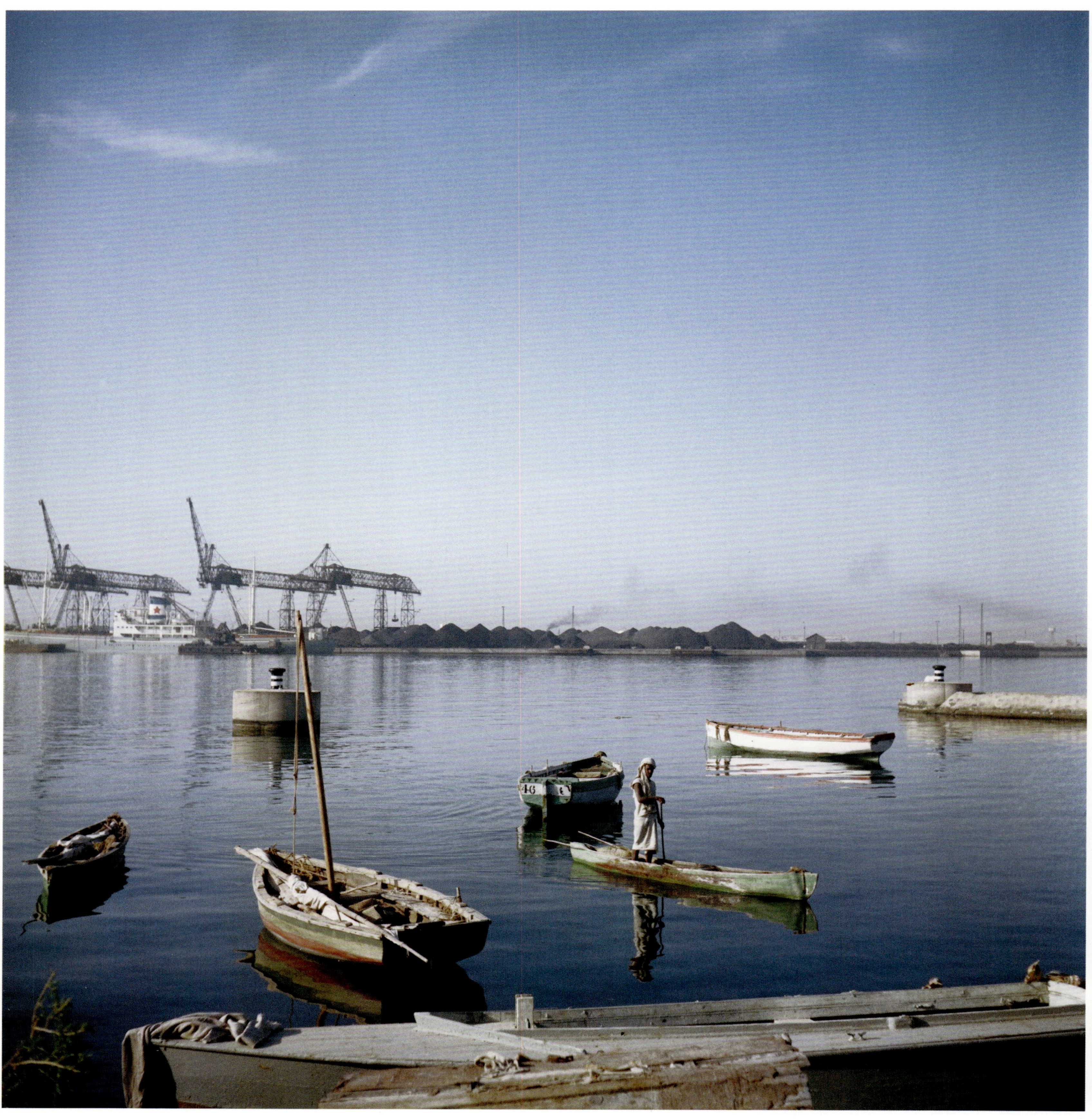

Todd Webb, *Untitled* (44UN-7961-222), Sudan, 1958
Man poling a boat through the harbor, with oil rigs in the background.

Color Photography in 1958

Webb photographed several rolls of color film in 1955, and when the UN's David Ritchie gave him 25 rolls of Kodacolor to work with in Mexico, it presented the perfect opportunity to experiment with color film, which he would later use for the majority of the 1958 commission. Webb worked simultaneously in color and black and white during his time in Africa, often carrying multiple cameras with him while he photographed. At the time, the more expensive color film was not widely used by photographers, except in advertising images and journals like *National Geographic* and *LIFE* magazine. Webb's friend Gordon Parks chose color film to document race relations in Alabama in a 1956 photo essay for *LIFE*, "The Restraints: Open and Hidden."[18] As a friend, Webb would undoubtedly have seen Parks' photographs, and perhaps realized the greater potential of this medium for his United Nations project. Most likely he received the color film from the UN as part of the African commission. Webb's images present the vibrancy of life on the continent at a time when most photographers were still using the more widely available and less expensive black and white film.

Todd Webb in Africa: Outside the Frame

This book invites viewers to explore the many layers of meaning in the images made during Webb's time on the African continent. Previously unseen, the photographs present a view of the countries Webb saw in 1958, where, as he suggested, "the old and new can still be seen."[19] They express the lushness of daily life enlivened through color film, the novel beauty he saw as a traveler, and the distinct cultural lens he brought to his journey, as well as the expression of individual people amidst the charged politics of the times. Webb's vision provides one perspective, while this book aims to critically engage with and contextualize the photographs through their rich history as multi-authored documents, and within the larger history of photography in Africa.

Todd Webb in Africa presents essays highlighting Webb's work in the context of the history of photography and colonialism, and includes interpretations of specific images from decolonizing, contemporary perspectives by scholars, artists, and writers from Germany, Ghana, Nigeria, Tanzania, Somalia, the United States, and Zimbabwe. The first few essays in the book provide contextual background on Webb's oeuvre and photography on the African continent. In her essay "The Myth of Africa," Aimée Bessire presents the complexities of Webb's preconceived notions of the continent and the photographs that often contradict these mythologies. Providing rich historical grounding in colonial-era photography, Christraud M. Geary presents Webb's images against a contextual backdrop of indigenous African photographers in Togoland and Ghana. The Ghanaian photographer, James Barnor, further illuminates what it was like to be a photographer working in Accra in 1958, revealing the many different image-making practices that overlapped to shape his own photographic career. Bessire further explores Webb's images in the history of color photography and considers the ways the inherent biases of 1950s color film presents a culturally coded view of the continent. Webb often focused his lens on landscape, documenting the human and industrial impact on African soil. Erin Hyde Nolan observes how Webb's photographs make landscape and industry inseparable, emphasizing the spatial dimension of these images, and how formative they were in shaping notions of place for the UN commission. Ali Jimale Ahmed explores what is visible and also hidden from view in Webb's images from the Trust Territory of Somaliland (Somalia), discussing the people in the photographs, and, synecdochally, a nation in the throes of deep social and political transformation. Writing about his place of origin, the Federation of Rhodesia and Nyasaland, Gary van Wyk employs Webb's photographs as a prism to reflect on the history of colonial occupation and racial oppression in the country. For van Wyk, these are decisive political moments that mark his own life's migratory path. Casey Riley examines the advent of the Civil Rights Movement in the United States, and how this political ferment shaped Webb's vision of the African continent. Rehema Chachage considers the complex status of Webb as an American outsider in a land that is not his own through his photographs of Tanzania, narrating the untold stories of the people in his images. In a creative response, Emmanuel Iduma writes about the poetics of Webb's photography through the lens of travel, migration, and tourism, allowing the images to be portals for imaginative and fictional stories about the continent. With this collaborative and inclusive approach, *Todd Webb in Africa: Outside the Frame* brings together a diverse body of research on colonial images of Africa to consider present-day responses to Webb's body of work. These contributions from individuals with connections to the countries Webb photographed actively intervene in the colonial (and postcolonial) metanarratives about Africa and African progress put forth by the United Nations.

We will never know what the Texaco worker was really thinking when he smiled for Todd Webb's camera. We can question the agency he had in the making of this photograph. As a representation of modernizing Africa, the image may be interpreted as full of 1950s optimism and possibility. But, as Gary van Wyk suggests in his essay, much of this progress was based on the colonial imposition of extractive industries, something that from today's perspective we understand as destructive and deeply unsettling. More than simply contrasting Webb's famous black and white imagery with this newfound color work, the authors' textual interventions in this book articulate a more human meditation on the power of seeing and being seen. These creative, and in many cases definitively local reflections attune Webb's images to a different frequency, where they vibrate with a new sense of visual sovereignty.[20] In so doing, the voices of people who may have been silenced by the colonial-era images are animated. It is our hope that, collectively, the text and photographs in this book make some noise.

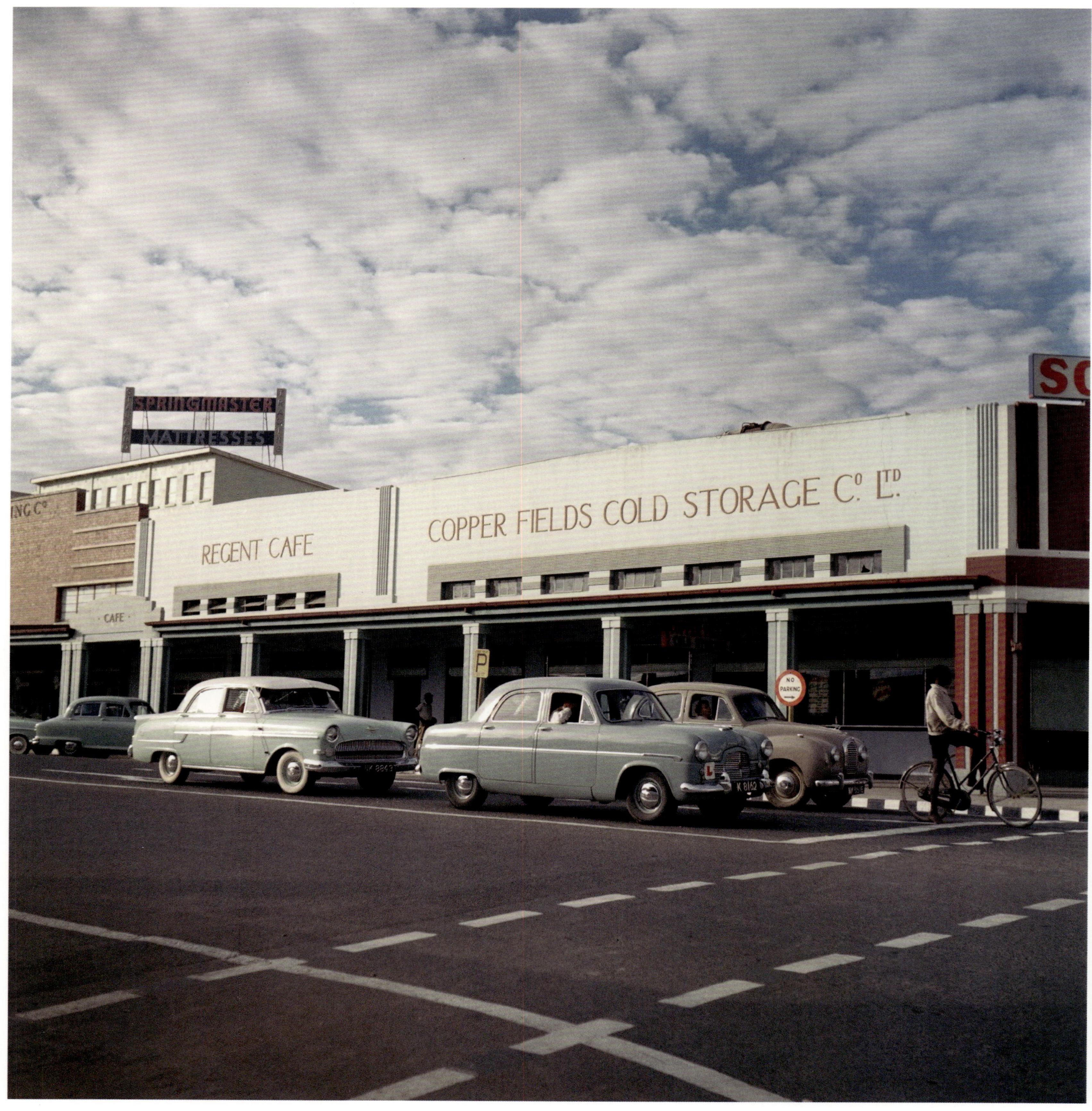

Todd Webb, *Untitled* (44UN-7982-127), Northern Rhodesia (Zambia), 1958
Street view of the Regent Café and Copper Fields Cold Storage Co., Ltd, Kitwe.

Lost and Found: Rediscovering Todd Webb's Photographs of Africa

Betsy Evans Hunt

On a single day, in a makeshift basement, Todd Webb's images of Africa were rescued. It's a stunning tale, a bit detective, a bit cat and mouse, and it has a happy ending. A short preamble is warranted.

Todd and Lucille Webb entered my gallery and my life in the fall of 1989. Fate, timing, and luck were all in play as we began a business relationship that quickly became more like family. As our friendship grew, I learned that Todd had had an unfortunate turn with an unscrupulous dealer in the 1970s, which had resulted in the loss of a large part of his archive. Todd never wanted to speak of it, and never wanted to "go after" the dealer; it was not in his nature. All I knew was that when he reluctantly mentioned it, he was truly bereft. At the time, I had no idea of the magnitude of his loss. I inherited Todd's reluctance, perhaps honoring his peaceful nature; but there came a time in 2015 when my curiosity was piqued by some online sales of Todd's photographs. I decided to do some sleuthing and tracked down a group of investors in Northern California who had purchased the collection from the original dealer. As it turned out, Todd had known these guys—I was able to dig up a file of correspondence between them. It was clear to me that they had also taken advantage of Todd's goodwill.

After figuring out how to approach the investors, I finally asked, "how much do you have?" The answer: "a lot." I never considered going after them legally, as Todd never did, and it wouldn't have rested well with him. But I did appeal to their better natures and asked that I might see their collection in order to be able to reunite the archive.

First stop: a Berkeley bungalow. Upstairs, through a home crowded with paraphernalia, to a bedroom with gorgeous photographs of Georgia O'Keeffe—an outstanding group. I thought that might be all, but then my host said, "there's more." Off we went to the Oakland Hills, where I met the next investor. We stood awkwardly in his living room for what seemed like forever, before I was led downstairs to the basement (thankfully a dry one), where I saw Todd's lost archive for the first time, locked in five old steamer trunks, unceremoniously scattered amongst the homeowner's other cast-off possessions.

As we opened the first trunk, I tried not to show my astonishment at the magnitude of what I might discover. My fingers were crossed that the contents were safe and sound, and miraculously, they were. I understood immediately why Todd had never really wanted to talk about this loss. Here before me was the sum of his life's work until 1976.

The investors left me on my own to sort through old photo boxes and manila envelopes with spectacular vintage prints; incredible early work that I had never seen. It was exhilarating and mind-numbing at the same time. I was beginning to be overwhelmed when I opened the third trunk—on top were several large manila envelopes labeled "Africa 1958." Todd rarely discussed this trip, from which only a handful of black and white images survived. Here was a cache of color, square-format negatives! I was thrilled but confounded. Todd had never spoken of photographing in color, and many of us assumed he only "saw" in black and white. It was dark, but I managed to get a sense of the beauty and scope of the work. Three trips and countless hours later we came to an agreement, and the trunks made their way to Maine.

My assistant Sam and I immediately started scanning the negatives. We spent about three days glued to our computers, somewhat delirious. We invited Aimée Bessire and Erin Hyde Nolan to take a look, as it became clear to all of us that we had uncovered special color photographs of a critical moment in African history. And the work was beautiful!

Todd would be honored to have such a talented group of voices contextualize and present his images of Africa. I am so happy that with fate, courage, and a bit of luck, it has come to pass.

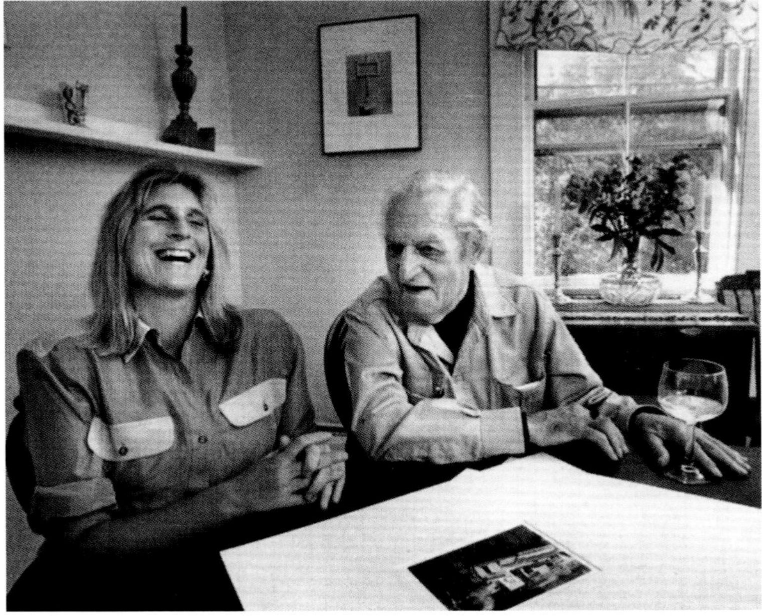

Betsy Evans Hunt with Todd Webb, Portland, Maine, 1991

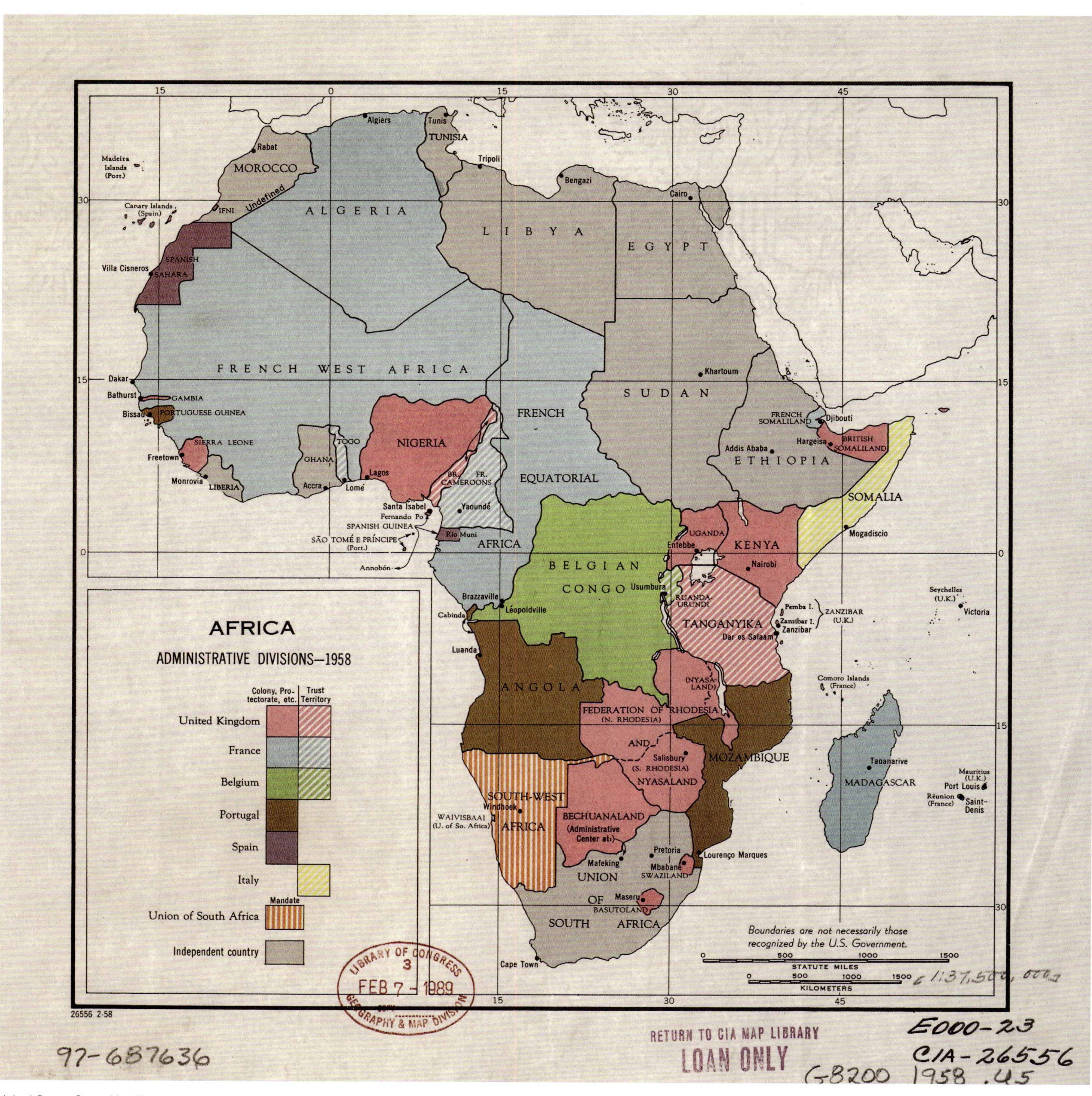

United States Central Intelligence Agency, map showing the political status of African countries, 1958

The United Nations Itinerary for Todd Webb, 1958

TOGOLAND (Togo)

April 11: Todd Webb flies from New York City to London, arriving on April 12
April 14: Leaves England for Accra, Ghana (via Lisbon, Portugal, the Canary Islands, Bathurst (Banjul), The Gambia, and Freetown, Sierra Leone
April 16: Flies from Accra, Ghana to Lomé, Togoland
April 21: Overnight in Sokodé, Togoland with a visit to Atakpamé, Lama-Kara, Aledjo, and Awanjelo
April 24: Trip to the countryside
April 25: Returns to Lomé
April 26–28: Lomé
April 27: Election Day
April 29: Day trip to Anécho (Aného)
April 29–May 4: Remaining days spent in Lomé

GHANA

May 5: Drives from Lomé, Togoland to Accra, Ghana
May 8: Day trip and stays at Government Rest House in Tafo
May 11: Takoradi (after traveling on previous days to Kumasi and to a gold mine at Konongo)

SUDAN

May 18: Arrives in Khartoum, Sudan
May 21: Train from Khartoum to Wadi Madani, Sudan[1]
May 23: Gezira, Sudan
May 26: Train from Wadi Madani to Kassala, Sudan
May 27: Kassala, Sudan
May 29: Port Sudan

TRUST TERRITORY OF SOMALILAND (Somalia)

June 5: Leaves Khartoum, flies from Aden Airport to Mogadishu, Trust Territory of Somaliland
June 5–19: Mogadishu
June 19: Flies from Mogadishu to Nairobi, Kenya

FEDERATION OF RHODESIA AND NYASALAND: NORTHERN RHODESIA (Zambia) AND SOUTHERN RHODESIA (Zimbabwe)

June 20–July 5: Flies Kenya to Salisbury, Southern Rhodesia and travels in Southern Rhodesia and Northern Rhodesia until July 5
June 24–25: Visits Kariba Dam (spanning the Zambezi river, between Northern and Southern Rhodesia)
June 26–28: Salisbury (Harare), Southern Rhodesia
June 29: Takes the train to Bulawayo, Southern Rhodesia
July 2: Flies to Ndola in the Copper Belt, Northern Rhodesia
July 3: Returns to Salisbury

TANGANYIKA AND ZANZIBAR (Tanzania)

July 6: Flies from Salisbury, Southern Rhodesia to Dar es Salaam, Tanganyika; stays at the New Africa Hotel
July 7: Moves to the Dar es Salaam Club to stay
July 8: Dar es Salaam
July 9: Dar es Salaam
July 10: Day trip to Bagamoyo
July 14: Travels to Zanzibar
July 15: Travels to Tanga, Tanganyika
July 16: Visits the Amboni Sisal Estate in Kingoni
July 17: Visits Pangani Falls
July 18: Visits the tea estates in the mountains east of Tanga
July 19–23: Moshi
July 24: Flies from Arusha, Tanganyika to Nairobi, Kenya

KENYA

July 24–August 3: Nairobi, Kenya
July 31: Day trip from Nairobi to Machakos, Kenya

EUROPE

August 3: Flies from Nairobi, Kenya to Athens, Greece
August 3–6: Athens, Greece
August 7: Flies from Athens to Rome and then Paris
August 15: Flies from Paris to New York

A Historical Synopsis of the African Countries Visited by Todd Webb in 1958

Jan-Lodewijk Grootaers

	Colonial history before 1958	Status in 1958	Political history after 1958
French Togoland	The German colony of Togoland was established between 1884 and 1905. In 1922, Great Britain received the mandate to govern the western part of Togoland and France the eastern part. In 1957, the residents of British Togoland voted to join the newly independent nation of Ghana.	French Togoland is an autonomous republic within the French Union, retaining its United Nations trusteeship status.	In 1960, French Togoland will become the independent Togolese Republic, later known as Togo.
Ghana	Known formerly as the Gold Coast, parts of the coastal area were controlled for centuries by Portuguese, Dutch, and British powers, until the latter established the Gold Coast Colony in 1874.	Ghana becomes an independent nation in 1957, under Prime Minister Kwame Nkrumah.	Kwame Nkrumah will be president during 1960–66. An advocate of pan-Africanism, he is one of the founders of the Organization of African Unity.
Sudan	The Anglo-Egyptian Sudan was established in 1899, a joint venture between Great Britain and Egypt, but in effect administered as a British Crown Colony.	Sudan becomes an independent nation in 1956, under Prime Minister Ismail al-Azhari.	Africa's largest country in surface area, Sudan will be plagued by internal conflict. In 2011, the country will split into the Republic of the Sudan and the Republic of South Sudan.
Trust Territory of Somaliland under Italian Administration	In the late nineteenth century, colonial powers established British Somaliland (in the north) and Italian Somaliland (along the east coast). After the Second World War, British Somaliland remained a protectorate, while the United Nations granted Italy trusteeship of Italian Somaliland—on the condition that it would be granted independence by 1960.	Italian Somaliland is a United Nations Trust Territory under Italian administration.	In 1960, British and Italian Somaliland will be united to form the Republic of Somalia. At the onset of civil war in 1991, former British Somaliland will declare independence, which is not recognized internationally.
Southern Rhodesia	The name Rhodesia came into use in 1895, in honor of Cecil Rhodes, the British empire-builder active during the British expansion into southern Africa. In 1953, the British created the Federation of Rhodesia and Nyasaland.	Southern Rhodesia is a British colony, part of the Federation of Rhodesia and Nyasaland.	The Federation of Rhodesia and Nyasaland will be dissolved in 1964, upon which the white-minority government will issue a Unilateral Declaration of Independence in 1965 and establish Rhodesia, an unrecognized state. The country will achieve internationally recognized independence as Zimbabwe in 1980.

	Colonial history before 1958	Status in 1958	Political history after 1958
Northern Rhodesia	In 1889, the British government agreed that Cecil Rhodes's company, the British South Africa Company, would administer the territory comprising Northern and Southern Rhodesia as a protectorate. Northern Rhodesia became a British colony in 1924.	Northern Rhodesia is a British colony, part of the Federation of Rhodesia and Nyasaland.	The Federation of Rhodesia and Nyasaland will be dissolved in 1964, upon which Northern Rhodesia will achieve independence as Zambia.
Tanganyika	Tanganyika as an entity originated as part of German East Africa, which existed from 1886 to 1919. After the First World War, it was transferred to Great Britain as a mandate by the League of Nations, later by the United Nations.	Tanganyika is a United Nations Trust Territory, ruled by the British.	The country will become independent in 1961, ruled by President Julius Nyerere, the promoter of an African socialism, during 1962–85. It will be renamed Tanzania in 1964, after its union with Zanzibar.
Zanzibar	An autonomous hub for the Western Indian Ocean trade, Zanzibar was part of the Portuguese Empire from 1503 to 1698, when it fell under the rule of Oman in southeast Arabia. In 1856 Zanzibar became effectively independent again, but the British took political control from the local Sultan in the 1890s.	Zanzibar is a British Protectorate, ruled jointly by the Sultan of Zanzibar and the British.	The island will become independent in 1963, and in 1964 will be subsumed into Tanganyika, renamed Tanzania. It will remain a semi-autonomous region.
Kenya	The British Empire established Kenya as the East African Protectorate in 1895. It became a British colony in 1920.	Kenya is a British colony.	The country will become independent in 1963, ruled by President Jomo Kenyatta during 1964–78.

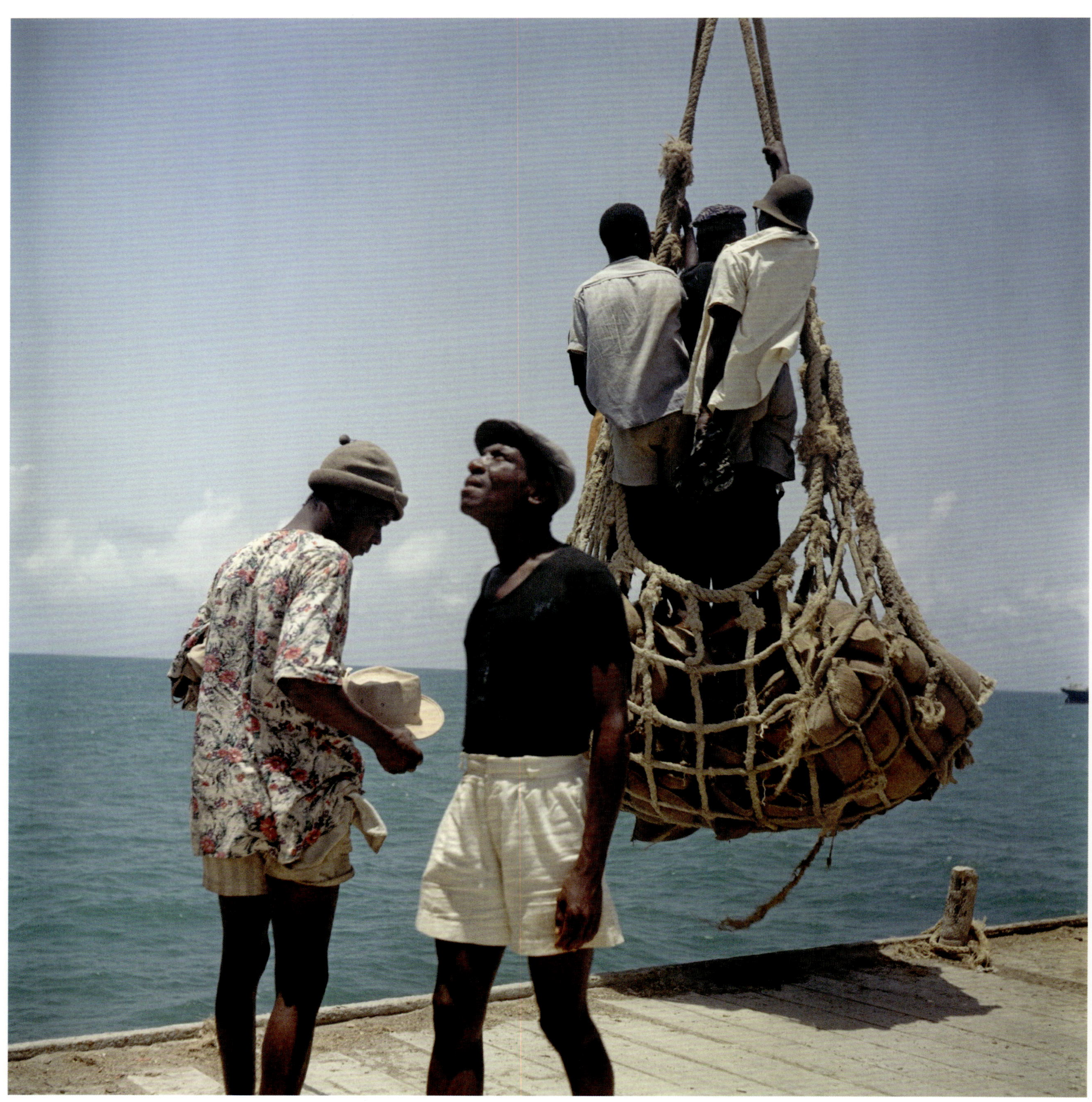

Todd Webb, *Untitled* (44UN-7916-069), Togoland (Togo), 1958
Loading people and goods at Lomé harbor.

TOGOLAND

(TOGO)

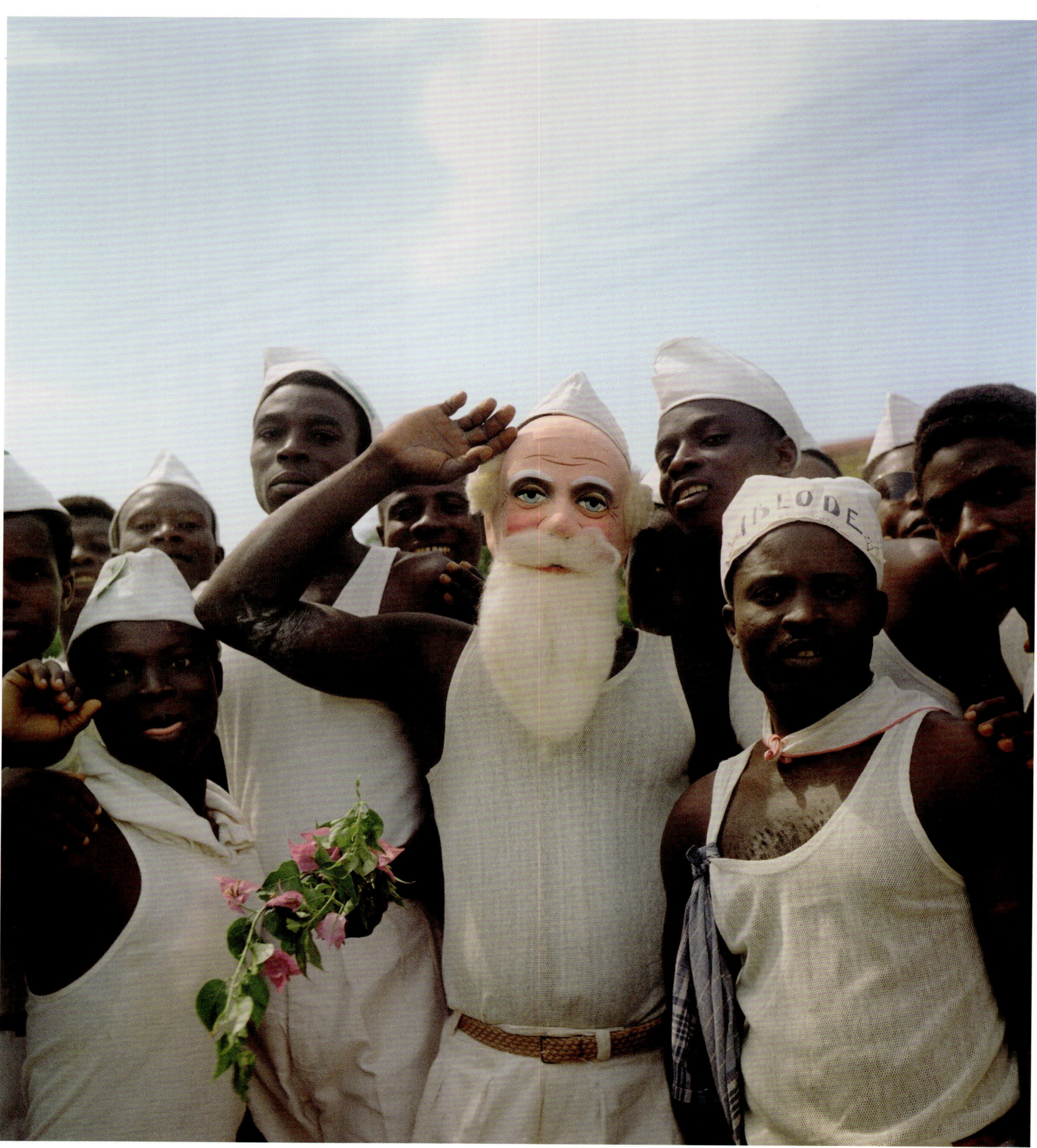

Todd Webb, *Untitled* (44UN-7925-071), Togoland (Togo), 1958
Group of men with white hats, one with the slogan "Ablode" (freedom), and another with a Santa Claus mask on election day, April 27.

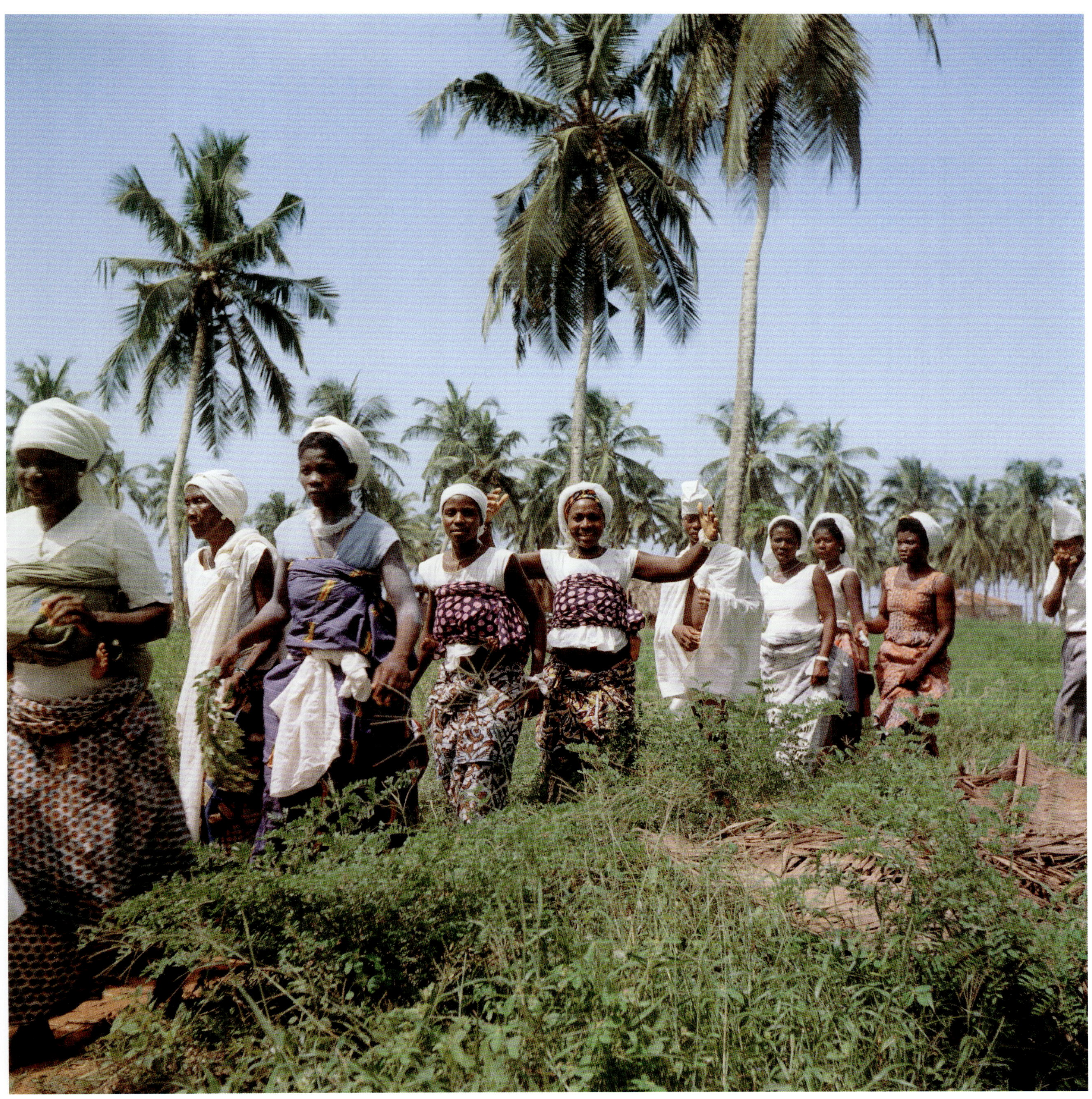

Todd Webb, *Untitled* (44UN-7915-350), Togoland (Togo), 1958
Women and men walking on election day, April 27.

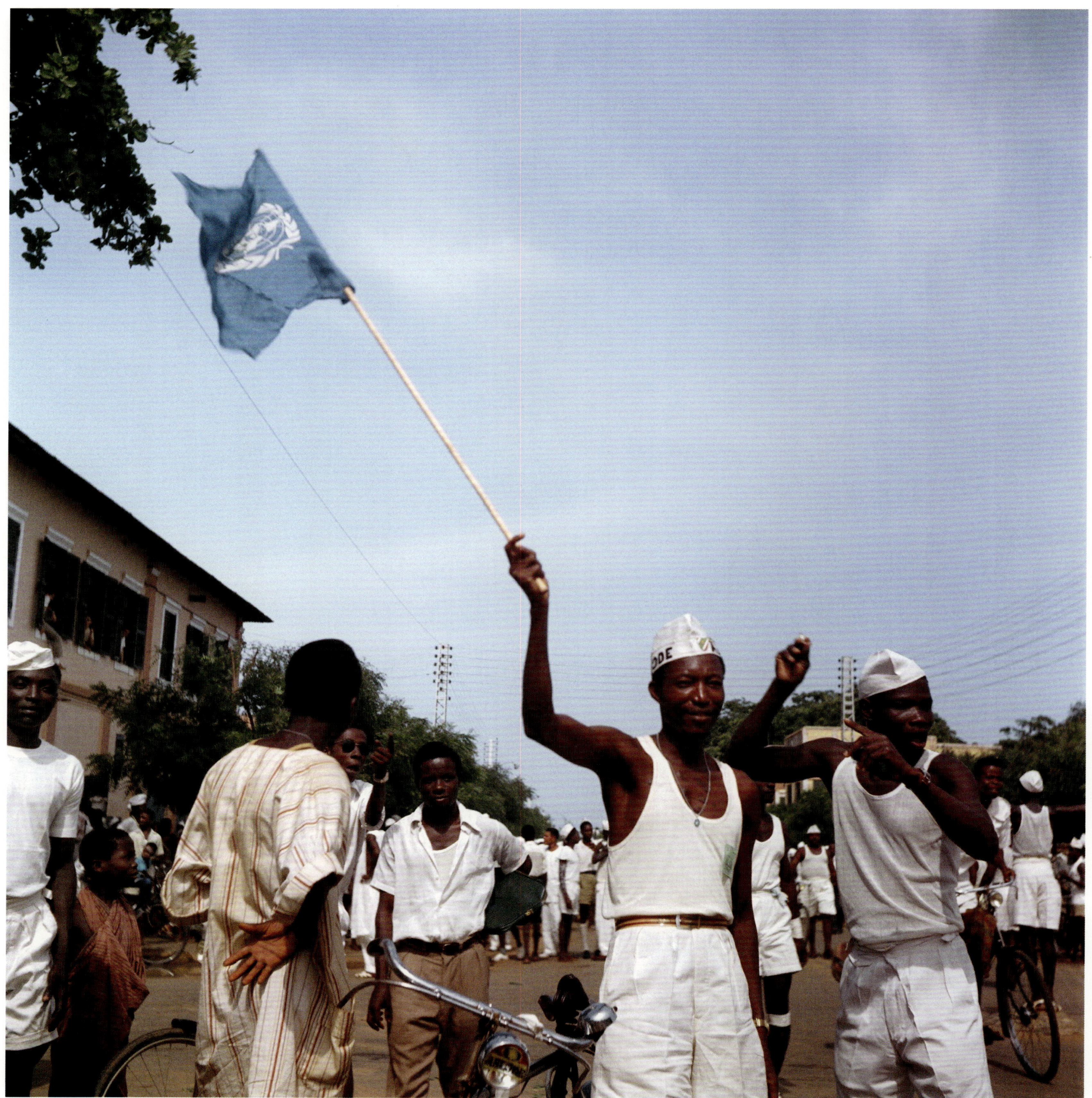

Todd Webb, *Untitled* (44UN-7925-070), Togoland (Togo), 1958
Waving a United Nations flag on election day, April 27.

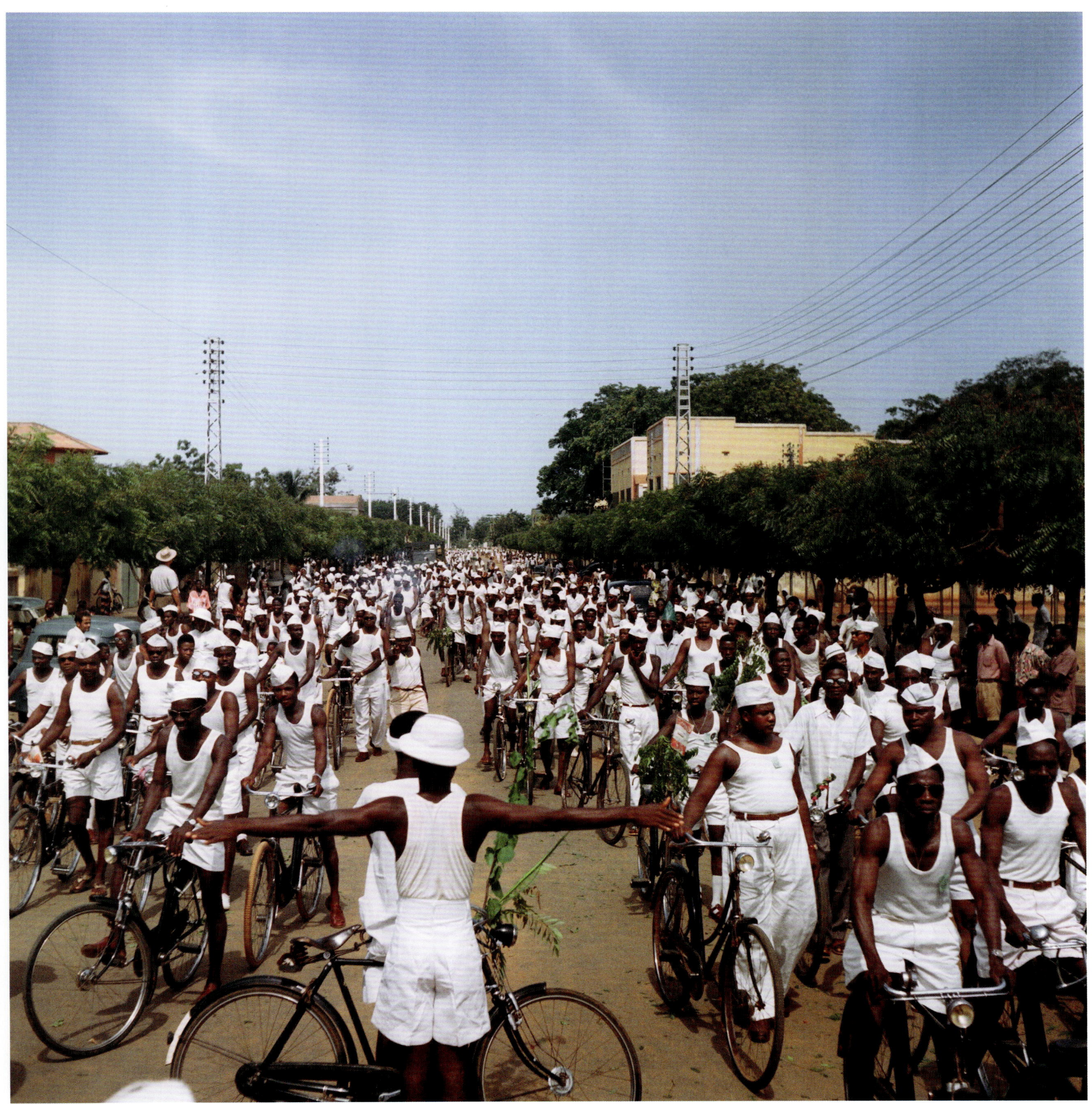

Todd Webb, *Untitled* (44UN-7915-365), Togoland (Togo), 1958
Crowds on election day, April 27.

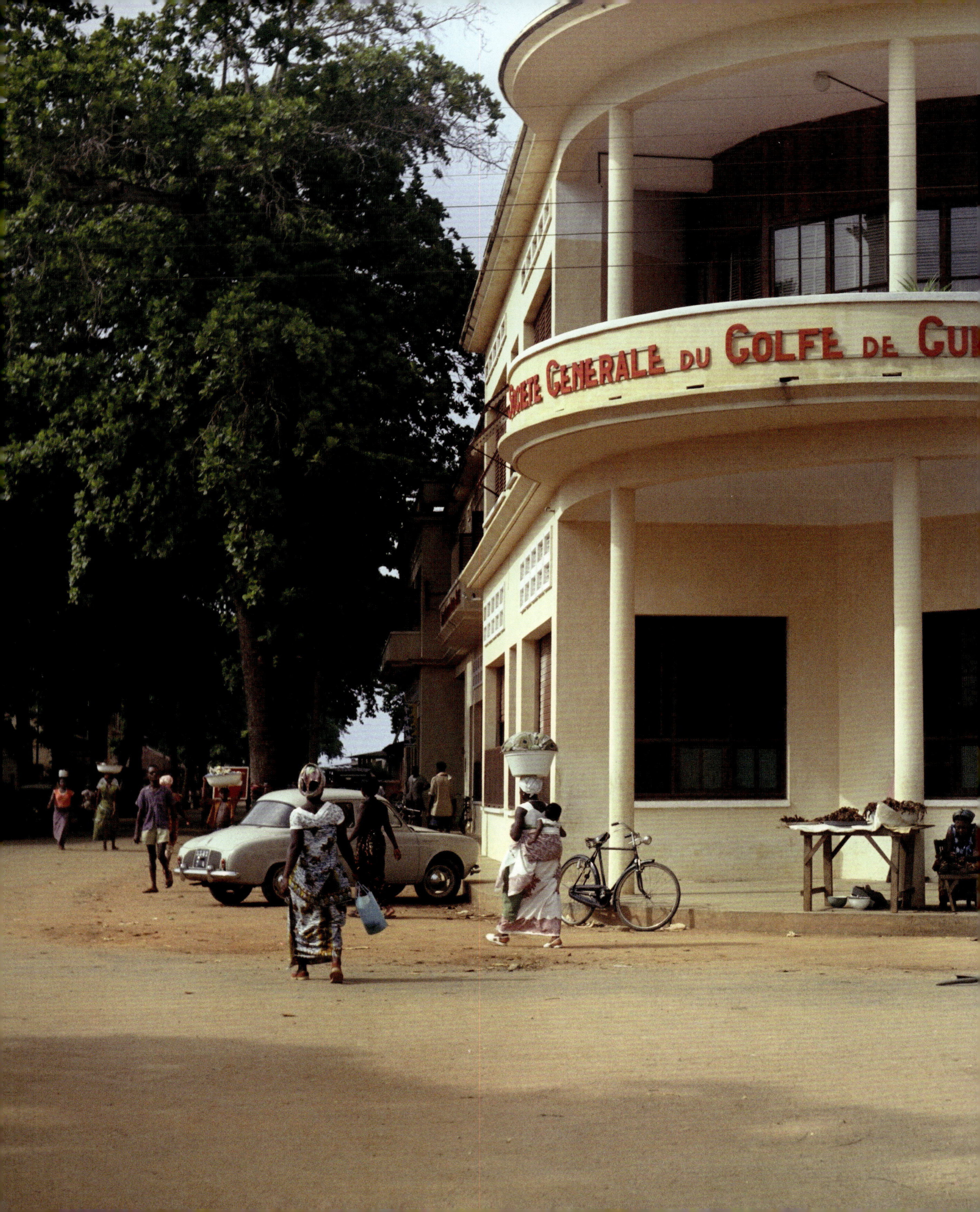
SOCIETE GENERALE DU GOLFE DE

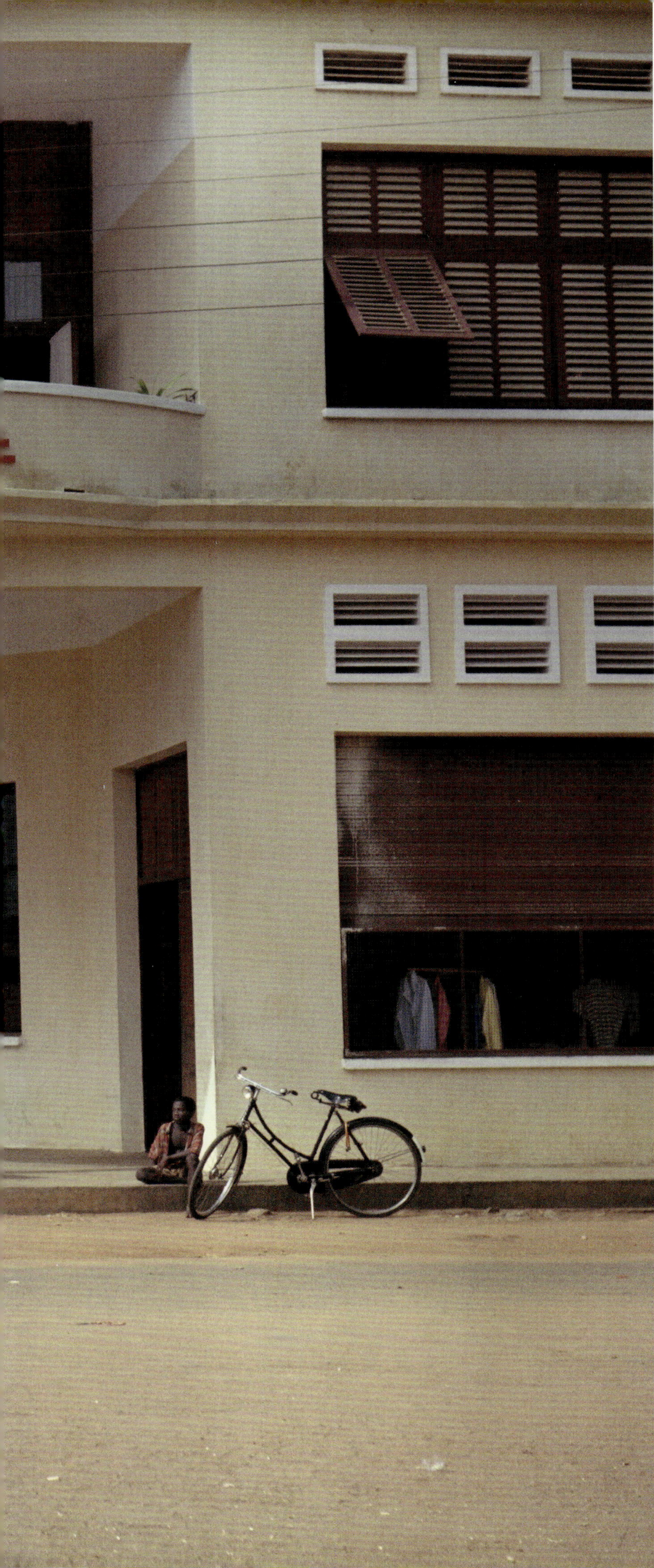

Todd Webb, *Untitled* (44UN-7908-004), Togoland (Togo), 1958
Offices of Société Générale du Golfe de Guinée, Lomé.

Todd Webb, *Untitled* (44UN-7909-072), Togoland (Togo), 1958
Women walking along a harbor quay in Lomé.

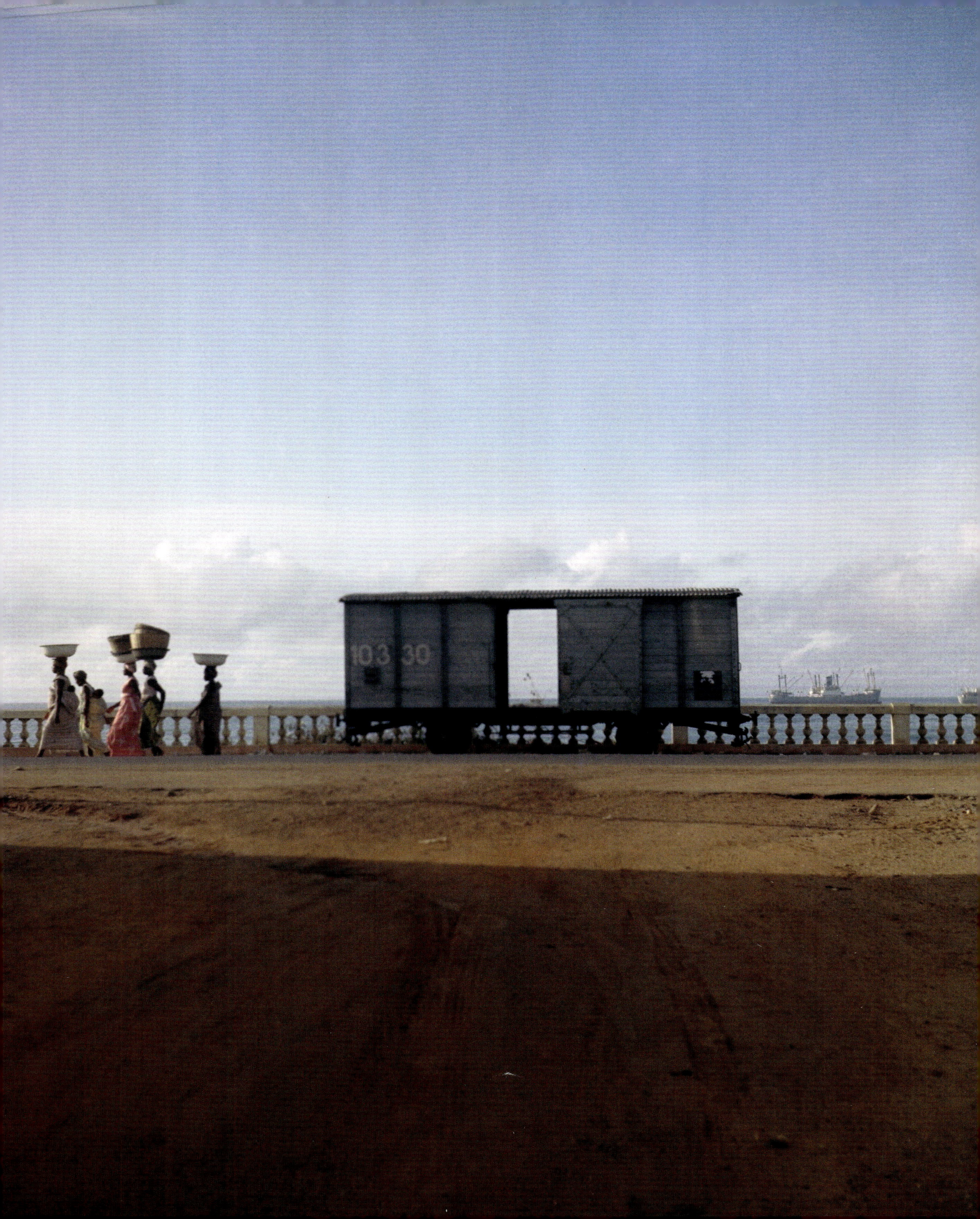
103 30

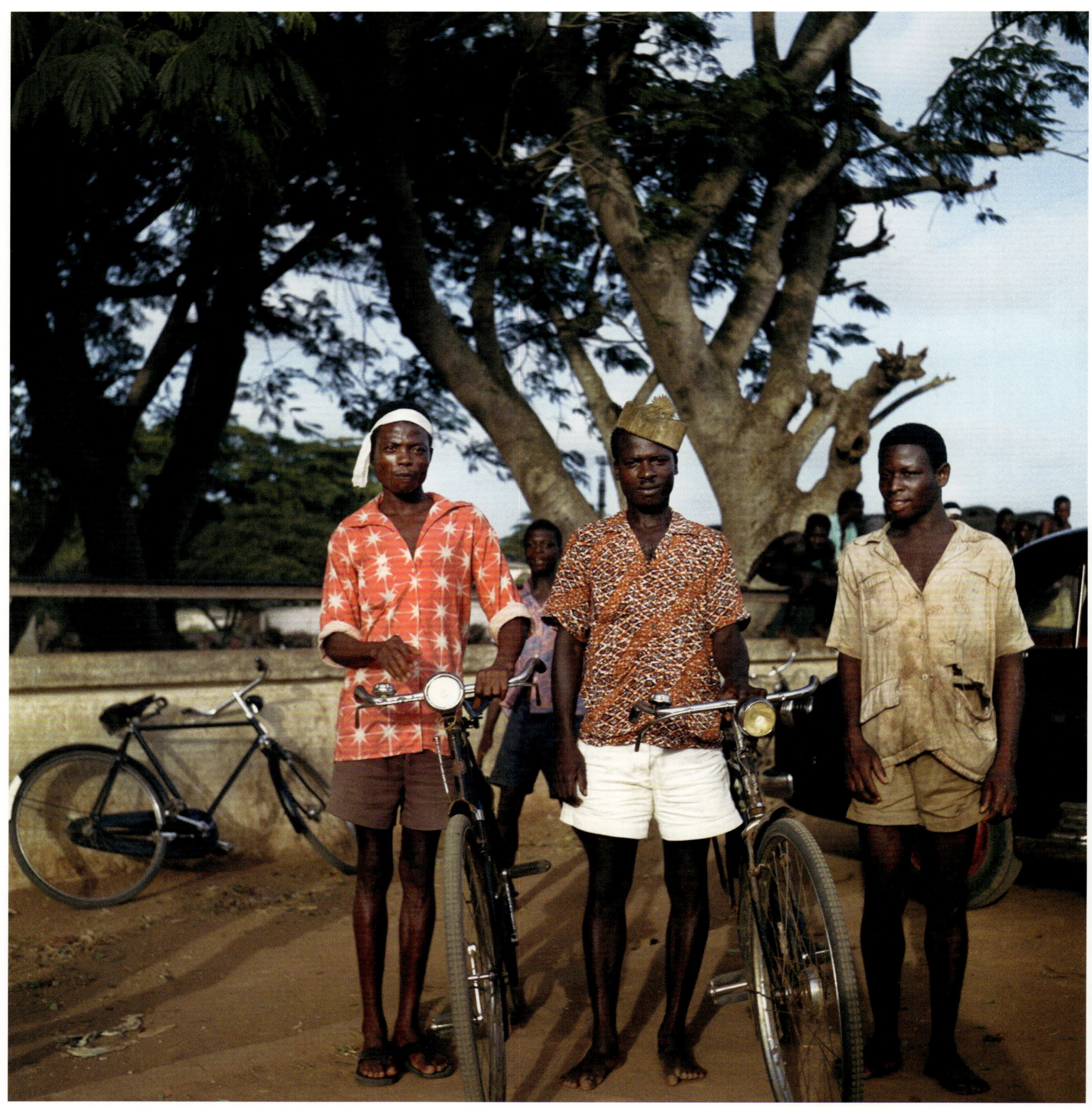

Todd Webb, *Untitled* (44UN-7911-378), Togoland (Togo), 1958
Men standing with their bikes, one wearing a tilted crown.

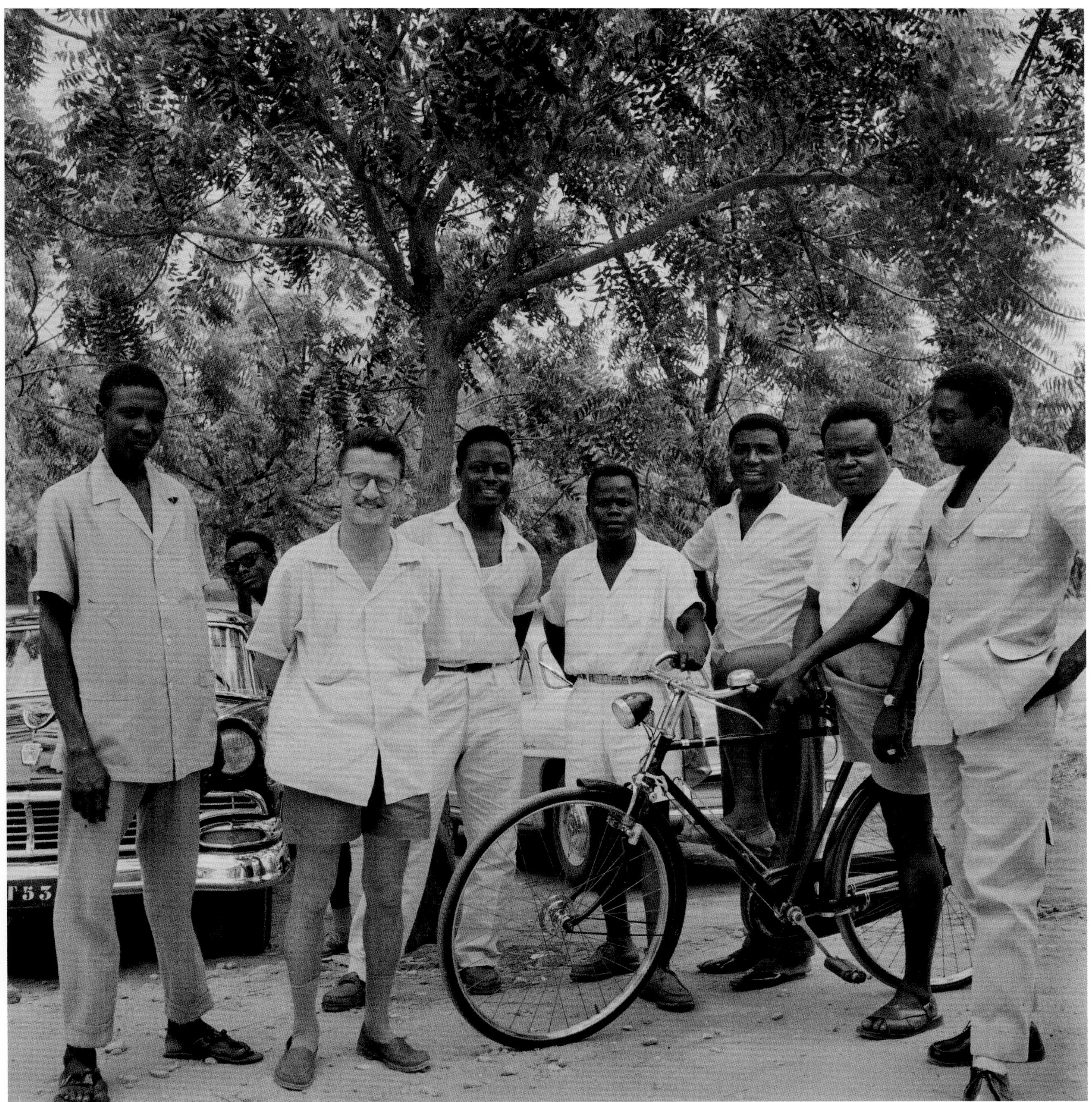

Todd Webb, *Untitled* (44UN-T5-R1-628), Togoland (Togo), 1958
Group of men posing with a bike near the car park.

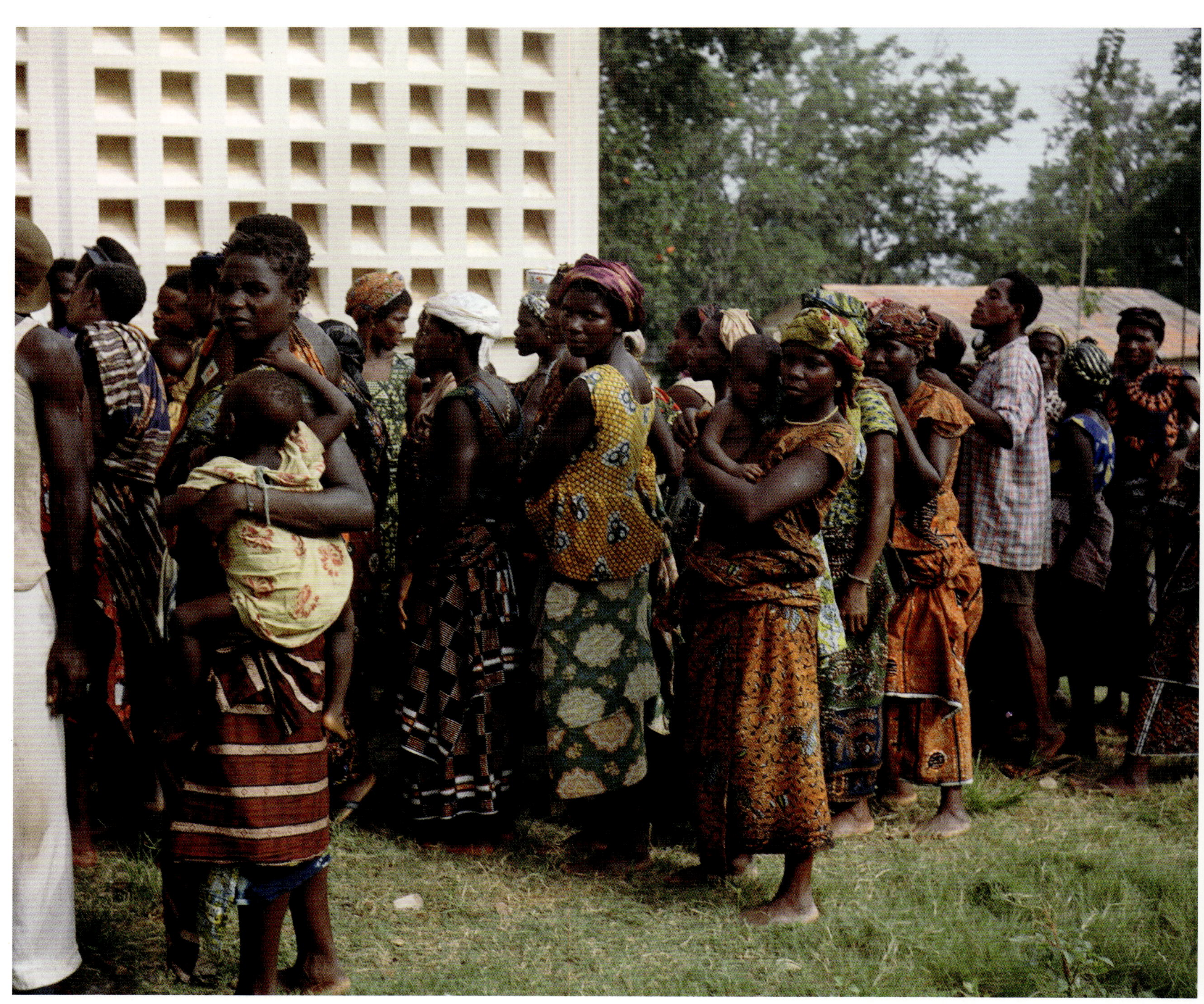

Todd Webb, *Untitled* (44UN-7914-203), Togoland (Togo), 1958
Women and men lining up to vote on election day, April 27.

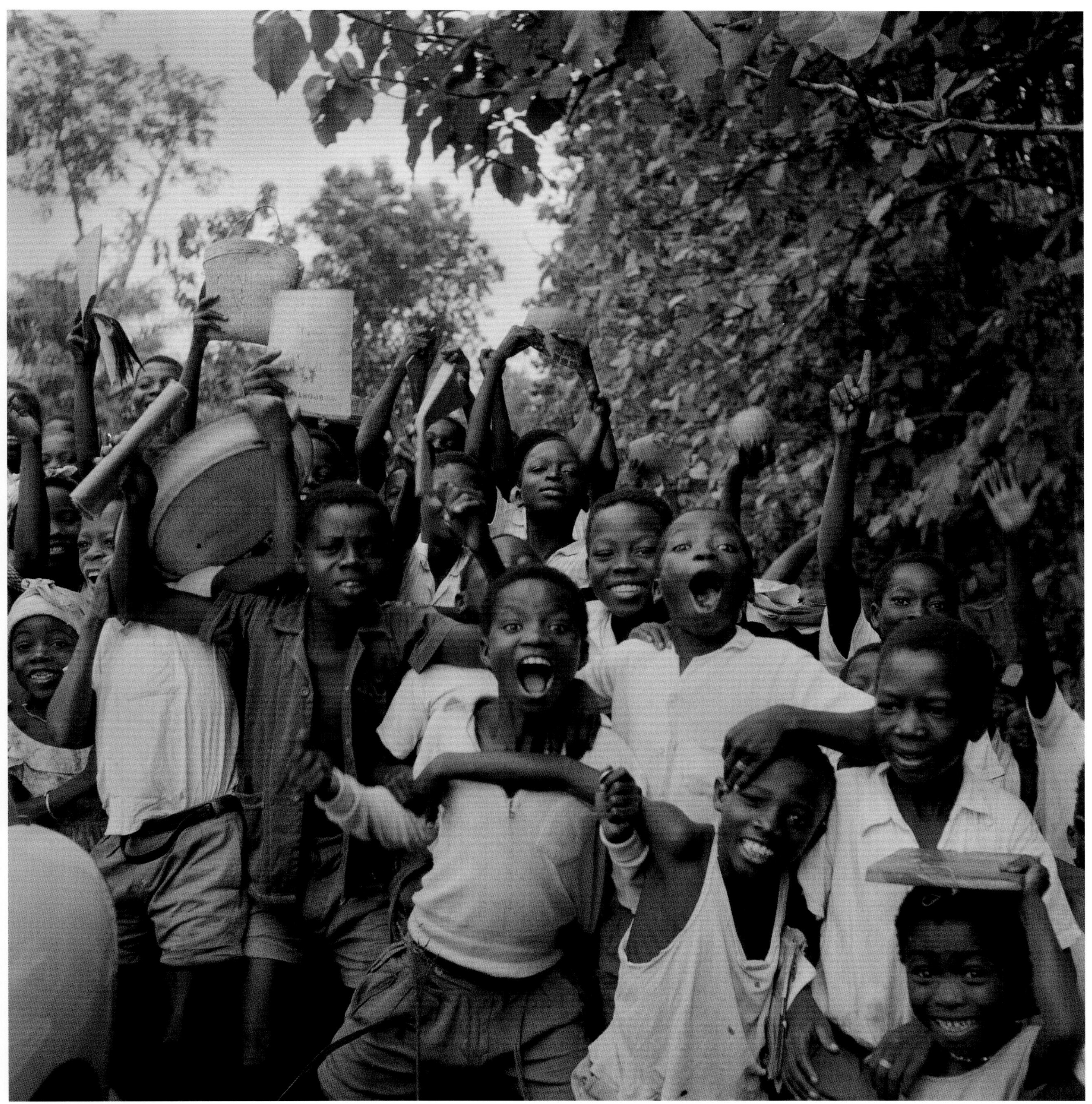

Todd Webb, *Untitled* (44UN-T3-R1-001), Togoland (Togo), 1958
Excited group of children with their school books and bags.

Todd Webb, Journal Entry, April 27, 1958

"A day of great surprise–and rejoicing. The opposition has won a landslide victory and now Togo is virtually free. The UN mission is vindicated and aside from the few here the country is in ecstasy. Everything is closed and the people in holiday mood. The cry of ablode! (freedom) rings in the streets–people have painted their faces white and donned outlandish costumes–almost impossible to photograph–the minute you stop you are jammed in by people wanting to shake your hand. I feel that I have seen history made–it was a good show."

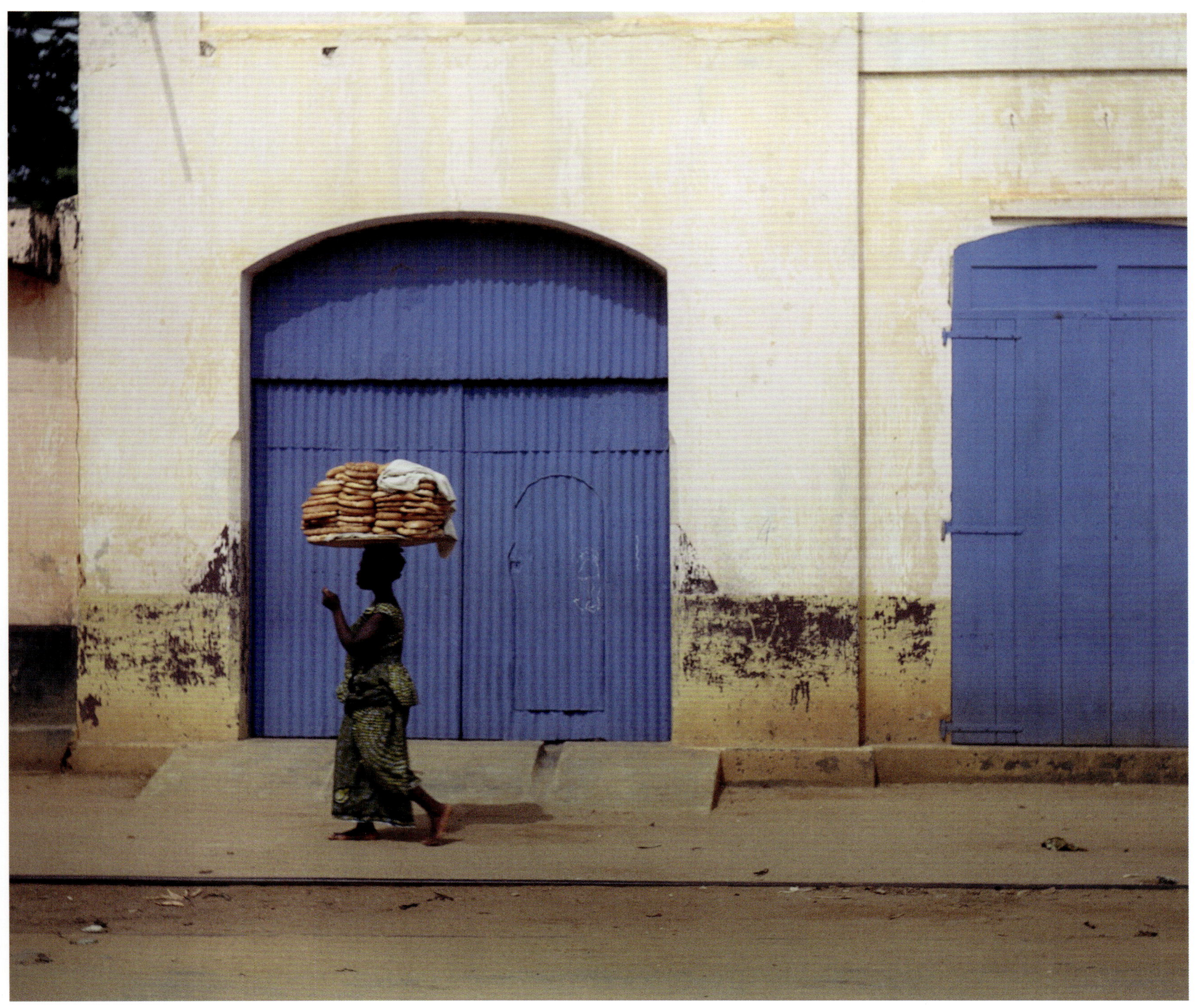

Todd Webb, *Untitled* (44UN-7907-001), Togoland (Togo), 1958
Woman carrying bread on her head, Lomé.

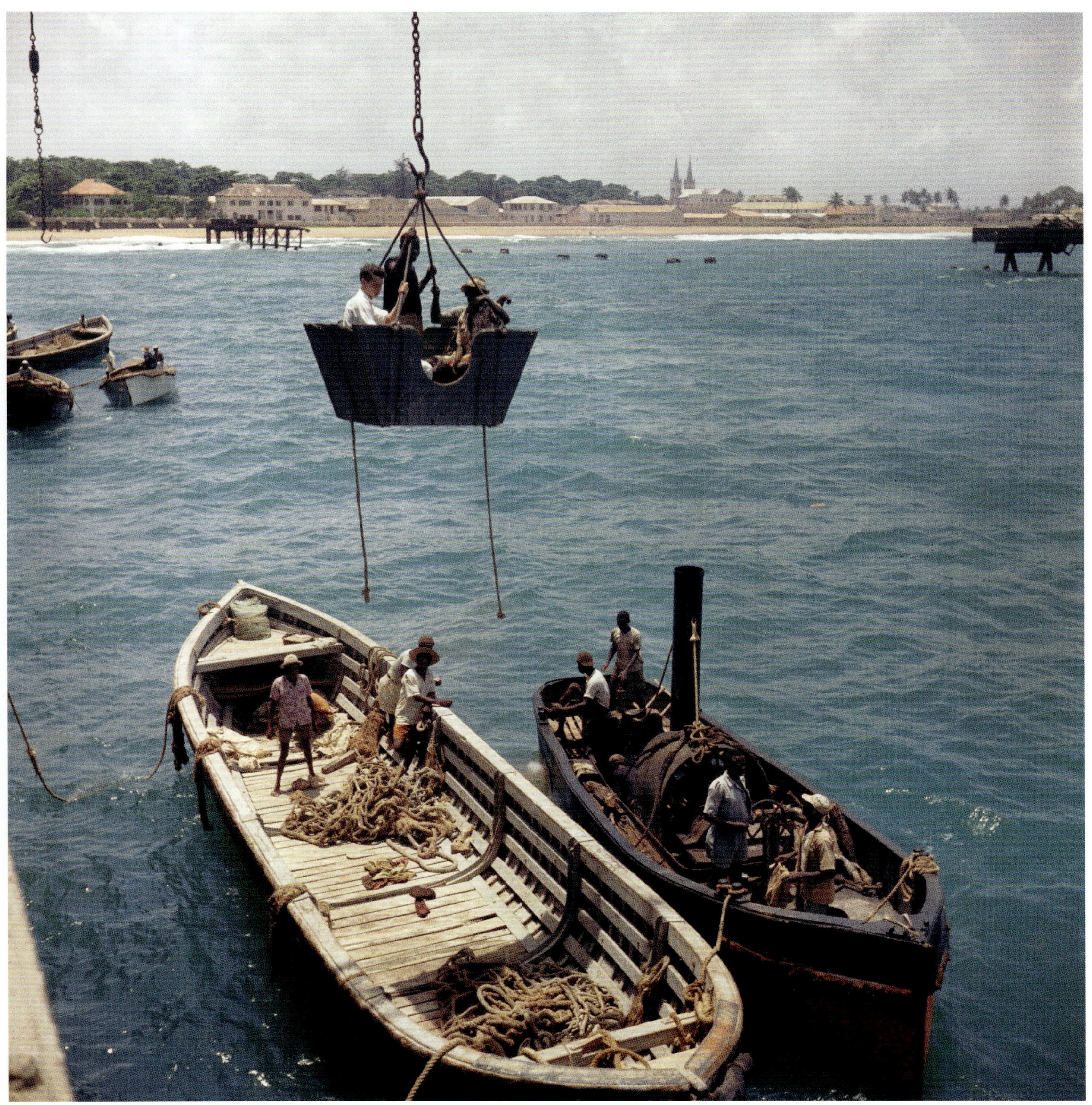

Todd Webb, *Untitled* (44UN-7916-068), Togoland (Togo), 1958
Loading people into the boats, Lomé harbor.

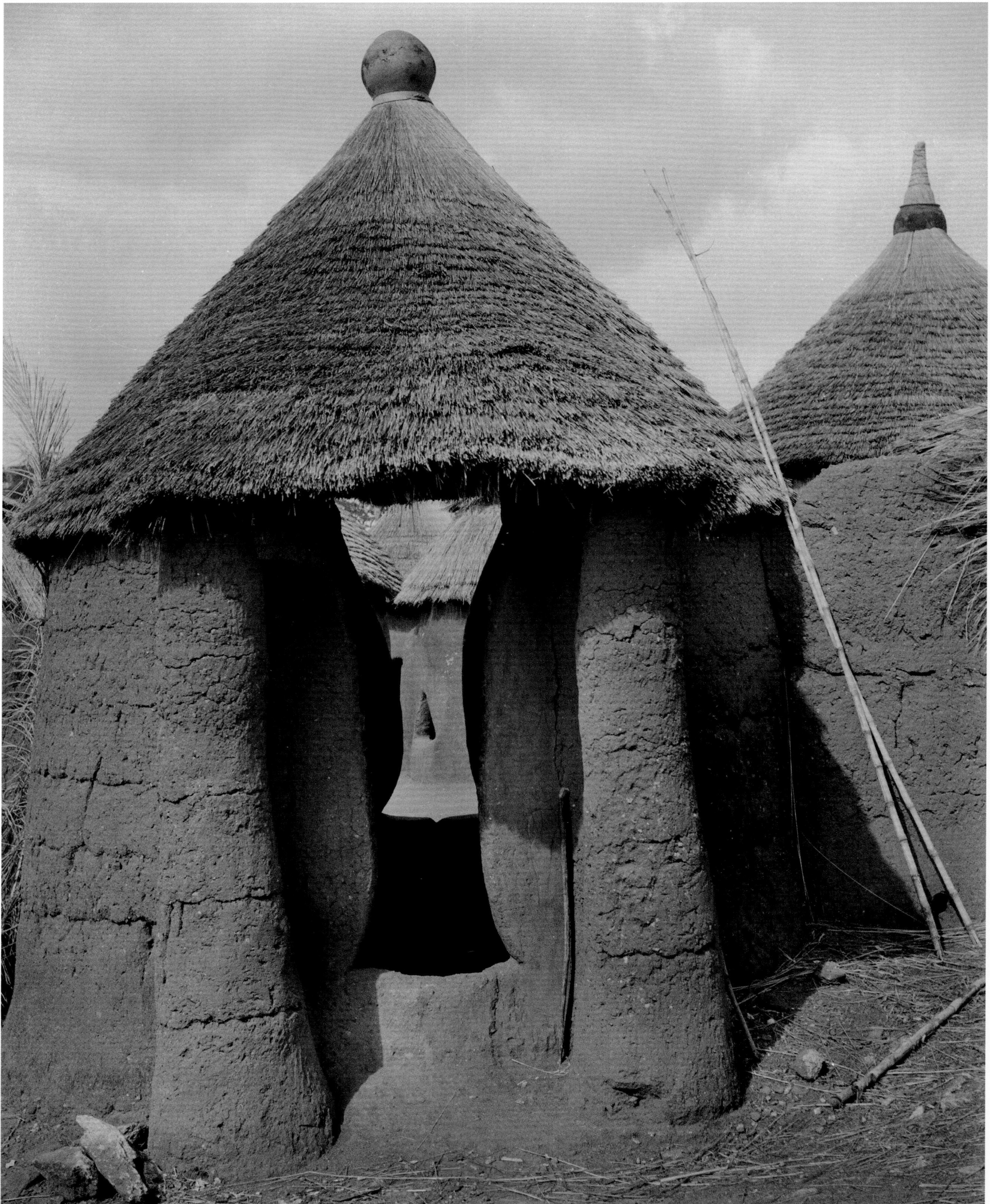

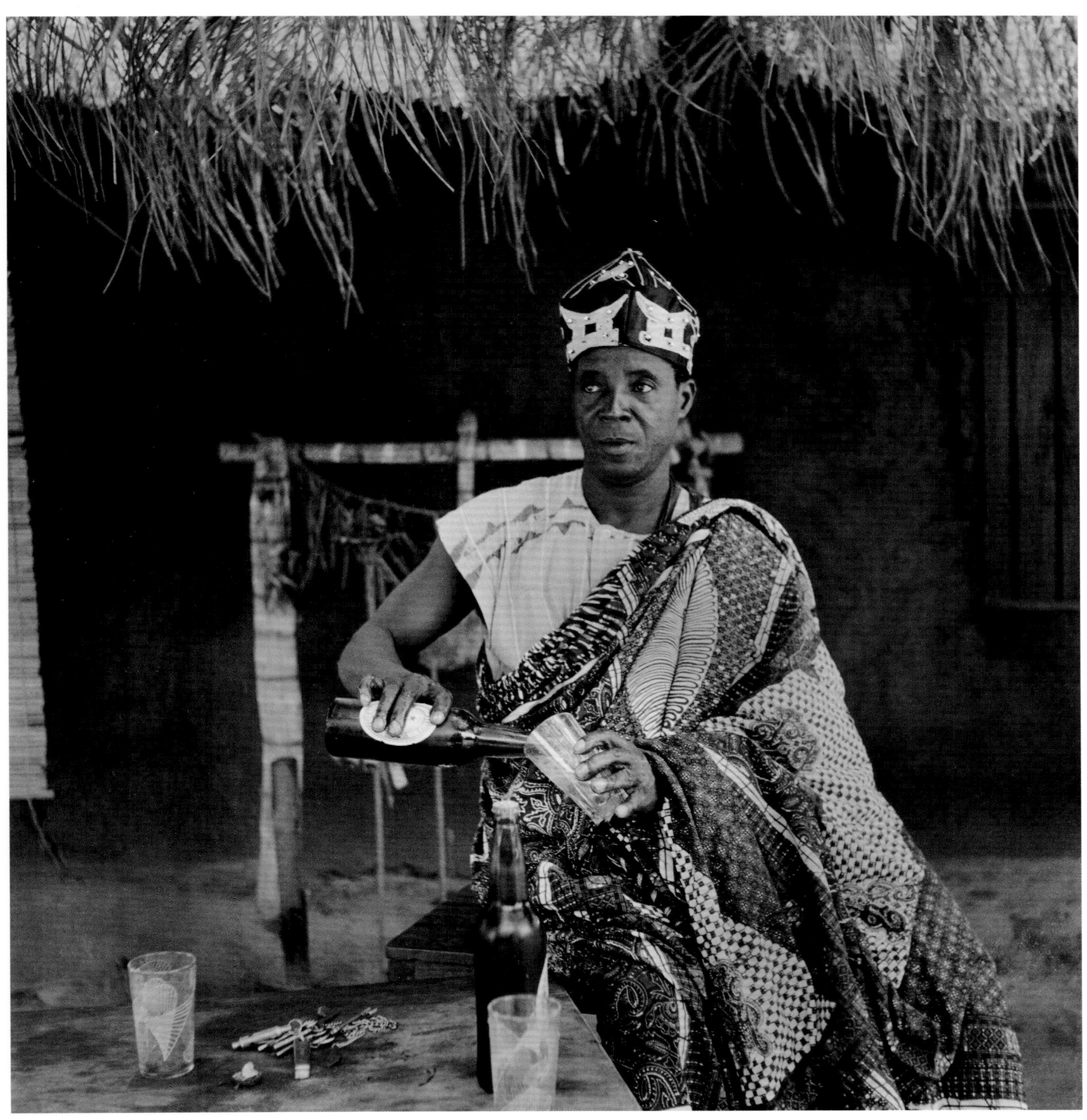

Opposite: Todd Webb, *Untitled* (44UN-BW-009), Togoland (Togo), 1958
Batammaliba dwelling.

Above: Todd Webb, *Untitled* (44UN-R3-001), Ghana, 1958
Chief wearing traditional Dahomean appliquéd hat and pouring a Heineken beer (photographed in Aflao, Ghana, on the Togo border).

A Snapshot of the Togoland (Togo) Election, 1958

Aimée Bessire

In April 1958, Todd Webb traveled to Togoland (Togo) to document the country's first universal suffrage election. A long chain of events and a great deal of change led to this historic United Nations-supervised parliamentary vote. In 1922, after the First World War, a League of Nations mandate split the German colony of "Togoland" into two administrative sections, with western Togo governed by Great Britain and the eastern part of the country by France. At the end of the Second World War, these became United Nations Trust Territories, and in late 1956, as part of the successive events happening across Africa leading to independence, residents of British Togoland voted to become part of the Gold Coast and officially joined the newly independent country of Ghana.

The trajectory of the French-governed territory was more complicated. In 1955, a French statute made French Togoland an autonomous nation, but still a UN trusteeship and part of the French Union. France instituted the *loi-cadre* in 1956, which ended the multiple electoral college system that had favored French nationals living in the colonies. But when French-backed parties won all of the parliamentary seats, with only eight percent of the population voting, indigenous citizens complained that the first election was highly flawed. A team from the UN visited Togoland in 1957 in response to these complaints, and highlighting the inconsistencies with the voting process, they called for the elections of 1958. Two political parties competed for parliamentary control: the Committee of Togolese Unity (CUT), today known as the Party of Togolese Unity (PUT), which advocated for the unification of the Ewe people,[1] and the Togolese Party of Progress (PTP), led by Nicolas Grunitzky.

The United Nations hired Todd Webb to photograph the election as the first part of his commission, and he accompanied the UN teams sent to observe the event (right). He provides a colorful, first-hand account of the days leading to the election and the actual event:

> The UN observers arrived about 2 months before the election and they made every effort to see that everybody had an opportunity to register. When it was understood that there was going to be a real election and that everybody was eligible to vote if they would come and register, business began to pick up. They came in droves to the registration points, bringing their whole families and often relatives and friends from neighboring countries to register. And some of them registered at a half dozen different places—and it was almost impossible to detect. Campaign speeches were made at rallies and meetings—political lines were drawn in all communities. The people campaigning for candidates not in favor of the French administration were called "the opposition." For days after my arrival in Togoland I traveled all over the country photographing operation registration. The twenty UN observers had been sent out to live in outlying territories where they could assist the local administrators in seeing that everyone was registered. Made one memorable trip to Lama-Kara, one of the northern towns a bit more than 400 kilometers from Lomé.... Most of the villages that we passed had a holiday atmosphere with impromptu dances and speeches. We were well received every place.[2]

Voter turnout reached almost sixty-five percent on April 27 and Webb's election images document crowds filling the streets, people standing in line to vote or waiting in tree-shaded areas, and joyful men and women waving flags, exuding the energy of what must have been an exciting occasion. The Committee for Togolese Unity won twenty-nine out of forty-six seats in the parliamentary elections and CUT candidate Sylvanus Olympio became the country's first Togolese Prime Minister, a key moment on the route to independence, which came just two years later.[3] Webb described the incredible joy he witnessed everywhere he photographed (opposite):

> A day of great surprise—and rejoicing. The opposition has won a landslide Victory and now Togo is virtually free. The UN Mission is vindicated and aside from the few French here the country is in ecstasy. Everything is closed and the people in holiday mood. The cry of Ablodé! (Freedom) rings in the streets—people have painted their faces white and donned outlandish costumes. Almost impossible to photograph—the minute you stop you are jammed in by people wanting to shake your hand. I feel that I have seen history made—it was a good show.[4]

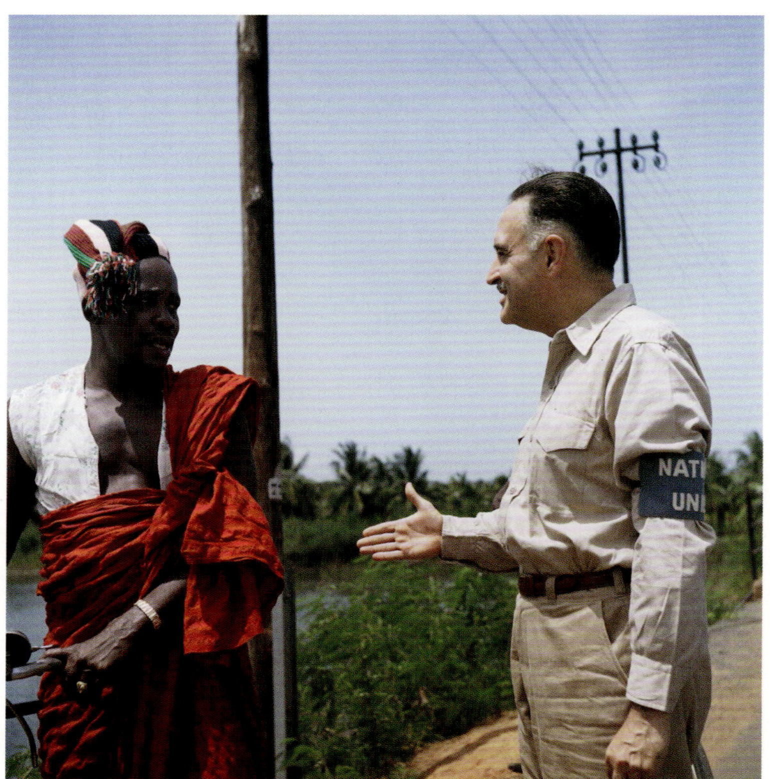

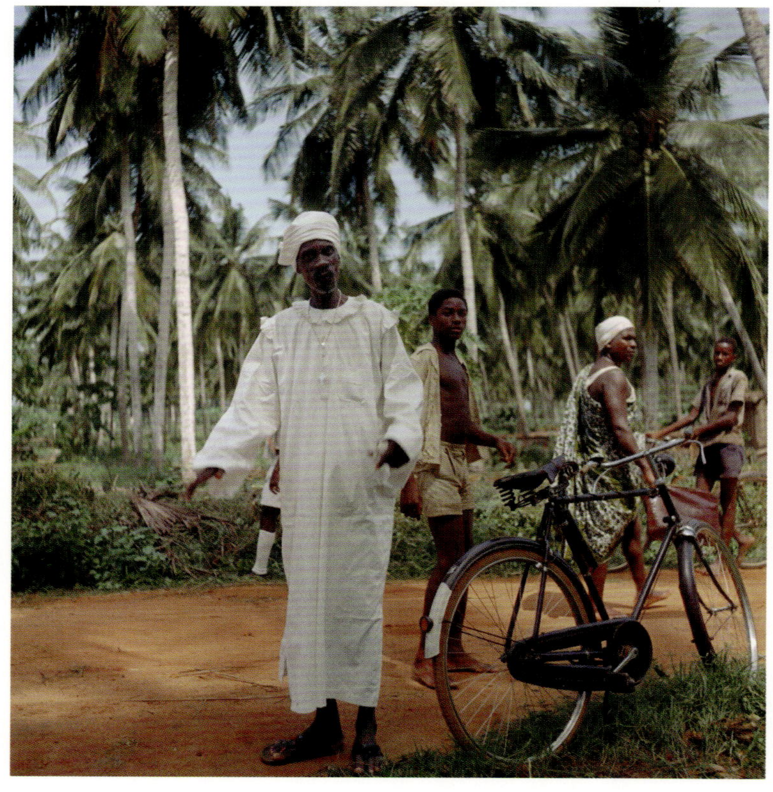

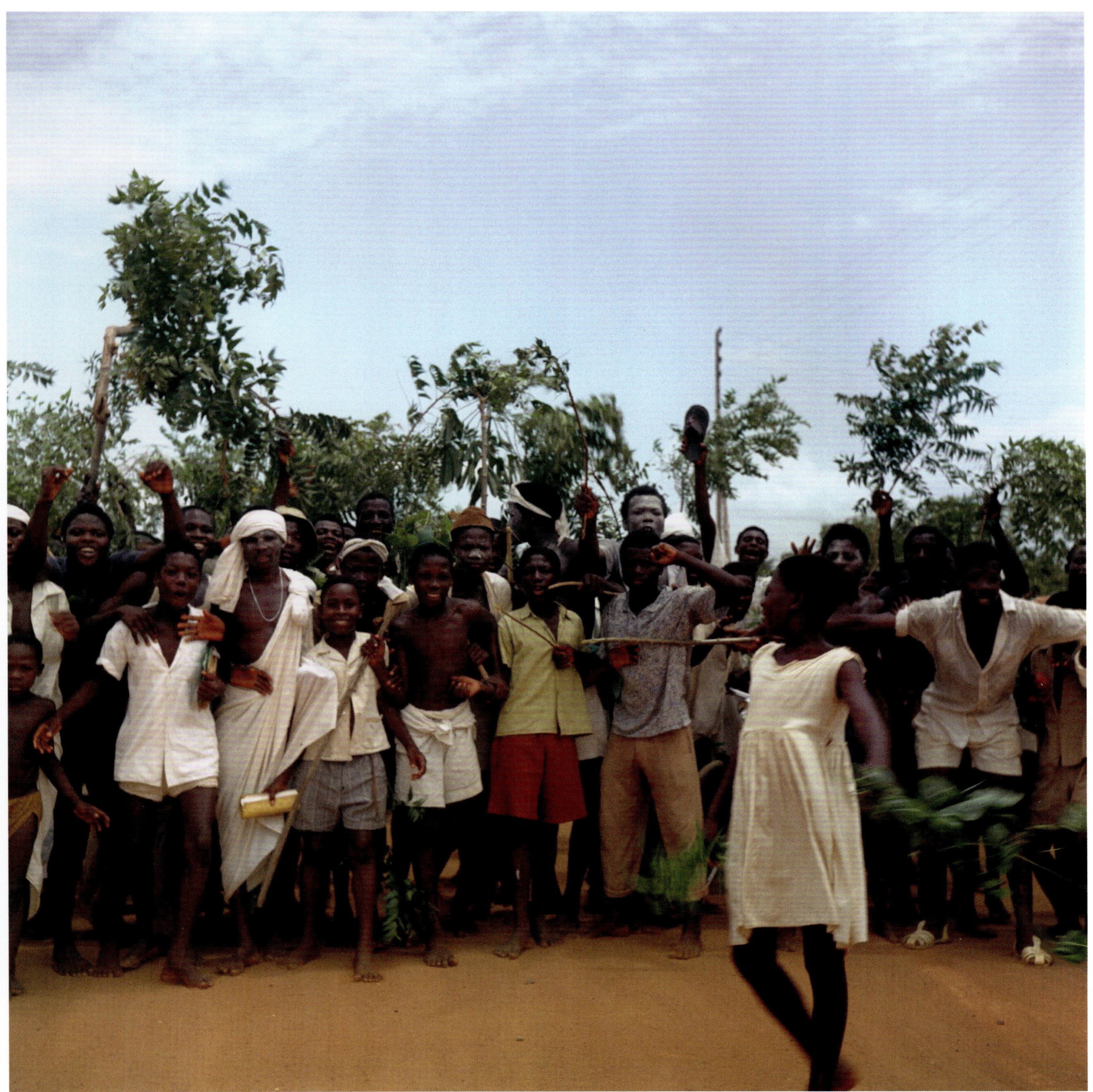

Opposite, top: Todd Webb, *Untitled* (44UN-7911-369), Togoland (Togo), 1958
United Nations election observer trying to greet a man.

Opposite, bottom: Todd Webb, *Untitled* (44UN-7915-348), Togoland (Togo), 1958
Man wearing celebratory white on election day, April 27.

Above: Todd Webb, *Untitled* (44UN-7910-187), Togoland (Togo), 1958
People celebrating on election day.

The Myth of Africa

Aimée Bessire

We choose which Africa suits our intentions, or, as it were, inventions. Each of these choices surely will correspond to a 'correct' representation. In this way, Africa ceases to exist as a concrete reality. Instead, it becomes phosphorescent like the proverbial will-o'-the-wisp, a dazzling dark ember in the figment of our imaginations.[1]
—Okwui Enwezor

Todd Webb's thrill in "seeing Africa" for the first time is palpable in his journal. Indeed, his excitement reads like a nineteenth-century adventure story: "I am breathlessly awaiting my first glimpse.... Minutes away from the realization of a dream—seeing Africa. It is hard to believe. At last! The sight of land."[2] Reading Webb's account allows one to see Africa through his eyes. His words add context to the trip and provide texture to our understanding of how he viewed the subjects of his photographs. It is clear, both through his journals and the letters he wrote to his wife, Lucille, that Webb had preconceived notions of "Africa." Yet his United Nations mandate to document a "changing Africa" situates his images in a unique place—one that attempts to contradict a romanticized and exoticized visual narrative of the continent, while still photographing through an outsider's lens. Webb's images are complicated by the fact that they are photographed with a new focus on documenting and aestheticizing modernization in the different countries, and yet at the same time are created through eyes taking in the continent for the first time, with a preconceived, constructed understanding of "Africanness." The UN photographs attempt to define the possibilities of a new narrative of Africa through their construction of a modern order presenting development and civilization,[3] disrupting and unsettling the visual myth of the continent that existed in 1958, and still in many ways exists today. As an image-maker, albeit one with a direct assignment, Webb focused his camera at the scenes that would tell a new story of the countries he visited, countering, perhaps, many of the primitivizing visuals that had informed his own perceptions of the continent.

Congolese philosopher V. Y. Mudimbe has written extensively on the "multifaceted 'idea' of Africa," as it is "invented" "through conflicting systems of knowledge" in the geographic North.[4] As he has suggested, "since the fifteenth century, the idea of Africa has mingled together new scientific and ideological interpretations with the semantic fields of concepts such as 'primitivism' and 'savagery'."[5] This construction of the idea of Africa as "less-developed" was reinforced in the visual narrative of postcards, photo albums, newsprint, *National Geographic* magazine, and other publications. The vast archive of early photographs by outsiders to the African continent often created strong dichotomies between naked vs. clothed, and connections to nature vs. industry, thus reinforcing false constructions of Africans as "primitive."

In his journal, Webb presented his anticipated idea of Africa, sometimes finding it challenged by the realities of the continent. At his first sight of land, he questioned what he was seeing: "We have reached the West African coast at Cape Verde and a few minutes later the red tiled rooves [sic] of Dakar, like a huge mosaic, and looking to my unpracticed eye, extremely unAfrican like."[6] He searched for a certain "Africanness" throughout his trip and described finding it in Togoland (Togo) and Tanganyika (Tanzania) more than in other countries. His own definition of what made up this greater "Africanness" is elusive, but in his journals and letters, the characteristics seem to hinge on cultural traditionalism and his experience of urban and rural environments different from those in the United States. He measured the countries by his own meter and found them either meeting or falling short of his expectations of what an African country *should* be. Webb wrote of his disappointment in Southern Rhodesia (Zimbabwe), finding it perhaps too close to American life to be "African." He suggested that "Salisbury is not anything like any picture of Africa I had ever imagined,"[7] and compared the city in letters and his journal to Topeka and Omaha: "The building boom, the wide streets, energetic crowds, the brand new architecture mixed with the fairly new, the number of cars and the variety of shops would seem about like Topeka, Kansas."[8] The closer the visuals and experience were to what Webb was accustomed to in the United States, the farther from his constructed idea of "Africa." He wrote to Lucille from Tanga, Tanganyika on July 17, 1958: "I have been enjoying Tanganyika—it is more as I think Africa should be.... Togo and Tanganyika are the best Africa so far. I had a hunch it would be like that."[9] But what was it about Togo and Tanganyika that he found more "African"? He never fully defined what made them "the best Africa," but he highlighted the ways that Togo "had the best music and sense of life that I have run into"[10] and inferred that "modern" aspects were more "unAfrican."

How was Webb's understanding of the continent informed by what he had been exposed to throughout his life? What were the dominant visual and written narratives in news media and magazines? As Okwui Enwezor and Octavio Zaya have suggested: "No medium has been more instrumental in creating a great deal of the visual fictions of the African continent than photography."[11] The image archive available to Webb, which included photographs of individuals in traditional clothing positioned as "noble savages," exoticized images of village settings, and constructions of false dichotomies positioning outsiders, colonial individuals, or missionaries as higher on an evolutionary scale, framed the continent in light of difference and foreignness.[12] As Enwezor has stated: "The manner in which photography frames the African body makes the body appear peculiarly defamiliarized.... To survey these photographic images—in newspapers, on television, in film documentaries and magazines—is to encounter an atlas of disorder."[13]

Countering the notion of "disorder," the UN mandate to photograph modernization in the countries presented visuals of an "ordered" Africa; Webb took very few photos that fall into the conventional image-narrative of a "primitive" continent. While documenting the registration of voters leading up to the Togoland election on April 27, 1958, he traveled to rural areas outside of the capital Lomé. In an April 21 journal entry, he described driving to Sokodé "on a single-track dirt road through gently rising and changing country...getting into higher country—passing through thick jungle and frequently through small primitive villages—the houses of mud with thatched conical roofs."[14] He took several photographs of women standing outside a family compound. In one photo, three women from the Batammaliba culture stand by a dwelling, wearing skirts with breasts exposed, conforming to the traditional attire of the time (see p. 47). The woman in front, who appears to be the matriarch, gestures an arm toward the other two women, one holding a baby, standing next to a toddler and teenager. Images showing exposed breasts reinforced the idea of Africa as less developed or more "primitive" in the dominant imagination of the geographic North, a narrative that was emphasized in *National Geographic* and other journals. Yet this type of image is unique among the photographs Webb took during his travels. He was not on the continent to reinforce a photographic understanding of Africa as "undeveloped," but instead to help the UN promote a notion of the continent as shifting and modernizing.

1958 was a moment of change in many of the countries Webb visited, especially in Togoland, where the election he photographed was a turning point toward the country gaining its independence from France only two years later. Three of the countries on Webb's agenda were trust territories of the UN Trusteeship Council: Togoland, Tanganyika, and Italian Somaliland. The Trusteeship Council was founded in 1945: "to promote the political,

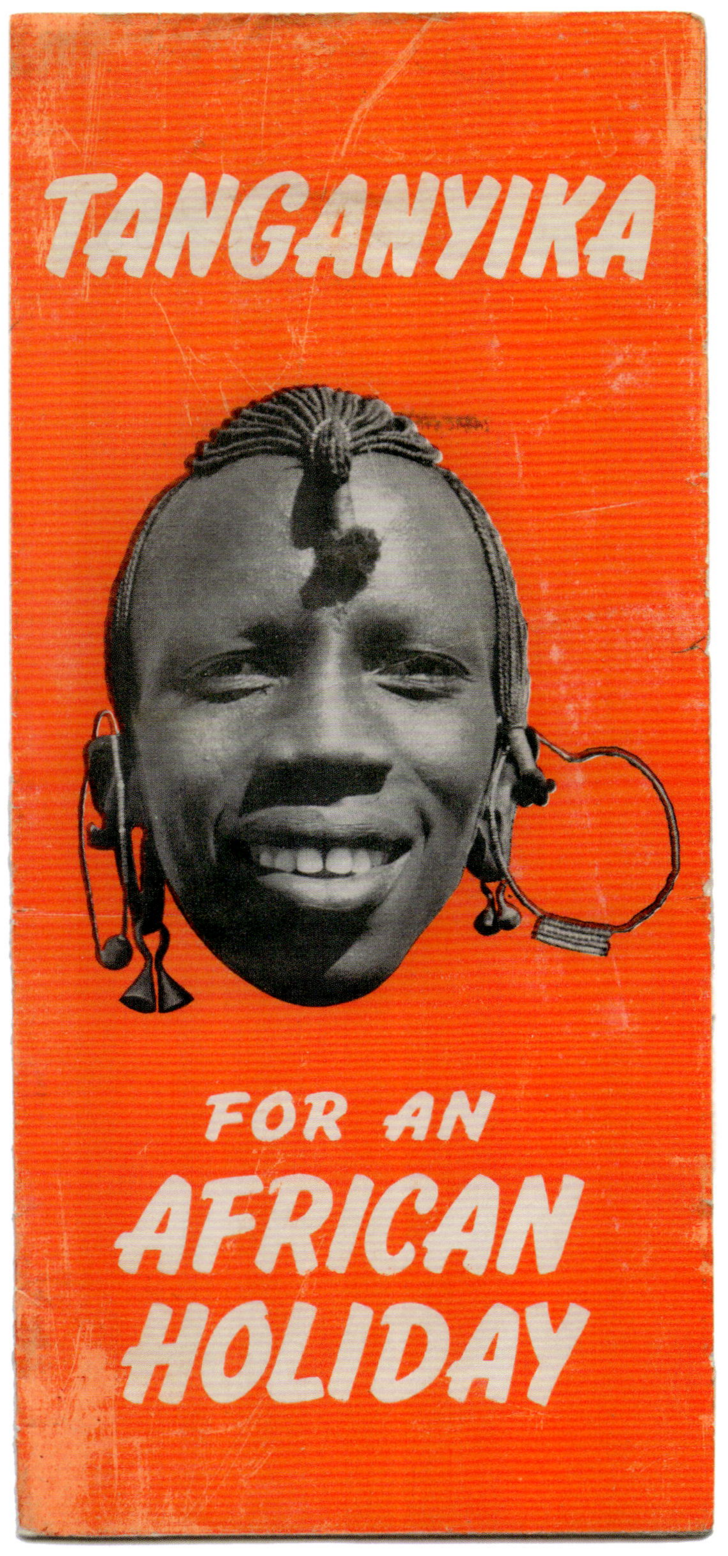

Brochure cover, "Tanganyika for an African Holiday," Tanganyika (Tanzania), *c.* 1958

economic, social and educational advancement of the inhabitants of the Trust Territories and their progressive development towards self-government and independence."[15] The UN played a role in supporting not only the trust territories in the Trusteeship Council, but many African nations in their move toward independence.[16] Webb's trip directly preceded the UN's designation of the 1960s as the "decade of development," which led to many African countries becoming independent nations.[17] Ghana had achieved its independence from Great Britain in 1957, and the Trust Territory of Somaliland and Togoland followed soon after in 1960, with Tanganyika in 1961, Zanzibar and Kenya in 1963, Northern Rhodesia (Zambia) in 1964, and much later, Southern Rhodesia in 1980. The UN had a vested interest in understanding the colonial dynamics at play in Africa and documenting the economic realities of the countries at a time of industrial expansion, all of which Webb attempted to capture through his images.

But Webb's own understanding of the continent complicated his depiction of the countries. At times the "myth" of Africa was reinforced during Webb's travels through encounters with expatriates and colonial officials, including some Americans he met in Tanganyika, who he said had "seen and been taken in by too many Hollywood films," romanticizing the continent.[18] This "myth" was even emphasized through the visual imagery of a brochure Webb picked up in Tanganyika, featuring the disembodied, smiling head of a Maasai *ilmoran* (warrior) with traditional hair braiding and beaded and metal earrings on a bright, orange-red background, with the words "Tanganyika for an African Holiday." The pamphlet reinforces the notion of cultural tourism, exoticizing the *ilmoran*'s plaited hair, the large beaded hoops pierced through the top of the ear and visibly stretched left ear hole, and claiming the smiling head as a main feature of a Tanganyikan holiday. This was perhaps part of what Webb believed he would find on the African continent, an essence of what he described in his journal as the "Africanness" of Togoland and Tanganyika, and a large part of what those traveling to the country would have anticipated when reading such a brochure.[19]

The majority of the images Webb took in Africa contradict this primitivizing narrative, partially because of his UN mandate to tell the story of industry and technology. The photographs were published by the UN Office of Public Information in a brochure "United Nations Photos, Supplement, No. 7" to document the "changing face of Africa" (see pp. 244–45). The brochure highlighted a dichotomy between what the UN described as a modernizing Africa and what they suggested had come before—thatched housing and ox-tilled farms:

> Across the whole continent of Africa vast changes are taking place—multi-storey buildings rise where before nothing but the thatch of an African village broke the long sweep of the golden veld—new cities, expanding industry and mining are powered from the harnessing of its mighty rivers—scientific, large-scale agriculture is taking over from the ox-drawn plough. The people of Africa are increasingly represented in the councils of the United Nations as more nations emerge from tutelage, and from UN Trusteeship. The UN Economic Commission from Africa provides a focal point for the expression of their economic needs.[20]

The dichotomies set up a clear "before and after" vision of primitive/modern, rural/urban, and traditional/industrial, with the brochure's written narrative supported by the photographs' focus on modernization. With only a few exceptions, Webb's images in the UN brochure, including a Tanganyikan surveyor, construction of a large-scale dam and city buildings, the shipping industry, and mining and factory operations, all contradict the conventional 1950s narrative of the African continent. Although four out of the thirty images inexplicably illustrate 1950s stereotypes of Africa—including photographs of lions, a woman sitting and winnowing grain, a Rift Valley landscape from Kenya, and a goat herder—the majority of Webb's photographs affirm the visual story of a "changing" Africa, reinforcing the UN's dichotomized narrative. A photograph of a shiny, new hydroelectric power station at Pangani Falls in Tanganyika is emblematic of the ways that Webb aestheticized modernity through his images (see p. 199). The bright silver frames supporting the conductors and voltage transformers rest atop white cement platforms on a pristine green lawn, presenting a sense of order and highlighting the sleek, cutting-edge newness of the space. This is not the exoticized Africa presented in such publications as *National Geographic*, but rather a different story—one of gleaming power transfer stations and the promise of an electrical grid spreading across the entire country. Another image presents a group of men working on a Somali oil rig (see p. 49). With a close focus on the central activity of five Black men winding chain around the metal pipe of the rig, while two white men watch in the background, the image displays the industrialization rarely seen in exoticized images of the continent. Webb captures the intensity of the activity and also, more subtly, the racial disparity between the white men overseeing the work and the Black men actively securing the chain and pipe. Images such as this reinforced the UN's narrative of a "changing" Africa while also presenting the racial and economic inequities persisting in the countries in 1958. They may even have offered a newly romantic vision of "modern" Africa, according to the standards of the UN.

While Webb's (and the UN's) focus on industry may have countered the visual expectations of the geographic North, Todd Webb was not the first by far to photograph such a narrative of the continent. From the development of the photographic medium in 1839, visuals of Africa have been presented both by outsiders looking in and by Africans imaging their versions of daily life.[21] Other Americans also photographed the African continent in non-exoticizing ways, as in the work of Moneta J. Sleet, Jr., a staff photographer for *Ebony* magazine, who traveled with Vice President Richard Nixon to document his 1957 trip to Liberia, Libya, Sudan, and Ghana, taking memorable images of Kwame Nkrumah at the country's Independence celebrations.[22] Early photo studios opened in many coastal cities, with African photographers such as George S. A. Da Costa, E. C. Dias, Francis W. Joaque, J. P. Decker, and the Lutterodt family, to name but a few, traveling to rural areas as itinerant photographers and producing studio portraits that in many ways replicated styles popular at the time in the geographic North.[23] These image-makers documented and celebrated life, providing a lens deeply distinct from the harmful racist misrepresentations and primitivizing images taken by missionaries, colonial administrators, traders, and expatriates.[24]

James Barnor's portrait of Evelyn Abbew, Sackey Mensah, and a friend, set against a painted cloudy sky at his Ever Young Photographic Studio in Accra, Ghana demonstrates the agency and flair of young Ghanaians in the 1950s (see p. 83). This group of friends having their portrait taken together presents a certain lightheartedness, even joy on a day in Accra, suggesting the hopefulness of youth at this moment in time.[25] The early 1950s photographers affiliated with the African magazine *Drum* also countered exoticizing narratives with their images describing the beat of everyday life in their countries.[26] Stories and images in *Drum* reinforced the vibrancy of daily life in many of the countries, and created a feeling of hope, as Okwui Enwezor suggested of the original *Drum* magazine in South Africa: "Brilliant, gorgeous, fabulous: these were the qualities used by many South Africans in the townships in the 1950s to define the substance of their lives, the peak of their coming to voice."[27] The images of cosmopolitan daily life published in *Drum* nurtured and even popularized this growing ideology through the magazine's "keen insight into Africa's popular culture, contemporary life, and emergent sense of modernity," according to Enwezor.[28] It is important to note here that *Drum* published these images of Africa *for* Africans, while Todd Webb's images were specifically focused on a United Nations audience through their final printing in a black and white brochure. While Webb's commissioned images did indeed, for the most part, counter the existing narratives of the continent, they did so for an audience specifically in the geographic North.

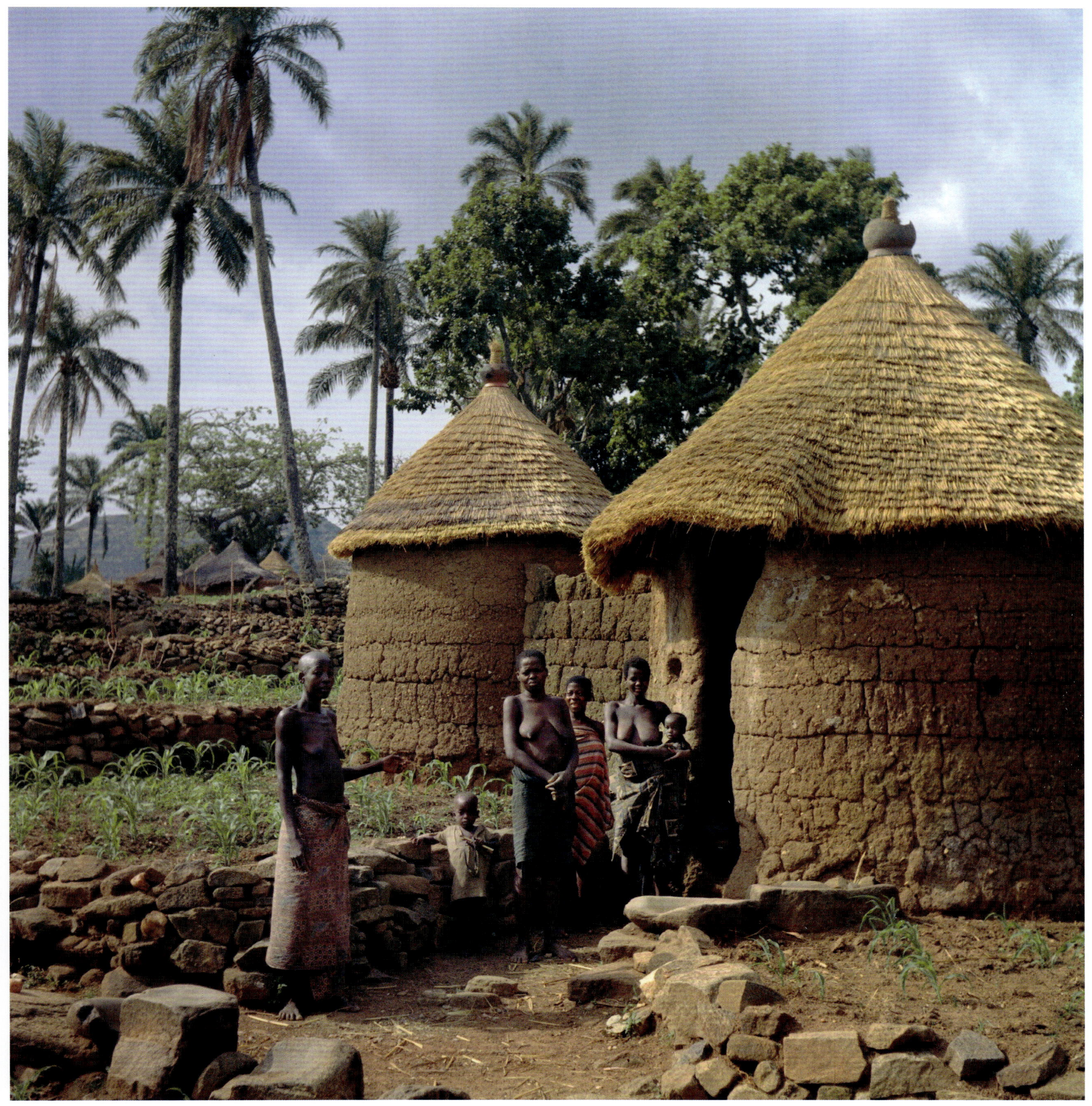

Todd Webb, *Untitled* (44UN-7906-038), Togoland (Togo), 1958
Batammaliba women and children outside their dwelling.

After he returned from Africa, Webb hoped to publish a book of the color photographs with his edited journal of the five-month trip included as text.[29] But he wrote in April 1960 that he was giving up on his dream of the "Africa" book because he could not find a publisher who was open to the unexpected images of industry and modernization: "The African book is off as a picture book—too expensive and limited by its interest in economics. I think they are wrong—I have an idea that they want a picture book full of Watusi [sic], Pigmys [sic], Ma[a]sai, Lions and women with exposed breasts."[30] Webb understood the larger context of what an American publisher wanted to show of Africa—an exoticized and primitivizing lens focused on cultural difference, part of what had perhaps informed his initial constructions of the continent. But this was oppositional to how the UN wanted to frame the countries Webb visited. Webb's images of the continent helped the UN construct and illustrate their story of a "changing Africa" at the decisive juncture between colonialism and independence in many of the nations. The images, aestheticizing modernization and industry, not only contradicted the 1950s "idea" of Africa, including Webb's own preconceived notions, they also reflected the work of a photographer negotiating multiple narratives during a critical moment in African history. It is ironic that while Webb followed his assignment to document "modernity" at the cusp of postcoloniality, he fell into the trap of defining what was "African" and "unAfrican" based on a dichotomy between his own constructions of the "modern" and so-called "traditional." In many ways, the photographs counter Webb's own early perceptions of the continent.

Today the images tell many stories. They provide insight into this pivotal moment of history in 1958 and exist as important visual documents of the UN's desire to shift dominant narratives of how Africa was perceived. They also highlight Todd Webb's subjectivities, and in many ways, how his understanding of the continent evolved through his visual journey. Above all, the photographs are a reminder of the complicated, multi-dimensional power of the visual to create or destroy the "inventions" of Africa in the imagination.

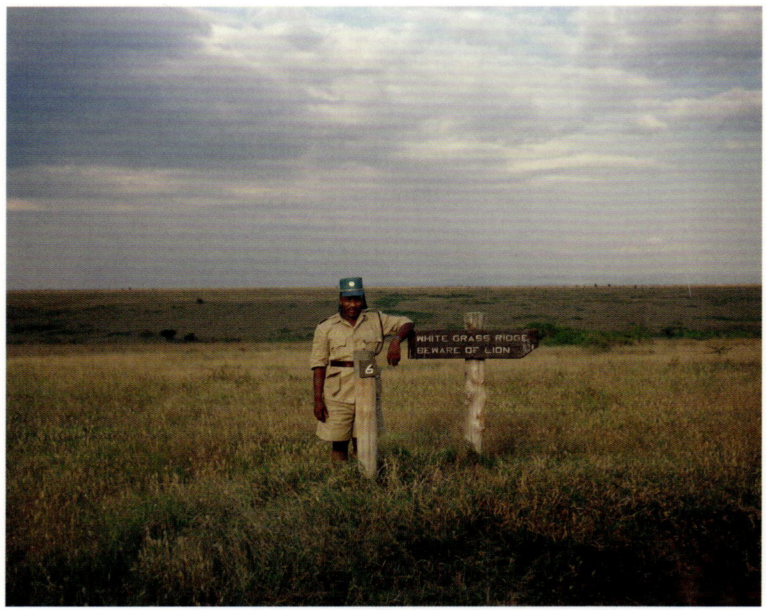

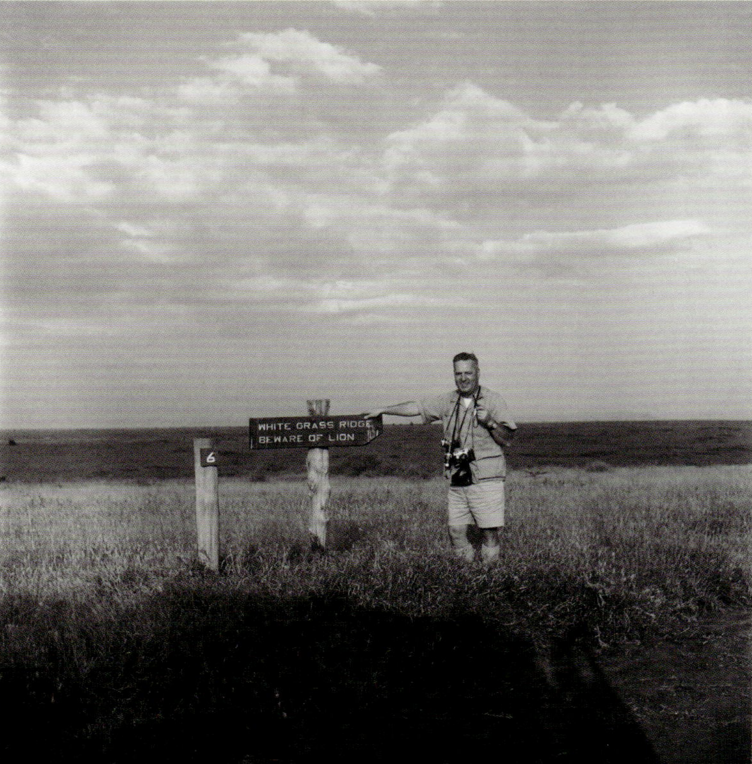

Top: Todd Webb, *Untitled* (44UN-7937-320), Kenya, 1958
Joseph (Nairobi National Park Ranger) standing next to "Beware of Lion" sign, White Grass Ridge, near Nairobi National Park.

Above: Unknown photographer (possibly a Nairobi National Park Ranger), *Untitled* (44UN-7705-622), Kenya, 1958
Todd Webb standing next to "Beware of Lion" sign, White Grass Ridge, near Nairobi National Park.

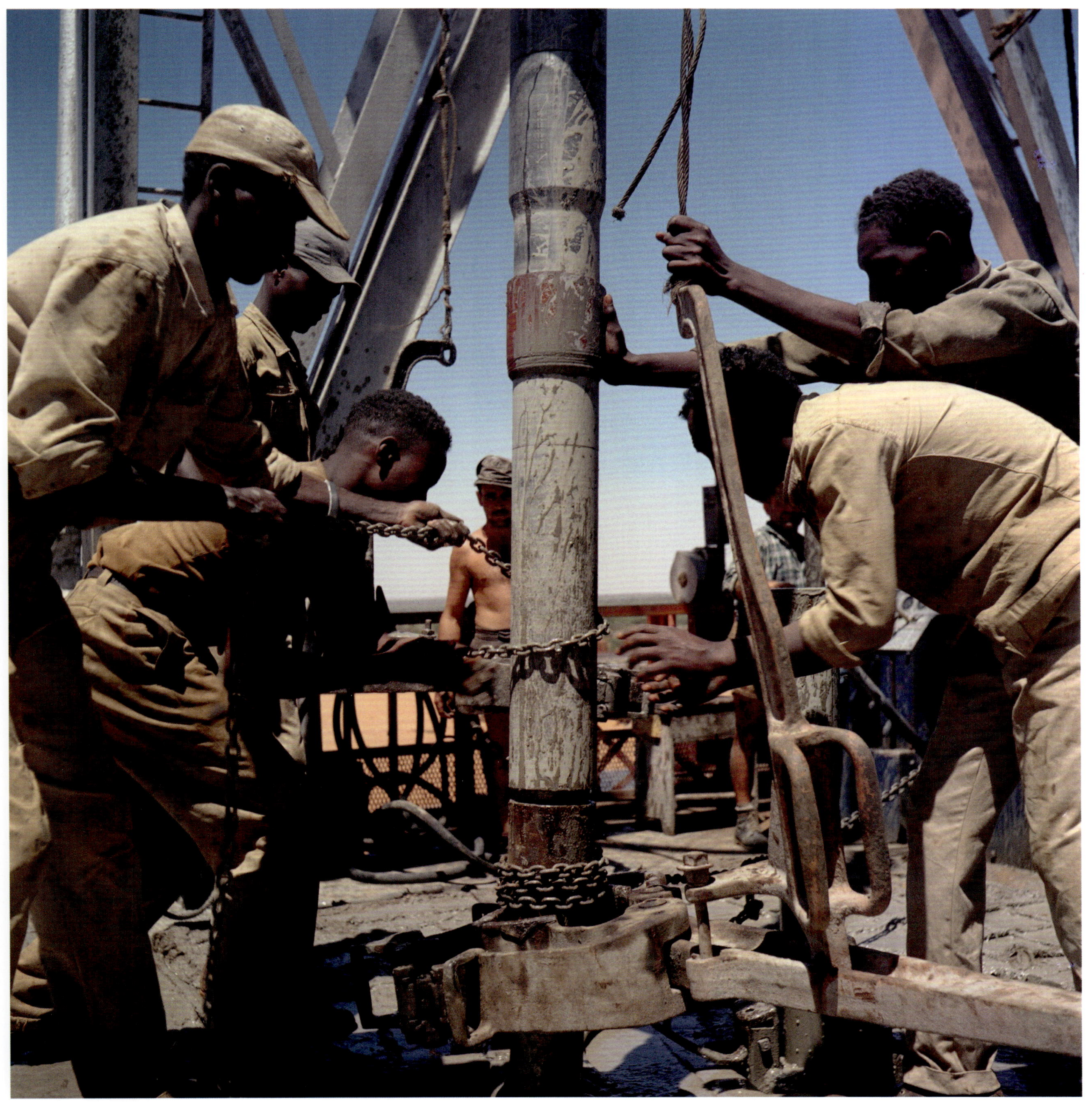

Todd Webb, *Untitled* (44UN-7920-283), Trust Territory of Somaliland (Somalia), 1958
Men working on an oil rig.

Eyewitnesses to History: African Professional Photographers in Togo and Ghana, 1880–1960

Christraud M. Geary

The year was 1925. His Royal Highness The Prince of Wales, Prince Edward, visited the Gold Coast Colony, now Ghana, from April 12 to 16, while en route to South Africa. During his brief stay, he appeared at a few official ceremonies, among them one on the polo grounds in Accra, where several African kings were presented to him. To this day, there are vivid memories of this "first ever [...] visit to our part of the world by a royalty of that stature," according to a 2018 account in *ModernGhana*.[1] Photographers and filmmakers documented the momentous event, and one photograph by an unidentified image-maker later appeared on a popular postcard (see opposite, top). Besides colonial officials and a large crowd of spectators, one notices a photographer or filmmaker with a camera on a tripod to the right of the picture. It is unknown whether either the photographer taking the shot or the one depicted in it were European or local African practitioners, but this picture attests to the active presence of image-makers on the continent by the 1920s.

Photography already had a long history on West Africa's Atlantic shores when, in 1958, the American photographer Todd Webb arrived in Togoland (Togo) and Ghana to begin his assignment for the United Nations. He may have been unaware of the scope of photographic production in the region, both by image-makers of many backgrounds who had worked there for decades before him, and by others who were active while he visited. Since the mid-nineteenth and well into the twentieth century, amateur photographers from Europe and North America, among them missionaries, ethnologists, and members of colonial administrations, had pursued their passion along the West African coasts. Throughout the time of imperial expansion and colonial consolidation, and well into the twentieth century, several professional practitioners from the geographic North also began to operate studios and photographic businesses in growing urban centers along the African coastline, and later in inland regions in today's neighboring countries of Côte d'Ivoire, Ghana, Togo, and Bénin, which share complex colonial pasts. These photographers kept up with rapid developments in photographic technology, from cumbersome cameras on tripods to hand-held ones, and from glass plates to roll film and finally color, introduced in the 1930s. At times, foreign professional photographers arrived for short-term assignments like Webb's, or for longer stays and return visits to carry out personal photographic projects. All of them depicted political, societal, economic, and infrastructural transformations, besides training their cameras on the peoples of West Africa. A few of their pictures circulated widely in print, and many more have found their way into archives, other repositories, and private collections around the globe.

In the last decades of the nineteenth century, some Africans, multilingual, educated in missionary schools, and mostly from privileged backgrounds among the large African populace, also took up photography as their profession. Some of these photographers enjoyed long careers marked by constant movement and crossed colonial borders along the West African coastline in search of clients and economic opportunity. They, too, kept up with the changes in photographic techniques and materials, although unlike practitioners from the geographic North they often did not have the means or access to the latest equipment and had to improvise.

This essay presents observations about the documentary work of several African professionals active at different times, chosen from among the many who could have been included. Their pictures remind us that they, too, contributed to the large visual archive of the momentous changes that gripped this region in the second half of the nineteenth and throughout the twentieth century. Pictures by these accomplished, technically savvy photographers appeared in early print publications, in books, on picture postcards, and in newspapers and illustrated magazines, as did images by expatriate practitioners. By the mid-twentieth century, towards the end of the colonial era and at the beginning of the postcolonial, picture agencies and information services in soon-to-be-independent African nations also began to distribute their photographs to worldwide audiences.

The oeuvre of these and other African photographers only gained recognition around the 1970s, when researchers in the fields of visual culture and art history, some of them photographers in their own right, began to focus on the practices of African professionals in the business. They visited local studios, documented their history and output, and interviewed practitioners who were active or had retired after long careers. In an archival turn, researchers also unearthed neglected holdings of pictures by these African image-makers in repositories and private collections in Europe, North America, and on the African continent.[2]

How peoples in the region adapted to the presence of photographers and dealt with image objects such as photographic prints on paper has been another focus of recent studies. Since the earliest days, residents in coastal towns, for example in Lomé, the capital of Togo, and Accra, the capital of Ghana, embraced two-dimensional pictures, in particular portraits, and integrated them into their everyday lives. Traditional rulers and high-ranking men and women in ancient kingdoms soon mustered the power of images for self-fashioning and furthering their own political agendas, both during European imperial expansion and in the colonial state. By the late nineteenth century, portraits of rulers by foreign and indigenous image-makers appeared in palaces, where they can be found to this day—for instance in the palace of Nene Sakite II, Konor of the Manya Krobo Kingdom, located in its capital Odumase in the south-eastern region of Ghana (see p. 52).[3] Such portraits also traveled to European metropoles and circulated in print.

Other African customers belonged to a growing elite, among them western-style educated businessmen, including the photographers themselves, or those who held positions in colonial administrations and the military. These local patrons posed for their likenesses in studios and outside settings and displayed the pictures in the parlors of their homes and in family albums. They exchanged and mailed them to family and friends in other parts of the continent and abroad, at times to former residents of the colonies who had returned to Europe. One such photograph, a silver gelatin print on postcard stock dated September 1931, shows a group of six men in Sokodé, a multi-ethnic commercial center in central Togoland (see opposite, bottom). The men, proudly dressed in locally tailored European-style attire, pose confidently and look at the camera, thus asserting their agency in this photographic encounter.[4] They may have belonged to the growing number of indigenous merchants and their employees, or they might have been in the service of the French colonial businessman Marcel Lefranc of Paris. The inscription on the back reads: "Sokodé, Lundi 7-9-31. Souvenir de votre ami Africain qui dans la photo est assis sur la chaise" [A souvenir from your African friend, who in this photograph sits on the chair]. There is an illegible signature, and "(Sokodé, Monday, September 9, 1931)." Portraits such as this, and others taken inside studios, constituted a major part of African professional practitioners' business. Ghanaian photographer James Barnor, whose pictures appear in this book, remarked in a recent conversation with Aimée Bessire (see pp. 82–91) that in his opinion photographs of "people are more important than

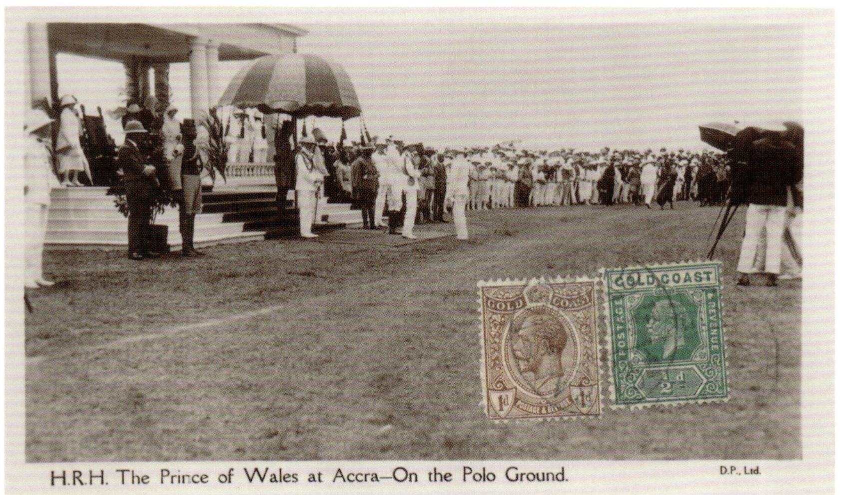

Left: Unidentified photographer, *H.R.H. The Prince of Wales at Accra–On the Polo Ground*, April 1925
Photographic postcard, dated February 20, 1926; published by D.P. Ltd

Below: Unidentified African photographer (possibly Alex Agbaglo Acolatse), *Portrait of six men in Sokodé* (back and front), Togo, 1931
Silver gelatin print on postcard stock

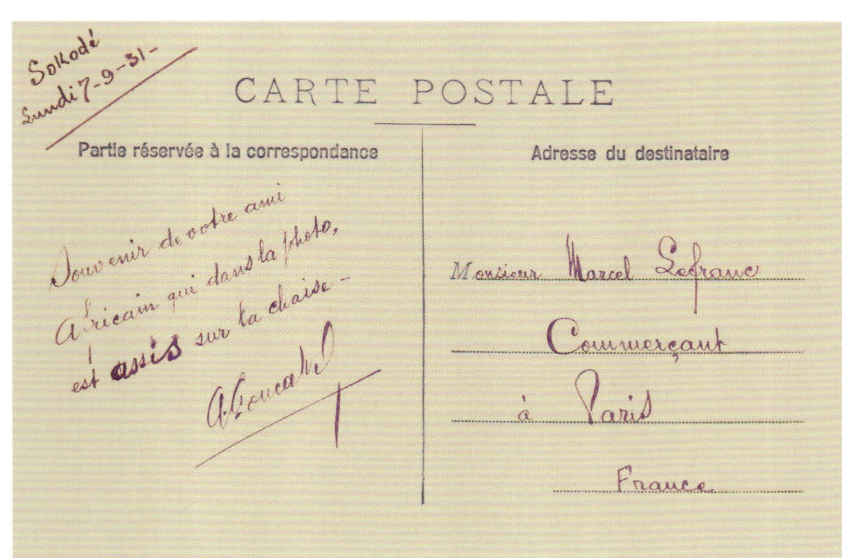

Sokodé
Lundi 7-9-31-

CARTE POSTALE

Partie réservée à la correspondance

Souvenir de votre ami
Africain qui dans la photo,
est assis sur la chaise -

Adresse du destinataire

Monsieur Marcel Lefranc
Commerçant
à Paris
France

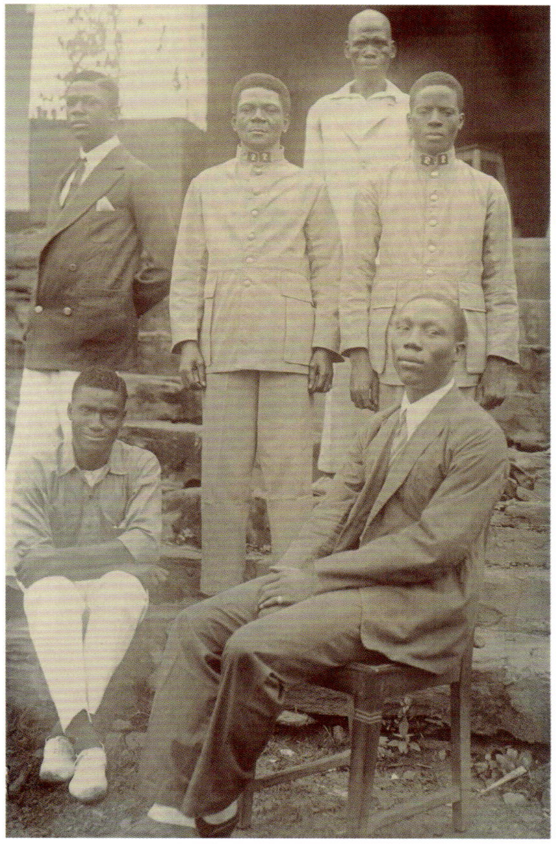

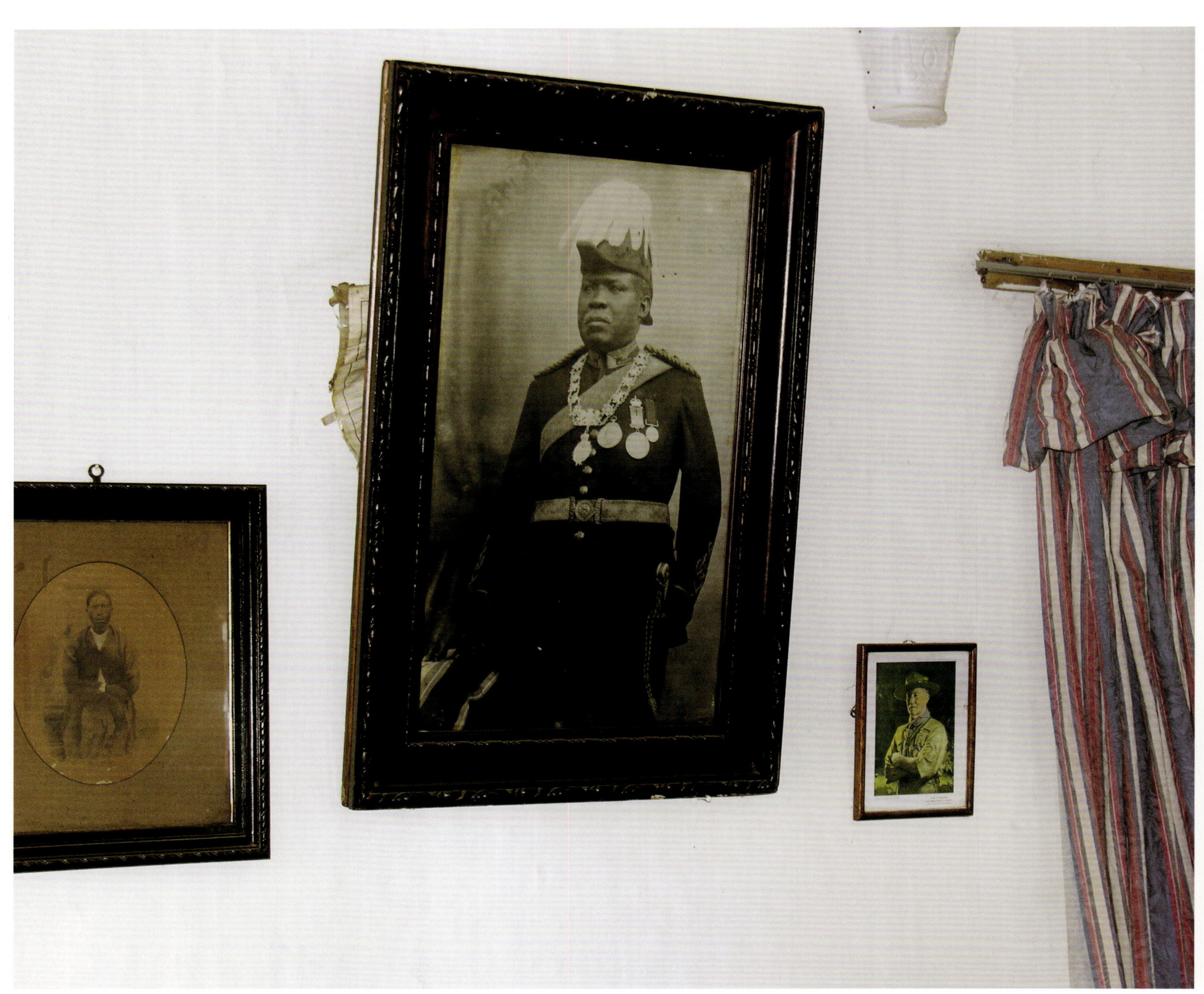

Early twentieth-century portrait of King Emmanuel Mate Kole I in the palace of Nene Sakite II,
Konor of Manya Krobo Kingdom, Odumase, Ghana, 2005

places."[5] But let us turn now to the photographers' other tasks, among them the documentation of the changing world around them.

Togo in Focus

Todd Webb arrived at the first stop on his African journey, Lomé, the capital of then-French Togoland, on April 16, 1958, a few days before the UN-supervised elections on April 27. Webb depicted elating moments during the final days of the election, and the celebrations–such as a festive parade of women–that followed its successful conclusion, before the winner, Sylvanus Olympio, a member of a prominent Togolese dynasty, became Prime Minister (see p. 54). In keeping with his assignment to document industry, infrastructure, and technology for his United Nations project, he was also drawn to the hustle and bustle of the port, where he depicted the way in which ships' cargo and passengers were unloaded at the time. Webb, along with photographers of all different backgrounds, was fascinated by this process; in the few harbors along the West African Coast, sandbars and lagoons made access to large ships difficult and required the use of surfboats (see related images by Arkhurst, p. 58; Barnor, p. 89; Webb, pp. 22 and 39). When not "on the job," Webb walked the streets of Lomé and took pictures in the manner of his previous work in New York, as an apt street photographer and flâneur who strolled through town and captured the scenes around him. He may have been unaware that his African colleagues had also been doing so for decades, since the introduction of photography.

Togoland was formerly a German colony, and some of the earliest African photographers documented rapid change during these times. One of them was F. F. Olympio, who like his relative Sylvanus, Togo's future president, was a member of the wealthy and influential Afro-Brazilian Olympio family. German printers reproduced some ten of Olympio's images on postcards. His views of Lomé, the capital of Togoland, document the growth of the town and newly constructed government buildings around 1900–2 (top right).[6] In 1922, after the First World War, Great Britain and France divided Togoland in two. The League of Nations awarded France the mandate to rule its eastern part, then French Togoland, now Togo. The western regions of the former colony were placed under British sovereignty, then administered through the Gold Coast, now part of Ghana; but locals, including photographers, continued to cross these new, artificial borders.

One of the major photographers to work in Lomé and beyond was Alex Agbaglo Acolatse (in other spellings Abaglo and Accolatse). Born on June 7, 1880, in Kedzi, German Togoland, today in Ghana's Volta region, he learned his photographic skills from German missionaries and African practitioners, among them Frederick Richard Christian Lutterodt (1871–1937), a photographer and member of a prominent Euro-African family in the Gold Coast who was active in the region.[7] Acolatse moved to Lomé in 1900 and may have acted as an official photographer for the Germans. After the First World War, he established a studio in town, and traveled the coast from Lagos, present-day Nigeria, to Accra, Ghana on photographic journeys. He was known as "Ametala," which means "the man who draws" in the Ewe language. An accomplished photographer and member of the local African elite, he was active in the community, a Freemason, and an eminent member of the Église Évangelique. Acolatse retired from active photography in late 1956 and passed away in Lomé in March 1975, at over ninety years of age. At the time of Webb's visit, Acolatse's family members were still operating his business in Lomé, by then named Ametala after its founder.[8]

Throughout his long career, Acolatse served an extensive clientele, including French colonials and British residents as well as African patrons. Besides portraying local people, he accepted commissions from rulers to photograph them with their entourages, as seen in a picture of an assembly

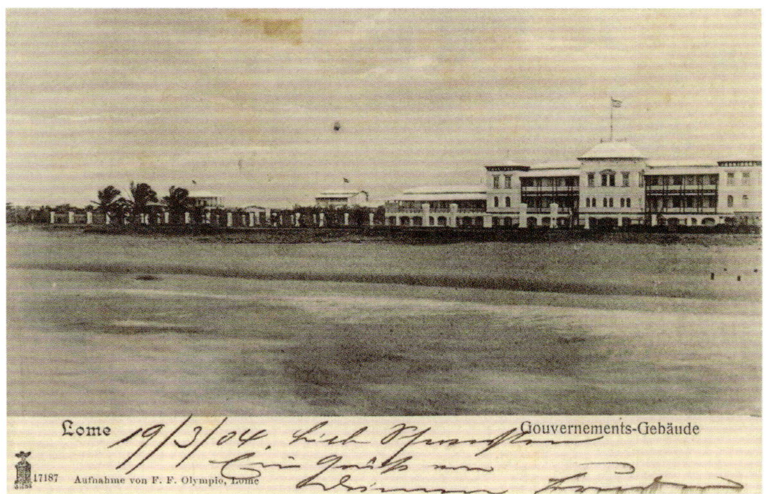

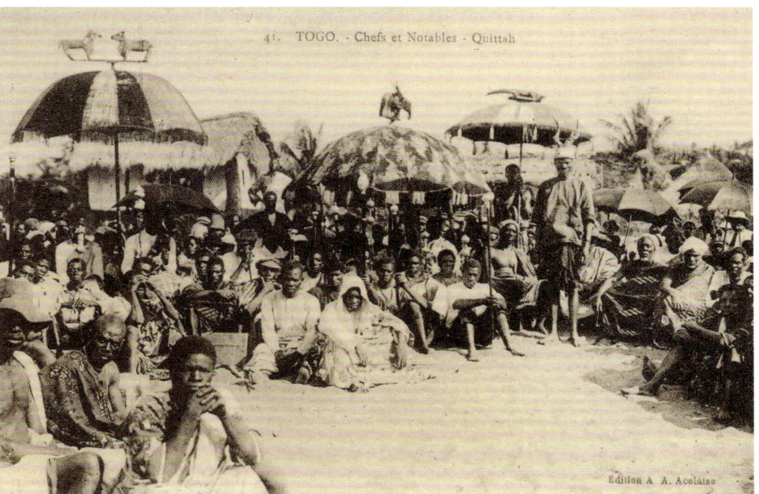

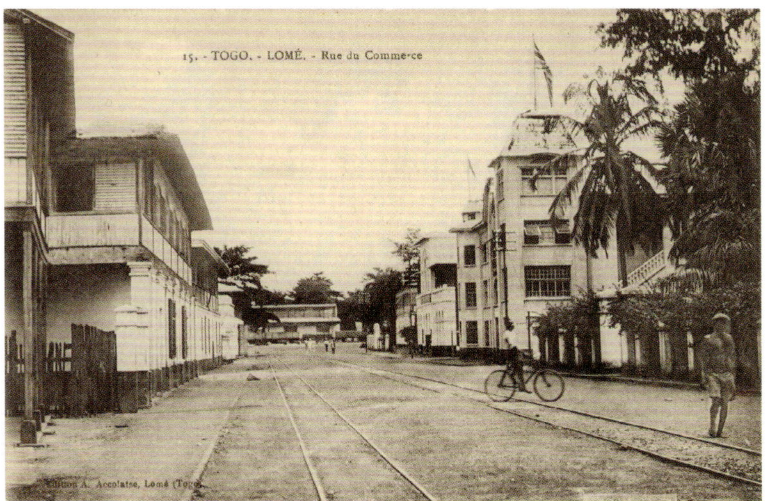

Top: F. F. Olympio, *Lomé Gouvernements-Gebäude* (Lomé Government building), *c.* 1902
Collotype postcard, postmarked March 26, 1904

Center: Alex Agbaglo Acolatse, *41. Togo.–Chefs et Notables.–Quittah* (Chiefs and dignitaries–Keta), *c.* 1920
Collotype postcard, dated April 6, 1929

Above: Alex Agbaglo Acolatse, *15. Togo.–Lomé.–Rue de Commerce*, *c.* 1920
Collotype postcard

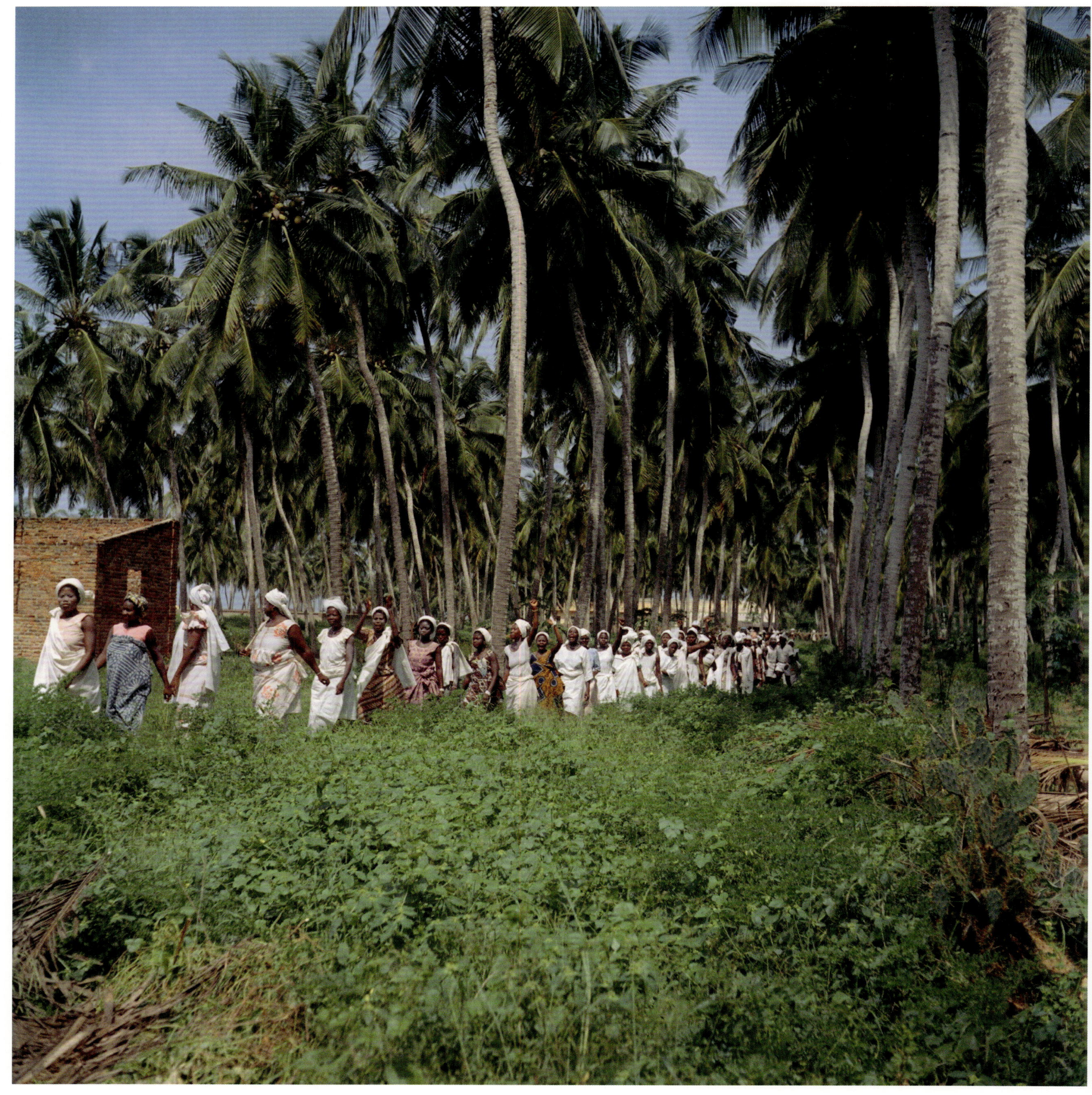

Todd Webb, *Untitled* (44UN-7915-346), Togoland (Togo), 1958
Women walking to vote, election day, April 27, 1958.

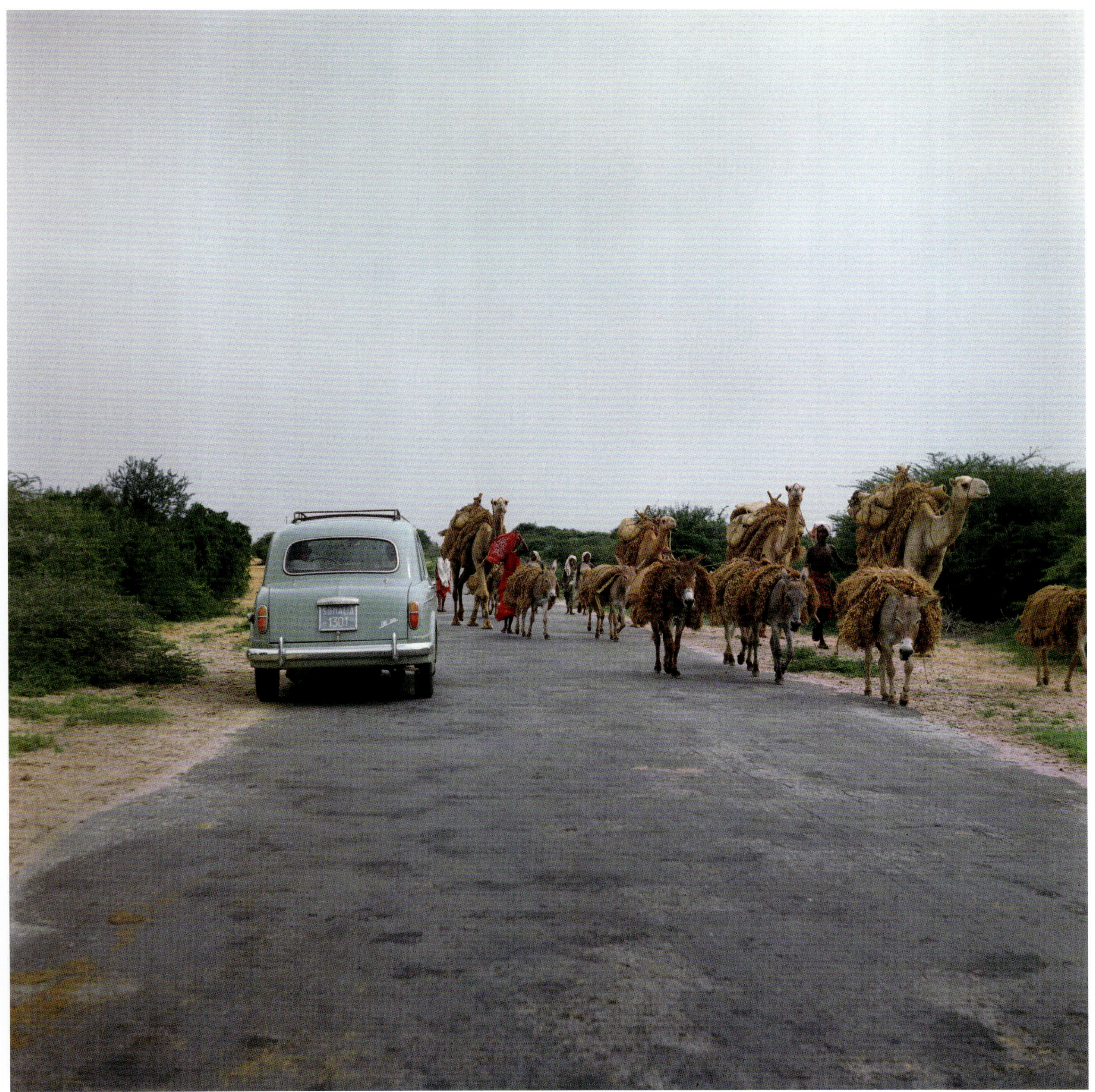

Todd Webb, *Untitled* (44UN-7971-310), Trust Territory of Somaliland (Somalia), 1958
Car with camel and donkey traffic.

of chiefs and noblemen in Keta, now across the Togolese border in Ghana and not far from Acolatse's birthplace (p. 53, center). Viewers may notice the various forms of dress, ranging from traditional to European-style garb, the imported umbrellas used as parasols, and several of the individuals gazing somewhat inquisitively back at the photographer and his camera on a tripod.

Acolatse also documented the growth of Lomé, with its colonial buildings and busy streets. One of his images from the 1920s shows Lomé's main commercial avenue, with rails for a small train that serviced trading companies along the street, such as the British John Holt establishment (see p. 53, bottom). One notices a passer-by, a bicyclist, and pedestrians in the distance. Todd Webb perhaps wandered the same street some forty years later, when the rails were still in place. The Catholic cathedral visible from the harbor at the time Todd Webb visited Lomé (see p. 39) remains a landmark to this day and appears several times in Acolatse's pictures (see right). A strong reporter and documentarian, Acolatse captured the comings and goings at train stations in and around Lomé and at the airfield in Sokodé, where a large crowd of spectators standing off to the right witnessed the arrival of French airplanes (see bottom right). Like Webb, years later and from a different perspective, he was fascinated by various modes of transportation (see p. 55).

On to Ghana

In the ancient port town of Cape Coast, on the Atlantic coast of today's Ghana, photography took hold among African professionals in the second half of the nineteenth century. Photographer Frederick Grant, a member of an Afro-British family, was born around 1850 and grew up in Cape Coast.[9] One of his earliest known photographs, now in the Basel Mission Archive, dates to 1873. Ten years later, on May 12, 1883, Grant, by then in Accra, advertised his services in the *Gold Coast Times*, offering photographic views including landscapes, group pictures, and "types of natives." He also stated that sitters could have their portraits taken in his studio on all workdays.[10] Wealthy local families, European residents, representatives of the colonial government and military, missionaries, and visitors may well have seen this and similar announcements he published over time. Among his contemporaries and competitors were members of the Lutterodt dynasty of photographers, which in later years included the aforementioned Frederick Richard Christian Lutterodt.[11]

Several of Grant's dry-plate photographs appeared as woodcuts and lithographs in contemporary publications. An albumen print mounted on cardboard in the Basel Mission Archives provides a good example of his documentary work (opposite, top). It shows a large English trading post in Accra, with a merchant in a dark jacket, white trousers, and a white hat posing on top of stairs leading to a courtyard, while African employees in locally tailored suits and hats stand on the flat roof behind him. In the yard below one notices wooden barrels of palm oil, a major export from the Gold Coast. Other workers and two women can be seen around the barrels in the foreground, and behind upright ones farther back. The impressive urban landscape of the vibrant harbor town appears in the background. An engraving of this image circulated in one of the publications issued by the local missionary society, and thus reached a wider viewership in German-speaking Europe (opposite, center).

Other African photographers active in the region were also keen observers of the many transformations that impacted local peoples, whether welcome or not. They included William Stephen Johnston, Jacob Vitta, and Frédérick W. H. Arkhurst. All three photographers, like Alex Agbaglo Acolatse, had Gold Coast roots or connections, and belonged to the growing African elite in the colonial state. Similar to their contemporaries and predecessors, they provided services to Europeans and worked within the respective colonial systems, whether they were

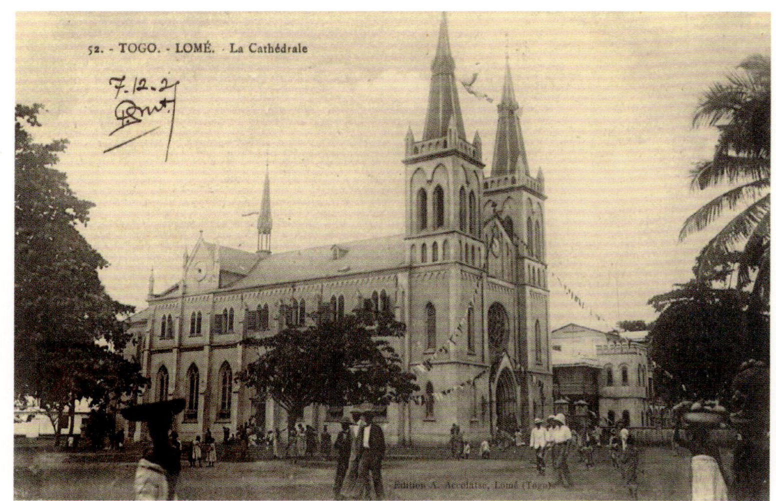

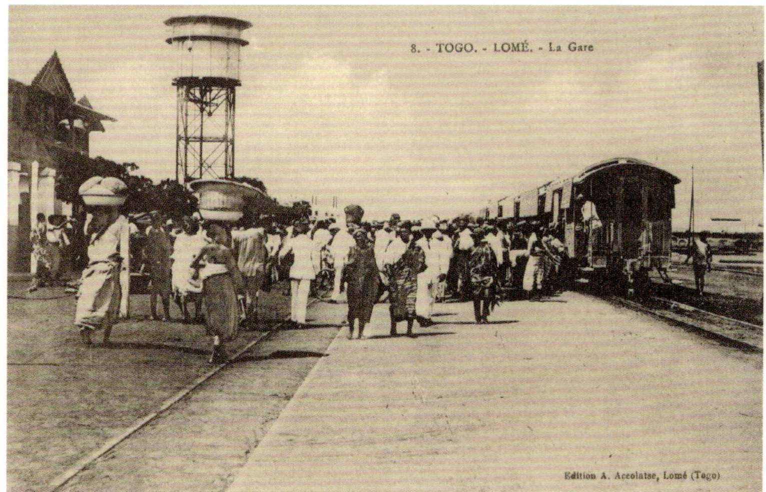

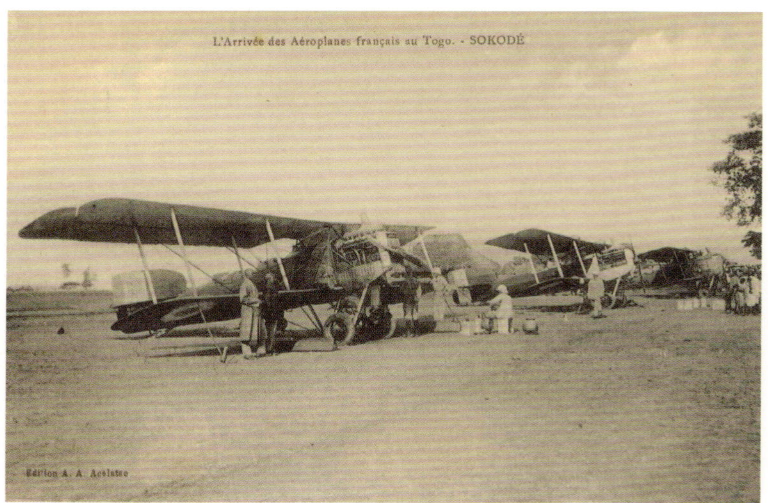

Top: Alex Agbaglo Acolatse, *52. Togo.–Lomé.–La Cathédrale*, c. 1920
Collotype postcard, dated December 7, 1921

Center: Alex Agbaglo Acolatse, *8. Togo.–Lomé.–La Gare* (The train station), c. 1920
Collotype postcard, dated May 22, 1925

Above: Alex Agbaglo Acolatse, *L'Arrivée des Aeroplanes français au Togo.–Sokodé* (Arrival of French airplanes in Togo.–Sokodé), c. 1920
Collotype postcard, dated May 22, 1925

critical of these repressive regimes or not. They had to conduct a business not only for themselves, but also to fulfill obligations to their extended families—and when printing techniques began to allow the reproduction of their pictures in postcard-format, they entered this lucrative market. They sent photographs and at times even glass plates to printers in Europe, who shipped the product back to them and also distributed the cards in their countries and beyond. At times, the photographers' work was appropriated by publishers in Europe without their knowledge or permission.

William Stephen Johnston began his career in the 1880s on the Gold Coast, and in 1893 he opened a successful studio and photographic enterprise in Freetown, Sierra Leone. His sons joined the business by 1900, and he remained active until 1920.[12] Johnston and his sons published numerous postcards, among them several pictures taken in the Gold Coast.[13] One of them depicts infantry soldiers of the Second Battalion of the West India Regiment standing at attention in formation under the watchful eye of British officers in front of Cape Coast Castle (bottom right). Johnston framed it carefully and took it under good light conditions—a prerequisite for a successful image, given the camera equipment at the time.

Jacob Vitta was a photographer and publisher who left a mark with his documentation of the economy and growth of urban spaces. By the 1890s he was working out of Tarkwa, a gold-mining town and major commercial center in western Ghana. Like his contemporaries, he traveled extensively in the Gold Coast Colony, as well as to areas in neighboring Côte d'Ivoire. His prolific postcard output includes hundreds of images and re-issues.[14] Besides portraits of local people, he also published picture postcards of towns, gold mines, and events in the region. Some of these photographs may have been requested by the British companies operating the mines, or by colonial administrators and missionaries. He took others to please his clientele, which included foreign visitors and members of the African elite. His pictures attest to the abilities and impetus of a documentarian, such as a view of the ancient harbor town of Elmina, Ghana, "Photographed and published by J. Vitta, Tarkwa. West Africa" (p. 58, top left). The sender, traveling on the SS *Patani*, a steamship in the fleet of the Elder Dempster Ltd in Liverpool, posted the card from Bonny, Nigeria, on August 22, 1910. Another card renders an animated view of mining operations conducted by the Obuasi Gold Fields Corporation, which exploited the Ashanti Mine in Obuasi, founded in 1897 by Joseph Ellis and Joseph Biney from Cape Coast. One of the richest gold mines in the world, it still exists today.[15]

In neighboring Côte d'Ivoire, Frédérick W. H. Arkhurst, another professional photographer and publisher from the British part of the Gold Coast, left an interesting body of work also preserved on postcards. Born around 1880, he arrived in the French colony by 1900 and ultimately established himself in coastal Grand-Bassam, the first French capital of Côte d'Ivoire. He took evocative studio portraits of local men and women, but besides this practice he also dealt in cocoa and tropical woods, an entrepreneurial background that influenced his selection of motifs. Several picture cards show how mahogany logs were stored on shore before transport across the sandbars to the waiting cargo ships that would bring them to Europe (p. 58, center left).[16] His acumen for documenting the transformation of workplaces and the establishment of infrastructure also appears in another image showing the interior of the railway company's repair shop in Abidjan, which by then had developed into a major urban center, with the first railway line opening in the region in 1905 (p. 58, center right). In this photograph, two French managers pose with and supervise two African workers, one in a white helmet, the other standing in the shadows, next to machinery and equipment on the far right.

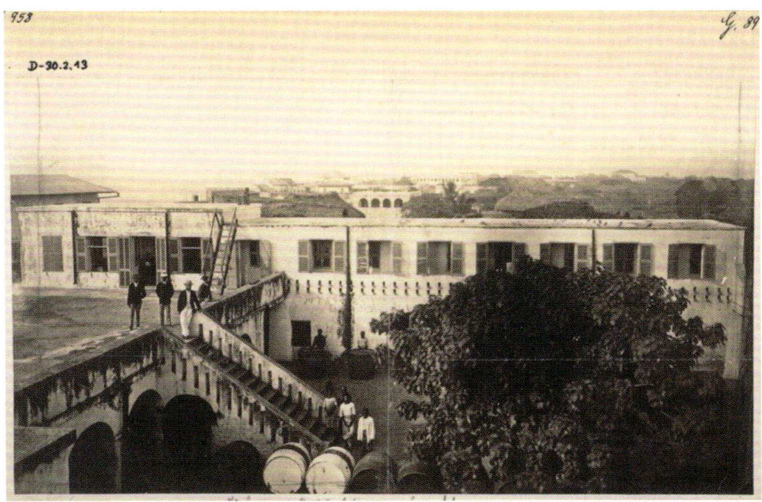

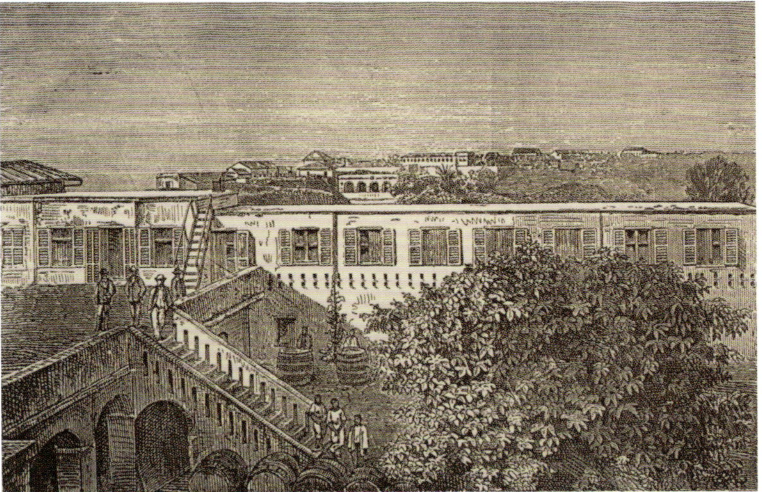

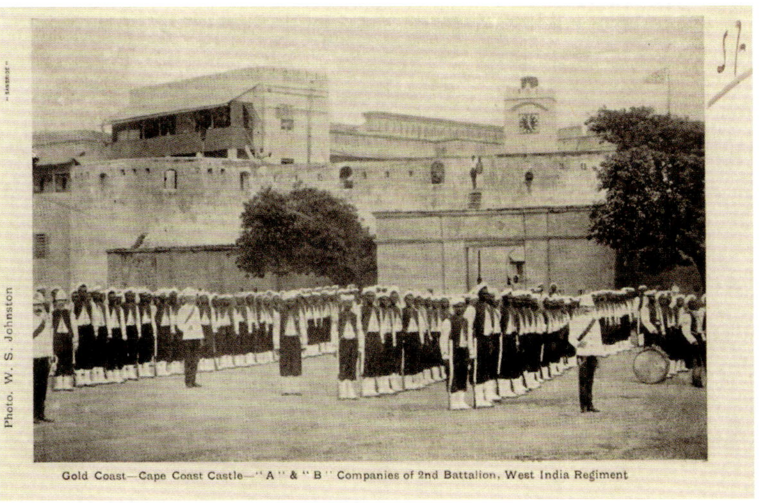

Top: Frederick Grant, *Faktorei in Akkra. Goldk[üste]* (Trading Post in Accra. Gold Coast), 1880s
Albumen print

Center: *Accra Engl[ische]. Faktorei* (Accra, English trading post), *c.* 1885
Print and wood engraving or line block, based on an albumen print by Frederick Grant

Above: W. S. Johnston, *Gold Coast–Cape Coast Castle–"A"&"B" Companies of 2nd Battalion, West India Regiment*, *c.* 1890
Halftone postcard, published *c.* 1902

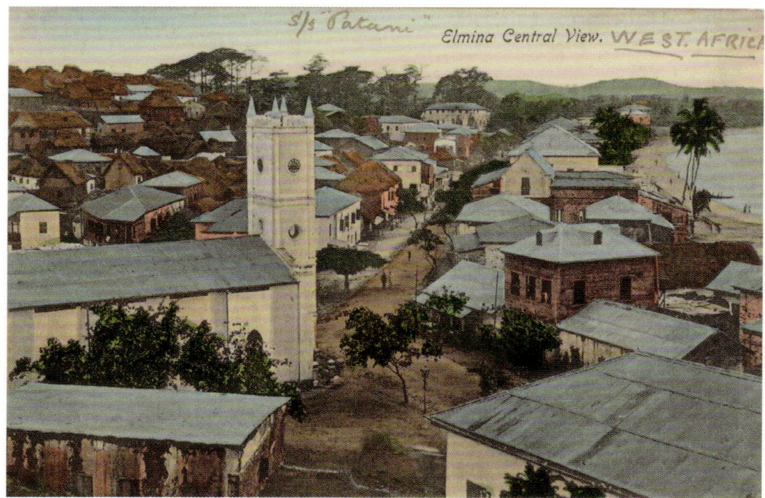

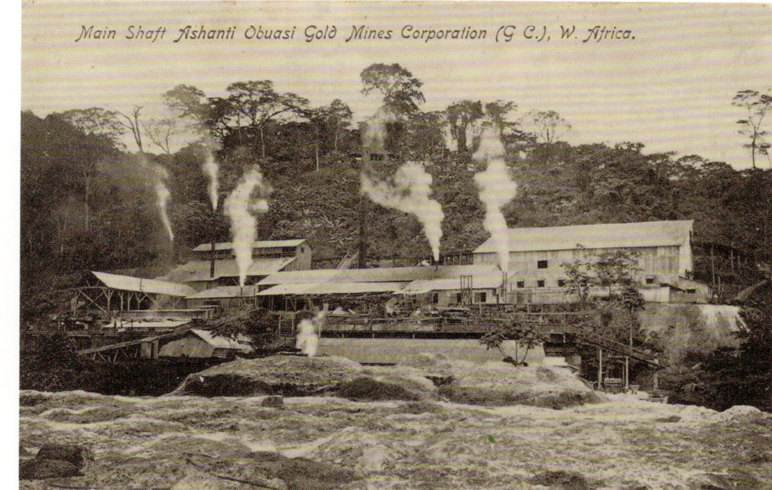

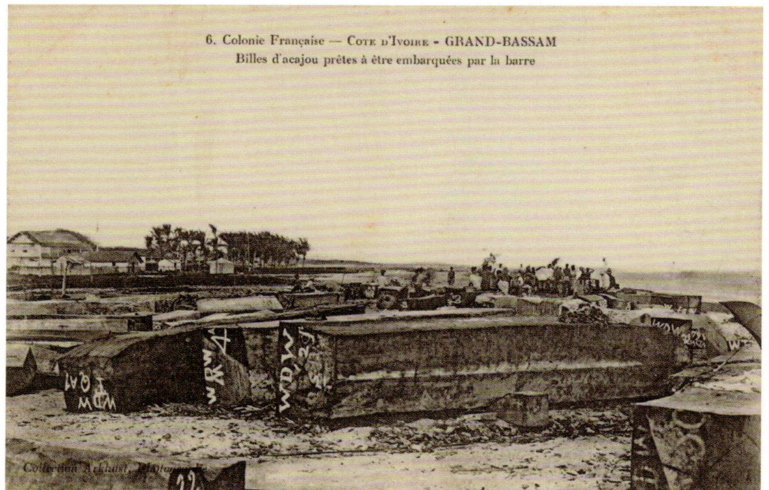

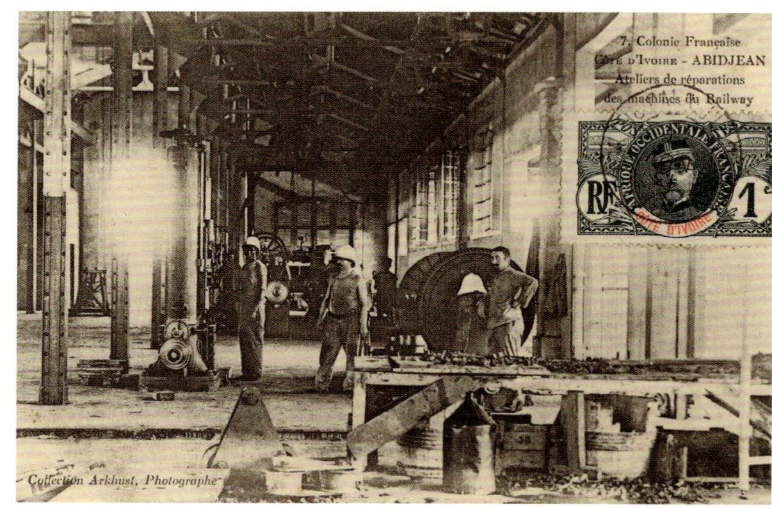

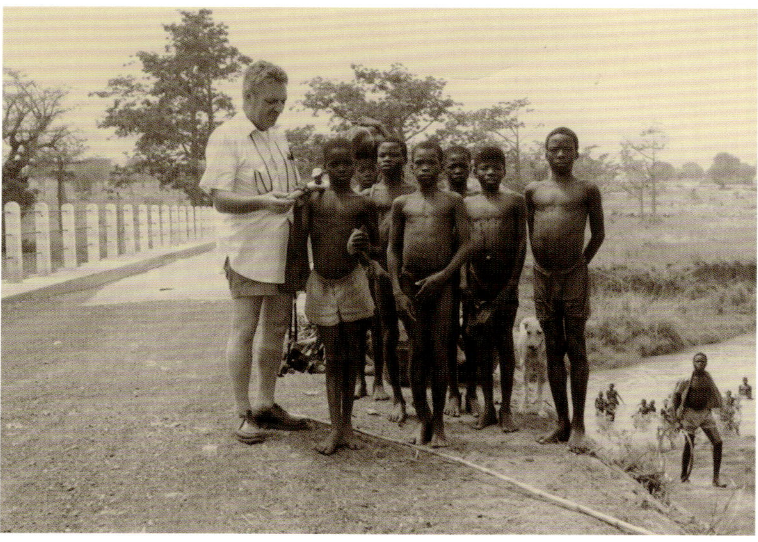

Top left: Jacob Vitta, *Elmina Central View*, c. 1907
Hand-colored postcard, published *c.* 1908

Top right: Jacob Vitta, *Main Shaft Ashanti Obuasi Gold Mines Corporation, G[old]. C[oast]., W. Africa*, c. 1908
Collotype postcard, published *c.* 1910

Above left: Frédérick W. H. Arkhurst, *8. Colonie Française–Cote d'Ivoire* [sic]–*GRAND-BASSAM. Billes d'acajou prêtes à être embarquées par la barre* (Grand-Bassam. Logs of mahogany ready to be shipped across the sand bar), *c.* 1910
Collotype postcard

Above right: Frédérick W. H. Arkhurst, 7. *Colonie Française. Côte d'Ivoire–ABIDJEAN* [sic]. *Ateliers de réparations des machines du Railway* (Abidjan. Repair shop for Railway machinery), *c.* 1910
Collotype postcard

Left: Unknown photographer, *Untitled* (44UN-58-063), Togoland (Togo), 1958
Todd Webb with a group of boys on a roadside in Niamtougou village.

Documentary photography in and around Accra by the mid-twentieth century

When Todd Webb arrived in Accra on May 5, 1958, several African professional practitioners were also active in the city. Just months before, in September 1957, the former British colony of the Gold Coast had gained independence within the British Commonwealth as the Dominion of Ghana, under now-legendary Prime Minister Kwame Nkrumah. Among the image-makers who documented the epic changes of the 1950s were James K. Bruce-Vanderpuije[17] and James Barnor, whose aesthetic visions, as well as some of the scenes they captured on film, echo one another.

A short 1989 essay by Tobias Wendl brought James K. Bruce-Vanderpuije's career and oeuvre to the attention of a wider reader and viewership outside of Ghana and Great Britain. More recently, websites and exhibitions have paid homage to this "master photographer," as his son, Isaac H. Bruce-Vanderpuije, who followed in his father's footsteps, described him in a 2016 interview.[18] Born in Accra in 1899, into one of the foremost families of the Gold Coast, Bruce-Vanderpuije traced his origins back to Jacobus van der Puije, an eighteenth-century administrator for the Dutch West India Company, which had established several trading posts along the Ghanaian coast. Bruce-Vanderpuije attended the Accra Royal School and worked briefly for the municipal administration, but rather than continuing a career as a lawyer, medical doctor, or businessman, which would have brought him greater financial success, he entered a three-year apprenticeship with Bright Davies, a successful African photographer. In 1922, he opened his own studio, named Deo Gratias–Latin for "Thanks [be] to God"–in James Town, the oldest business district in the Accra urban area, next to its first harbor. Besides taking many portraits, initially outside in bright light and then, when electricity arrived, inside his studio, Bruce-Vanderpuije also worked on commissions for local businesses and published picture postcards. According to his son, he was meticulous in the darkroom, processing and retouching black and white pictures of sitters in his studio and elsewhere.

One of Bruce-Vanderpuije's early works of reportage documents the aftermath of a devastating earthquake that hit the Ghanaian coast, including Accra, on June 22, 1939. Twenty-two people died and many had to seek shelter. After the Second World War, his studio and photographic activities in town thrived. He was called upon to document political and other official events, parties of the upper class, weddings, and funerals. By the 1950s, if not earlier, the photographer must have become aware of Modernist and documentary images as they appeared in the newspapers and illustrated magazines from Europe and North America available in the Gold Coast. It is likely that British employees of the nascent Ghana Information Service and its film unit, headed by Roland James Moxon, an administrator with a long career in the Gold Coast, acquainted local practitioners with the work of overseas photographers, whose pictures appeared in *LIFE* and other magazines. According to Isaac H. Bruce-Vanderpuije, his father's studio was actually in the same building as the Ghana Information Service's headquarters, but he ultimately refused to work for the Service because he wanted to remain independent.

By then Bruce-Vanderpuije had begun to use a Rolleiflex, the camera of choice for many documentary photographers around the globe, outside of the studio. His son commented: "It is very easy to operate, and you can use it from different angles to get good results. You don't have to have it close on your eye to view what you want to shoot. So if you are somewhere where there are many people, and you cannot focus, you raise up the Rolleiflex and see what you want to shoot."[19] Indeed, by the mid-1950s Bruce-Vanderpuije's aesthetic approach, which included excellent framing, unusual camera angles, and close-ups, echoed the Modernist style of Europe and American photojournalism.[20] Around 1955, for instance, Bruce-Vanderpuije captured waiting chauffeurs at Accra's

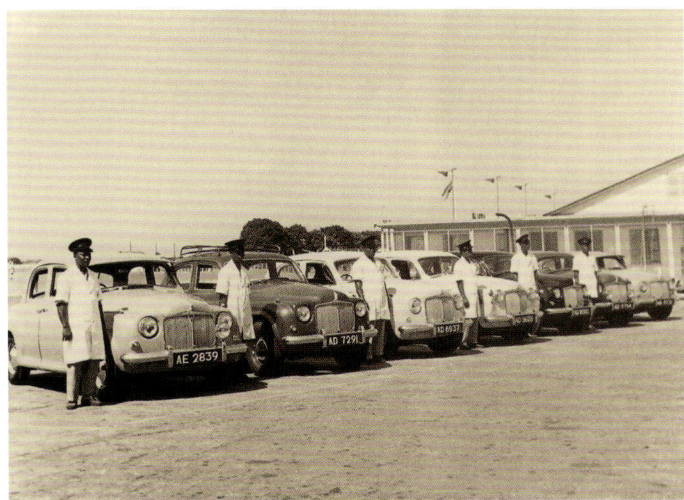

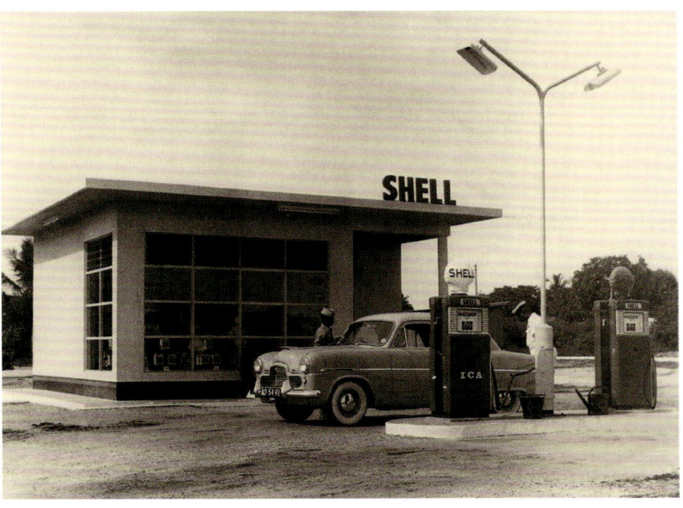

Top: James K. Bruce-Vanderpuije, *Chauffeurs at the airport*, c. 1955
Silver gelatin print

Above: James K. Bruce-Vanderpuije, *Gas station*, c. 1955
Silver gelatin print

airport; he also photographed a Shell gas station with two uniformed attendants filling the tank and cleaning the windshield of a car, having been hired by the Shell Oil Company for advertising campaigns promoting their products in Ghana (see p. 59). One of his most gripping images depicts a young man at a bus station, pensively and hesitantly awaiting the moment when he will be able to board the bus. Taken from a low angle with his Rolleiflex around 1960, its atmosphere can now be read as a metaphor for things to come, as the newly independent Ghana entered politically turbulent times (opposite). After Bruce-Vanderpuije's passing in 1989, his son Isaac and granddaughter Kate Tamakloe have continued to operate the studio in Accra and preserve many of his photographs.

James Barnor has received international acclaim for his photographic oeuvre, with exhibitions in Ghana, Europe, and North America, and a 2015 monograph in English and French. He himself has been outspoken in interviews–as seen on p. 82, in conversation with Aimée Bessire.[21] Born in 1929, Barnor's family belonged to the local elite of the Gold Coast and included several members who engaged in photography. A young Barnor received his first camera, a Kodak Brownie 127, from the headmaster of the missionary school he attended, and at the age of seventeen he became an apprentice in the studio of his cousin, photographer J. P. Dodoo, who specialized in portrait photography. By 1953, he had opened his 'Ever Young' Photographic Studio in James Town, Accra, the same district as Bruce-Vanderpuije's Deo Gratias (see pp. 92–93). Barnor faced challenges such as procuring state-of-the-art cameras and photographic supplies, but soon became known for his skillful pictures, which included dignitaries, hip young Ghanaians, and portraits of local families. His studio turned into "a social place, community center, where everybody came to."[22]

British and Ghanaian members of the Ghana Information Service were among his many visitors and friends, including the aforementioned Roland James Moxon and other British heads of Service departments. One of Barnor's photographs shows a British member of the Service's film unit at work during a durbar, an official welcoming and greeting ceremony in Cape Coast (see p. 84). The filmmaker holds a camera, while Sir Charles Arden-Clarke, the last governor of the Gold Coast Colony from 1949 to 1957, who maintained his close connection to Ghana, walks by in his parade uniform waving at the spectators. A royal state umbrella, used for Ghanaian dignitaries, indicates his rank. One barely sees the umbrella carrier; only his bare foot is visible next to the governor's expensive leather shoes.

Competition among local photographers was fierce, and though they were neighbors and often present at the same occasions, professionals kept their techniques and connections secret. Barnor trusted only his relatives in the business when seeking advice. His cousin Julius Aikins, also a photographer, worked as a lab technician at the Service and had experience with printing pictures from negatives, a critically useful skill that he taught Barnor. It was also from Aikins that Barnor heard for the first time about Ansel Adams, whose black and white photographs he began to admire. Unfortunately, not many of Aikins's own photographs survive, and few were published.[23]

Barnor was the first Ghanaian photojournalist to work for the *Daily Graphic*, a newspaper published in Ghana, and he is best-known for his photographs in the pan-African magazine *Drum*. His association with *Drum* began when he was introduced to James Bailey, the South Africa-based editor of the magazine, while Bailey visited Accra.[24] A spread of pictures taken by various *Drum* photographers in Ghana around the time of independence appeared in *The Short Century: Independence and Liberation Movements in Africa 1945–1994*, edited by Okwui Enwezor, in 2001. It includes one photograph by Barnor, captioned "Photo James Barnor and Deh, Long Live Ghana: The first minutes in the life of Ghana at Accra's Old Polo Ground. Prime Minister Nkrumah and his cabinet speak to crowd from the podium. March 6, 1957."[25] It captures an earth-shaking moment in Ghana's history. Barnor's other photographs of this event and the celebrations happening all over town reflect the joy, excitement, and enthusiasm of the newly independent nation (see pp. 62–63, 88).

Many of Barnor's photographs depict everyday life around him. His studio in James Town was near Accra's old harbor, and he only had to step out into the sunlight and walk a short distance to get to the beach. He would watch crews of young men waiting to row out in boats through at-times heavy surf to load ships, while other boats could be seen at the pier in the distance. This grueling work, for which the men were paid so little that they could barely survive on their wages, becomes evident in another photograph, showing workers unloading heavy flour bags in the harbor (see p. 89). Todd Webb was documenting activities in harbors along the Ghanaian coast at around the same time, as did many photographers before and after him (see pp. 78–79). In December 1959, Barnor left Accra for England, where he continued to freelance for *Drum*, and began the next chapter in his distinguished career. He returned to Ghana in 1970 and practiced there until 1994, when he once more relocated to Great Britain. He is now London-based.

*

This brief essay has mentioned only a few of the many African professional photographers who documented major transformations along the West African Atlantic shores from the last decades of the nineteenth century to the 1960s and beyond. They served clients of different backgrounds and were active through different eras, witnessing and depicting not only the tremendous changes of colonial and postcolonial times, but also necessarily keeping up with advances in photographic technology and equipment. At a disadvantage compared to their counterparts from the geographic North, African professionals made up for this through ingenuity. All started their careers at a very young age, took opportunities to further their education, and often spoke several indigenous languages as well as German, English, or French. If necessary they crossed the arbitrarily drawn colonial borders in search of business. Through different channels, these professionals also had connections with the metropole in occupying European countries. They were internationally linked, as seen in the printed products that circulated their images, be they pictorial postcards, newspapers, or illustrated magazines. Some photographers traveled to Europe themselves, and connected with African diasporas and photographic communities in places like London.

At the time Todd Webb stayed in Togoland and Ghana, photographs by African practitioners were available to him in print publications and on the picture cards offered to travelers in hotels and bookshops of major towns. Webb may have even encountered local professional photographers who, like him, were documentarians, though there is only one reference to such engagements in his journal, relating to the photographer Mohinder Singh in what was then Tanganyika (Tanzania).[26] But could it be possible that an African took this picture of Todd Webb, which shows him with a group of boys in the Togolese village of Niamtougou (see p. 58, bottom). It seems that Webb had handed his camera to someone accompanying him on the journey, as he did in a few other instances. At the time, photography had made inroads even in smaller places in Togoland, and a few enterprising local people had learned how to operate cameras. Unfortunately, we will never know the identity of this image-maker. After his short sojourns in Togoland and Ghana, Webb, subject to a strenuous traveling schedule and an all-consuming assignment, continued on to several other regions of Africa.

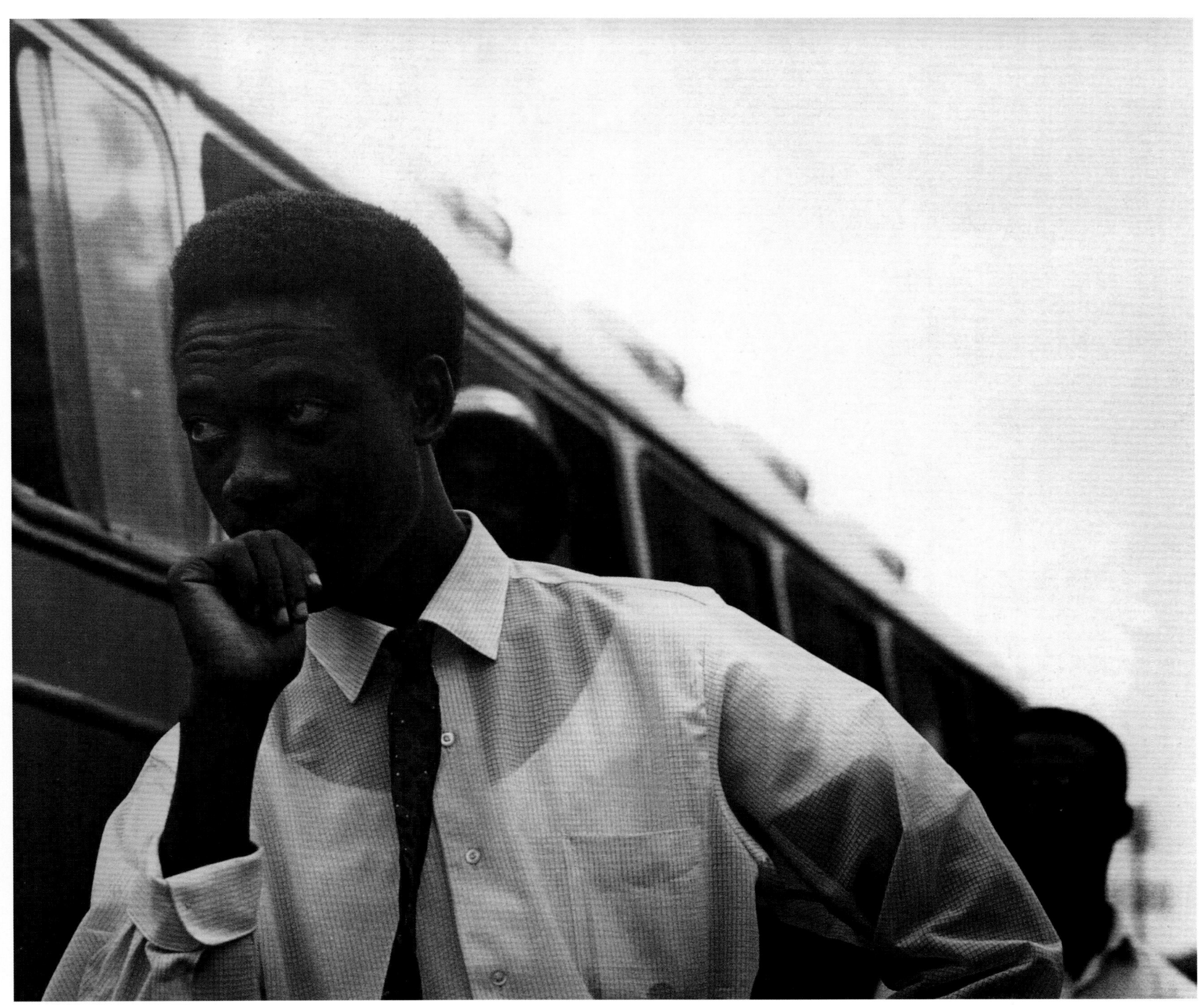

James K. Bruce-Vanderpuije, *At the Bus Station*, c. 1960
Silver gelatin print

Author's Note: *First and foremost I would like to express my thanks to editor Aimée Bessire, who contacted me about the important Todd Webb Archive and asked me to contribute to this book. She and Erin Hyde Nolan, the co-editor, shared some of the tremendous research they had conducted with the director and staff of the Todd Webb Archive. The nature and scope of Todd Webb's oeuvre and the pictures he took during a critical time in African history are indeed impressive. As the writing of my essay progressed, Aimée and Erin helped me with comments and edits. Without their input this essay would not be the same.*

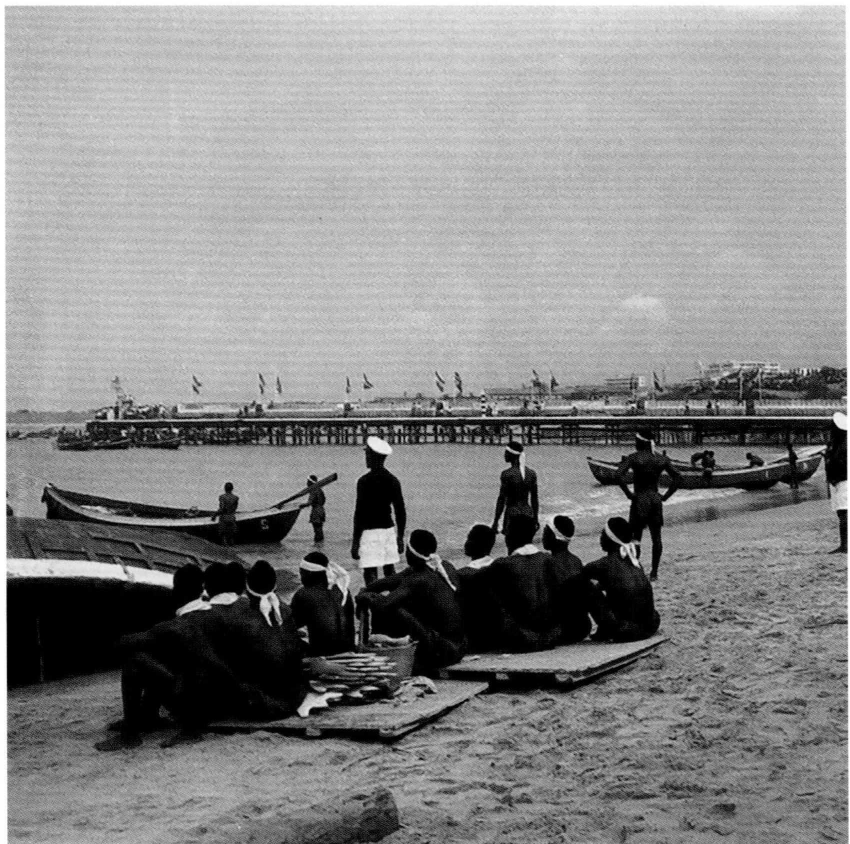

James Barnor, *Old Harbor in Accra*, March 5, 1957
Harbor boat race during Independence celebrations at Accra beach.

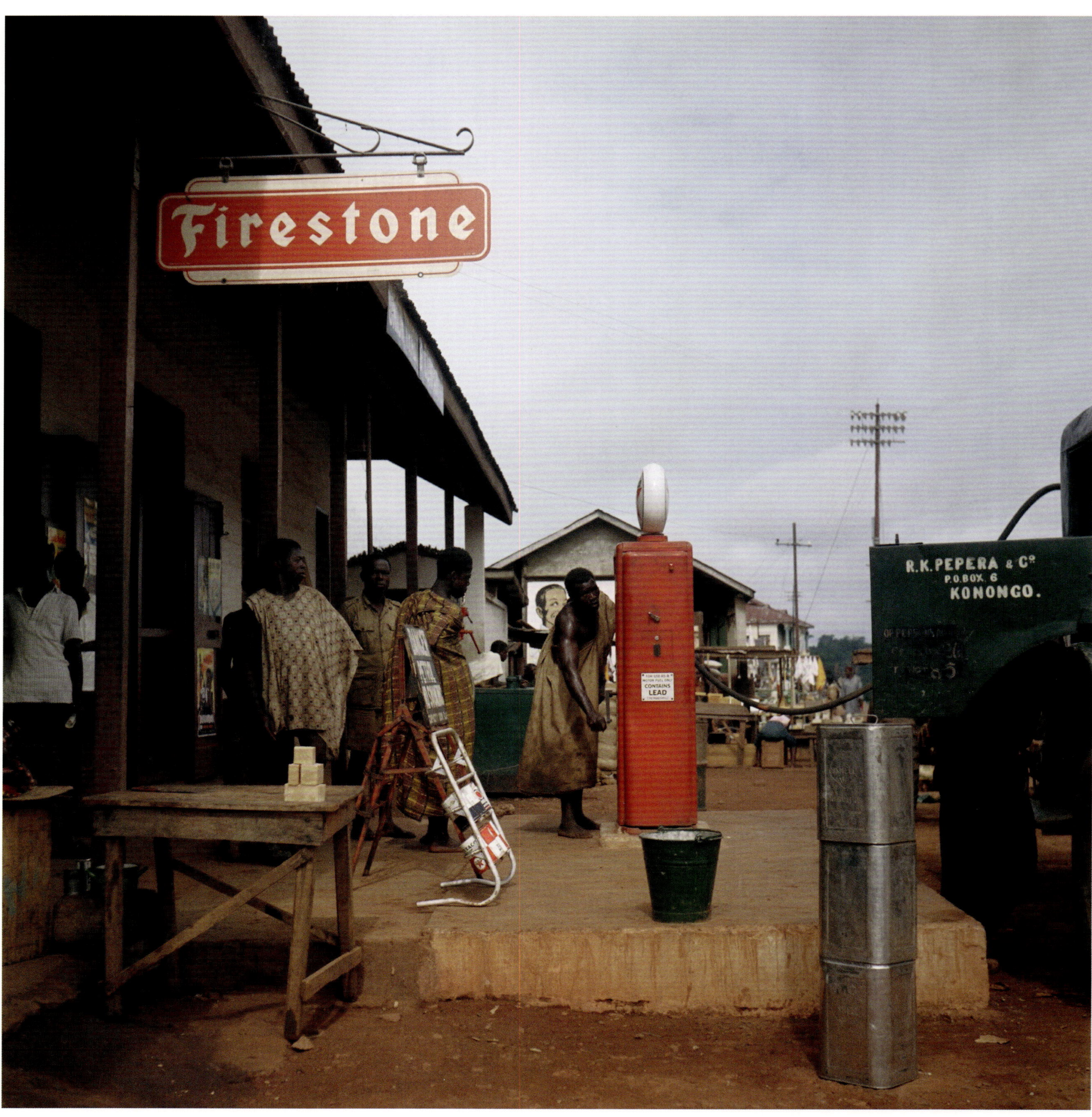

Todd Webb, *Untitled* (44UN-7978-547), Ghana, 1958
Filling up at the Firestone station.

GHANA

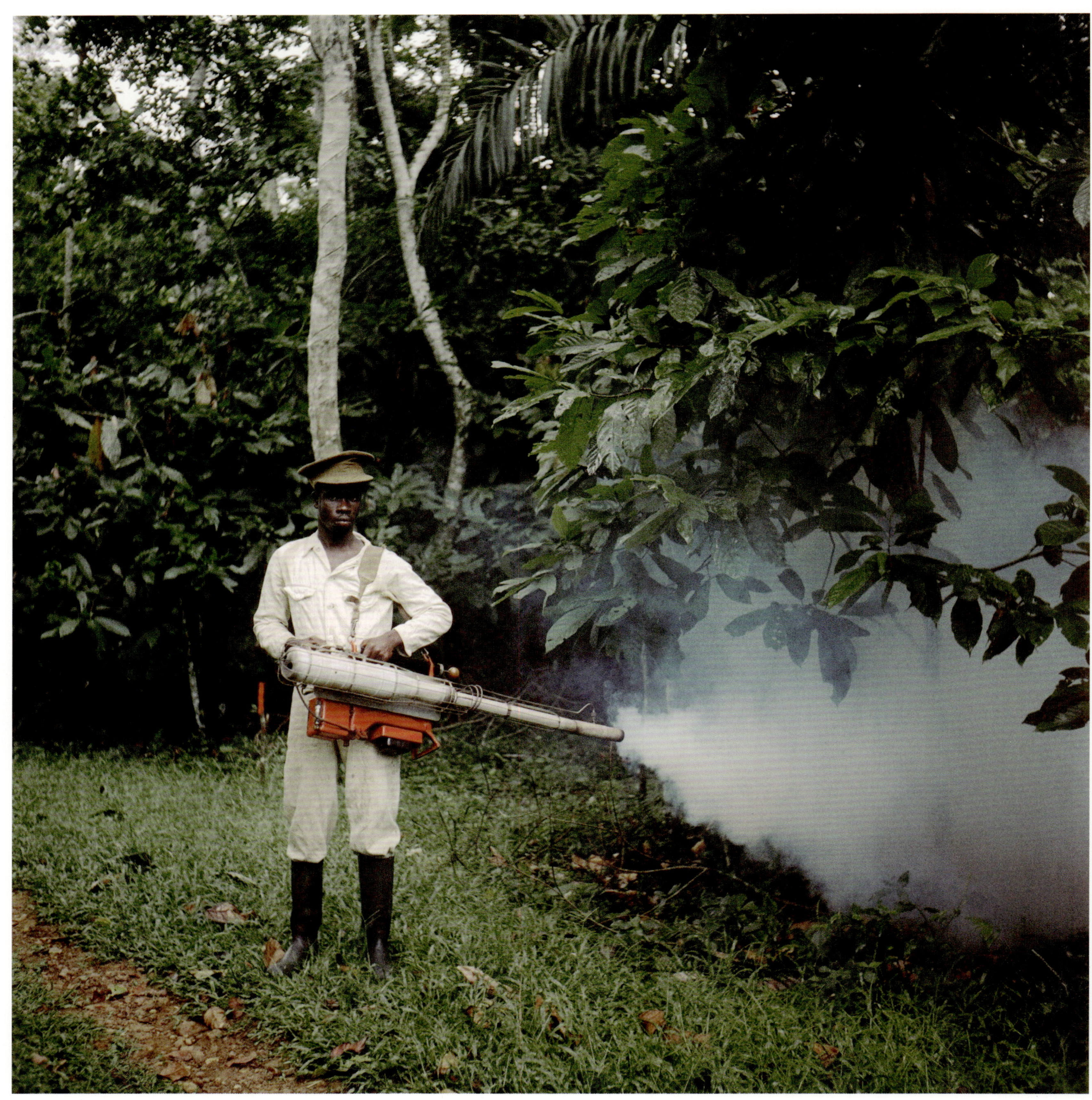

Todd Webb, *Untitled* (44UN-7776-038), Ghana, 1958
Spraying pesticide on cocoa crop.

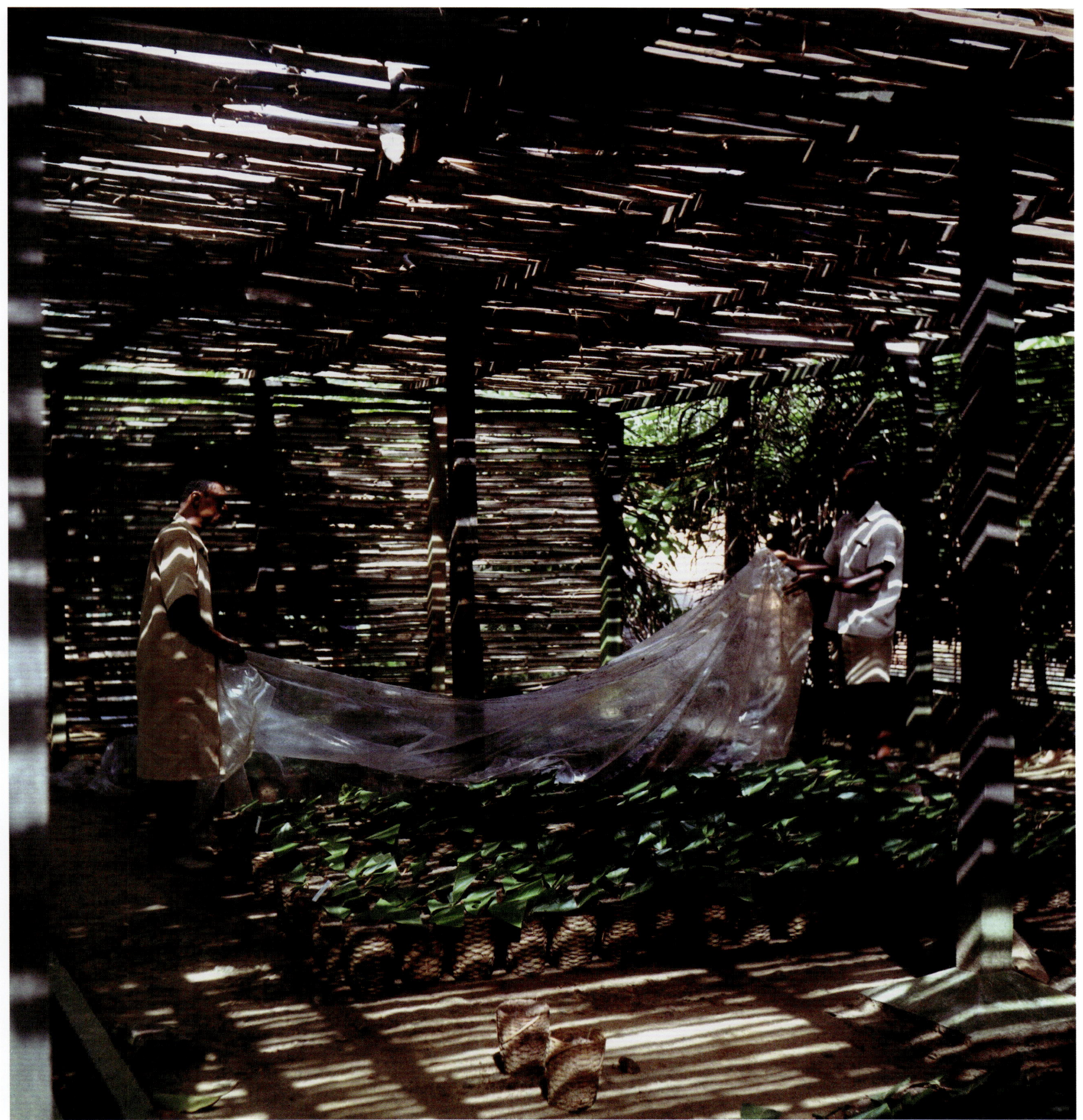

Todd Webb, *Untitled* (44UN-7976-042), Ghana, 1958
Cocoa seedlings at the West African Cocoa Research Institute, Tafo.

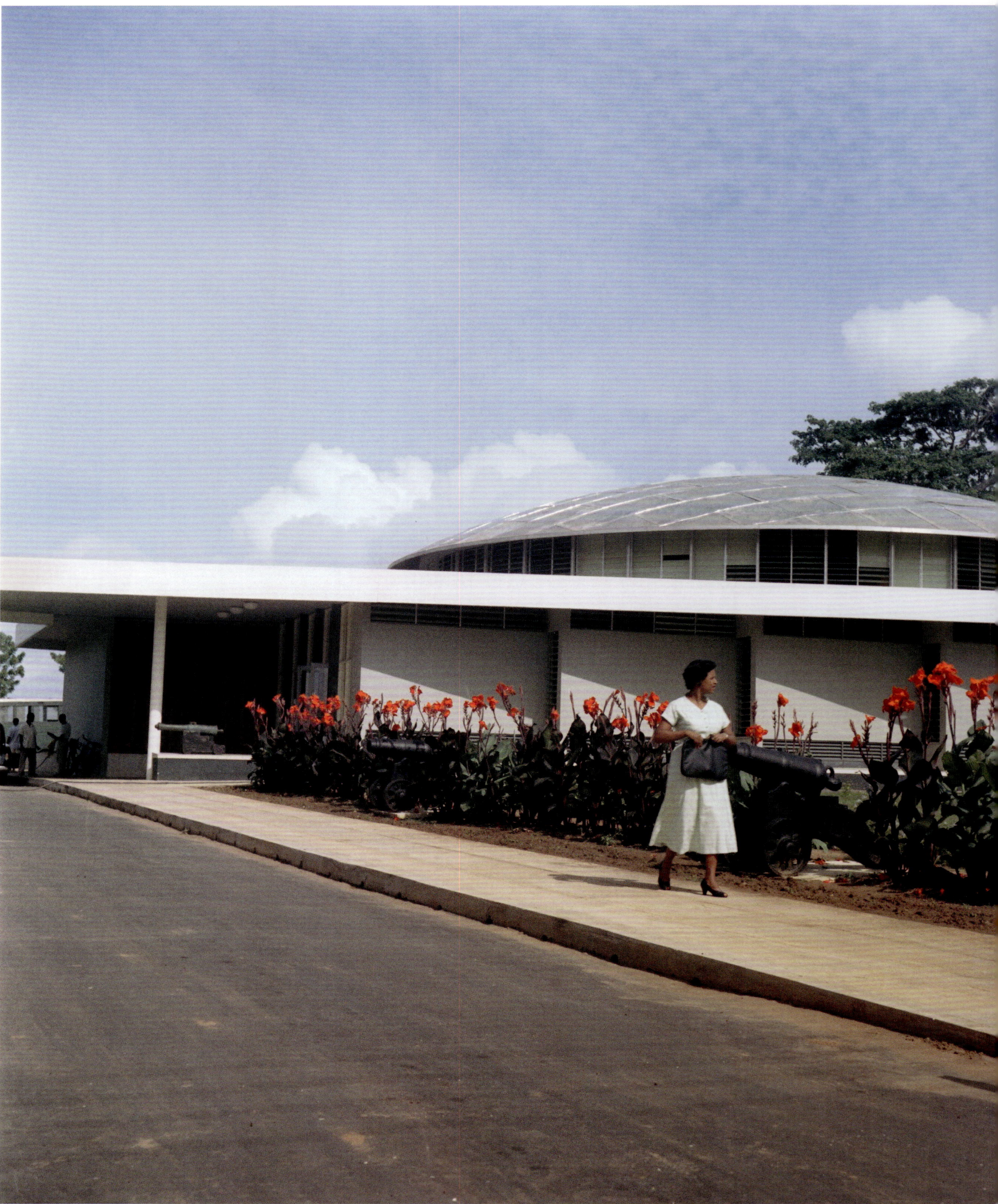

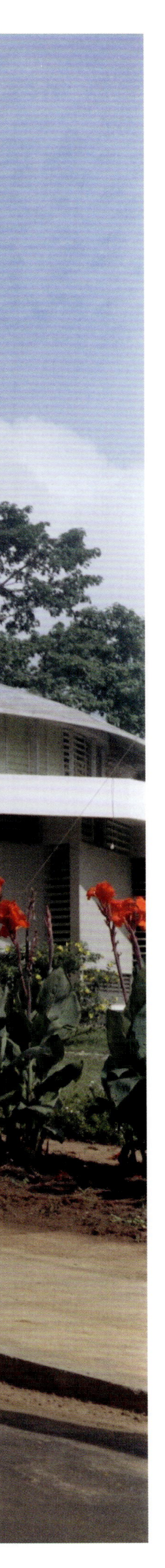

Todd Webb, *Untitled* (44UN-7977-291), Ghana, 1958
Woman leaving the National Museum of Ghana, Accra.

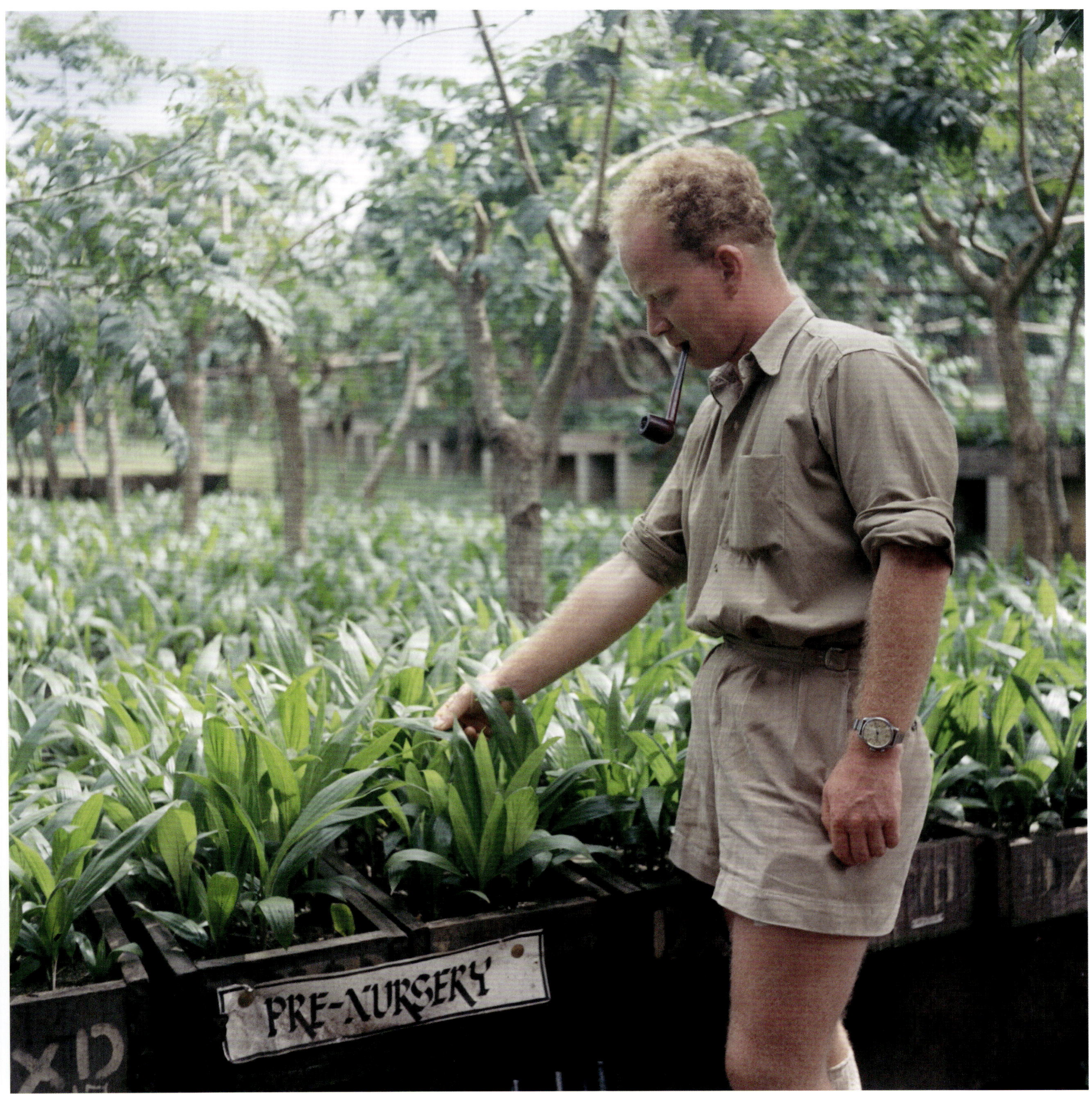

Todd Webb, *Untitled* (44UN-7978-552), Ghana, 1958
Man with pipe examining a farm nursery.

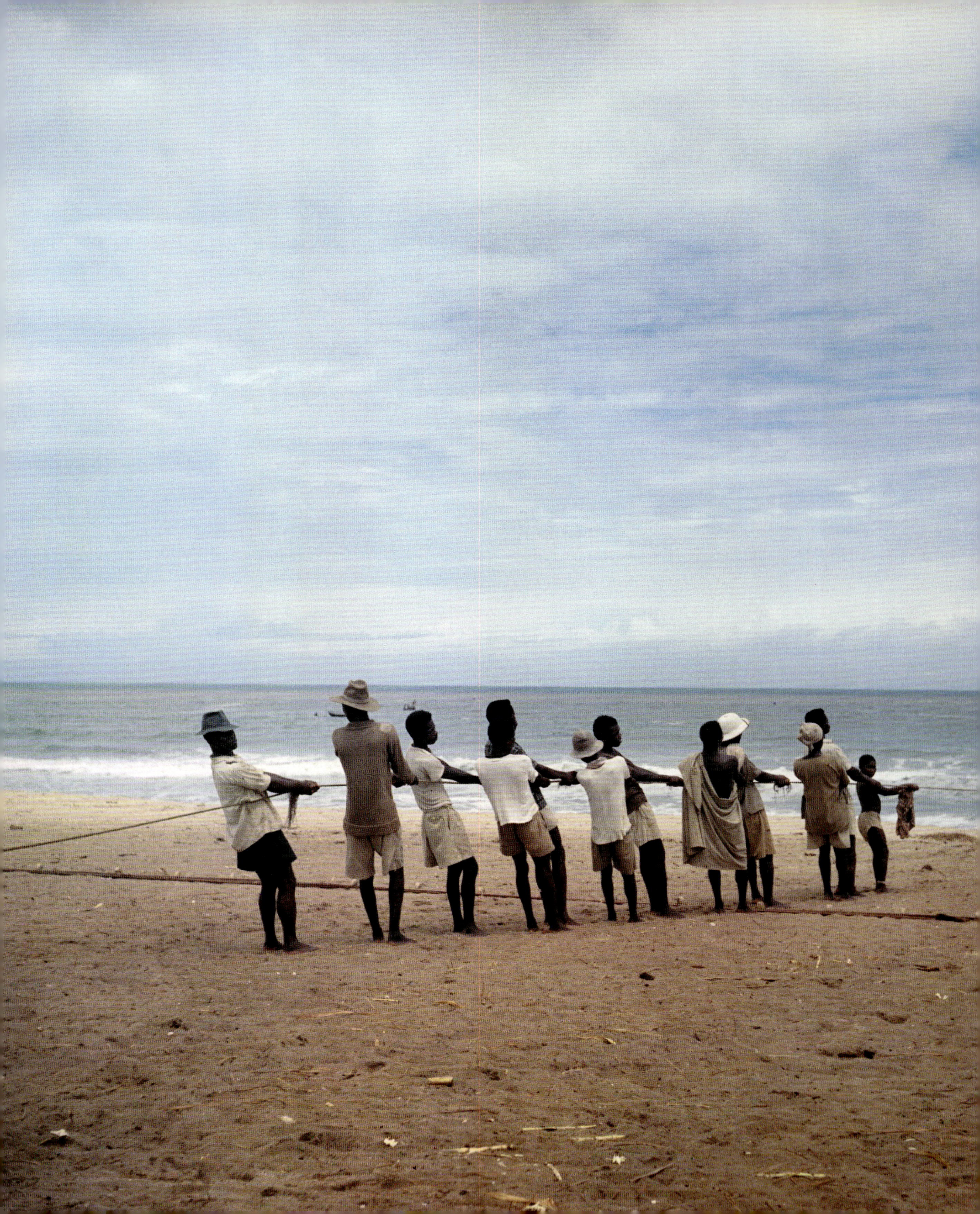

Todd Webb, *Untitled* (44UN-8003-155), Ghana, 1958
Fishermen working together to bring in their nets.

Todd Webb, *Untitled* (44UN-7998-110), Ghana, 1958
Moving logs at Takoradi Harbor.

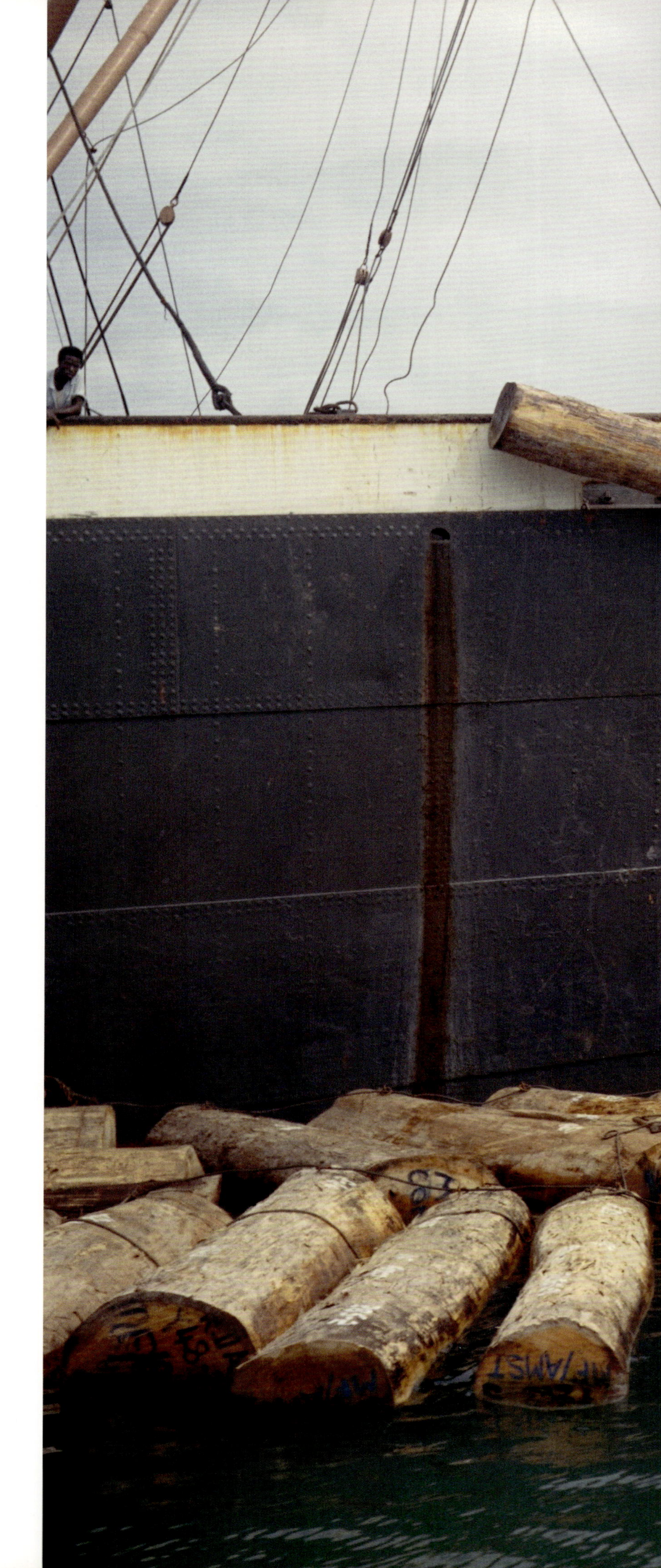

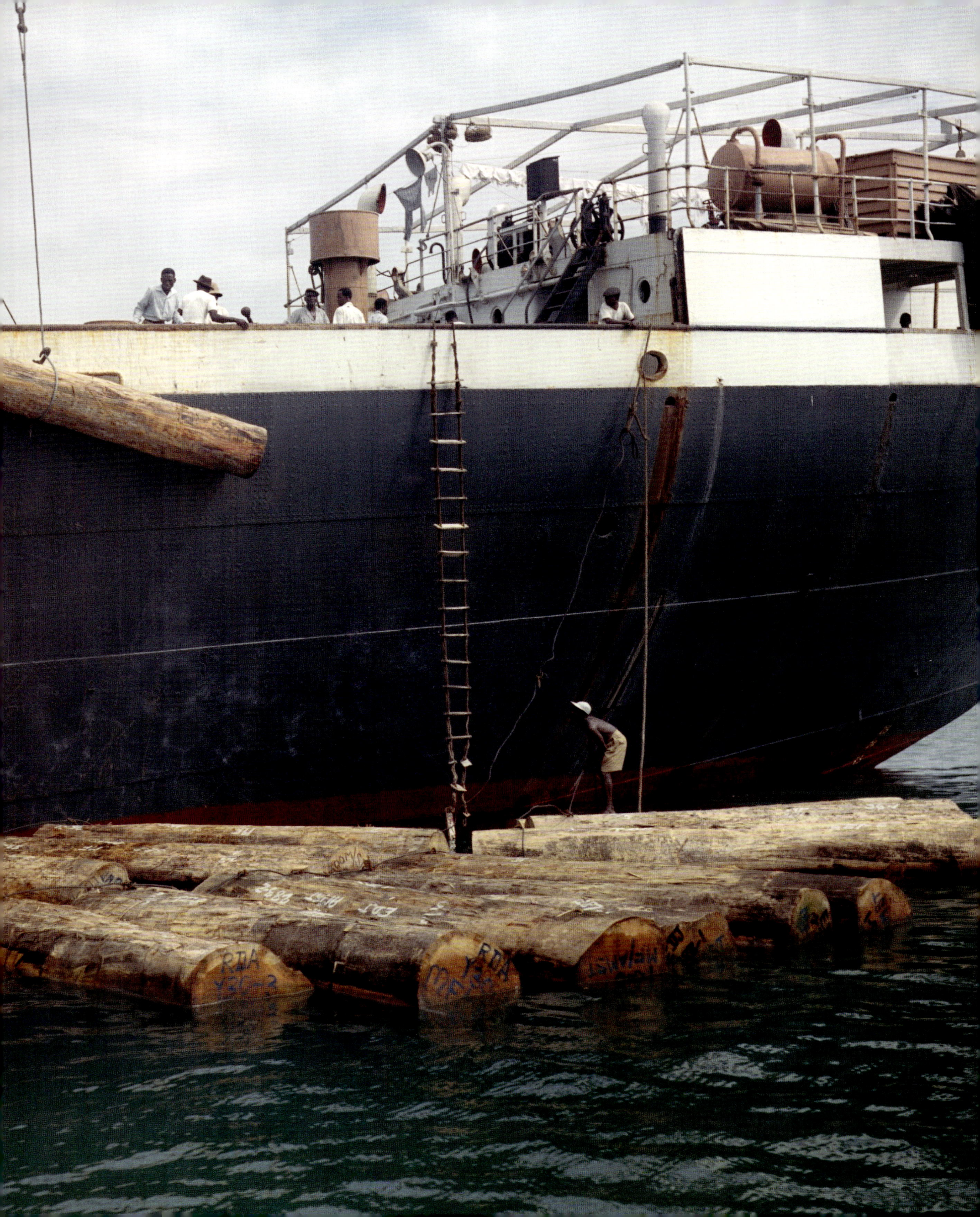
RDA
RDA

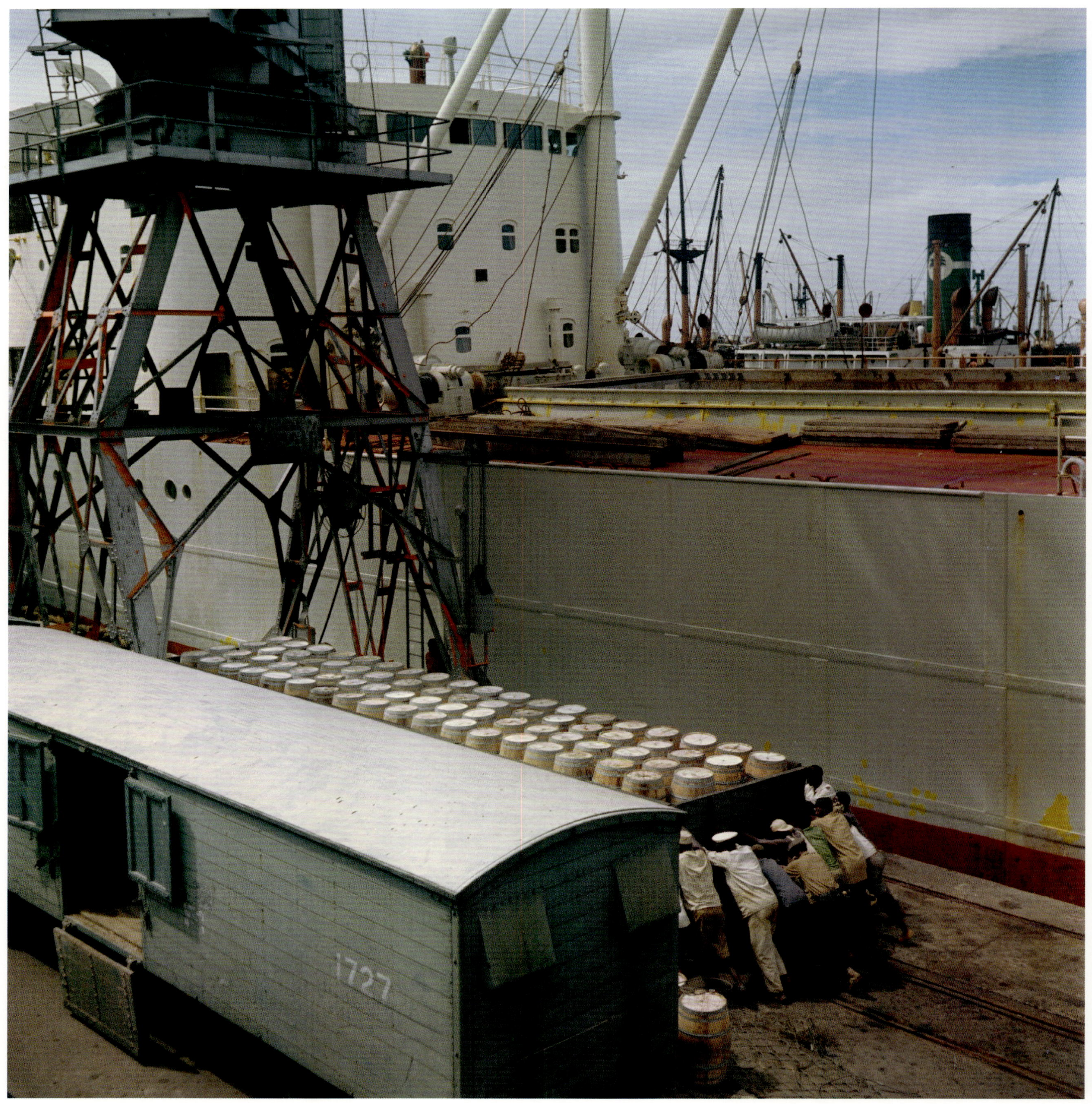

Todd Webb, *Untitled* (44UN-7996-115), Ghana, 1958
Men pushing a railway car with barrels, near the shipping harbor.

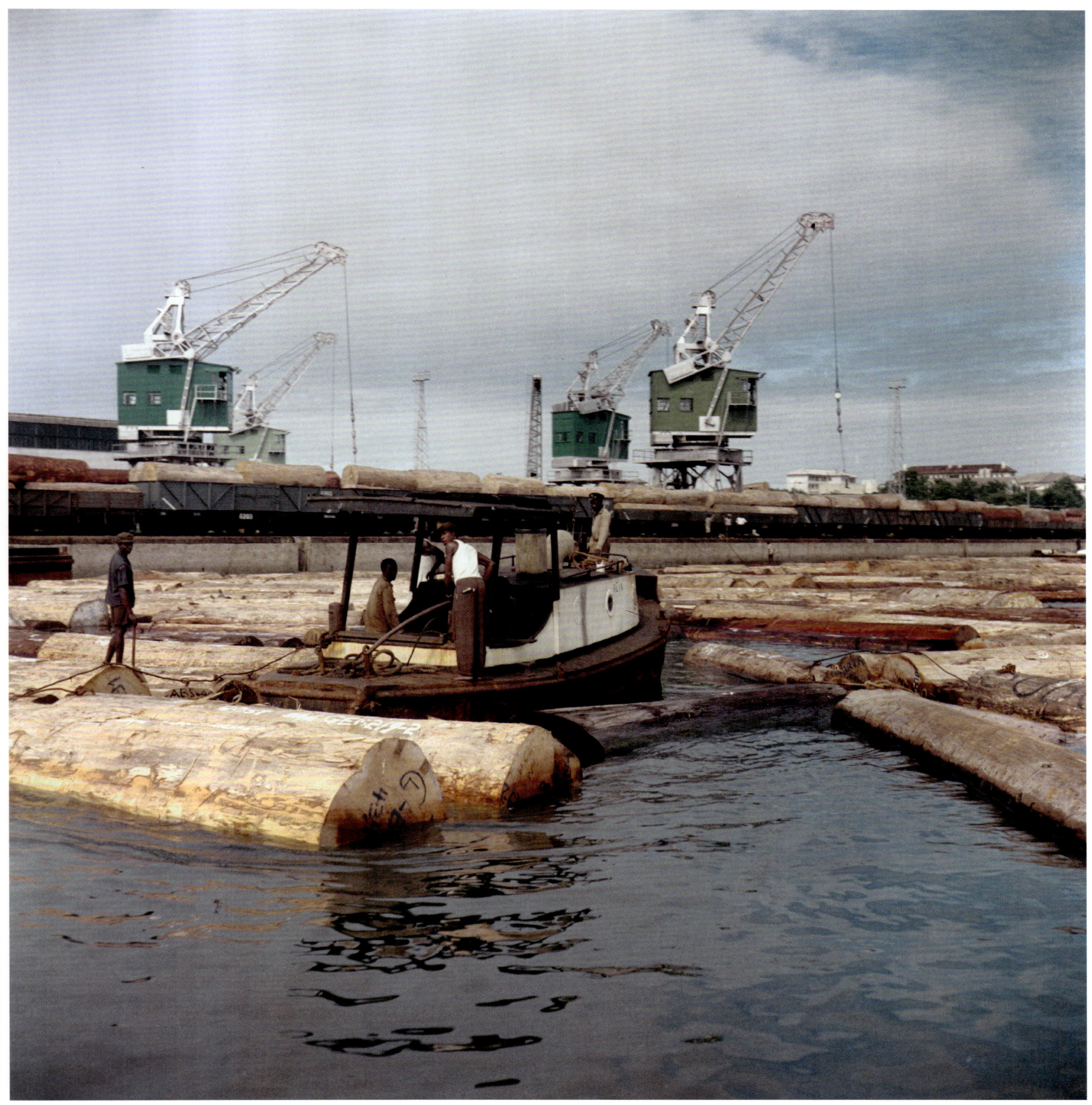

Todd Webb, *Untitled* (44UN-7996-114), Ghana, 1958
Moving logs at Takoradi Harbor.

Todd Webb, *Untitled* (44UN-7997-226), Ghana, 1958
Unloading cargo with Customs House and Ghana Railway and Harbours in the background, Accra.

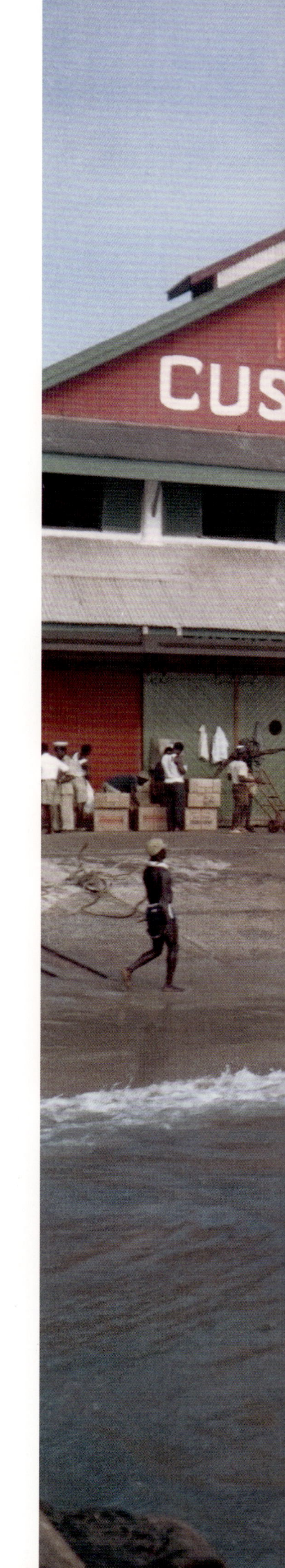

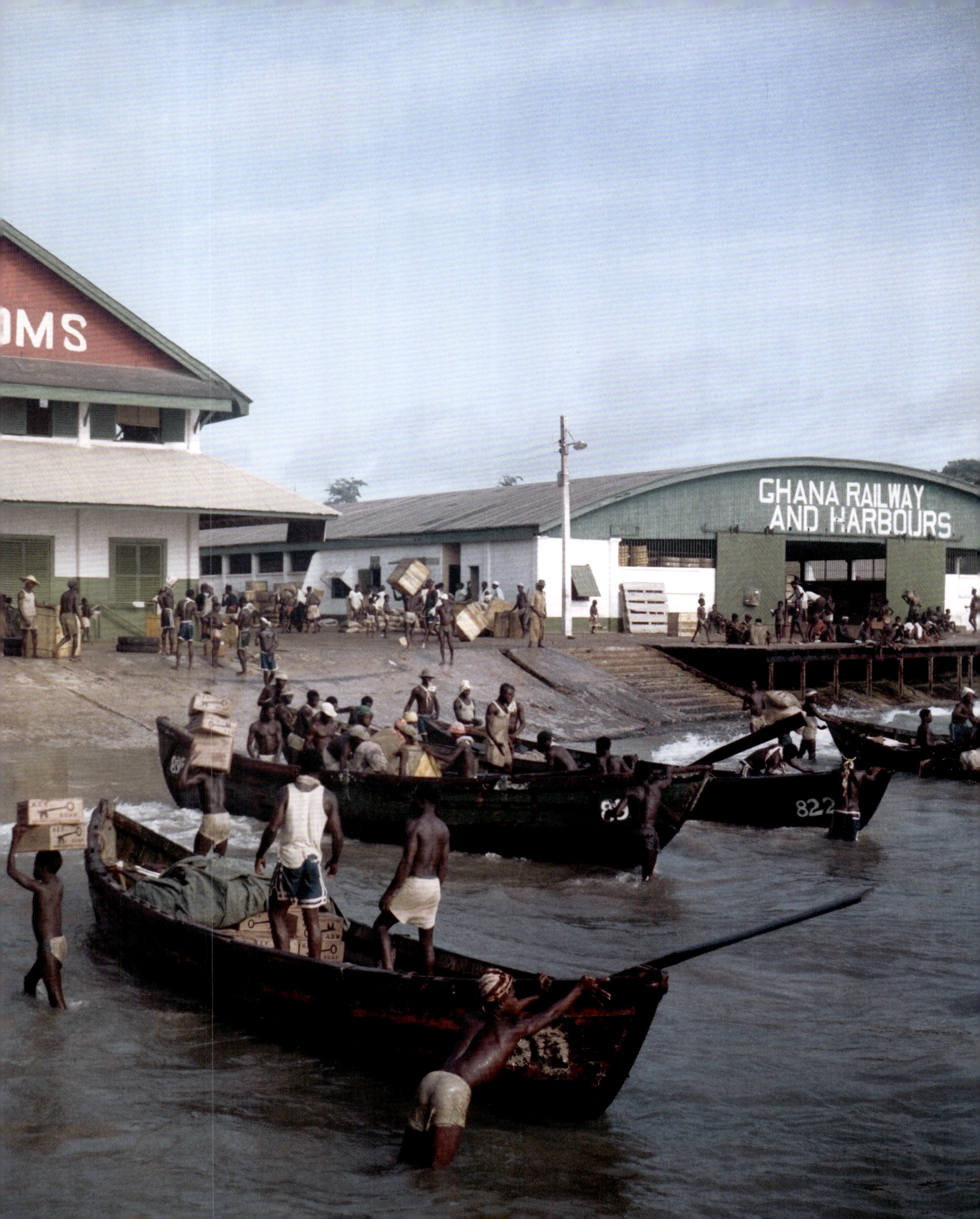
OMS
GHANA RAILWAY
AND HARBOURS
822

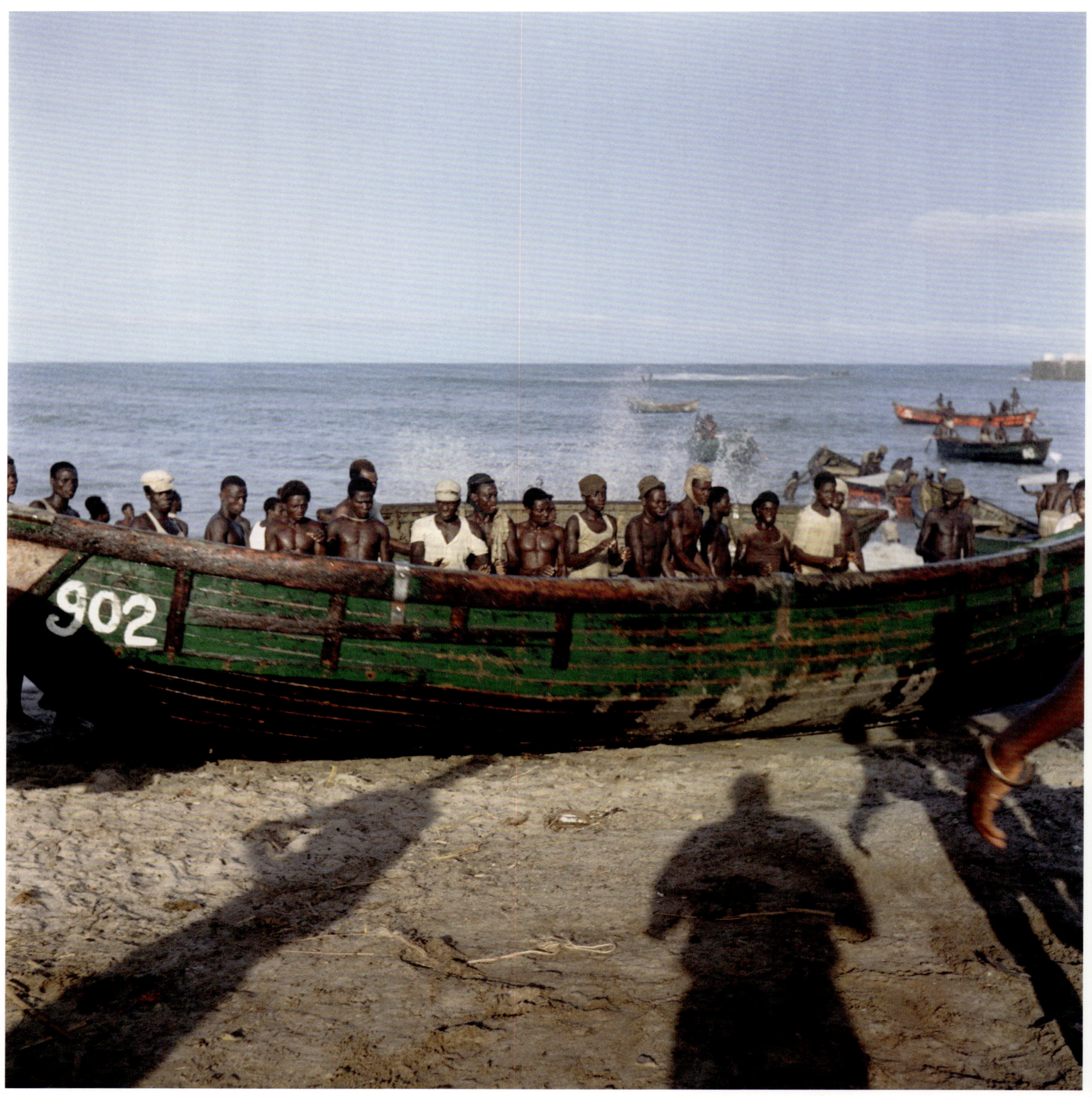

Todd Webb, *Untitled* (44UN-7997-231), 1958
Todd Webb's shadow at the center, as he photographs men in a boat.

Todd Webb, Journal Entry, May 8, 1958

"Have had quite an exciting three days in Ghana. Much too much to do here for a ten-day stay. Seems to me that Ghana is a going concern. Much progress has been made since Independence Day."

James Barnor on Photography in Ghana in the 1950s

James Barnor in conversation with Aimée Bessire

In this conversation, James Barnor reflects on his active role in the Ghanaian photographic community in the late 1950s. Although James Barnor and Todd Webb never met, Webb visited Ghana at a time when Barnor was working in his popular Ever Young Photographic Studio. James Barnor was part of a thriving local photographic community who were actively involved in representing Ghana's transition from colonialism to Independence. He was a photographer for The Daily Graphic *and* Drum *magazine, and opened the first color-processing laboratory in Accra in 1970, working with Agfa-Gevaert. Now based in London, James Barnor frequently works between England, France, and Ghana.*

Aimée Bessire: What was it like to photograph Ghana in the 1950s?

James Barnor: In the 1950s there were quite a lot of photographers, amateurs as well as some professionals. I saw one or two in Cape Coast and one or two in Kumasi and other regions, but most were based in the capitals, especially Accra, because there was electricity and shops selling photographic things. People [outside of the cities] had to travel a long distance to Accra to buy film. There was that backwardness, in a way, but photography was quite popular in the 1950s.

We had two [types] of photographers, professional photographers with studios, doing portraiture, and [itinerant photographers working mostly outside]. The [professionals] used large glass plates [with a] minimum size of 6½ x 8½ [in.], which we call full plates, for taking groups of offices, work establishments, people, weddings, instances where you have large groups or large buildings for architectural purposes. The [professional photographers] used wooden field cameras and also practiced retouching on the negatives. Those who did were different from those who didn't. I went through an apprenticeship with a cousin of mine, even though it seemed boring, because you [had] to spend a lot of time working on a negative for thirty minutes to an hour to fill all the gaps, blemishes, and so on.

The other type is [an itinerant photographer] who has a camera and [travels] taking pictures. A few of these had kiosks on the roadsides. I used the services of one that I remember very well. He didn't have electricity, but he developed and printed my frames for me outside in the kiosk. Sometimes I would sit and [I could see] there was a part of the kiosk with light and [another area where he went] into the darkroom. I would sit outside; he would go in and [develop] it and [then] come and show it to me.

That was when I was doing pupil teaching, sort of an untrained teacher with the camera. I used to send my frames to him. He was very nice. I used him as the one to do all my [developing] and I was satisfied with his work. I got to know him.

Also, there was a type of photography at the time, we called it "wait and get," something like instant photography. They were in the markets; they did passports [and] used paper negatives. They didn't use plates or film at all. I didn't get to study it, but they put their hand in a dark area and manipulated when they made the exposure. They developed and brought it out, dried the paper negative and then copied it [sometimes] using another paper to cut in four and produce the four passport or driving license pictures for you. You didn't need to go to a studio and get them; these people were outside.

In fact, when I was working for *Drum* magazine I intended to [work on] a story [about] them, but I [never did]. I regret it until now. It was fascinating. That [technique] was even more popular because their work was cheaper. And they were outside; they were always sitting there.

There were also other photographers with roll film cameras that they finished and sent to studios to be developed and printed. Those who were professional photographers underwent apprenticeships and operated their own. Even these were tools, some did not [use] lighting in a studio, they took the pictures outside. Even among the studio photographers, only [a] few had lighting set up in the studio where they could take photographs at night as well as day.

Not all photographers [used lighting], and my cousin who trained me didn't do it. I think I started [first] and had done it for a long time before he started. I would say he didn't even come to my standard in lighting. The thing is that you don't have to pay for electricity when you use daylight to take your pictures. Especially, those who print without electricity, they get it cheaper still. If the daylight is there [when] a customer comes, we take him outside, we put the backdrop on the wall outside and [shoot the photo]. The light was favorable most of the time; but again, when I started studio photography it became a novelty at the time. Especially, in the early 1950s, it was a novelty and people wanted to do it, they brought their girlfriends and partners.

I lived near two important night spots. One was one of the best hotels in Accra, called Sea View Hotel. I was just two doors from the Sea View, so people who visited there came to my studio. There was a nightclub and drinking place about a quarter of a mile from me with dances and bands and so on and so forth. People from there came to me, or I could take my camera and go there and take pictures.

It was exciting. But I think only Kingsway Chemists and Agfa-Gevaert, were ordering and selling photographic materials. The source of supply was a bit limited, but people still enjoyed it.

In the 1950s, even right from the beginning of 1958, when you are talking about Todd Webb's work, and even 1959, photography was buoyant, I would say. But before I come to that question, I didn't see much color and I didn't work in color at all during my time in Ghana. That doesn't mean that no one [photographed in] color. There were people who had the means or the facilities to try color. Europeans and so on, and they sent them overseas for processing. My cousin Julius Aikins, who also helped me to be what I am now, he started developing in color. [He did] not do negative-positive, not developing the negative and then printing; he did reversal. What intrigued me was that when he was going to do it, he would start collecting ice blocks. He would buy ice blocks from the ice company and put them in buckets in his room for a period to reduce the temperature of his darkroom. He brought the temperature down to the required temperature, but this is what I haven't got time for [laughs]. But he experimented in everything and anything. He was able to process. I know he did, but I wasn't interested.

[Julius] worked for the Information Services long before the war and during the war. Through the war, there was the West African Photographic Service, a company [founded] I think by the British government to process or handle photographic work done in West Africa at the time. They would develop films and make prints. After the war, it was given to the Ghana government. So it became the basis of the Information Services of the government. [Julius] worked there as a technician, developing and printing.

I don't know how he studied photography. I don't know anybody who taught him. He taught himself everything. He was the one who introduced me to small camera works, which has benefited me today, because the printing sheet that I had for two years or more was for plate negatives. I wasn't allowed to handle a roll film. His instructions were: "If you double in those, you will start to make money and you will concentrate on learning what I'm going to teach you as soon as you start taking photographs and charging people. Like in doing small camera work, you will learn the retouching. That will make you the man that you are going to be."

Honestly, I did ten years work from 1949, when I started on my own, to 1959, when I left and went to Britain. All the plates that I do, and even during that period, we shifted from plates to sheet films, flat films, the same

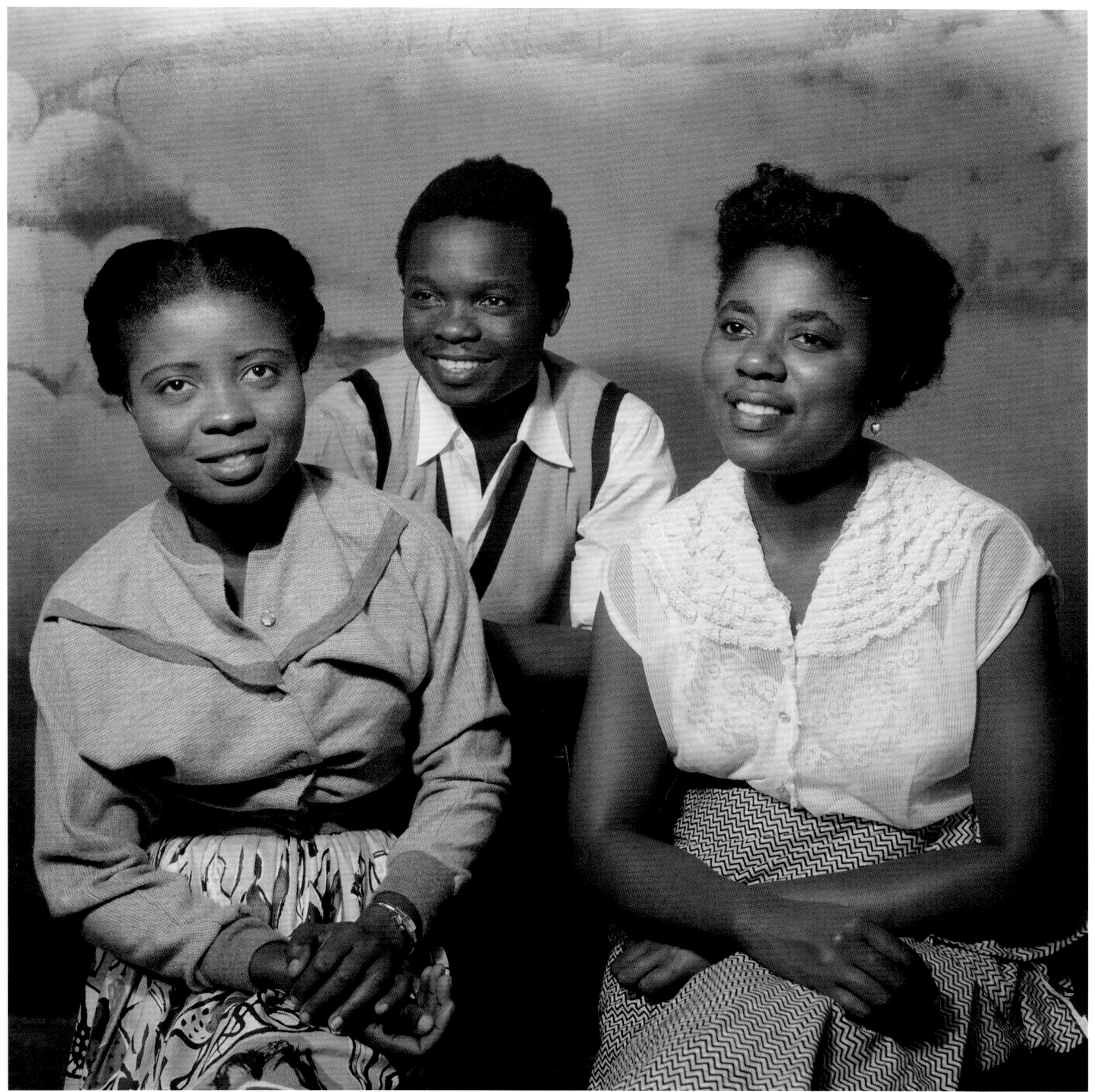

James Barnor, *Evelyn Abbew, Sackey Mensah and a Friend, 'Ever Young' Studio*, Accra, 1950s

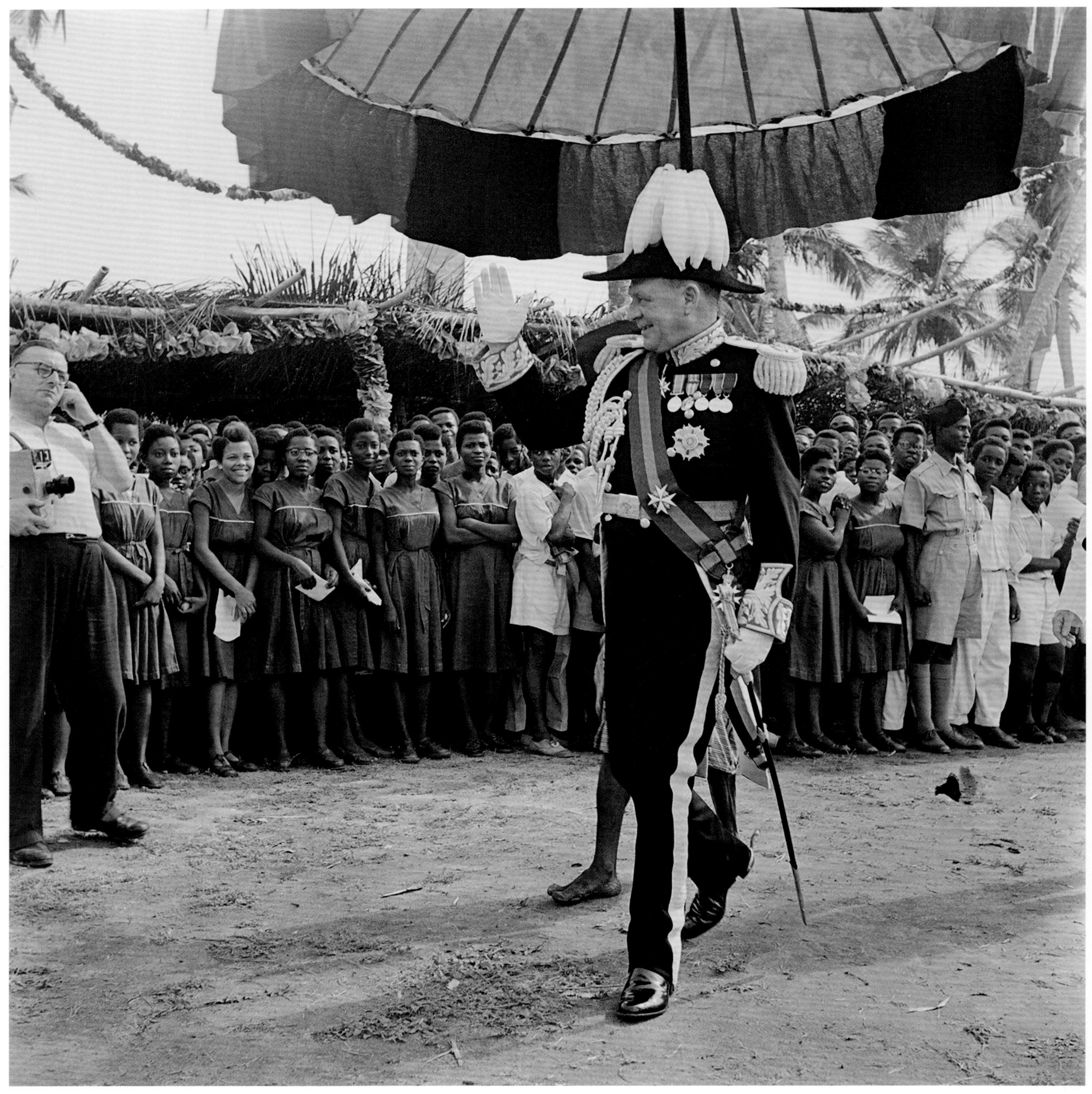

James Barnor, *Sir Charles Arden-Clarke, Last Governor of the Gold Coast, Attends a Durbar in his Honor Before Leaving Ghana*, Cape Coast, 1958

size, but on film. When it falls from your hand it doesn't break. You pick it up again. Sheet films were started when I was an apprentice, and I did both.

You know the size of sheet films or plates and the weight? Ten years work took up a lot of space. And traveling to England, I couldn't take them. I couldn't take anything. In fact, I didn't think or plan to live in Europe. I just wanted to go for a couple of years and come back. But things change.

So, when I lived [there] for 10 years, [the plates] were in the way of the person to whom I left them, and they were all thrown away. I'm not saying this for you to cry for me, you know, because I'm alright [laughs]. But I lost all the retouching. I lost all the portraits, the important people who came to my studio and the work that I did.

I actually said I was somebody who didn't fear any competition, because I had my own way and I didn't bother [with that]. And so, I employed a retoucher who was better than me, an assistant, so some of the retouching was excellent, but I lost all of these [when I was away in London].

But I also [learned from Julius] Aikins, who didn't bother about retouching. And it was Aikins who made me hear of Ansel Adams, who is crucial in this story. His cameras and his way of taking photographs and his sense of technique, perfection in technique, was something that I learned from Julius Aikins from my infancy. Even though I didn't achieve it, fifty percent, it's part of me and that has also helped me.

Aimée: He sounds like a wonderful mentor.

James: I wish the Ghanaian photographers who are coming [today] would think like that. When I was working as a photographer, because we never had enough education, the Ghanaian photographers especially, we feared competition. If you are well educated and you are working, you would rather not compete as such but cooperate with your neighbor. And you go on because your outlook on life and your experience and your purpose will be different, and you need to share these.

You enjoy when somebody has read law and you've done psychology and you meet, and you're talking, it's quite different. Photography is only a small part, but it brings you together. [But some photographers] fear that when they expose their work or themselves, their competitors will steal their customers. Or what should I say, steal their techniques. But I didn't fear anybody, because I'm always experimenting.

If that fear would go and the photographers would have come together to critique one another, or even ask non-photographers who perhaps [had a good eye] to come and look at your pictures and tell you what they thought about them...if they would do that, within a short time their mentality would change. In my time, we didn't have that. Everybody kept to themselves. If they would think that I'm a mentor, they would listen to what I tell them. And then within two or three years, their work will start to be exposed outside as mine.

That brings another sorrowful case. Mr Aikins was also my cousin. When he died, later I went and asked his children about his negatives. They had been thrown away. And I said, "What? The man who taught me and today my work is being shown at Harvard University, and what about him?"

He did a lot of work, and he was always ahead of anybody in Ghana with a camera. He ordered the first Linhof I ever saw. When he applied to the Information [Services] for a grant or advance to buy a car, he used it to order the Linhof. He brought it to show me. I've got a picture of him, standing with the Linhof near my signboard. Recently, I found that picture and I'm adoring it like a statue. This man, if I could expose his negatives, he would be a millionaire, and his children have thrown them away.

Later, they gave me his MPP [Micro Precision Products Ltd], the American type of press camera, which he ordered, and I got the Linhof from him. He came and told me, "I'm selling this because I bought this." And I said, "No, this camera is not going out of the family." And I got it. I used it a bit and took it to England, and I used it at college. It was after college that I traded it in and bought a Mamiya C3. But I did a lot of work with the Linhof. In fact, I couldn't use it fifty percent, because the Linhof is the leading technical camera. You can get all the movements, you can get everything with it, and I didn't have to use it [laughs].

I would like to be a mentor if that is how people will [remember] me. When I die, when I am no more, if people will say, "Well, this man inspires the young people to be this or that," I would love that more than anything else [laughs].

Aimée: What cameras were you using in the 1950s?

James: I started around 1949 with my uncle's field camera–the old plate camera with a wooden tripod, with three double dark slides. You load six parts. Essentially, when you go out of your studio, your limit is six. With these, you have carriers that enable you to use other sizes of plates, like half plate, quarter plate, those kinds which are normal or usual in a Ghanaian studio for everyday shots, [and also those for] passports, driving licenses, which would use 2½ x 3½ [in.]. We have carriers for all these sizes.
We still have the two-plate slide, but when you go into the darkroom you load a carrier in it to take the size of plate you want. That is what I got from my uncle. In fact, what led me to it when I was teaching was somebody gave me a baby Brownie. It uses 127 film, and it takes 8 exposures. That was what I started with and then I progressed to Kodak 620 and 120 Box and so on. I think I also had the chance to use a folding camera.

Sometimes you get away with pleasure and passion. For some reason, because I was poor, I didn't get the opportunity to use expensive or good cameras. I used whatever I could get. I made it an aim to study my camera, know how to use it, know its limits, and make it serve me.

I didn't worry about the camera. The only time that I pursued a camera was when my uncle said, "Oh this camera, I'm selling it." American engineers, who employed him to take process work of a building project at Tema Harbor, convinced him to get rid of the Linhof and get an American camera. That's where I also got the chance to take the Linhof. I got the Linhof. That was the only time when I got an expensive camera.

There was an occasion where I had to buy a camera which was better than what I was using. I was covering activities at the assembly, you know, parliament. Every morning, I would take [photos of] parliamentarians, whatever they were doing, visitors coming in. I used to sell the pictures then, as well as use them for the press.

I was busy one day and one minister was coming with his secretary. He said, "Give him my camera." They gave me a camera, so I thought it was mine, and I started using it. It changed the quality of my pictures. I didn't quite notice until one day he said, "Where is my camera?" I had to give it up. Then I found that I was forced to go and buy a similar camera. I bought an Agfa Isolette, which was similar. I noticed that change very well. Then I noticed a change when using the Linhof. Otherwise, I take any camera that goes. I don't bother, you know. I didn't have money to buy a good camera.

I covered the Ghana Independence for the Black Star Picture Agency. That was the first time I saw a Hasselblad, because the world press, the people who came, had all sorts of cameras. One day, I was taking photographs, and I realized one was hanging on the shoulder of another [photographer]. It even appeared in my picture. I couldn't get anywhere near.

Believe it or not, I trained somebody who was later employed by the West African Cocoa Research Institute in Ghana. I trained him and he was employed by their star photographer. He used the Linhof.

There was another shameful experience that nobody knows. I was doing an assignment for *Drum*, who asked me to do a feature on Roy Ankrah, who had won the Commonwealth Featherweight Boxing Championship and had come to Ghana on holiday. I planned and took him out jogging and shopping and so many things. I was [taking photographs] of him and his family eating breakfast, when Nkrumah [Ghana's first Prime Minister] sent his driver to invite him over. We agreed on two o'clock, and I asked the driver to pick me up from my studio.

Then I didn't have a studio. In fact, the studio that everybody knows was opened after the coronation of Queen Elizabeth in 1953, because I remember how I got odd jobs to get some money and borrowed a little bit in addition to renovate the whole place before moving in to start work. I know that very well. At this place I took pictures with daylight and so on and so forth. I asked the driver, he knew the place. He picked me up and we went to Nkrumah. In fact, the pictures that I took are on exhibition in Paris now. With me, Nkrumah, Roy Ankrah, and his wife.

Nkrumah said, "I have a camera." He went and brought the camera and gave it to me to take pictures. I had film, it was a Rolleicord or something. I didn't know how to load it.

Yesterday at my Paris gallery, we saw the negative. We scanned it, but I didn't want to divulge this [story]. So, I didn't. With a Rollei, you pass the film and the paper through, which stops when the film gets streamed and starts to count. I didn't know that. I put it in, and started, and it wouldn't stop. I did take some. I had double exposures, and I couldn't get on. This is the first time I'm telling anybody. I knew very well that if I used that camera, I would have taken it from him. He would have given it to me.

The atmosphere that we created, how we took pictures. If I'd taken that picture with that camera from him and taken it home, I wouldn't have returned it to him again, because he would get another one. Somebody from Germany gave it to him.

When it comes to cameras, I didn't worry. I had to get what my money could buy, and then I made it serve me by knowing how to manipulate it and do things for me.

The other difficulty I had, all Ghanaians had, was time and temperature development, because our place is very hot all the time. Even the water, nobody had running water, and when you go out to fetch water, it's hot. You don't bother about thermometers and so on in development. Most of our negatives, my negatives, especially the bleached ones, were overdeveloped. I've never told anybody this, but you look at the negative and it's dark.

Either then you learn to reduce it by Farmer's Reducer to a printable degree, or you use a suitable paper. You have grade 1, grade 2, grade 3, even grade 0. Some manufacturers, they have 0, 1, 2, 3, 4. You pick the grade that will match the negative. You've got [to find] a way. When I look at my negatives, I say, "How did I work through this?" after going to England and learning and sticking to time and temperature development, and also using an exposure meter to read and then taking the exposure.

Now, [when you have] an automatic or built-in exposure, you just do it. Today's photography is easy, but we went through something interesting and we managed.

Aimée: It's very different. I once used a camera from 1952 and there are so many more steps to consider.

James: It is very, very different. Today you can even decide to keep the picture or delete it while you're on the assignment. Today we are lucky. I think they can stop and transmit the picture to their editors or to their office while they're still on the assignment.

My uncle, J. P. Dodoo, my mother's senior brother, who was a photographer, gave me all his old equipment. He had a traveling box and it was also a darkroom. When he traveled to places where there was no electricity, no darkroom, he already had a changing box. This same box is what he [used to] arrange, develop, rinse, and print. At that time, you didn't use a lot of rinse, but with a stop bath, you could have the developer, because it was a very small space. You developed it, stopped it, and then fixed it. You could feel the smell of the chemicals. This was a box with an in-built lining, of something like, not trampoline [fabric], but plastic that is black. You put it on the table, and you put your head in it, cover everything, and then start with your developer. At the time, there was no chromatic film. We were using autofilm, only sensitive to a limited range. There was a ruby light, very thick—a red light at the top, with a cover, which you opened and you could see what they were doing.

I traveled with this because when I went out in to [the] country, I had to make sure the negatives were alright, especially if it was a group, especially confirmation groups. At Christmas, all of the children get confirmed. That's the best year in their lives, and they all want copies.

You made sure they were all good, the plates are out. I did all of this, and took orders before I returned to Accra and printed [them] and sent back. This was from the beginning of the 1950s until I opened the big studio, and then [no longer] traveled much.

Aimée: What year did you open the big studio?

James: 1953. In fact, I wouldn't have opened the big studio. I didn't care about it, because I had a darkroom specially built for this. I remember the working table was designed for the space that I had. It was erected in the darkroom.

I had everything that made it a darkroom built in a small veranda. I had the corner to work and the corner to sleep. The corner to work was more important to me than the sleeping area. In fact, if I have money one day, I'll do a replica of the working garage that I copied from my master, because he had something similar, where the table was a hole and a box, like a printing box, specially designed to take the plates and to take diffusing paper in between the bulb, the light source and the diffuser to make all the light even, and not spotlit.

I designed the same thing. You can change the printing frame, a half plate, and a quarter plate. Guys, interesting. When I think of this, I wish I [could] make a replica for archiving, so that people can see how we printed—contact printing. That was contact printing. He enlarged with daylight. Can you imagine? He and my uncle both made their enlargements by daylight, using the same full-plate camera they used in taking the picture.

Through Julius Aikins I ordered a vertical enlarger for 9 x 12 limits, and I'm sure I ordered one for my cousin as well. I used an enlarger like that where everything was done by daylight. I know how to make enlargements using daylight in the darkroom.

As far as when I started working in my aunt's room—I know this is more of my life than what you wanted [laughs]—I copied Mr Julius Aikins's way of printing. He did a lot of developing and printing. There was something like a box with a safelight. You have a safelight and you have a screen in front to make the room safe. You have your bulb and there is an opening in front; you have the safelight. You set everything up, contact, frame, everything, and then remove the safelight and expose your target frame to the time. Then share it and develop, and then develop and fix. That's how I did it and it was so simple. I used the same light as my room light. When I wasn't working, I would just take it out to have light in my room.

These are some little things that future photographers, or even today's photographers, can't imagine—how we went through with the basic photographics, emerging equipment, and other things. The enlargement with daylight is something that nobody I have met knows how to do, but I did it.

All these old things, even Aikins honored the first automatic contact printer by GNOME, an English company manufacturing photographic dishes, tongs, and all these. They produced a frame, a box that has a sliding mask. If you wanted to do full plate, you would just slide one side, and if you wanted a passport photo you would just slide and get your wide margin. The light source was under it and you had a timer and the controls.

Honestly, I forgot about it until recently when I saw a negative that I shot of somebody, but the printer was on the stage, on the corner because I knew when I was printing, I would crop. I didn't worry about things around, and I saw it there. It's interesting, the time we're talking about, and how they learned and how they managed and the slow, slow emulsions that they used. Did you ever hear of gaslight paper? Can you imagine that today?

Aimée: What was the social and political climate like in Ghana in 1958? It's just a year after Independence. What was the community of photographers like? Did Ghanaians interact at all with foreign or visiting photographers?

James: There was only one American photographer that came in fact to settle. He must have been introduced to the country by either the Public Relations Office (PRO), the government PRO [officer], called James Moxon, or the *Drum* proprietor Jim Bailey. They introduced him to me at one time when he was doing a book, *The Road Builders*. I think it was published in 1960 or 1961. It's a very good book on Ghana, and beautiful, too. I remember when he was introduced to me, I saw the plan of the book. He was the one who in fact came there and settled.

When I went back in 1970 to start the color [processing lab], he was one of my number one customers; he shot color and we would develop and print for him. He opened his doors to me. Normally, no Black photographer would be allowed to see how he planned it.

I didn't meet many photographers from overseas working there. There was a Syrian, a Lebanese photographer, he came to settle when I was a schoolboy. I was still very young.

Overseas photographers were always moving. If anything, they got in touch with us and we showed them around. Ghanaian photographers are always happy to meet foreign photographers and exchange ideas, because they know they will not steal their ideas, and, if anything [laughs], they might get the chance to go overseas. That's very cordial and inviting. Ghanaian photographers don't shun any overseas, foreign photographer.

Aimée: Were there many British colonial photographers in Accra or in other cities?

James: Honestly, I didn't see British photographers. I didn't have any interactions with them. I was close to these two people, Jim Bailey, then the *Drum* proprietor, and James Moxon. When Jim Bailey came to the country to see the establishment of *Drum*, he was introduced to me and I think he even came to live in the hotel next to me. We saw one another, we went out, and we became very close. Also, James Moxon, the Information Services was not very far from my studio. My studio was in the center of town and like a community center.

Aimée: So, everyone came to you?

James: The head of the Public Relations Office would leave his office and come and spend some minutes in my studio. It was very social. Again, before independence and a little bit after, the heads of the graphic department [of the Public Relations Office] were all English. It was later that Ghanaians took over. I think it was also because white people advanced much in education. They wanted to be lawyers, politicians, doctors. Photography is far down the ladder. If you're doing photography, you didn't take your time to go to high school and then go and do photography. We didn't have universities until after Independence.

I was saying that somebody like Webb was a self-made man already before he took [up] photography. When he went to Africa, he could talk about the United Nations. A man like [Webb], when he is commissioned, he is already on the same mind with those who gave him the order, the assignment. When he goes, he knows what to do. The technique of taking and producing is only a small part of his job.

Aimée: Todd Webb photographed in black and white throughout his life, but it's interesting that he shot in color during his UN trip to Africa in 1958. He also was visiting a continent he'd never ever seen before. How do you think he represents Africa, Ghana specifically, in the images?

James: First of all, Ghana has a lot of color. Africa is colorful, but in Ghana color is the normal thing. People don't put on color, it is there all the time. People are cheerful, and it's nice to capture them in color. The sun, the light is there and luckily, he had a film at the time. The subjects attract you. It even makes you regret if you didn't have color in your pack. You will say, "Ah, why didn't I take this color? Why didn't I?"

[At] that time, color was a new thing. Kodak and Agfa, they all want to experiment and improve on their production. There's one thing, color in Ghana normally is very attractive, and much more so at the time [in the 1950s]. People were not conscious of themselves and what they were wearing. You felt like [shooting] it in color.

I was apprenticed to a black and white-conscious photographer with no money to buy color [film]. I didn't realize it at the time, but if I had ventured into color then, I would have reverted to black and white. Webb was right in taking [the color images], and I think he treasured them so much that he locked them up.

When I arrived in London, I met Dennis Kemp, who worked for Kodak and was engaged in a special lecture service at Kingsway. Kodak had an elite group of three or five photographers. They went around talking about photography, equipment, type of films, and so on. They didn't sell directly, but they had knowledge and background on photography, including color.

Dennis went round schools talking about his experiences and his interests, based on the Kodachrome pictures that he had taken. During the time I met him, he was preparing to go to Nigeria to cover the Queen's visit at Independence. He went to the Ghanaian Embassy to [do research for this trip] and look at images. He was told that, "Our photographer has arrived from Ghana, he wants a job, can you help him?" He said, "No, I can't give him a job, but let him come and see [what I do]." That changed things for me. It was then that I was first introduced to color. I studied even the techniques of taking the pictures, and I started taking one Kodachrome roll a week.

Dennis went with me to Nigeria to cover Independence. While we were there I suggested we go to Ghana. He agreed, and I told him: "All right, you carry on with your work, I will go to Ghana and get things ready."

Within a year, I had been to Africa and back and talking about color. When he came to Ghana, I arranged a shoot at this Cocoa Research Institute. That time my apprentice wasn't there, but I just went to ask [permissions from] my uncle at the Public Relations Office and he invited us to come. I took him to our own traditional cocoa farm to see how the Ghanaians also did their work. You can imagine the work that he had in color, in Kodachrome, cocoa in green, brown, and every color, it was wonderful. He covered the scientific way of producing cocoa.

Aimée: What year was that?

James: 1960, after the Independence. It was in 1960 that Dennis Kemp came and we also went to a gold mine and I told them, "Oh, I've brought an Englishman photographer who wants to take pictures." They gave [permissions], because I'd done some work and they knew me. We went into the boat [at the mine] and you could see the color of gold. When we returned [to England], he took me to a photographic exhibition, I think it was at the Royal Albert Hall, a photographic exhibition that was held there

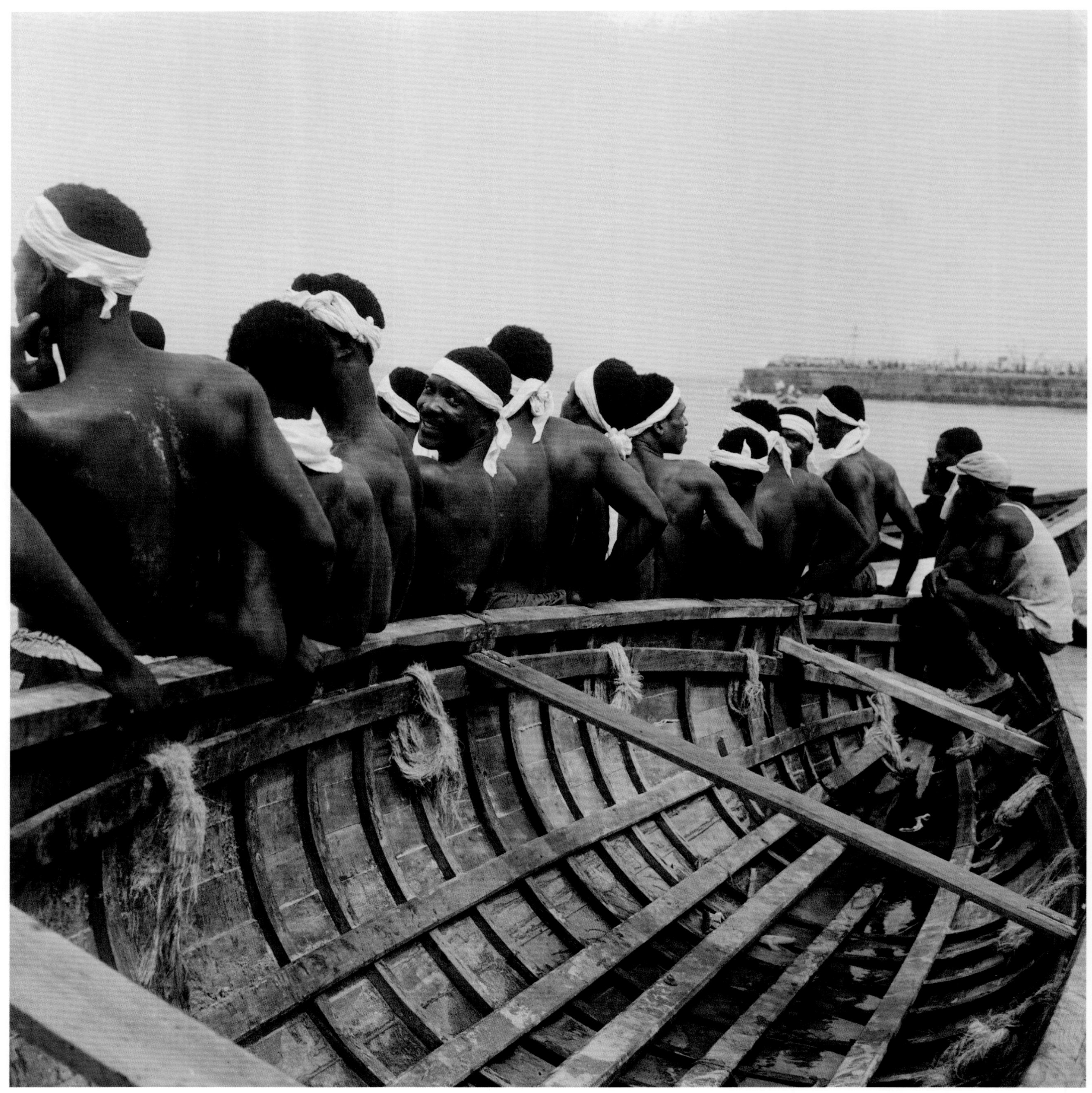

James Barnor, *Regatta, Independence Celebration*, Accra, 1957

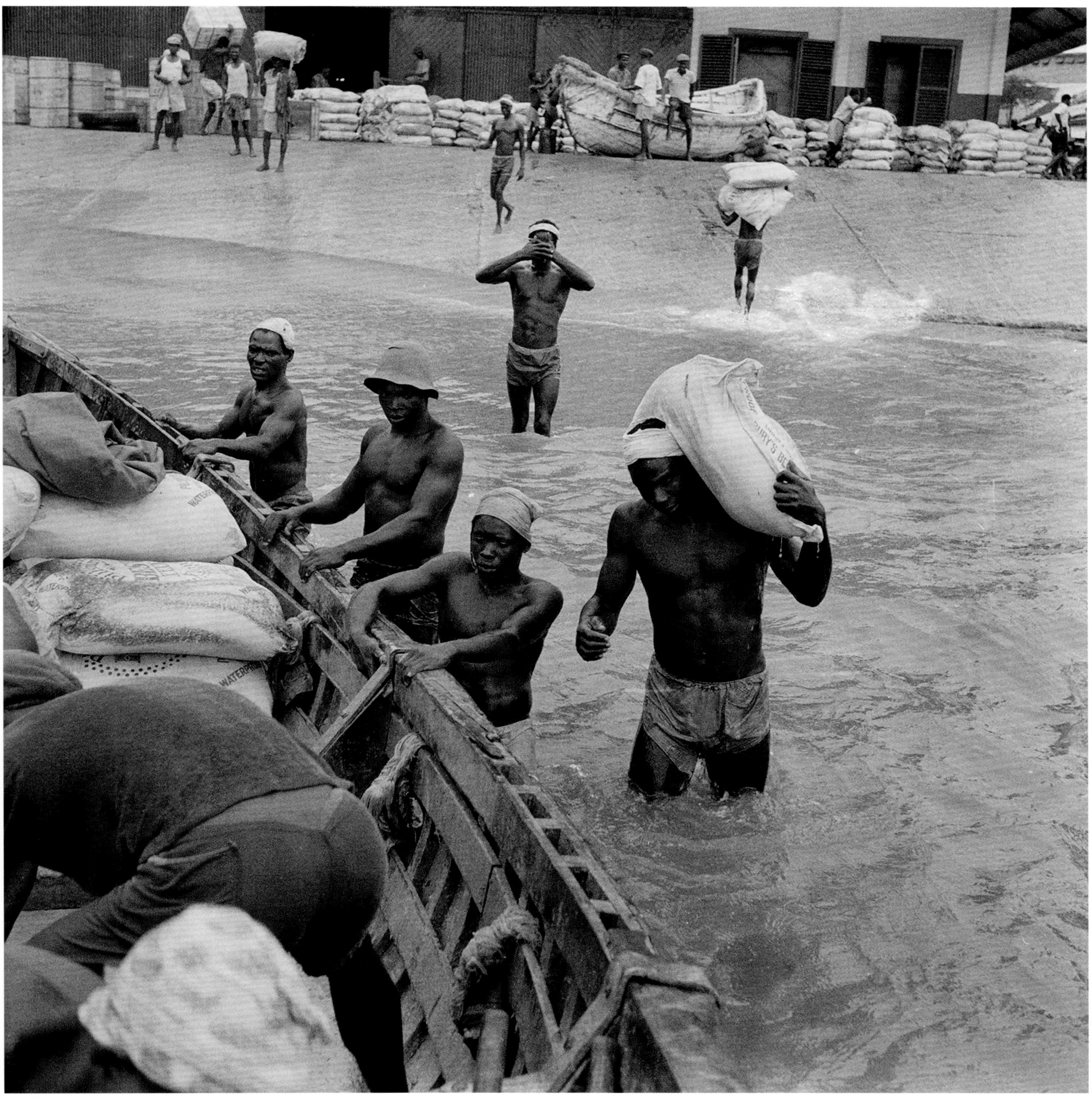

James Barnor, *Unloading Flour, James Town Harbour*, Accra, 1955

and I saw an exhibition of color [work]. Big prints in different colors. I went and told the man in charge, "I want to learn this." He asked me where I came from, and when I said Ghana, he asked if I knew [a friend of his]. And I did. I had photographed him before he came to England. Then he said: "Oh, then you can come [and learn color]."

That's how I went into color. Yes. In the sixties, straight from Ghana. From there I went to the Medway College of Art, and they introduced color into the scheme. I was employed as a technical assistant, and so it continued. Later and it was [at] the same color-processing laboratory that I got the hint to apply for the job to come back to establish color, because Agfa was thinking that, "Oh, color is the 'in thing'. If we can get the processing centers in Africa, people will order more." That's how I returned [to Ghana]. My life and color and photography and *Drum*. *Drum* is another thing altogether.

Aimée: How did you first get connected with *Drum*?

James: Anthony Smith was the one who came to establish *Drum* and later Jim Bailey came to see how the work was going on. He was brought to my studio. How it happened I don't know, but it clicked straight away and we were friends.

I remember the eve of Independence, Jim came from his hotel and passed my studio and said, "What are you doing?" I said, "I'm going to sleep." He said, "You, a Ghanaian, on this day? No, take your camera let's go out."

We walked and ended up at the place where Nkrumah declared that, "Tonight Ghana is free." We were standing right in front of him. We walked around before we went back.

At one time he bought a motorbike for the press and it was kept in my studio. When I came to London, his was my house, [and he was] my savior. Every day I was there, they did everything for me like [giving me] a lead for a job, showing me where to go, helping me with transport.

Aimée: What were some of your most memorable assignments for *Drum*?

James: So many little ones, but there's one that is very memorable. I never worked for anybody; I worked mostly freelance for *Drum*. Then one month, I was there full time, and normally the editors do their own thing and they tell you, "I want this picture." One editor was planning to photograph a hanging, and I said: "That's my line." He opened his eyes and said, "What do you mean, that's your line?" And I told him: "My studio is facing the James Fort Prison, where the hangings take place in Ghana. From my studio I can see the gate." The process of sentencing and charging and all the actual process of hanging and the documentation are handled by the CID [Criminal Investigation Department, Ghana Police Service].

When the time came for hanging, they came with all the documents and made sure that the same person who was sentenced was the same person who was going to be hanged. They took fingerprints, and then you were hanged. It took one hour.

I had that story already. The editor was surprised I knew this and said "let's do the assignment." I got a special bonus after the job as I knew so much about it. I watched and used the motorcycle to follow the van to the cemetery. This is only one of the assignments I did [while full time] for them.

Aimée: Just to document that is also such a traumatic event, to watch someone's death, but it sounds like you were able to follow the whole process.

James: Yes, I thought later that I was lucky, because the warders had their guns. It's the prisoners who carry the body and do everything. The warders have to guard the prisoners so that they don't run away or something.

They looked at me from outside. I didn't have a special camera with a telephoto lens where you could hide in a tree and use a zoom to take your pictures. I followed them and they could have done anything to me. "Where do you come from? Why do you follow us with a motorbike?" But I got away with it.

Aimée: Were you scared?

James: I don't think I was at the time. Maybe only later when I realized what I had done.

Aimée: What is it like to look through your photographs from this period now?

James: Now I wouldn't be able to teach photography; photography is on another level. But I can talk about how I did my work at the time. If it inspires somebody, well, good. Luckily, we are archiving all my work.

Every time we see some new images, I get excited, because I had forgotten all about them. Each and every one has a story. I wish I could get five more years in addition to my ninety. So that I can look at the archives on the road to work.

At my gallery, we saw a picture similar to one of Todd Webb's taken in Togo, where somebody was wearing a mask (see p. 24). I just saw a similar one of mine, but it is more cultural and traditional, and of an animal mask and not a human face.

I tend to concentrate on people more than other things. People are more important than places. Most of my pictures are of people, but I took some that are similar to Todd Webb's images. I also photographed men loading and unloading goods from a ship in Accra harbor (see p. 89). I'm proud of this; it's in black and white. I know where Webb stood to take this image (see pp. 78–79). I photographed [a scene of] unloading from another angle; I've got the Customs building and the beach scene, but not as good as that.

Aimée: Where was Webb standing to take the image?

James: There's a breakwater, something that was built to make the village safe. It's cement and goes about some yards into the sea. Today, [laughs], the birds sleep on it because it's not used anymore since the harbor was moved to Tema. They haven't invested properly in that area and now it's an eyesore. They're trying to change it and make it into a boat-building port, where they build boats for fishing, possibly a fishing area as well.

In the 1950s, it was the wholesale area, where imported things were stored before being delivered to the owners and offices for the workers. That was a very, very busy time when [Webb] went there. You could photograph this all day. The boats were numbered. I lived just a stone's throw from the harbor. Even then, there was no restriction on whether you could go there or not. Most of the workers lived around where I lived and had my studio. You see this one, I think where the boat is in the middle somewhere, apart from the breakwater (see p. 233). I think Webb took this picture from somewhere where the boat is out of the water. There is a boat on top there, out of the water. It's somewhere in the middle of the picture, but there's a white boat there. It was the front of the warehouse where people worked and even lorries could drive into the warehouse and take deliveries. There's where he stood and took the picture.

Aimée: What do you think of the images Todd Webb took in Ghana?

James: One thing, Ghanaian people don't object [to being photographed]. Sometimes they say, "Oh, you are going to sell my pictures so give me this or that." As soon as you give a penny or something, they are themselves. They let you take [the photograph].

In fact, I would have taken the same type of pictures as Webb, except that perhaps I might have been able to go [places] he couldn't. But again, Ghanaians prefer foreigners. We give home to foreigners easily.

I approve of [Webb's] pictures, because they were for development, they were for industry. But you cannot go away from the human aspect of Ghanaian life, whatever your aim or your subject. You will see people acting between themselves or doing things, like he said, "You are going to a new country." Things were so different, so strange.

Basically, if anything, if you were a foreign photographer, you had all the equipment and the background. We Ghanaian photographers didn't have the money to equip ourselves and never traveled. I think I'm one of a few who had the chance to go out like that. Within Ghana we didn't travel. I followed my uncle and started traveling around. I had the facility and I could develop. I don't know where they got that idea of the dark tent with the filter at the top. We first used it as a changing bag, like today's changing bag, and also as a developing facility. [My uncle], at one time, printed using a number of matchsticks around the printing frame. They took the match, struck it, once or twice to give the exposure, and printed it. You could smell the inside of the tent. I am telling you, because I inherited that tent.

Aimée: Looking at what Webb photographed as part of his UN commission documenting industry and technology, can you think of other things you would have photographed in 1958? Was there anything Todd Webb missed?

James: For that, I would say yes. Educational developments, schools, science pursuits. He photographed a man standing there, an agricultural inspector, somebody in uniform and hat. I would say this is Ghana, possibly the Ministry of Agriculture or Department of Agriculture. You can see the size of the knickers were typical of that era in Ghana. The art, or the flower, is common in Ghana. All parts of the country. That's another Ghanaian, because all the other official employees are doing this scientific work or overseeing these works. You can see the pockets, the size of the pockets. It takes me back to my childhood days.

Aimée: Did you ever wear clothes like that?

James: I didn't work for anybody where I wore a uniform. When I was at school, when I was teaching, I wore my own clothes. We didn't have a uniform as a school teacher. That's the only work I did. That [and] I went into photography. From school, after the war, 1945 and then 1946, I tried to get a job, but I couldn't. The school was waiting for me.

At school I learnt to weave baskets. This is the first university in Ghana, based in Legon (right). These are some of the things that Webb could have photographed in more depth, the infants or secondary school, before university. I would have liked to photograph the life of children who would carry Ghana in 1958. It was just one year after our Independence.

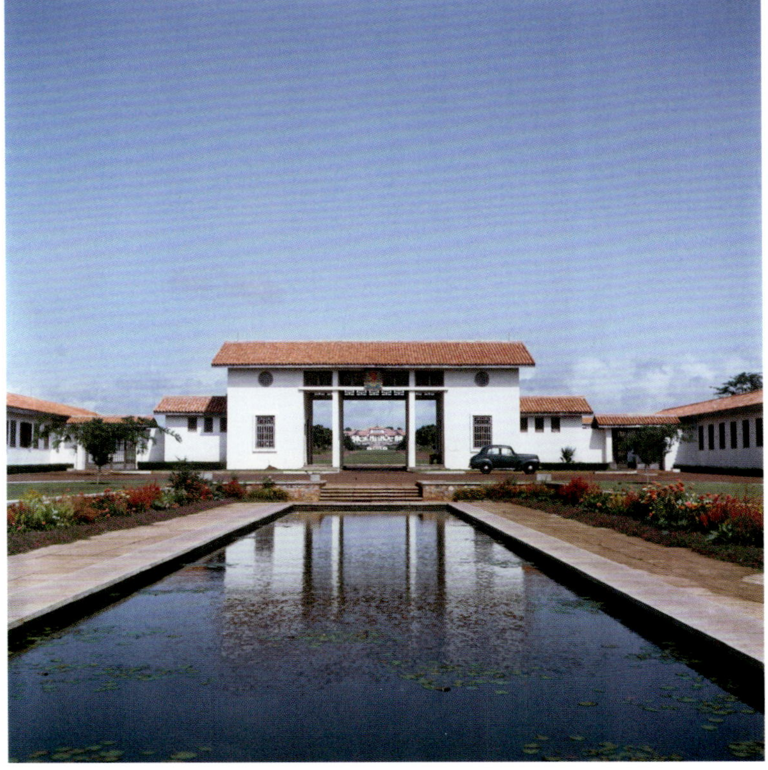

Todd Webb, *Untitled* (44UN-7977-296), Ghana, 1958
Entrance to University of Ghana, Legon, Accra.

Overleaf: James Barnor, *The 'Ever Young' Photographic Studio in the James Town neighborhood*, Accra, 1956

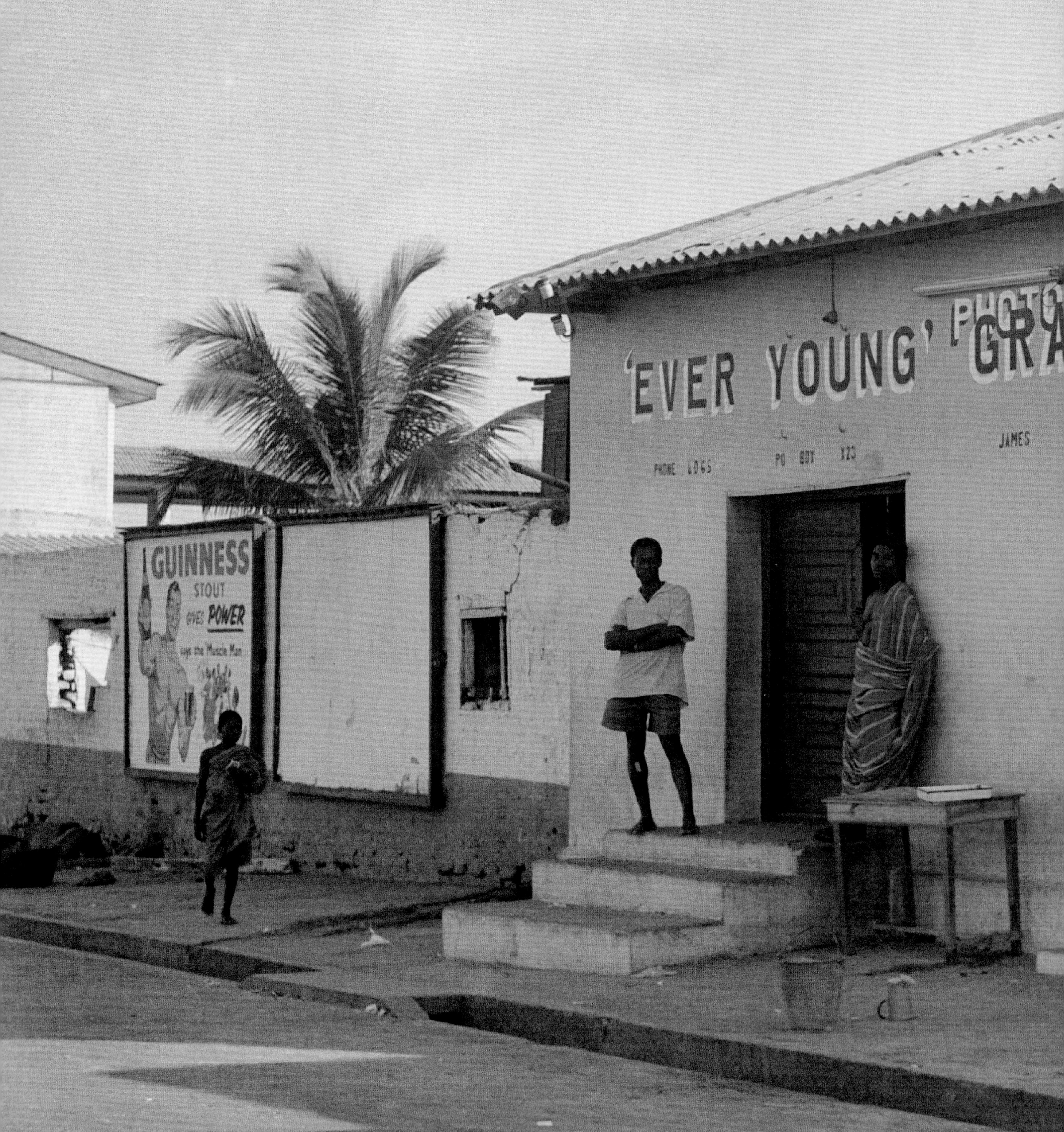
GUINNESS
STOUT
gives POWER
says the 'Muscle Man'
'EVER YOUNG'
PHONE
PO BOX
JAMES

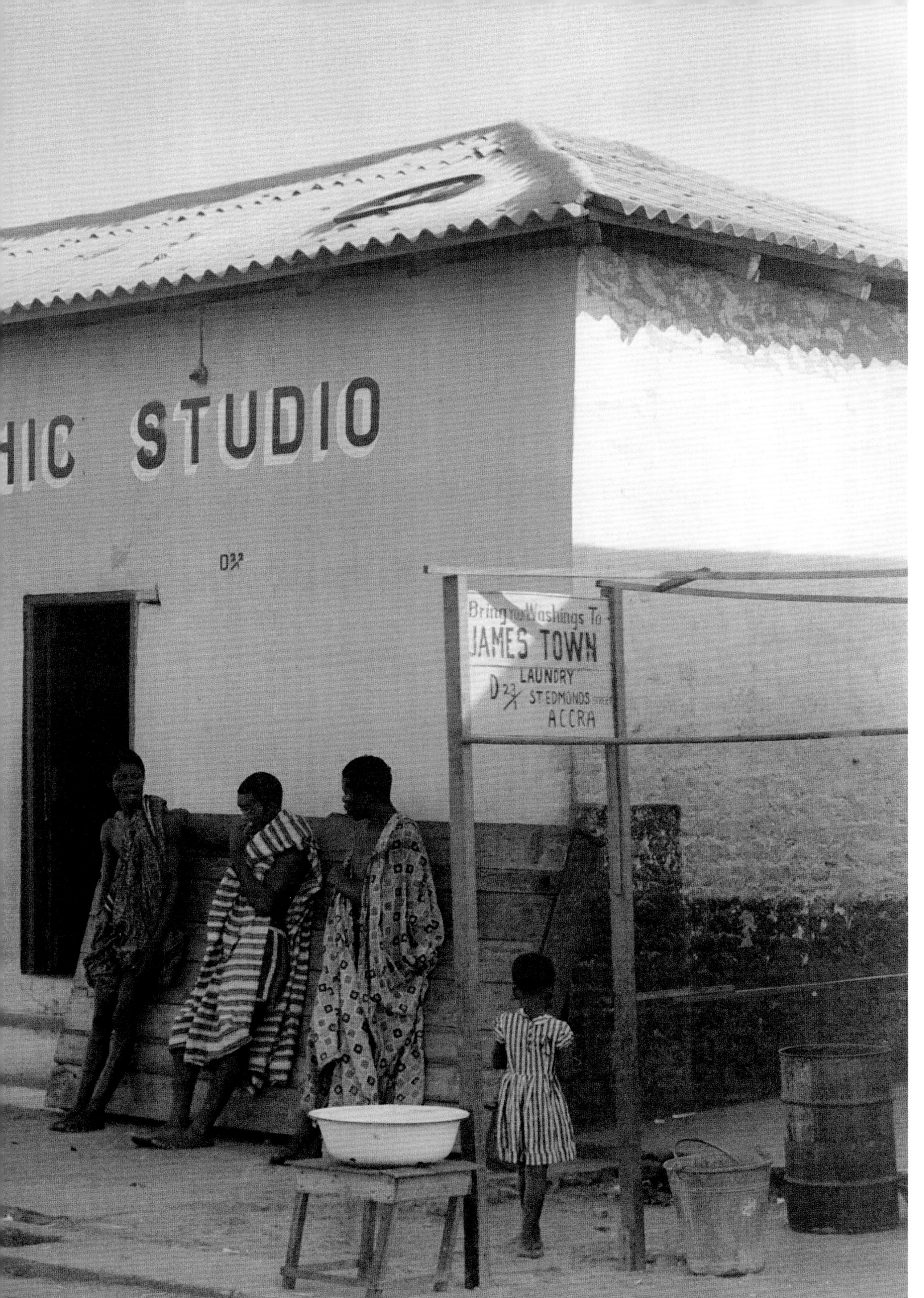
HIC STUDIO
JAMES TOWN
LAUNDRY
ST EDMONDS
ACCRA

Seeing in Color: Todd Webb's Color Photography and the United Nations Commission

Aimée Bessire

Ghanaian photographer James Barnor suggested that the vibrancy of Africa lends itself to being captured with color film: "Africa is colorful.... People don't put on color, it is there all the time.... It's nice to capture them in color. The sun, the light is there and...the subjects attract you."[1] It is clear that Todd Webb thoughtfully considered how to photograph the bright colors he saw during his five-month United Nations commission. Visiting at a time when film and processing equipment for color photography were not readily available in many of the countries, Webb's images present early color documents of urban and rural Africa. Some of the photographs display the vibrancy of daily life through clothing and architecture, while others frame people within or against backdrops of breathtakingly bright skies, aestheticizing the everyday and capturing the atmosphere and environments in many of the countries.

Color photography is widely viewed, and perhaps even judged, by its presumed relationship to "reality"–both the reality of the colors and, by default, the veracity of the actual image. It is important to note that color film has been widely criticized for its inherent racial biases and inability to capture and record all skin tones equally.[2] While Webb's color photographs may offer a reflection of the colors he saw on his trip, the film available in 1958 was not able to document all people equitably. Where one might presume the "realism" of the images, it is important to register their subjectivities–both through Webb's own selection process, and the ways that the colors of individuals and scenes are determined through chemical processes on sensitized surfaces. Do Webb's color photographs represent the reality of life in these countries, or an "intangible mirage of color," to borrow photo historian Michel Frizot's phrasing?[3]

Webb's color images presume a certain connection to the specificity of the moment in which the shutter was pressed. Color adds a dimensionality to the scene, where the description of the setting's colors, apparently as the eye would see them,[4] animates the vernacular. Where black and white photographs suggest a certain timelessness, Webb's color images intimate a "present" moment. While this may be a false supposition, the colors of the photographs act as potential "codes" to Webb's perception of space, and they also activate culturally coded representations of Africa during the time in which they were photographed. This is seen, for example, in Webb's image of a Dar es Salaam street scene, which presents the presumed realities of colors he saw while in Tanganyika (Tanzania) (opposite). The green truck parked at the acacia tree-lined street curb provides a colorful frame for the bicycle balancing a basket of pineapples and sun-reflecting oranges. The fruit colors resonate with the yellow shirt and yellow dress of the two pedestrians walking toward the viewer, all exemplifying the presumed "realities" of a vibrant, sunny day in Dar es Salaam. A closer look reveals some of the signs embedded within the image that provide a sense of the cultural life on the street. The barefoot man in the bright shirt, ripped pants, and traditional Swahili coast kofia (hat) walks confidently on the city sidewalk as he passes a boy in school uniform to his far right, almost out of the frame, suggesting the movement of city life during the colonial era. Does the photograph capture the specifics of the pedestrians' skin tones? We will never know. All of these subtle and overt cultural codes complicate our reading of the image's significance and this moment in time on a Dar es Salaam sidewalk.

Todd Webb and Color Photography

Often carrying multiple cameras–a Leica 3, a Rolleiflex, and a Simmon Bros. Omega 6x7 medium-format–Todd Webb worked in both black and white and color while in Africa. His black and white images present a conscious awareness of contrast, tone, shadow, and shape in the framing of compositions, as in the photograph of a door in Zanzibar, where the contrasting dark gray tones emphasize the wooden frame and traditional carved door (see p. 213). The contrasts allow the cracks in the wall to present as interesting textures and the black graffiti on the right to draw the viewer's eye. Webb wrote of how he approached images differently when working in color as opposed to black and white, having to adjust to "seeing" in color and considering the play of colors in the image frame.[5] For a white outsider photographing individuals and settings in African contexts, "seeing" in color may also have had subconscious or overtly racialized implications. Although it is not clear if Webb directly considered race when photographing a woman and infant in Northern or Southern Rhodesia (Zambia or Zimbabwe), one might envision his process of concentrating on the colors in this tightly focused image (see p. 170). Webb is likely to have understood that the natural lighting on this close-up portrait was ideal to capture some of the subtleties of the skin tones of the woman and child, partially making up for the inherent flaws of 1950s Kodak film. As he turned his lens to look slightly upwards at the pair, he might have appreciated the ways that the woman's red dress and white head wrapper and the child's green and red striped sweater and hat would enliven the image, creating an engaging document of life in the Federation. The vibrancy of these colors in close-up, along with the woman's direct gaze and smile and the child's focused curiosity, draw the viewer in.

In the United States, during the 1950s, color photography was becoming more accessible to professionals and amateurs alike. Although color film and processing were still considered expensive, the technologies had come a long way since the first commercial availability of color with the Lumière autochrome in 1907, and the introduction of lush color advertising and fashion photographs to entice consumers in print journals in the 1920s and 1930s. Kodak played a central role in changing how the public engaged with color photography. With their introduction of color slide film in 1936, color photography became more accessible to a broader public despite the relative expense. Yet, at that time, the public still associated color with commercial practices such as advertising and fashion, and it wasn't until the 1960s that color film became more readily adopted by amateur photographers.

Kodak advertisements from as early as the 1930s marketed the new color film to capture "fleeting personal moments, artistic aspirations, and naturalistic colors," as Katherine A. Bussard suggested in her historical overview of color photography.[6] Extensive advertising campaigns promoted the idea of "color" in the broader imagination, with taglines such as "Add color with Kodachrome" (1936) or "Lifelike in black and white.... It *lives* in Kodachrome."[7] Yet such advertisements did not illuminate the inherent racial discrimination of color film. Early available film stock, printing, and processing techniques privileged white over other skin tones.[8] In the mid-1950s, Kodak famously created a card featuring a pale, white-skinned woman with dark hair, to be used to calibrate skin tones when printing and processing film. Called the "Shirley Card," after the original model in the image, Shirley Page, the so-called "standard" created clear racial biases when calibrating printing colors for photographs of individuals with darker skin tones. It was only when, in the 1980s, furniture and chocolate manufacturers complained about color photography's inability to capture the intricacies of their products' distinct brown tones that Kodak created new film stock that attempted to more equitably record the specificities of dark colors.[9] They did not produce a Shirley Card presenting multiple racial skin tones until 1995.

Photographers and critics debated the Kodak advertisement's claims that black and white photography presented more "lifelike" representations, while color brought "reality" to life. In her essay "Real Color," photo historian Lisa Hostetler traces the trajectory of black and white and color photographs in the broader public's understanding of what were considered representations of reality: "As color photographic technologies developed, discussions about the realism of black and white versus color emerged. At times, color photography was deemed too artificial to be real; at others, it

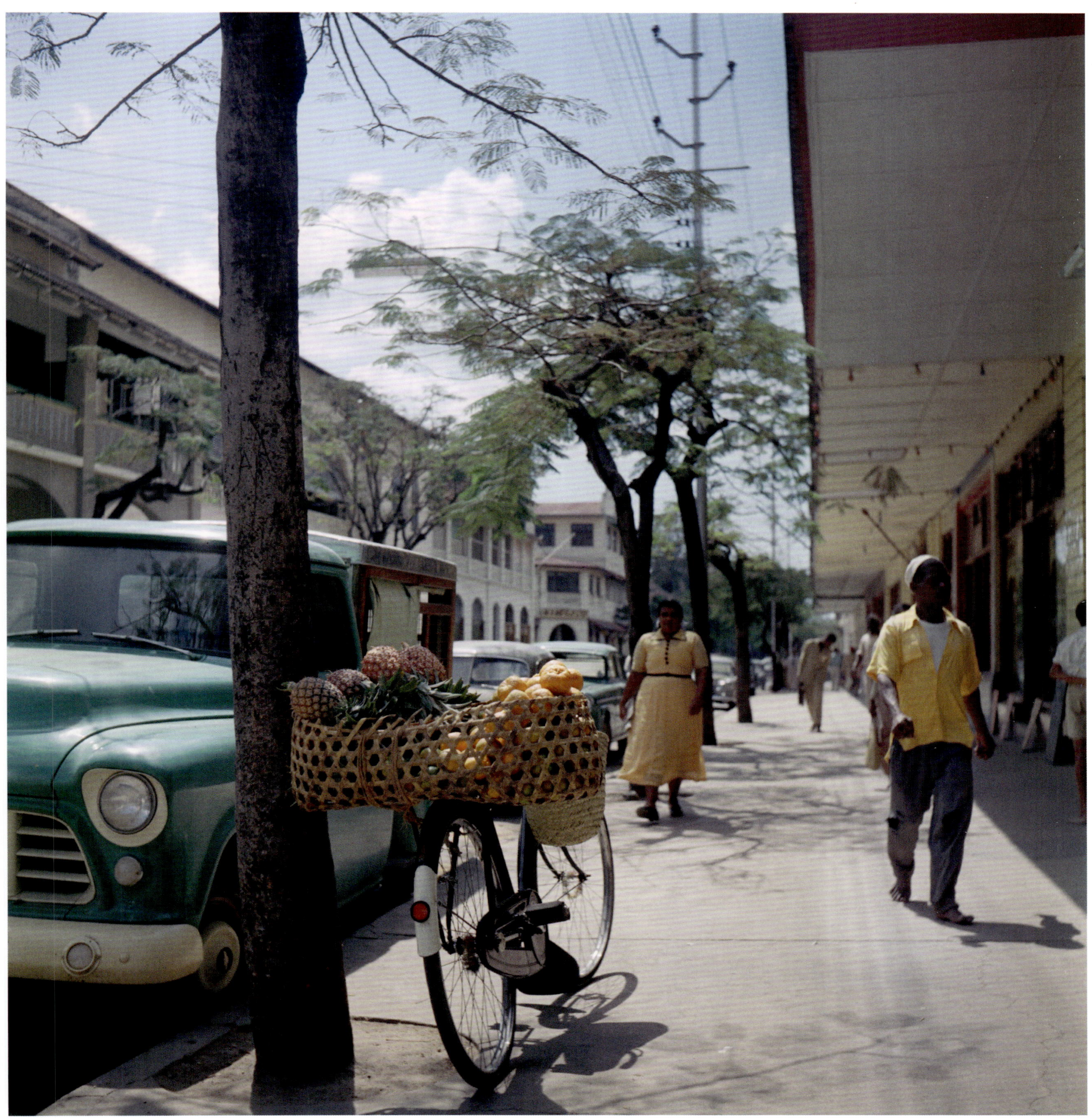

Todd Webb, *Untitled* (44UN-7940-008), Tanganyika (Tanzania), 1958
Pedestrians on a city street, Dar es Salaam.

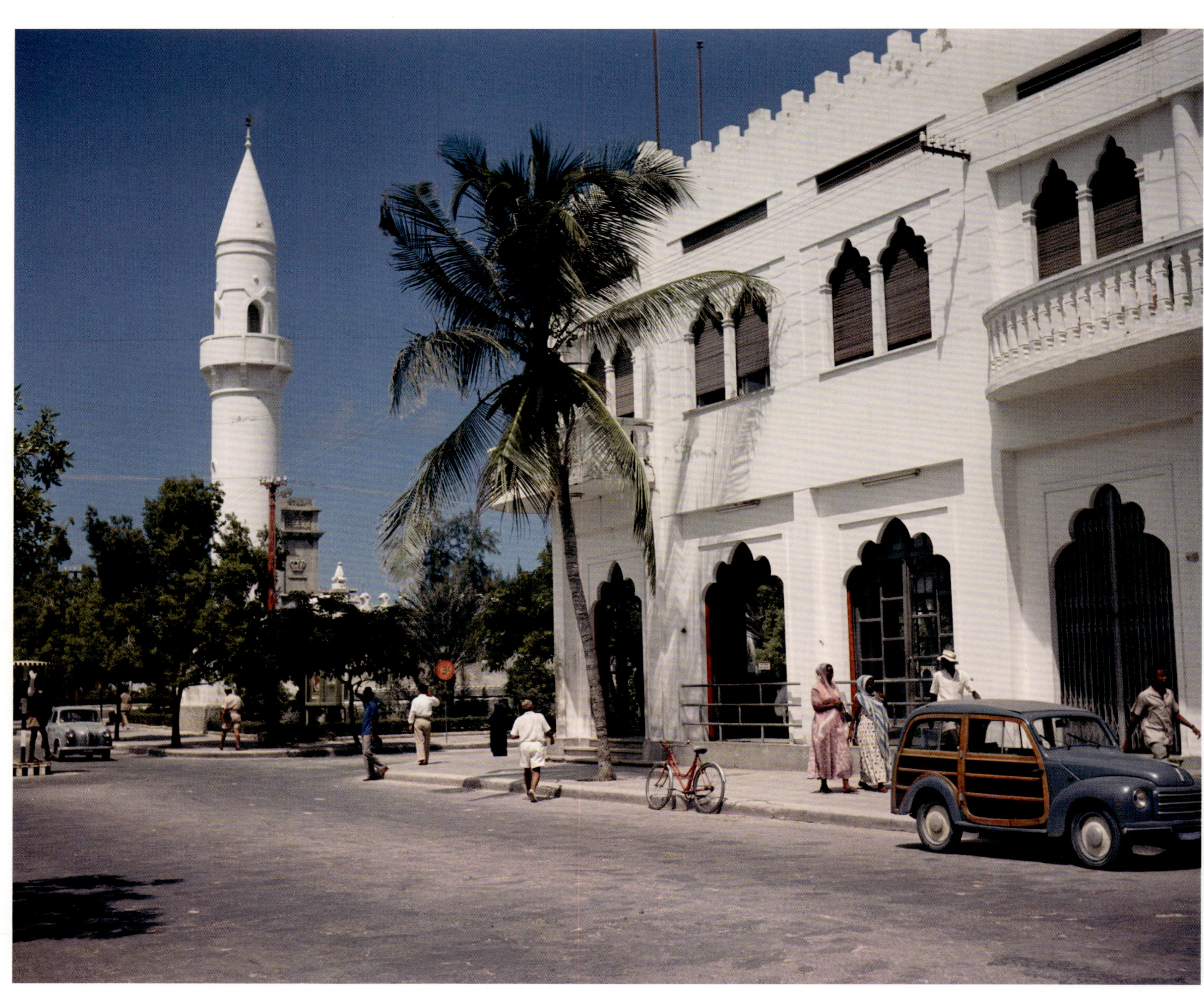

Todd Webb, *Untitled* (44UN-7921-003), Trust Territory of Somaliland (Somalia), 1958
Street scene with the Arbaca Rukun (Arba'Rukun) Mosque in the background and the Cinema Hamar at the right, Mogadishu.

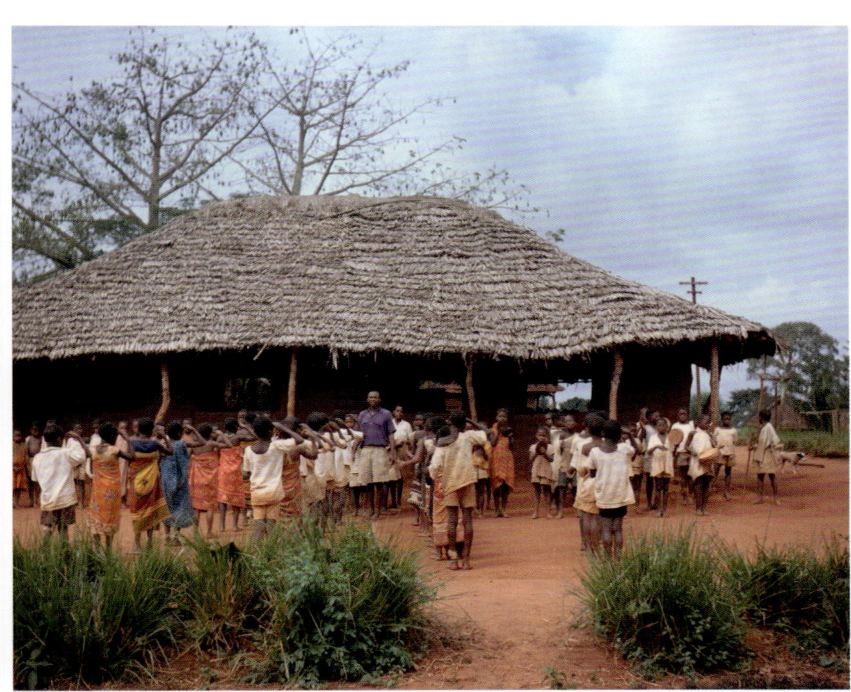

Todd Webb, *Untitled* (44UN-8015-455), Tanganyika (Tanzania), 1958
Students during outdoor music practice at a primary school near Tanga.

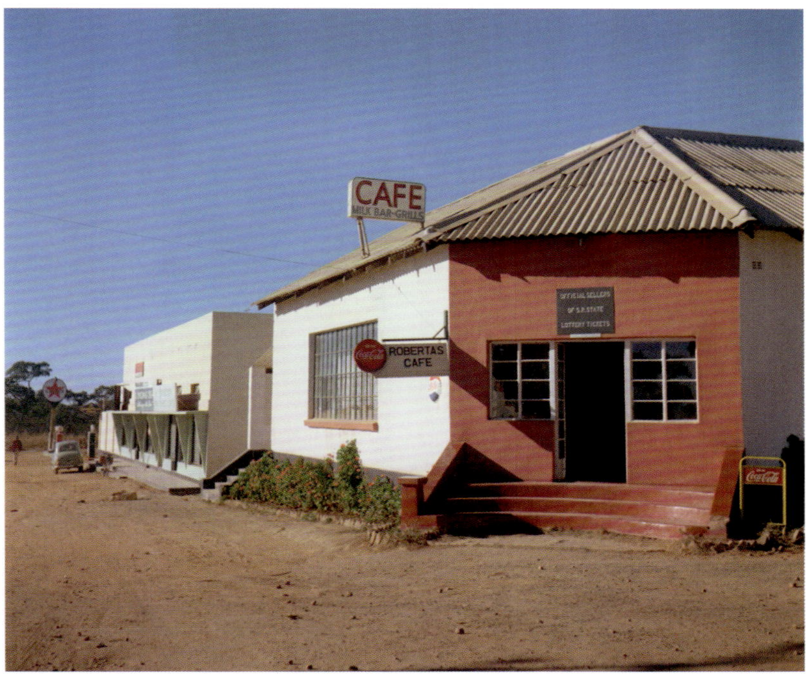

Todd Webb, *Untitled* (44UN-8022-015), Northern Rhodesia (Zambia), 1958
Caltex station and Roberta's Café.

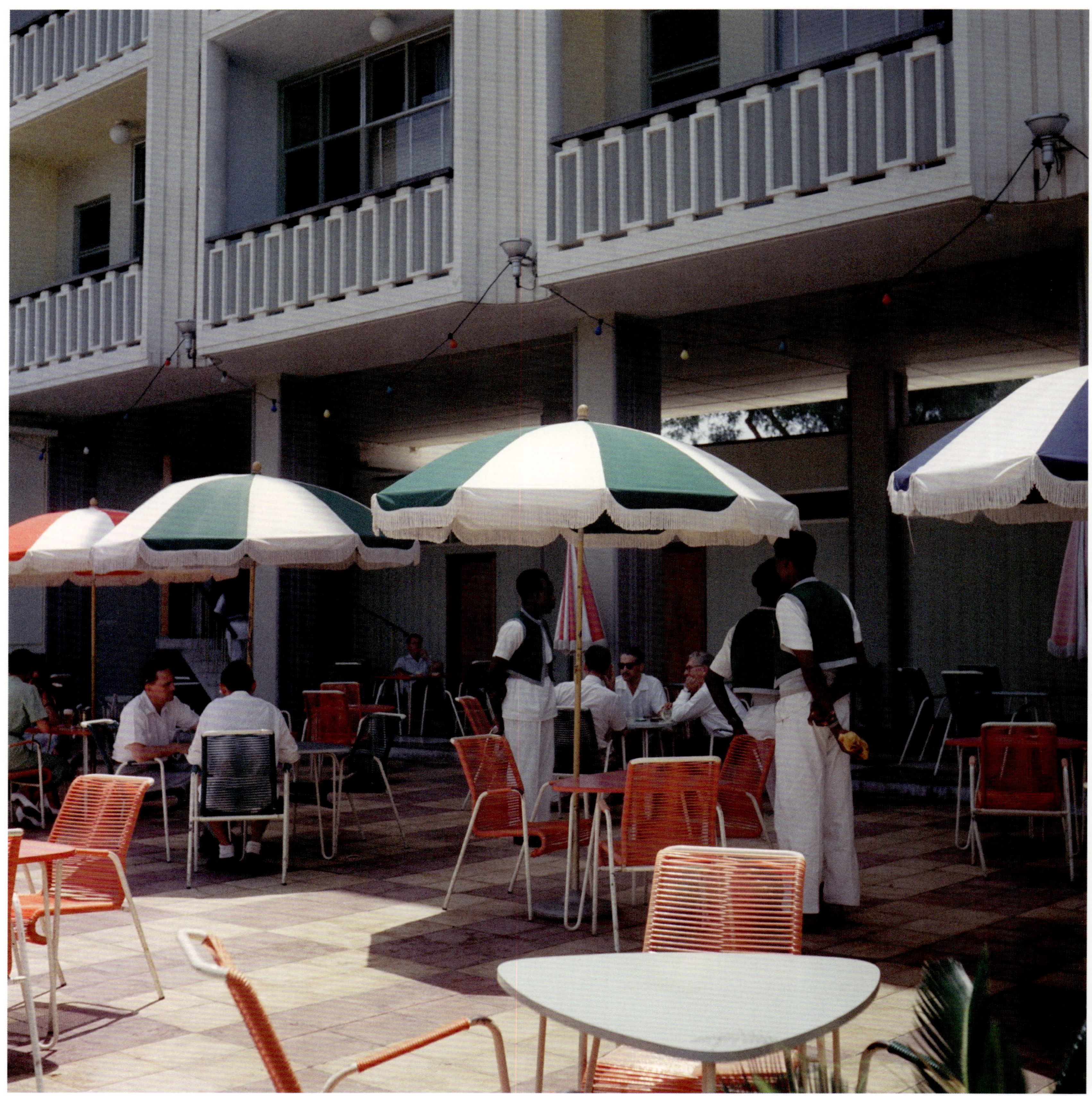

Todd Webb, *Untitled* (44UN-8003-001), Ghana, 1958
Patrons and waiters at the Ambassador Hotel in Accra.

was too literal to be artistic."[10] Webb would have been aware of the debate surrounding black and white as more realistic and color as "too literal," and of the potentially complicated relationship between color photography and documentary work. As Hostetler suggests, "in the documentary era–the 1930s and early 40s–monochrome photography's association was with reality and truth, while color photography was usually associated with superfluous fantasy and commercial extravagance."[11] Webb was highly influenced by these ideologies, especially through his work with Roy Stryker at Standard Oil Company, and through Farm Security Administration photographers like Walker Evans and Dorothea Lange, whom he revered, and who in many ways codified documentary photography as a black and white practice.[12] Webb associated black and white photography with greater reality and artistic expression, and deemed color more "superfluous" and less serious;[13] yet, his color photography of Africa presents a vivid document of the colors he experienced during his travels, describing or even "enlivening" individual contexts and opening up the possibilities of seeing the "reality" of life on the continent, even if this was in fact an illusion created by Webb's own subjectivities and the play of color on light-sensitive surfaces.

In his journal entries on color from the 1940s, Webb talks about its newness and his own experimentation with color film, mostly for advertising and commercial fashion work.[14] During the mid-1940s, he discussed its value for his commissions and the higher pay it brought in.[15] He also delineated his early views of color in a journal entry from August 19, 1946: "I don't know that I will ever want to do it for myself–there is a big demand for it here and they pay very well for it. Maybe concentrating on color work for earning a living could more or less divorce my work from my love."[16] The suggestion that at this point he viewed color photography as "work" and black and white as his "love" is telling. In 1954 he noted that his experimentation would help him "produce some good sellable color," and he "might even make some good things" for himself.[17] As he continued to photograph in both monochrome and color, it is interesting to consider how Webb may have distinguished between "work" and "love" in his images taken in the African countries.

In December 1957, Webb began making color photography experiments for David Ritchie at the United Nations.[18] It is possible that Ritchie, the Chief of the Photographic and Exhibition Services at the UN, wanted to see Webb's color results before he left on his five-month trip to Africa. Arthur Tyrrell, also with the UN, gave him twenty-five rolls of Kodacolor to photograph with in Mexico in February 1958.[19] The trip to Mexico presented a perfect chance for Webb to experiment with his cameras and color film in potentially similar light conditions to Africa. The bright sunshine he found in many of the African countries provided ideal conditions for photographing in color, quite the opposite of trips Webb had taken to London and the American South in 1948, where he was unable to photograph with color film on cloudy days, lamenting "the sun must come sometime."[20] But while the African sun may have contributed to the supposed ease with which Webb took color images, it is also interesting to consider what may have influenced Webb's larger understanding of color photography in this context.

Seeing the continent for the first time, Webb's perspective would have been largely informed by monochromatic images he had seen published in newsprint and magazines.[21] But like most Americans, he would also have been aware of the ways that news publications[22] and journals such as *National Geographic* and *LIFE* were making color images part of daily life.[23] In 1953, *LIFE* invited Ernst Haas to create a color photo-essay on New York City, the magazine's first ever full-color spread.[24] They also included Eliot Elisofon's "Voyages to Paradise," color images of the South Seas in 1955, the same year the magazine paid for the film for Webb's 1955–56 photographic walk across the United States with the intention of publishing the images.[25] On September 24, 1956, *LIFE* published Gordon Parks's important photographs of segregation in Alabama, in the article "Restraints: Open and Hidden."[26] This lush color essay documenting the deep racial divide in the South appeared only a year and a half before Webb left for his UN-commissioned Africa trip, and it is highly likely that Webb would have seen his friend's piece. What he may or may not have been aware of, however, are the dangers Parks faced as a Black man photographing the story in Alabama, including fleeing the local White Citizens' Council, and the assault of Sam Yette, a young Black reporter, for drinking out of the whites-only fountain at Birmingham Station to help Parks get a photograph.[27] Todd Webb would not face such discrimination when photographing in Africa.

Photographing Africa in Color

Throughout Webb's images, color film provides context for the bright environments and vibrant patterns of African daily life amidst the inequities of the colonial era. Color photography was still not prominently used in Africa, and Webb took his images twelve years before James Barnor opened the first color-processing laboratory in Accra, Ghana. The colors of the photographs present a certain "mirage" of reality as they animate or even "activate" specific moments in time, often adding texture through culturally coded representations. Todd Webb began his UN commission documenting the first open election in Togoland (Togo), then traveled to seven other countries to photograph industrial expansion and technological developments. Throughout the project, the color images present a sense of the "reality" of the settings in 1958, but one that may be called into question considering the inherent subjectivities of the medium. Many capture the atmosphere of the environments: the brightness of sun against blue sky backdrops, and an almost palpable feeling of heat and humidity or arid desert conditions. An image from the Trust Territory of Somaliland (Somalia) of a teenage boy carrying three fish wrapped in straw atop his head presents the distinct feeling of a hot day, with the boy walking along under glaring sun against clouds, on the "magnificent sand beach" Webb described in his journal (see p. 143).[28] The breathtaking blues of the image create a picturesque backdrop for the perhaps mundane activity of the boy, whom Webb photographed looking straight ahead, seemingly unaware of the camera. Most likely, the boy's skin in the photograph is darker against the background sky than it may have been in reality. In many ways, the aestheticization of the scene, drawing the viewer's eye to the indulgent colors, highlighting the contrasts, and providing a strong sense of the heat and haze of the sun against the clouds and sky, supersedes the potential reality of a hard day's work for the boy.

Color functions in a similar way in a photograph of a man riding his bike on a dirt road in Kassala, which Webb described as "a center for the desert nomadic tribes of Sudan and surrounding countries" (see p. 2).[29] The image gives a sense of the bright sun and desert environment, where the average high temperature in May, when Webb was visiting, is 106 degrees.[30] The sun casts the man's shadow on the sand-colored road, and the long shadows in the front right corner hint at the buildings lining the opposite side of the street, just outside of the frame, all projecting an indexical sign of a particular time of day. Color enlivens the context of the image, highlighting the almost unreal blue that frames the mountains in the background. The green leaves of a thin neem tree to the left create a burst of color against the sky, and a man's white djellaba stands out against one building's subtle mint-green walls. This photograph presents the flow of daily life within a sharp, somehow impossibly bright environment, color enhancing the viewer's perception of Webb's indication of time and temperature.

In another photograph, this time in Mogadishu, Trust Territory of Somaliland, the colors similarly demonstrate the vibrancy of street life (see p. 96). The white minaret of the historic Arbaca Rukun (Arba'Rukun) Mosque is framed against a bright blue sky. The colors of the photograph–the green trees and the palm fronds against the white side of the Cinema Hamar; the dark, reddish wood lining the interior frames of the theater's windows, echoed in the red bike leaning against the sidewalk and the red street sign; the blue shirt of a man looking right to cross the street; the women in pink and blue patterned dresses and head coverings; and the blue and wood paneling of the "Woody" station wagon–all enliven the context of this image. Photographs such as this capture the spirit and movement of a Somali city, perhaps even bringing the illusion of the scene to life, as the early Kodachrome advertisement posited. Such movement is absent from another image, of a Caltex station and Roberta's Café (see p. 97, right). The photograph instead depicts the colors of a still moment on this dirt road near Northern Rhodesia (Zambia). The open door and terracotta color of the front of Roberta's Café draws the viewer in, and the red of the distant Caltex star in the background visually plays with the reds of the "Cafe Milk Bar–Grills" sign, the Pepsi bottle cap and Coca Cola logos, and the "specials" sandwich board to the right of the café steps. The green shrubs with orange flowers planted to the left of Roberta's entrance are covered with dirt, hinting at the dust kicked up by passing car tires, enhancing a feeling of desolation in this quiet setting. Here the colors not only present Webb's possible perception of the scene, they also animate dirt from unseen passing cars, creating a palpable sense of absence.

Other photographs highlight the play of color, the bright clothing of daily life, and the fashion styles of 1958, providing cultural context and marking a specific moment in history. In one image of the Trust Territory of Somaliland, a man in his bright red suit stands out against the light sand color of the buildings (see p. 136), while in another, two women in matching yellow dresses hold hands as they walk on the beach, gazing directly at the viewer (see p. 128).[31] The color photographs draw attention to the vibrancy of clothing and fashion in Somaliland in 1958. The diaphanous, sleeveless yellow dirac dresses signify a time before styles shifted and more conservative dress "became the norm," according to Ali Jimale Ahmed, "towards the end of the Siyaad Barre regime...and especially after the defeat in the Ogaden War in 1977–78."[32]

In an image from Tanganyika, color photography delineates the subtleties of gendered representation. The photograph of an outdoor school music assembly shows students with a school band and a smiling teacher in a blue shirt (see p. 97, left).[33] The girls wear patterned cloths, made in East Africa and named kangas during the colonial era, when traders brought colorful gingham and other printed cottons to East African ports. The imported fabrics were compared to the dotted patterning on guinea fowl–kangas in Swahili–and are said to have inspired these local patterned cloths, with a border around the edges and often a Swahili phrase at the bottom. In the photograph, the girls' kangas stand out against the boys' school uniforms of white shirts and khaki shorts, creating a visual divide and suggesting the gendered division by which the education of boys, the ones privileged with uniforms, was valued over that of girls, shown without uniforms–a distinction reinforced from the colonial era to today.[34]

Webb equally captured the bright colors of the daily lives of colonial administrators, tourists, and expatriates. An image of the Ambassador Hotel in Accra, Ghana, shows a mostly white, male clientele (see p. 98). Seated in red chairs under white umbrellas striped with green, red, or blue, the patrons are socializing and appear to be enjoying a relaxing afternoon. Colored lightbulbs hang from the upper balcony and three Black waiters in uniforms of white pants and shirts and bright green vests stand by to take orders, giving the viewer a sense of the racial and socio-economic disparities in 1958. Here, the colors present an insight into the leisure available to those with privilege during the colonial era. They also express the inherent racial biases of early color photography. This photograph illustrates the ways in which color film available in 1958 privileged white skin, permitting a greater detail of the white facial features than it was possible to capture in the Black skin of the workers, who appear almost featureless. Unlike other images, this photograph communicates a frozen moment; a pause between breaths while the faceless attendants await their next orders from the hotel's privileged clientele; a specific "reality" of Ghana in the year after its independence.

At the Kitwe mine in Northern Rhodesia (Zambia), Webb photographed rows of worker housing, suggesting the large numbers of people brought to work there (see opposite). Two men on bikes ride toward one another, silhouetted against the repetition of bright houses in white, blue, and yellow with identical tan roofs–a feature that no doubt would have motivated Webb to photograph the scene in color. This display of a local economy meets the UN mandate to document industry and technology, but its appealing aesthetic risks glossing over the harsh realities of the workers, who had no choice other than to live there and work within an inequitable colonial system. Webb comments on this in his Africa journal: "the differences in educational background and the habits of cheap labor formed through the years [of colonial domination]...is one of the most difficult problems that has to be solved in Africa."[35] Another image provides a more intimate view of people at the worker housing in Northern Rhodesia (see p. 102). The red dirt road, with a row of white houses running along one side and fencing on the other, directs the eye to the distant factory and people walking, standing, and talking. A woman wearing a peach-colored sweater, flower-print skirt, and red hat carries a white bundle on her head. Next to her a woman in a print dress rides a bike. A boy leans on a fence, perhaps separating the worker housing from the larger, brick dwellings of management, and in the near distance, groups of men are standing together or walking. This image provides insight into daily life at the worker housing, possibly on a day off or after work has ended for the day. It does not, however, tell the whole story of the workers' lives, or reveal the harsh inequities they and others like them experienced during colonial rule in Northern and Southern Rhodesia.

Despite the vibrancy of the images, the United Nations Office of Public Information only published the photographs in black and white. No color images were circulated. The UN brochure "United Nations Photos, Supplement, No. 7" promoted "the changing face of Africa" and the expansion of industry and technologies during a colonial moment across the continent. Webb's cover photograph, published in black and white, of a Somali herder walking behind his goats toward an open-air market, has a very different feeling than the original color image (see p. 103). In monochrome, the viewer has a sense of the brightness of the sun emphasizing the deep shadow of the herder and creating the light tones of the dry landscape. The background trees create a contrast against the dry land and the wedge of deeper gray suggesting blue sky against clouds. In color, the same image provides the detailed textures and hues of the landscape, with the reddened earth blending with the herder's tan shirt, hat, and wrapper, and the trees and green grass providing a burst of color beneath the white and gray clouds, with a small wedge of bright blue peeking through. The color image gives a stronger sense of the atmosphere and feel of the environment at a moment in time when the sun shone brightly toward the oncoming clouds. Perhaps Webb would have viewed it as "too literal" or perhaps commercial and "superfluous" in its description of time and place. Perhaps he would have regarded the black and white image as more poetic in its tonal depiction of the scene. It is ironic that, while Webb had adjusted to "seeing in color," as he described, his color images were only published in black and white–a retranslation of his focused, color lens.[36] Indeed, after being commissioned to shoot color for the UN, Webb all but abandoned color photography after 1960, photographing with color film only a few times through the 1970s. Would Webb have imaged the African countries differently in black and white?

The UN's black and white publication drains the life from the color images, positioning the African individuals in a racialized "timelessness," frozen in space outside of modernity, exactly the opposite of their mandate to document the "changing face" of the continent. While the decision to print the photographs in black and white may have been a financial choice, the results dismiss the vibrancy of the color images and indeed of African life in 1958. They do not make it "live" through color as Kodak would have suggested; nor do they highlight a proposed veracity of the continent's colors. But the monochrome brochure also does not highlight the racial biases of color photography seen elsewhere in the commission. Webb's color photographs present not only his own subjectivities and perceptions of space and color, they also expose the inherent biases of 1950s color film while imaging culturally coded representations of Africa on the cusp of postcoloniality.

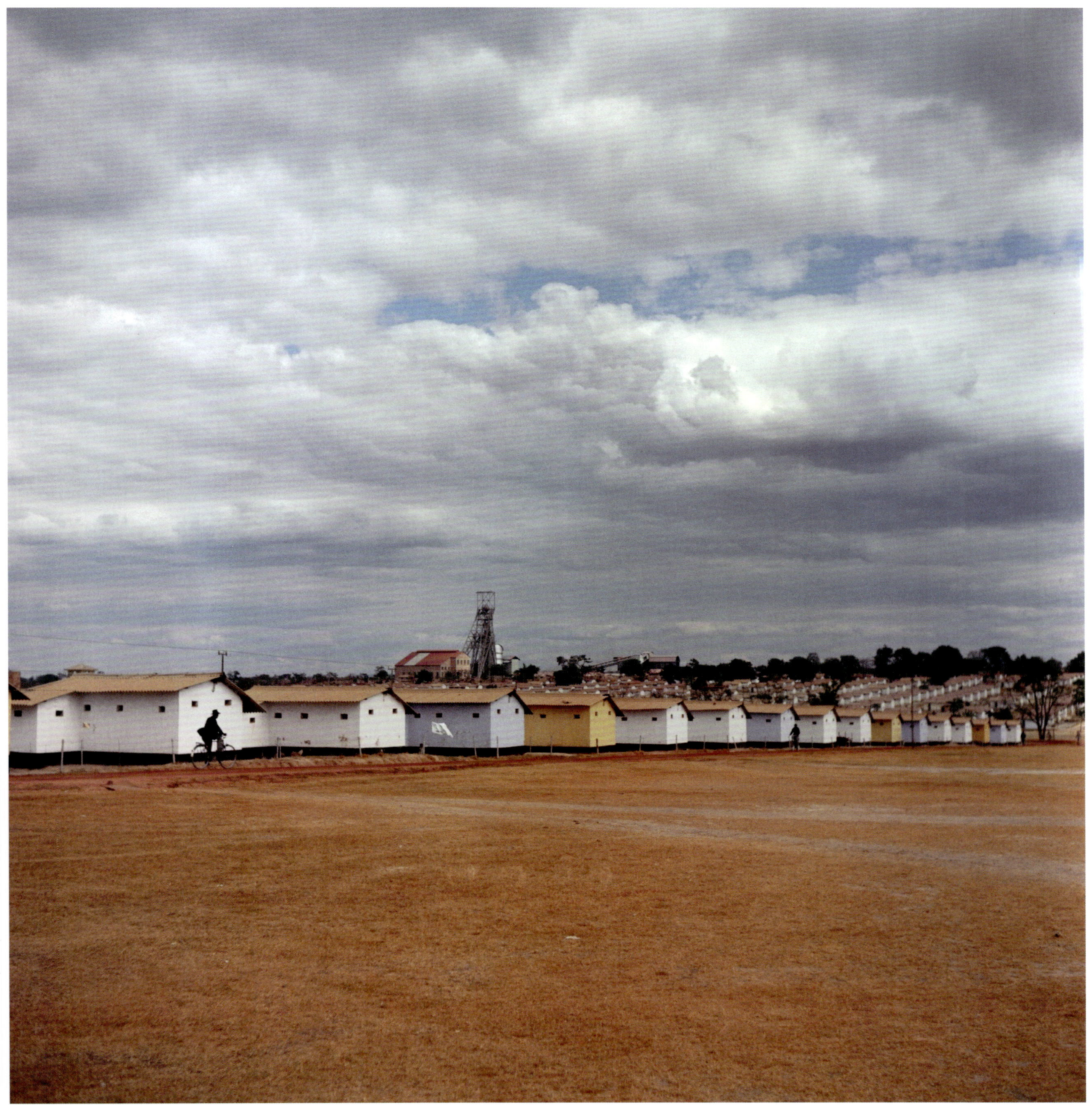

Todd Webb, *Untitled* (44UN-7983-037), Northern Rhodesia (Zambia), 1958
Worker housing at the copper mines, Kitwe.

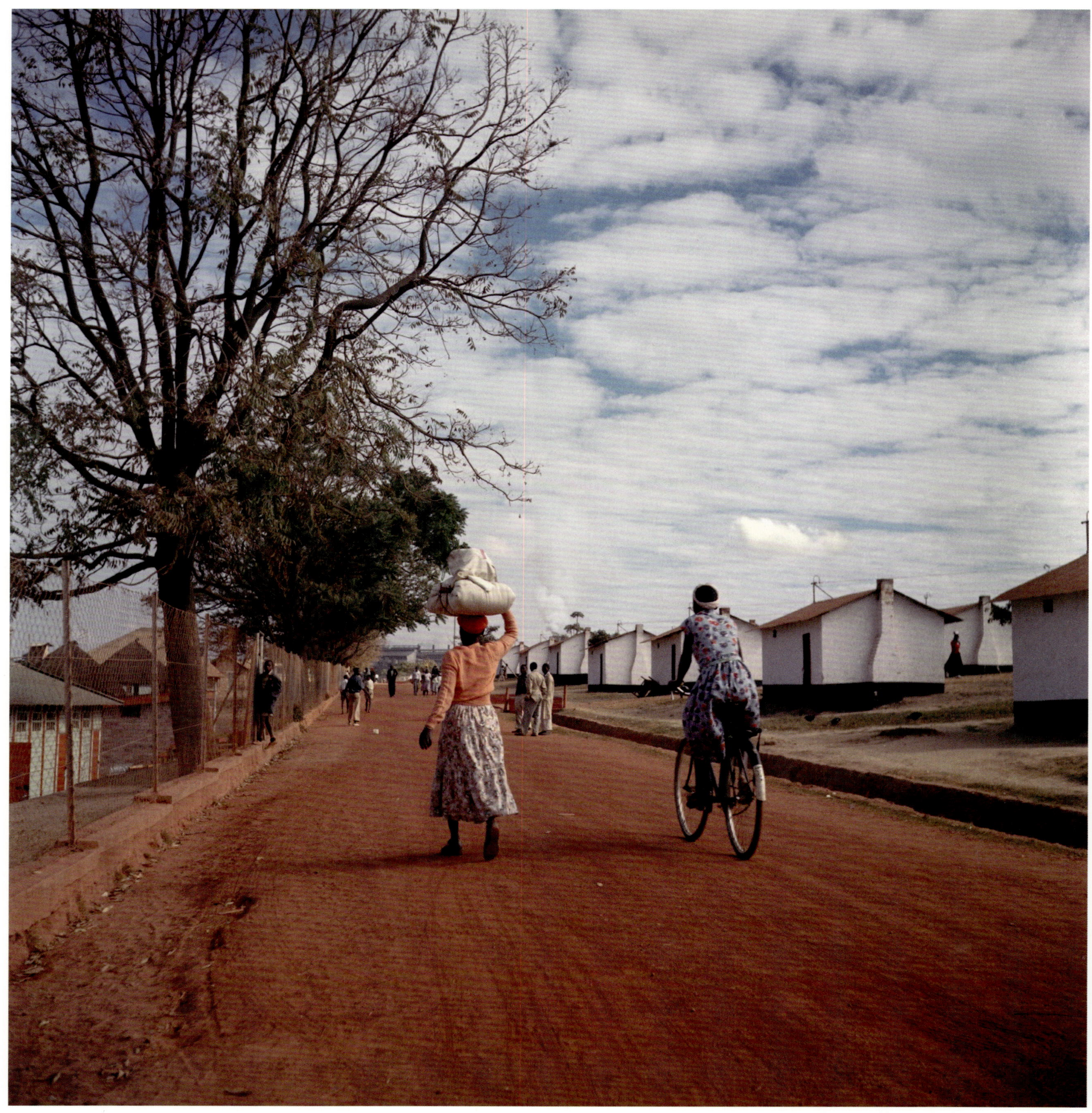

Todd Webb, *Untitled* (44UN-7981-181), Northern Rhodesia (Zambia), 1958
Workers on a day off at a mine in the Copperbelt.

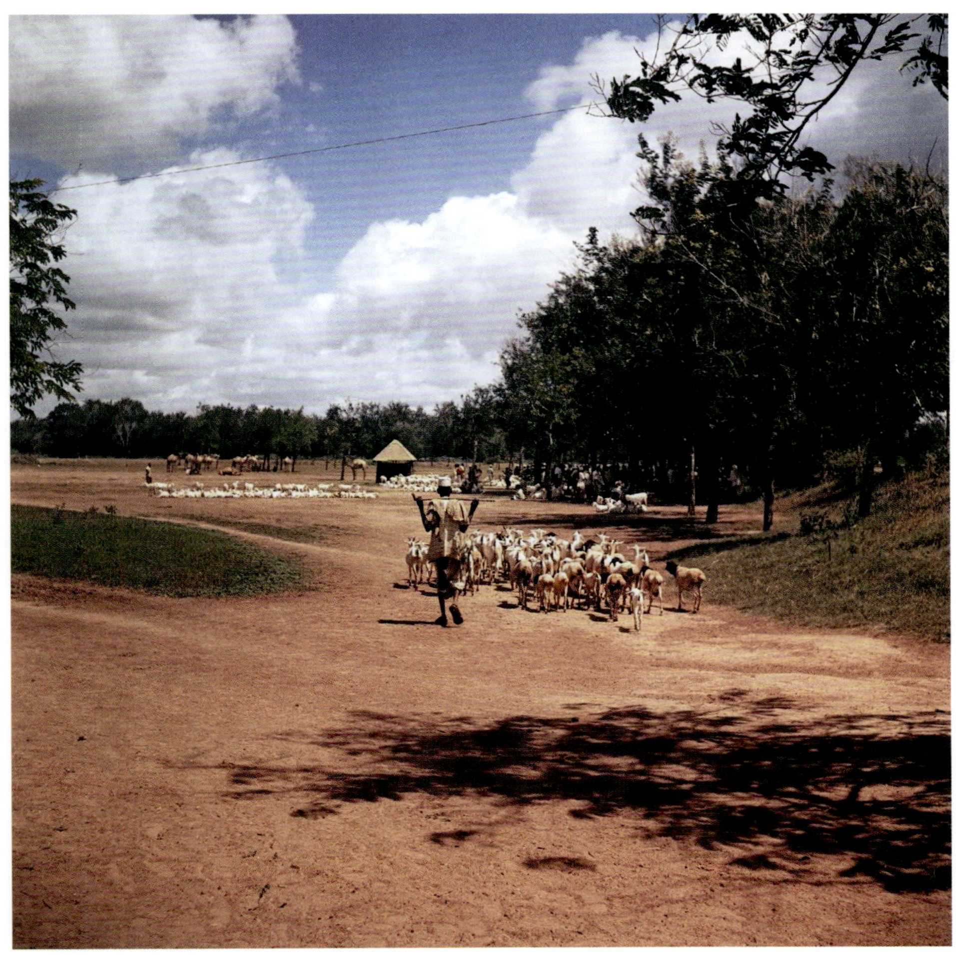

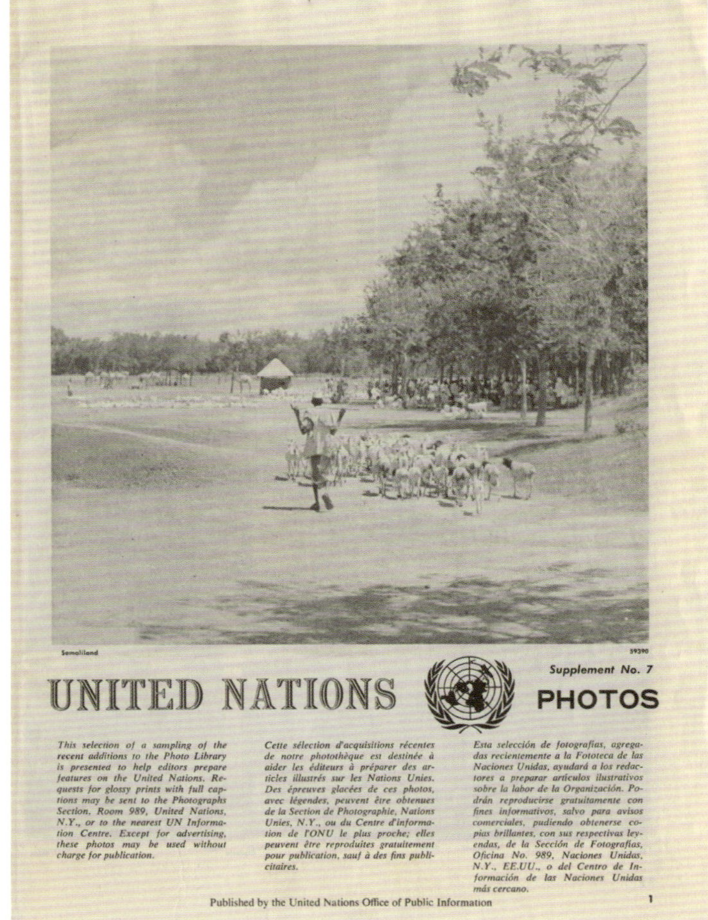

Somaliland 59390

Supplement No. 7

UNITED NATIONS PHOTOS

This selection of a sampling of the recent additions to the Photo Library is presented to help editors prepare features on the United Nations. Requests for glossy prints with full captions may be sent to the Photographs Section, Room 989, United Nations, N.Y., or to the nearest UN Information Centre. Except for advertising, these photos may be used without charge for publication.

Cette sélection d'acquisitions récentes de notre photothèque est destinée à aider les éditeurs à préparer des articles illustrés sur les Nations Unies. Des épreuves glacées de ces photos, avec légendes, peuvent être obtenues de la Section de Photographie, Nations Unies, N.Y., ou du Centre d'information de l'ONU le plus proche; elles peuvent être reproduites gratuitement pour publication, sauf à des fins publicitaires.

Esta selección de fotografías, agregadas recientemente a la Fototeca de las Naciones Unidas, ayudará a los redactores a preparar artículos ilustrativos sobre la labor de la Organización. Podrán reproducirse gratuitamente con fines informativos, salvo para avisos comerciales, pudiendo obtenerse copias brillantes, con sus respectivas leyendas, de la Sección de Fotografías, Oficina No. 989, Naciones Unidas, N.Y., EE.UU., o del Centro de Información de las Naciones Unidas más cercano.

Published by the United Nations Office of Public Information

1

Above: Todd Webb, *Untitled* (44UN-7930-619; UN number 409114), Trust Territory of Somaliland (Somalia), 1958
Goat herders at the livestock market in Villa Bruzzi.

Above right: Cover image, "United Nations Photos, Supplement No. 7," United Nations Office of Public Information.

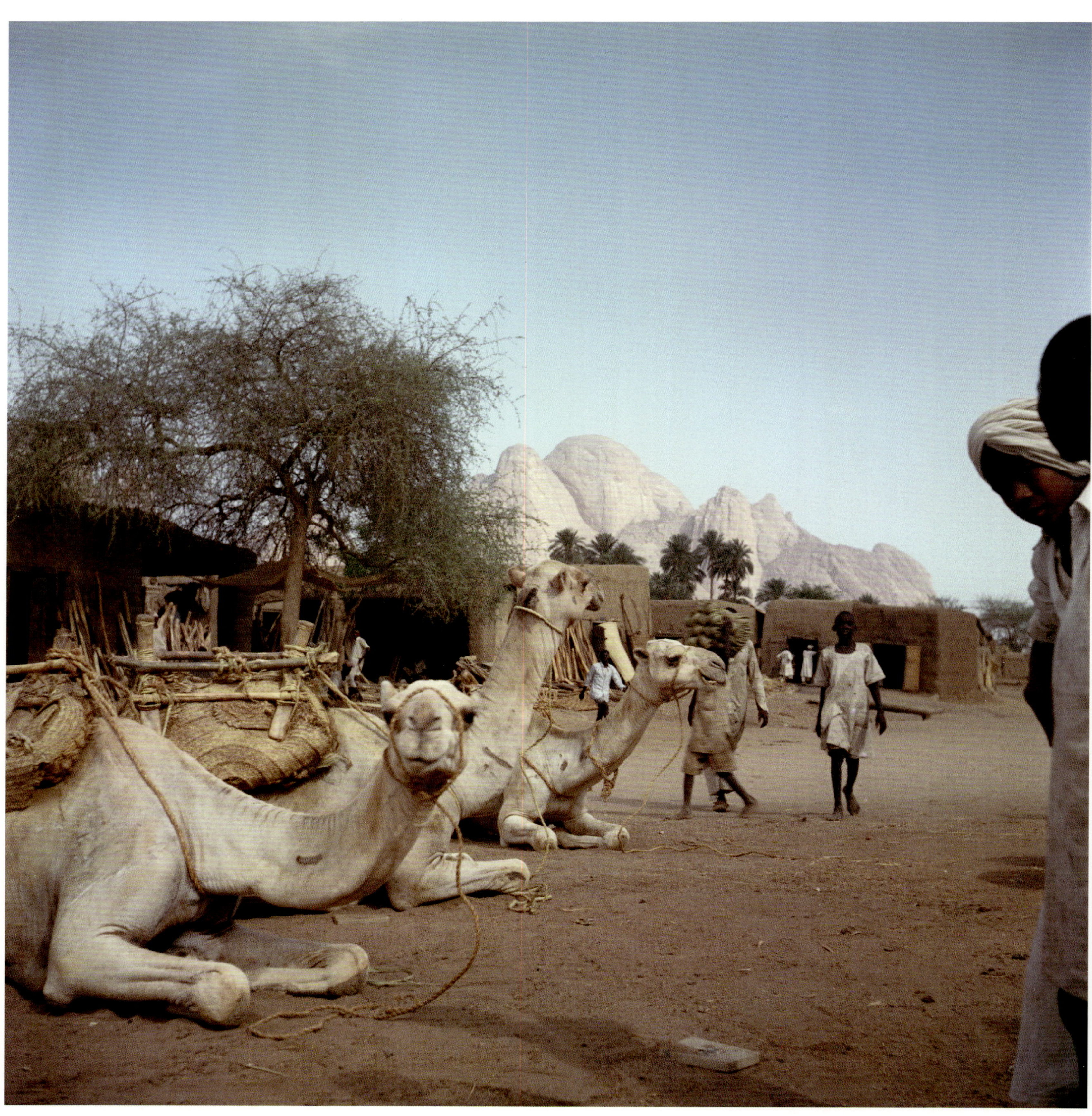

Todd Webb, *Untitled* (44UN-7960-595), Sudan, 1958
Camels resting with the Kassala hills in the background.

SUDAN

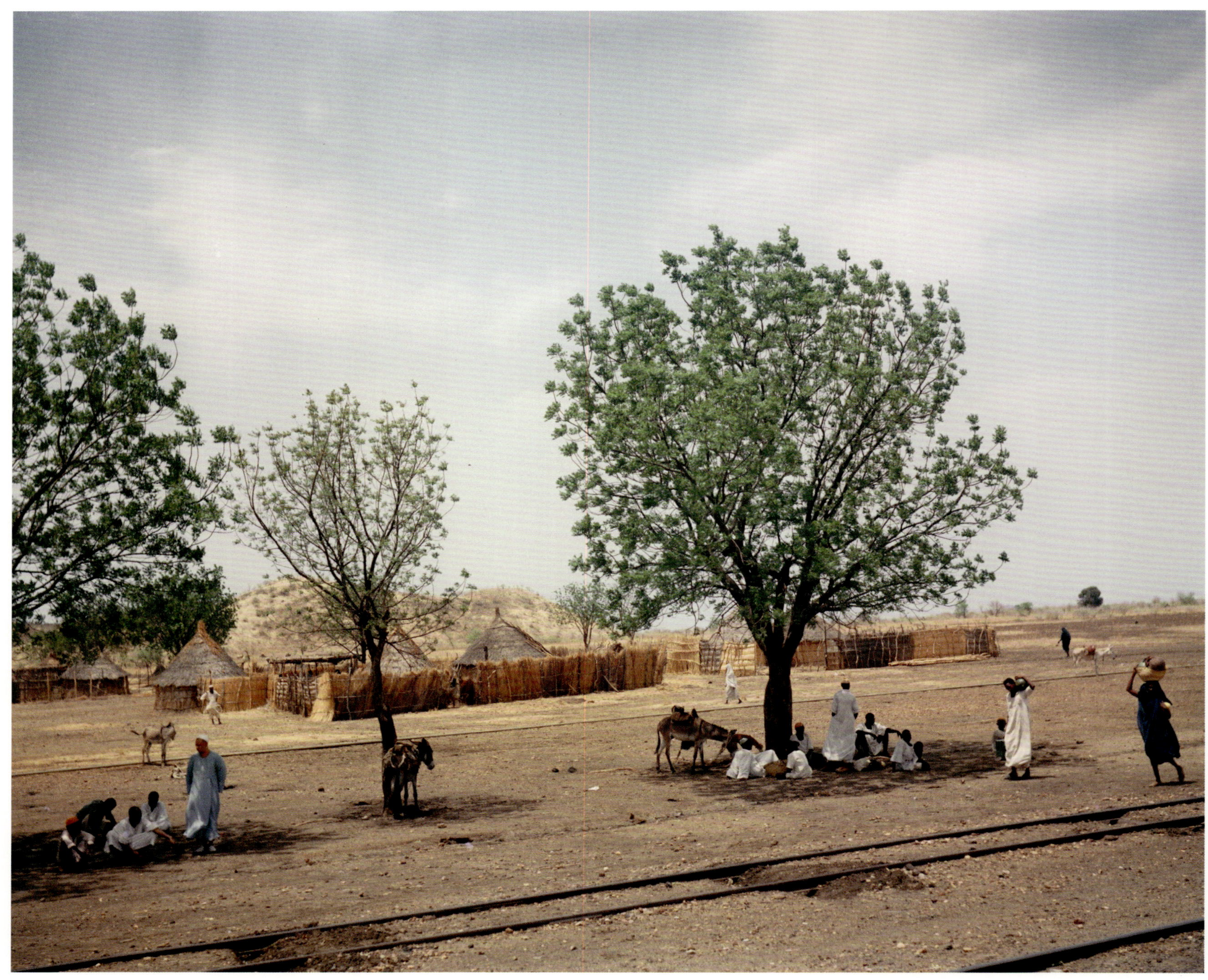

Todd Webb, *Untitled* (44UN-7957-607a and 607b), Sudan, 1958
Diptych of daily life at the train station.

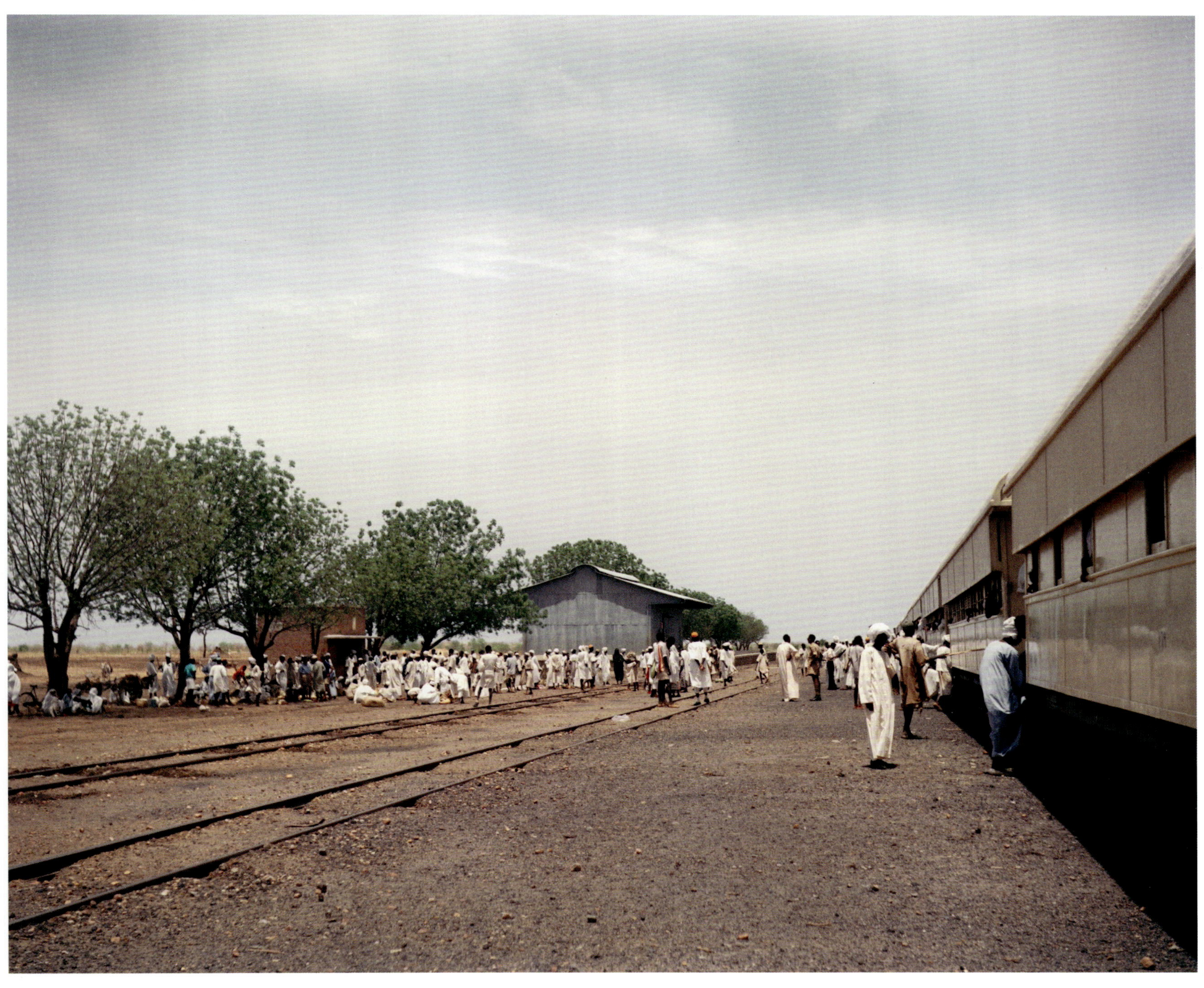

Todd Webb, *Untitled* (44UN-7959-579), Sudan, 1958
Nomadic tents in the desert, Kassala.

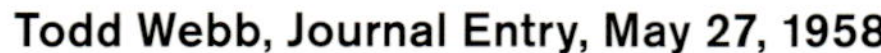

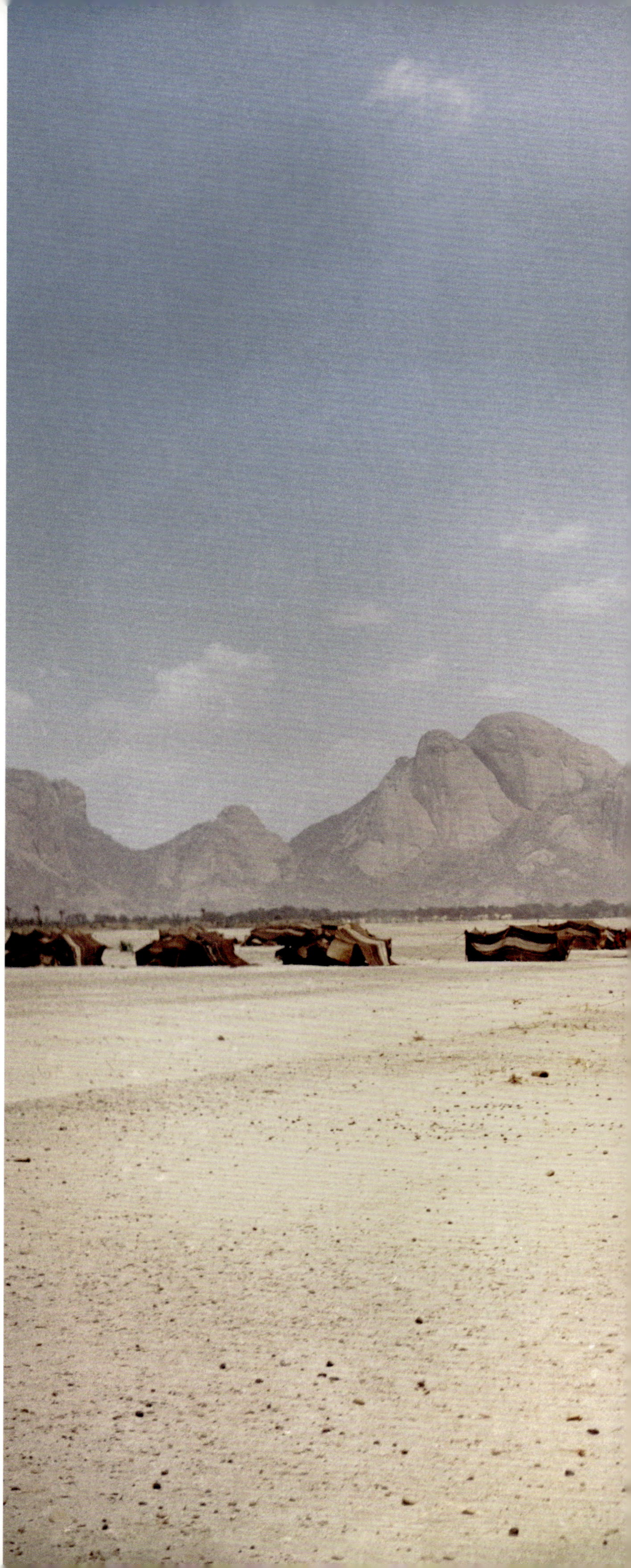

Todd Webb, Journal Entry, May 27, 1958

"Kassala is most interesting–the most exciting place I have seen in Sudan. It is a meeting place for the nomad camel-raising tribes of the desert and with its mountain background it has color."

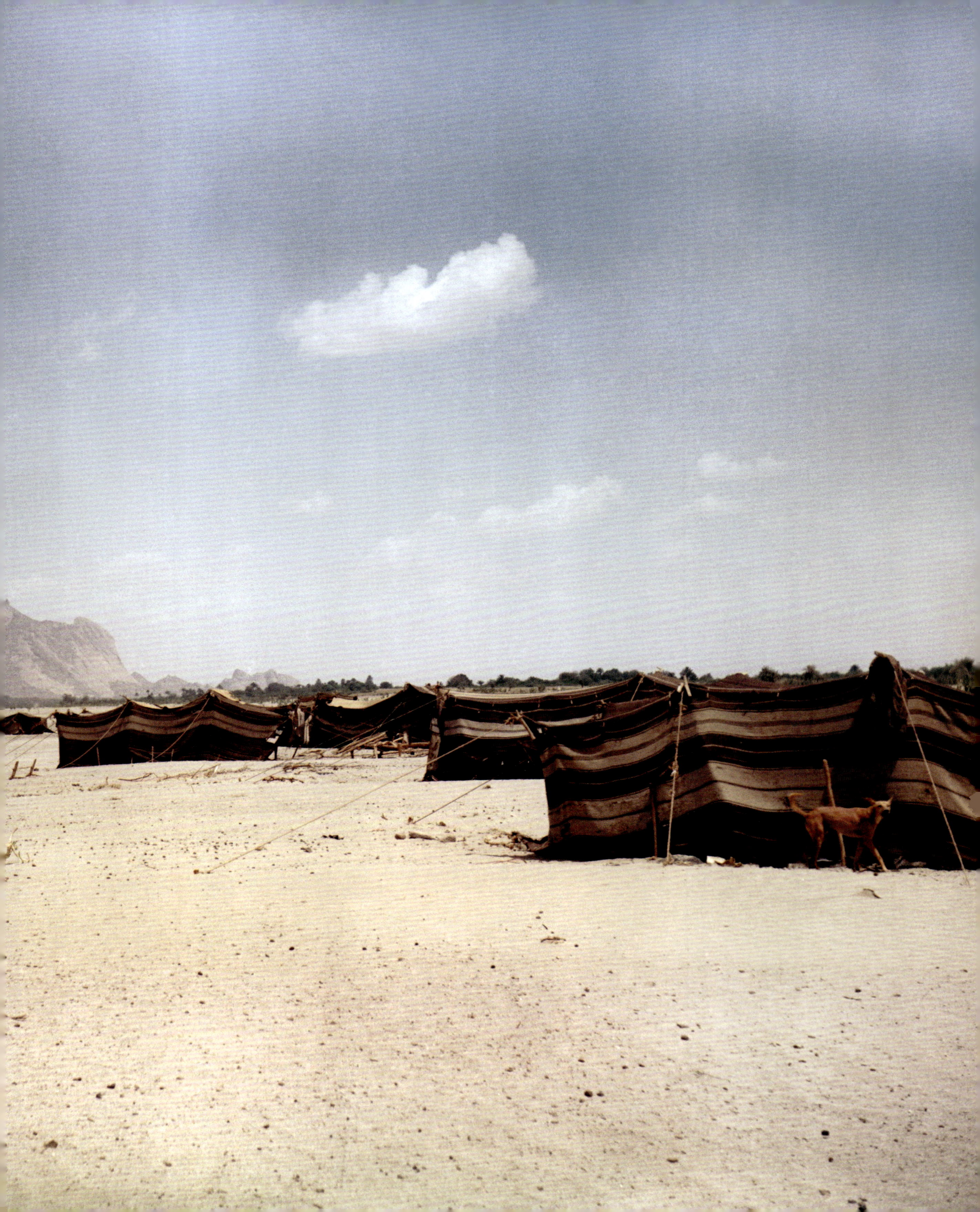

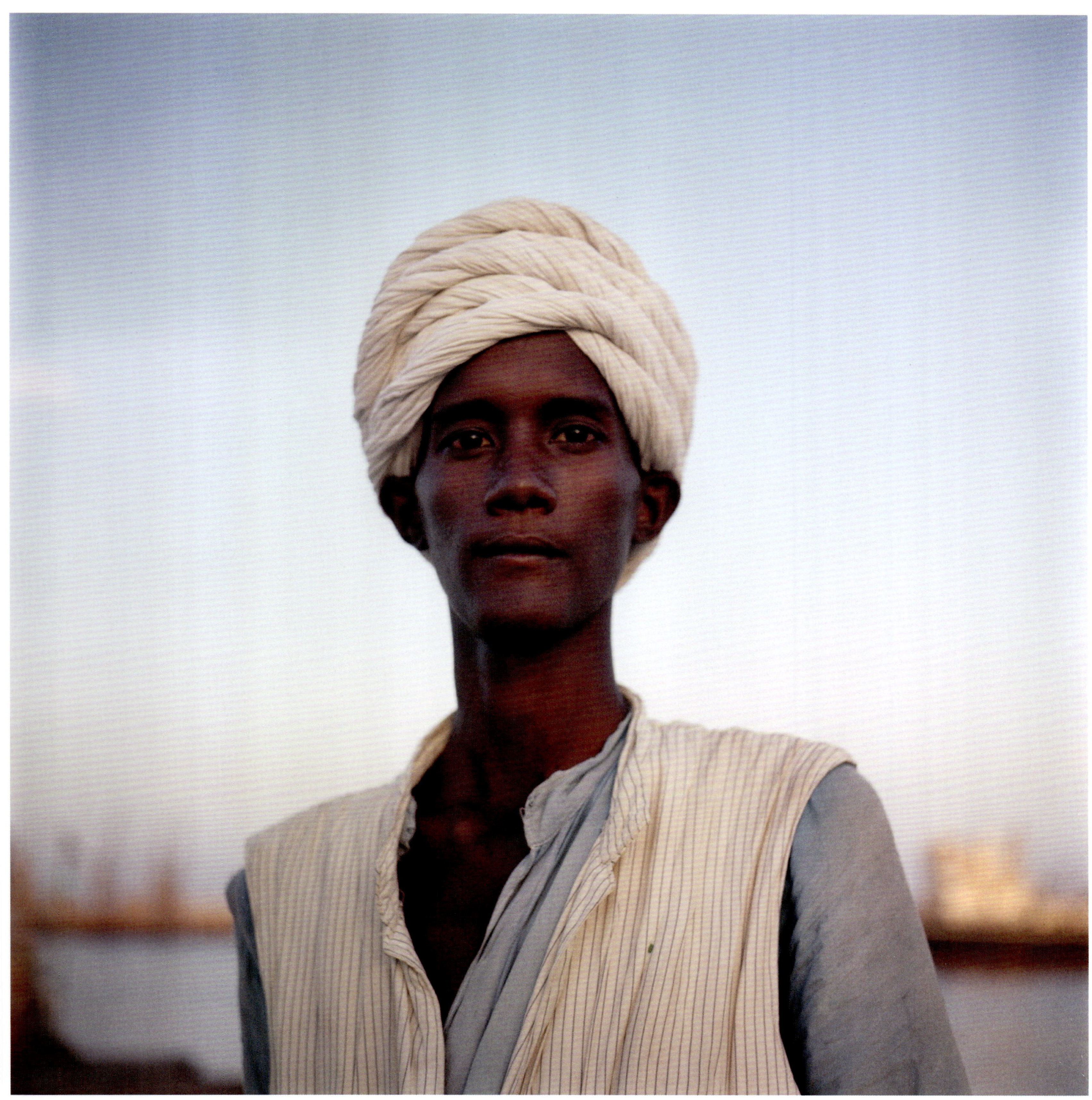

Todd Webb, *Untitled* (44UN-7963-162), Sudan, 1958
Portrait of a man with a turban near the port.

Todd Webb, *Untitled* (44UN-7970-001), Sudan, 1958
Men and boys in front of a passenger truck.

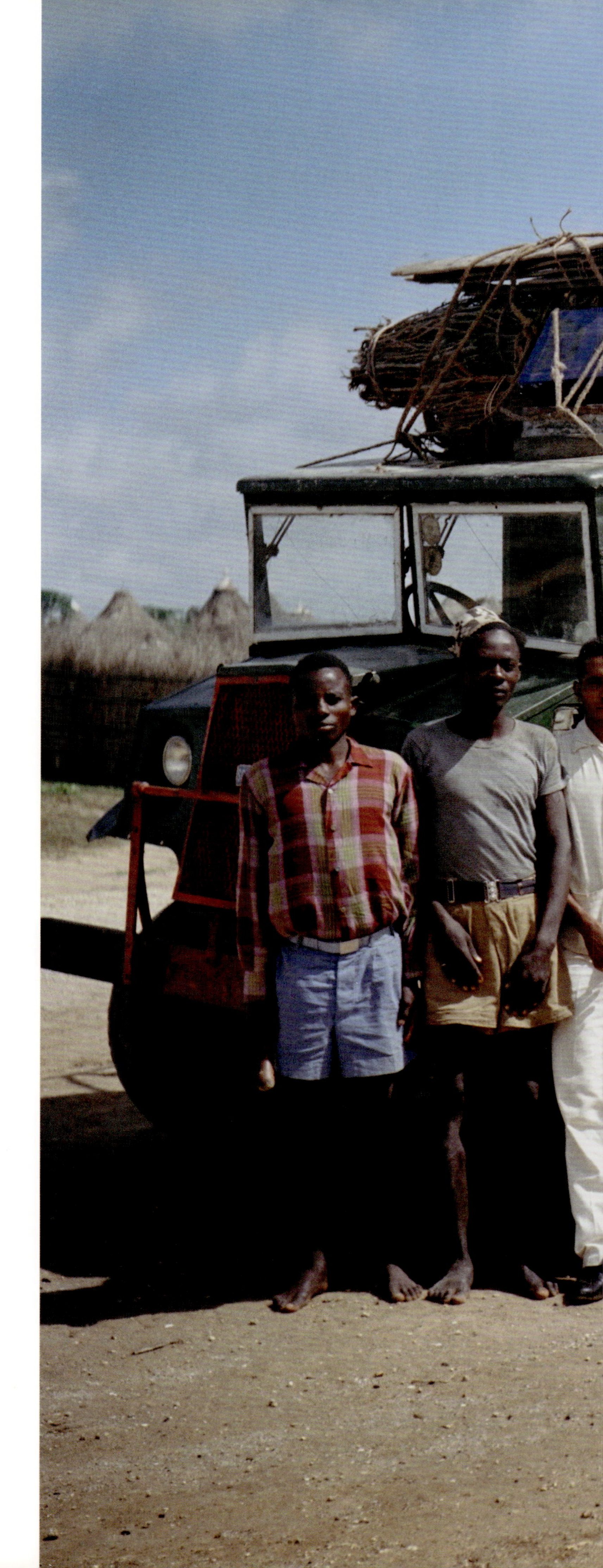

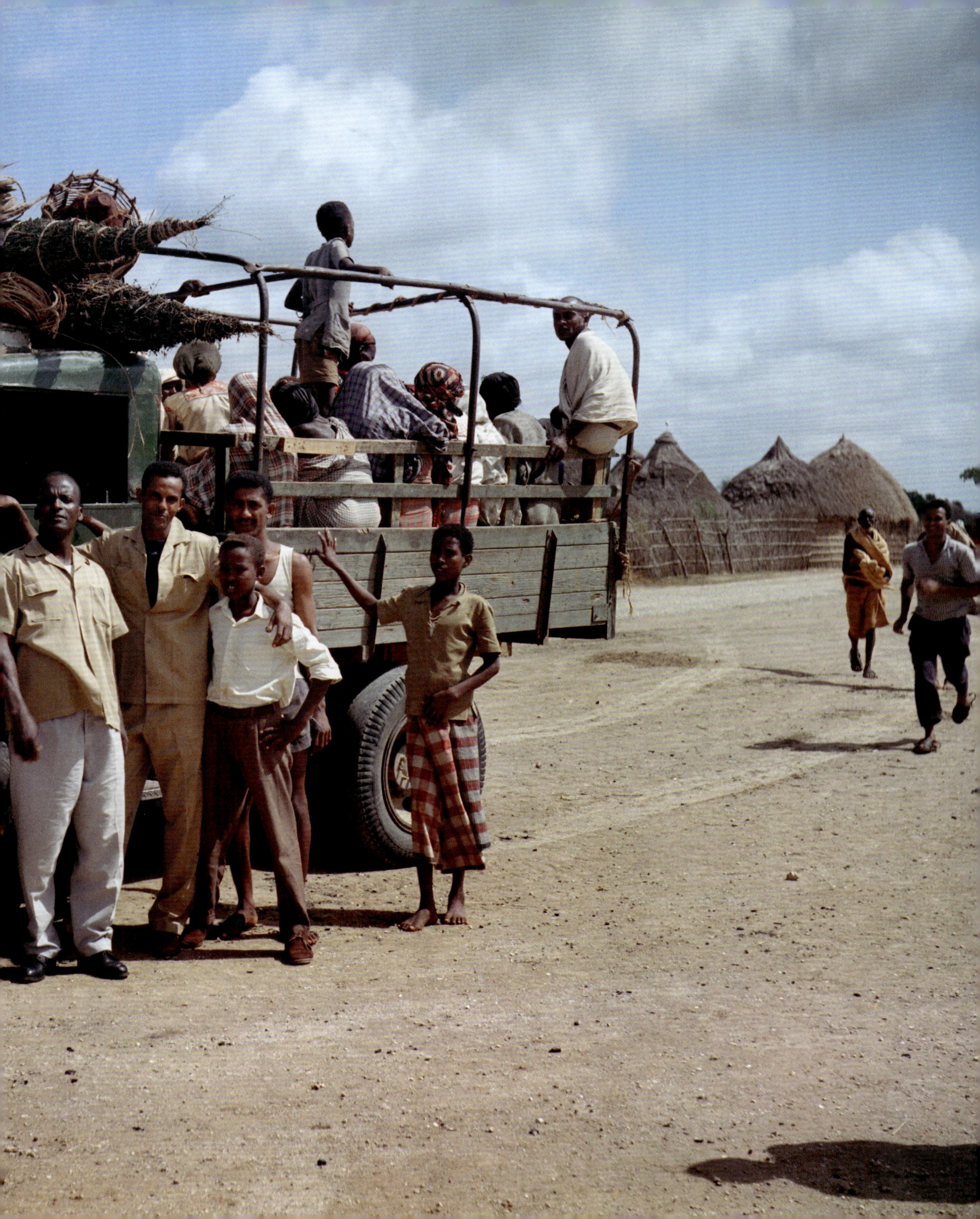

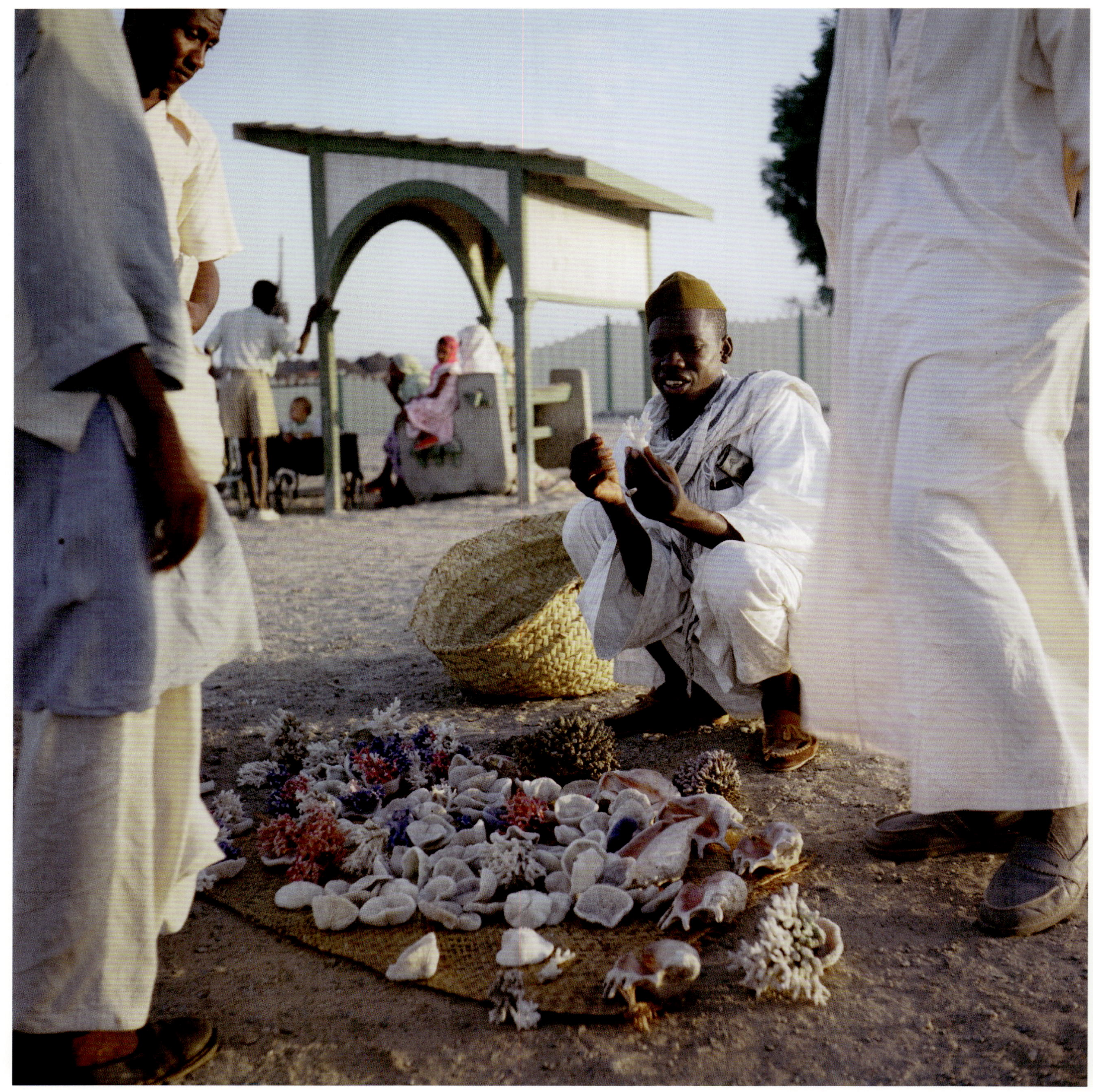

Todd Webb, *Untitled* (44UN-7963-001), Sudan, 1958
Selling seashells and coral at the beach.

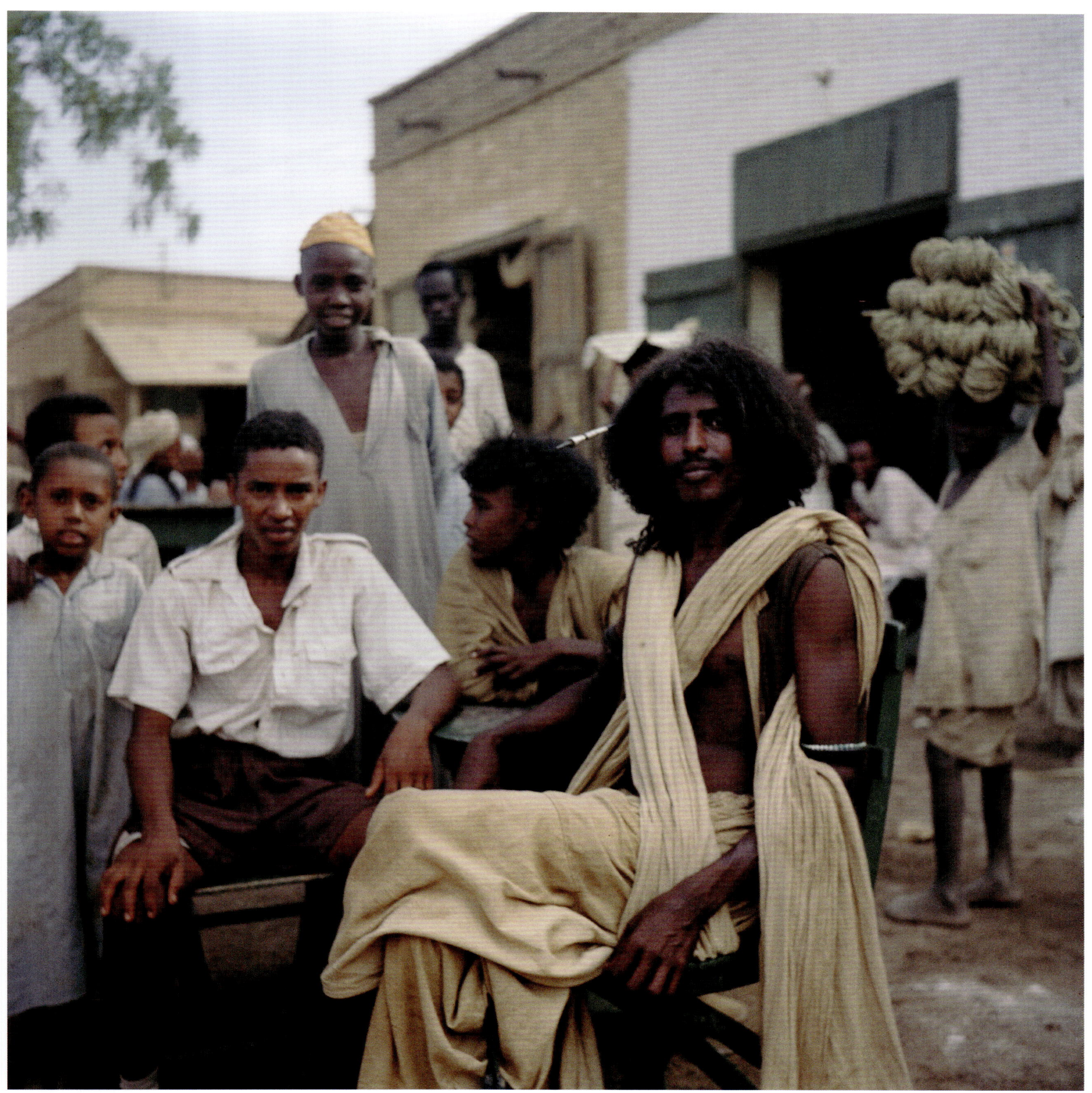

Todd Webb, *Untitled* (44UN-7960-594), Sudan, 1958
Man and boys relaxing outside the shops.

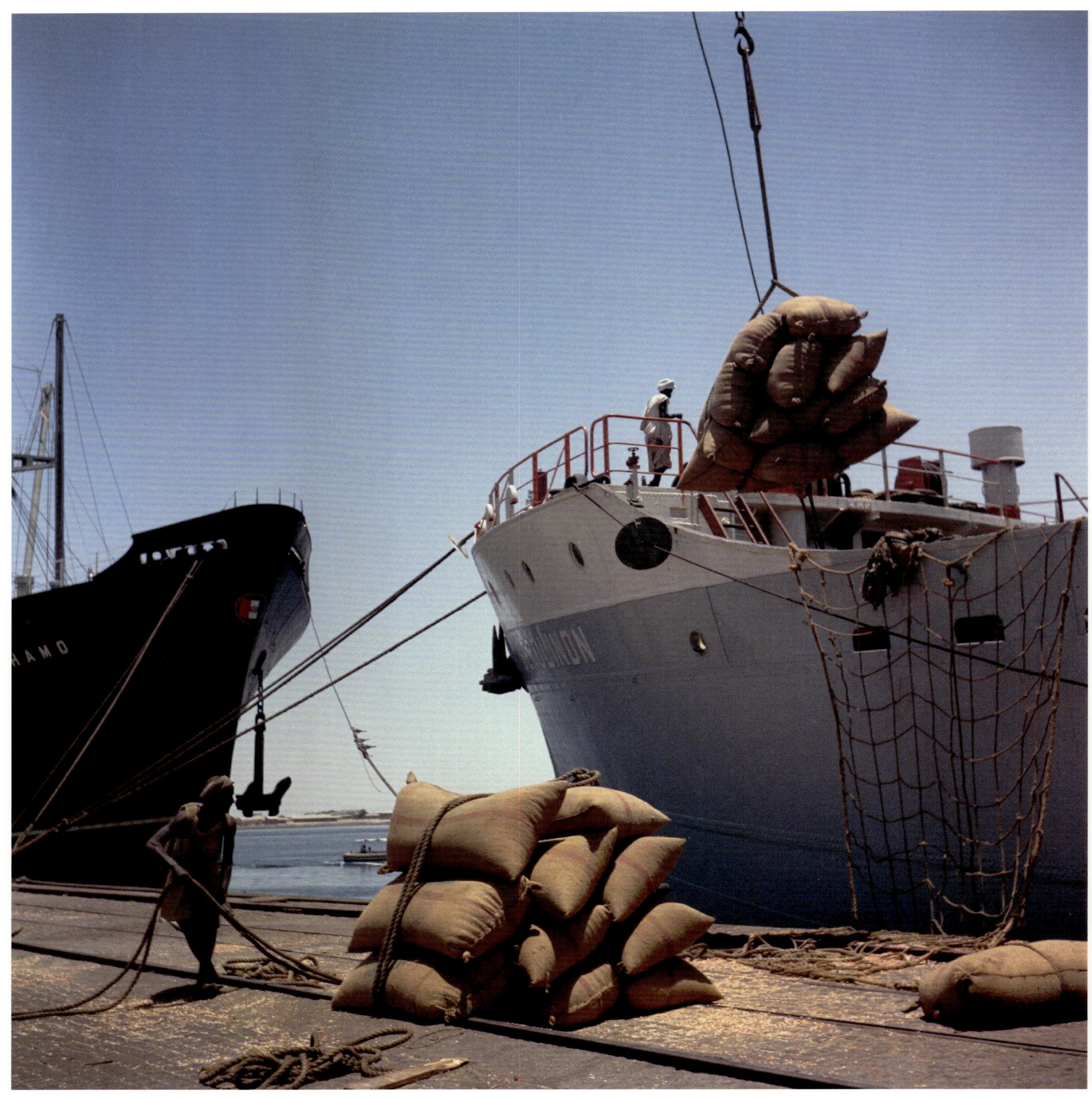

Todd Webb, *Untitled* (44UN-7975-565), Sudan, 1958
Unloading cargo from boats in the harbor.

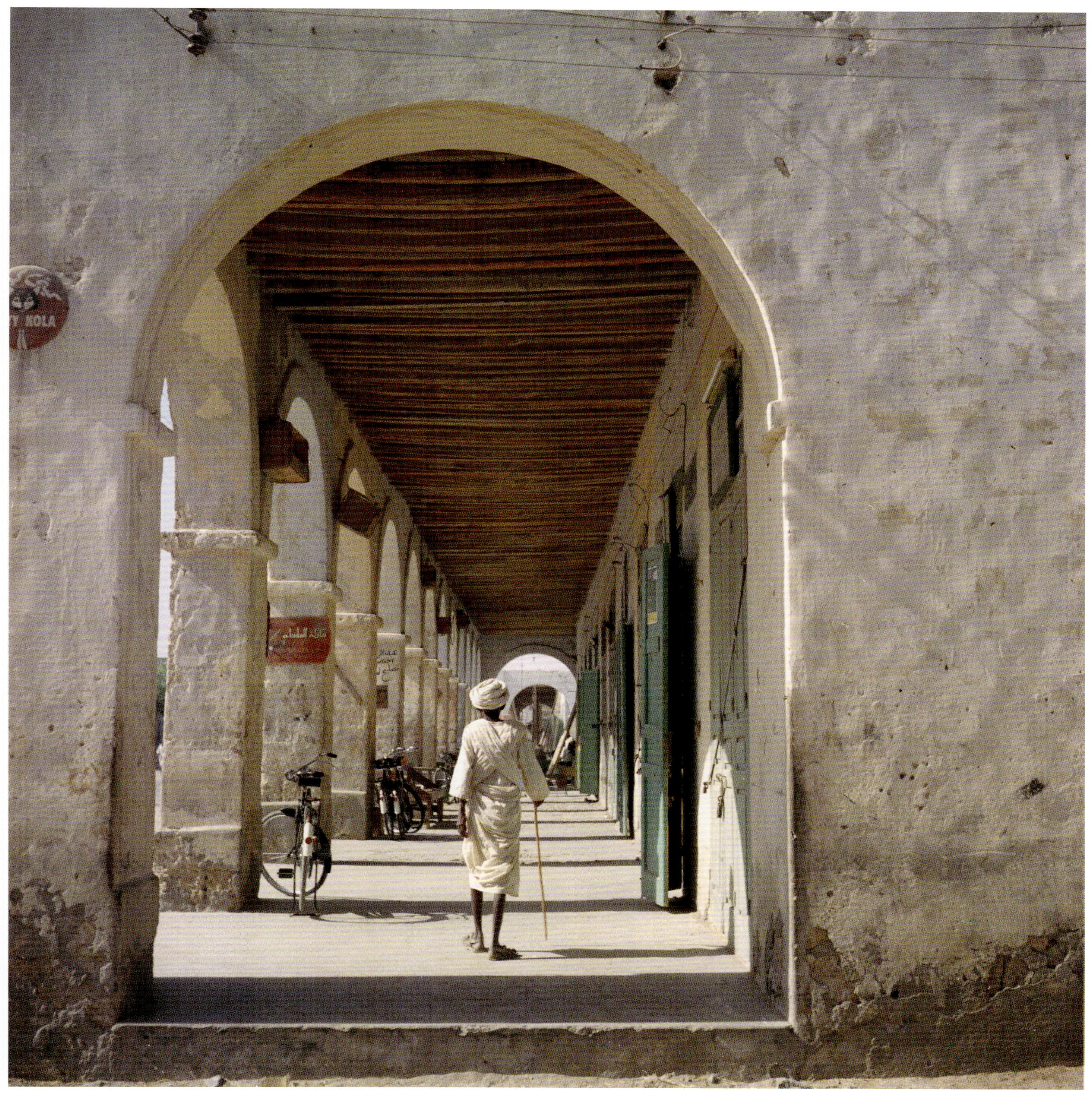

Todd Webb, *Untitled* (44UN-7961-002), Sudan, 1958
Man walking by stores along an arched colonnade.

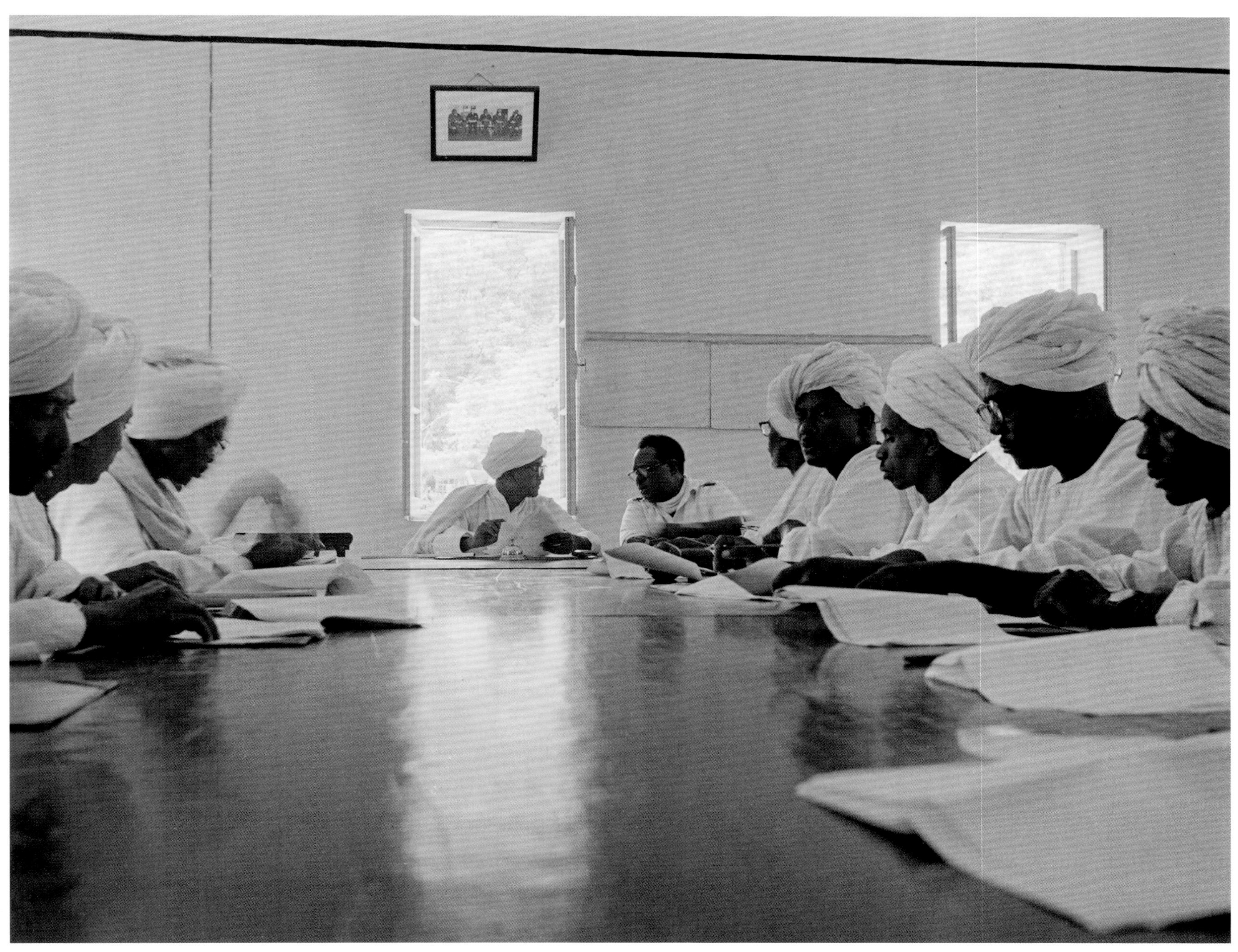

Todd Webb, *Untitled* (44UN-58-074), Sudan, 1958
Webb's handwritten caption reads "Council Meeting Cotton Growers of the Gezira Wadi Medani, Sudan."

Landscaping: Todd Webb's Representations of a Changing African Topography

Erin Hyde Nolan

Photography furnishes evidence. Something we hear about, but doubt, seems proven when we're shown a photograph of it.[1]
–Susan Sontag

Photographed by Todd Webb on July 19, 1958, a snow-capped Mount Kilimanjaro shimmers above the purple horizon, its peak a phosphorescent phantasm (see opposite). The mountain hovers over a field populated by hundreds of plants whose spiny tentacles unfold wildly in the afternoon light. This image seems to depict unspoiled terrain, majestic in its natural state. Yet the composition also reveals a landscape altered by human agency, all but constructed as a result of colonial intervention. A small patch of land in the foreground, overrun with weeds, gives way to a row of muscular sisal plants. Like a troop of delinquent soldiers who have stepped out of line, the disorder in these first rows quickly organizes into a vista marked not by organic environmental principles but gradually mapped by Cartesian control.

To *landscape*–virtually or materially–is to assert an order, to take hold, to control.[2] Taken amidst an ostensibly boundless plantation of sisal–the oldest commercial crop in Tanzania–the edges of the photograph struggle to contain the plants as they fan out at the base of Kilimanjaro. Indeed, sisal crops were nearly uncontainable in the country's warm, arid climate, where they grew rampant after being introduced from Mexico's Yucatán Peninsula by Dr. Richard Hindoff in 1893 to what was then German East Africa.[3] By 1961, the year Tanganyika became independent from Great Britain, the country reigned as the world's largest sisal exporter. Rather than an army of European soldiers or even bureaucrats, in this photograph, the plants themselves act as foreign colonizing forces, invading the field and disrupting the health of indigenous species.

Webb made this image during his five-day sojourn to Moshi, Tanganyika (Tanzania). Transfixed by the sublime apparition of Kilimanjaro, Webb wrote on July 19–the same day he made the image–that it was "pretty unreal looking and I have to pinch myself to believe I am seeing it."[4] The mountain's grandeur, however, is not the subject of his photograph. With its conquest of pictorial space, the sisal (and its commodity value on the international market) eclipse Webb's moment of transcendence. A series of photographs taken just three days earlier at the Amboni Sisal Estate instead illustrate the labor-intensive production on an agro-industrial plantation, which included the drying of the fibers in a covered barn, revealing the practical use-value of Webb's photographic narrative (p. 127). With the United Nations' vested interest in supporting newly independent African states, perhaps Webb's images encouraged the General Assembly to declare in 1960: "[T]he necessity of bringing to a speedy and unconditional end colonialism in all its forms and manifestations...all peoples have the right to self-determination; by virtue of that right they freely determine their political status and freely pursue their economic, social and cultural development."[5] Webb's photographic record–which was itself also conceived of as a modern and modernizing technology–of colonial institutions and their intervention in Tanganyika's landscape was certainly deployed by the United Nations to support independence and enable emerging nation states.[6]

Within a single photographic frame, Webb binds a romantic reverence for landscape–as championed by his teacher Ansel Adams–to the capitalistic obsession with mechanized progress. Such synthesis is explicit in another image of Kilimanjaro, lustrous on the horizon (see p. 124). Here, the image delights in the opacity of mountain mist and the ambiguity of distance, both of which accentuate the crisp focus of the cityscape in the foreground. These dichotomous forces, the hazy yet awesome mountain crest and the clinical geometry of the Ford workshop in the foreground, present different aspects of landscaping–unaltered terrain and man-altered terrain–as distinctly intensified by each other. This is similarly true in one image of the Sudanese desert–just outside of Kassala–where brown tents dot the sand in front of a mountainous outcropping (see pp. 108–9). If, as stated above, "to landscape" is to assert order, this is established here through a symbiotic cohabitation built by naturalizing the land itself (through colonial forces) and Webb's photographic mediation of that tamed (colonized) space. Landscape, in the 1958 United Nations commission, functions as an active cultural and transcultural practice.[7]

Taking such a framework as a starting point, this essay critically evaluates Webb's landscape photographs during his five-month trip across the African continent. It is not intended as a comprehensive survey of African topographies nor of UN photographic projects; rather, it highlights key images in order to explore the legibility of photographs as visual texts, which are, to borrow Nicholas Natanson's words, "supremely compelling and supremely slippery" in their readability.[8] Although this argument relies heavily on the photograph's aesthetic features to instill social significance, especially in how landscape naturalizes social and cultural conventions, it also considers the status of these images as documents. The photographs themselves capture a slippage between what is real and what is rendered, questioning the documentary form and how that was used to justify and authenticate oppressive forms of colonialism on the continent.

Webb's photographs blur the line between what W. J. T. Mitchell calls "a represented and a presented space, both a signifier and a signified, a frame and what a frame contains," illuminating the special expectation that we have of documentary photography: to tell us the truth.[9] This tension materializes in an image of a painted house in the village of Kingoni, Tanganyika (see p. 126). Here, the windowless side of a house is painted with two trees. Leafed in green, their gnarled branches creep across the gray wall. Perched on the right side of the building are four birds, including a vulture, owl, and eagle, their sharp talons wrapping tightly around the limbs of the tree.[10] On the left side a leopard crouches; its pink tongue wags in anticipation and front paw lifts, ready to pounce. The mural transforms a rural scene into a theater of simulacra. The tight cropping of the photograph presents the painted wall as a stage upon which an archetypal scene of predator and prey plays out. What disrupts this performance is the transformation of the painted trees into real trees. Two papaya trees, lush with unripe fruit, emerge from behind the wall, their broad, serrated leaves reaching over the roof of the house and outside of the photographic frame. The incorporation of these trees–both painted and real–raises questions: Which came first: the mural or the trees? Where does representation end and reality begin? What is the difference between what we see and what we know? This space, produced through an intersection of imagination, attitudes, and natural formations, reflects not only relationships between the cultivation of land, home, and property, but also how representations of these become sites for the interrelational.[11] Like the dramatic animal/tree mural, the landscape itself is a dynamic medium, a theater where the performance of place confuses the relationship between presentation and representation, and entangles the positions of viewing and photographing.[12]

This dynamism gives Webb's photographs a structure, one that explores the borders between natural and man-made worlds. In one photograph of a mining operation in Northern Rhodesia (Zambia), a barbed-wire fence defines such a boundary. This image asks: was it erected to keep the viewer out, functioning as a barrier even in its transparency, a threshold between an industrial and pre-industrial world? The fence separates the sandy, undeveloped foreground from a deluge of water sprinklers and the steaming mining enterprise that occupies the middle ground of Webb's photograph. Here, a cylindrical stack puffs dirty, sulphurous smoke that

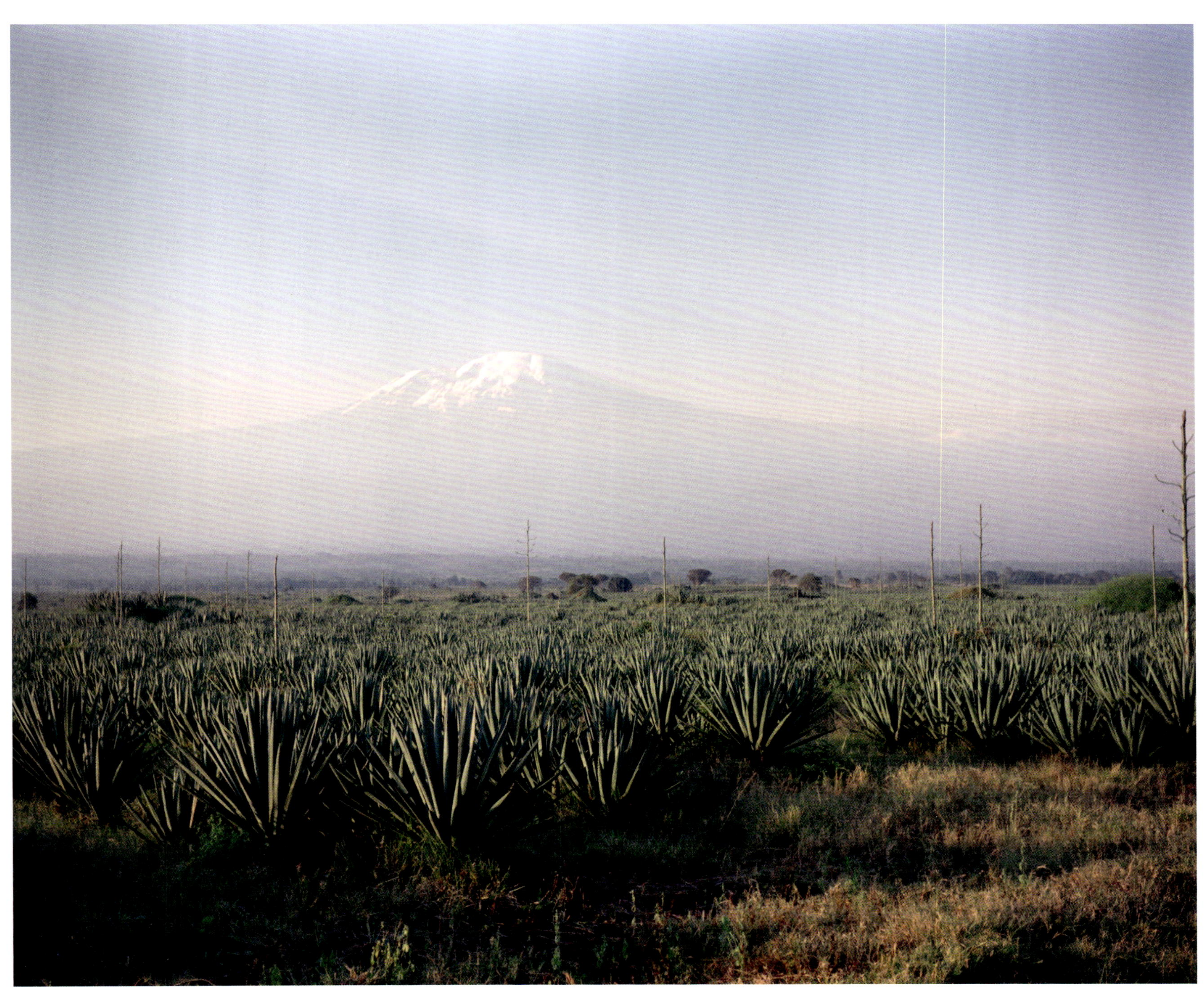

Todd Webb, *Untitled* (44UN-7943-006), Tanganyika (Tanzania), 1958
Sisal fields with Mount Kilimanjaro in the background.

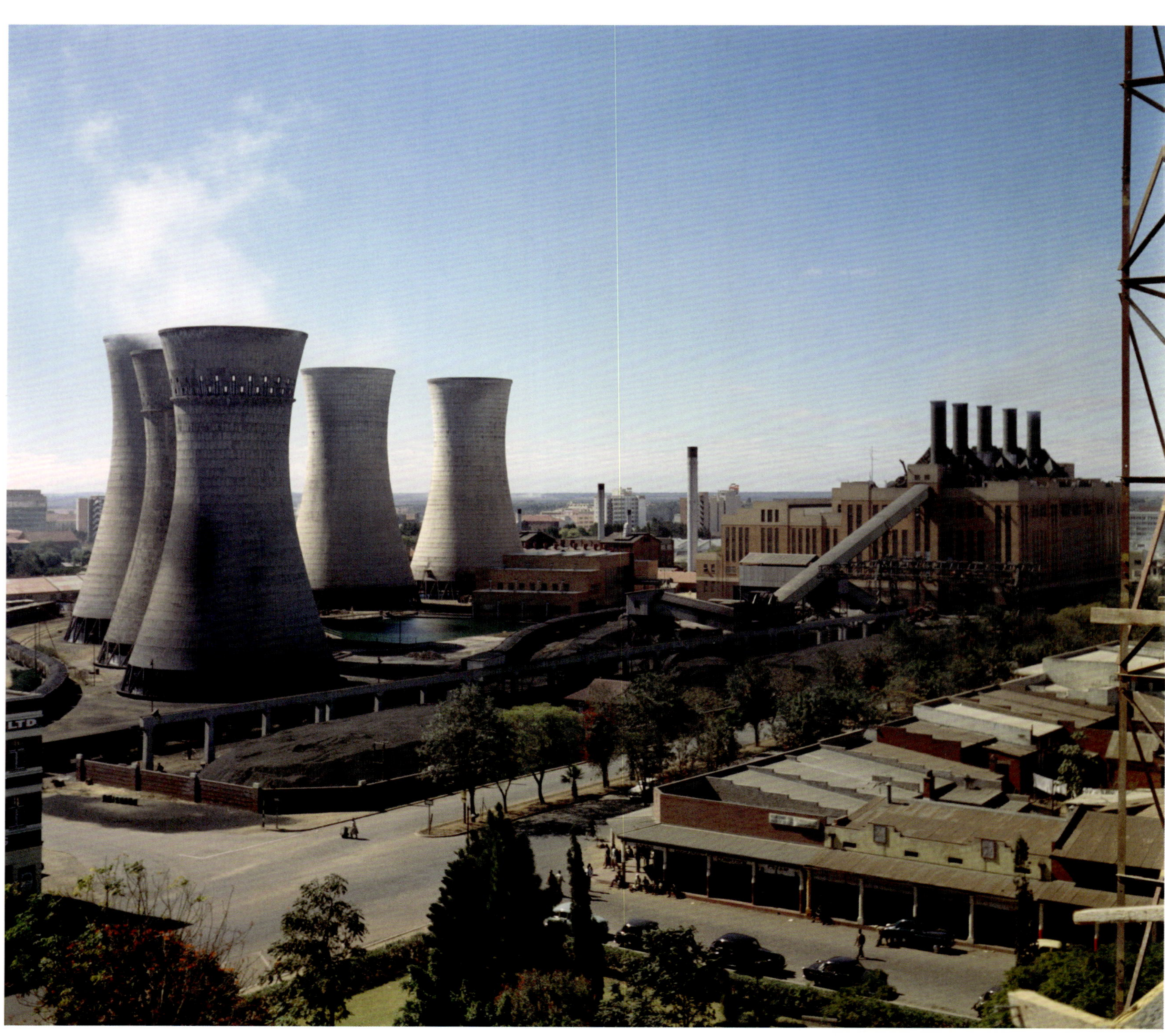

Todd Webb, *Untitled* (44UN-7991-099), Northern Rhodesia (Zambia), 1958
Coal-fired power at the copper mine, Kitwe.

dissipates into the white clouds and blue sky (see p. 125). A smaller stack in the distance echoes this emission, while a black car drives out of the frame. Just beyond the fence stands a tree, budding with greenery, its branches silhouetted against the sky, witness to a world where innovation and industry exist alongside decay and destruction. Perhaps symbolic in its vitality, the tree might also suggest, as the UN charter states, that this investment in innovation and industry promises independence for Northern Rhodesia.[13]

An image of the coal-fired power plant at the Kitwe copper mine presents a similar dichotomy (opposite). Five hourglass-shaped stacks penetrate the sky, mirroring a five-pronged smokestack opposite an aquamarine pond. Delicate lines of scaffolding frame the right side of the image. The edge of a wood plank, just out of focus, reminds us that Webb positioned his camera from the roof of a building, overlooking the geometric cityscape. A median strip with a single row of trees divides the copper plant from a commercial complex. The roads are empty of cars, but not without people. Like Charles Sheeler's photographs of the Ford Red River Rouge complex from 1928, Webb's image glorifies the man-made machine, but not the human process of labor. Here he illustrates the UN Charter's commitment to show both modernizing and mechanical technologies in Africa, but simplifies and obscures the local worker.[14]

Webb's photographs deliberately blur otherwise established notions of "the documentary," confusing boundaries established by his contemporaries at the Farm Security Administration, Magnum Photos, and the New York Photo League. The active qualities of landscape—not what the landscape *means* but what it *does*—can be read like calligraphic inscriptions, etched into the earth of the Zambezi River basin (see pp. 166–67).[15] Contours plowed into the porous, sandy soil snake down the hillside. The crescent-shaped cement-slit dam at the base of the hill mirrors these switchbacks. Webb described this scene in his journal: "The [river] flowing toward the Indian Ocean after its tumbling cascade over Victoria Falls enters the Kariba Gorge where its waters were compressed to such an extent that it was a rushing torrent."[16] Capturing the concrete arch of the then-ongoing Kariba Dam project, which opened in 1960 and was originally owned by the Central African Power Corporation, Webb points his lens into the gorge at a sprawling worksite, littered with trucks, buildings, water barrels, turbines, scaffolding, machinery, and people. From his high vantage point, Webb shows the land being carved up and into, a sight of environmental and ecological destruction pursued in the name of discovery and progress.

In its indulgence of monochromatic colors, Webb's photograph might at first appear monotonous, what Joel Snyder calls a "disinterested report," presenting a generic perspective that is detached from any individual viewpoint.[17] Such institutional and collective vision promises neutrality—but photographs are never neutral, and what this image of the Kariba Dam neutralizes are the very complex stories of displacement, exile, and resettlement for the Tonga people.[18] 57,000 Tonga people were moved off of their indigenous territory because of the expansion of Lake Kariba, marking one of the worst dam-resettlement disasters in the continent's history.[19] Webb's visualization of a place that was reshaped to generate hydro-power for the Federation might appear benign; but the coercive dispossession of the Tonga people was enforced in order to gain control of these resources. The absence of this information from the United Nations report reveals how firmly tethered representational practices are to cultural and aesthetic conventions.[20] Through the violent inscriptions on the earth's surface—both ripping apart the topography to gain power and ripping a cultural group apart from their homeland—the land at the Kariba Dam site quite literally bears witness to entanglements of power, control, and innovation. By choosing to represent this colonial violation, Webb questions what kind of witness the surface of the earth can be, especially when that witnessing is performed in the service of modernization.[21]

One week after visiting the Kariba Dam, Webb traveled 500 kilometers north in Northern Rhodesia to photograph the copper mines near Ndola. In a photograph from this trip, molten slag cascades down an ash-covered hill, so hot and viscous it seems to barely touch the ground, as if burning from the inside out (see p. 169). Vermillion, it surges downward, curving toward a sandy outcropping. In contrast to his panoramic view of the Kariba Dam, here Webb turns his camera upward, exalting industrial progress. Yet, as one of his letters suggests, he found the site dull: "I thought the copper mine would be [exciting] but it was quite tame."[22] In this case, the shocking beauty of Webb's photograph does not correspond to its complicated political inferences. This image does not complement romantic fantasies of the African landscape, but instead challenges such myths, especially in the face of postcolonial Zambian history. Rebecca Solnit's astute observations about the photographer Richard Misrach resonate here: "The surrounding facts undermine the aesthetic appreciation these images elicit, making such pure response almost an act of complicity."[23] For Webb, photographic meaning is formed outside of the frame, and for the twenty-first-century viewer in particular, this meaning tarnishes the image's beauty; its seductive surface belies more traumatic, even violent, and invisible truths of the subjects of colonial rule in the Federation.

In Todd Webb's landscape photographs there is a protracted attentiveness to what is real and what is represented; the logic of the documentary as a truth-telling form exists here in a precarious balance.[24] As seen in an image of temporary worker housing installed in the desert over 300 kilometers outside of Mogadishu, Webb repeatedly presented the landscape as altered through colonial intervention (see pp. 148–49). His photographs reveal that systems of seeing (and being seen) operate through established visual codes.[25] In the photographs produced for the United Nations Office of Public Information, and especially in this image of a Sinclair Oil Corporation remote work station, these conventions manifest as a distinctive horizon line, clear one-point perspective, and concrete framing device, seen in the silver trailers and light posts lining the pathway. Here, industry-making and picture-taking become congruent activities. They are, in the same stop-time moment, simultaneously in harmony and at odds with one another, forcing the viewer to question the ability of documentary photographs to tell the truth. By photographing worker housing at the Sinclair outpost, Webb "furnishes evidence," making Somali industry visible and, therefore, knowable to the United Nations, and by extension, the world.

Across Webb's larger body of landscape photographs, the possibilities of the photograph as a political device collide; it emerges both as a hegemonic weapon of colonialism and a tool of postcolonial-era reconstruction. These images display moments of tension and collision, representing a transitional period in history when so many African states were moving towards independence.[26] Webb's photographs are not radical, nor are they revolutionary. Their greatest power is not simply as material (and sometimes unstable) representations of the rapidly changing topography of the African continent, but perhaps as tools used for landscaping the postcolonial imaginary.

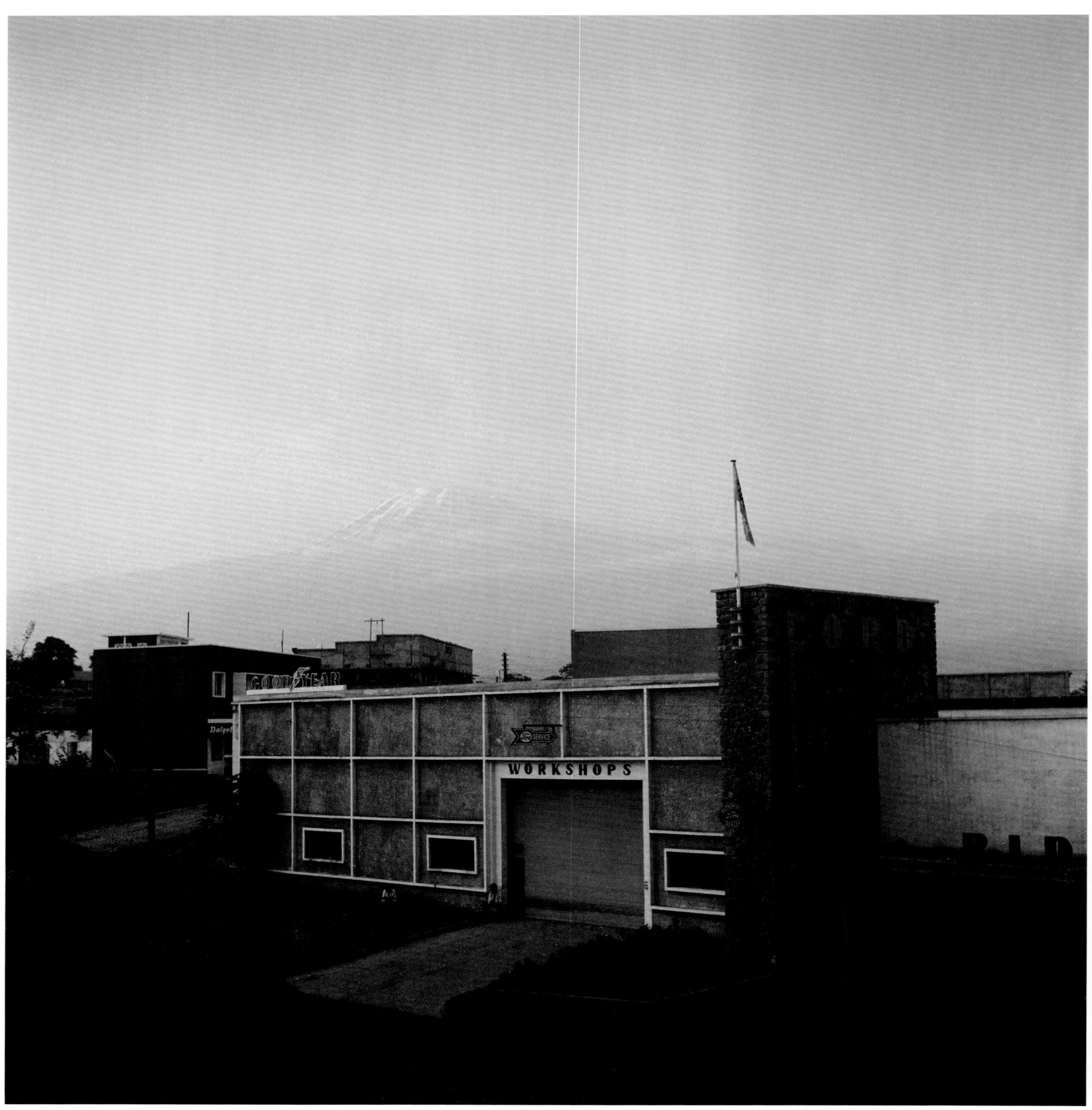

Todd Webb, *Untitled* (44UN-T2-R17-671), Tanganyika (Tanzania), 1958
Ford workshops building with Mount Kilimanjaro in the background.

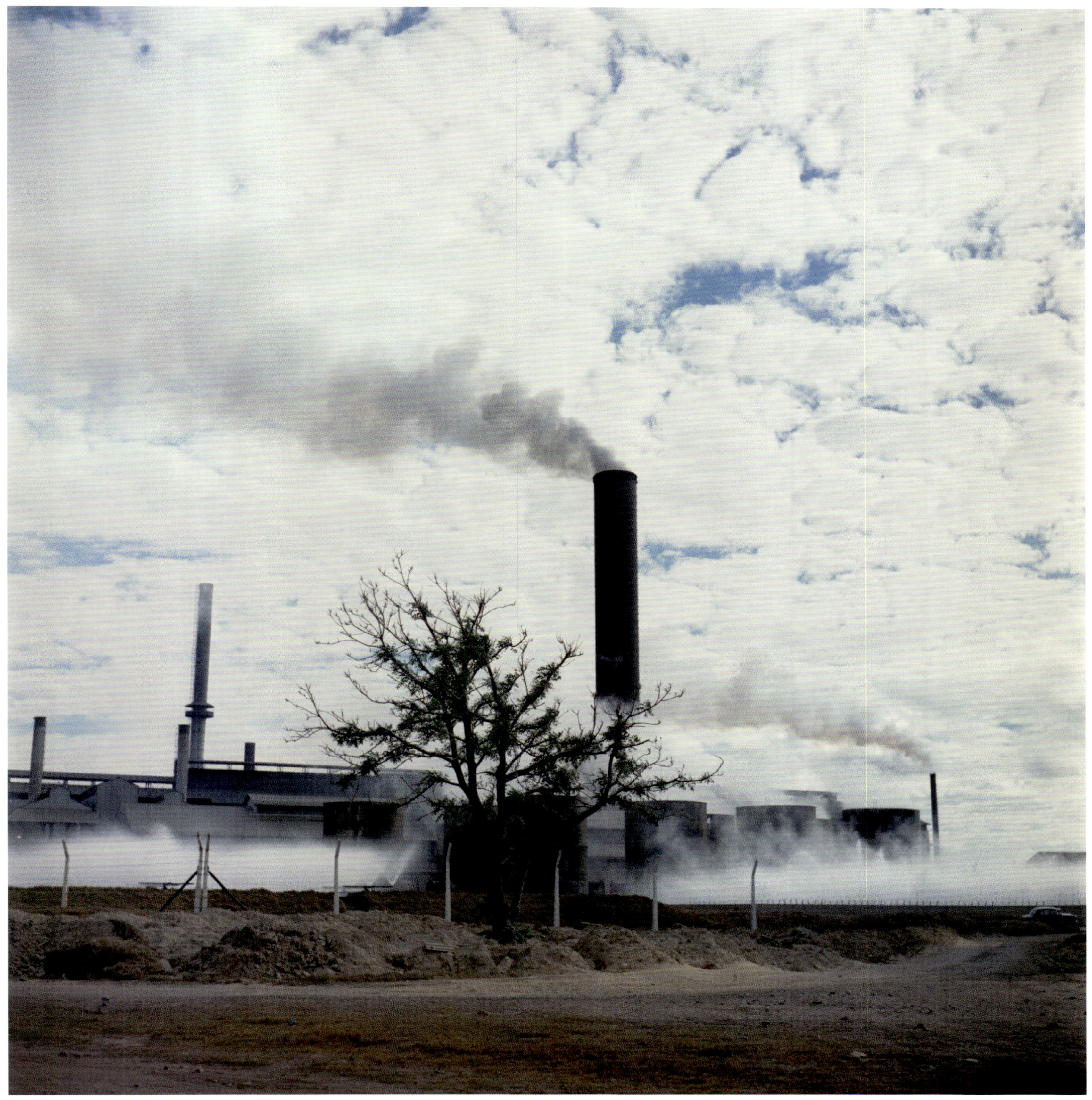

Todd Webb, *Untitled* (44UN-7995-131), Northern Rhodesia (Zambia), 1958
Mining company's smokestacks behind a fence.

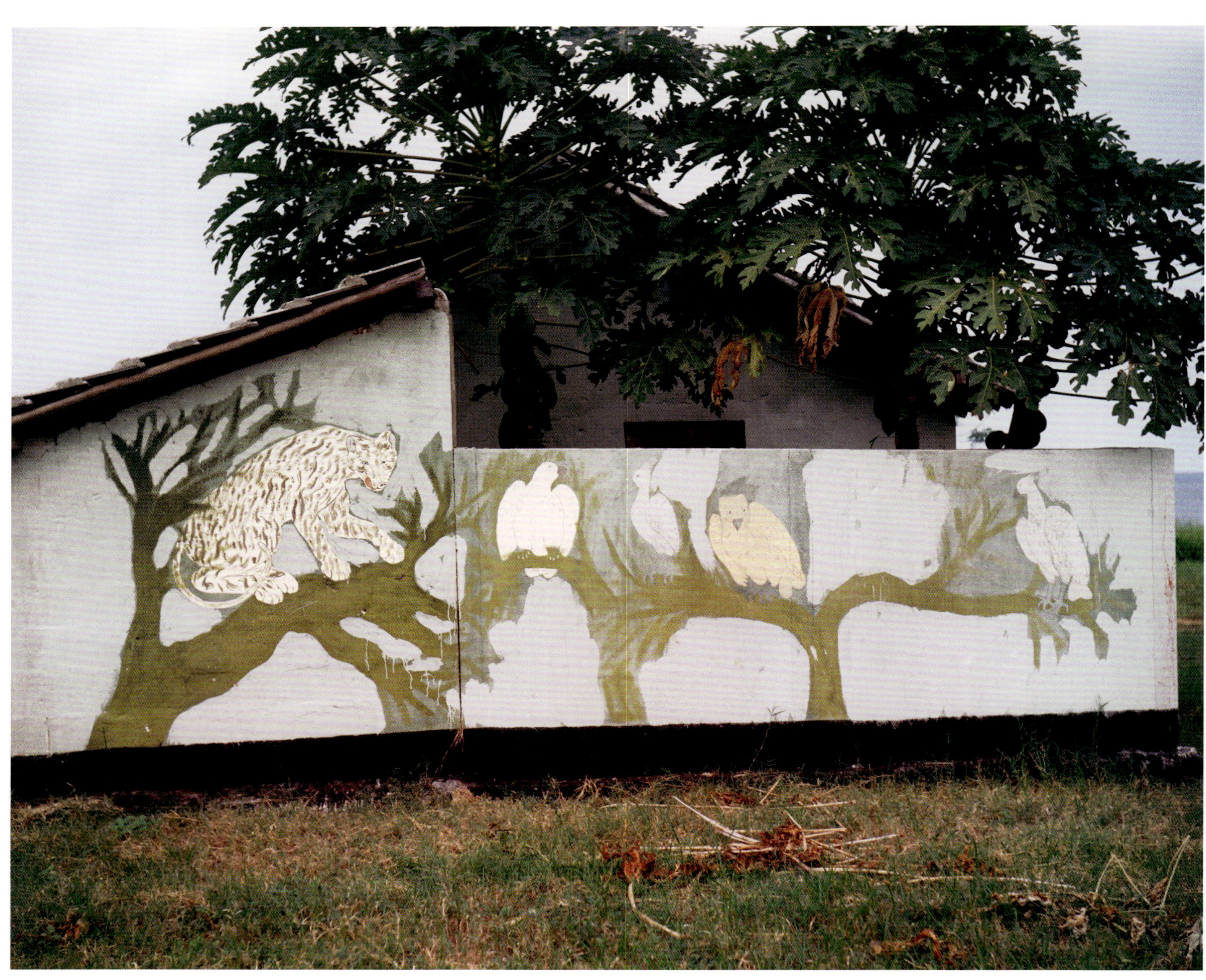

Todd Webb, *Untitled* (44UN-7931-017), Tanganyika (Tanzania), 1958
House mural painting with birds in trees, Kingoni village.

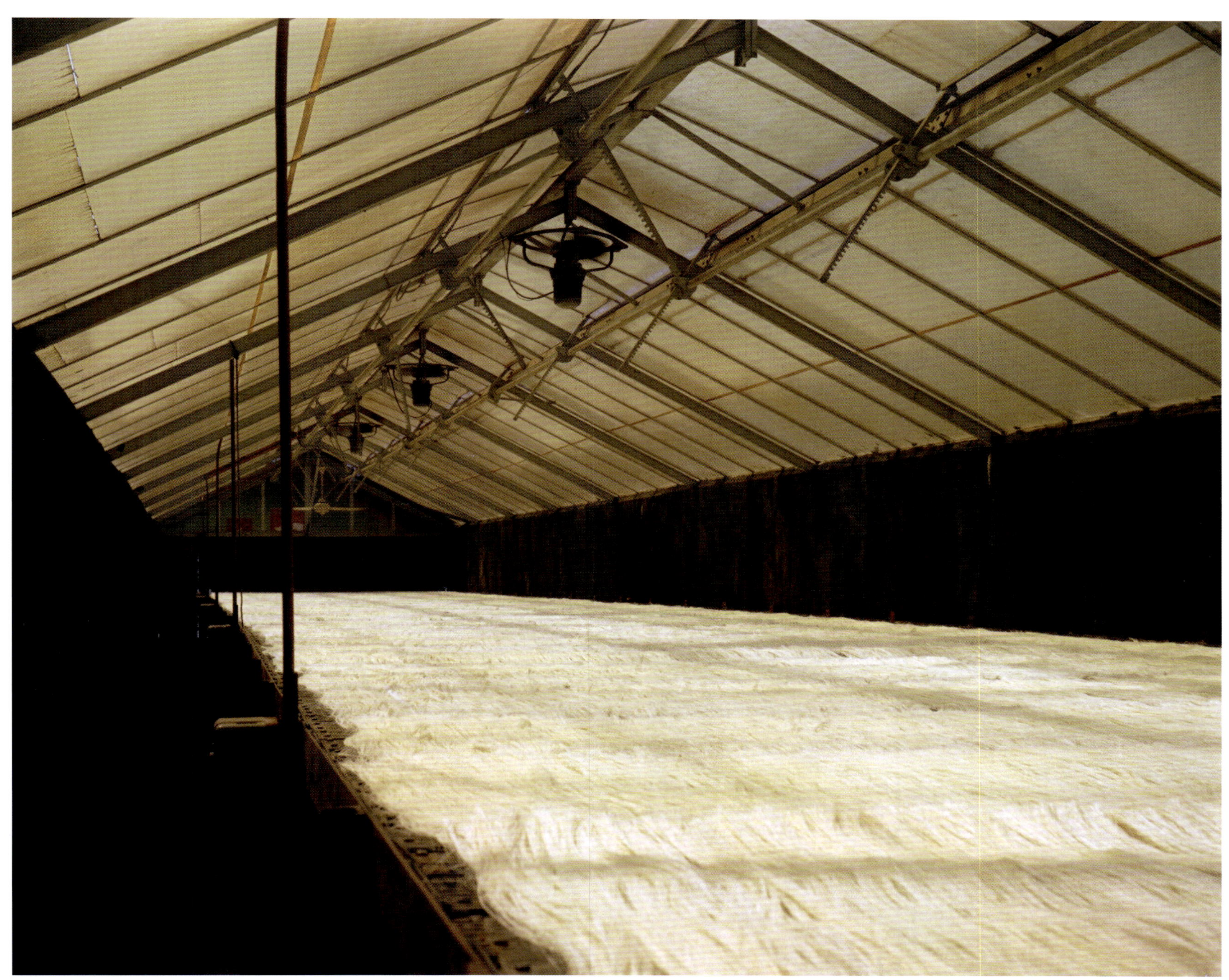

Todd Webb, *Untitled* (44UN-7934-325). Tanganyika (Tanzania), 1958
Drying sisal fibers at the Amboni Sisal Estate.

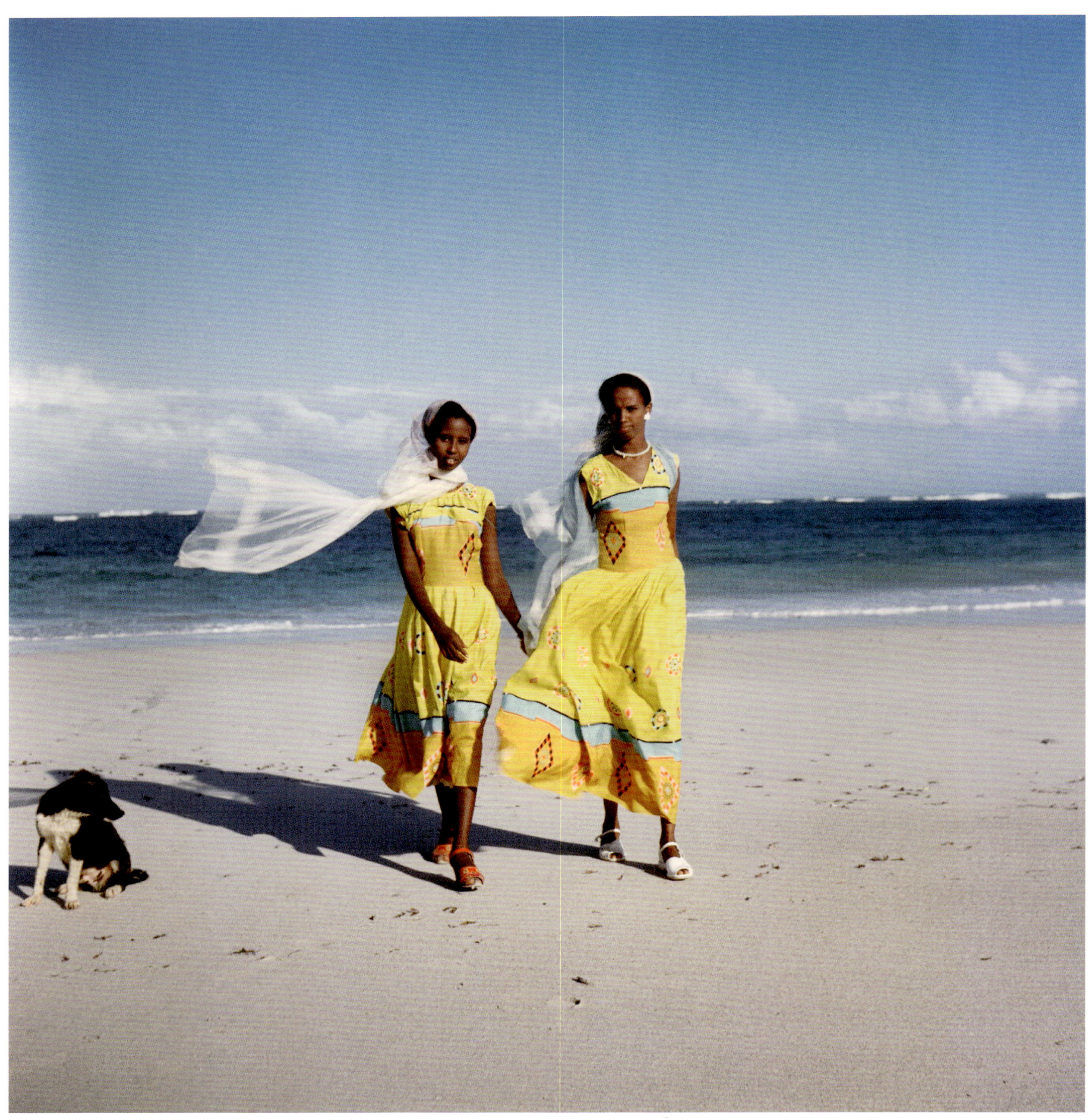

Todd Webb, *Untitled* (44UN-7930-609), Trust Territory of Somaliland (Somalia), 1958
Two women walking on the beach, with a dog to their right.

TRUST TERRITORY OF SOMALILAND

(SOMALIA)

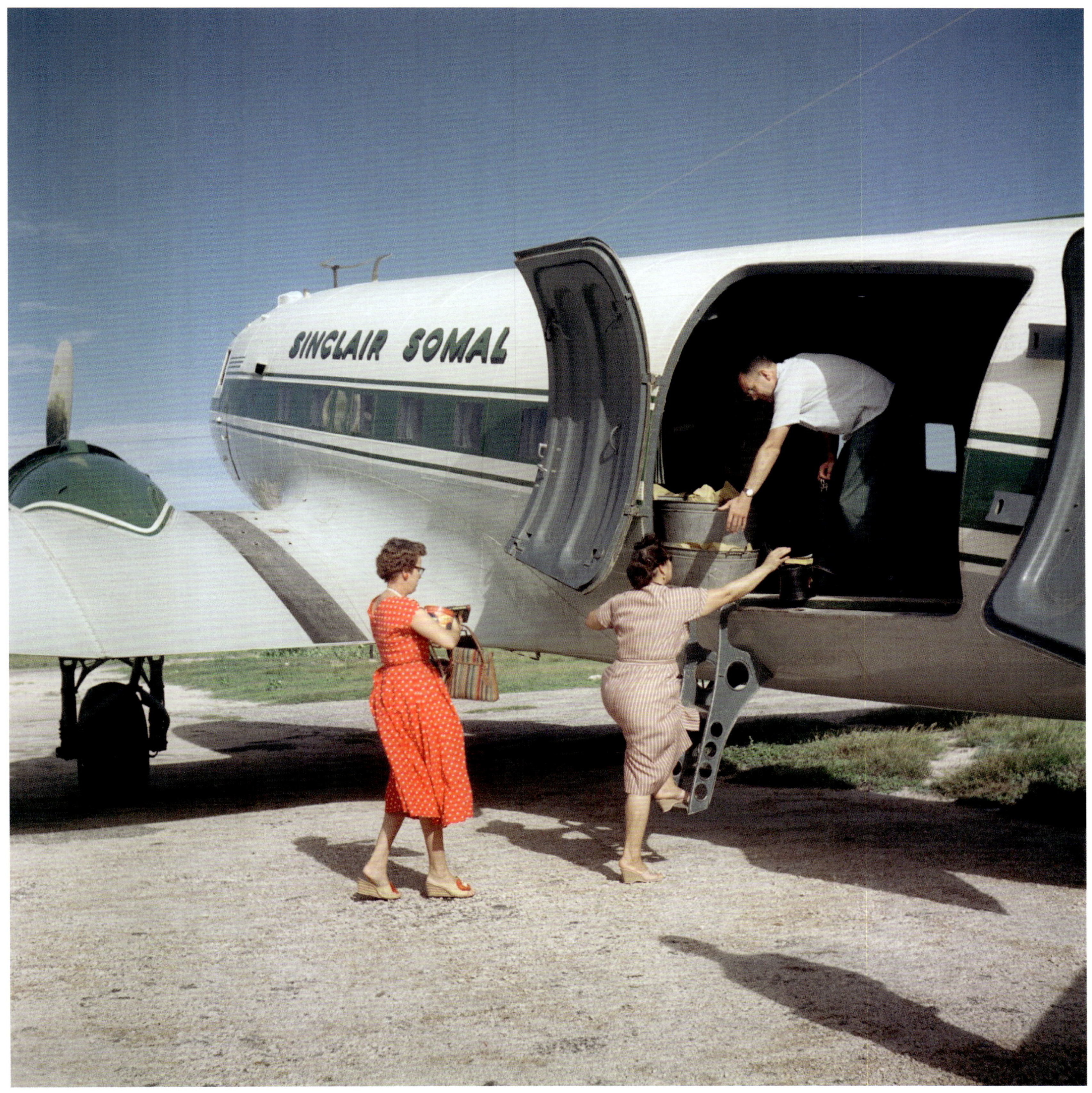

Todd Webb, *Untitled* (44UN-7968-C01), Trust Territory of Somaliland (Somalia), 1958
Women stepping up into a Sinclair Somal airplane.

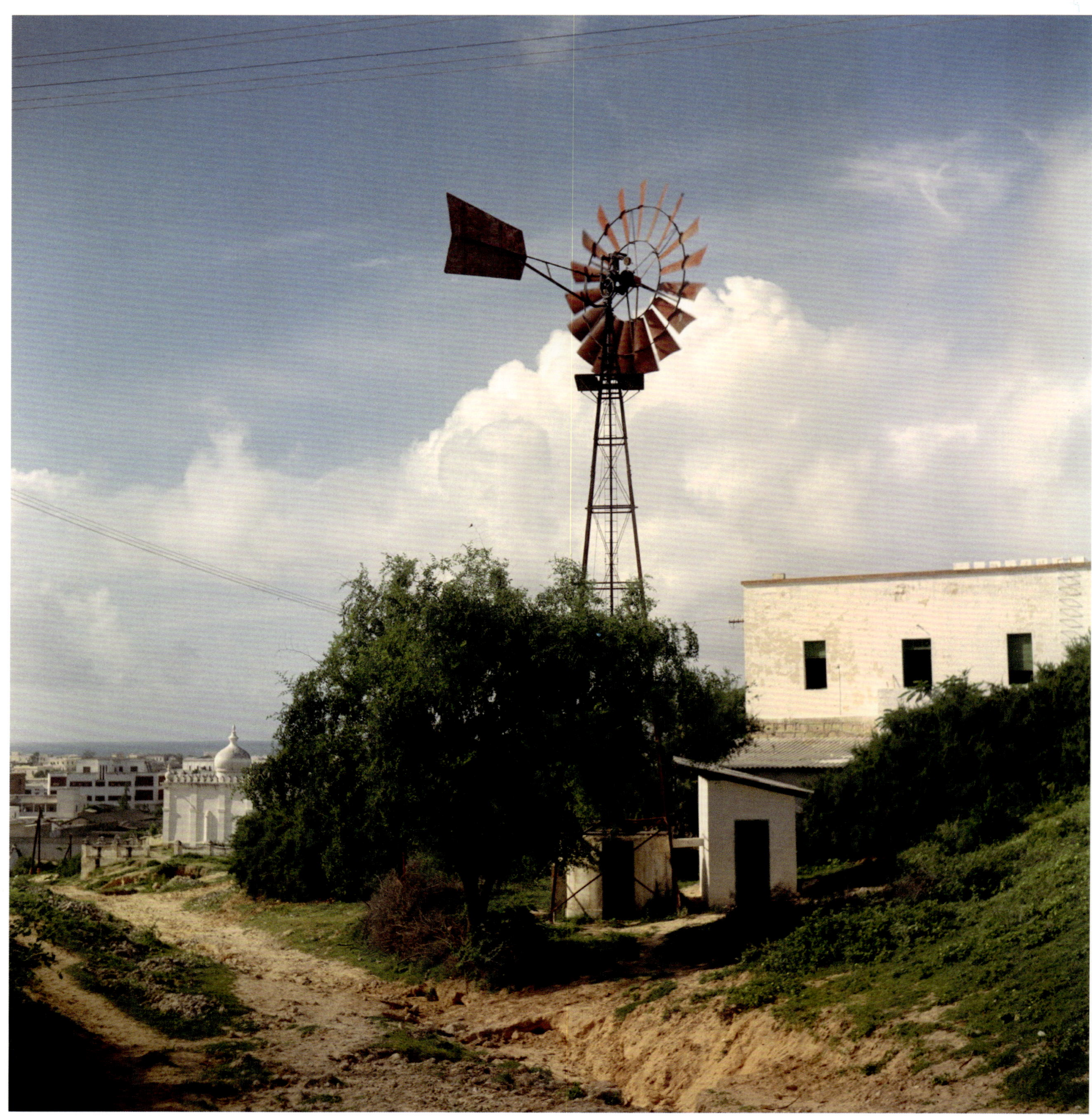

Todd Webb, *Untitled* (44UN-7774-044), Trust Territory of Somaliland (Somalia), 1958
Windmill with mosque and city buildings in background.

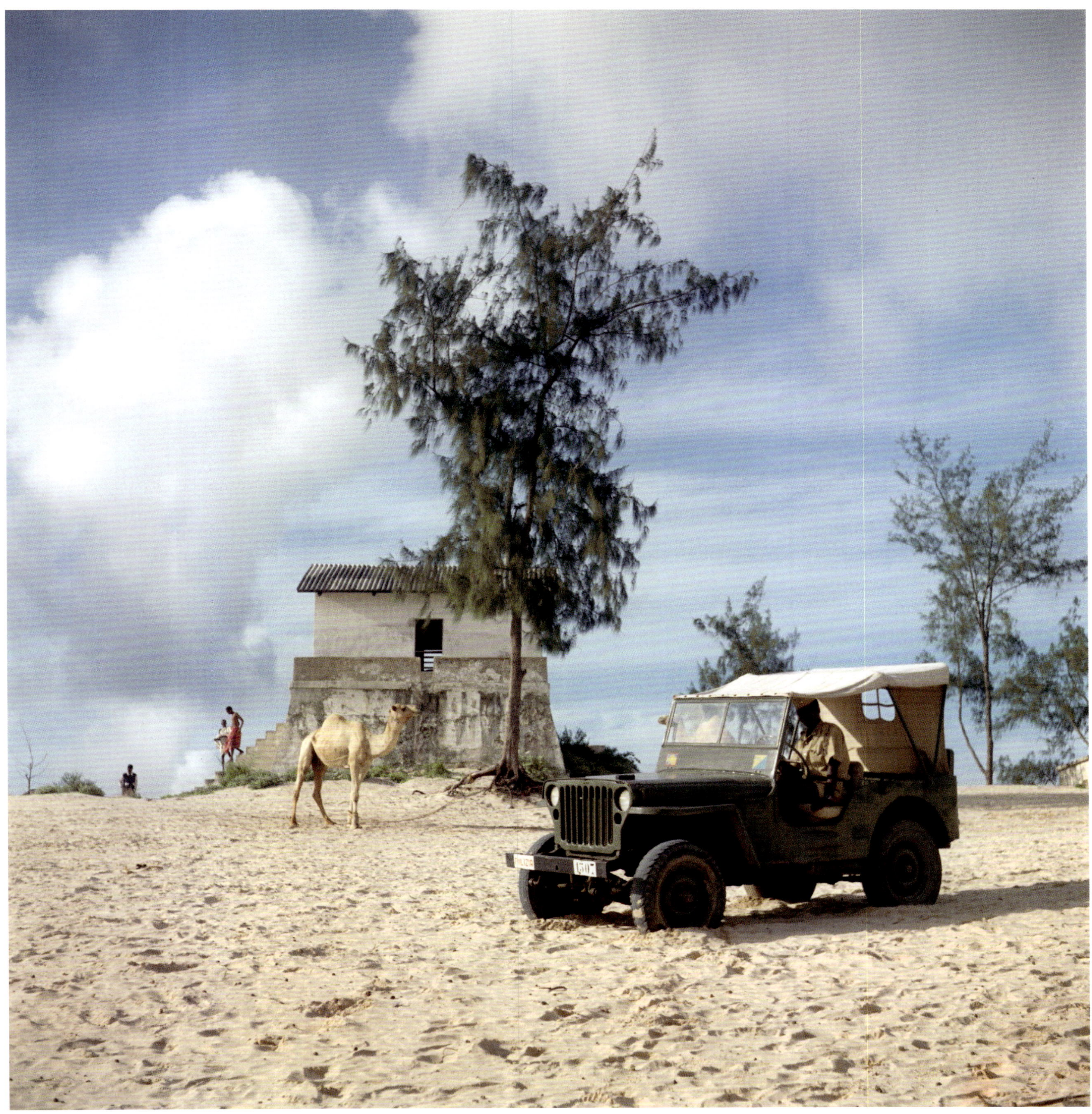

Todd Webb, *Untitled* (44UN-7928-267), Trust Territory of Somaliland (Somalia), 1958
Police jeep and camel on the sand.

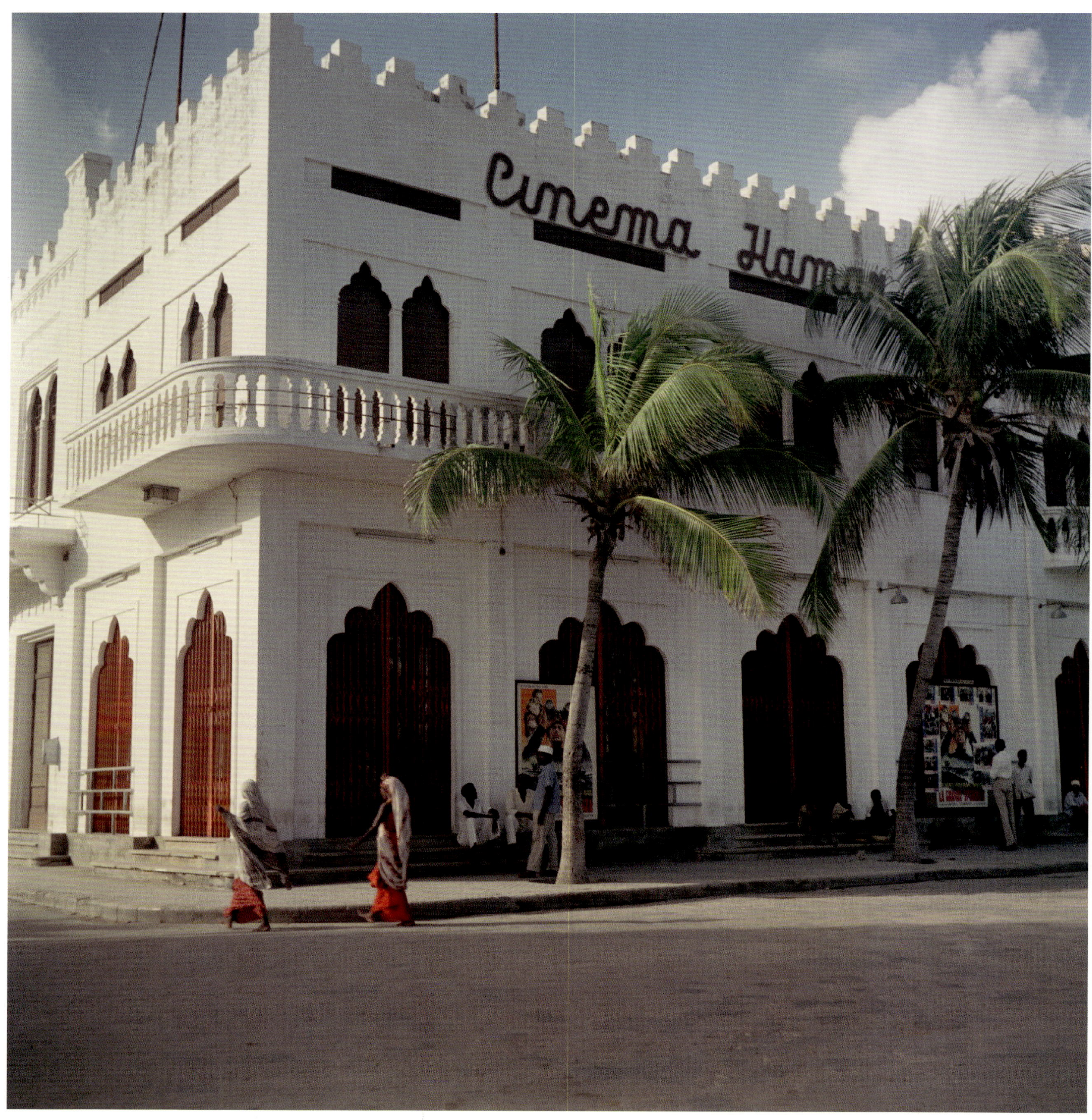

Todd Webb, *Untitled* (44UN-8007-281), Trust Territory of Somaliland (Somalia), 1958
Cinema Hamar, Mogadishu.

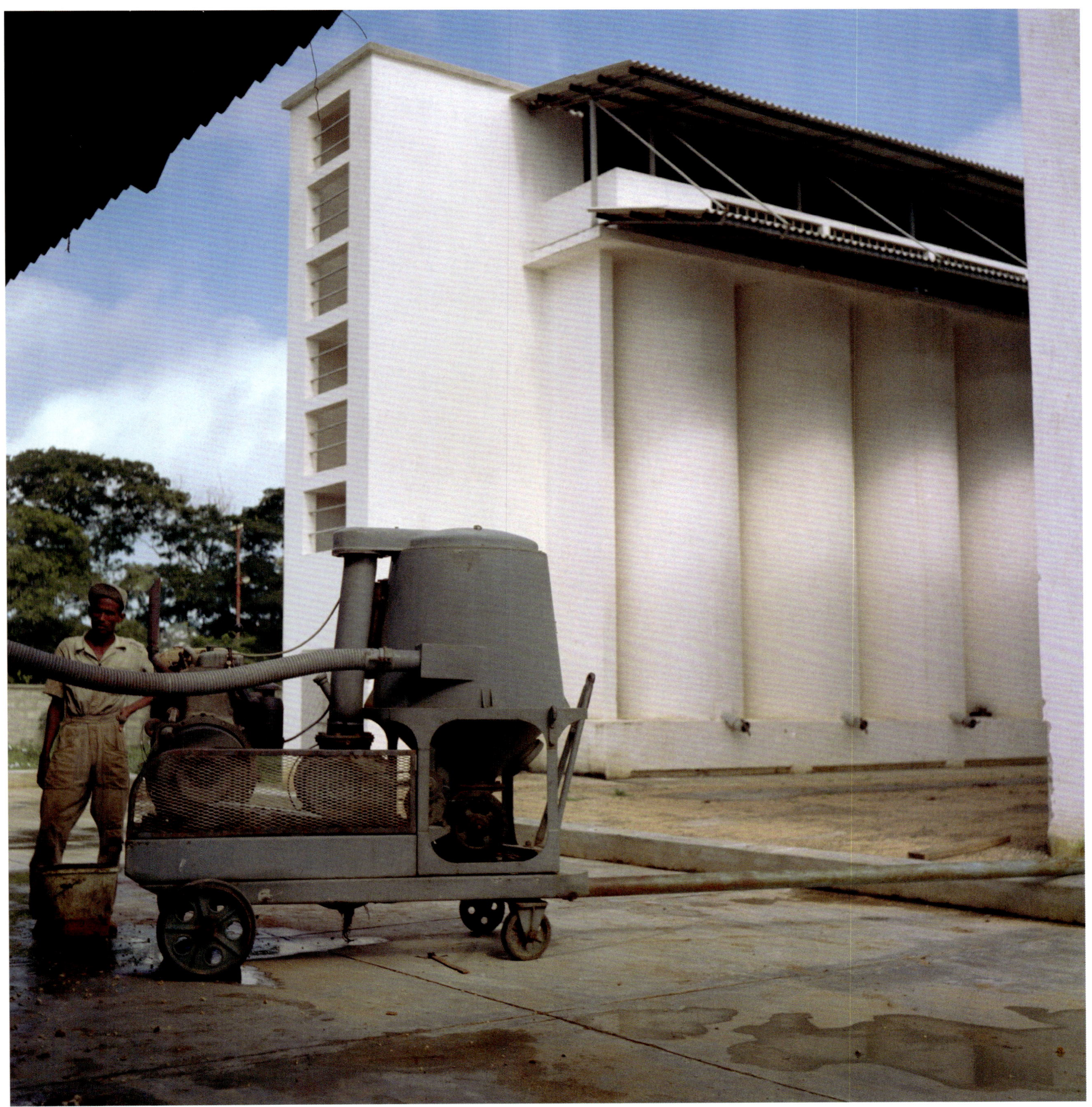

Todd Webb, *Untitled* (44UN-7907-149), Trust Territory of Somaliland (Somalia), 1958
Worker using machinery at the factory.

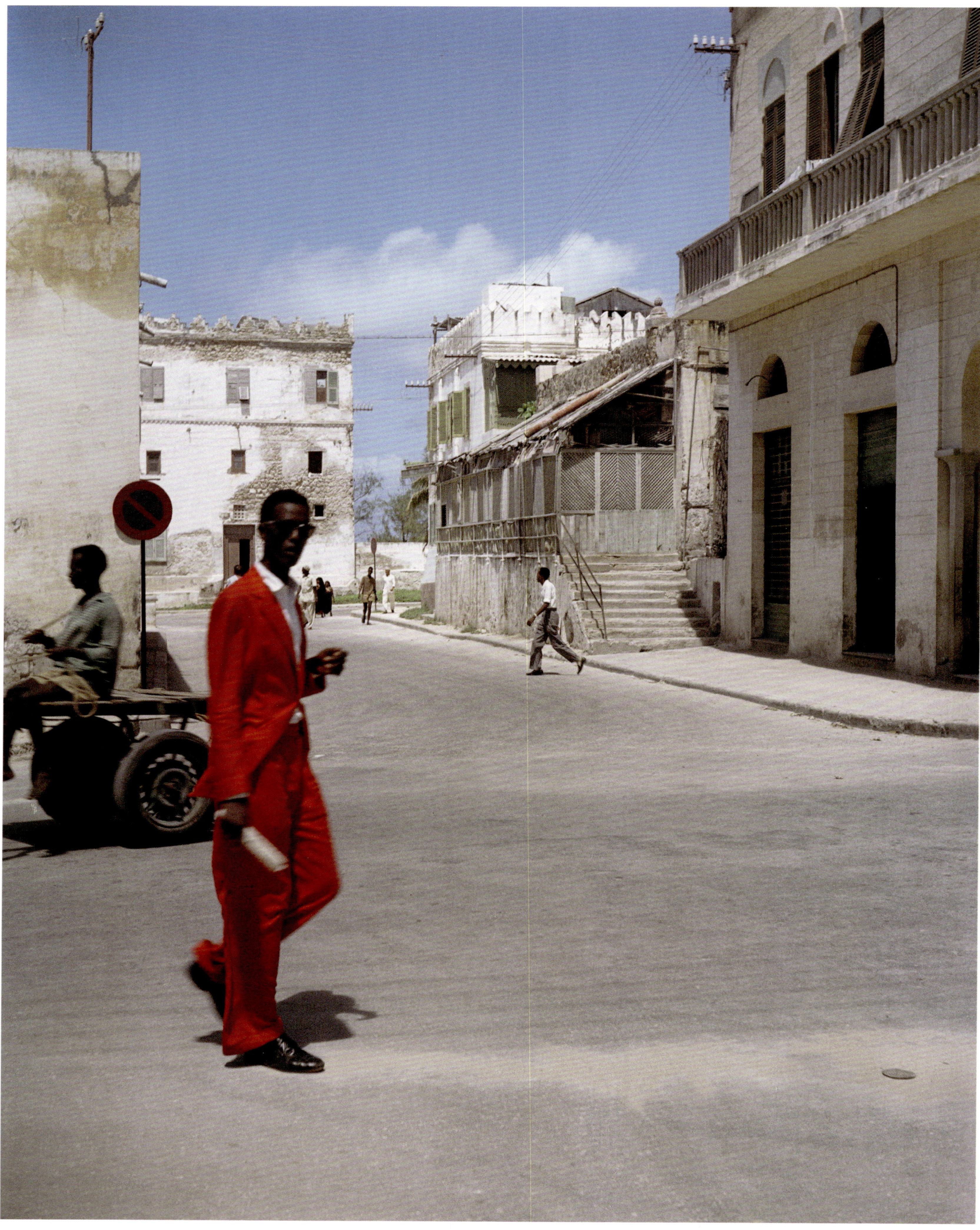

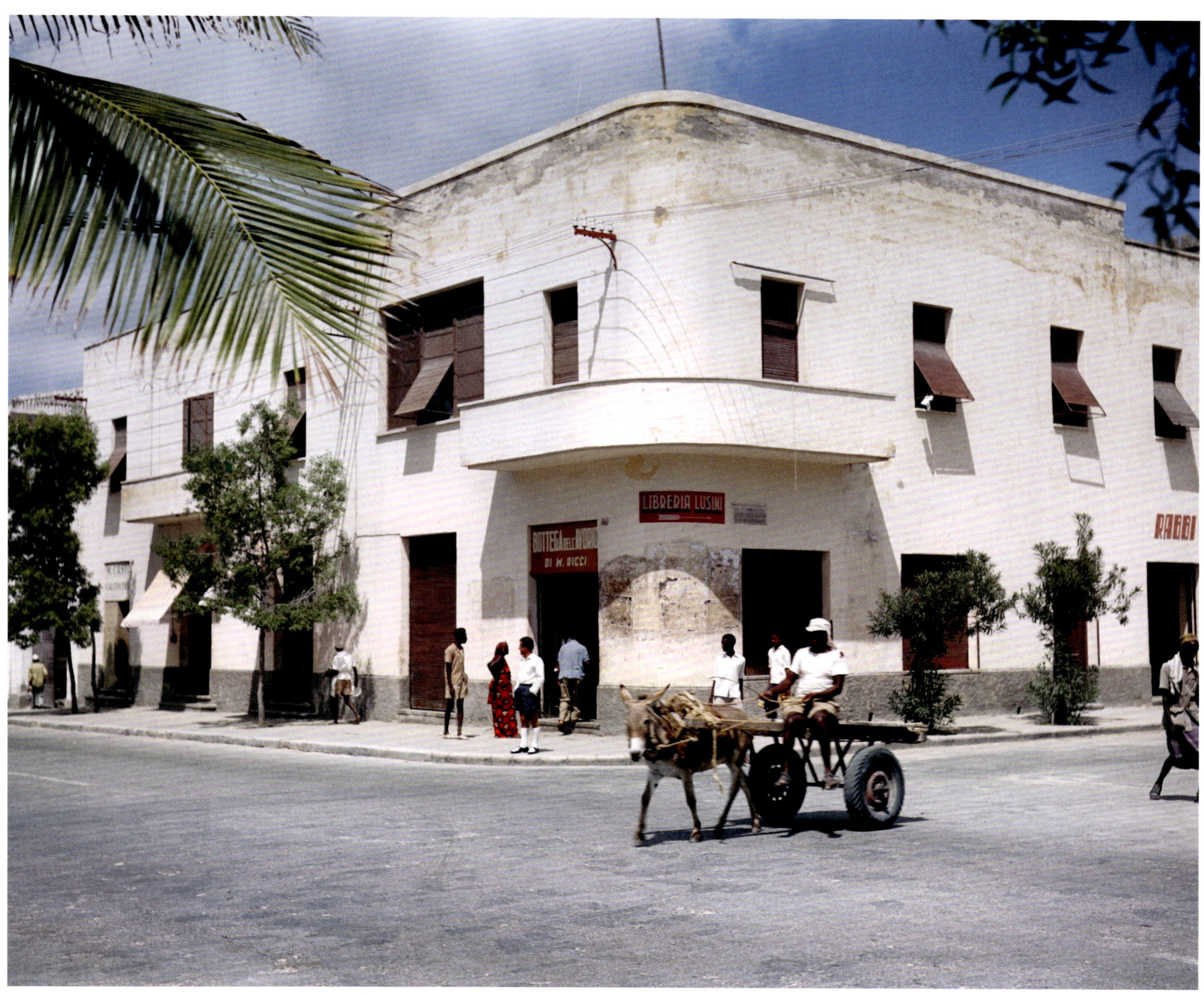

Opposite: Todd Webb, *Untitled* (44UN-8001-496), Trust Territory of Somaliland (Somalia), 1958
Man in red suit walking in Mogadishu.

Above: Todd Webb, *Untitled* (44UN-7921-002), Trust Territory of Somaliland (Somalia), 1958
Donkey cart passing a city corner near Bottega dello Avorio (Ivory Store), Mogadishu.

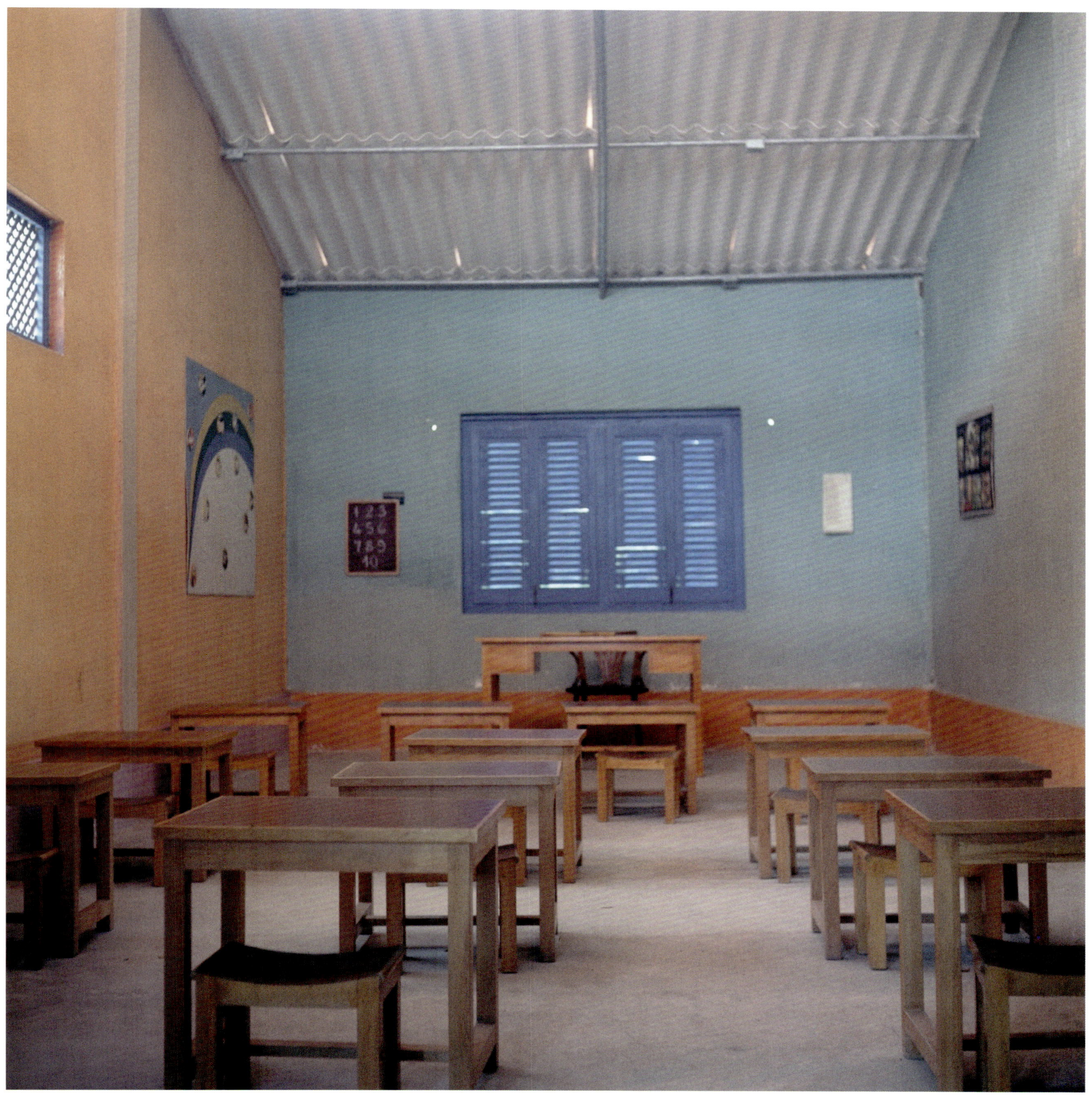

Todd Webb, *Untitled* (44UN-7764-083), Trust Territory of Somaliland (Somalia), 1958
Classroom interior.

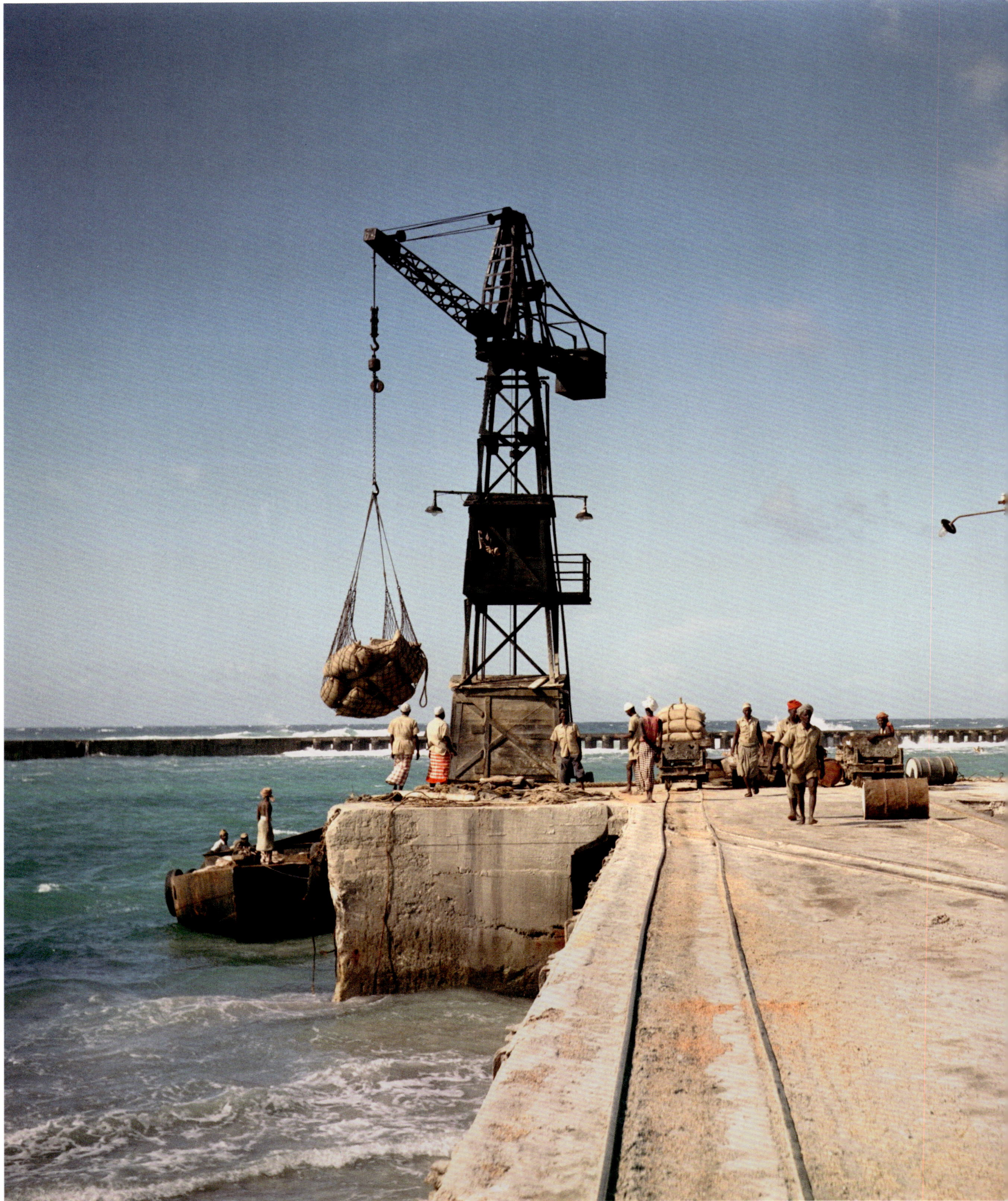

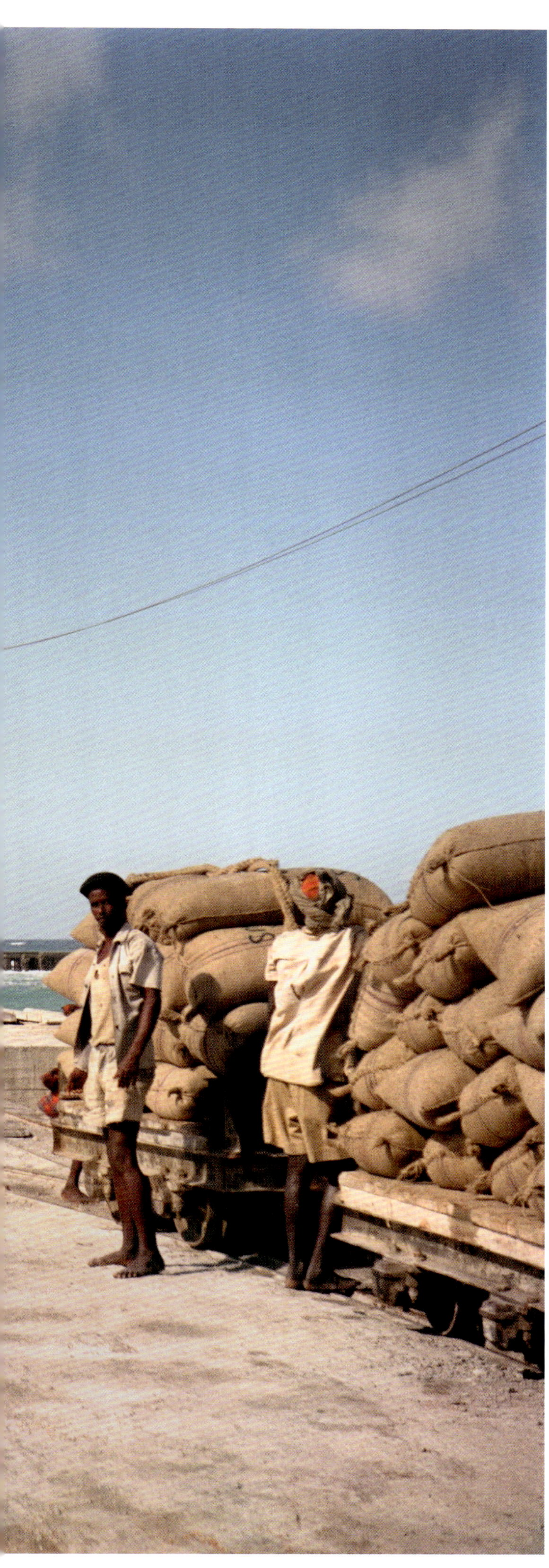

Todd Webb, *Untitled* (44UN-7953-003), Trust Territory of Somaliland (Somalia), 1958
Loading and unloading cargo at the harbor.

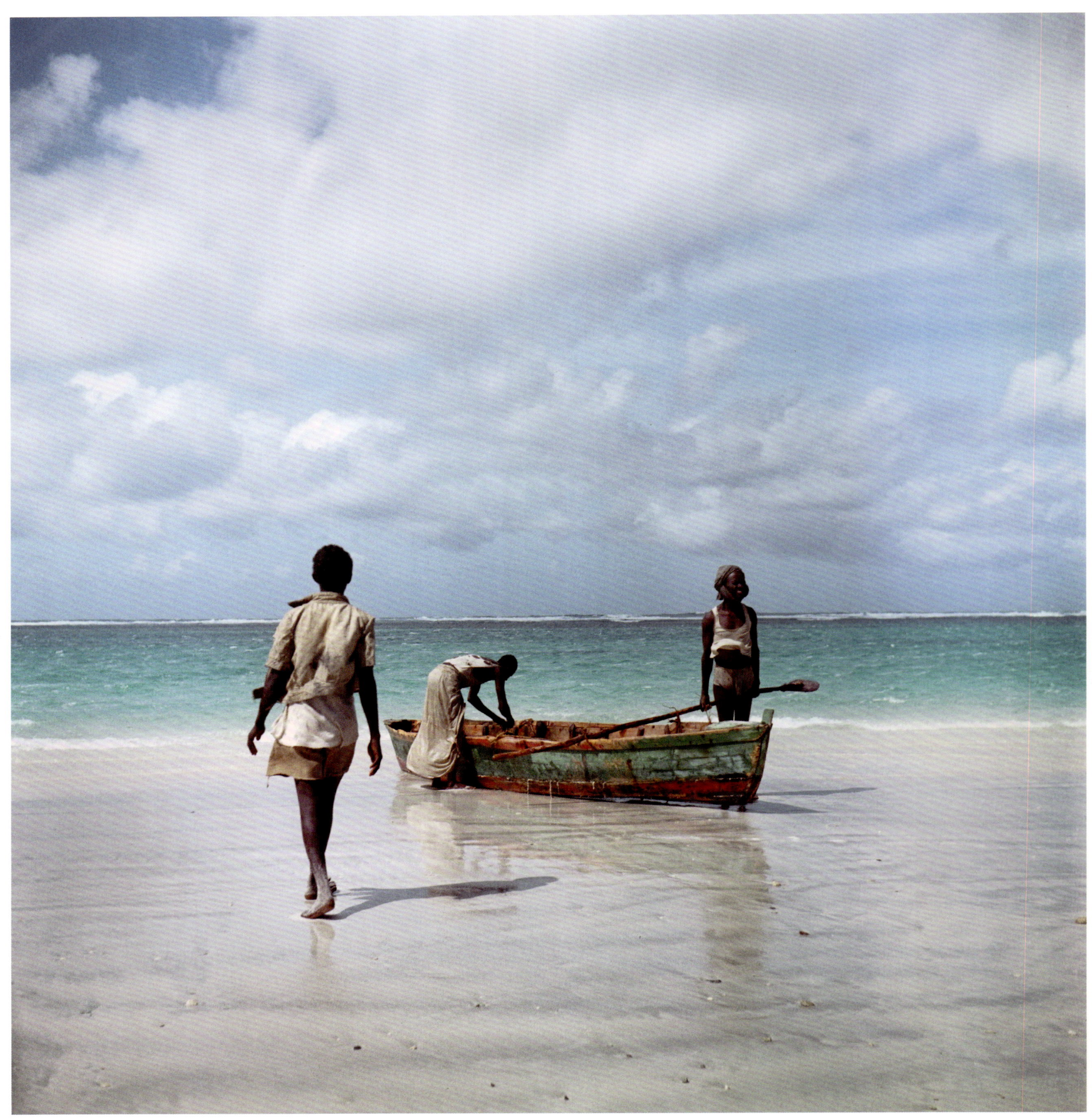

Todd Webb, *Untitled* (44UN-7967-001), Trust Territory of Somaliland (Somalia), 1958
Men with fishing boat, near Mogadishu.

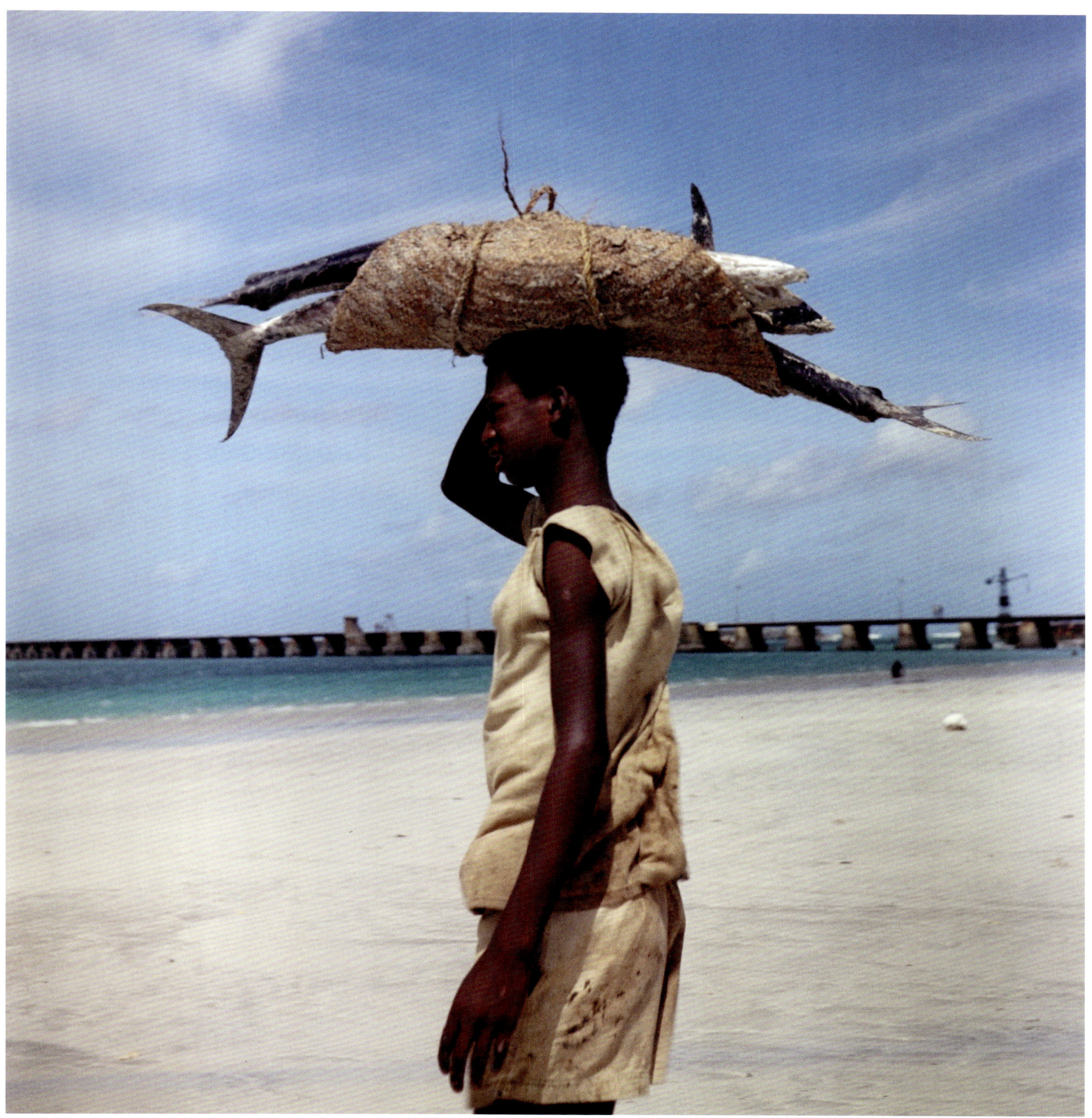

Todd Webb, *Untitled* (44UN-7967-002), Trust Territory of Somaliland (Somalia), 1958
Boy carrying fish on his head, near Mogadishu.

Todd Webb, Journal Entry, June 19, 1958

"I liked Somalia–made friends–fleeting ones–but firm–and I regret the fleetingness and the hopelessness of never seeing them again. The Somalis are most hospitable and generous."

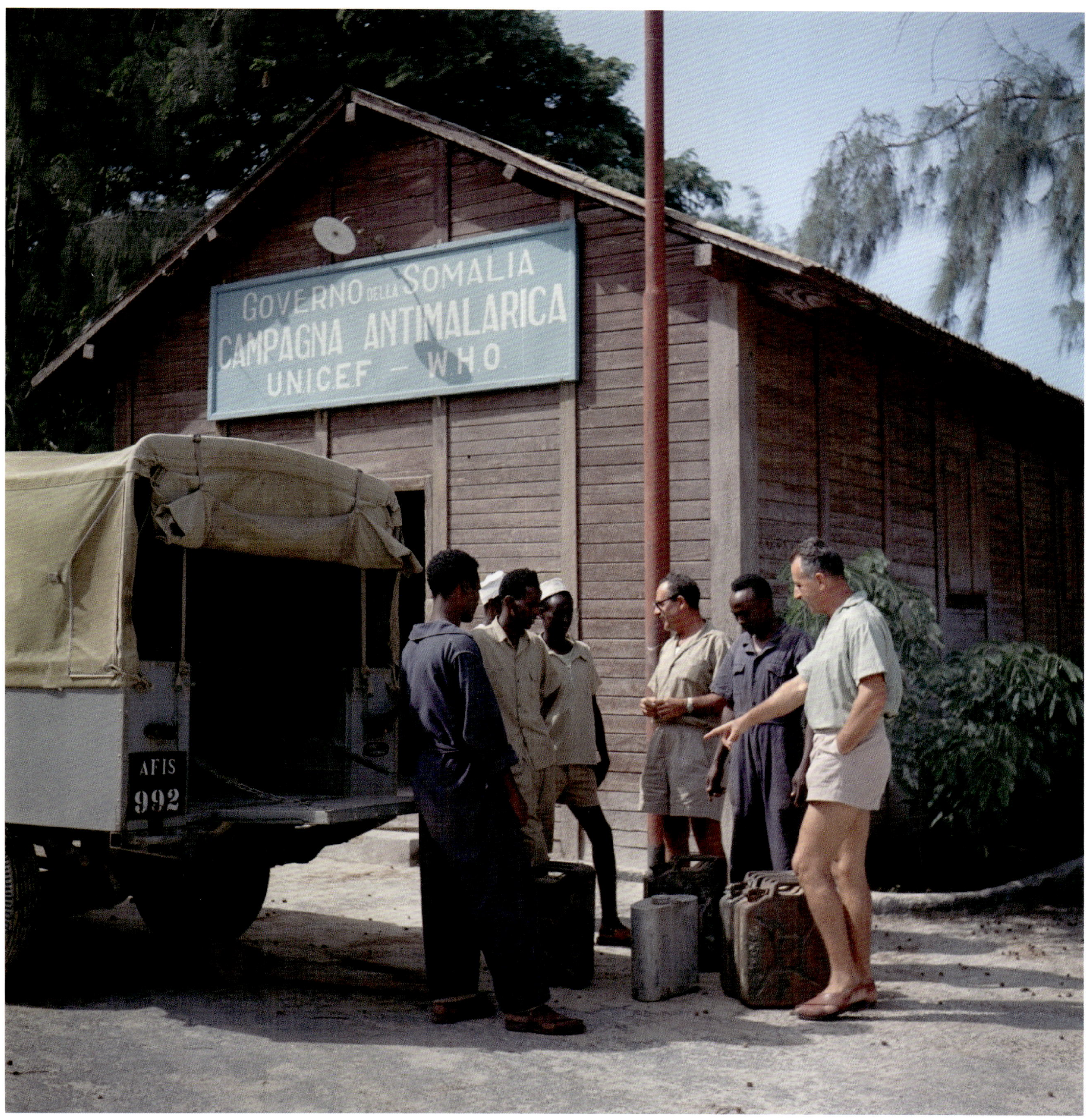

Todd Webb, *Untitled* (44UN-7969-049), Trust Territory of Somaliland (Somalia), 1958
Men with supplies at truck outside the Somalia Governor's Campaign against Malaria, Unicef and WHO.

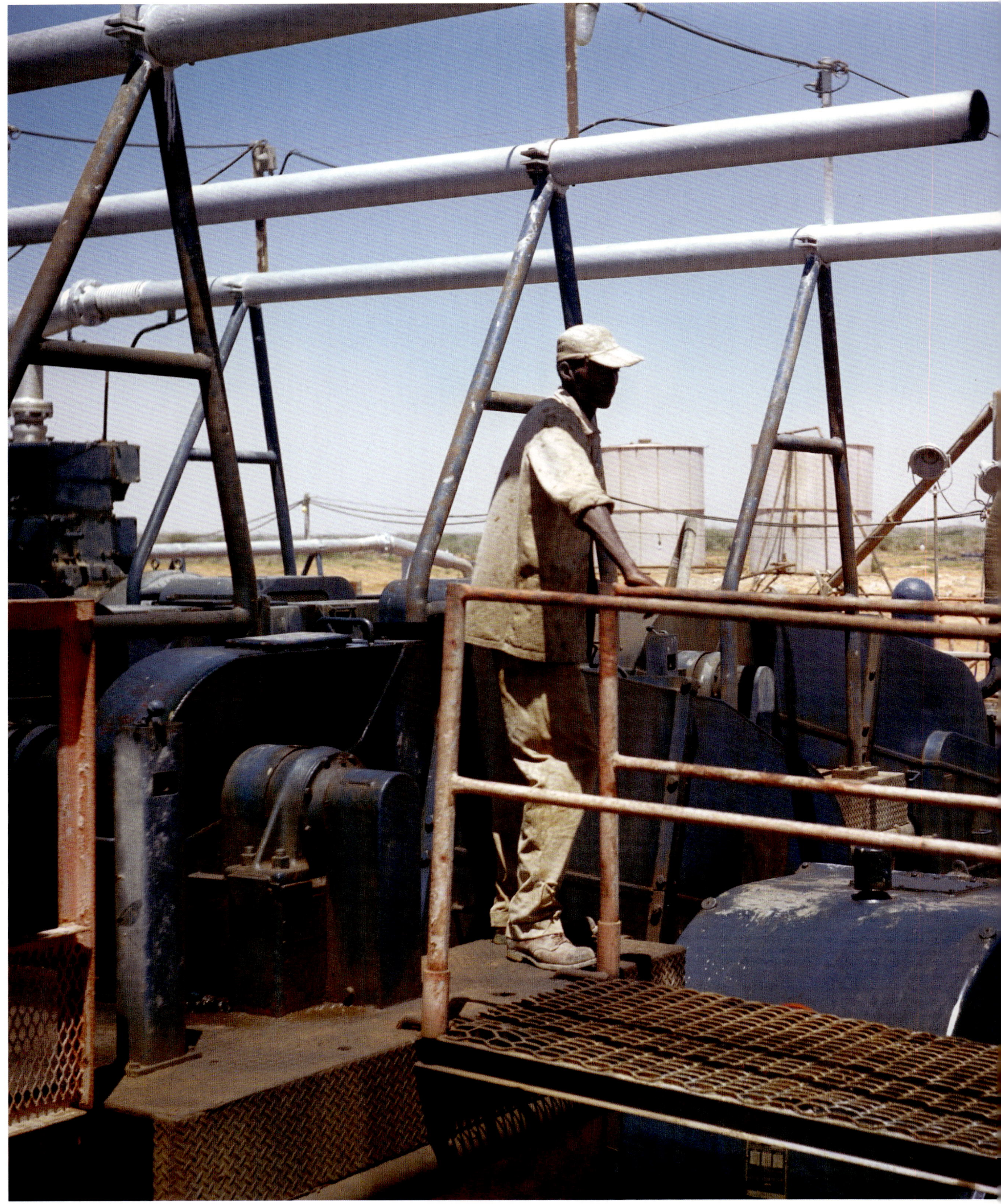

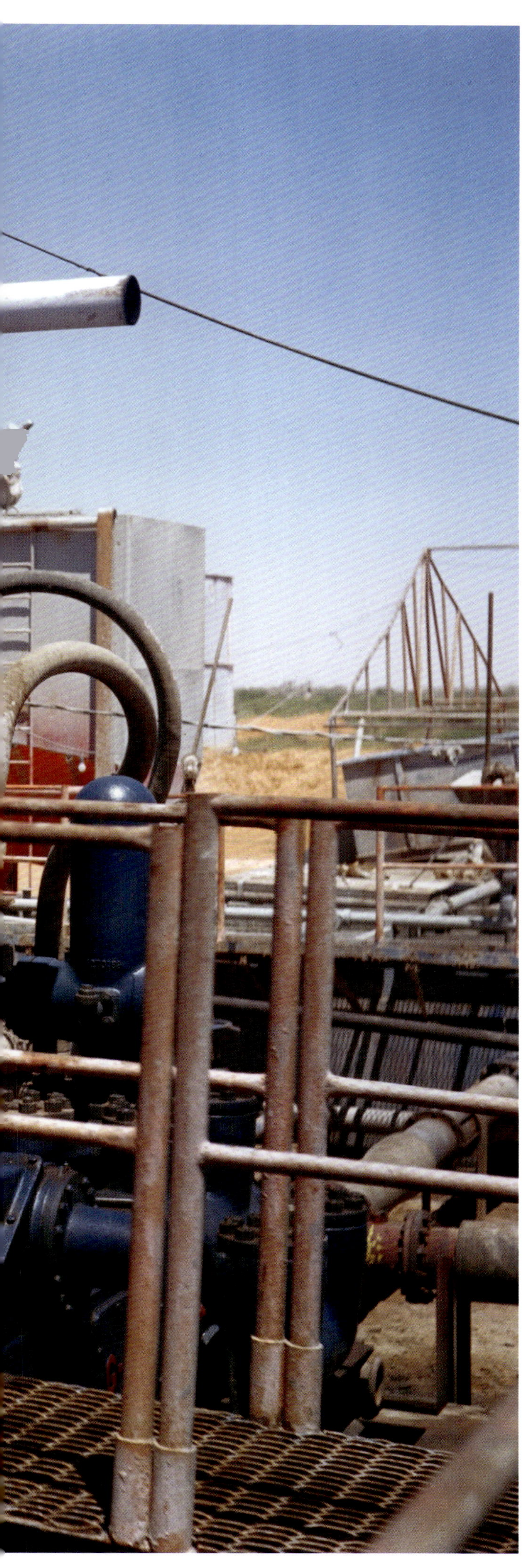

Todd Webb, *Untitled* (44UN-8000-007), Trust Territory of Somaliland (Somalia), 1958
Men standing on an oil rig.

Todd Webb, *Untitled* (44UN-8001-498), Trust Territory of Somaliland (Somalia), 1958
Trailers at the Sinclair Oil Corporation site, 320 kilometers north of Mogadishu.

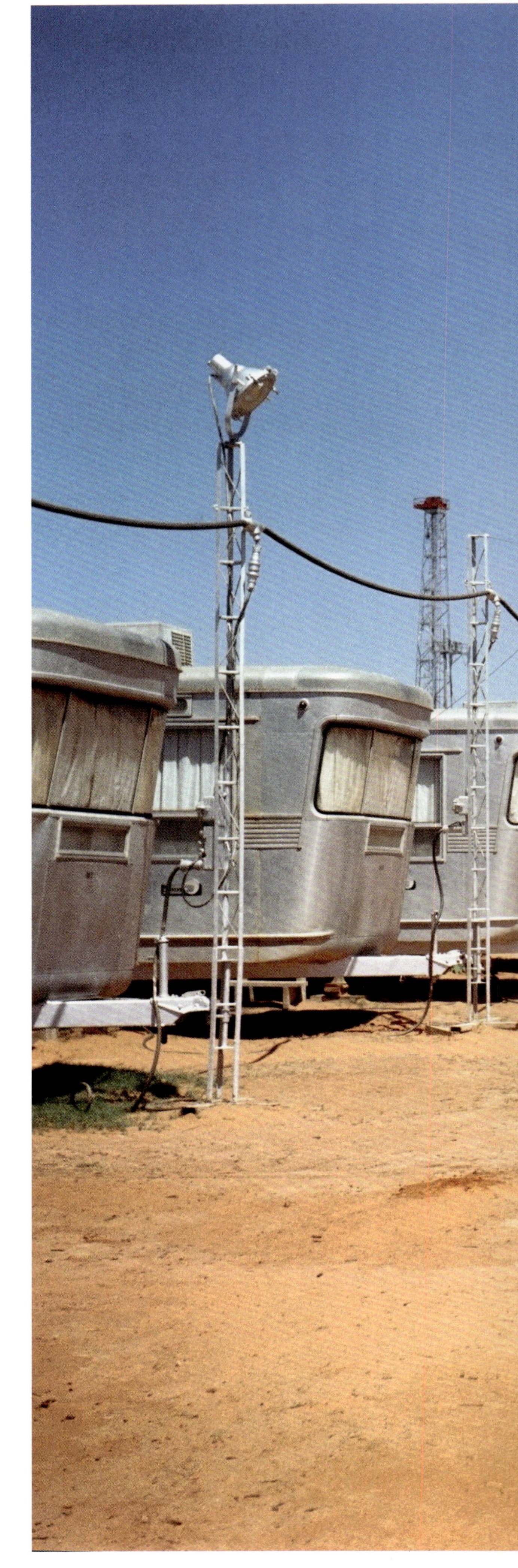

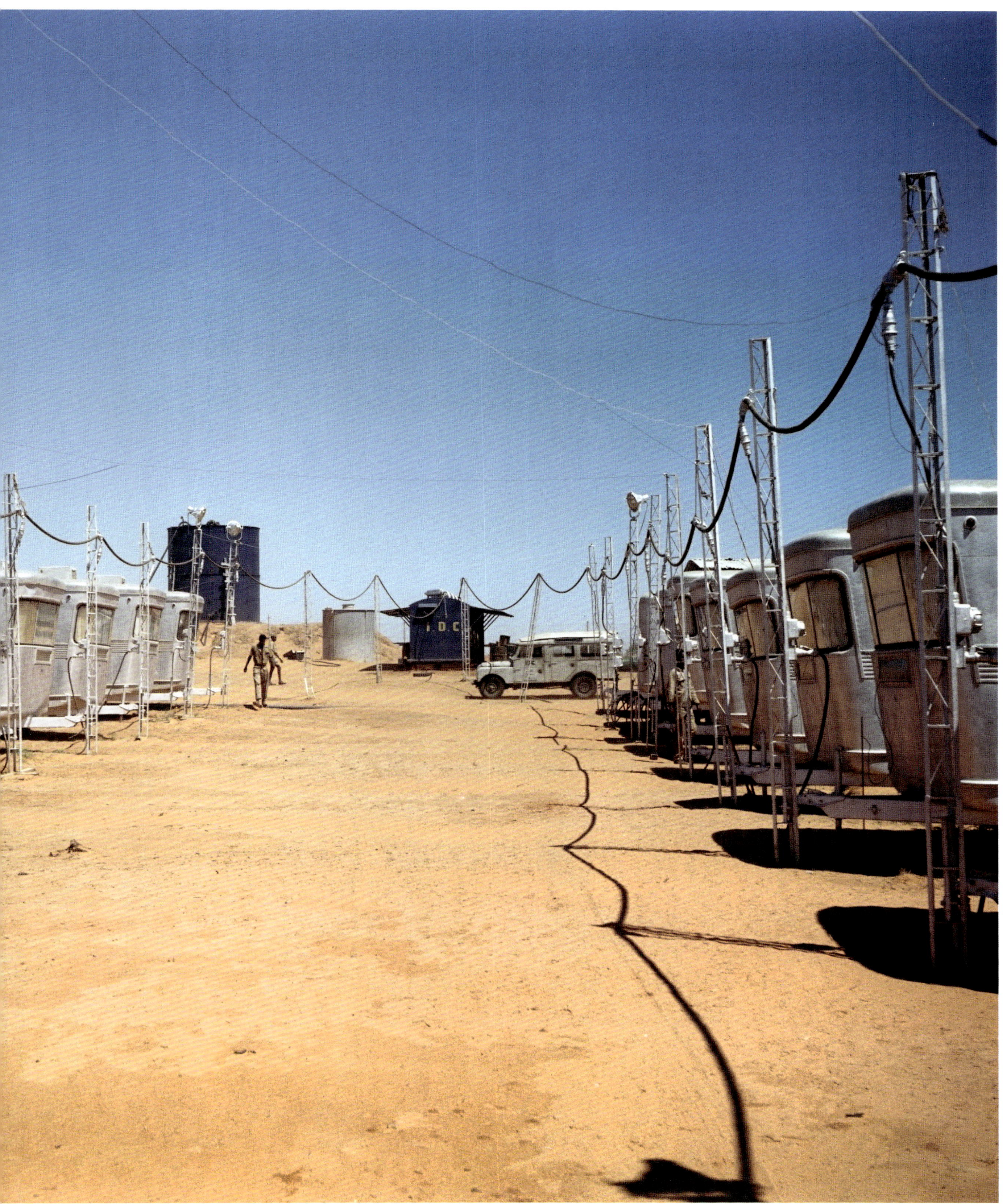
I.D.C

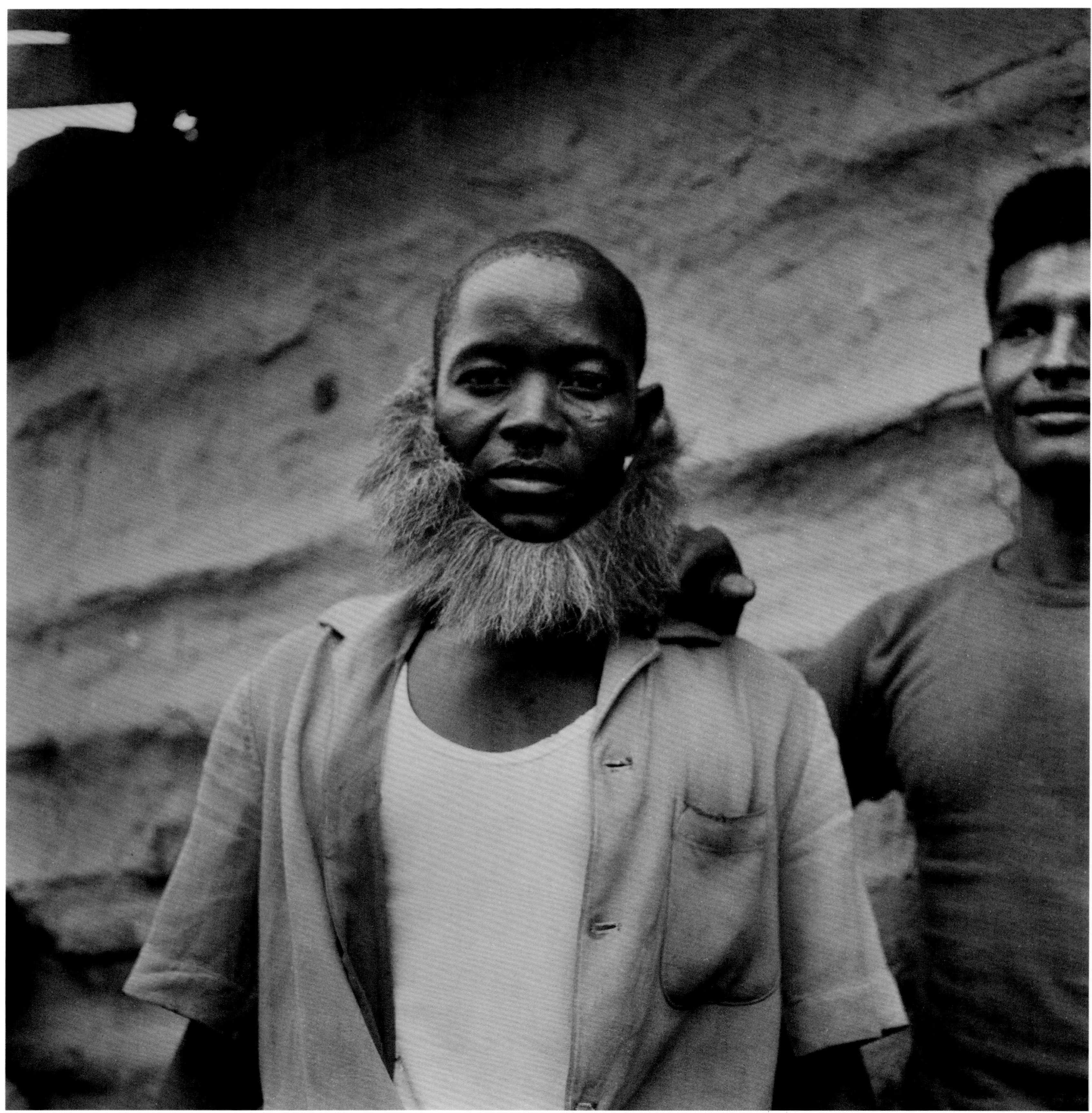

Todd Webb, *Untitled* (44UN-SOM-2-1-002), Trust Territory of Somaliland (Somalia), 1958
Man with a faux beard.

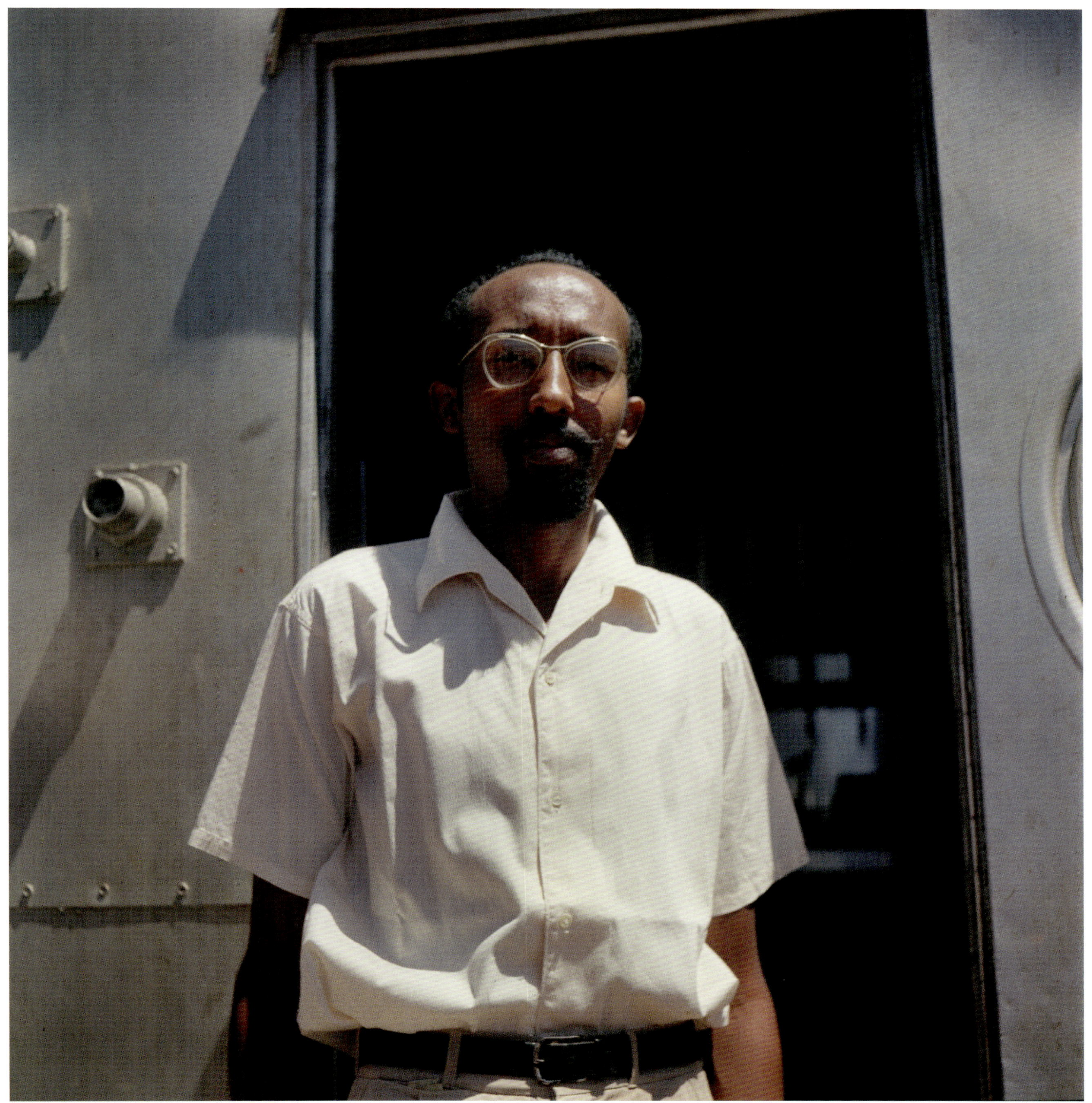

Todd Webb, *Untitled* (44UN-7920-288), Trust Territory of Somaliland (Somalia), 1958
Somali man standing outside office door.

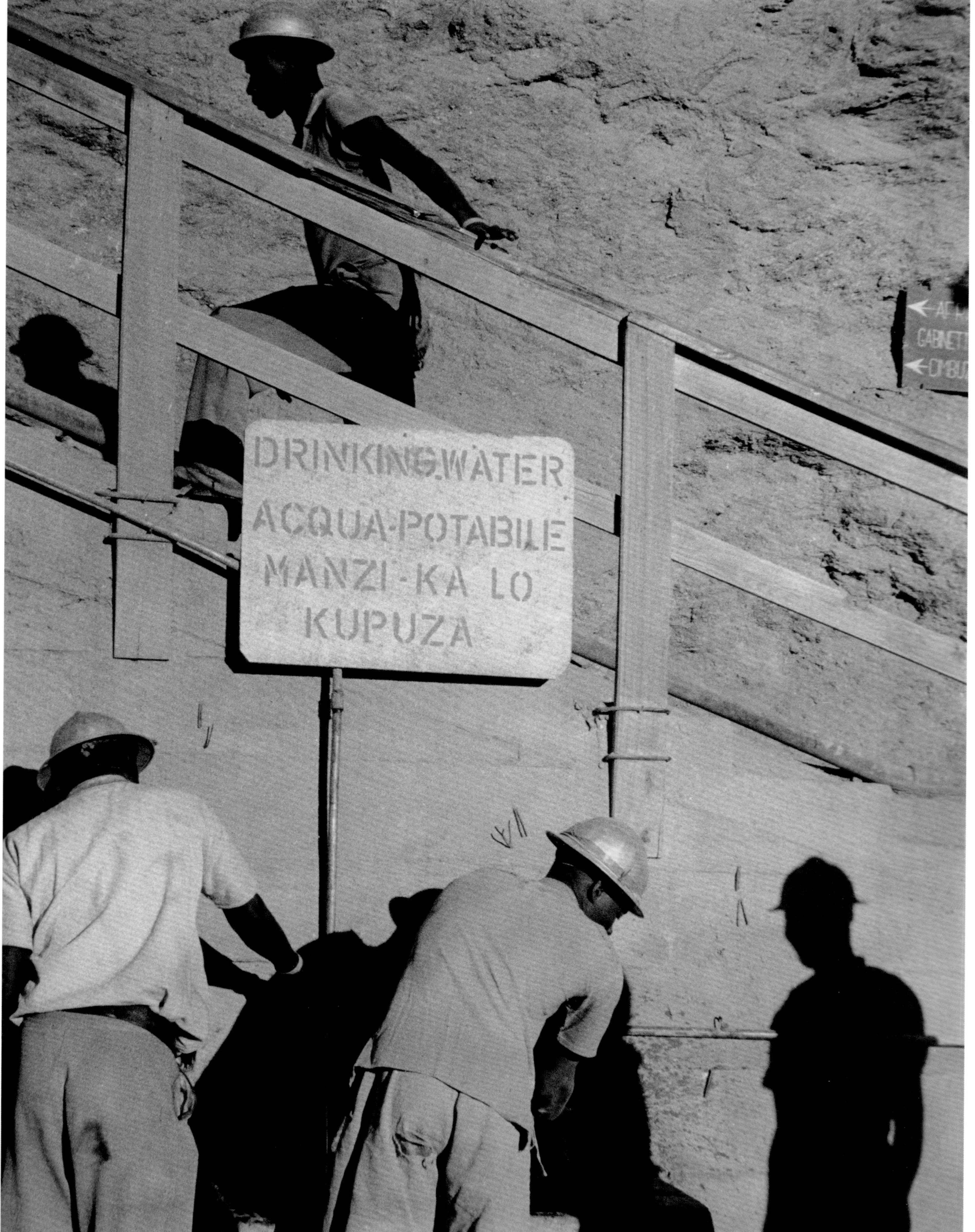
DRINKING WATER
ACQUA-POTABILE
MANZI-KA LO
KUPUZA

Todd Webb, *Untitled* (44UN-58-064), Trust Territory of Somaliland (Somalia), 1958
Drinking water sign at a work site.

Todd Webb's Excursions into Somalia (or, Todd Webb in Somalia)

Ali Jimale Ahmed

What are the possible relations between images and text?
How can we approach the reader together?[1]
– John Berger

Seeing Todd Webb's photographs from his 1958 trip to the Trust Territory of Somaliland (Somalia), I instinctively began reminiscing about iconic places and landmarks that had, for years, defined the landscape of the Somali capital. Two images that capture Webb's testimony to a rife contradiction in transition are the future Parliament building and the Arch of Triumph, constructed by the Italian colonial regime during its heyday (see opposite and p. 157). The Parliament building points to a nation in the process of becoming; the Arch points to a past that is coming to an end. Webb astutely documents the impending "winds of change."

All that I know about photography comes from reading books, including works by John Berger and Susan Sontag. But for practical and technical terms, before clicking the shutter on the camera, I always sought help from "Camera for Dummies" brochures. That said, I have always been drawn to the photographic image and its near-infallibility as an evidentiary "text." I use "text" here as something that is spun, and the camera as an instrument that spins a simulacrum of an image whose beauty and believability depend on the artistic acumen of the craftsperson. The photographic image relies on its ability to have the viewer accept the veracity of its purported authenticity. Yet, that image depends upon external choices that frame and shape its believability, namely upon the photographer's intentions as well as the sitter's predisposition or lack thereof. In short, I posit that all photographs approximate Samuel Taylor Coleridge's characterization of "truth as a divine ventriloquist."[2] And Todd Webb's photographs from Somalia are no different. They too present as "truthful," while in fact we can question that truth. As through a ventriloquist, an outsider's voice speaks through them. But before we delve into any discussion of the photographs, a cursory note to contextualize the photographer's excursion into Africa, and specifically the Trust Territory of Somaliland, is in order here.

On November 21, 1949, the General Assembly of the United Nations agreed in principle to place Somaliland (a former Italian colony) under Italian trusteeship. The decision dovetailed with robust and rigorous discussions in several other UN member capitals of what was to be done with the former colonies of those countries who were vanquished in the Second World War. Before that war, Italy, under the fascist government of Mussolini, had three African colonies: Eritrea, Libya, and Somaliland (South Somalia). The Somaliland case seemed to be the most intractable in that a number of countries–Britain, France, the United States, the USSR, Egypt, and Ethiopia–had a great deal of vested interest in the colony. Its geographic location necessitated that these countries have a say in any final decision regarding the fate of the colony. A majority at the General Assembly voted to put Somaliland under a UN trusteeship, with Italy as the administering country, and Colombia, Egypt, and the Philippines functioning as a United Nations Advisory Council. The Italian administration, called Amministrazione Fiduciaria Italiana in Somalia (AFIS), began its ten-year administration of what is now Somalia on April 1, 1950. And that is how and why in 1958 the United Nations Information Services included the Trust Territory of Somaliland in its list of countries they commissioned Webb to photograph. At the time of his commission, Italian Somaliland had only two years left before the country would eventually gain its independence. The United Nations, no doubt, wanted to showcase its operations there, and to document its successes in helping the country achieve quantifiable progress in all sectors: human, social, and economic. As the UN brochure accompanying the pictures demonstrates, Webb was commissioned to document the following: 1) construction projects such as electrification; 2) development of human resources; and 3) the changing face of a rapidly modernizing Africa.

Webb's spectacular photographs of the Trust Territory of Somaliland on the cusp of independence show, in the main, the spirit of a nation represented by its people and its chief or capital city, Mogadiscio/Mogadishu. In several captivating moments–for instance the alluring picture of two young women in yellow dresses, perhaps the image that draws us in the most, Webb captures the gaiety and ebullience that suffuses the faces of those he photographs (see p. 128). Walking on the beach with a gait that shows confidence, arms swinging and a corresponding cadenced or accented leg movement–what the Somalis call "laafyo isla helid"–the women exude elegance and beauty. Their rhythmic movement of limbs is accentuated by the shared color of their dress, which denotes close friendship. The "sign-language of clothes," to borrow from John Berger, points to what the Somalis call "isku dooq" ("same taste").[3] This is perhaps a symbol, a presage, of the trajectory of a nation about to come into being. Yet surprisingly the two women share a space with a dog that also seems to be confident of itself and its surroundings. This is strange, since people and dogs in Somalia would rarely come in such close proximity to one another. As Muslims, Somalis do not keep dogs as pets. Indeed, in most circumstances dogs run for their lives; rarely does one witness a dog chasing down an adult. This juxtaposition of the two in such close proximity in Webb's photo is intriguing, in that it casts doubt on the veracity of the picture: is it staged? Are the women the maidservants of some expatriates who are not in the frame? Or did Webb perhaps get lucky at this one moment? After all, the beach was a favorite place of his, as he wrote to his wife Lucille in a letter of June 16, 1958: "Here I take my siesta on the beach along with a swim, which is wonderful."[4] The letters contribute to our understanding of the photographer's drift and intention, giving the photographs the requisite context. But we have to remember the dialectic between the historical past of the image and the historical present of the viewer. It is important that the viewer wrestle with the meaning of the image from their present vantage point, while at the same time keeping in mind that the image is tied to its historicity.

Also alluring is the photograph of the young man in the red suit, perhaps an early specimen of the confident dapper (see p. 136). His sauntering gait suggests that he is aware of being photographed. Webb mentions that Somalis, on the whole, did not easily acquiesce to being photographed, but with some patience and a smile, he could secure a willing "victim" (my word, not Webb's). In the same frame, we see a man with his donkey cart and, at the far end, another man crossing the road. Also inspiring some real hope is the photograph of the female road-builder (opposite), who, ironically, has her back turned to Somalia's future parliament–though her action is part of the daunting preparations for the country's independence. That she has carved out her niche in a male-dominated profession is important, for after Independence, women all but vanished from the construction business.

In addition to these photographs are some that deal with work undertaken by both the AFIS and UN agencies: a case in point is the photograph of the men with jerrycans on the ground and a Land Rover parked in front of a shed (see p. 145). The sign on the shed, all in capital letters, reads: "Governo della Somalia, Campagna Antimalaria, UNICEF-W.H.O." (Somali government, Campaign against Malaria, United Nations International Children's Emergency Fund and the World Health Organization). The license plate shows that the Land Rover belongs to AFIS, the Italian Trusteeship administration. The jerrycans most likely contain DDT and other anti-malarial sprays. Webb also photographed a Cessna plane with the insignia of the American Sinclair Oil Corporation, contracted to prospect oil in Southern Somalia and parts of the Ogaden, the Somali-inhabited territory inside Ethiopia (see p. 131).

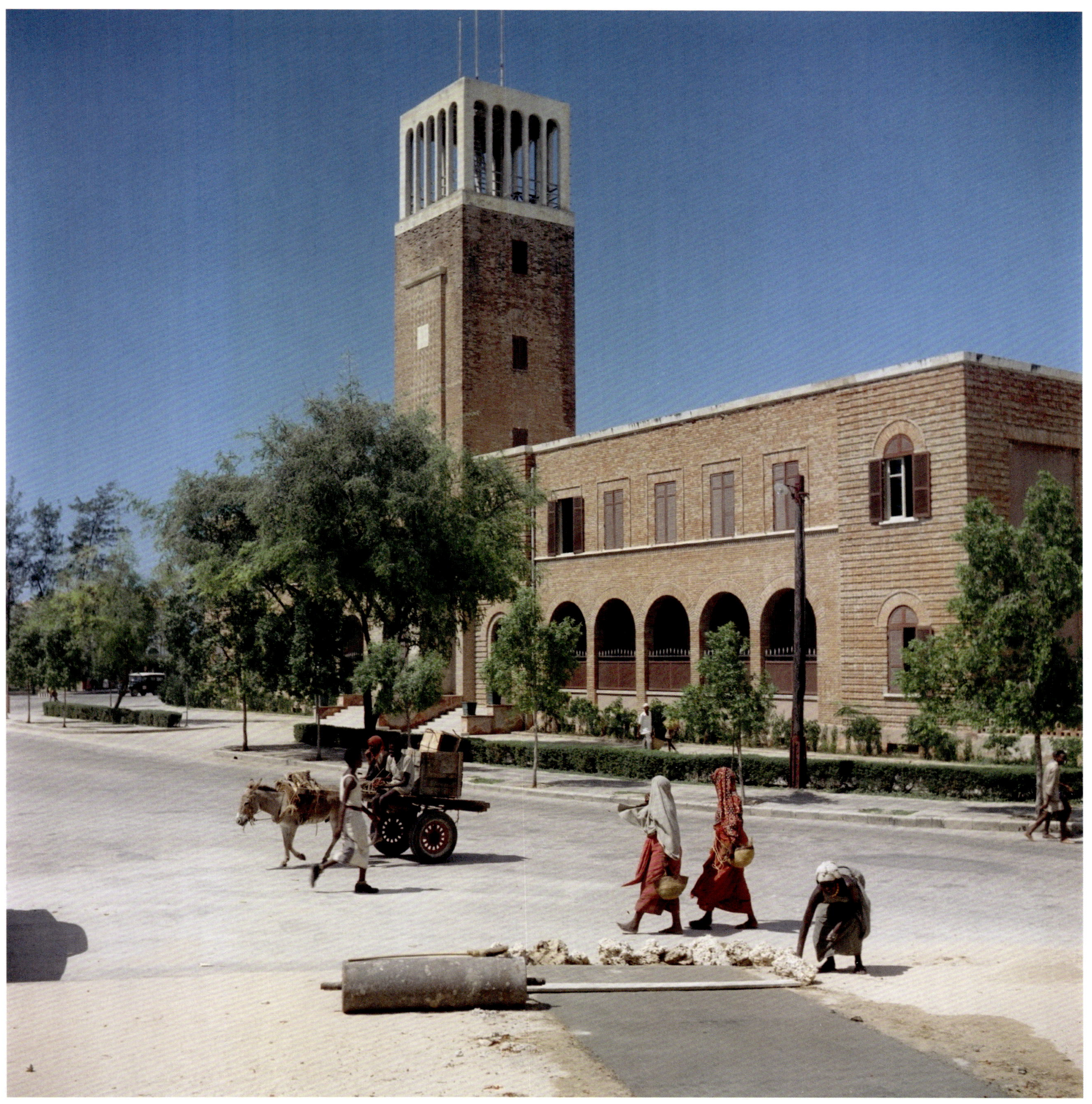

Todd Webb. *Untitled* (44UN-7966-359), Trust Territory of Somaliland (Somalia), 1958
Woman road builder and pedestrians in front of the future Parliament building, Mogadishu.

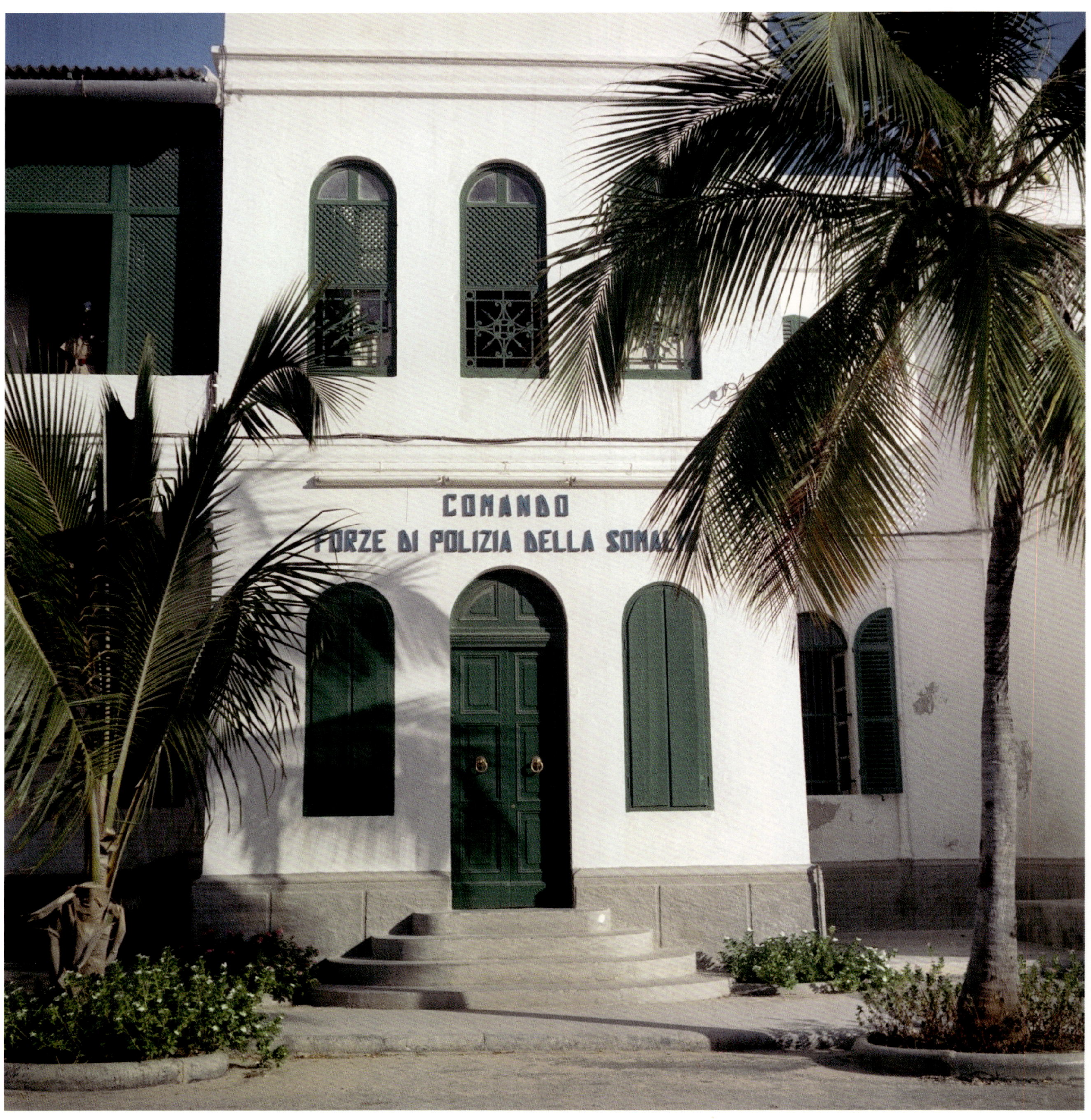

Todd Webb, *Untitled* (44UN-8007-273), Trust Territory of Somaliland (Somalia), 1958
Somali Police Force Command building.

The company did not find any oil in either place; but it reaped a great deal of controversy in Somalia. One of the company's staunchest critics was the Somali Youth League's president, Haji Mohamed Hussein, a fiery populist leader who had a large number of supporters in the city.

When Webb arrived in Mogadishu, there had already been a meeting of the League, the party that for all practical purposes was going to lead the country to Independence. The upshot of their meeting was the expulsion of Haji Mohamed Hussein from the Party, a serious decision when the country was in the throes of civil strife. Yet it seems that the AFIS and the UN did not bother to inform Webb of the situation, which might explain why he went to empty classrooms (see p. 139) and found the streets mostly uncrowded. Even the Cinzano liquor bar is deserted (see p. 158). Perhaps customers–both local and expatriate–felt it unwise to show their faces. At times it seems that Webb was on a short leash, held up by the political situation in and around Mogadishu, which explains why his photographs are taken in the vicinity of Shangani and Hamar Weyne districts, both in the heart of the city and very close to AFIS and UN offices.

That said, Webb did manage to document contrasting views of the city. Take the photograph of the three women, who seem to share a space. The physical distance between them is palpable and axiomatic of the power differential (see p. 160); the well-dressed white women contrast starkly with the blurred image of the Somali. All three are standing in front of decaying buildings. In general, the photographs–those of dilapidated buildings, a relatively well-kept government building (opposite), the Italian-owned Albergo Croce del Sud (the Southern Cross Hotel) in the center of town where Webb stayed (see p. 159), a classroom without any trace of students or even a blackboard (see p. 139), or a police jeep on the beach or in the desert (see p. 133)–all present a macrocosm of a world and a city either in an inchoate state or in disrepair. The photographs seem to possess prescient insight, a premonition. The Sinclair Somali saga is repeated in today's political discourse–oil prospecting is bringing back memories of the past, including the cacophony that mired the discussions of the Somali Youth League some sixty-one years ago. Now as then, oil prospecting injects incivility into the national discourse. It also rekindles old rivalries among nations in the Horn of Africa. The past is brought back. The more things change, the more they stay the same.

Todd Webb's photographs offer the viewer a coherent map of 1958 Somalia. Webb looks and observes–with the somewhat attenuated gaze of the foreigner–at something similar to a Somali "quotidian," and in the process compels us to reflect on its contours and map it onto a horizon, an uncharted territory. The photographs attest to what is, as well as what is absent or hidden from view. We reflect on the semantic and semiotic drift of the photographic image. And while Webb's images are mostly without captions, the people in the photographs represent both themselves and, synecdochally, a nation in the throes of deep social and political transformation. At times you crane your neck to see what is beyond the photographic image on offer, out of curiosity, out of a nagging belief that wishes it could see what the photographer was looking at the very moment he clicked the shutter on his camera. That, of course, is an impossible wish. You would wish to eavesdrop on their conversation or be privy to the silent thoughts of the Somali woman. One would like to trail the thoughts of the lone gentleman with the walking cane, passing by the Arbaca Rukun (Arba'Rukun) Mosque (see p. 161),[4] one of the oldest mosques in Mogadishu, located near the Arch of Triumph (right). What is possible is to extrapolate from the photographs what they do not willingly share with us, while respecting their distance, their context, their prior existence, their future configurations and trajectories.

Author's Note: *Thanks are in order to Aimée Bessire and Erin Hyde Nolan for their impeccable comments and valuable edits. Also, my thanks to Professor Abdalla Omar Mansur, a leading Somali linguist and a revered cultural historian.*

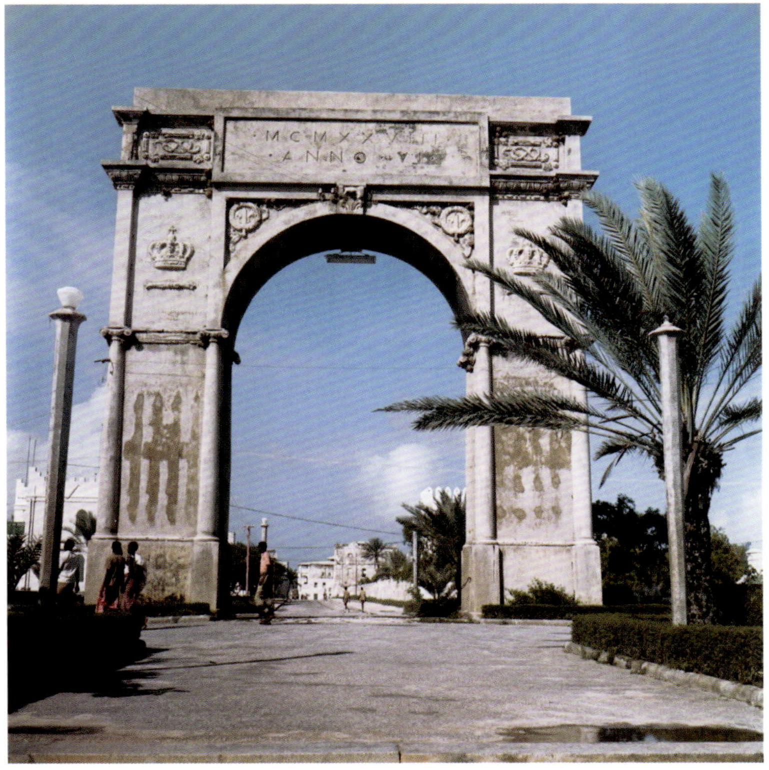

Todd Webb, *Untitled* (44UN-7966-313), Trust Territory of Somaliland (Somalia), 1958
Italian-built Arch of Triumph, Mogadishu.

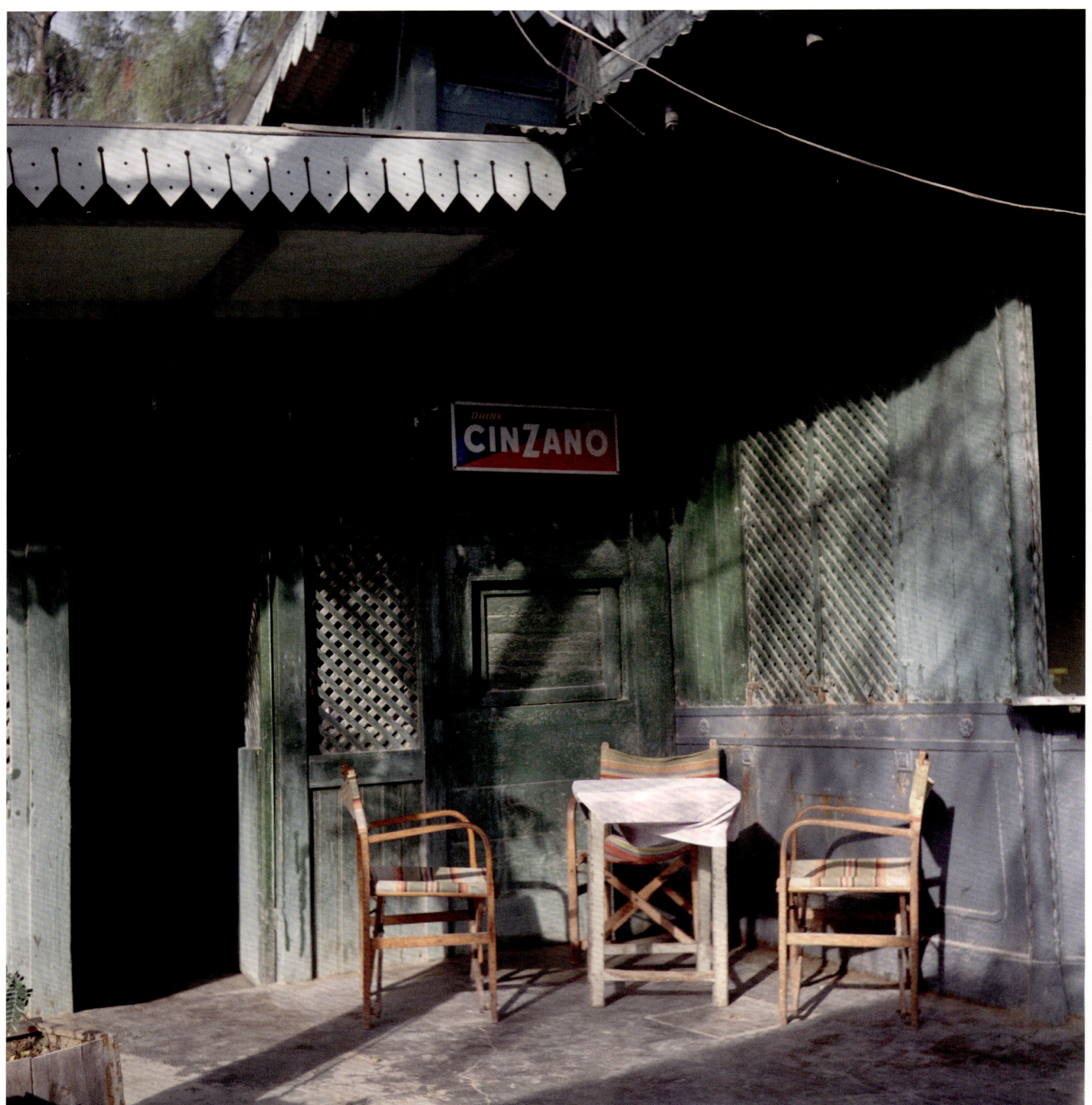

Todd Webb, *Untitled* (44UN-7971-308), Trust Territory of Somaliland (Somalia), 1958
Outdoor café seating with Cinzano sign.

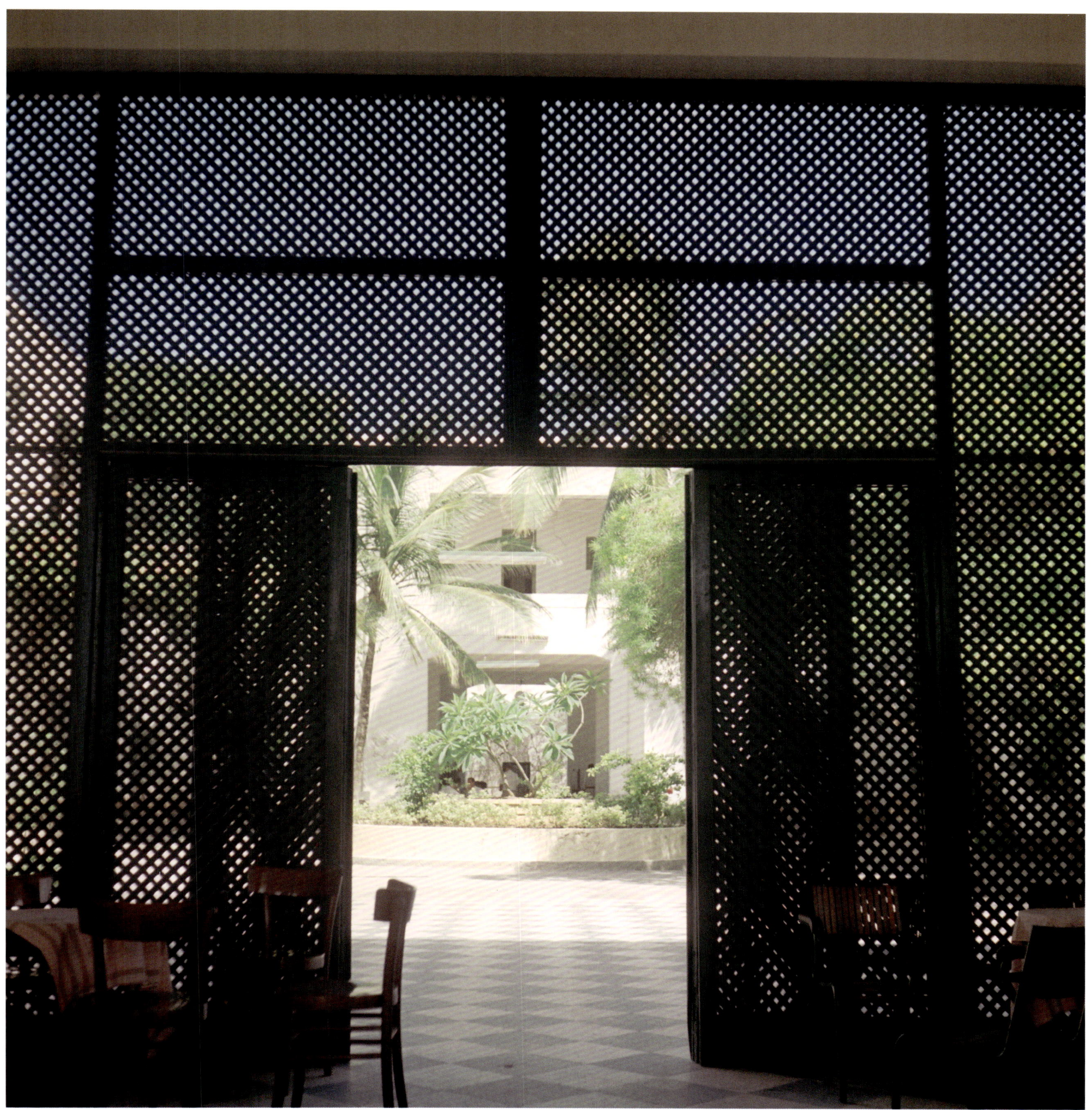

Todd Webb, *Untitled* (44UN-7966-358), Trust Territory of Somaliland (Somalia), 1958
View through lattice screening into a courtyard at the Albergo Croce del Sud (Southern Cross Hotel).

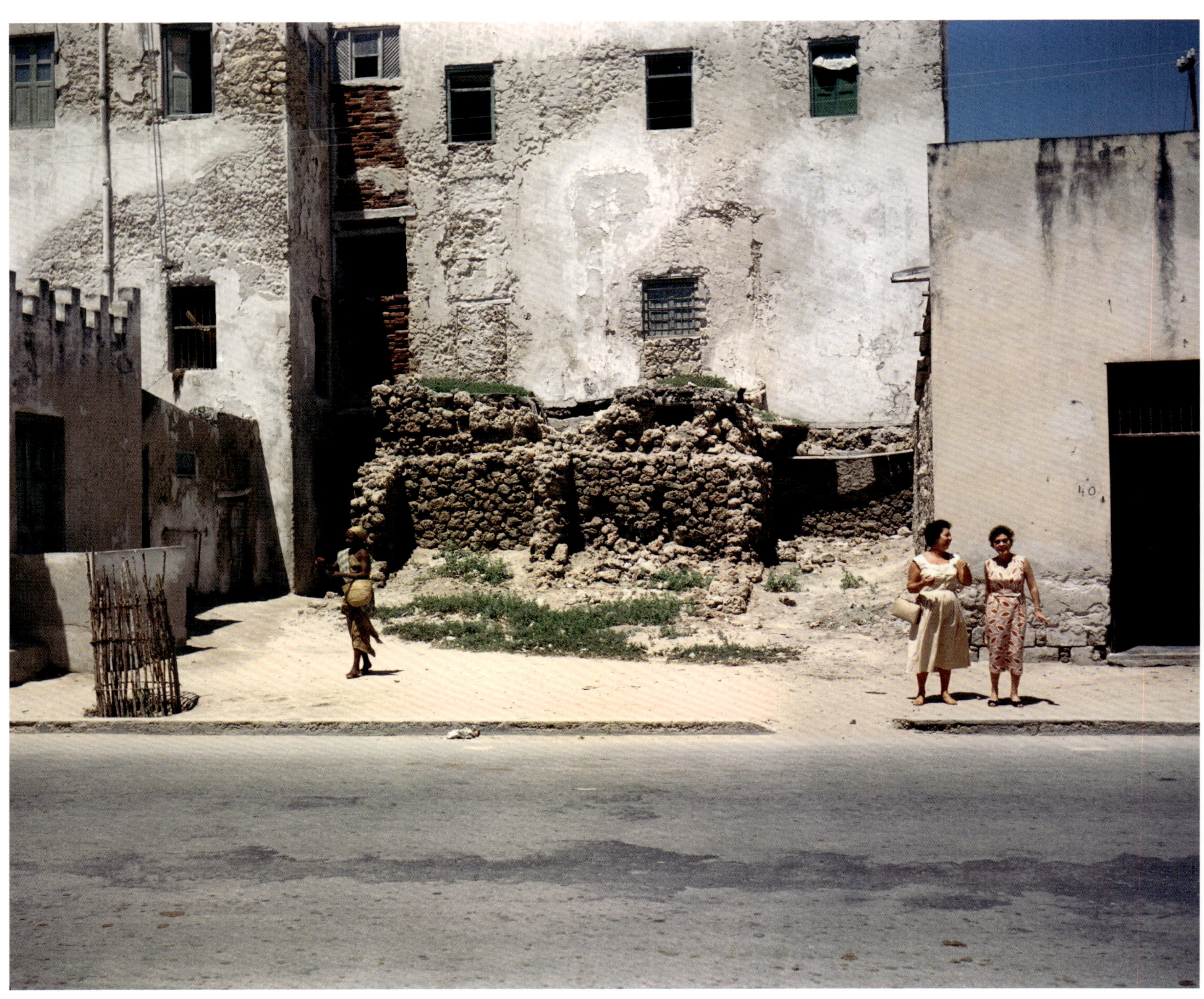

Todd Webb, *Untitled* (44UN-8001-500), Trust Territory of Somaliland (Somalia), 1958
Somali woman wearing a traditional guntiino (fabric draped over one shoulder) and two Italian women on a Mogadishu sidewalk.

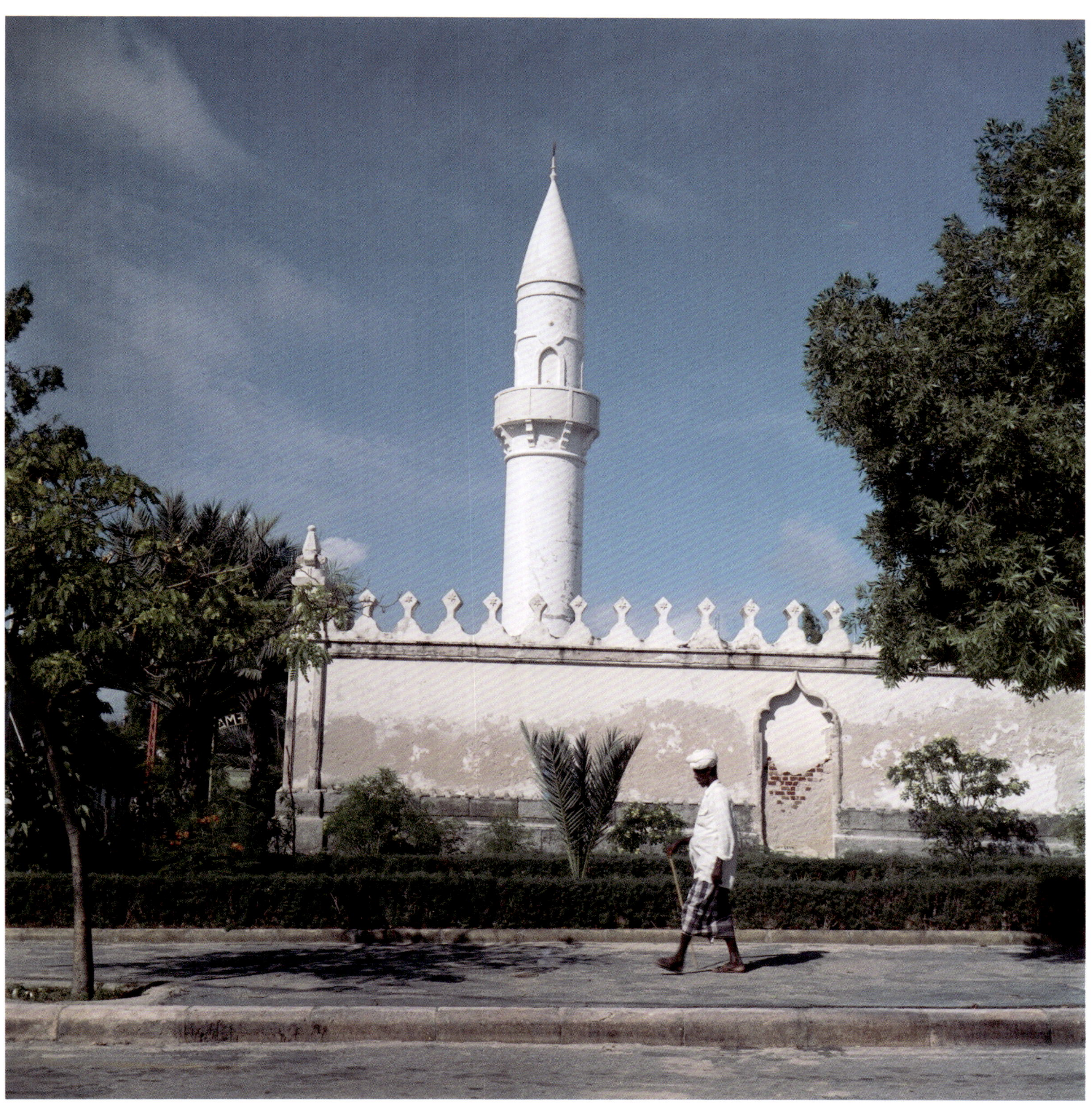

Todd Webb, *Untitled* (44UN-7966-316), Trust Territory of Somaliland (Somalia), 1958
Man walking past the wall of the Arbaca Rukun (Arba'Rukun) mosque, one of the oldest mosques in Mogadishu.

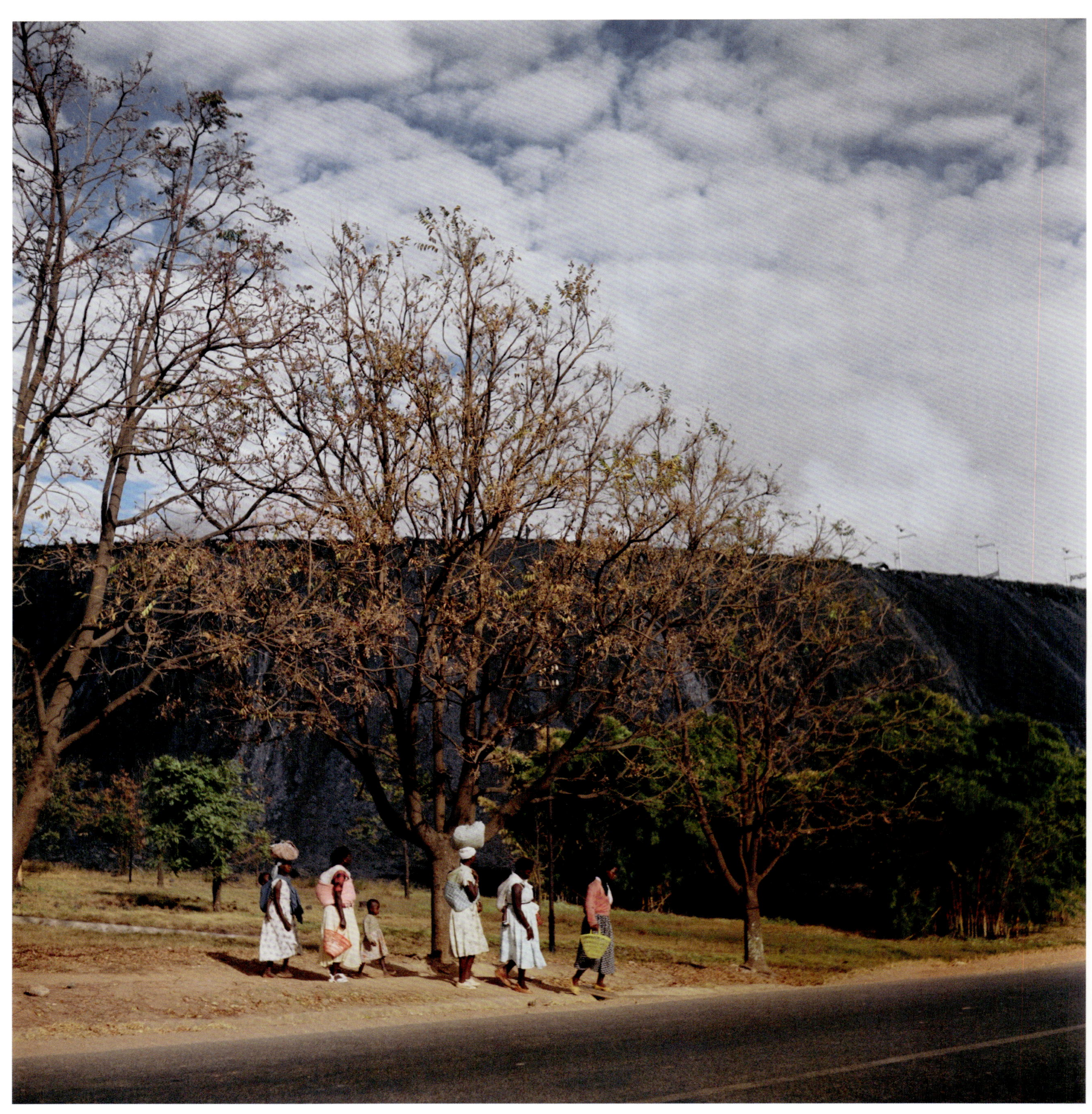

Todd Webb, *Untitled* (44UN-7982-129), Northern Rhodesia (Zambia), 1958
Women with children walking near the copper mine hill, in Ndola District.

FEDERATION OF RHODESIA AND NYASALAND

(ZAMBIA, ZIMBABWE, AND MALAWI)

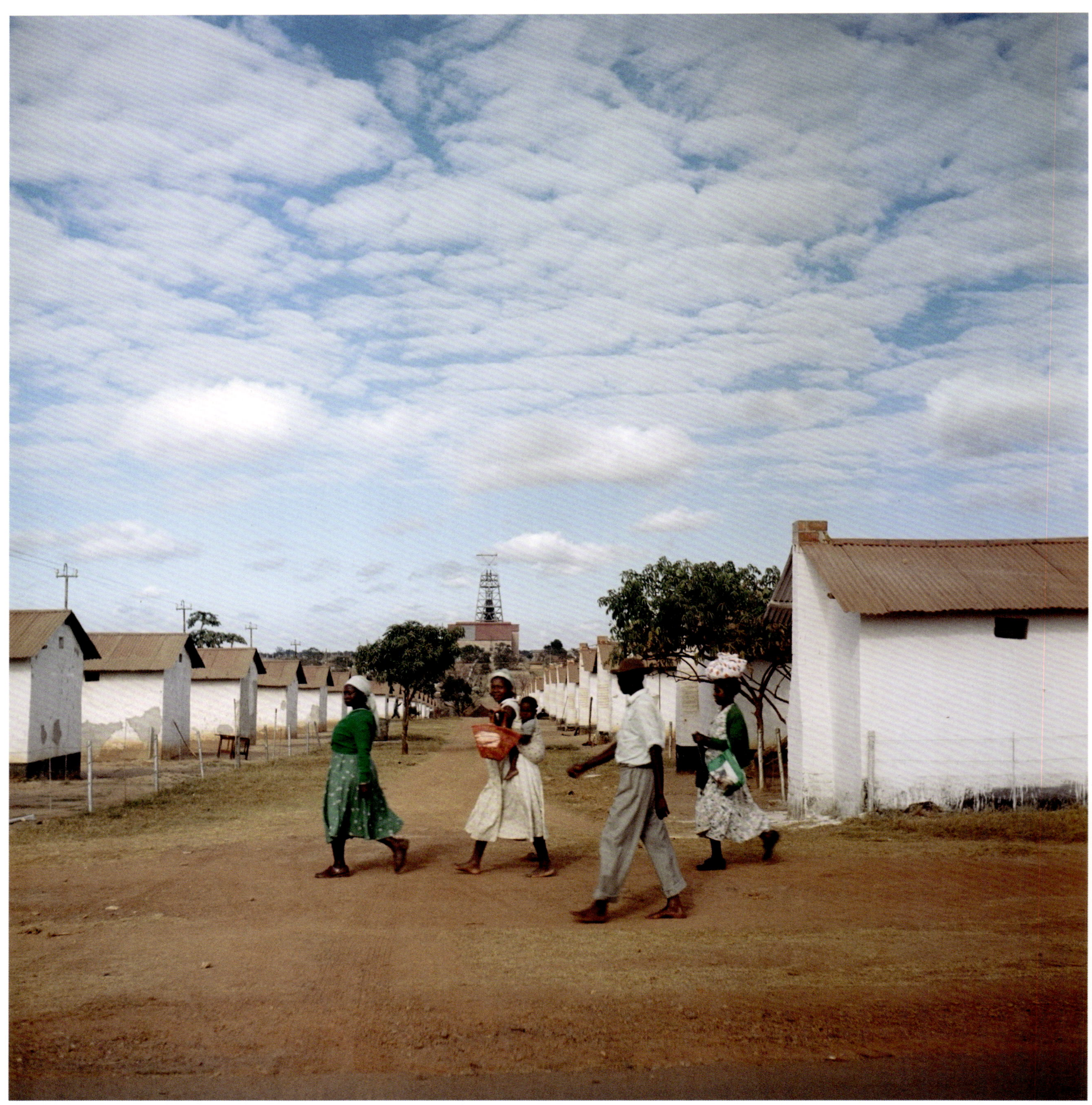

Todd Webb, *Untitled* (44UN-7982-126), Northern Rhodesia (Zambia), 1958
Man and women walking by worker housing at the copper mines, Kitwe.

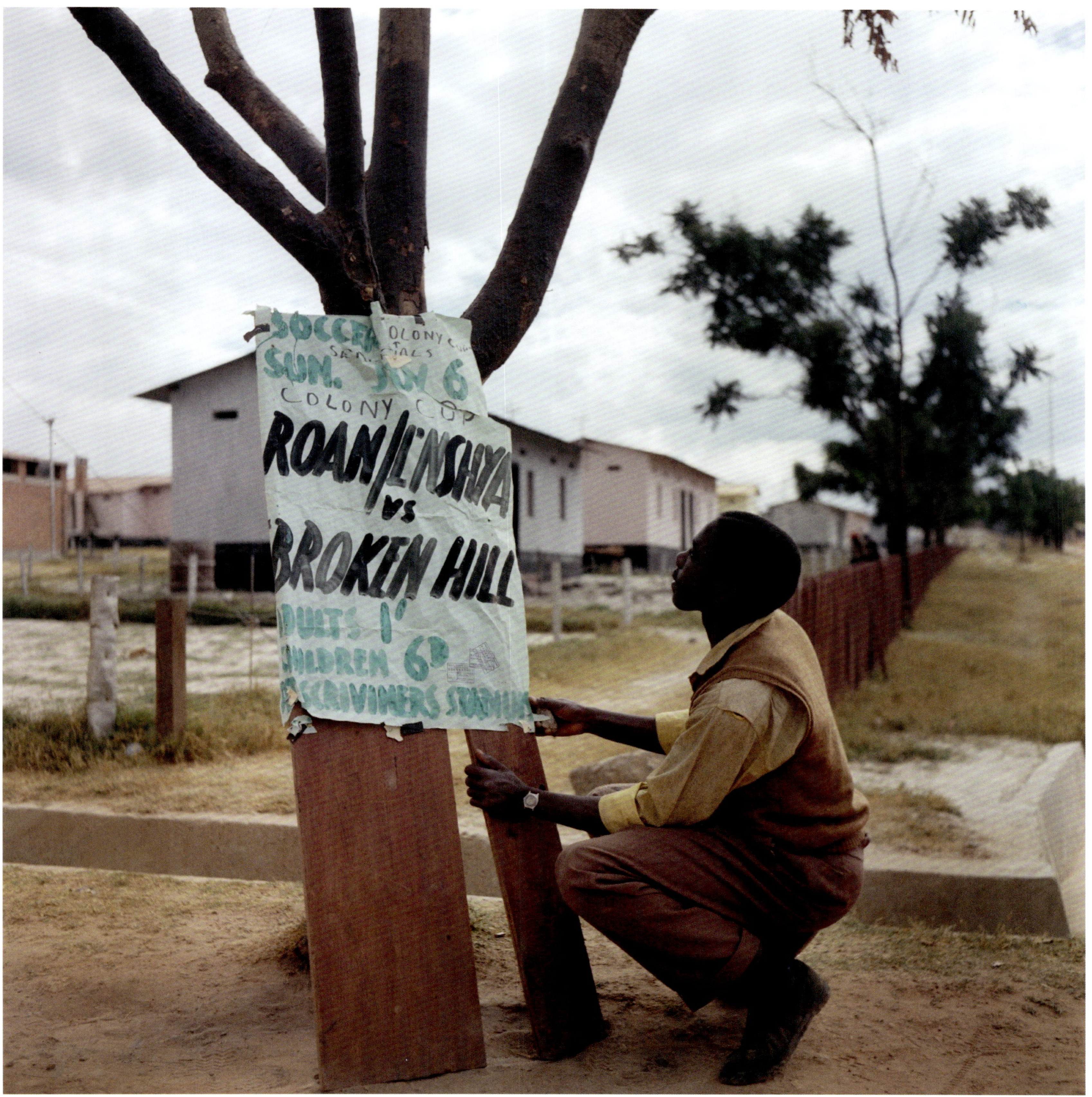

Todd Webb, *Untitled* (44UN-7983-034), Northern Rhodesia (Zambia), 1958
Man putting up a sign for the Sunday, June 6 soccer match between Roan Youth League (Luanshya) and the Broken Hill Warriors (Kabwe).

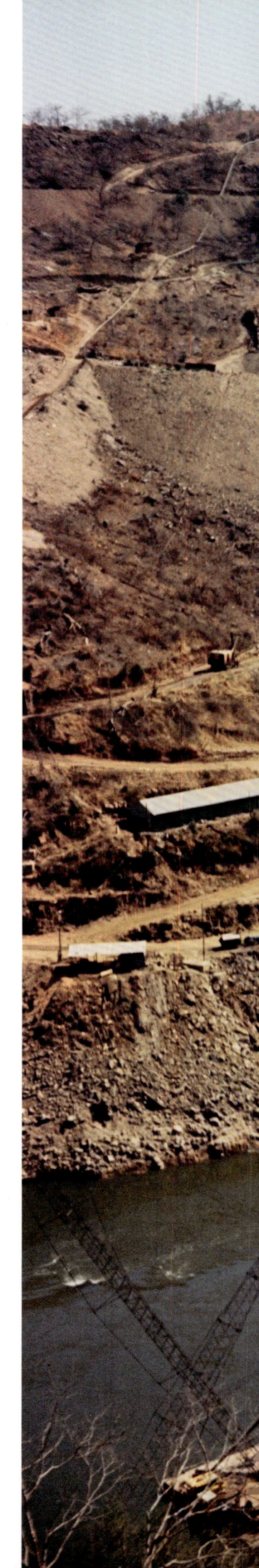

Todd Webb, *Untitled* (44UN-7890-241), border of Northern Rhodesia (Zambia) and Southern Rhodesia (Zimbabwe), 1958
Contours cut through the Zambezi River basin to create the Kariba Dam.

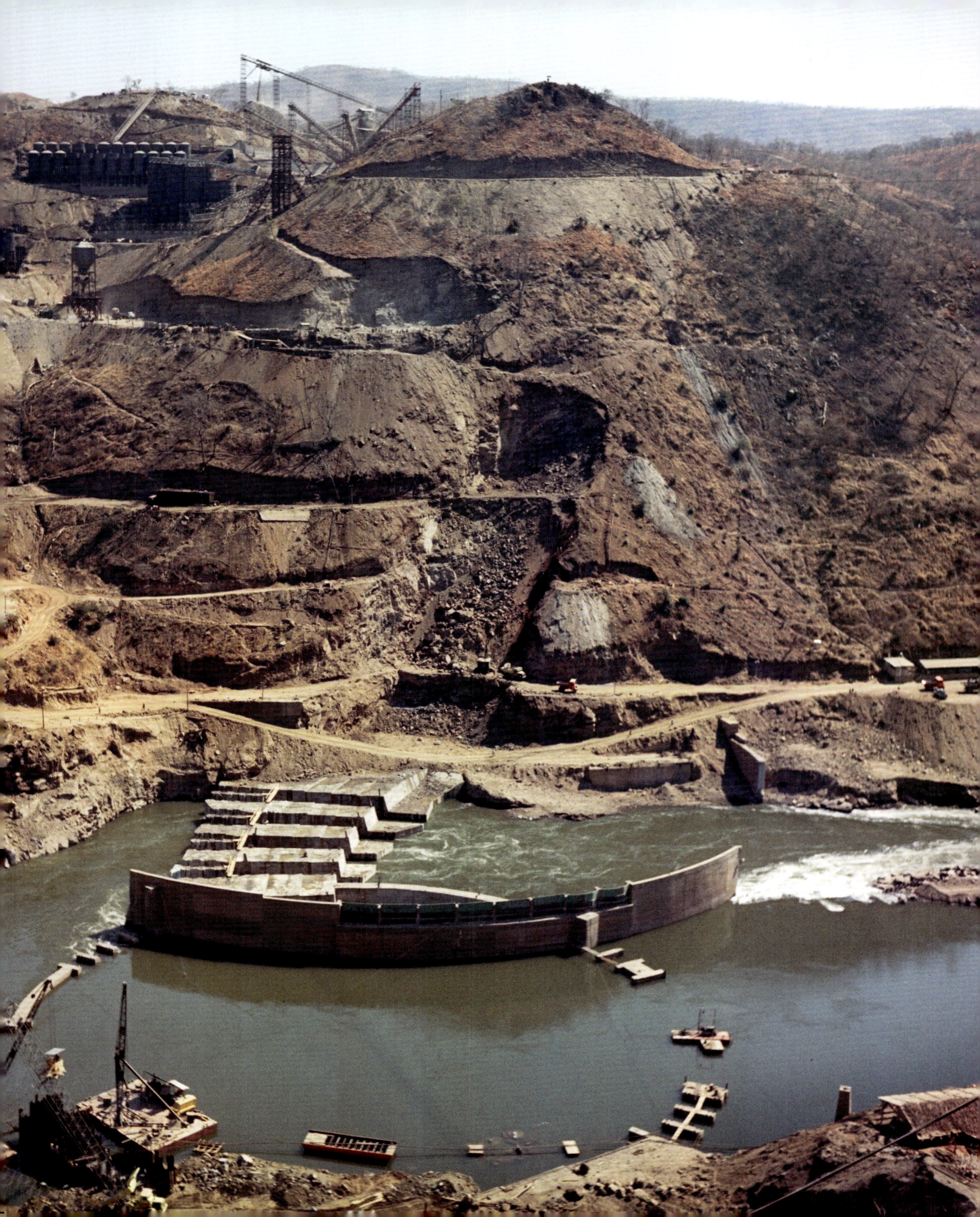

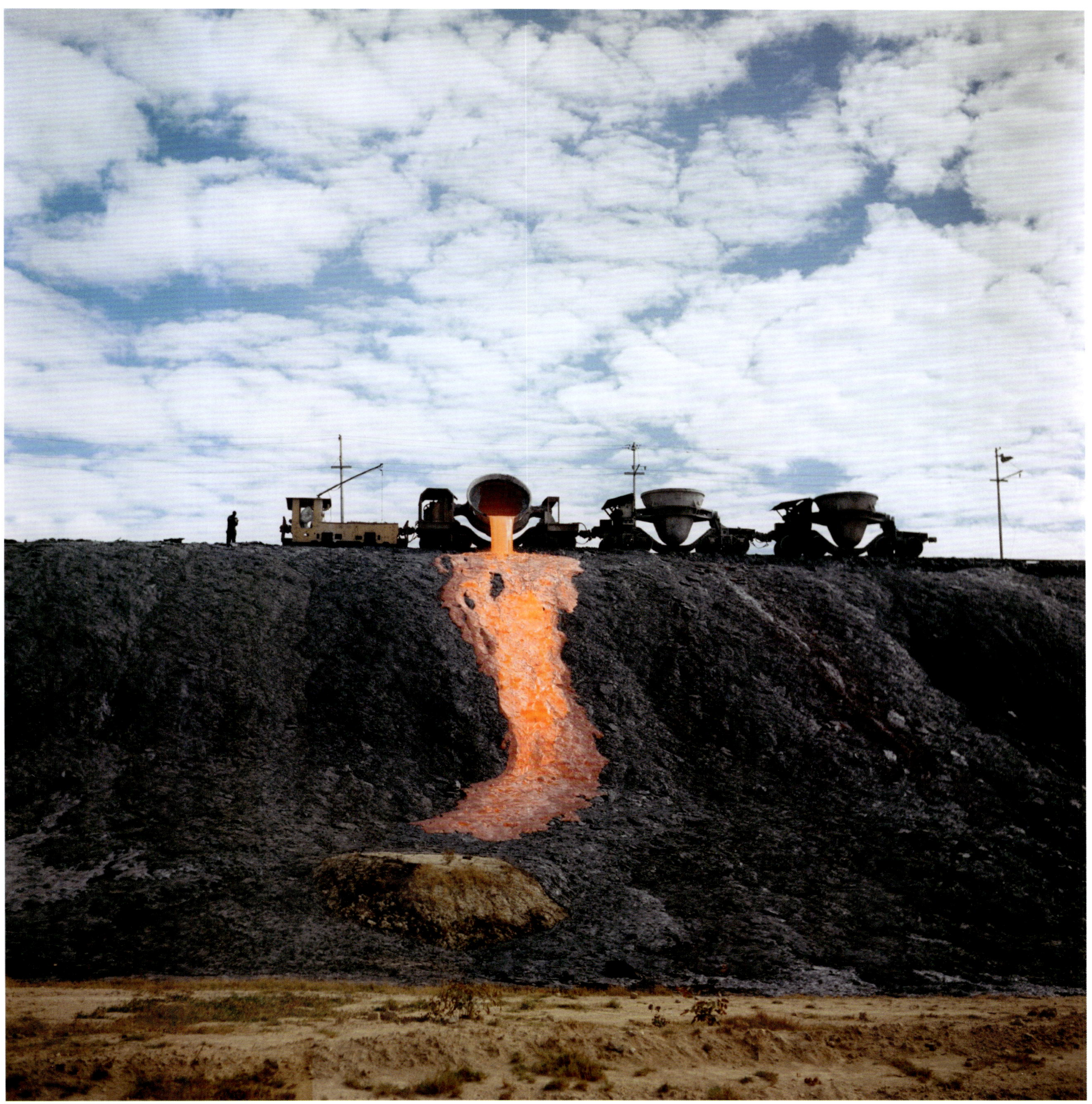

Todd Webb, *Untitled* (44UN-7981-177), Northern Rhodesia (Zambia), 1958
Molten slag running down a hill at a copper mine in Ndola District.

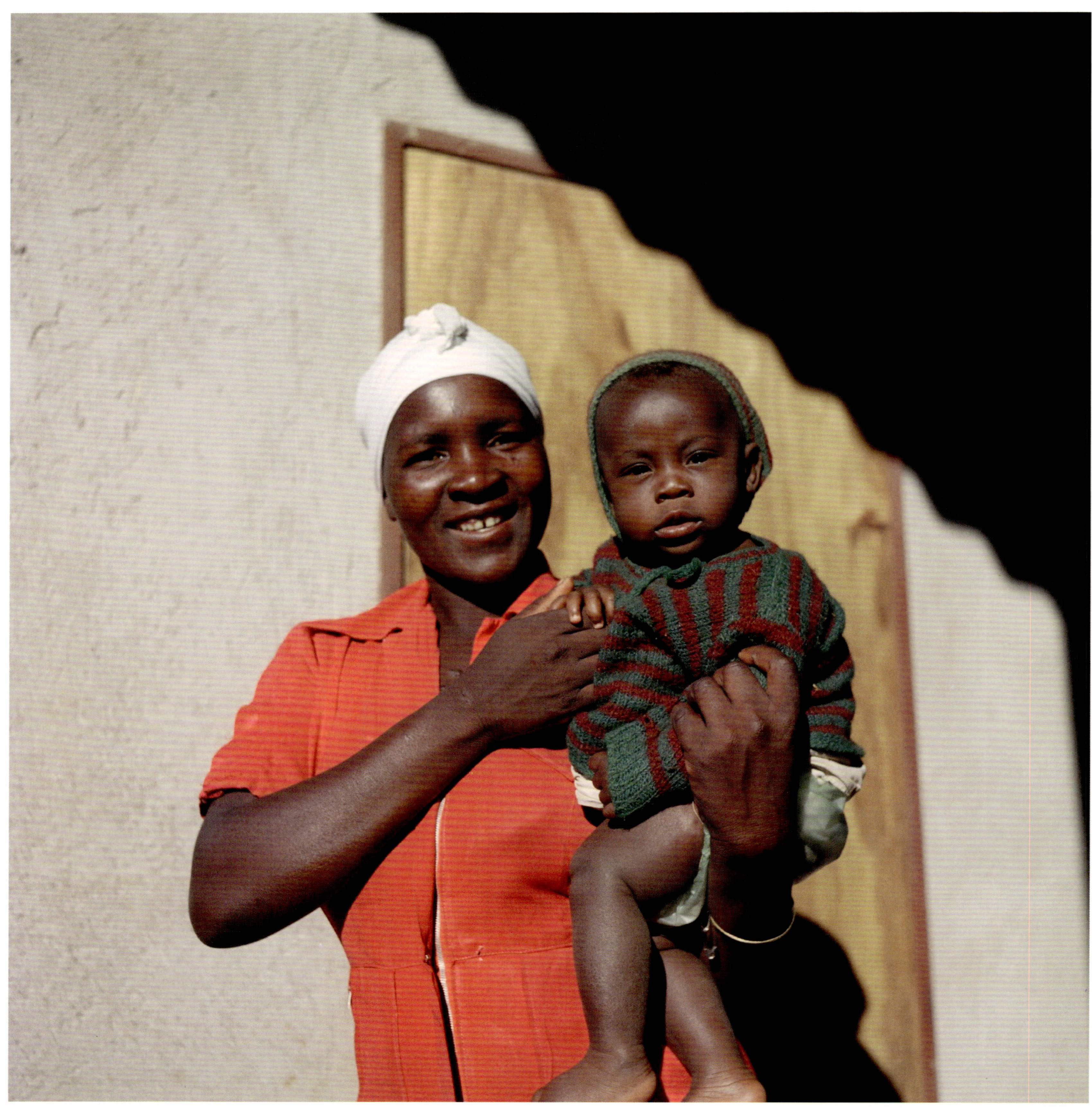

Todd Webb, *Untitled* (44UN-7994-515), Northern or Southern Rhodesia (Zambia or Zimbabwe) [exact location unknown], 1958
Woman in red dress holding an infant.

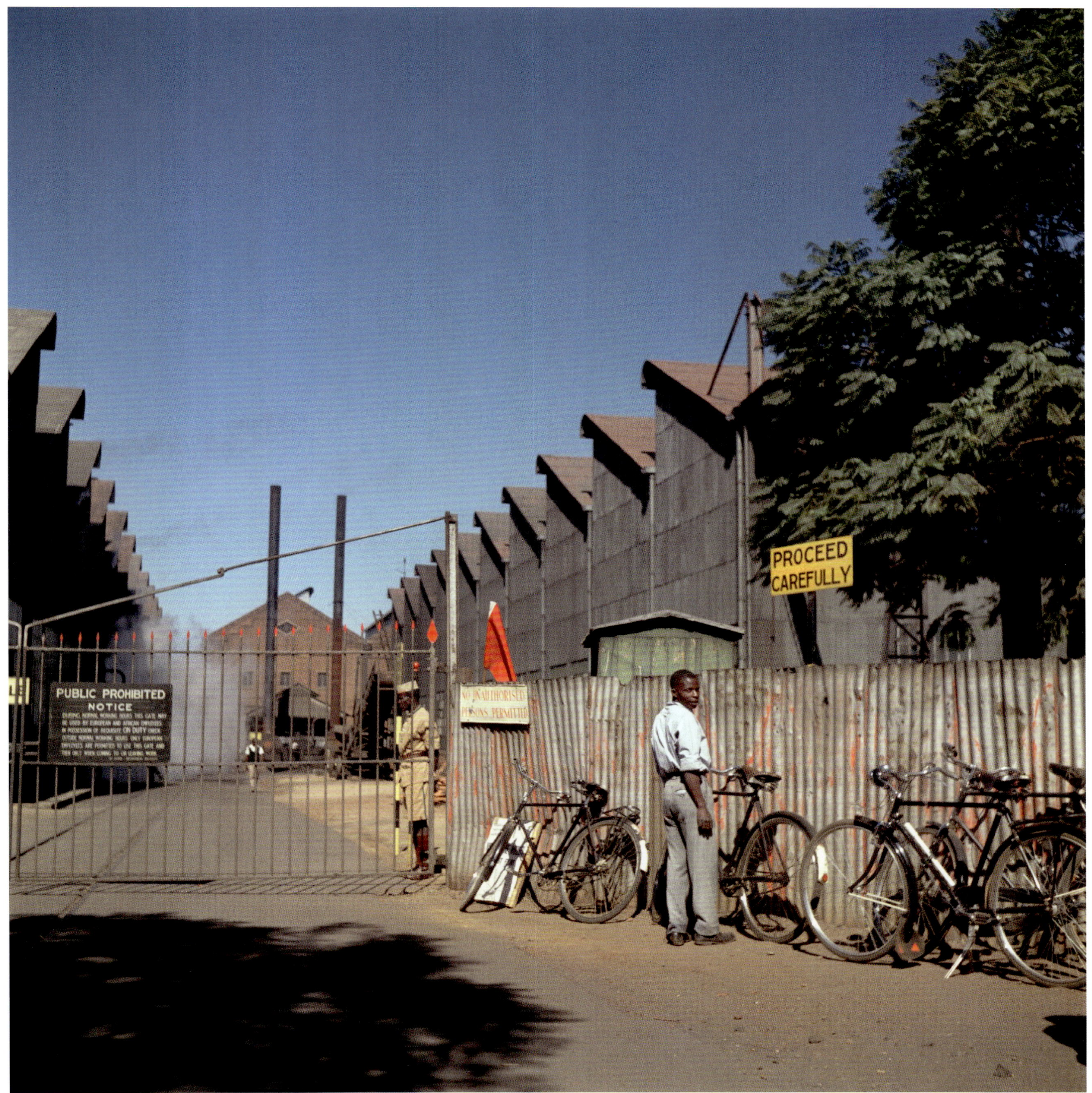

Todd Webb, *Untitled* (44UN-7991-093), Northern or Southern Rhodesia (Zambia or Zimbabwe) [exact location unknown], 1958
Man parking his bike outside the factory gate, where a sign highlights different restrictions of entry for "European and African employees."

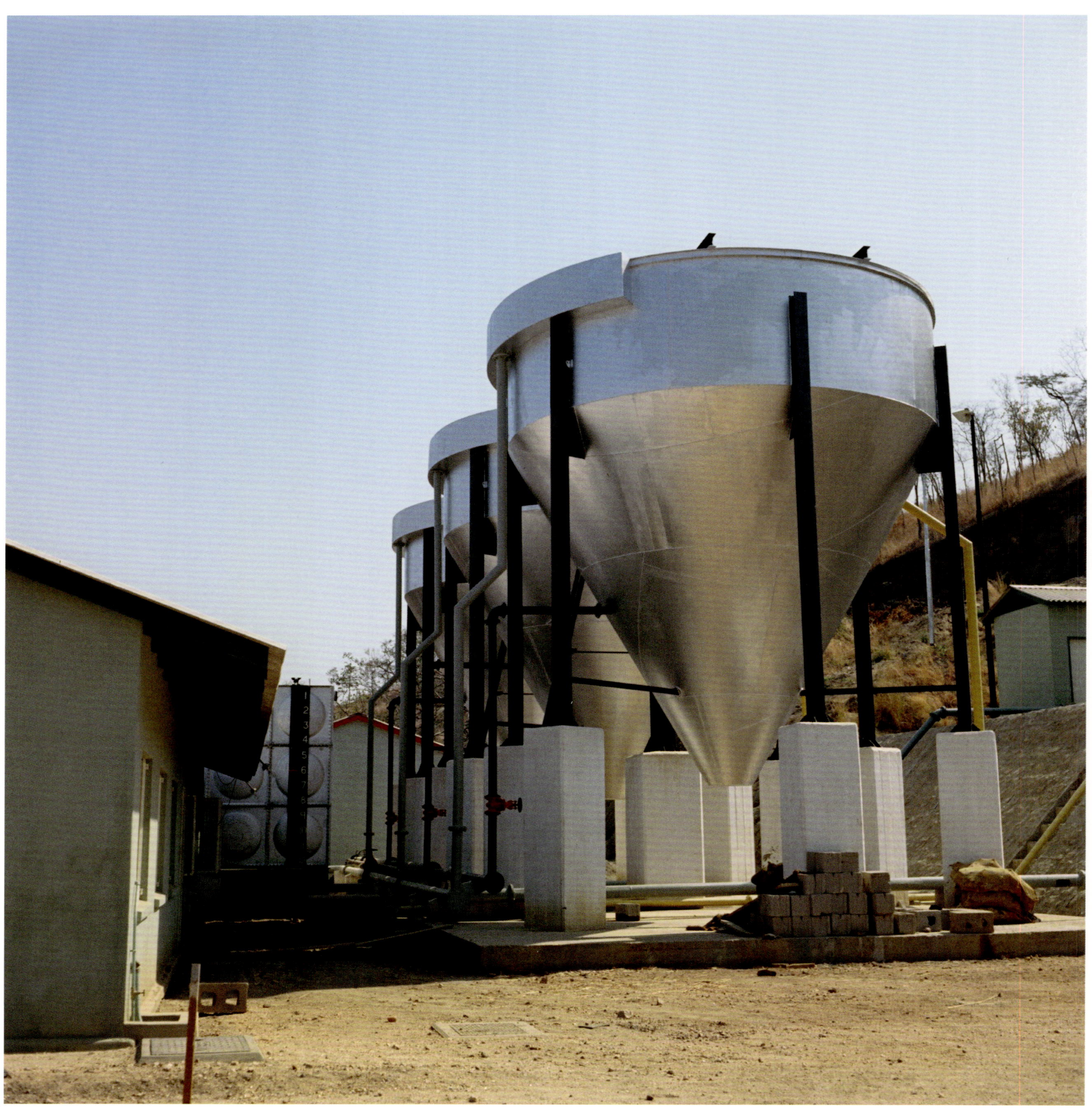

Todd Webb, *Untitled* (44UN-7995-119), Northern Rhodesia (Zambia), 1958
Storage silos at a copper mine.

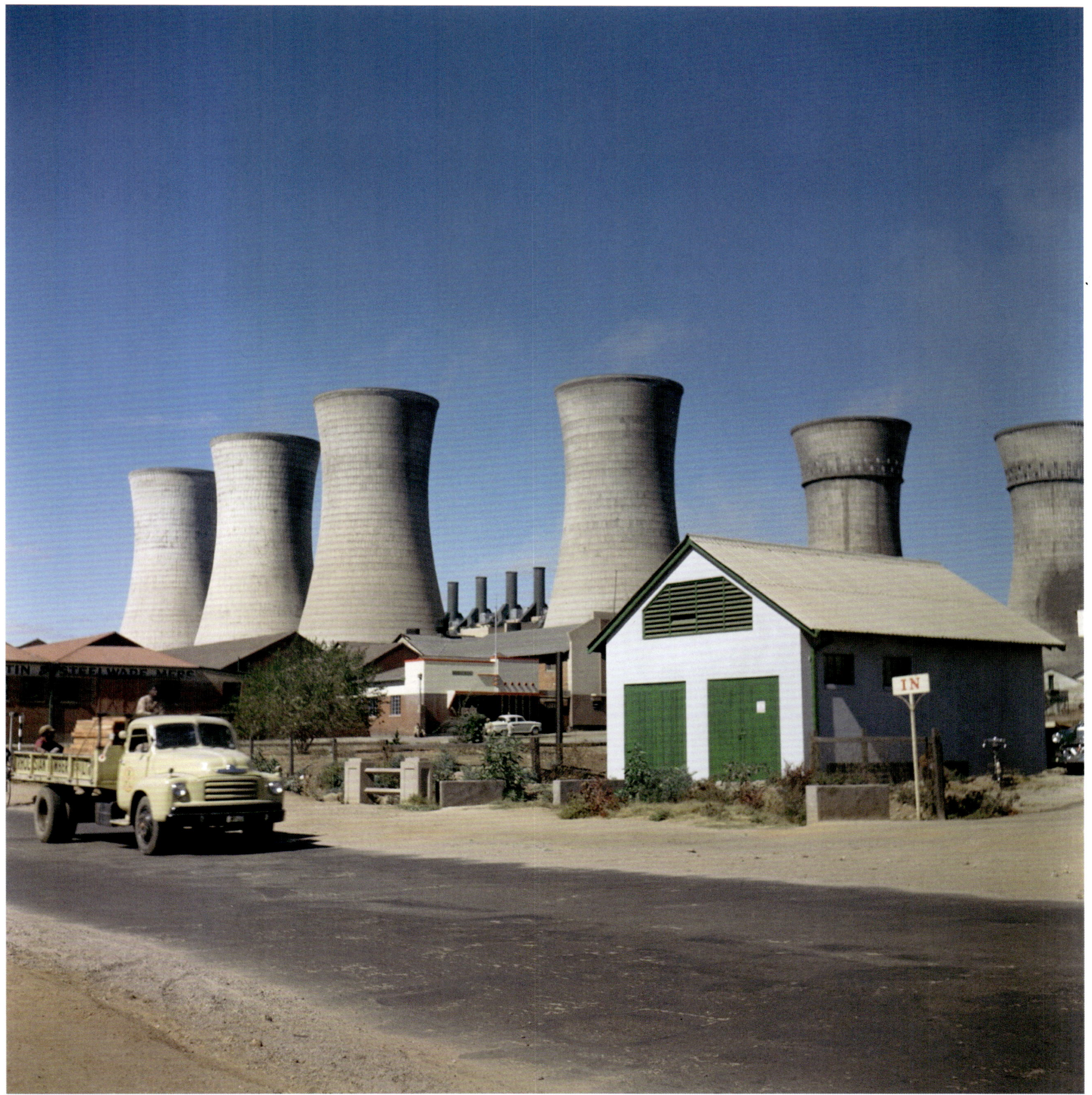

Todd Webb, *Untitled* (44UN-7991-097), Northern Rhodesia (Zambia), 1958
Rhodesian Timber company truck delivering wood to a copper mine.

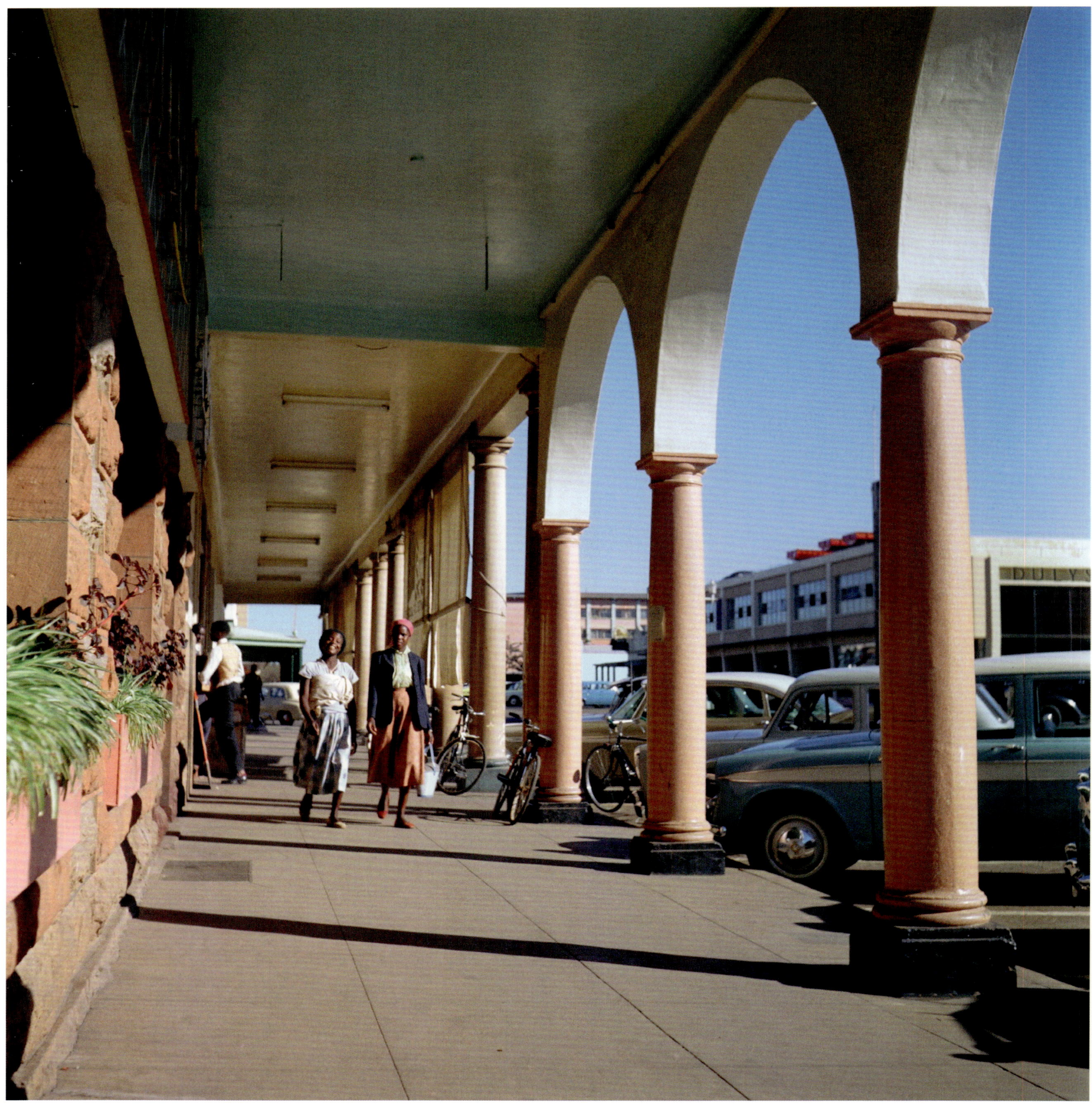

Todd Webb, *Untitled* (44UN-7990-211), Southern Rhodesia (Zimbabwe), 1958
Women walking along a sidewalk colonnade, Bulawayo.

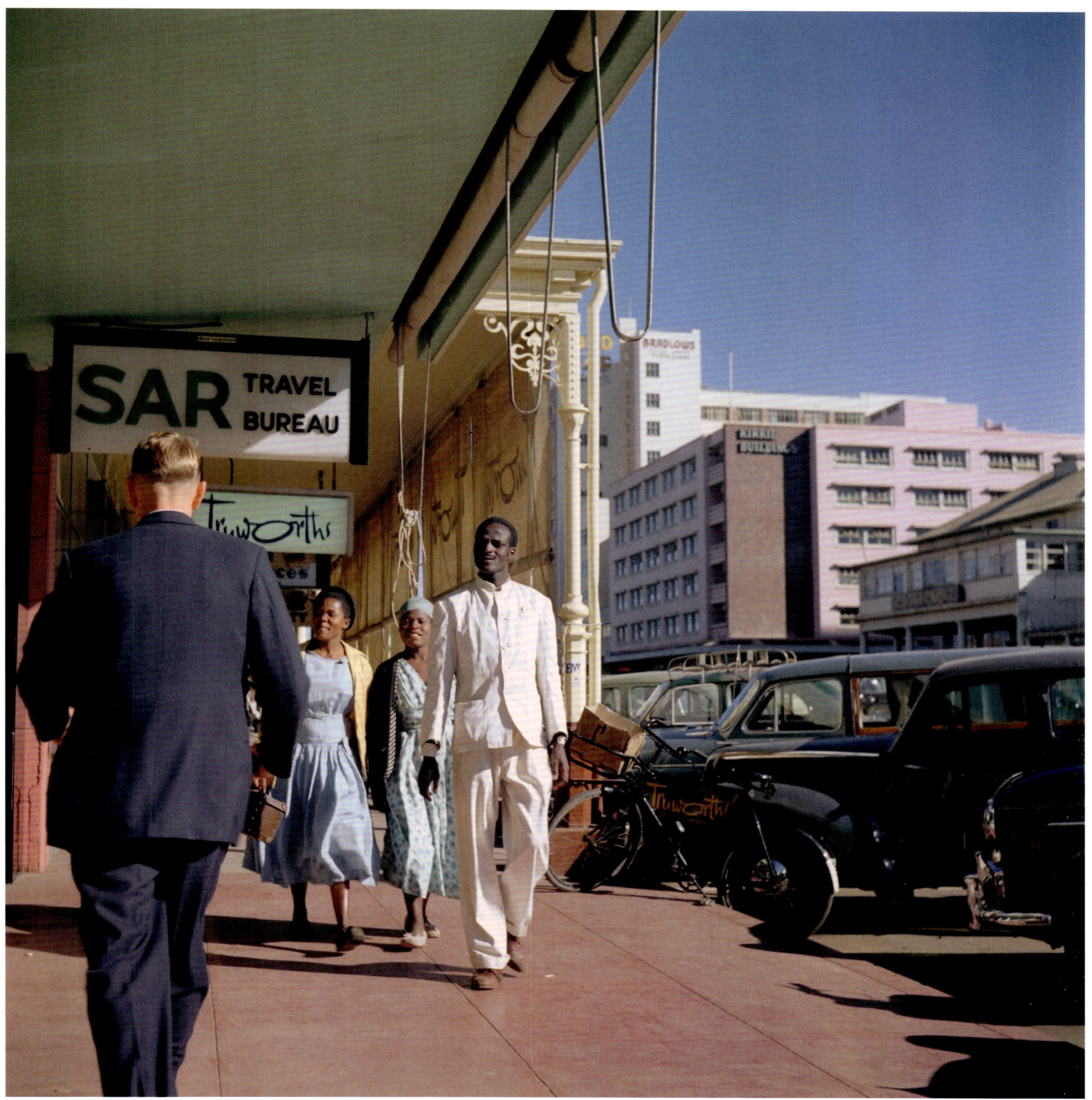

Todd Webb, *Untitled* (44UN-7990-212), Southern Rhodesia (Zimbabwe), 1958
Pedestrians walking past SAR Travel Bureau, Truworths, and other shops, Bulawayo.

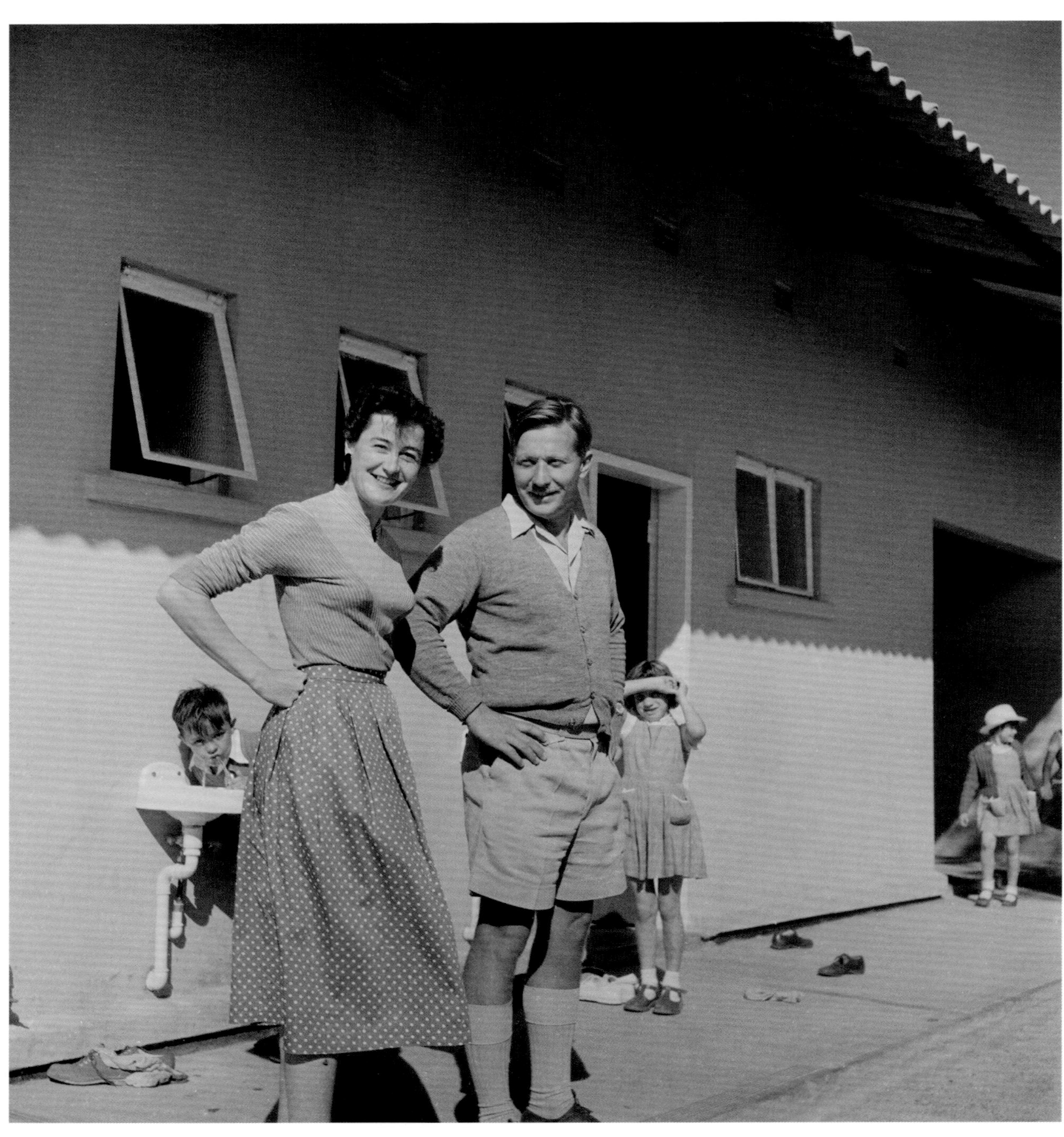

Todd Webb, *Untitled* (44UN-T1-R4-637), Northern or Southern Rhodesia (Zambia or Zimbabwe) [exact location unknown], 1958
Man and woman with children outside of school.

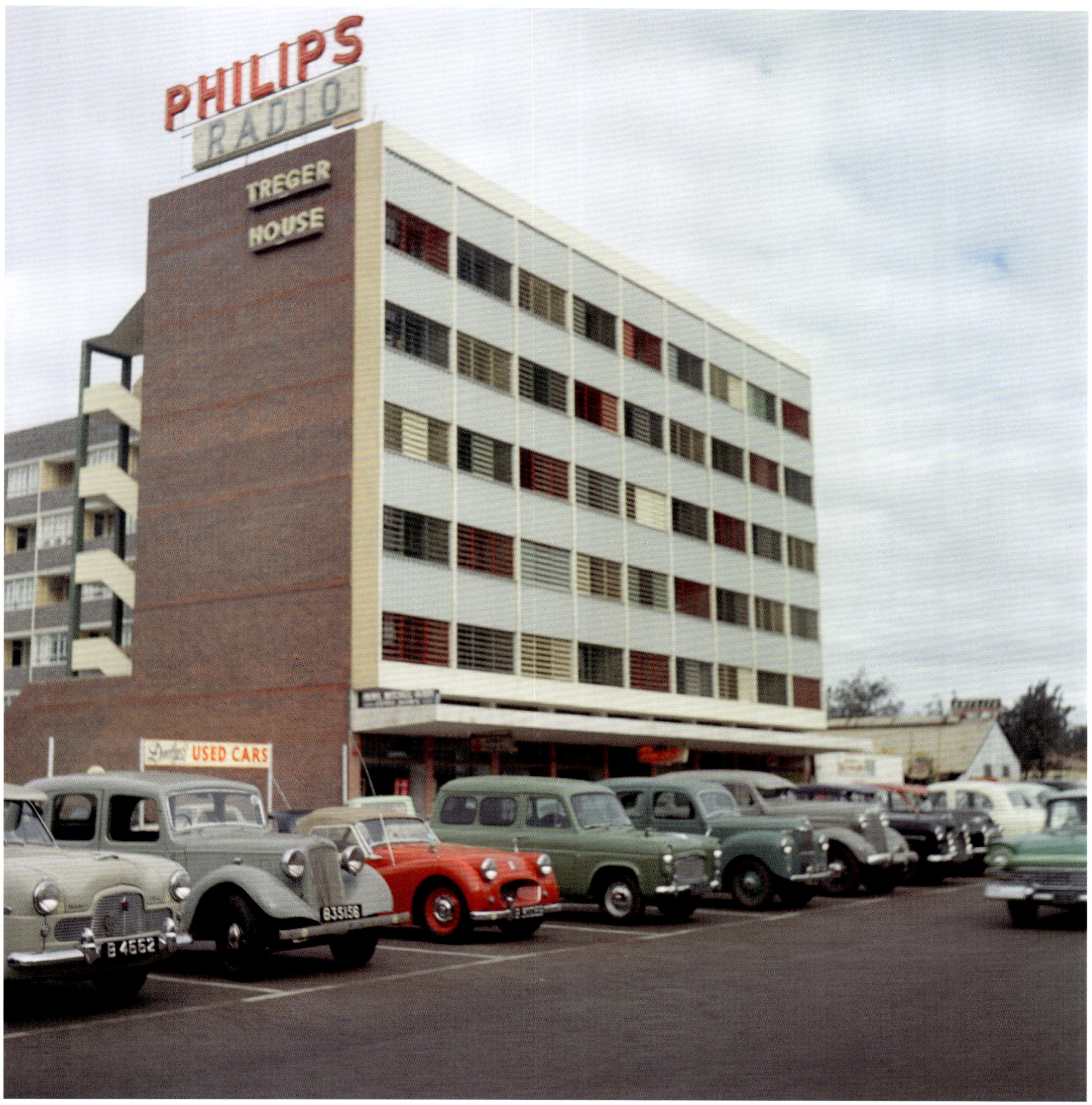

Todd Webb, *Untitled* (44UN-7985-545), Southern Rhodesia (Zimbabwe), 1958
Philips Radio sign at Treger House, Bulawayo.

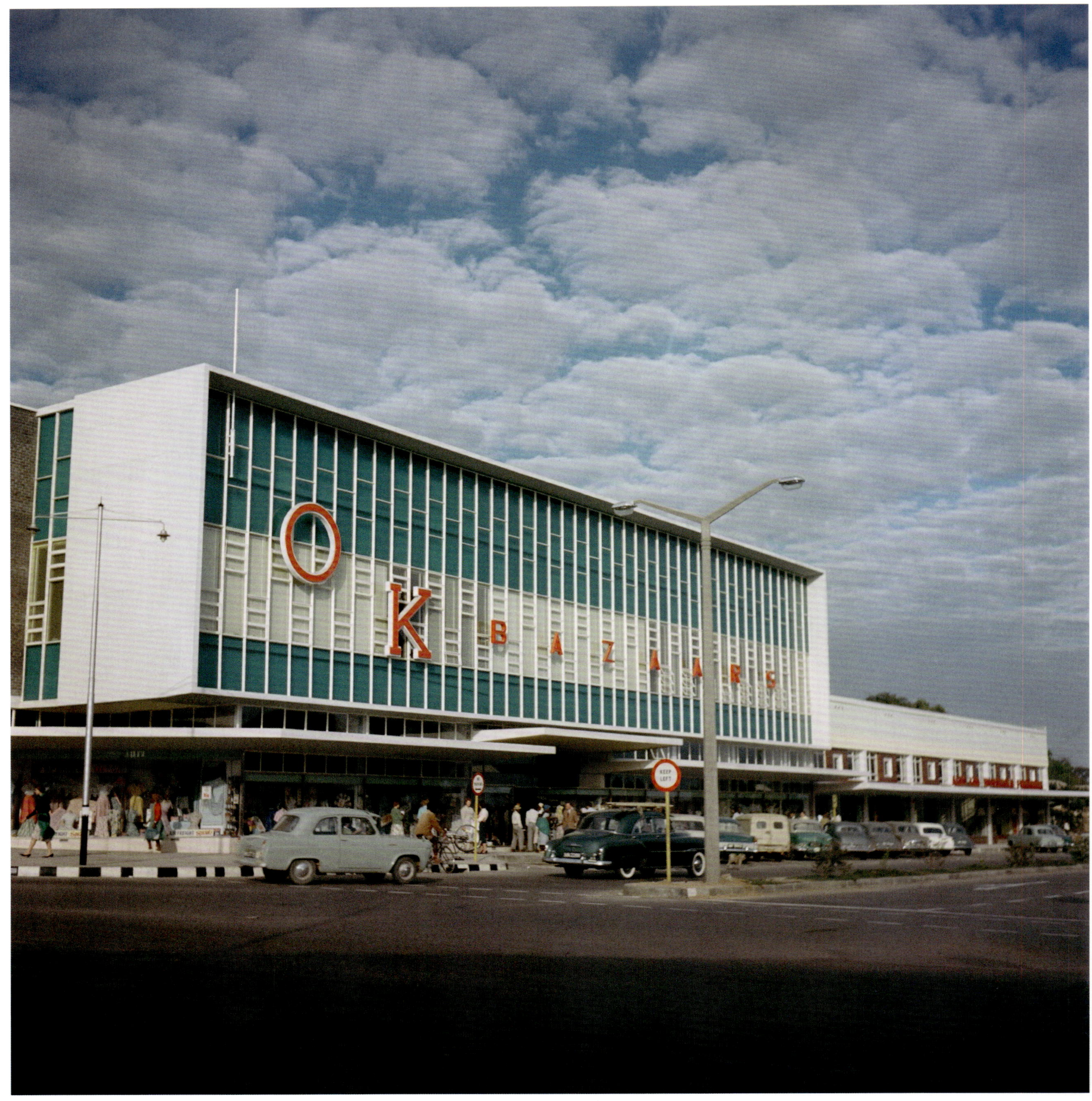

Todd Webb, *Untitled* (44UN-7982-128), Northern Rhodesia (Zambia), 1958
OK Bazaars, in Kitwe town center.

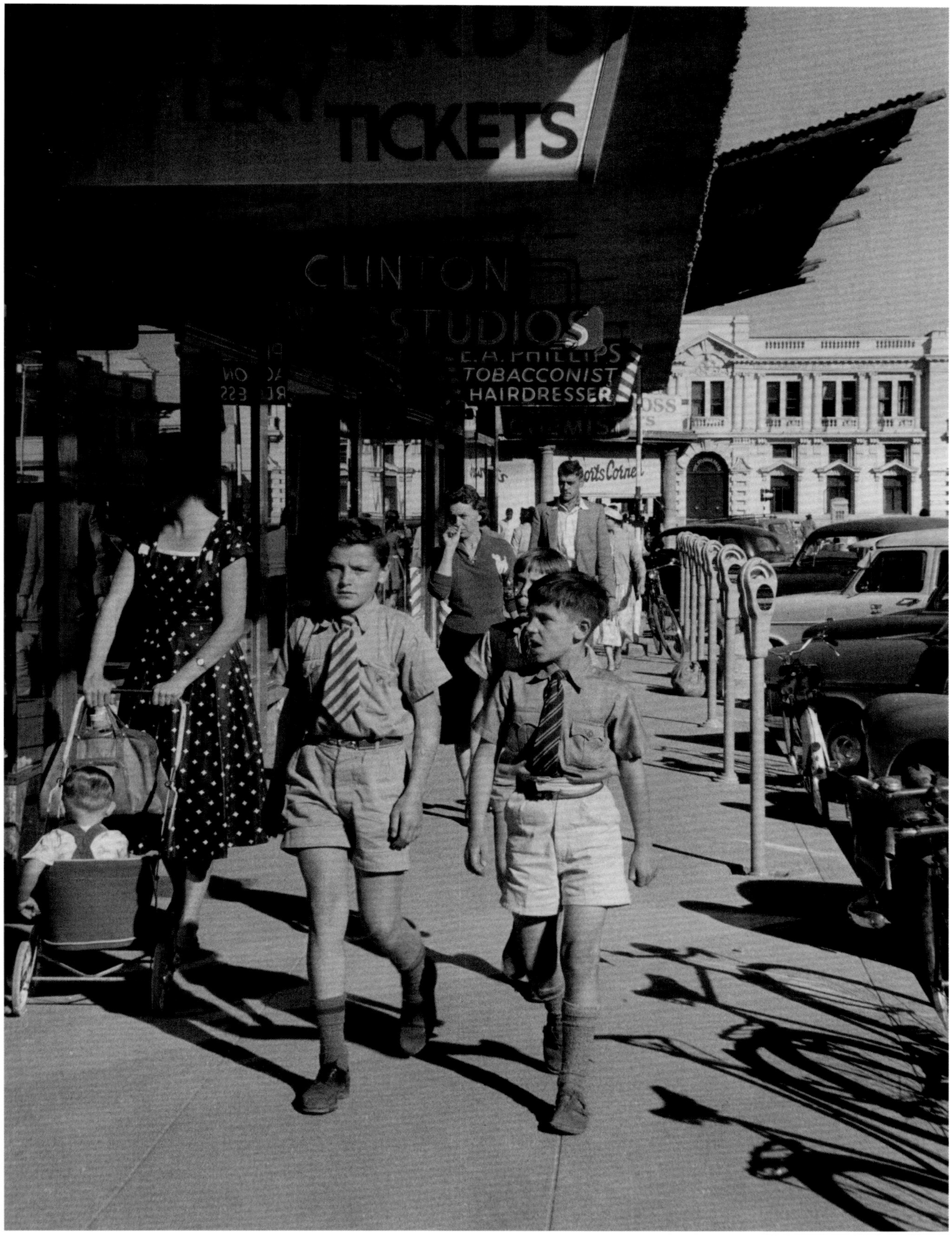

Todd Webb, *Untitled* (44UN-58-067), Southern Rhodesia (Zimbabwe), 1958
Two boys walking past a row of shops, with the Standard Bank on Manica Street in the background, Salisbury.

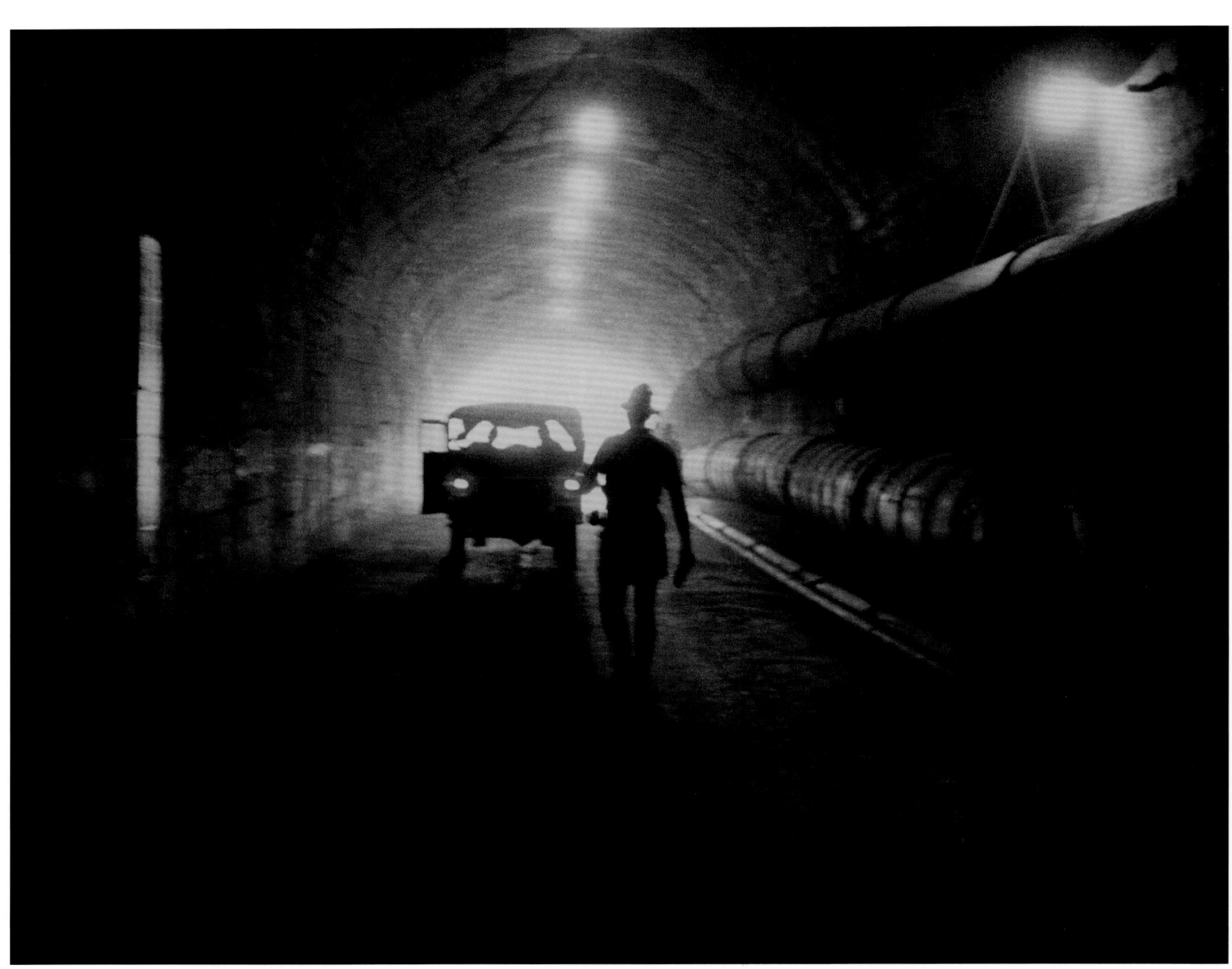

Todd Webb, *Untitled* (44UN-58-065), Northern Rhodesia (Zambia), 1958
Jeep in a copper mine tunnel.

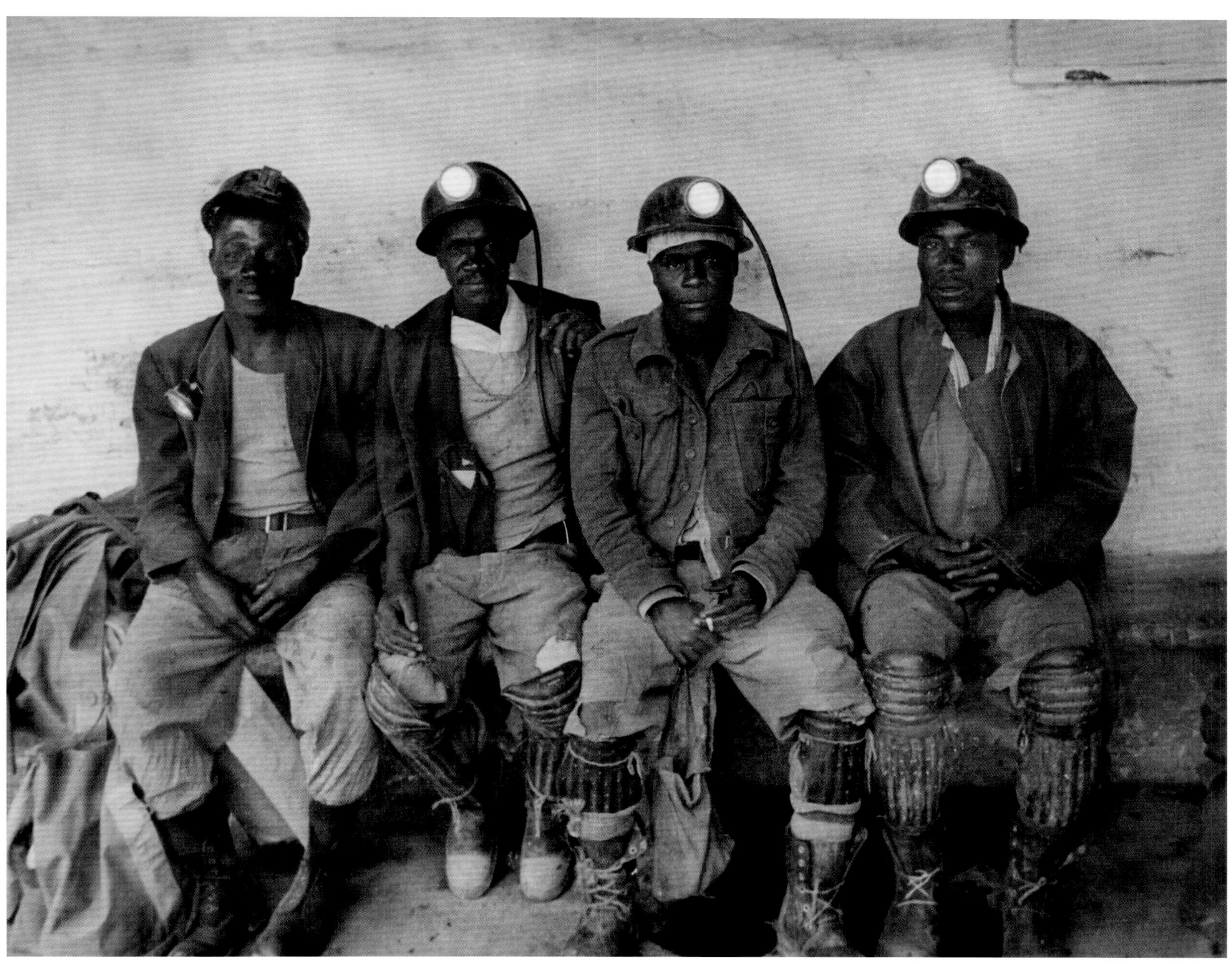

Todd Webb, *Untitled* (44UN-58-066), Northern Rhodesia (Zambia), 1958
Miners wearing headlamps outside a copper mine.

Yesterday Today Tomorrow Bush – Shooting in the Federation

Gary van Wyk

I browse through Todd Webb's 1958 images of the Federation of Rhodesia and Nyasaland (Zambia, Zimbabwe, and Malawi), slivers of time, with familiarity and unease. I recognize my motherland. I know its history. I've tasted its future. I know that the present "order" we see in Webb's photographs is a colonial order; all the "construction" is a subset of the structural violence of colonialism. All the "development" Webb photographs flows from extraction, the exploitation of labor and of the earth, harnessing the power of water and the power of people, whether to mine and smelt minerals or to grow the gold-leaf tobacco we see advertised against the sky atop the tallest building in one of Webb's pictures of Abercorn Street, Bulawayo, above a hanging rope (opposite, top left).

In 1958, that golden leaf is Southern Rhodesia's (Zimbabwe) chief export, rolled into British and American cigarettes, it connects the world, going up in smoke (opposite, bottom).

I know the rich smell of a tobacco barn, that tobacco came from Native Americans, is wrapped up with Francis Drake, the colony of Virginia, plantations of enslaved Africans, and that it was rolled into cigars on Cuban thighs to be smoked by fat cats. Redolent of plutocrats' expensive scents. The redolence of plutocracy surrounds me today, an African living in the United States; it wafts among the fantastic window-dressing on Trump's Fifth Avenue and seeps down into the subways where the huddled homeless stink.

Looking at Webb's 1958 images of the Federation, I know what is coming. The Bush War. But first the Federation will fail. In 1965, right-wing racists will take control of Southern Rhodesia through an illegal Unilateral Declaration of Independence from Britain, trying to echo the United States, and rename the country "Rhodesia." Ian Smith's regime will lose the Bush War in 1980, and when Rhodesia becomes independent Zimbabwe, I will become Zimbabwean.

By 1958, the Federation has run one half of its ten-year lifespan. The Federation combined the self-governing colony of Southern Rhodesia, which was its white-dominated powerhouse, and Northern Rhodesia (Zambia) and Nyasaland (Malawi), which were constituted as British protectorates under the Colonial Office, to protect and promote the indigenous populations. At best, the Federation was a liberal dream. The idealistic Prime Minister of Southern Rhodesia, Garfield Todd, "envisaged a growing harmony between all the peoples with standards of living rising steadily as complementary economic forces built up that strength which develops from a new unity of states. The Federation, as a united people, would then move steadily towards full nationhood within the Commonwealth."[1] Too little, too late. Garfield Todd led Southern Rhodesia from 1953 until 1958, when his own party drove him out of office for being too liberal. Todd saw the white population divide into what he described as two camps, "those who see salvation for the country in white supremacy and those who see our future as a non-racial state in which men are honored for their worth, not passed over because of their color."[2] My parents, counting themselves among the latter, left when the Federation failed in 1962 and Ian Smith's party took power.

Countering the Federal dream, African nationalists demanded independence for each of the three territories–Southern Rhodesia, Northern Rhodesia, and Nyasaland–viewing the Federation as intrinsically perpetuating the economic dominance of Southern Rhodesia, underpinned by racial discrimination. In Southern Rhodesia, white men called the shots. Whites, though a miniscule minority, owned the better half of the land.[3] Job reservation excluded Black people from many job categories, such as on the railroads, where Webb captures white workers manning a locomotive while a Black man washes it (see pp. 184 and 185). There were no Black pilots (and no women pilots). Laws enforced the color bar, separating living areas, schools, and facilities, as with apartheid in South Africa or Jim Crow in the United States. Black nationalists like Joshua Nkomo, elected president of the African Railway Workers Union in 1952 and president of the Southern Rhodesian African National Congress beginning in 1954, had been speaking out against racial injustices even before the Federation was formed. My mother told me how she had gone to listen to Nkomo speak in Bulawayo and agreed with his views. She thought socialism a marvelous ideal.

The popular bar at the Palace Hotel, next to Charter House in one of Todd Webb's photos of Bulawayo, would have had Black men in white suits, like the man we see walking toward us down the arcade, serving white men in dark suits, like the man who walks away from us (see p. 175). Most hotels had a separate "ladies bar" where white women could socialize with white men, if they chose. During the era Webb photographed the Federation of Rhodesia, women's liberation had not yet dawned.

In 1958, a South African is crowned Miss World. She is white. In 2019, a South African is crowned Miss Universe. She is Black and an advocate against gender-based violence, but the beauty contest is still with us.

Webb, too, senses tension mounting. On July 3, 1958, he writes to his wife, Lucille, from Southern Rhodesia's capital, Salisbury, "This is settlers [sic] country and the Africans are quite detribalized and it is nothing like the other places. Quite dull I find and great effort being put forth to keep the African down has made a situation that will be anything but dull before very long. There is an underlying feeling of fear that is quite apparent."[4] It's not that Webb possesses uncanny clairvoyance about the wave of African liberation, having just photographed Togo's election; but before his letter even reaches Lucille in New York, Nyasaland is in an uproar over the return of Dr. Hastings Banda, who rejects the Federation as "stupid," and advocates independence.

In 1958, the people of Togo vote for the first time; Guinea and Central African Republic gain their independence from France; and Gabon, Republic of the Congo, and Chad become self-governing–yet all of these countries, except for Guinea, will remain tied to France by the apron-strings of a common currency.[5] What is the currency of freedom? How does African freedom look for a white American like Webb in 1958, for whom Rhodesia feels "too much like home," as the great battle for Civil Rights intensifies in the United States, whose wealth was built on the backs of African slaves, on land taken from Native Americans, but where the term colonial is only applied to white American colonists fighting white British overlords?[6]

Webb spends just two weeks in the Rhodesias. He tells Lucille that his host Ranger Tyrrell's garden holds such novel delights as the "Yesterday, Today, Tomorrow bush." Day one the flower opens violet, for yesterday, today it is lavender, and tomorrow it fades to white, before it drops. He omits to mention that the yesterday, today, and tomorrow bush emits an enticing perfume. It was this scent that made it my mother's favorite, stirring nostalgia for the gardens of her childhood. Yesterday, today, and tomorrow is native to Brazil.

Ranger Tyrrell is the older brother[7] of Arthur Tyrrell, Acting Chief of the Photographic and Exhibition Service in the New York headquarters of the UN,[8] which has spent that office's 1958 budget on Todd Webb's African assignment.[9] While Todd Webb was staying with Ranger Tyrrell, Lucille Webb socialized with Arthur Tyrrell and his wife.[10] They were part of the same set in Connecticut.

On June 23, 1958, Webb tells Lucille, "I am getting eager to get home...I am getting blase [sic] about sights. I may even miss seeing Victoria Falls. I don't mind too much–it is just a bunch of water flowing over some rocks."[11] You can't sense a river's power when you stand on its dam wall. Webb's brief from Arthur Tyrrell is to picture "development," particularly copper mining in Northern Rhodesia and the link with the

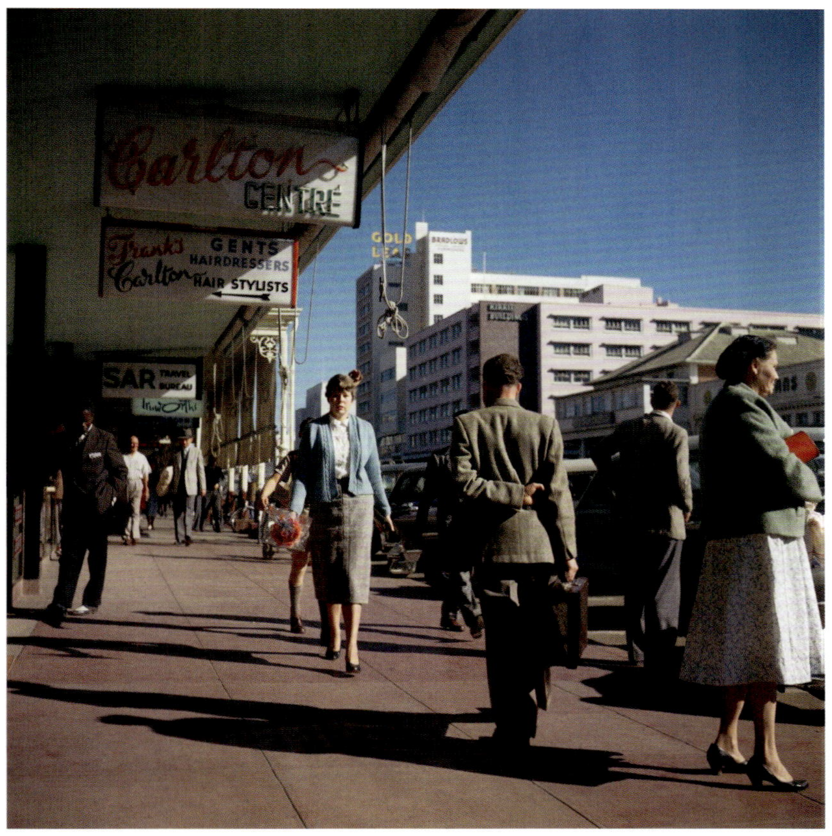

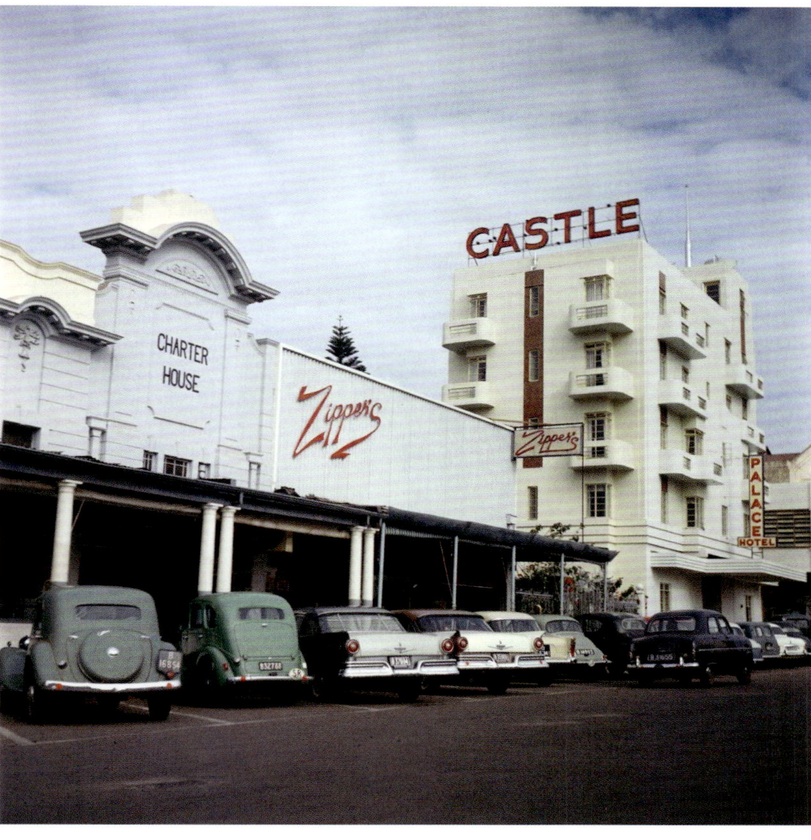

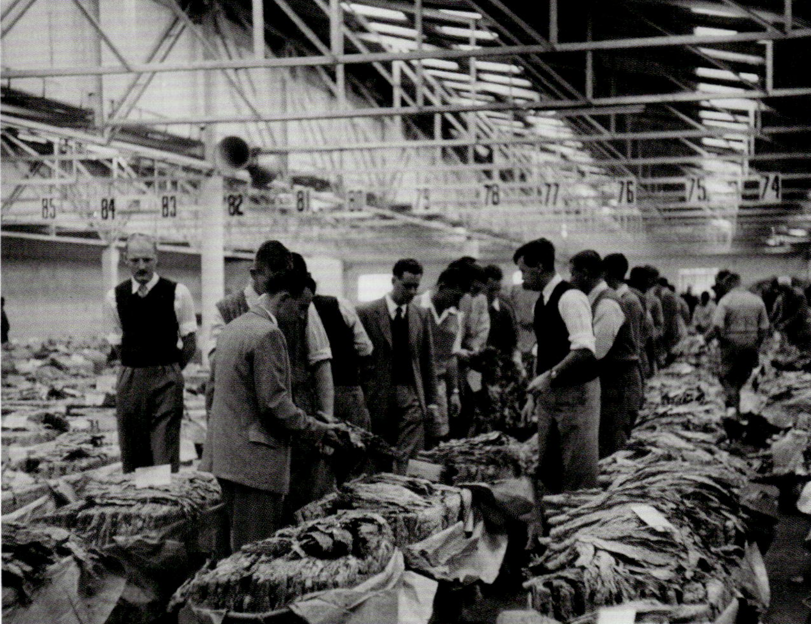

Above left: Todd Webb, *Untitled* (44UN 7990-210), Southern Rhodesia (Zimbabwe), 1958
Pedestrians walking along the sidewalk colonnade, Bulawayo.

Above: Todd Webb, *Untitled* (44UN-7985-534), Southern Rhodesia (Zimbabwe), 1958
Zipper's Store at Charter House and the Palace Hotel, Bulawayo.

Left: Todd Webb, *Untitled* (44UN-58-068), Southern Rhodesia (Zimbabwe), 1958
At a tobacco auction.

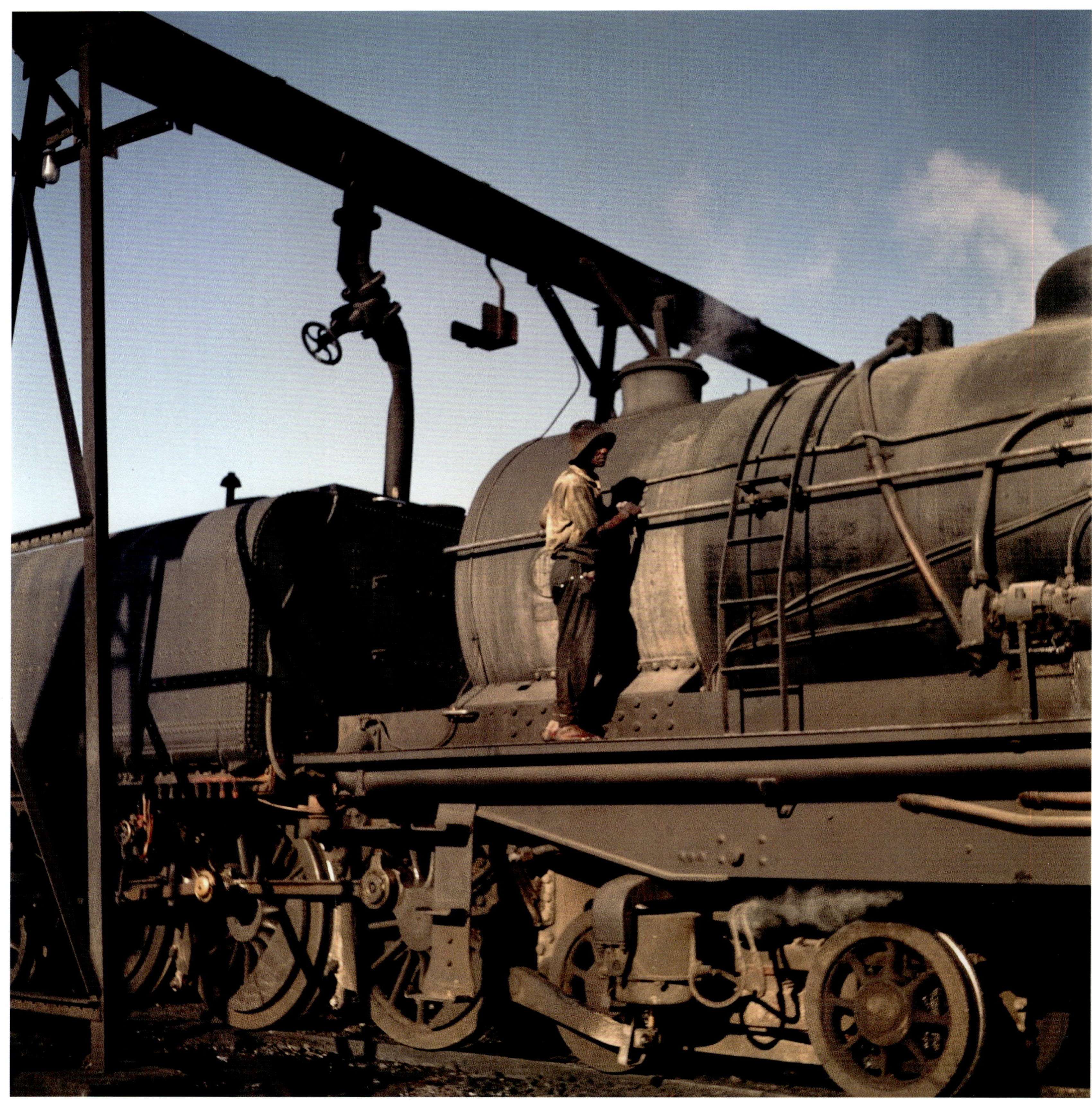

Todd Webb, *Untitled* (44UN-7990-208), Northern or Southern Rhodesia (Zambia or Zimbabwe) [exact location unknown], 1958
Rhodesia Railways worker maintaining a train.

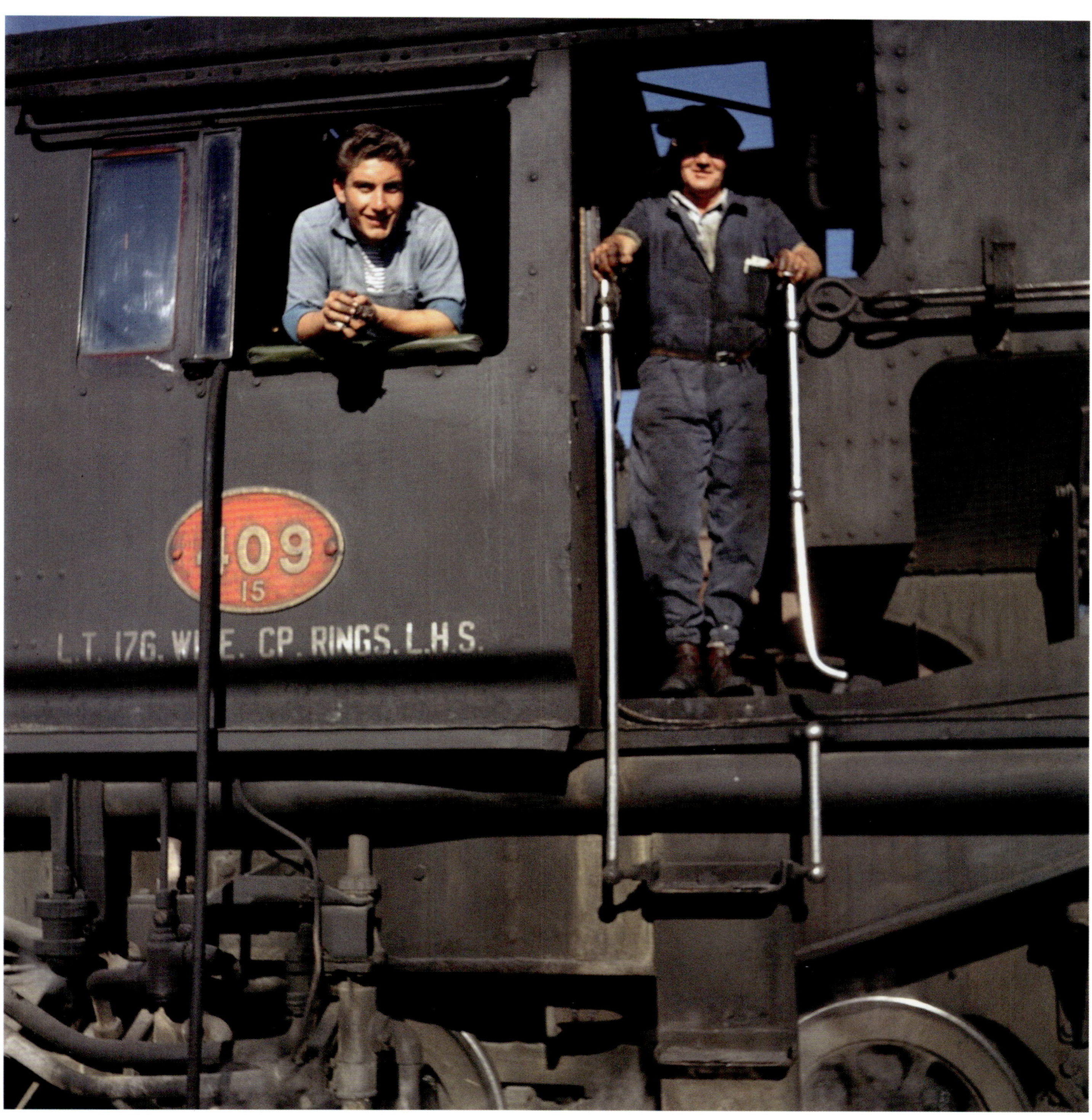

Todd Webb, *Untitled* (44UN 7990-205), Northern or Southern Rhodesia (Zambia or Zimbabwe) [exact location unknown], 1958
Rhodesia Railways workers on the 409 train.

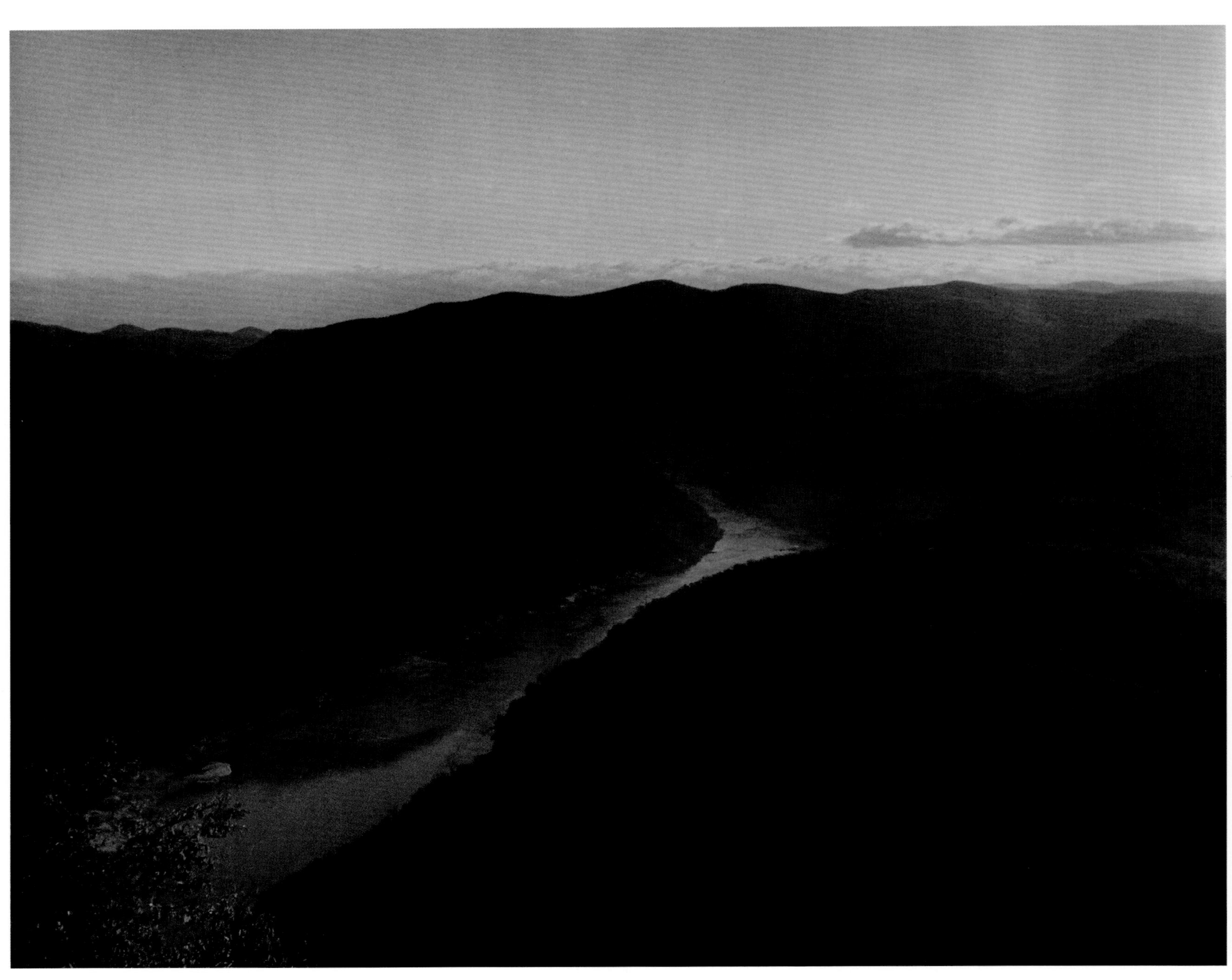

Todd Webb, *Untitled* (44UN-58-069), border of Northern and Southern Rhodesia (Zambia and Zimbabwe), 1958
View of the Zambezi River, between Northern and Southern Rhodesia.

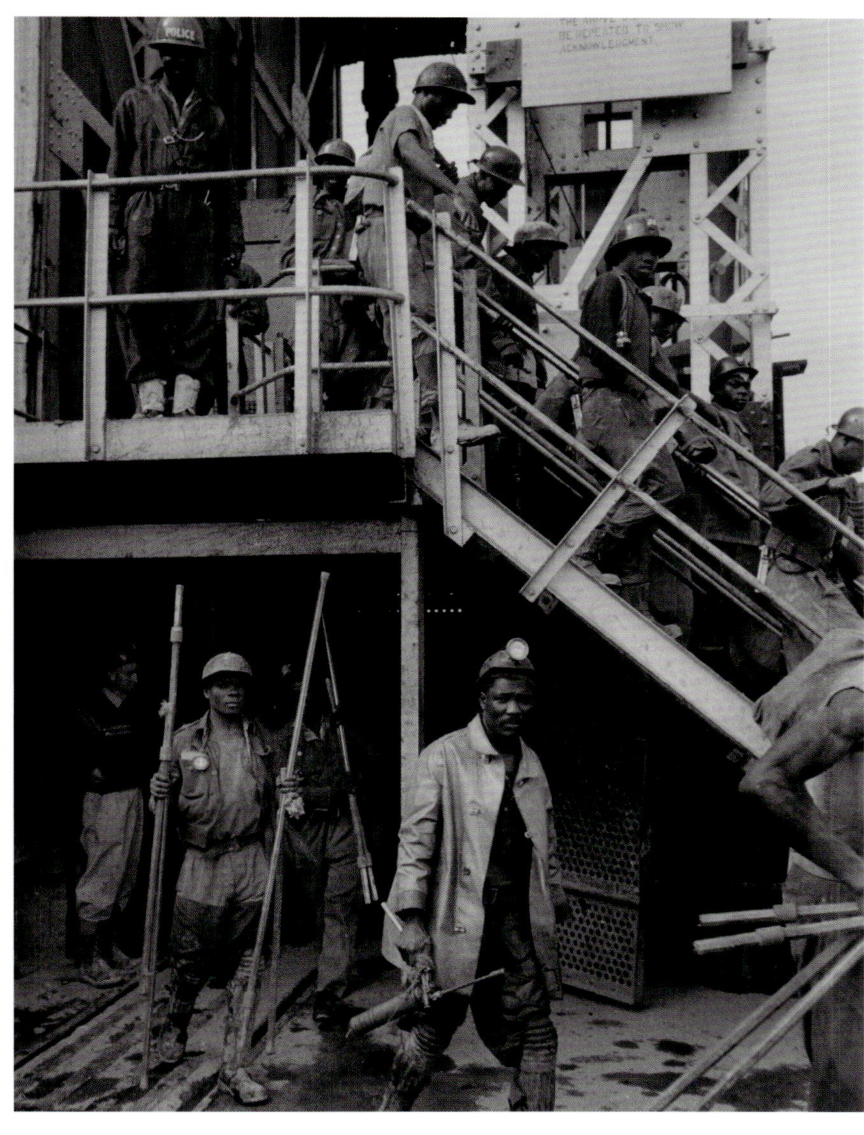

Left: Todd Webb, *Untitled* (44UN-58-071), Northern Rhodesia (Zambia), 1958
Copper miners at work.

Below: Todd Webb, *Untitled* (44UN 7992-529), Southern Rhodesia (Zimbabwe), 1958
OK Bazaars, chemist, and Truworths on Abercorn Street (Jason Moyo Street), Bulawayo.

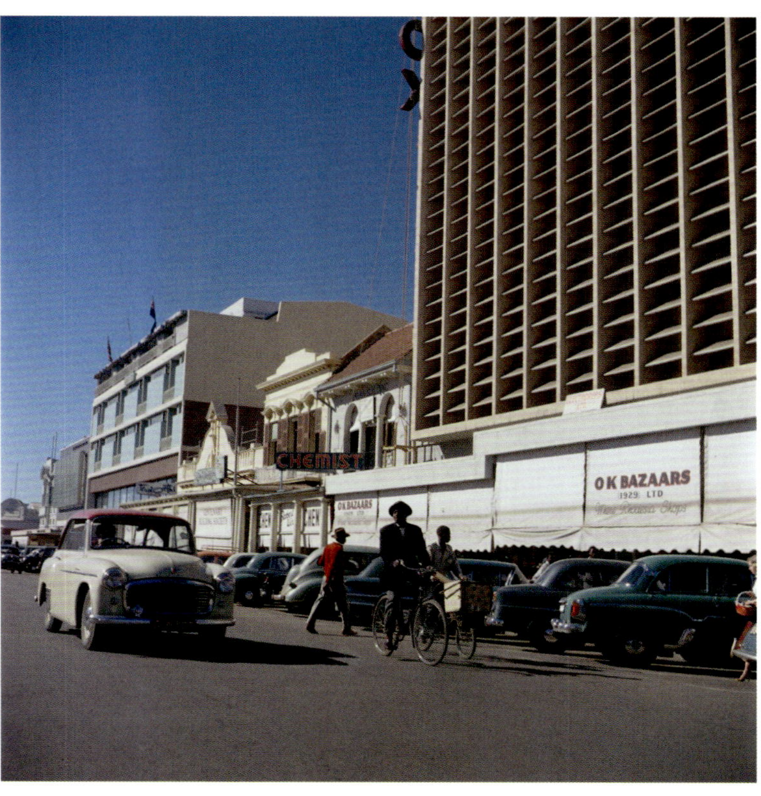

electrical power required to smelt it. Megawatts are about to be brought online by the Kariba Dam hydroelectric project, formed by damming the Zambezi River, which curves between Southern and Northern Rhodesia, creating what was then the world's largest dam and one of its biggest man-made lakes (see p. 186). In 1958, more than half of the Federation's foreign exchange earnings are from copper.[12]

In the copper fields, Webb photographs a scab of molten slag, the "model" workers' houses with red roofs, the white workers and the Black workers coming off shift separately (see p. 187, top). In the small town of Kitwe, he photographs a hulking, modern OK Bazaars, a South African department store supplying commodities that soak up the miners' wages; this is a building with great expectations in the hinterland (see p. 178). OK Bazaars also edges into another picture of Abercorn Street (see p. 187, bottom). SAR (South African Railways) and Truworths, a South African clothing chain, appear in other shop signs, advertising links of commerce and capital routing through Abercorn Street.

Today, Abercorn Street has been renamed in honor of Jason Ziyapaya Moyo, born 1927, assassinated in 1977 in Zambia by a parcel bomb after calling on African countries for more military aid in the liberation struggle. His comrades called him JZ. He trained as a carpenter and a builder and was issued a permit to work in Bulawayo during the building boom after the Second World War. But the barriers JZ encountered against Black builders from white competitors spurred his leadership in the African Artisans Workers Union of Southern Rhodesia, which led to increasing political involvement. At that time, my grandfather, James Victor Cowden, Jr, or JVC, headed the construction company that his father had founded in Bulawayo in 1897. As president of the Southern Rhodesia Master Builders' Association as well as the National Federation of Building Trade Employers, JVC must have had dealings with JZ's African Artisans Workers Union of Southern Rhodesia. Perhaps they met.

Webb doesn't visit Nyasaland—Land of the Lake—it reflects little "development." To many, this represents its beauty compared to the extractive/constructive system Webb is documenting. The possibility of one world entails the expulsion of the other. There are no animals in Webb's pictures; yet, the story of this land and this water is also the story of animals. Water wells behind the rising walling of Kariba Dam. The pressure builds. As the Zambezi Valley floods, bewildered animals are marooned on shrinking islands that were once hilltops. Operation Noah, one of those heroic colonial salvation projects, begins in 1958 to ferry animals to the mainland. Eleven men, "three white rangers and eight native trackers," as *Time* magazine put it in a dramatically illustrated feature,[13] save thousands of panicked animals, from the deadly mamba to the spiteful buffalo, ungrateful leopards and indifferent tortoises—all except for the birds, they fly free. Many drown. The crocodiles feast to prodigious, prehistoric lengths. The women of Rhodesia donate nylon stockings to knot nets and to bind the legs of the animals, instead of rope that cuts the hide.

To escape the flooding, 57,000 Tonga people, maybe more, must be resettled from the lands of their ancestors in the Zambezi Valley. That operation was less photogenic for the magazines. In the guestroom of our home we keep a Tonga stool. Across the top of the seat are paintings of matchbox houses like those Todd Webb photographed. The stool is carved in the shape of one of the speedboats that the Tonga can now watch skimming over what was once the sky above their villages. This boat is carved without an engine. The stool, a tradition of the ancestors, is painted red and black, colors of spiritual power.

Writing from Salisbury, Webb complains to his wife that he is cold and bored. He knows it shows in his photographs. They seem bland and detached, his human subjects in the distance. Apart. He tells Lucille he finds Rhodesia too "un-African…it no longer seems like Africa. First of all this city is a modern and very up-to-date place and it could be Rochester or Syracuse. The Africans have become citified and are just poor colored people."[14] We see these "citified" Africans on Webb's sidewalks, but they don't look poor. They all wear shoes and appear gainfully employed. What is at stake in this "citified" modernity—whether in Rhodesia or in Rochester—is the distribution of its prosperity; that is the question that is going to play out. Apparently, "modernity" does not gel with Webb's preconceptions of Africa, but neither is he sensitive to the Africanness in this context. He doesn't realize that every Black person in the city or working a job, that man with the two-tone shoes, that overlapped man wearing a suit and hat who we can tell is Black only by his right hand (see p. 183, top left), the Truworths' messenger who rides that bicycle, each one is linked to a family in the rural countryside, where their ancestors are buried. Tomorrow, that is where the war for hearts and minds will be waged and won, in the bush.

I'm uneasy viewing Webb's images because development is linked to displacement, construction requires excavation, foundations are unstable; but especially because civil war is coming, and a bush war is the antithesis of what Webb is shooting. The undulation of forces has commenced in 1958, though the climax will be twenty years in the future, when that man hawking baskets woven by the blind has his retirement disturbed because the government relocates his village into one of the PVs, the "protective villages" built like concentration camps, which fail to isolate the rural population from the guerillas who draw on them for support—like Vietnam. When that golden-haired child in the stroller (see opposite) turns out to be a white teenager forbidden to leave Rhodesia in 1978, because he must stay and fight his Black countrymen, the "terrorists." That Black woman smiling at Webb on the sidewalk, is her nephew or niece the "comrade" who will come upon him, with guns in their hands (see p. 174)? Who remembers the people Webb has captured, their real stories?

In 1958, there are race riots in Notting Hill, UK. The Ku Klux Klan bombs Bethel Baptist Church in Birmingham, Alabama. In American courts, Southern states attempting to preserve segregation lose case after case. In North Carolina, a KKK rally at Hayes Pond is attacked by Lumbee Native Americans, whom the KKK leader had declared a "mongrel" race of largely African origin. He intended offense, but given a moment to consider, isn't that what we all are, humanoids of African origin migrating and mixing and moving on again, mixing some more? Freedom is motility. What does Freedom mean in the United States, where more Black people *today* are in prison than ever were enslaved?[15]

*

My parents marry in Bulawayo in 1958. The *Bulawayo Chronicle* runs several photographs of the couple. During his visit, Todd Webb features on the front page of the Salisbury *Herald* as a photographer in the "Family of Man" exhibition, along with other news of the day. Perhaps they looked at each other's pictures in the newspaper or passed on the street.

In a letter dated June 23, 1958, Webb asks Lucille if Arthur Tyrrell has mentioned him covering the Brussels World's Fair, Expo 58, a destination included on my parents' honeymoon. My father shoots color transparencies. One of Webb's works is exhibited there, a composite panel of eight images of Sixth Avenue, New York. The Belgian pavilion has a Congolese Village, replete with a bust of Leopold, where contemporary Congolese act "primitive" for the edification of visitors, with whom they are forbidden to communicate. Capitalism, championed by the United States of America, might seem to be winning the "progress" race, but the American economy is in recession, and in 1958, the Soviets get the first satellite into space. The Soviets exhibit a model of Sputnik at Expo 58, and blame the Americans when it is stolen. The US creates NASA in 1958. Shoot for the moon. The Great Famine begins in China.

Soon, the US and the USSR will be fighting proxy wars in this part of Africa. In the Rhodesian war of liberation, the USSR will back ZAPU

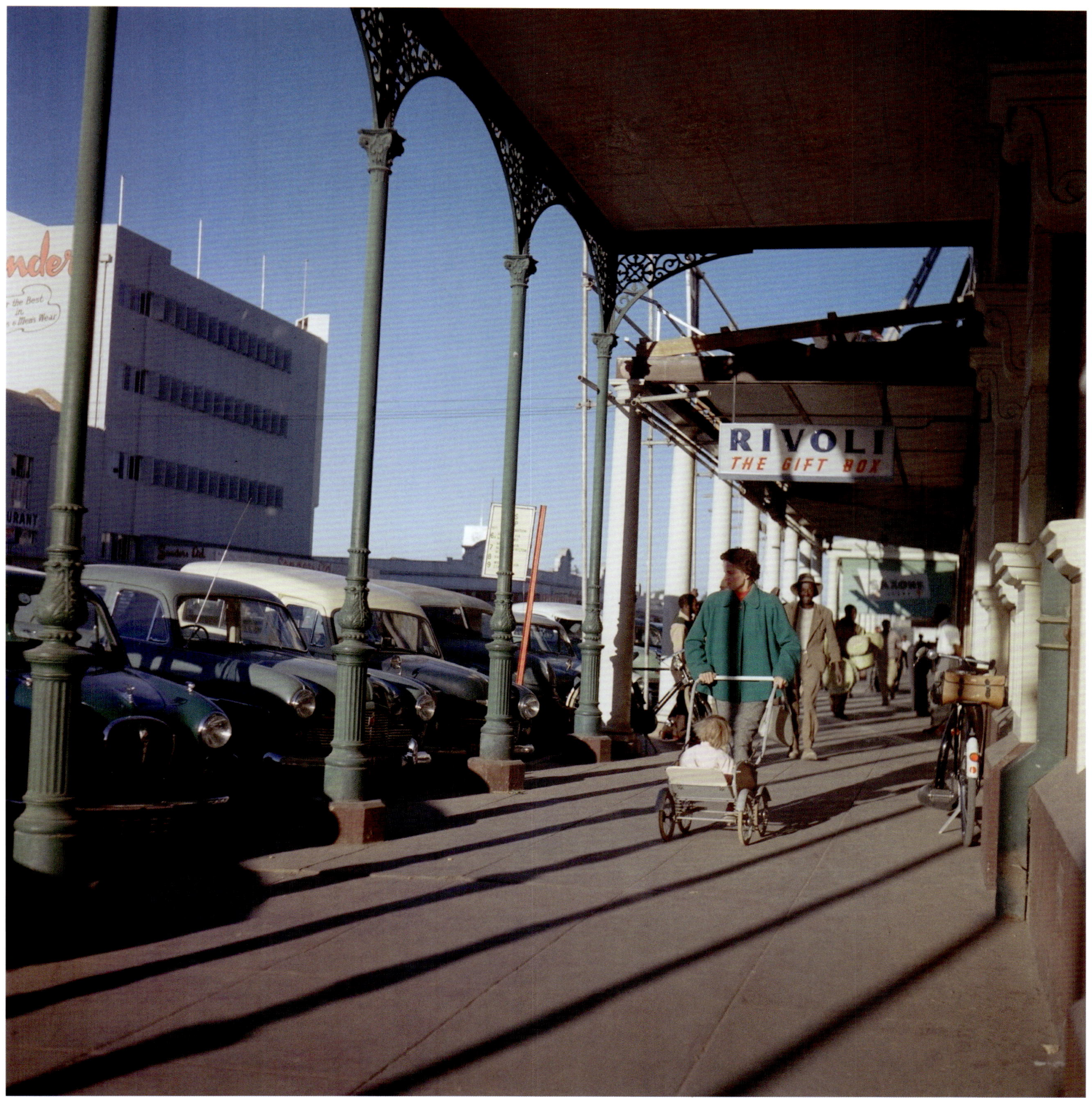

Todd Webb, *Untitled* (44UN-7985-538), Southern Rhodesia (Zimbabwe), 1958
Woman pushing baby stroller by the Asbestos Building (today the National Gallery) at the corner of Selborne Avenue (Leopold Takawira Avenue) and Main Street, Bulawayo.

(Zimbabwe African People's Union), led by Joshua Nkomo, with JZ Moyo in charge of the military wing, ZIPRA (Zimbabwe People's Revolutionary Army). China will back a breakaway group, ZANU (Zimbabwe African National Union), with the military wing of ZANLA (Zimbabwe African National Liberation Army), whose leader, Robert Gabriel Mugabe, educated by Catholics, will rule Zimbabwe for thirty-seven years. The United States will covertly prop up the Ian Smith regime during the war of liberation, from the Unilateral Declaration of Independence in 1965 to 1979. Some American mercenaries with experience in Vietnam will fight alongside Smith's forces, importing their derogatory slang, such as "gooks."

Rhodesia began as an enterprise. Cecil John Rhodes had leveraged his wealth and power from mining to become Prime Minister of the Cape. Then, despite dubious proclamations fit for "the prototype of the modern dictator,"[16] he obtained a Royal Charter from Queen Victoria authorizing his British South Africa Company (BSAC) to occupy the territory that became the eponymous Rhodesia on the basis of mineral concessions granted by Lobhengula,[17] king of the people then known as the Matabele, today Ndebele.[18] In 1890, a BSAC regiment raised a British flag at Salisbury (present-day Harare), in Mashonaland, heartland of the Shona people, who had been partially subjugated by the Ndebele in the early 1800s. Within two years, the Cape press, in which Rhodes had financial interests, began calling the country Rhodesia, and the BSAC made that name official in 1895.

James Hamilton, Duke of Abercorn, is the first person named in the Charter: "WHEREAS a Humble Petition has been presented to Us in Our Council by the Most Noble James Duke of Abercorn, Companion of the Most Honourable Order of the Bath...."[19] As well as being Chairman of the BSAC, Abercorn was Lord of the Bedchamber to the Prince of Wales from 1866 to 1885, then Groom of the Stool until 1891. One of Webb's photographs shows Charter House in Bulawayo, next to the Palace Hotel, named for this foundational document (see p. 183, top right).

The Palace Hotel in Webb's image was originally built to coincide with the 1897 opening of Bulawayo's rail link to Kimberley, and hosted its inaugural banquets.[20] That man in the white suit probably has a steady job there. Perhaps, like nearly half of the employed Africans in Southern Rhodesia, he too is an immigrant, sending a portion of his wages home to Nyasaland or Northern Rhodesia.[21] Perhaps he served my great-grandfathers, my grandfather, my uncles at the Palace bar, each, of course, on their side of the "color bar." Both of my mother's grandfathers were immigrants to Bulawayo. Her father's father, James Cowden, was born in Australia to Scottish parents, and established a construction company in Bulawayo in 1897. Her mother's father, George Peiser, came from South Africa and opened the first branch of the Standard Chartered Bank in Rhodesia in a tent in 1892. His father was a diamond field pioneer in Kimberley with Rhodes, and one of the original shareholders of Rhodes's diamond cartel, De Beers, which still monopolizes the world's diamonds.

With this history in mind, I see Todd Webb's pictures of 1958 as "decisive moments,"[22] exactly halfway between James Cowden's arrival in Matabeleland in 1897 and my being here in the United States in 2019.

Bulawayo was Southern Rhodesia's financial and industrial center, a pragmatic place, and the country's most important constituency. James Cowden served as mayor for an unprecedented four terms, from 1919 to 1923, when the population of Bulawayo numbered well under 10,000, and surely nearly everybody in the small, white settler community knew who was who. Later, after his party, which opposed union with South Africa in favor of preserving their "British character," led the country to self-government in 1923,[23] he represented Bulawayo in the all-white parliament until 1939. He must have epitomized what white Bulawayo voters valued and trusted. He helped shape their world. Bulawayo's High Court, Barclay's Bank, and many other civic and commercial structures were built by my great-grandfather—which is to say, by his construction company and, like so many imposing buildings still standing today, with the use of Black labor, whether enslaved as in the case of the American White House, or poorly paid, as Rhodesian workers were, trapped by taxes to enter an oversupplied and exploitative labor system.

The Bulawayo Barclay's Bank stands at the intersection of Eighth Avenue and Joshua Mqabulo Nkomo Street, formerly Main. Bulawayo's main streets were planned wide enough for a full span of sixteen oxen to U-turn a wagon, so there was ample place at that intersection to erect a massive stone plinth for a bronze statue of Rhodes, right by the Barclay's Bank. In 2013, on that plinth, President Robert Gabriel Mugabe unveiled a sculpture of Joshua Nkomo; irony upon irony, after Mugabe had killed so many of Nkomo's supporters in Matabeleland in the years following Independence.

The Shona say, "Who kills the intruder? The stranger." In 1983, Mugabe set his North Korean-trained Fifth Brigade, the "Red Berets," controlled directly from his office, against his former allies in Matabeleland. The operation was called Gukurahundi, which is when the first rain after winter floats the chaff out of the fields and washes it out of sight. The Ndebele killed were "chaff"—how many we will never know exactly, but the International Association of Genocide Scholars puts the number at 20,000. To end the conflict, in 1988, ZANU and ZAPU fused into ZANU-PF (Patriotic Front), but this erased neither the differences nor the history. When Mugabe went to unveil Nkomo's statue in the heart of Matabeleland, where once Rhodes's stood, of course people remembered. Mugabe admitted that that had been a time of madness—a remarkable remark, since Mugabe admitted little, and there had been so much madness.

All civil wars are vicious, leaving lasting scars. When I returned to Zimbabwe to live there in 1986, to avoid participating in civil war in South Africa, blood was still flowing in Matabeleland as if there was no escaping civil strife. By 1986, two-thirds of the whites had left Zimbabwe, including the most bitter of racists. Fewer than 100,000 whites remained.

Ninety years separate Rhodes's founding of Rhodesia in 1889 and Independence in Zimbabwe, in 1980; over forty years have passed since Independence. What have development and freedom delivered for the people in Webb's images and those yet to be born in 1958, like me?

When I took up permanent residence in Zimbabwe in 1986, the Zimbabwe and US dollars were officially at par, though on the black market you could get eight-to-one. Today, on my desk I have a Zimbabwean banknote from 2008 (opposite). On its face is the logo of the Reserve Bank of Zimbabwe: a pile of balancing rocks that one scholar has described as "a metaphor demonstrating the importance of balancing development and the preservation of the fragile environment."[24] On the rear are two giraffes and a line of grain silos to hold the wealth of the land, provided contented ancestors have delivered the rain. The denomination on my bill is 50 billion Zimbabwe dollars. The issue date is May 2008, when the exchange rate to one US dollar was 777,500,000 Zimbabwe dollars, so my note was worth a little over $50US. By July 2008, fifty years since Webb took off from Salisbury/Harare on a Central African Airways Viscount (opposite, top), which could have been piloted by my father, the exchange rate to the US dollar was 758,530,000,000, meaning that, three months later, my bill was worth only five US cents. In August 2008, the Zimbabwe Reserve Bank recalibrated the currency at 1,780 to one US dollar. Within three months it fell to Z$669,000,000,000 to one US dollar. Meanwhile, in 2008 the economy was losing US$5 billion daily due to corruption.[25] Imagine the universal chaos of that economy...

My Z$50,000,000,000 bill is an Agro-Cheque, which might be paid to a grain farmer selling to a government silo. By 2008, Mugabe had delivered on a populist promise to take back the land from the white farmers by encouraging land invasion.

*

According to scholar David Lan, it is Zimbabwean ancestral imperative that: "the ultimate test of the legitimacy of any political system is its ability to provide fertility, to ensure that the crops grow, that the people prosper and are content."[26] It matters whether people have enough money for shoes, perhaps for a suit and even a hat, not to mention their "daily bread."

In June 2008, British newspapers estimated that only 280 out of 5,000 white farmers remained on their land,[27] plunging the country into food shortages. A famine followed. The poor suffered most; the rich got richer. Mugabe enriched his cronies—his own family foremost—with everything from prime farmland to diamonds; extractive industries are the most prone to corruption. In search of a better life, Zimbabweans streamed over the South African border, even risking the crocodile-infested Limpopo River.

I had asked my mother to get me one of these Zimbabwean bills with an unimaginable number as a memento of my origins and my migrations through the land of our birth, and as a perpetual reminder of the crazy relativity of calculations of fortune.

My unease about Webb's pictures also emanates from their programmatic glorification of progress. I suspect all representations of "progress" and "development" of being justifications for exploitation that fails to deliver what really matters: an equitable distribution of wealth. Contrasting yet equally false narratives of progress have swirled around me all my life, from my birth under African colonialism, living through apartheid South Africa, right up until today, raising our son within view of Wall Street's Freedom Tower while Donald Trump boasts that he could shoot somebody on Fifth Avenue with immunity, enriches himself off the US presidency—irony upon irony, like Mugabe—inflames racism and xenophobia, and rails against immigrants, like Mugabe did. Whether it be "progress" in capitalism's narrative of trickle-down prosperity and rising boats, or "progress" in socialism's metanarrative of liberation, what counts in the end is who owns what, and how much. When there is plenty, none should ever want. That is what my mother saw in socialism.

Yesterday, Today, Tomorrow. The best time to plant that bush was twenty years ago; the next best time is today; failing that, tomorrow.

Enough. It is time to plant.

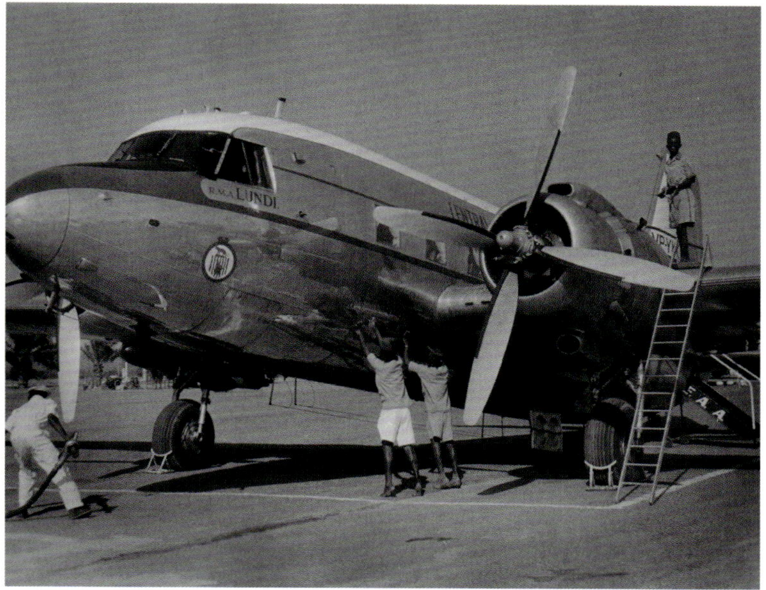

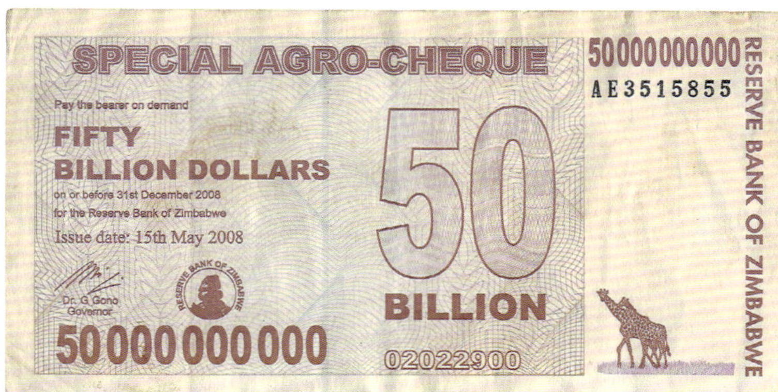

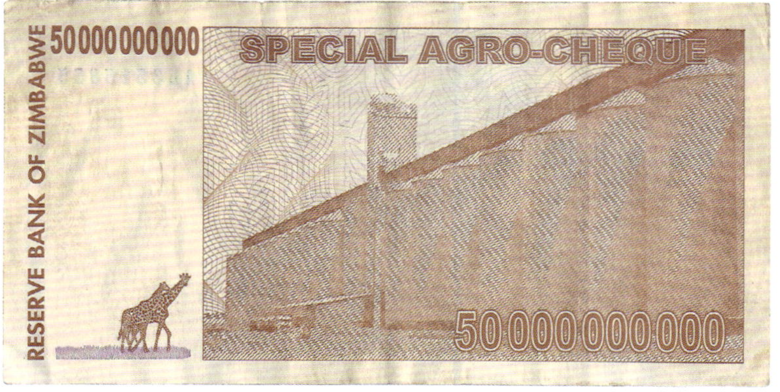

Top: Todd Webb, *Untitled* (44UN-58-070), Southern Rhodesia (Zimbabwe), 1958
RMA Lundi, Central African Airlines Viscount, Salisbury.

Above: Fifty billion Zimbabwean dollars, banknote, 2008

Of Color: Todd Webb's Images of Africa in the American Civil Rights Era

Casey Riley

The three years in which Todd Webb worked as a consultant and photographer for the United Nations coincided with a critically important period within the American Civil Rights Movement. During this brief span of time, numerous landmark developments shaped the course–and the international impact–of the movement. In September of 1957, President Dwight D. Eisenhower ordered a newly federalized National Guard and United States Army troops to support the desegregation of Central High School in Little Rock, Arkansas. Throughout this crisis–during which nine Black high-school students faced political obstruction, public harassment, and repeated threats of violence as they pursued their education–American media outlets exposed the grotesque ramifications of so-called Jim Crow laws, which segregated the public and private lives of United States citizens by race. That same week in September, Eisenhower also signed into law the first federal civil rights legislation, the Civil Rights Act of 1957. Although these laws would ultimately be superseded by the passage of the Civil Rights Act of 1964 and the Voting Rights Act of 1965, the concurrent establishment of the United States Commission on Civil Rights and the Civil Rights Division of the Department of Justice in 1957 laid the foundation for future anti-racist legislation.

Federal entities were responding to a well-organized resistance movement coordinated by Black Americans and their allies across the United States. Arguably the most important development within this three-year period occurred in February of 1957, when Civil Rights leaders met in Atlanta, Georgia, to form the organization known as the Southern Christian Leadership Conference. This powerful group, which would organize and support numerous acts of civil disobedience to dismantle white supremacy, named Dr Martin Luther King, Jr as its first president. Having recently led the successful desegregation initiative known as the Montgomery Bus Boycott, from March 1955 to December 1956, King commanded national headlines as he promoted nonviolent resistance as the most effective collective action against systemic racial oppression. Under his guidance, the Southern Christian Leadership Conference would become a leading voice for justice and equal treatment under the law of the United States, reaching the consciences of millions of Americans.

In this same period, King galvanized a generation of political and social activists within the United States. In 1958, students affiliated with the National Association for the Advancement of Colored People (NAACP) organized sit-ins to protest segregation within dining establishments. Youth marches in Washington, DC in both 1958 and 1959 called for school integration. The young minister's legendary eloquence stirred individuals to collective action and encouraged a critical approach to systems of governance. King could be particularly stern in his own assessment of Euro-American geopolitics. In an important address to his congregation at the Dexter Avenue Baptist Church in Montgomery, Alabama, in November of 1957, he presented a forceful critique of the status quo:

> Democracy is the greatest form of government to my mind that man has ever conceived, but the weakness is that we have never touched it. Isn't it true that we have often taken necessities from the masses to give luxuries to the classes? Isn't it true that we have often in our democracy trampled over individuals and races with the iron feet of oppression? Isn't it true that through our Western powers we have perpetuated colonialism and imperialism? [...] We must face the fact that the rhythmic beat of the deep rumblings of discontent from Asia and Africa is at bottom a revolt against the imperialism and colonialism perpetuated by Western civilization all these many years.[1]

Linking the destructive forces of colonialism and imperialism with the rise of Communism in both Africa and Asia in his sermon, King deftly illuminates parallel failures within the borders of the contemporary US. These assessments would prove to be controversial–the Federal Bureau of Investigation monitored King from the mid-1950s onward, erroneously suspecting him of Communist sympathies–but ultimately underscored the increasing public debate surrounding the morality of Euro-American interventionism.

While direct connections between the above debate, the American Civil Rights Movement, and Webb's goals for engagement with the citizens of African nations might prove elusive, we can assume that he carried some knowledge of these events into his framing of the diverse cultures he encountered while on assignment. Webb's social conscience was refined through his work with Roy Stryker, and he possessed no small awareness of systemic racial oppression, especially during and after his travels in the American South in the late 1940s and 1950s. Webb noted many instances of racial injustice while in the South, as well as his indignant responses to these events, in his diary. One entry describes his disgust at "the ridiculous code of white supremacy" he observed in Natchez, Louisiana, stating that the "whole pattern of living here is to cherish the evil and worn-out traditions of the pre-Civil War South."[2]

Yet how Webb might have understood his own role within the context of these events as he pursued his work in Africa remains an open question. As a representative for the United Nations, his work to document processes of decolonization, democratization, and self-rule ultimately supported the oversight of these systems by elite global forces. Would King's critique of these structures have resonated in his imagination throughout his journey? Perhaps not. Yet a photograph of an integrated college classroom, taken during his travels in Tanganyika (Tanzania), suggests that the dynamics of race–especially as they are embedded within cultural institutions–were never far from his visual imagination (opposite). Seated in rows of five, with their work spread before them, students of different racial backgrounds work dutifully, signaling to otherwise resistant American eyes something extraordinary through the very ordinariness of their attitudes. As a sign of educational progress within a developing country, Webb's photograph also functions as a window into a potentially more promising future–for Tanzania, and for the United States of America.

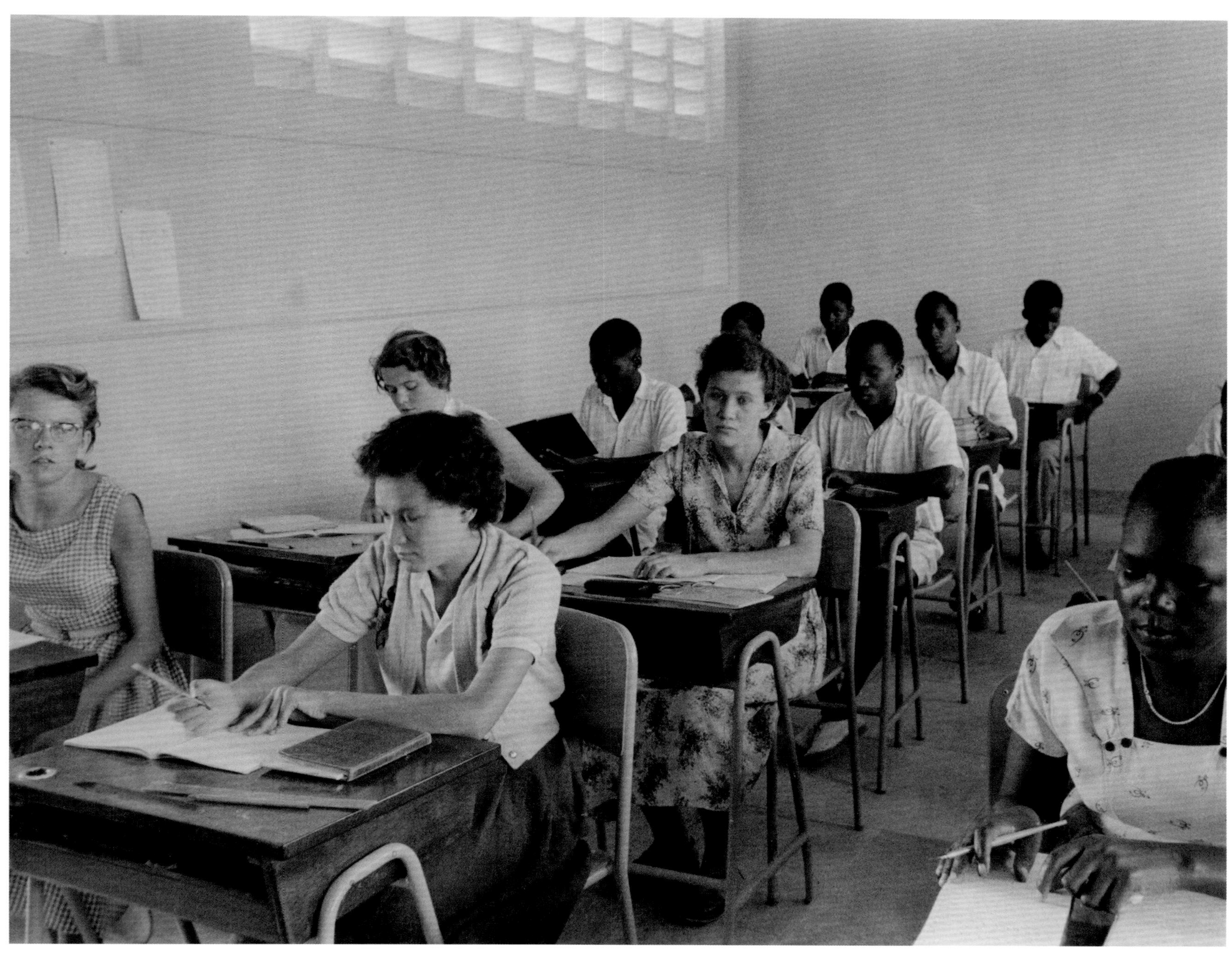

Todd Webb, *Untitled* (44UN-58-072), Tanganyika (Tanzania), 1958
Students at the Kilimanjaro Native Cooperative Union College of Commerce, Moshi.

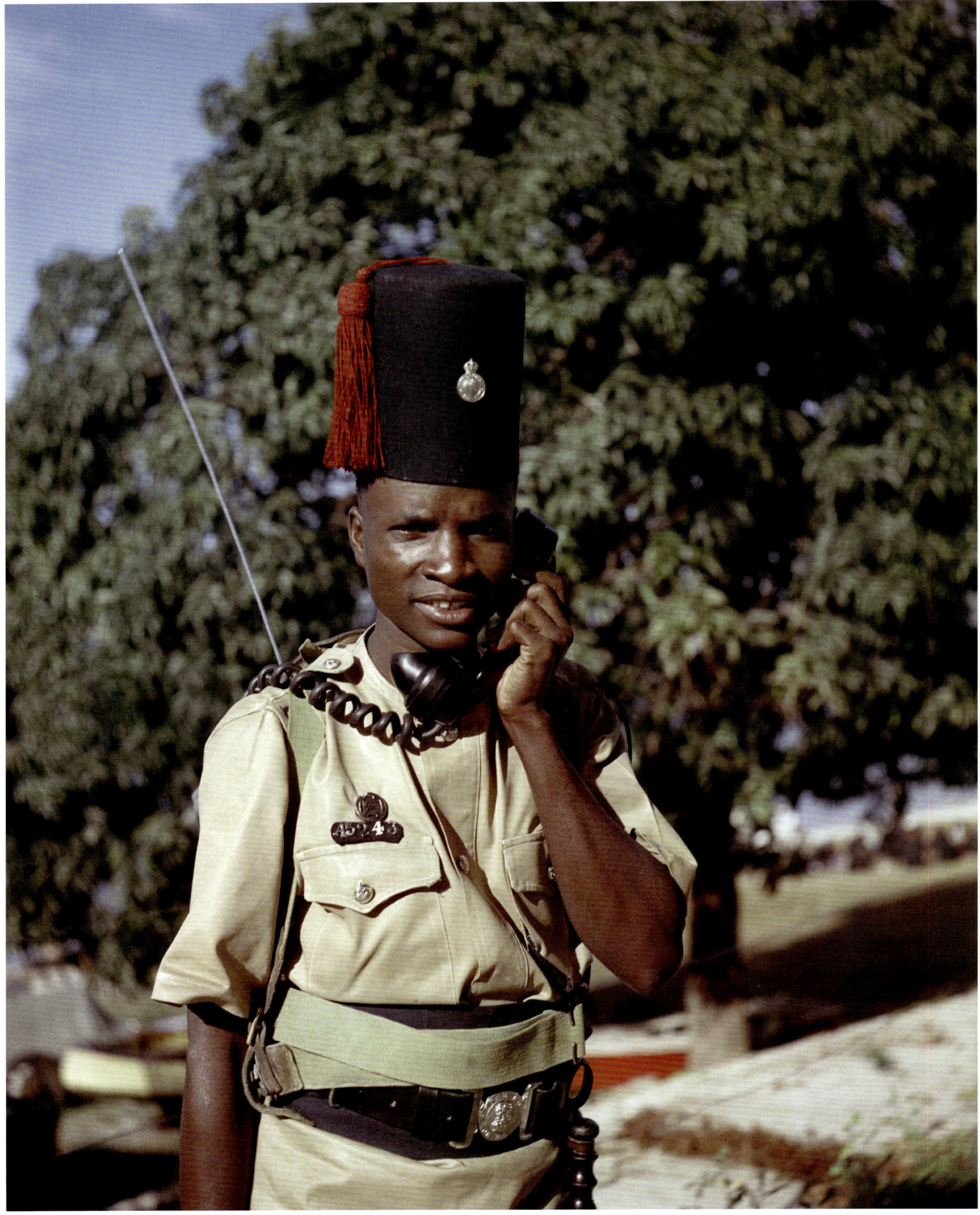

TANGANYIKA, ZANZIBAR, AND KENYA

(TANZANIA AND KENYA)

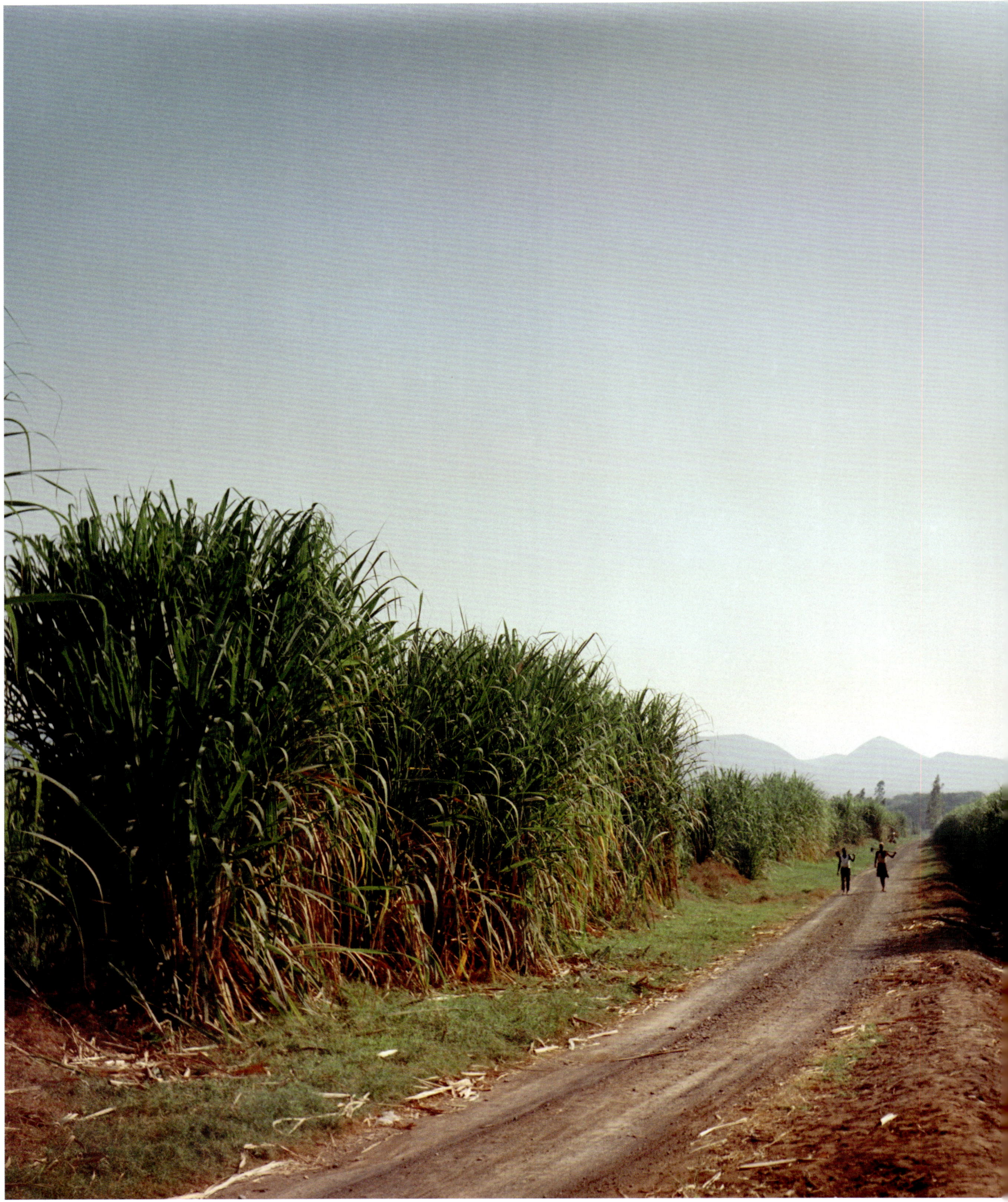

Previous spread:
Todd Webb, *Untitled* (44UN-8021-415), Tanganyika (Tanzania), 1958
Tanganyika Police Officer using a field telephone.

Todd Webb, *Untitled* (44UN-7943-003), Tanganyika (Tanzania), 1958
Farmers with hoes walking on a rural road.

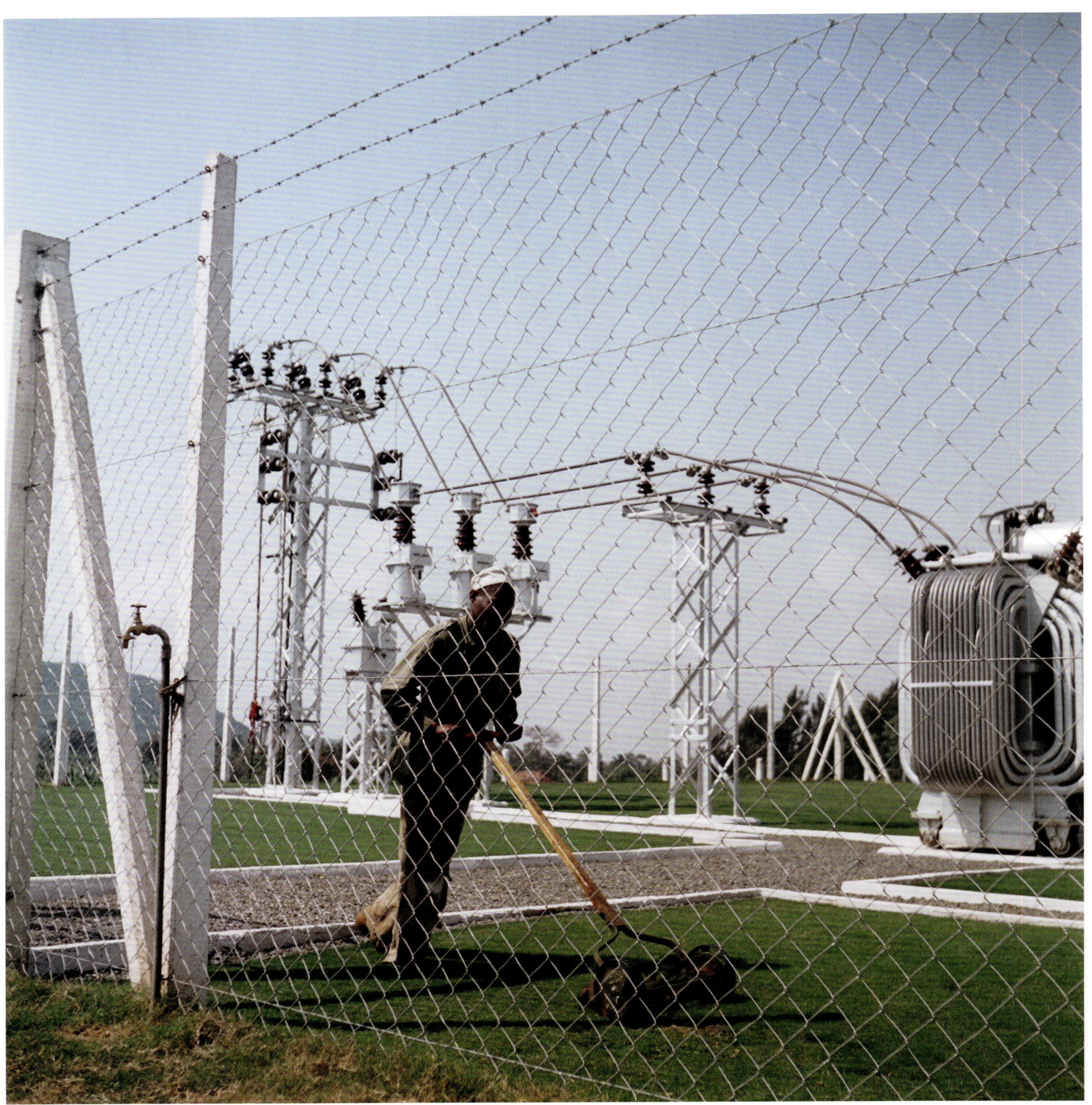

Todd Webb, *Untitled* (44UN-8011-469), Tanganyika (Tanzania), 1958
Man mowing the lawn at the Pangani Falls hydroelectric power station.

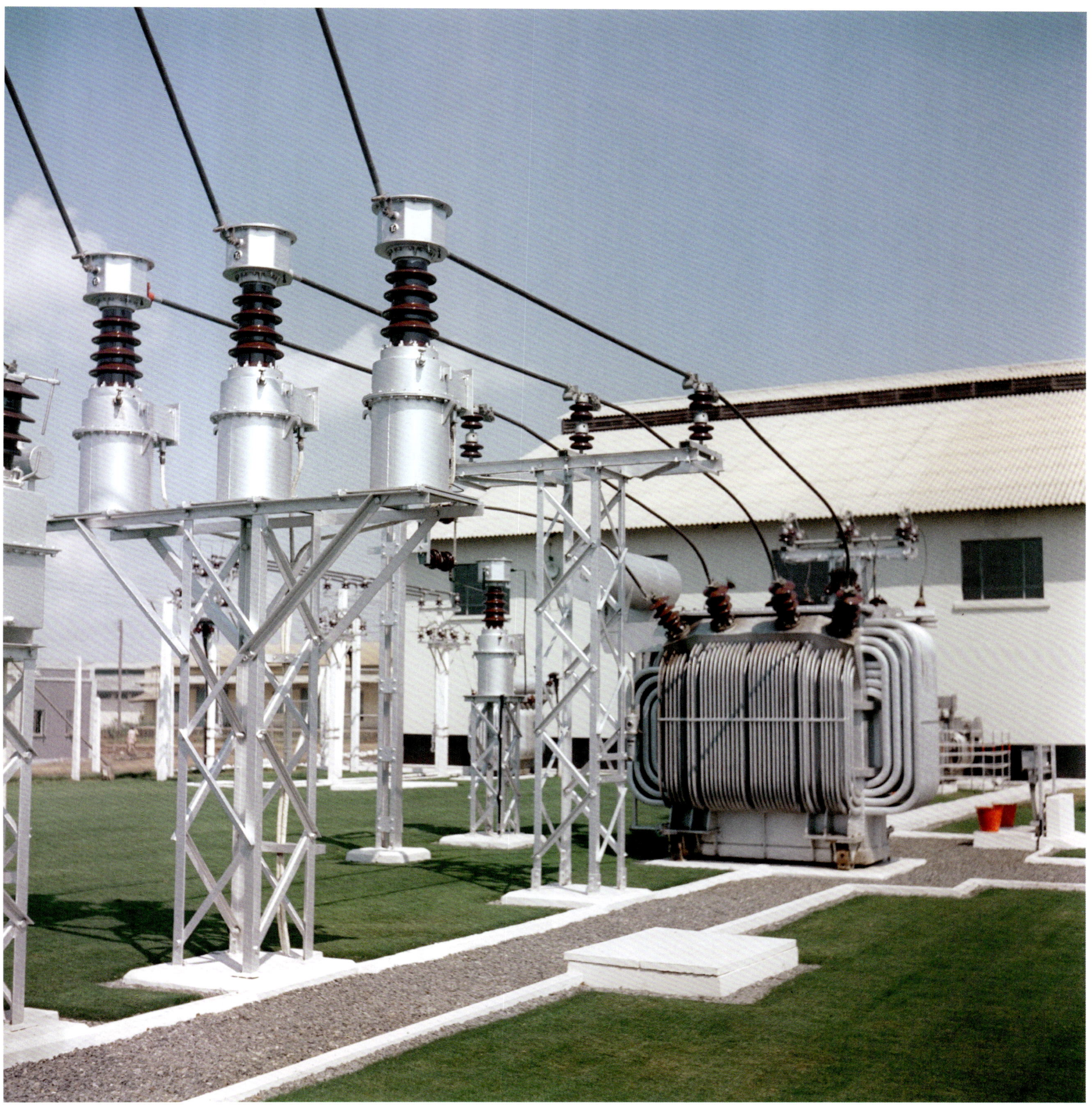

Todd Webb, *Untitled* (44UN-8011-477), Tanganyika (Tanzania), 1958
The sleek lines of the Pangani Falls hydroelectric power station.

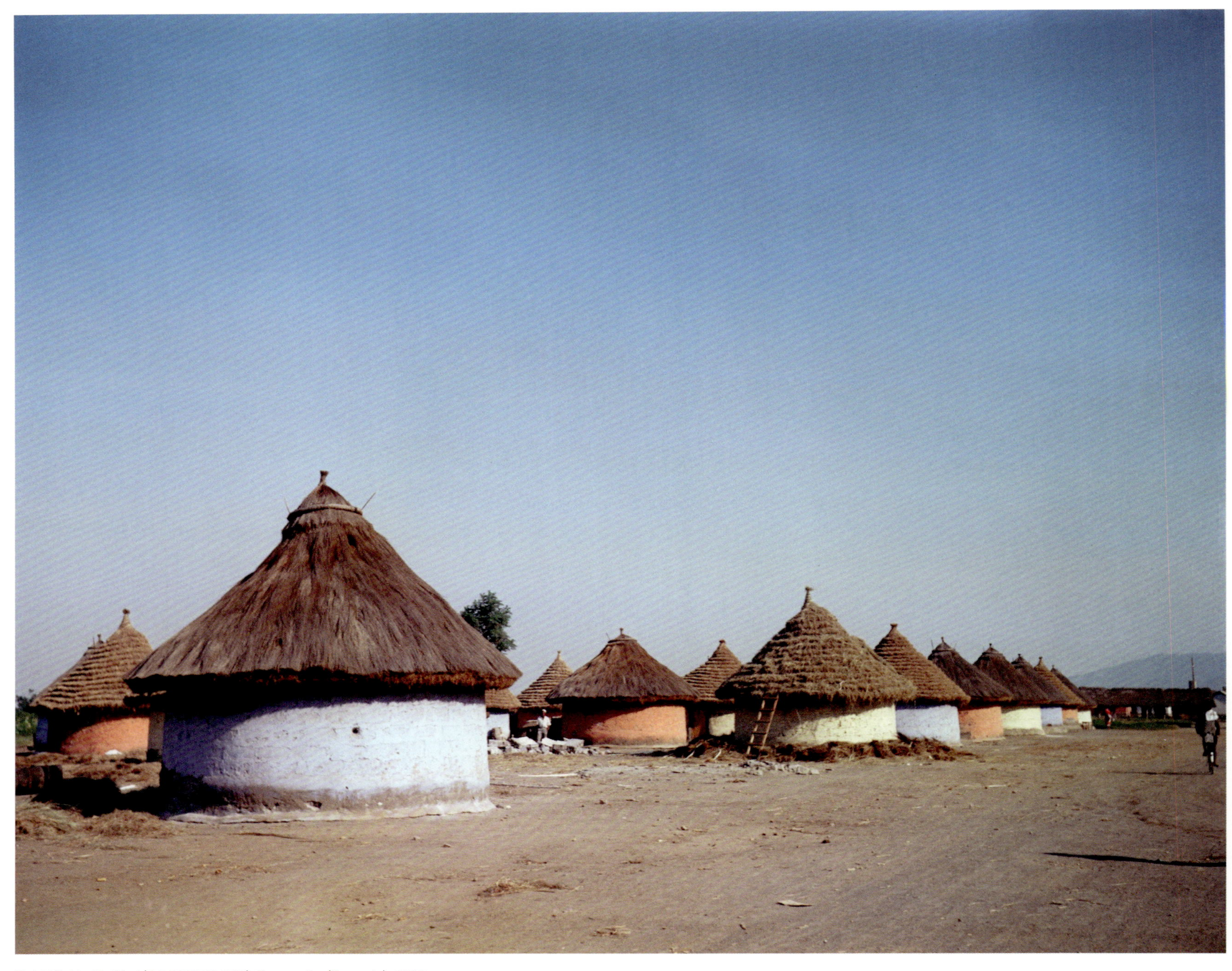

Todd Webb, *Untitled* (44UN-7943-001), Tanganyika (Tanzania), 1958
Painted houses near Tanga.

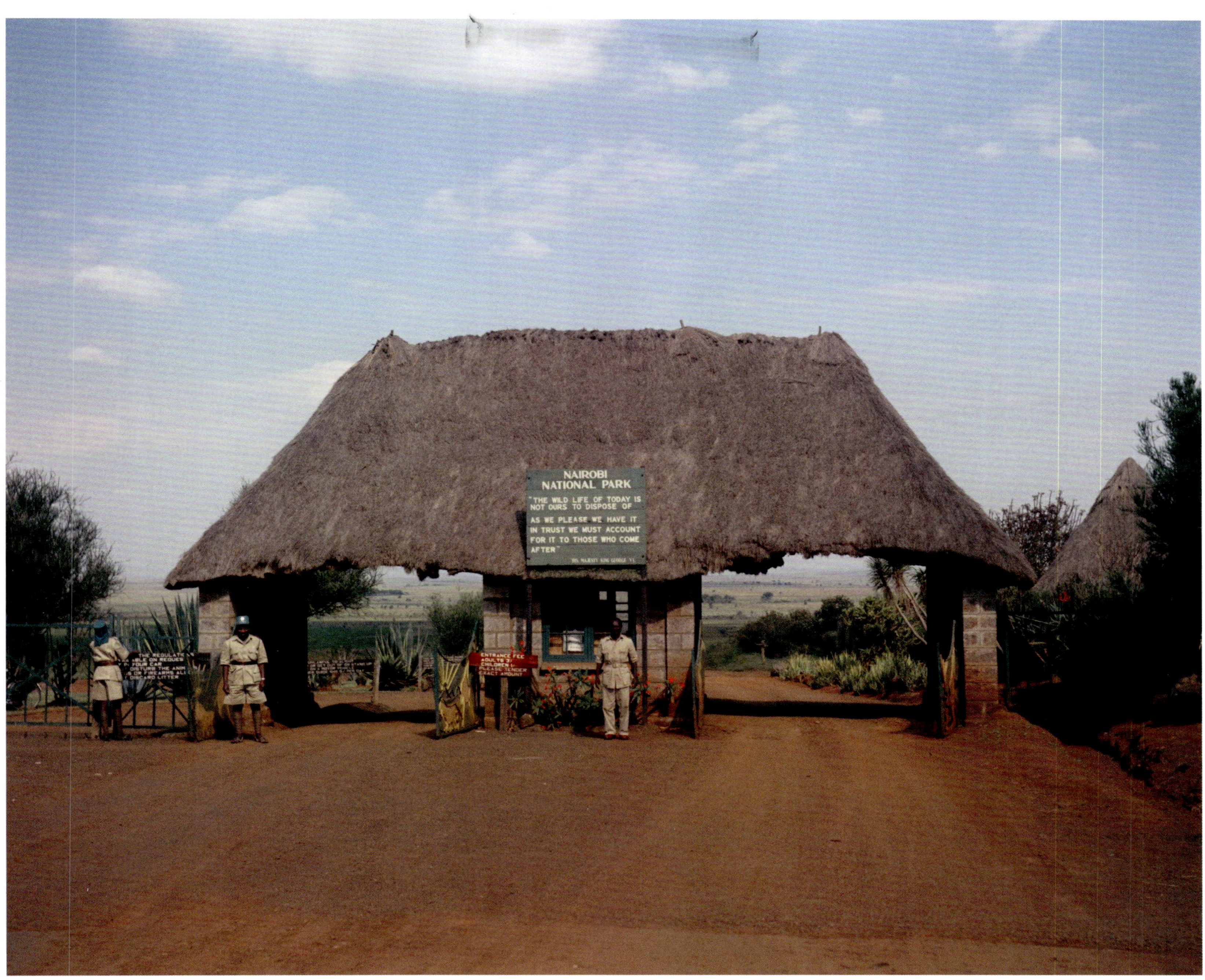

Todd Webb, *Untitled* (44UN-7937-319), Kenya, 1958
Entrance gate at Nairobi National Park.

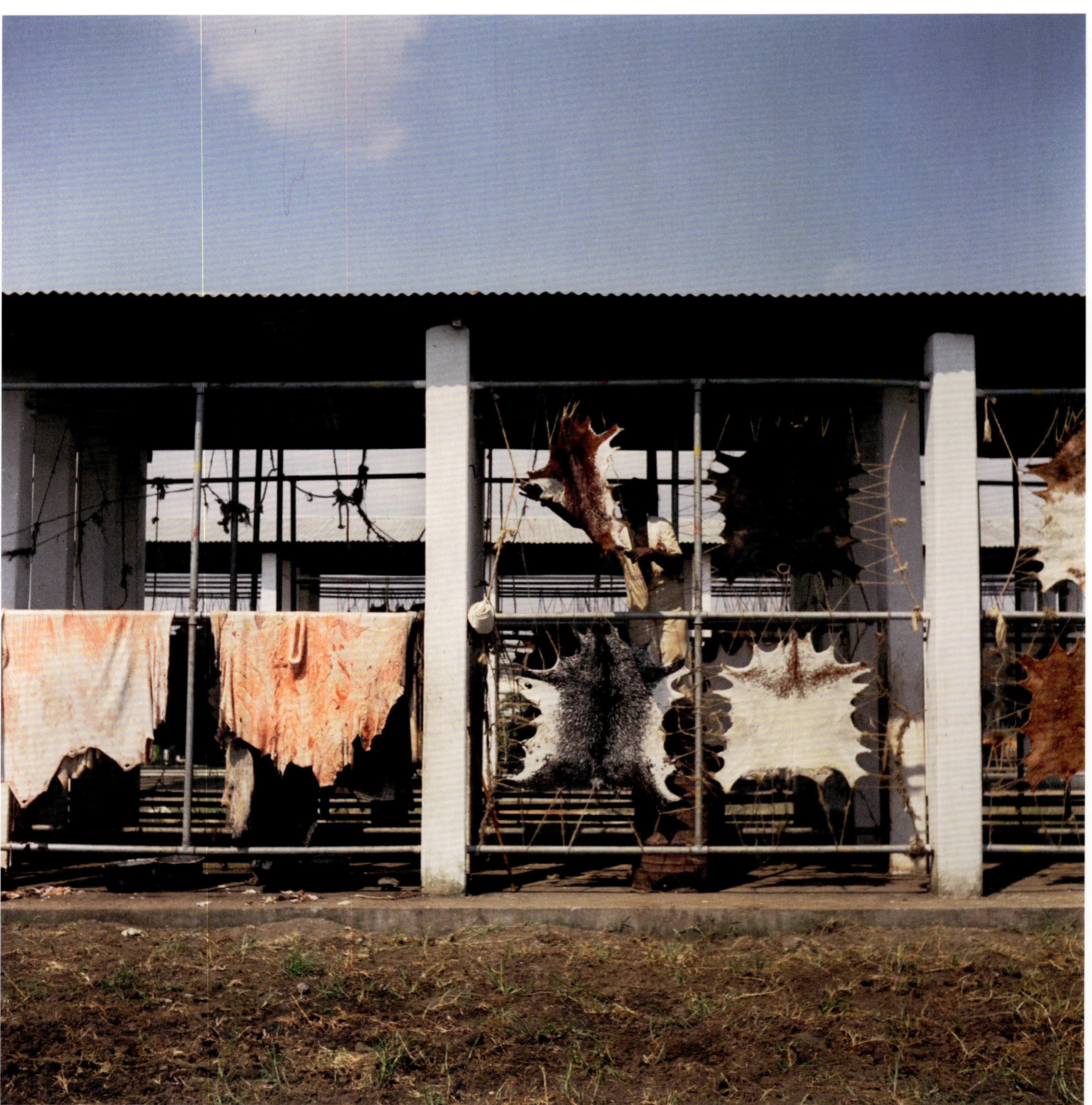

Todd Webb, *Untitled* (44UN-8011-475), Tanganyika (Tanzania), 1958
Cow and goat hides drying at a leather-processing factory.

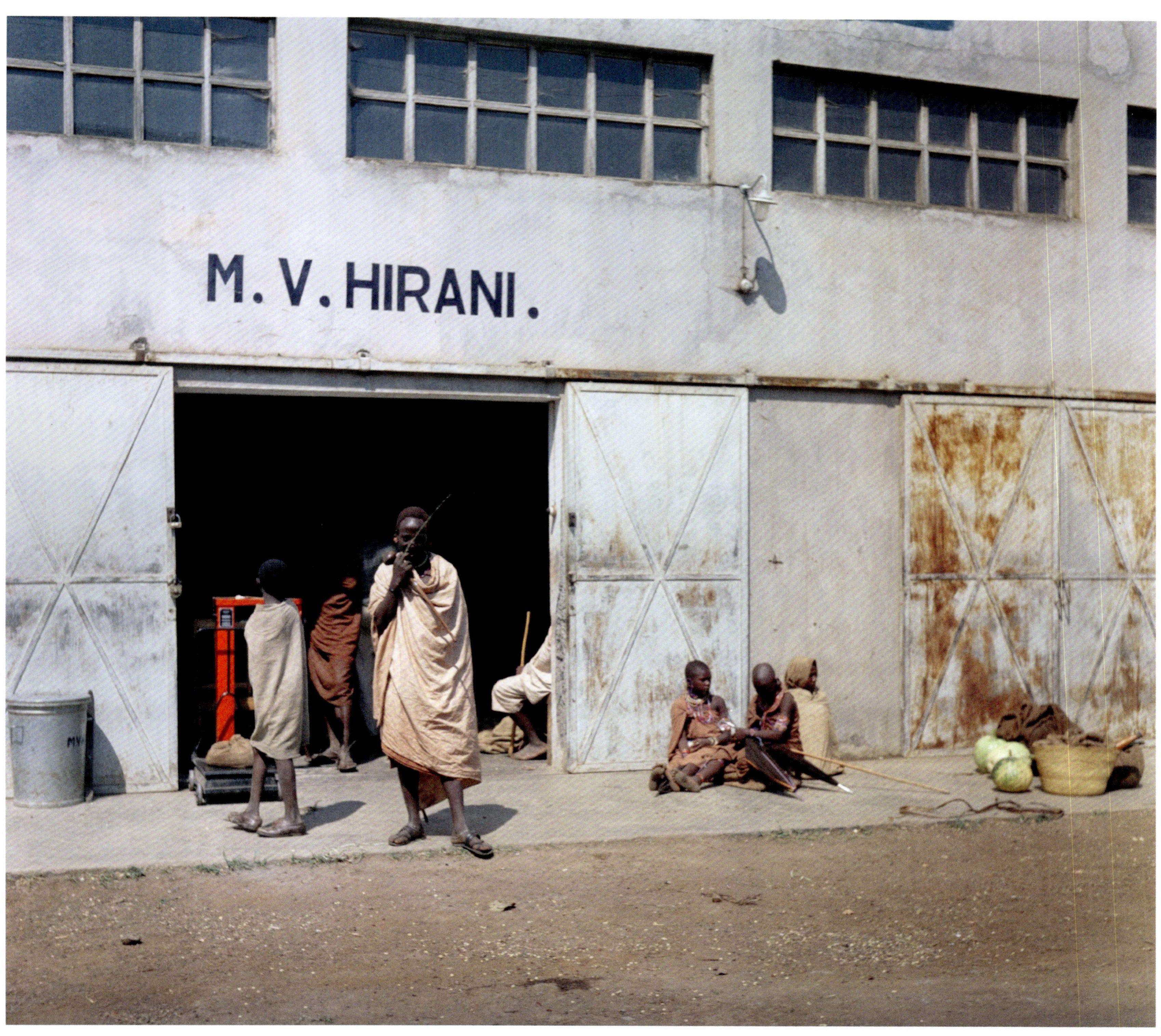

Todd Webb, *Untitled* (44UN-8013-470), Tanganyika (Tanzania), 1958
Patrons in front of the M.V. Hirani store.

Todd Webb, *Untitled* (44UN-7732-029), Tanganyika (Tanzania), 1958
Mural of an outdoor tailor measuring a woman painted on a building in Kingoni, Tanga Region.

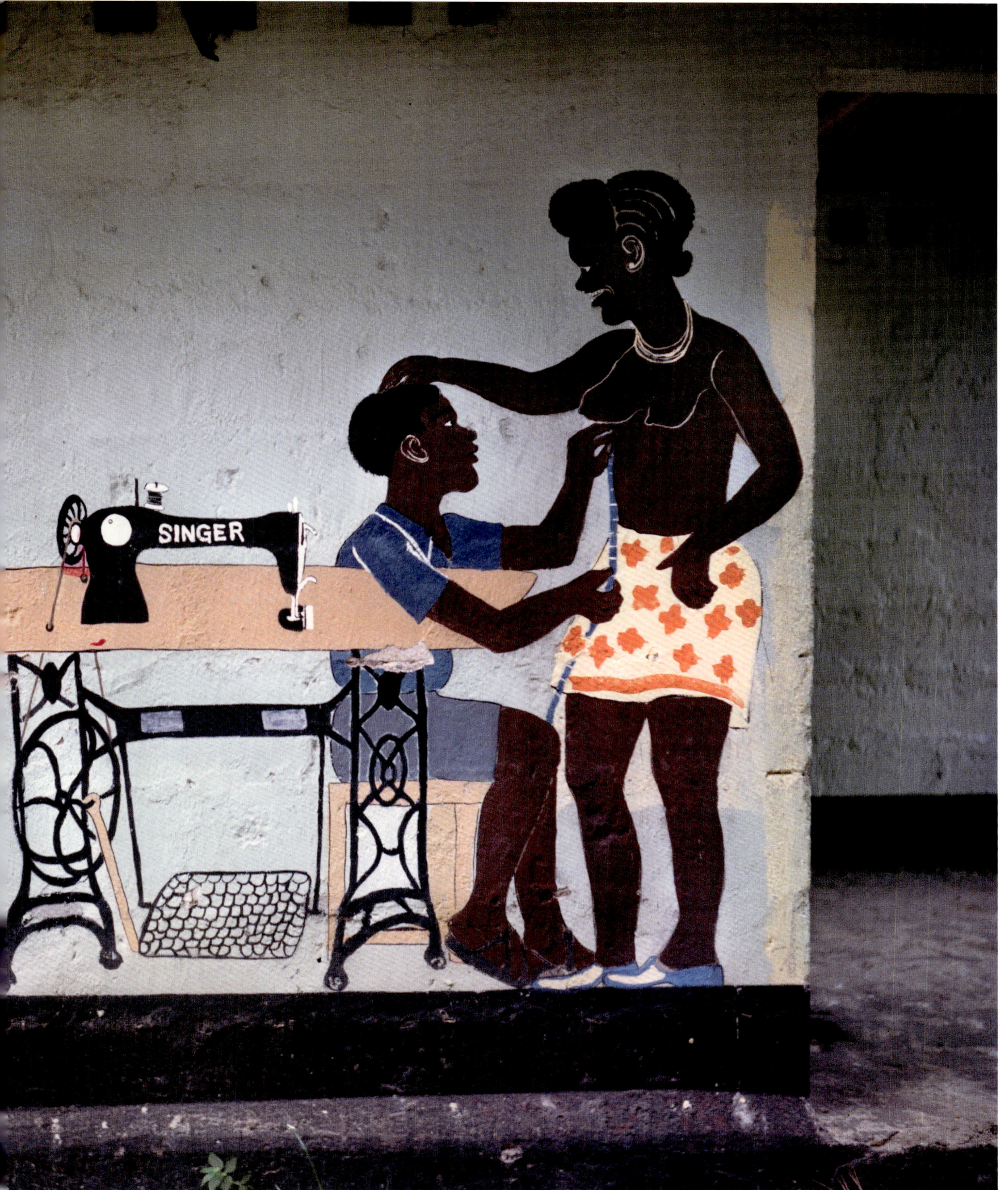
SINGER

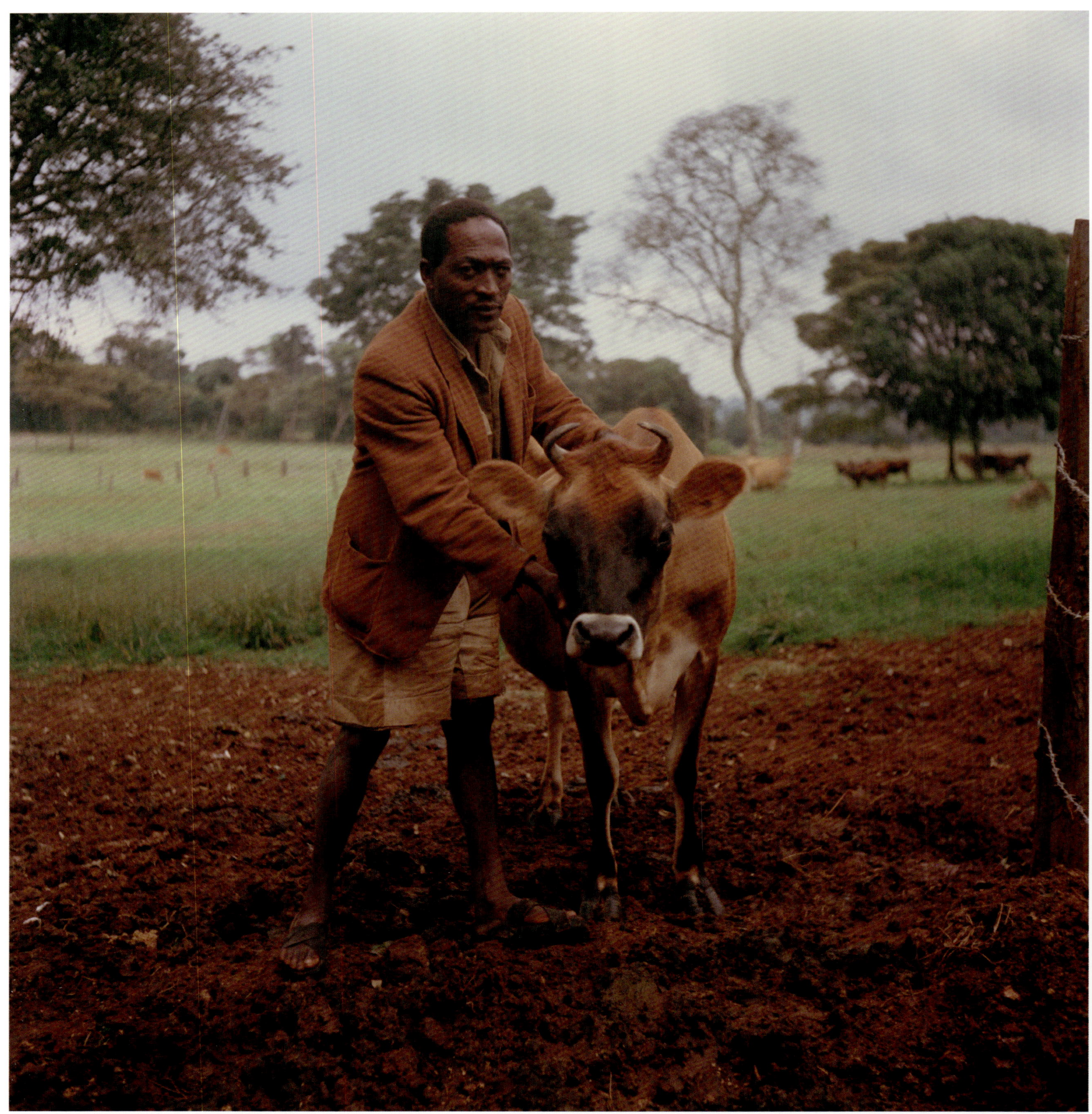

Todd Webb, *Untitled* (44UN-7903-388), Kenya, 1958
Veterinary field worker examining a cow.

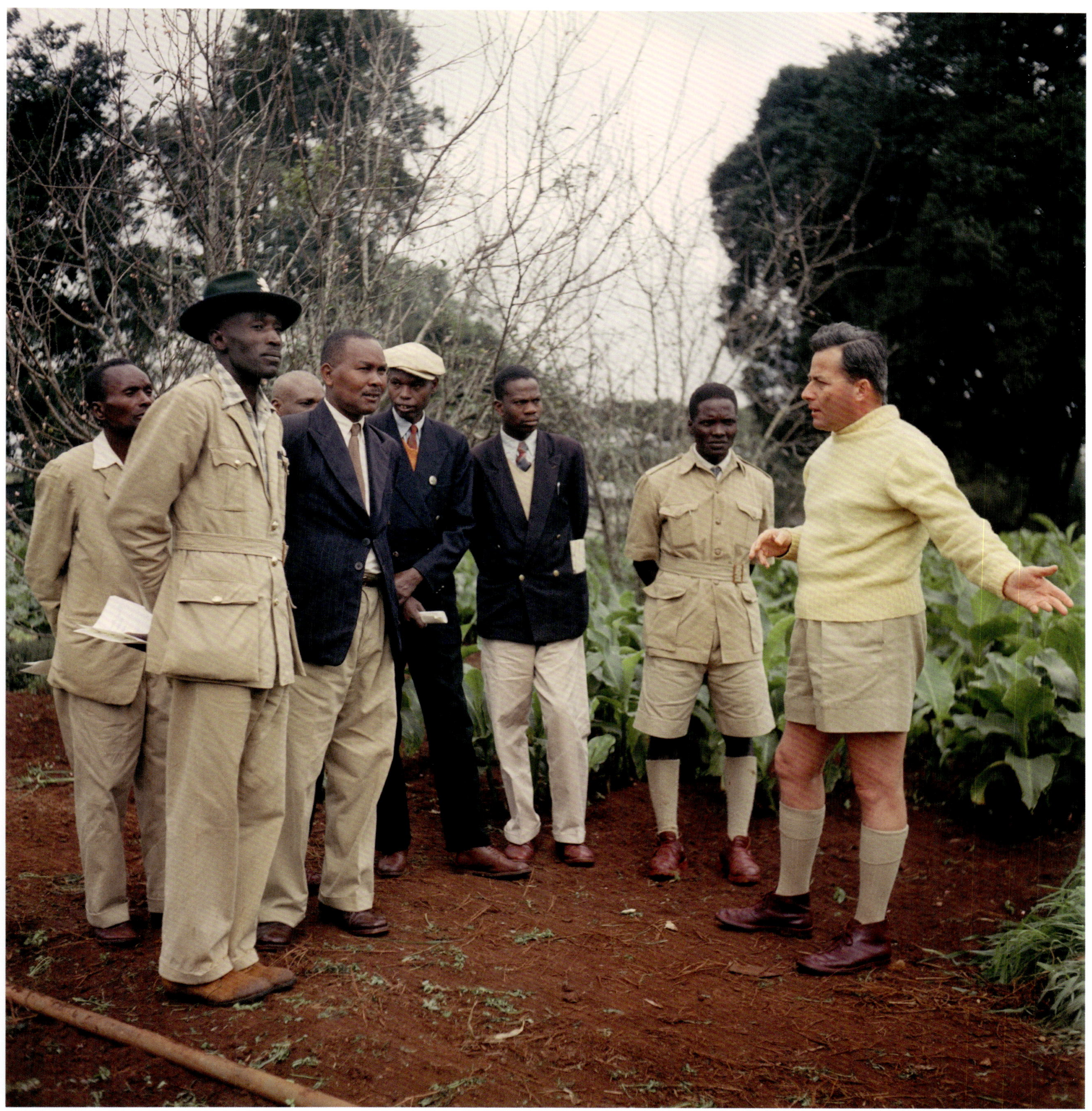

Todd Webb, *Untitled* (44UN-7903-389), Kenya, 1958
Group of Kenyan farmers visiting a British colonial-run farm, July 30.

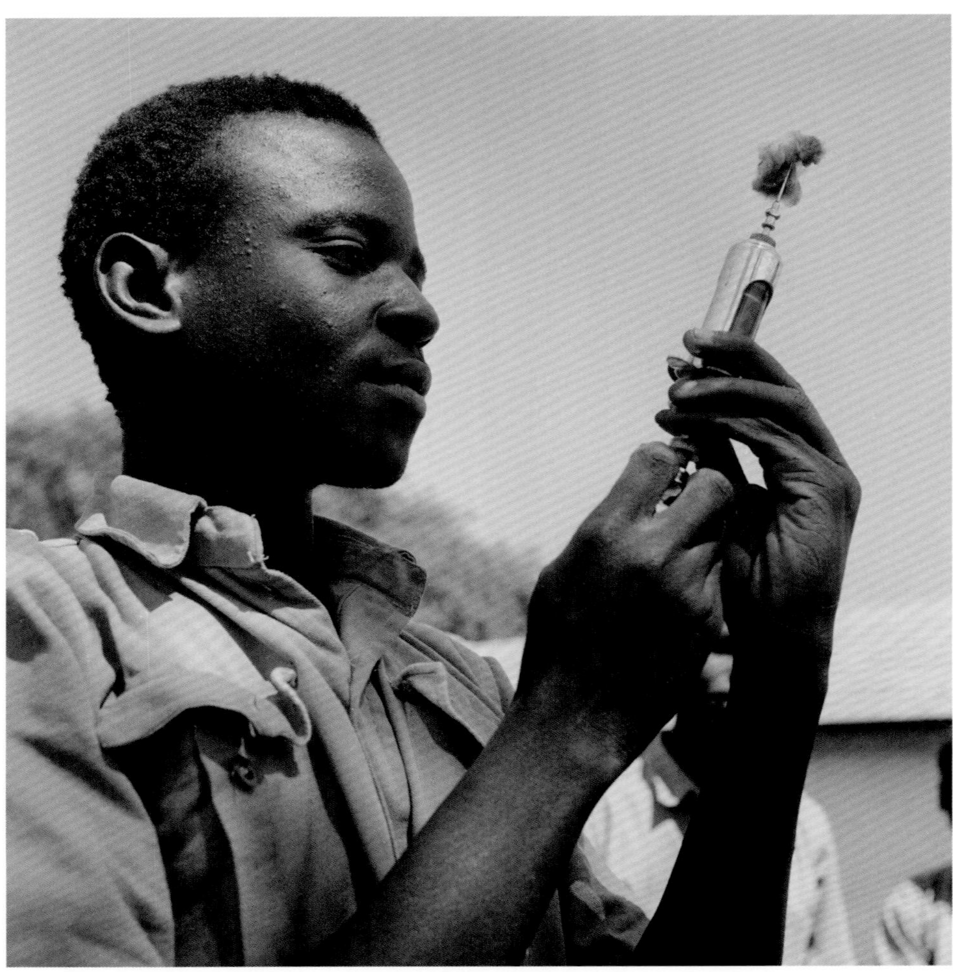

Todd Webb, *Untitled* (44UN-T2-24-656), Tanganyika (Tanzania), 1958
Veterinarian field worker with vaccination syringe.

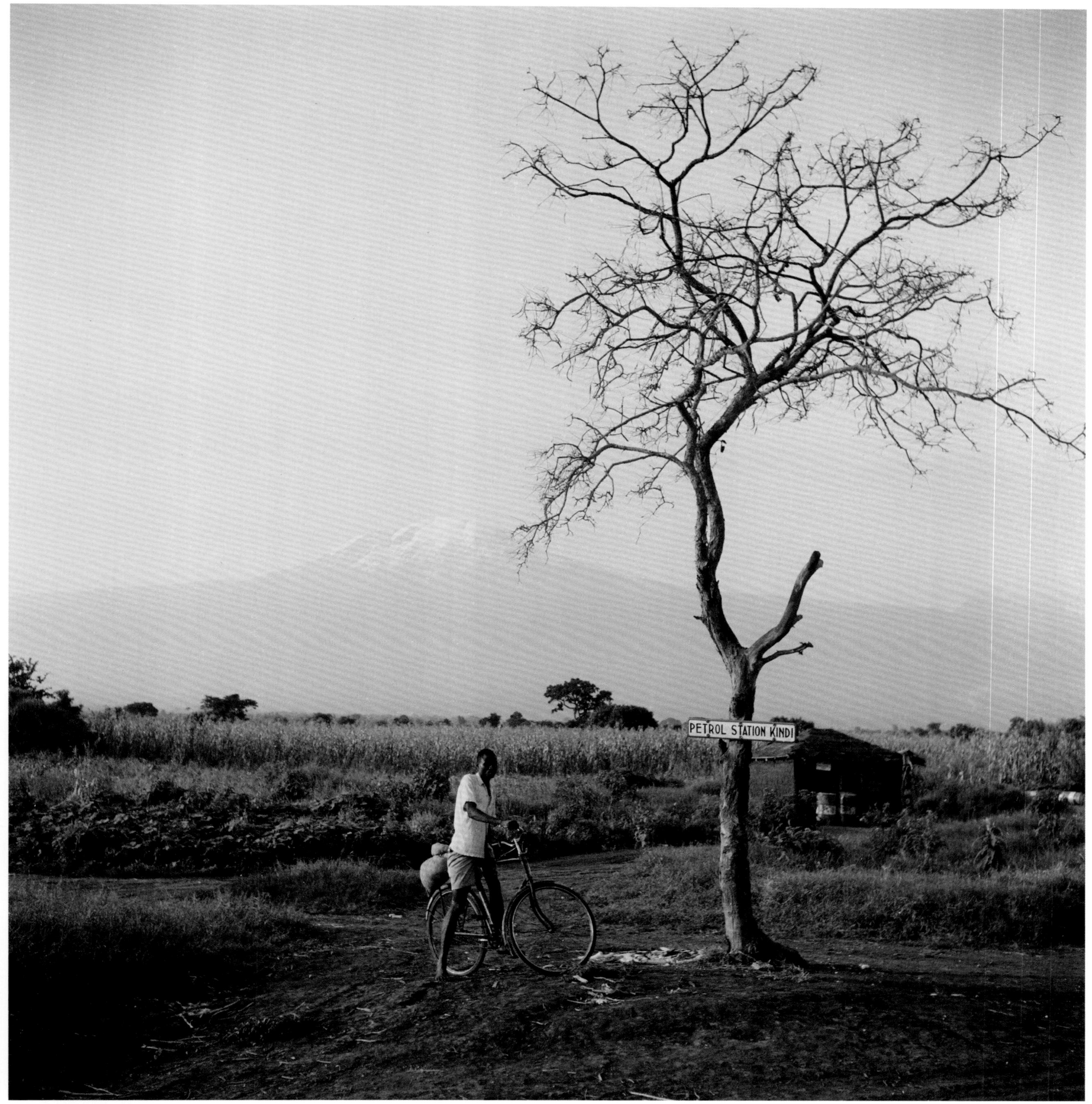

Todd Webb, *Untitled* (44UN-T2-R21-679), Tanganyika (Tanzania), 1958
Man pausing on his bike next to the rural "Petrol Station" with Mount Kilimanjaro in the distance, Kindi.

Todd Webb, *Untitled* (44UN-7942-003), Tanganyika (Tanzania), 1958
Mosque, with Kilimanjaro in the distance.

Todd Webb, Letter to Lucille Webb, Dar es Salaam, July 8, 1958
"...I like Dar. It has character.... Good architecture here—quite Moorish—or Middle East. But a beautiful sea. And it is soft—the whole feeling—the winds—the light and the spirit of the people. No rush or bustle—everything moves deliberately."

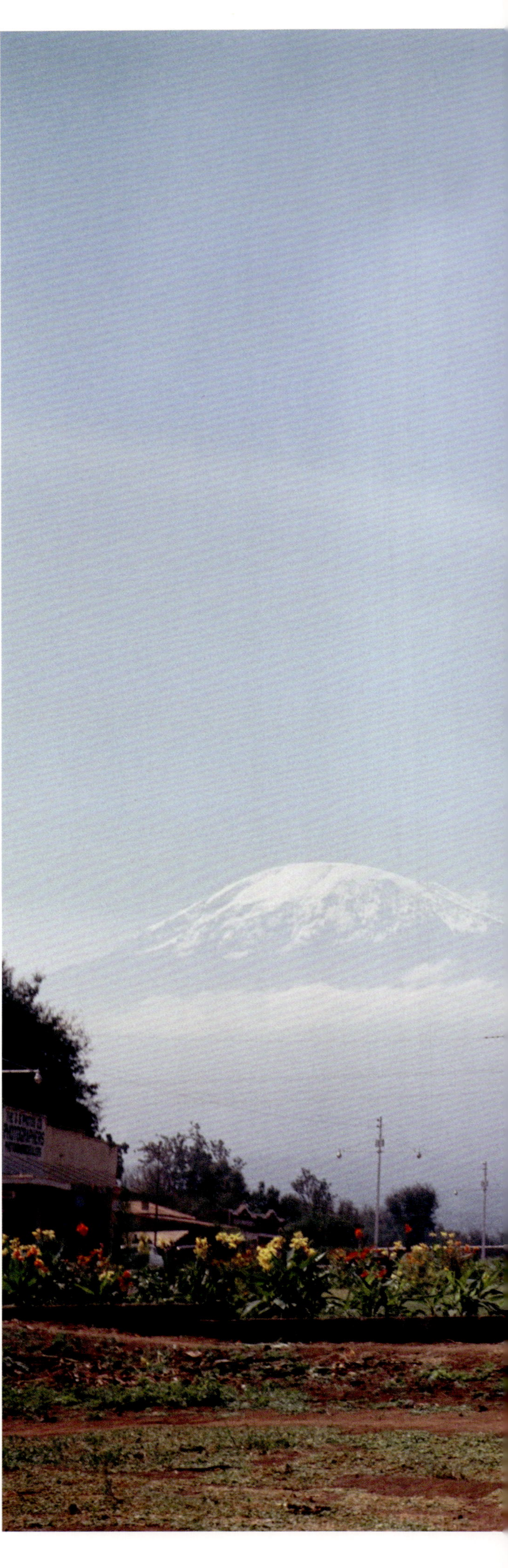

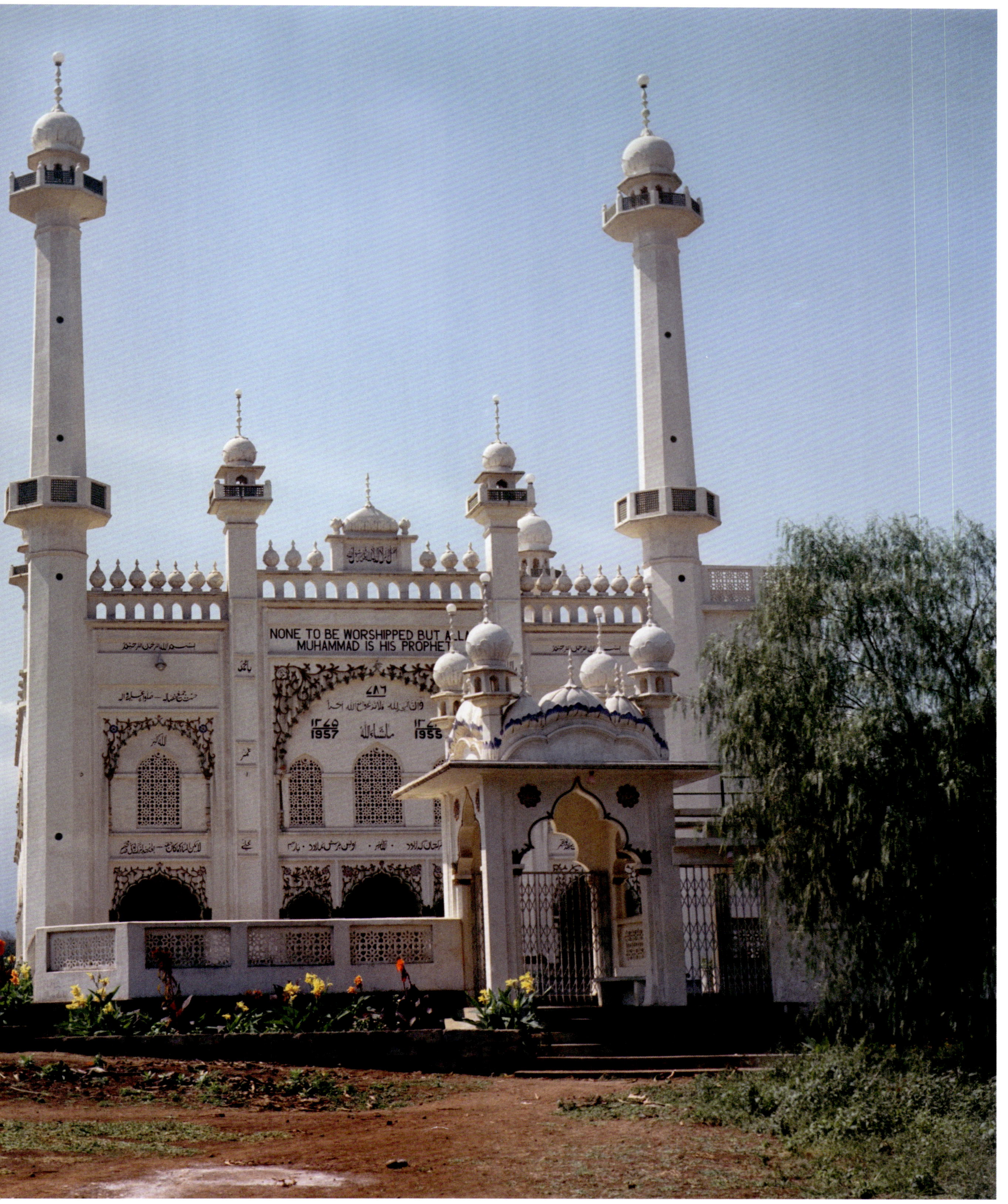
NONE TO BE WORSHIPPED BUT ALLA
MUHAMMAD IS HIS PROPHET
1957
1955

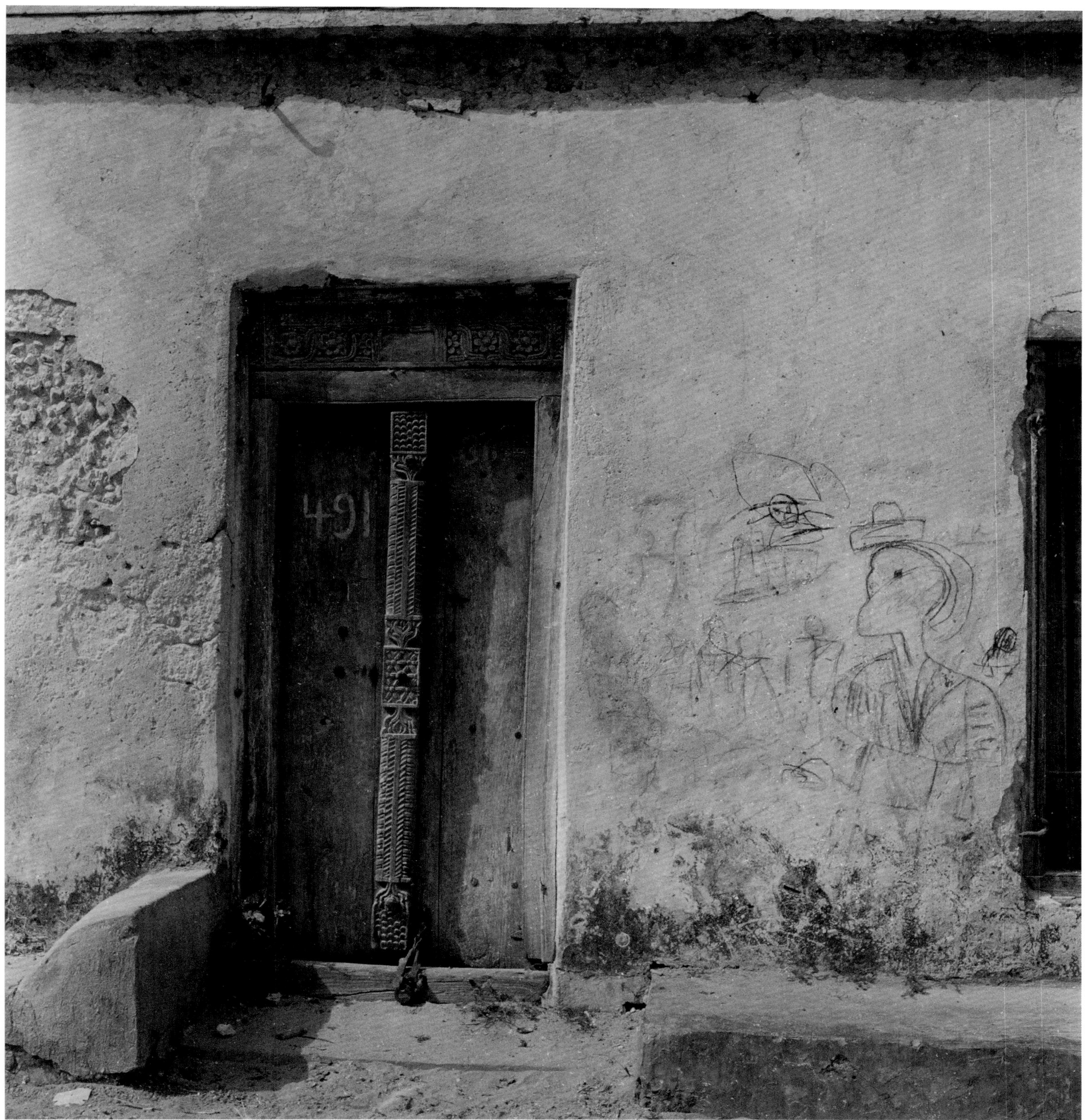

Todd Webb, *Untitled* (44UN-T1-R3-658), Zanzibar (Tanzania), 1958
Traditional wooden door and frame with graffiti on wall, Stone Town.

Listening to Todd Webb's Images of Tanganyika and Zanzibar

Rehema Chachage

Uncomfortable stares, lush landscapes, men in uniform, mowed lawns, colonial structures, projects, murals, ruins, order, silence. These are some of the things I was immediately confronted with upon my encounter with Todd Webb's images of what was the Tanganyika territory of British East Africa, as well as the Zanzibar protectorate.[1]

Encountering these images as a Tanzanian and as an artist, I view them with curiosity.

Webb captures these spaces in 1958, only three years before the country became independent and almost thirty years before I was born. In them, I see a time in history I have only encountered in books, images seen while researching for my own art practice, as well as heard and envisioned through oral stories. Despite this, and maybe mostly because of this, viewing these images also felt like a practice of revisiting a time in history that I once knew but can no longer recall. They feel familiar.

They are familiar in their portrayal of people that I recognize and yet don't recognize. Of people I am acquainted with through stories passed on across the generations—and those I don't know because their faces, names, and (hi)stories have disappeared into the pit of historical amnesia.

I see some of my relatives in these photographs. I feel the disparity in the reality the images capture. I am reminded of my Bibi Mkunde, of the smell of her warm, delicious baked goods, of her love, and her resilience.

Ultimately, what I am able to hear from listening to these images, in exercising Tina Campt's methodology of *listening* rather than looking at images, is a narration of two tales—that of the outsider and that of the insider. This essay attempts to bring a fresh perspective to these two tales and these two worlds. It also suggests the human and generational stories embedded within the images, and in so doing it activates these narratives in a new way.[2]

1. The Outsider's Tale

The outsider in this tale is the American photographer, Todd Webb.

Unlike the white, British colonial officials and settlers in Tanganyika (Tanzania) at the time (who Webb himself encountered and mentions in his letters and journals), Webb was visiting Tanganyika as a photographer on a commission from the United Nations Office of Public Information.

At the time of his assignment, Tanganyika was considered a trusteeship territory of the United Nations, administered by the British colonial government.[3]

Webb spent a few weeks in July 1958 traveling across Tanganyika and Zanzibar, photographing industry and technology and people in their communities.

The people of Tanganyika and Zanzibar are comprised of Africans (from over 120 ethnic groups), as well as people of South Asian (especially Indian and Pakistan) and Arab descent.

For his commission, Webb's directive was to document people in their communities with a "focus on workers and industries."[4] At the time, Tanganyika was a racially segregated society with white, colonial settlers at the top, those of Asian and Arab descent in the middle, and the African majority at the bottom, sustaining this uneven structure through their meagerly compensated labor. It is no wonder, then, that in Webb's charge to focus on industry, the Africans became a main subject of his camera's gaze. Arabs and Asians are missing from his images, with one exception in an image taken in Zanzibar, where he captures a man who appears to be of Asian origin.[5]

Webb's portrayal of Tanganyika's people and near-total exclusion of the Asian and Arab minority is worth mentioning here, since it exposes a very significant hierarchy that defined the country's race relations at the time—and to a large extent, continues to influence the complex dynamics of race and religion in the country today.

His images not only highlight these hierarchies, which placed Africans at the very bottom of the social ladder; they also participate in positioning the Arab and Asian people of Tanganyika as "outsiders," a position which has been problematized by many over the years.

The historical realities of these groups were indeed not comparable in the sense that the African majority of the country were unable to access the same opportunities as those of Arab or Indian descent; however, all groups are connected through the history of conquest and form part of contemporary Tanzanian identity—an identity characterized by hybridity and diverse origins.

By asking a question that is both sociological as well as historical, "when does a settler become a native?," Mahmood Mamdani reminds us of the interdependency that exists between the different groups of people who are often distinguished by "native" and "settler" labels.[6] These distinctions relate to the context of Tanzania when considering the positionality of Africans in relation to that of Arabs and Asians; and, I think, they might perhaps have been relevant to the thinking behind the UN's directive regarding whom Webb should photograph while in Tanganyika.

Webb's time in Tanganyika began in Dar es Salaam. He further described his travels in a letter to his wife Lucille: "my stops will be Zanzibar, the clove capital of Africa and island in the Indian ocean—supposed to be a sight, Tanga, a port town and center for tea and sisal, and Moshi, the coffee country...at the foot of the Kilimanjaro with opportunity for camping, safaris, and many animal sightings."[7]

Traveling under the aegis of the UN Office of Public Information, Webb finds himself a participant within these hierarchies—his race privileging him with experiences known only to those at the top of the social ladder. But one can safely conclude that although he was couched within these hierarchies, he was not completely blind to them. In one of his letters to Lucille, we see that Webb in many ways positioned himself as an outsider to both the British colonials and American expatriates, writing:

> Some of the English people out here are very funny. Lots of hyphenated names, monocle-wearing blokes. They are public servants, but they are so intent on upholding the prestige of the British crown that they have illusions of royalty. I like some of them in spite of the airs, but some of the American needlers are hard to bear. They have seen and been taken in by too many Hollywood films. They are the first to brag about paying the cook 30 shillings a month ($4.20) and they are also the first to point at me with a nasty sneer and say, "How about Little Rock, Yank."[8]

From his letters and journals, Webb describes working and making friendships with British civil servants, enjoying the hospitality that was offered to him by the British colonial government, and living well in big, clean rooms, some with balconies and views. He watched the sun set behind Kilimanjaro, rode a rickshaw in Zanzibar, enjoyed a safari traveling from Moshi to Monduli, "Ngurdoto" [sic] (Ngorongoro) Crater, Karatu, and Lake Duluti, and enjoyed all that the land had to offer, from the fresh food that was cooked for him at the hotels where he stayed, to the tropical fruits, some of which he had never tasted before.

These experiences were not new to the expatriates of colonial times or even present-day Tanzania. In *Life in Tanganyika in the Fifties: My Reflections and Narratives from the White Settler Community and Others*, for instance, Godfrey Mwakikagile narrates life in colonial Tanganyika. He includes narratives from the white settler community, many of whom grew up and are nostalgic for the life they had in colonial Tanganyika. Describing their experiences, which in many instances do not differ much from those

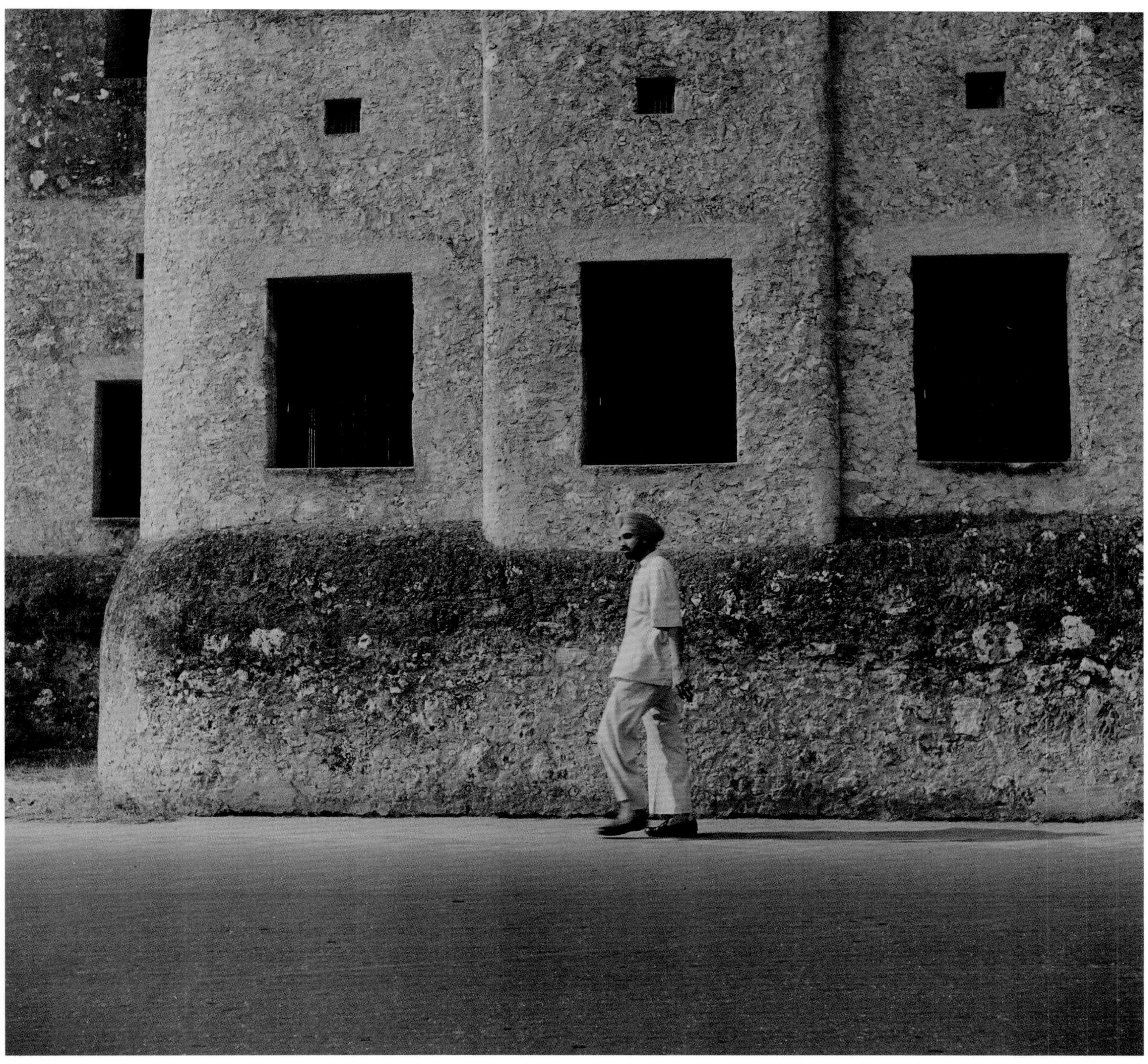

Todd Webb, *Untitled* (44UN-44A-58), Zanzibar (Tanzania), 1958
Man walking on a street in Stone Town.

Webb describes, the overall consensus for many of them is that life in colonial Tanganyika was one of freedom and possibilities, with terms like "good," "safe," "happy," "care-free," and "privileged" recurring.[9]

In total, Webb had traveled to eight African countries. He traveled from Togoland (Togo) to Ghana, Sudan, Trust Territory of Somaliland (Somalia), and Southern and Northern Rhodesia (Zimbabwe and Zambia respectively), then arrived in Tanganyika and Zanzibar, and afterwards ended his trip in Kenya. He notes more than once that of all the African countries he visited, he had by far the best experiences in Tanganyika. Repeatedly comparing his experiences of Tanganyika to that of Rhodesia, Webb wrote while in Dar es Salaam: "...Tanganyika. I like it much better that Rhodesia in spite of the crude facilities...of course, the race business was much worse there than here. This is more like I feel Africa should be."[10]

2. The Tale from the Inside

The majority of Tanganyika's people, whose labor was exploited for the sustenance of the colonial project, were dispossessed of Webb's grand colonial experiences.

Webb captures these people in their roles as cleaners, farmers, security guards, lawn mowers, street cleaners, factory workers, and so on (see p. 198). From the images, it is unclear whether or not they were aware of his presence or asked to pose for the camera. However, from the awkward and at times *tense* poses and stares the individuals give in some of these images, it is quite obvious that not all of them were entirely comfortable with being photographed.[11]

In the image of a police officer with a portable telephone, for example, one can feel the discomfort communicated through this man's smile, which does not appear to be a complete one (see p. 194). Rather than *trying* to smile, he looks like he was instead about to say something but stopped from doing so as the shutter of the camera released. His slightly furrowed brows, as well as the half-open, half-closed eyes are further evidence of his unease. Holding the phone, his arm communicates a tension through its grip.

This man was photographed twice by Webb, but the awkwardness and discomfort are more visible in the first image than in the second (opposite). In the black and white photograph, his eyes, brows, and grip on the phone appear to be a little more relaxed, but his smile is less so. This image also captures a man in the background, who seems to be communicating his own discomfort through his stern stare and an intense furrowing of the brows.

In *Listening to Images*, Tina Campt argues for ways to bring sound and dignity to the people without voices in historic photographs through the process of *listening*. She invites us to embrace a different understanding of photographs by listening to and not just simply looking at what she refers to as "quiet photography."[12] It is through this method, Campt argues, that we are able to open up the "radical interpretive possibilities of images and... archives that we are most often inclined to overlook."[13]

Noting the quiet stasis displayed by many of the images discussed in her book, Campt identifies the frequency vibrated by such images as that of a "muscular tension," which encourages its viewers to approach the subjects' poses as "visible manifestations of psychic and physical responses (rather than submission) to colonization and...ethnographic gazes."[14]

Listening to Webb's images, one can see how the "muscular tensions" Campt describes, such as the man's grip of the telephone, were mobilized as a display of "an effortful balancing of compulsion, constraint, and refusal that vibrates unvisibly yet resoundingly through these images. They are tensions that are not necessarily accessible when we focus on the visualization of stillness. They become perceptible only when we attend to the quiet frequencies of stasis."[15]

For many of these people, tension may have been a form of rebellion, albeit subtle, which refused the very terms of photographic subjection that Webb's commission was perhaps engineered to produce. As if they were saying, "we are much more than this photograph."

And indeed, they were so much more than what Webb's camera was able to capture. They were also mothers, fathers, sons, daughters, husbands, wives, sisters, brothers, neighbors, lovers, friends, confidantes.... Their lives were filled with love. They had hopes. They had dreams.

Listening to the two images Webb took of building murals in a rural village, which also exist as "living-proof" in bell hooks's sense of the word, we are able to catch a glimpse of the overlooked stories of these people's lives, of this side that makes them so much more than what Webb's photographs (*of* them) were able to capture.[16]

Painted in the murals are several scenes from what appears to be everyday life. Traditional beer is prepared and shared, a woman drinks beer while sitting on a man's lap, another woman feeds beer to a man who is playing the guitar (see p. 220). A healer, or perhaps an elder, feeds what appears to be medicine to a man. Goods are exchanged in the market. Tasks are shared in the kitchen between a mother and daughter, or perhaps between two sisters, or an aunty and niece, or a grandmother and grandchild. A man and woman, perhaps man and wife, walk side by side. A woman wears a buibui (abaya). Men wear kanzu and kofia, traditional long robes and hats.

In the murals we see the expression of community, joy, love, relationships, friendship, camaraderie, family, prayer, art, and music. These are some of the things that have been largely excluded in the canon of history, as well as in archived material, and are the nuances which, I feel, are missing in Webb's portrayal of Tanganyika's people.[17]

3. A Real Tale

The two women painted in the murals (the ones who share tasks in the kitchen) remind me of my many visits to Bibi Mkunde's house and of her kitchen (whose activities often extend to the outside, just like in the mural), which we treat as an intimate space where bonding between members of the family and the passing down of stories, recipes, as well as the spirit of generosity, can occur.[18]

Triggered for me by this memory of my Bibi's kitchen is also a longing for her cakes, which are so distinctive in taste. I still have not managed to find anything similar anywhere else.[19]

You see, my Bibi was excellent at baking.

Excellent is a relative term of course, but she was excellent by my standards and those of my family. In fact, my Bibi is still quite good at baking, but given her age, her craft is now not as polished as it once was. Instead, the mantle has been passed onto the next generation. Taking after my grandmother in many ways including her given name, my sister is also an excellent baker!

I have often asked my mother and other members of my family for the origin story of Bibi Mkunde's baking skills. For me, baking is a science that requires precise measurements of weight, volume, and temperature. For this reason, I had never associated the craft as something "god-given," but rather as a transferrable skill that one has learned and perfected over time. This was my assumption anyway. And it must have been the understanding for several members of my family, because Bibi Mkunde's craft has always been traced back to her background as a worker for the local mission and the women's program run by her church.

As I have relatively recently discovered, my Bibi was a domestic worker.

From the age of thirteen to the age of seventeen, Bibi Mkunde went from her mother's house to the Christian mission to do domestic work in harsh and discriminatory conditions—performing duties that were degrading and well below her worth as a human being.

Bibi Mkunde walked to work from her mother, Bibi Orupa's house, located in Suji, a village in the Pare mountains, in the Kilimanjaro region. The house, along with those of many other people in the village, was separated by a

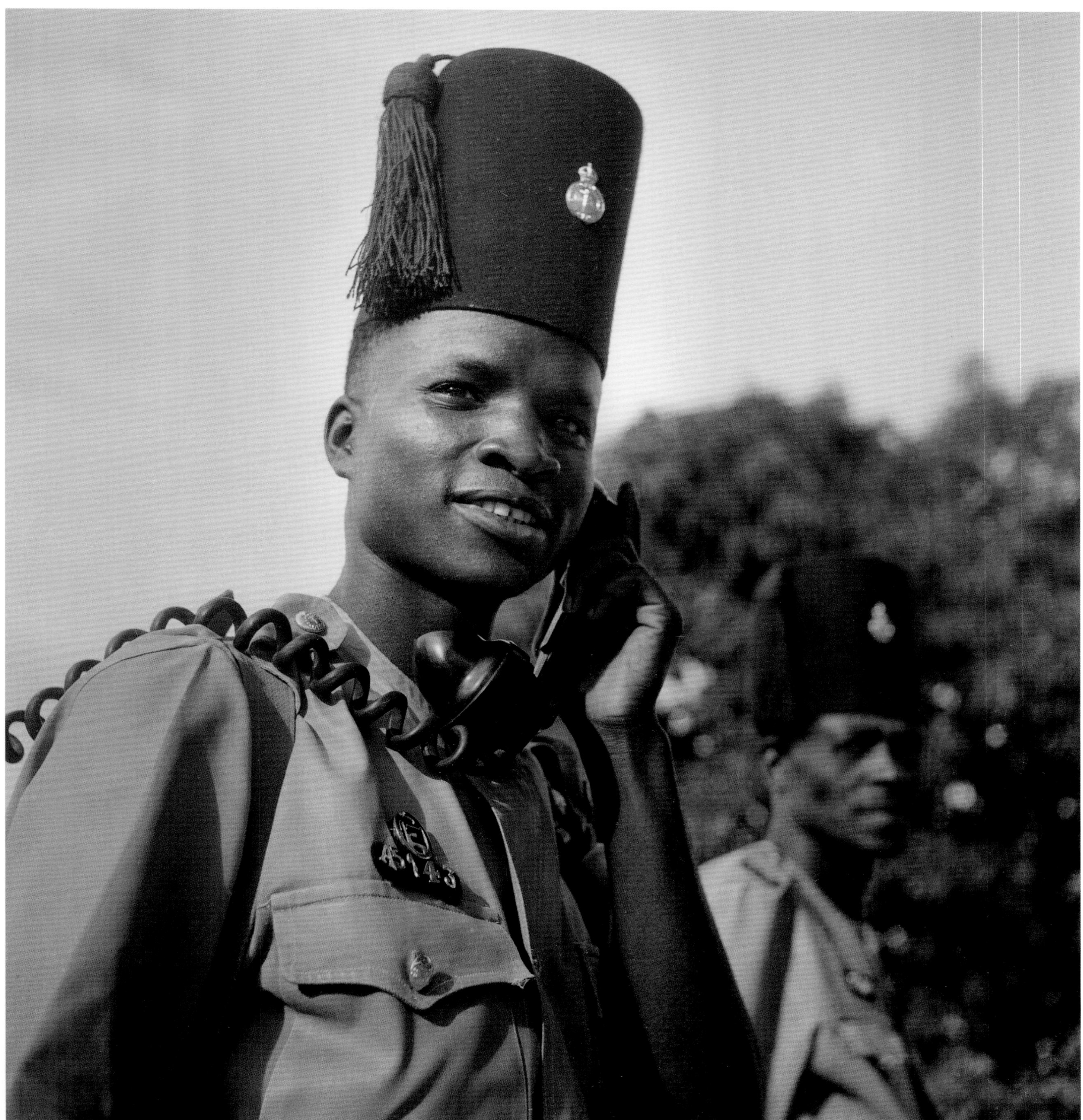

Todd Webb, *Untitled* (44UN-R4-001), Tanganyika (Tanzania), 1958
Tanganyika police officer using a field telephone.

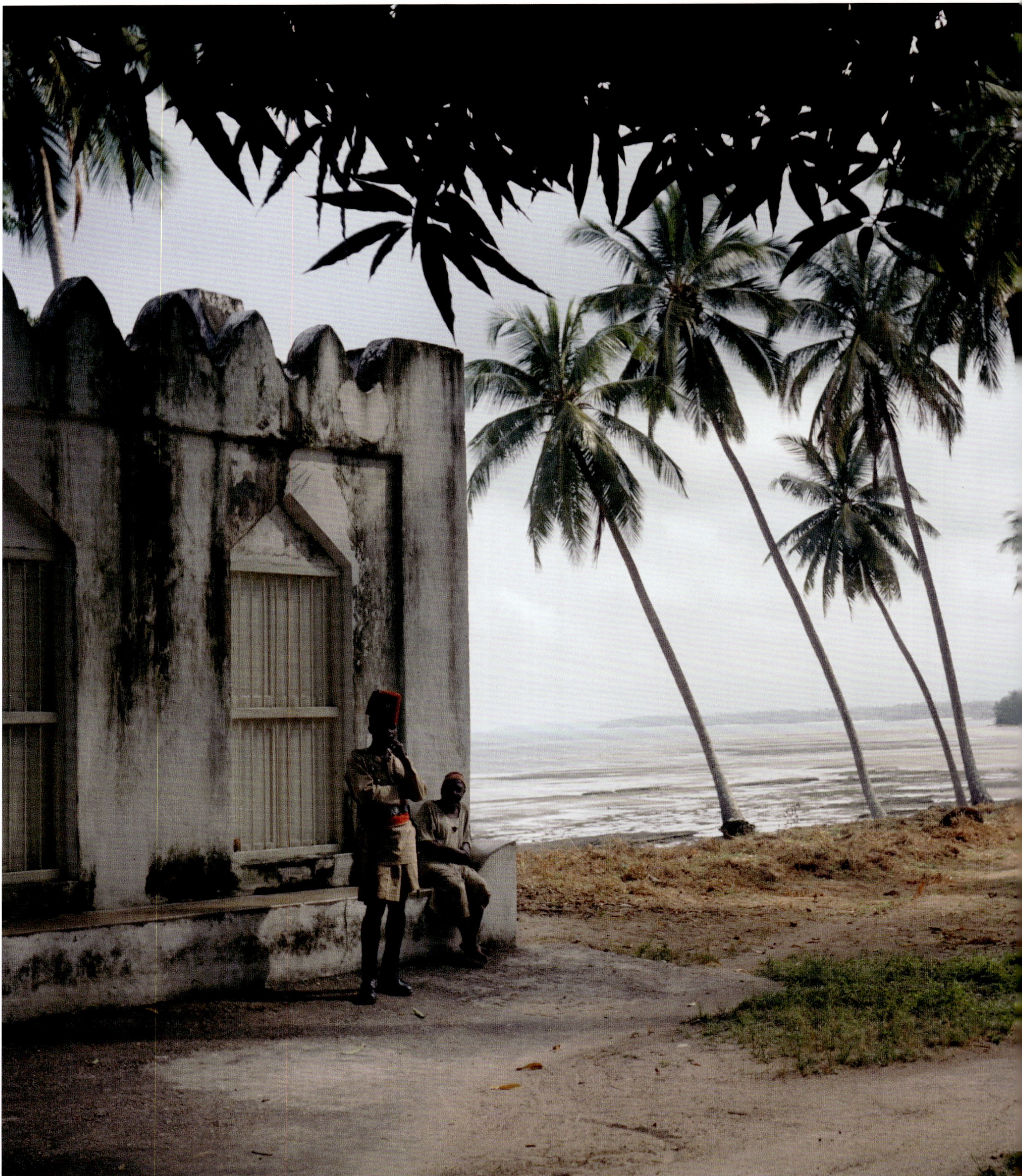

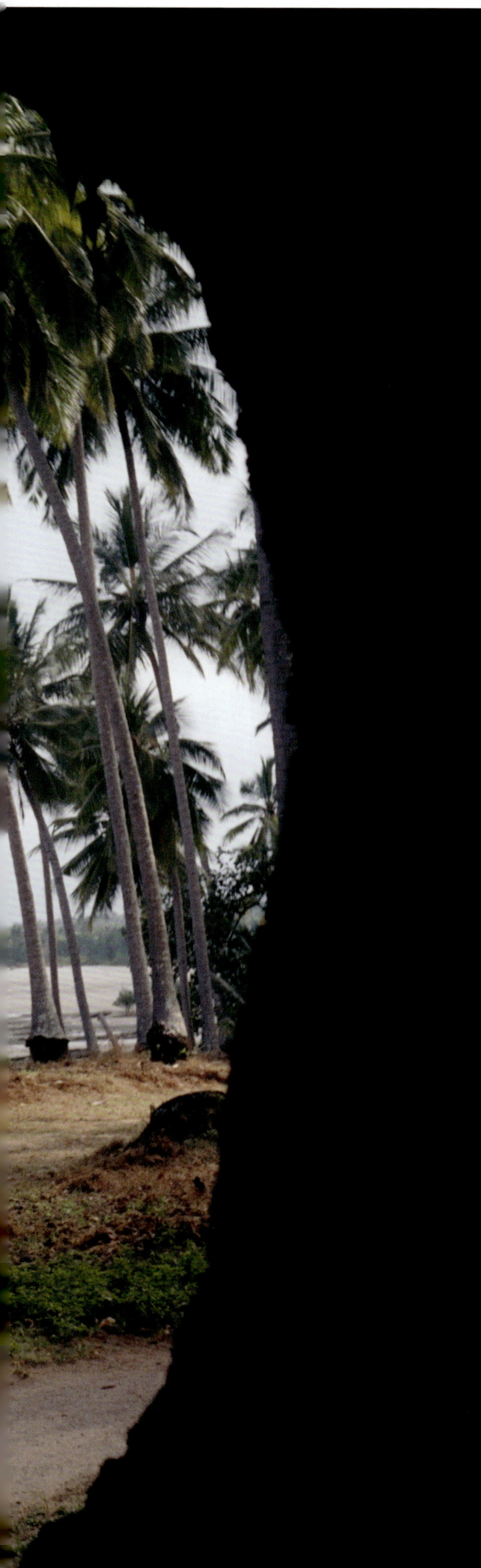

street from the Seventh Day Adventist mission, which was distinguished by its clean, European-style plan, which included a school, dispensary, church, several two-story houses, and the white Christian missionaries who inhabited them.

For five years of her life Bibi Mkunde performed domestic work for this mission. When she married my Babu, both of them were absent from home.[20] Working as a district authority employee as a veterinarian field worker, Babu was regularly posted to different villages, which meant extended periods of absence from his home.

Baking is a science. But it is also an exercise of care and love—sometimes enough to be a form of survival.[21] For many years of her life, my Bibi had turned a skill she had acquired (and perfected) from her background as a domestic worker into an exercise of care and love, presented as warm delicious baked goods carried in her basket whenever she traveled to visit her people—her mother, siblings, children, husband, friends, and us, her grandchildren.

I believe that personal stories like that of my Bibi are the unheard narratives of the people Webb captured in his images. These are the stories we do not fully hear in the photographs, the ones that capture the active, resilient spirits, possessing the dynamism to employ whatever means necessary to not only accommodate but also subvert the very systems designed to dispossess them as a people. They are the stories I wish I could have seen and heard more of.

Through Webb's commission, we experience first-hand some of the mechanisms behind silences that enter the process of historical production, making some narratives worthy enough to pass as history while others remain overlooked. It is precisely in response to such silences that I take the opportunity to speak my Bibi's name in this essay (as I have often done in my artworks), as well as the names of the many women and men who have walked this earth before me (and paved the way for me). I do so because history and historians have overlooked the (hi)stories tied to people like my Bibi and Babu for long enough.

Todd Webb, *Untitled* (44UN-8014-463), Tanganyika (Tanzania), 1958
Tanganyika police officer and man next to a wall near the Indian Ocean coastline.

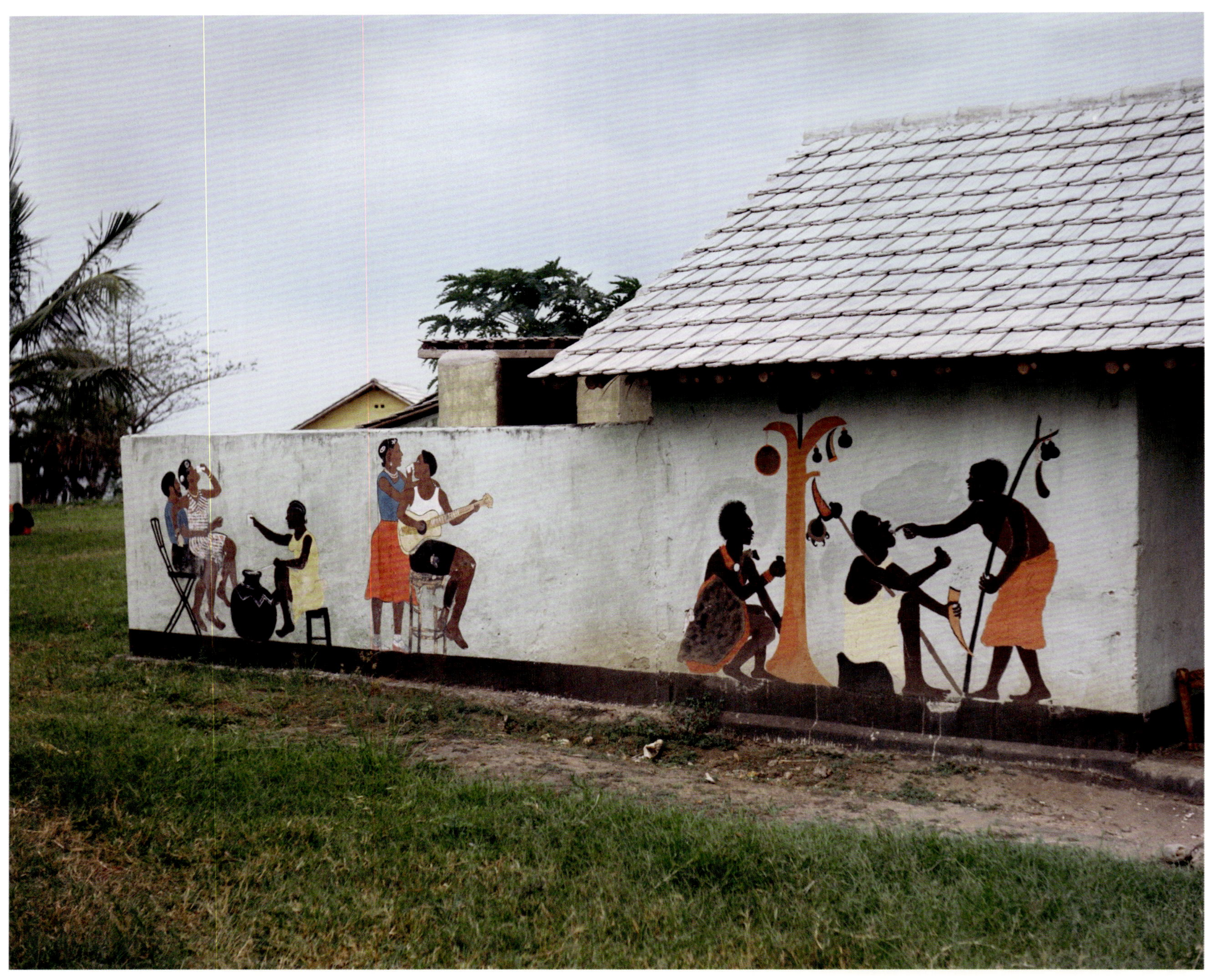

Todd Webb, *Untitled* (44UN-7732-030), Tanganyika (Tanzania)
House with wall mural showing a bar scene and indigenous healer at work, Kingoni village.

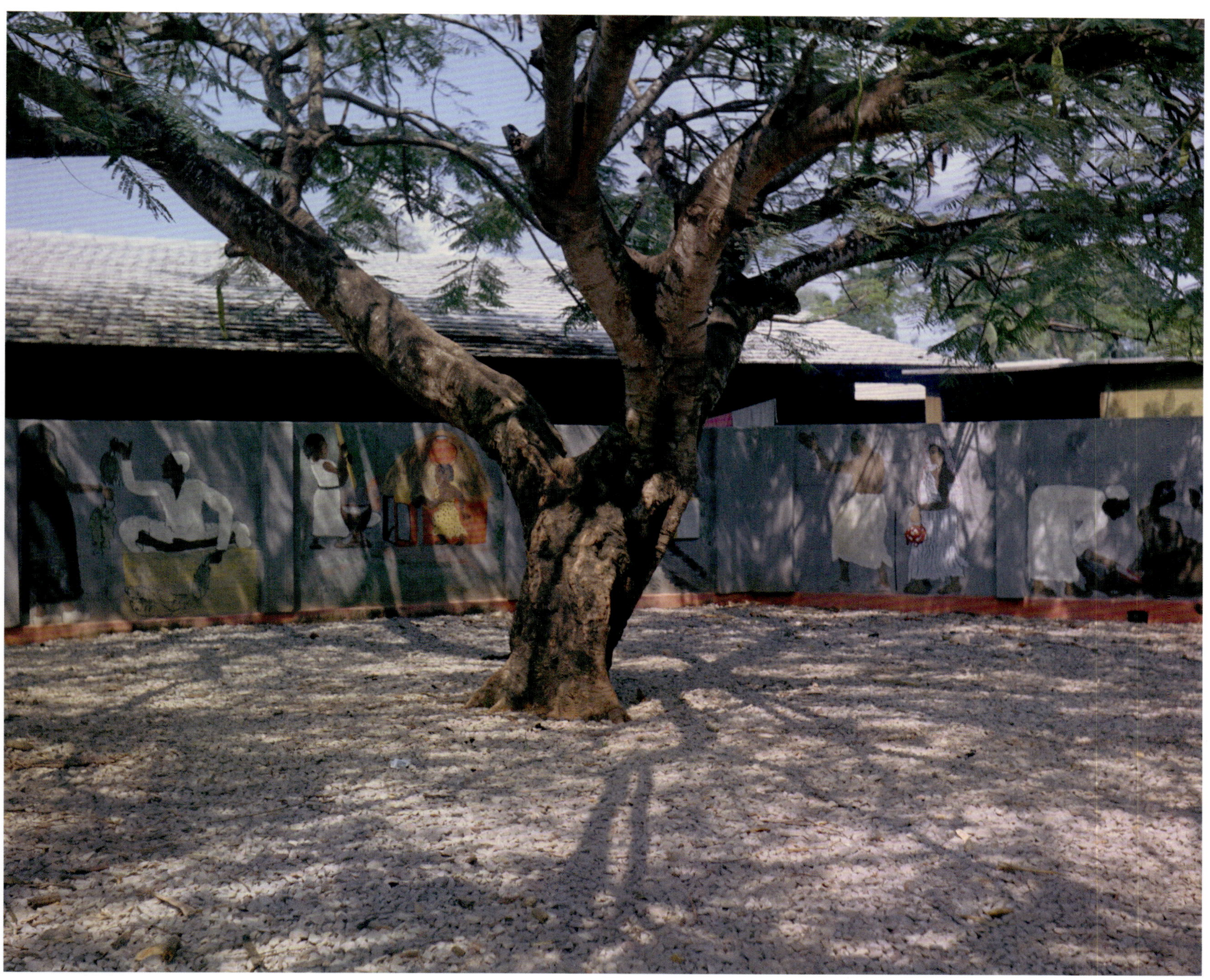

Todd Webb, *Untitled* (44UN-7733-021), Tanganyika (Tanzania), 1958
Tree in courtyard with a wall mural, Kingoni village.

Mileage from Here: Nine Narratives

Emmanuel Iduma

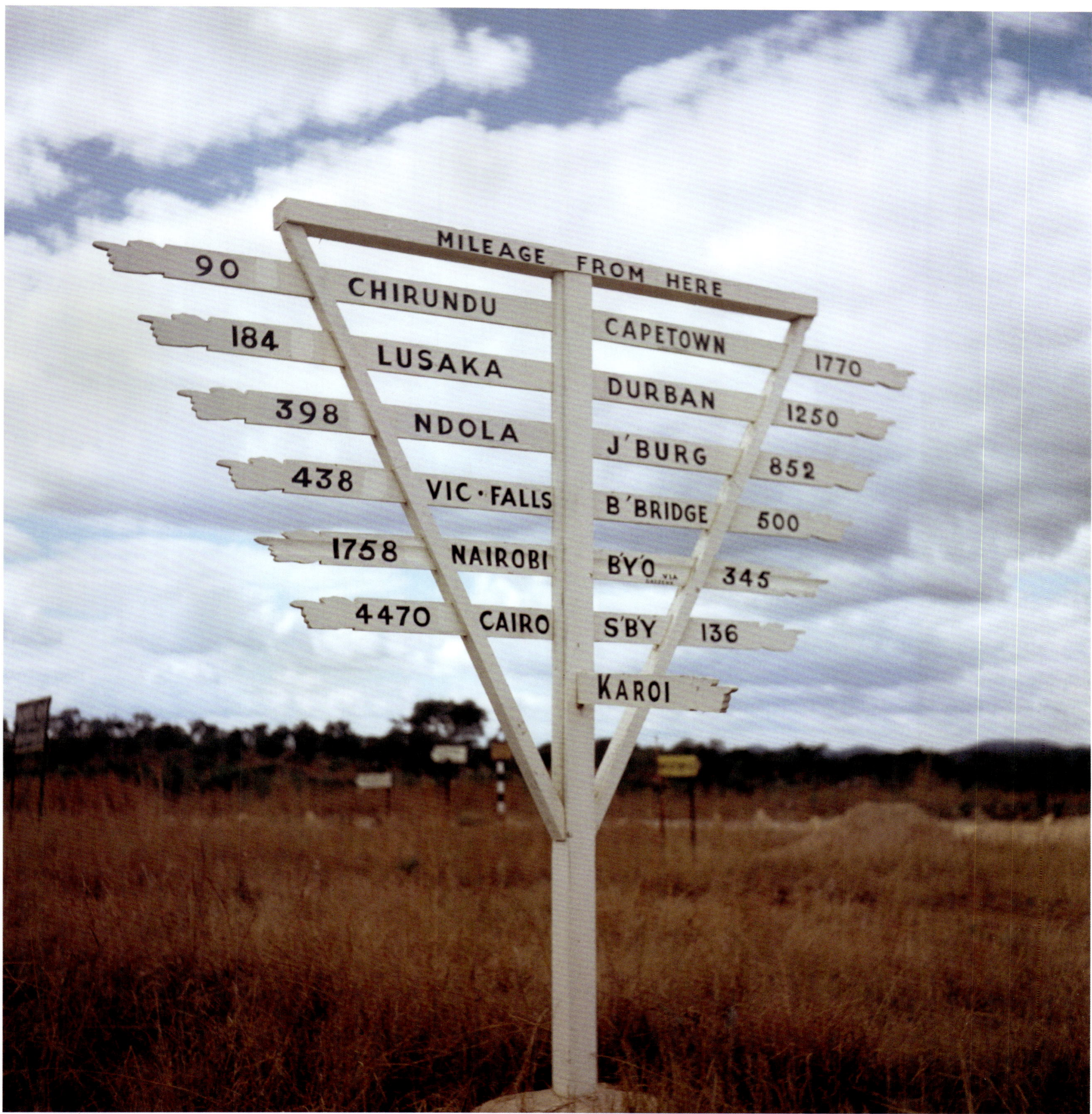

Todd Webb, *Untitled* (44UN-7994-506), Southern Rhodesia (Zimbabwe), 1958
"Mileage From Here" sign near Karoi.

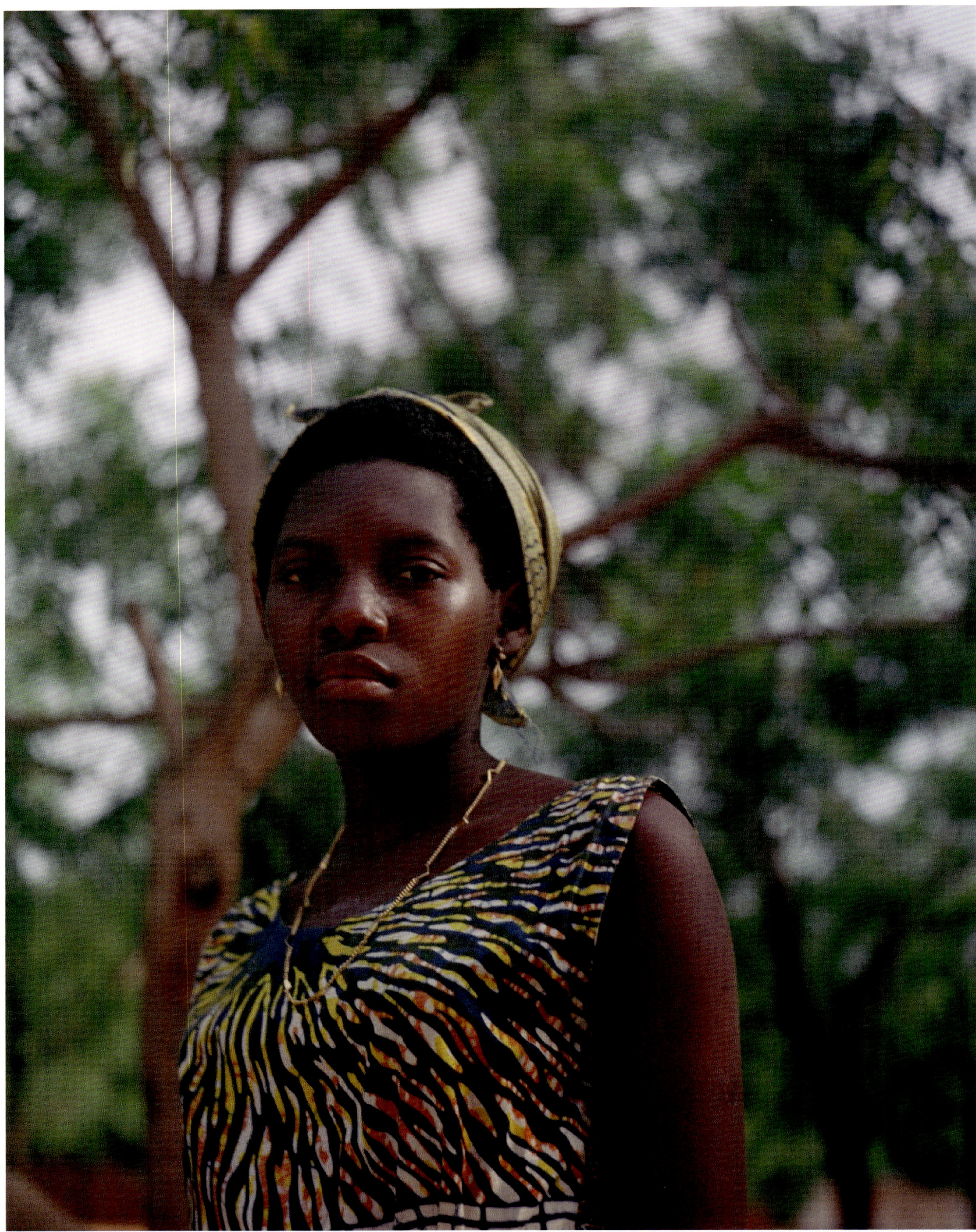

KEEPSAKE

B.'s wife is gone.

While in New York for graduate school, she sent him several dozen photographs of herself. In the summers she'd ask a passer-by to take a photo of her for him, and the city would seem to enfold her in a wide embrace, her smile like a pockmarked glint. During the winters she'd bring her face so close to the camera he could sometimes see crumbs of food on her upper lip, as if she held a half-eaten sandwich in her free hand. In either case he was amused by her need to send keepsakes to him. He would have that thought long enough to feel guilty for not measuring up, at which point he would send back a photo of himself, sometimes the same one he'd sent the previous week. She never complained.

All that fussing over keepsakes has become unnecessary.

Once when they lay on the asphalt, those years ago when neither had declared love for the other, they tried to distinguish one star from another. Once—again when their love was undeclared—she let him take selfies of their faces together, so close he wondered if she would flinch from the bristles of his closely shaven skin. One day he remarked that she hadn't smiled in any of their pictures together. She warned, in response, that he mustn't assume that her unsmiling face was an expression of disdain. Instead, a measure of feeling. This is what he remembers of what she said, and he is unconcerned that in her absence he has produced new versions of their past. What matters is that to linger on any portrait she left behind is to wait for the moment grief reenters a cosmos of tenderness. Lying on the asphalt they believed they could mark the pathways made by stars as they fell to their resting place.

He remembers everything. What occurs to him is like an album of old photographs, peopled with strangers in remote places, to whom he may allot their past. He has become insomniac from a slideshow of memories.

To hold in esteem is not necessarily to be in love. But no one in love will shy from looking as if they hold their beloved, or hope to be held, in esteem.

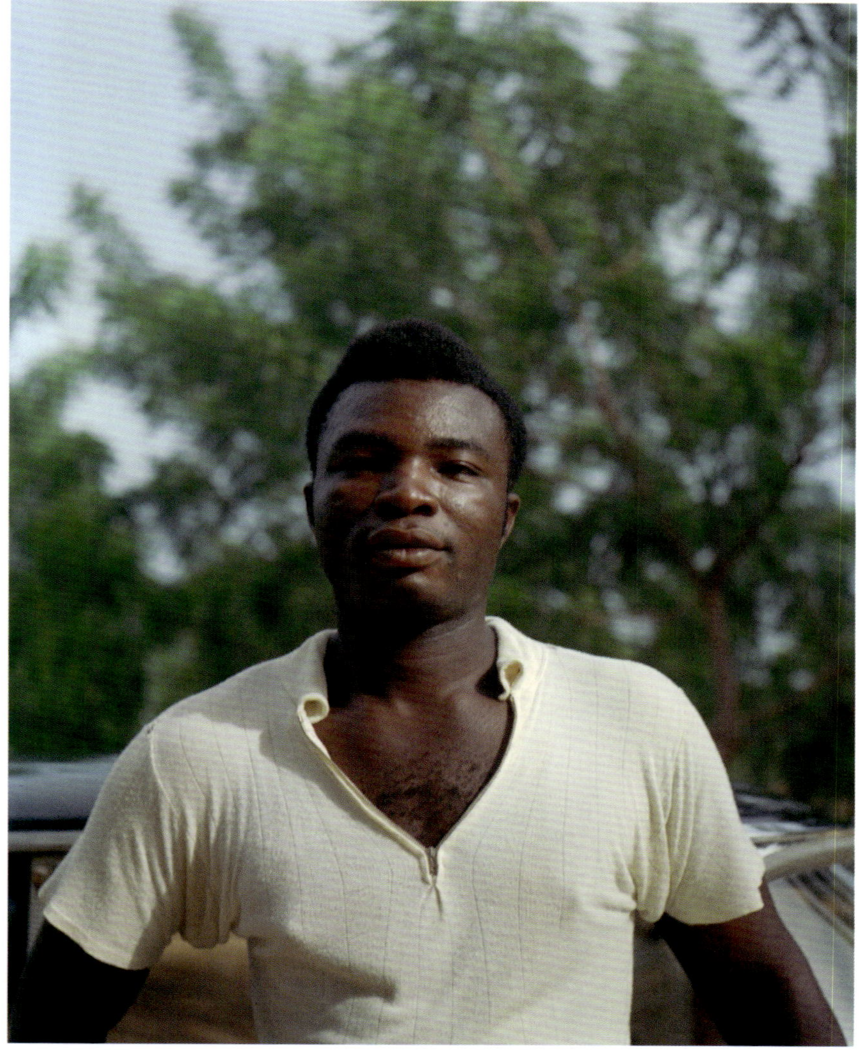

Opposite: Todd Webb, *Untitled* (44UN-7907-144), Togoland (Togo), 1958
Portrait of a woman.

Above: Todd Webb, *Untitled* (44UN-7907-145), Togoland (Togo), 1958
Portrait of a man.

A FACE IN PROFILE

If anything came close to a ritual the first year of their marriage, it was weekend trips to Labadi Beach to draw. She owned a Volkswagen then, a Beetle, and they hauled easels into the trunk. But the large rolls of paper she would hand to him, once he sat firmly in the passenger seat.

During the hours of working they paid little attention to each other. If the corner of her eye searched him out it was only to confirm his work hadn't been hampered. The ocean was difficult to please. There were days when the first stroke of her drawing was made with the edge of a brush and the last with the tip of a blunt pencil. He does not remember a yacht or surfer appearing in any of her pictures—only waves.

Once, when he watched her draw, he saw that she had stayed unmoving, and her head was pressed close to the sheet in front of him. No word or utterance, but breath. She was poised that way for no less than a minute. He wished to call to her, but feared that if he did, he would foil her concentration.

After two years he stopped going with her. By then he had come to understand that her need for persisting in depicting the onrush of waves wasn't his. He made sketches of the touch of skyscrapers against the sky, as far as his eyes could see. But he'd rather be painting squares with restrained tones. Not so for her. It didn't seem to matter how long she kept looking at the ocean. If the ocean repeated its scurrying, so would she. If the ocean's form appeared unerring, so would she, her hand seeking natural forms. He didn't have her patience, her pact with longevity.

Weeks after he stopped accompanying her, he noticed a new obsession. She returned with sketches of a face, drawn in profile. The ocean had led to a face. Once he let her go alone, she changed the subject.

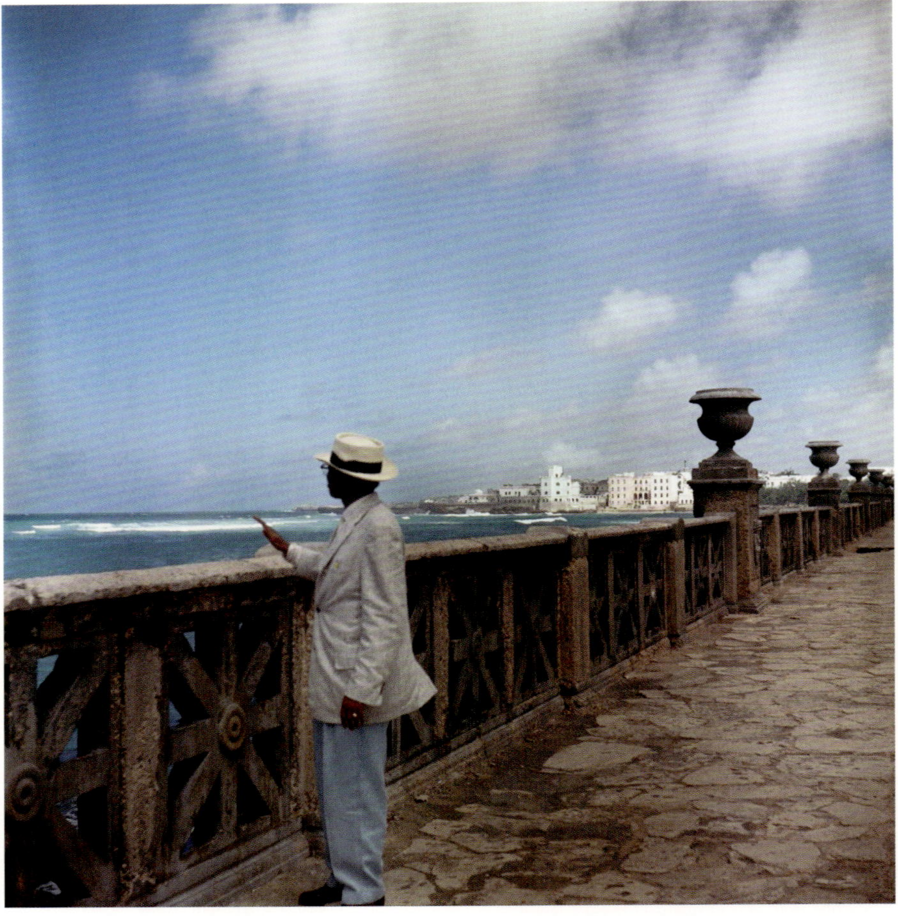

Todd Webb, *Untitled* (44UN-7966-352), Trust Territory of Somaliland (Somalia), 1958
Man in a suit and hat looking out over the fishing harbor, Mogadishu.

His studio has changed in form. Crowded with shelves when she was still here, it is now cleared of all except a large worktable, one against which he can work standing. And besides the settee where he often sits, and a little stool at a corner, he's allowed no other furniture. On the worktable there are several paper types—crepe, matte, manila—laid out on a grid. From the distance of the doorway a passer-by could see on each the outline of a face.

Alone he returns to the quayside, to watch from afar a view of the beach. Sometimes, absent-minded, he holds out a hand, letting it hang awhile. On most visits he thinks of the faces she had drawn. None had looked like him, even in profile, as though she had aimed to preserve his anonymity.

PRESENCE

He never met his father. But once, in his early thirties, he was waiting in a corner of a railway station, for what or whom he couldn't recall. He had his back to the window, and the sharp evening light had thrown an outline of his head against the adjacent wall. The light played a trick on him. His head became one of many. The illusion was so startling he swears to have seen faces of all the men he had ever known for more than a casual hello. Where was his father's face? He reached for a personality he knew for certain and found it obscure. Not just a face; a manner of appearance. Yet, face and gesture were repressed, and he struggled with hints of a presence. How could this be? What is the memory of a face that has never been beheld?

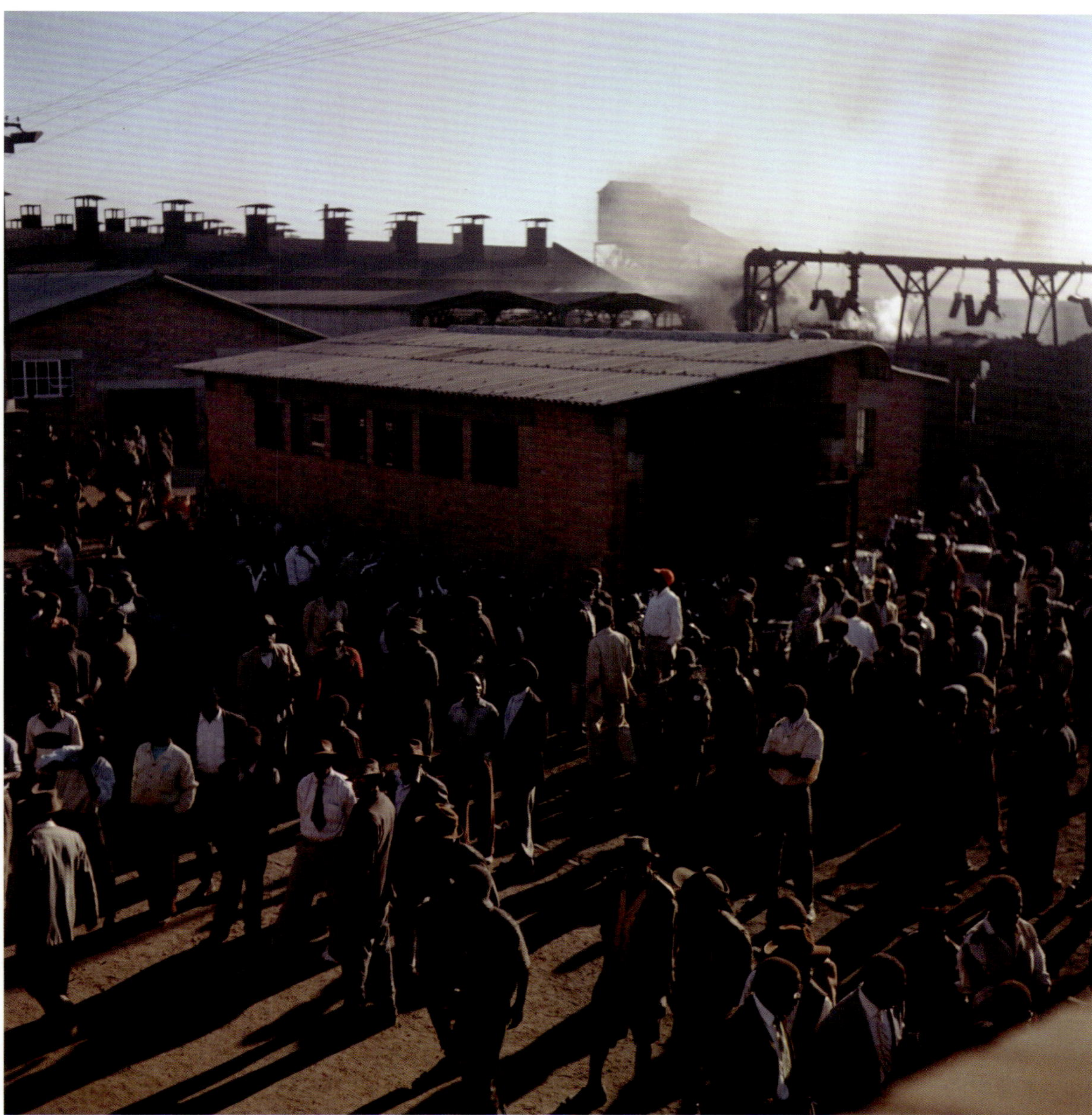

Todd Webb, *Untitled* (44UN-7990-207), Northern Rhodesia (Zambia), 1958
Workers awaiting the train near a copper mine.

ETERNITY

In the dream B. has a week before her funeral, he is with her relatives, and they have encircled her corpse. They are checking for the onset and extent of rigor mortis. He is pulling the upright arm downwards; someone is trying to relax the jaw, another to shut the eye, the other to straighten the legs. They go about this unspeaking, each to their assigned region of the body. He wakes with dread.

Then, days after the funeral, while in a car, he closes his eyes awhile, swimming in that state between dream and mirage. He sees his wife's smiling face and at once snaps his eyes open. It is brief, the snatch of a vision, a slight distance between eye and eyelid. He fears he'll return to his earlier dread if he'd kept his eyes shut any longer. But what he perceives, most of all, is that no matter how slight the distance between his eyes and her smiling face, it is difficult to understand how a soul is held in abeyance.

I am worried about B., now that his wife is gone.

"For patience joins time to eternity." I found this in a poem by Wendell Berry, which one morning I read aloud to B. Days later he said my poem reminded him of a sentence by Thomas de Quincey. "Before I read," he said, "I like to remind you of de Quincey's relationship to eternity, revealed at the moment of his death, as we read in Fleur Jaeggy's hypnotic biography of the nineteenth-century writer: 'A semblance of youth came over his face. He was seventy-four years old but seemed a boy of fourteen.'" Then, exhausted by this rigmarole of thinking, he paraphrased, instead, that sentence by de Quincey: "Between us and eternity, there is but a minute and a half."

In the Book of Ecclesiastes, what you could call the Biblical toolkit for existential meditations, we are told, "For everything there is a season, and a time for every matter...." A time to be born, and a time to die. Time to weep, and a time to laugh. It is one life-season set apart from its counterpoint. Only it isn't merely so. The Biblical existentialist considers sorrow in relation to joy, death as parallel to life. This is cosmic, mysterious truth. Each time we repeat it, there is a sense of hope, hope smuggled through the borders of despair. There is time for every matter. There is time for a glance to contain the eternal.

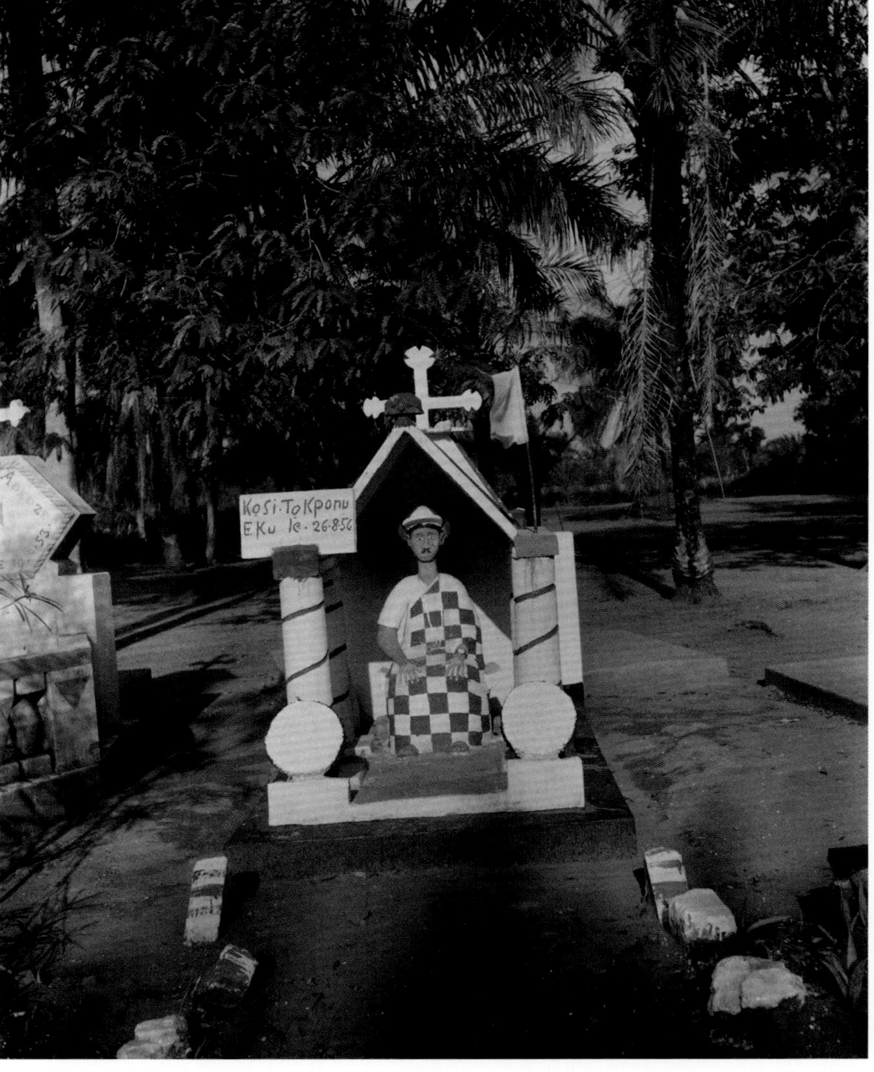

Todd Webb, *Untitled* (44UN-44A-7), Togoland (Togo), 1958
Grave of Kosi Tokponu, who died July 28, 1956.

IN TRANSIT

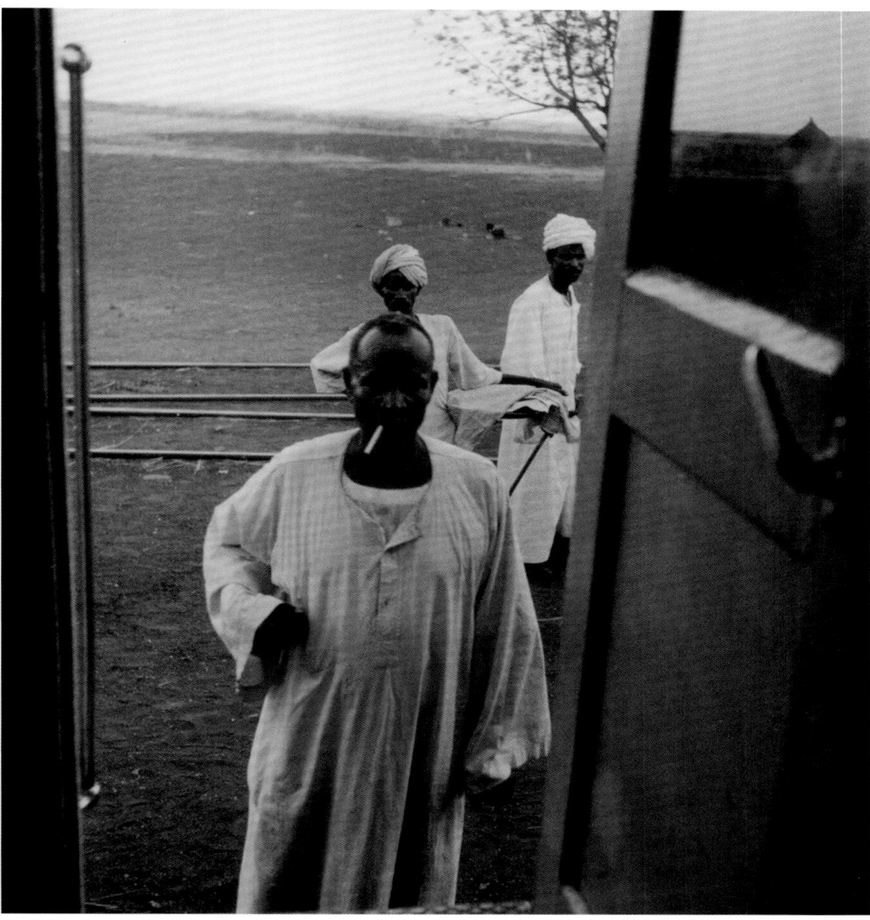

Todd Webb, *Untitled* (44UN-R6-631), Trust Territory of Somaliland (Somalia), 1958
Man with a cigarette about to board a train.

Suppose I live on a space station. It barrels along at twenty-two times the speed of sound, four hundred meters above Earth. In addition to livable room larger than a five-bedroom house, two bathrooms, and sleeping quarters for crew members, there is a 360-degree bay window. From this window, as the station orbits the earth, a journey that takes an hour and a half, entire continents, entire oceans, can be seen in one glance. Onboard, in the course of those ninety minutes, the sun rises and sets.

The first mystery is of time compressed. Observing from a certain perspective, moving at a certain speed, the normal flow of time is disrupted, as if I step into a whirlpool of consciousness.

The second mystery is of life compressed. What would it mean for the past and future if time were measured differently, an hour and a half between sunrise and sunset? Seen from that vantage, what is the unit for quantifying experience?

To travel is to experience both mysteries. All modern forms of transportation focus on speed. As indubitable as both propositions are, they might seem clichéd to most humans today. Yet no other form of engagement with the world highlights the mystery of transition without obfuscation as travel does. Whether on a train, airplane, or spaceship, or a car, the traveling body knows itself in flux.

Consider, then, those who see others while they are about to embark on journeys, or are in transit—acknowledging faces against which the entire gamut of human expression might be found. In the hurry of their glance they notice all the people who were and are yet to come.

It is not too lofty to declare that those faces signify a virtuous form of human exchange: when all is fleeting, and nothing is said or replied to. We hold each other in possibility.

CO-INCIDENCE

In *The Invention of Solitude*, Paul Auster's book on his father and the nature of memory, there are several sections–"commentaries"–on the nature of chance. They are often stories of coincidences, sometimes absurd. For instance, during the Second World War, a man hid in a room in Paris. His son, having moved to Paris, rented the same room. Only when he writes his father to tell of his new lodgings is the significance of the room disclosed.

Take for a second example a story I was once told.

W. owns a Mazda truck. It is old and beat-up, frequently requiring repair. Every now and then she calls a mechanic. She works outside the city, using the Mazda each time she travels. The mechanic can only work on the truck when she is in the city, and in her city house there is a maid. One day the maid tells W. she is pregnant, and the mechanic is responsible. We are getting married, the maid says. Everyone is happy; the maid moves out of W.'s house, pregnant, married to the mechanic.

Time passes, a new maid is employed. The Mazda truck needs repair, and again a mechanic is hired, different from the first. The new maid again tells W. she is pregnant. The second mechanic is responsible. Everyone, again, is happy. The new maid moves out of the house, pregnant, married to the second mechanic. When the Mazda is in need of repair again, W.'s husband says, "Warn your mechanics!"

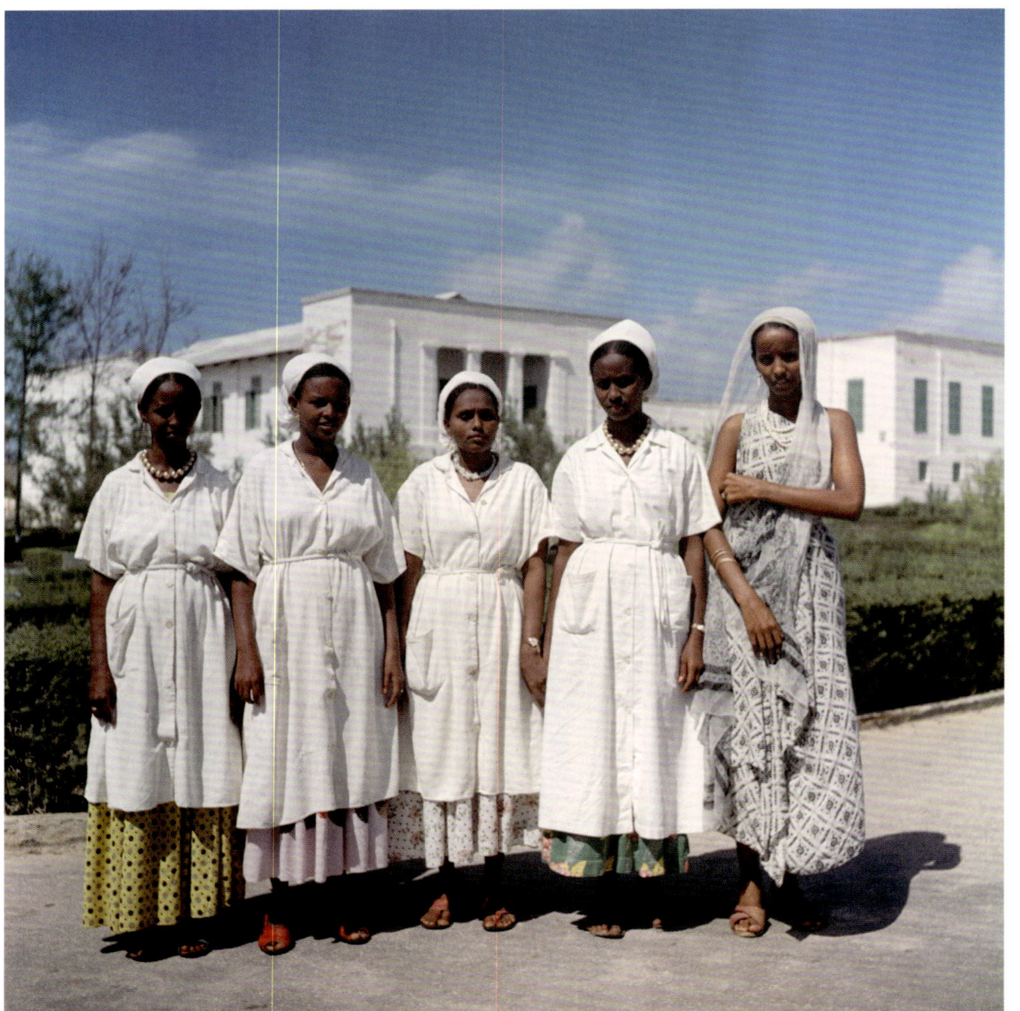

Todd Webb, *Untitled* (44UN-7965-107), Trust Territory of Somaliland (Somalia), 1958
Women in Mogadishu.

NO-PERSON-LAND

The photograph of the border station is not as I remembered the event, but I'll let the disjuncture stand: late afternoon, nearly a decade ago, leaving Ethiopia *en route* to Sudan. I was traveling with a group of artists, and none of us had realized that we carried single-entry visas for Sudan. We got out of Ethiopia alright, but once we presented our passports to the Sudanese officials, they shook their heads and turned us back. We found out soon enough that it was a terrible, not to mention impossible situation—having been stamped out of Ethiopia, and refused access to Sudan, we only had rights of stay in the no-person-land, a patch as long as a quarter of a mile.

We waited and wondered. Then the leader of the group recalled that while in Ethiopia, we had met with the ambassador of Nigeria to Ethiopia. When he called the ambassador, we were in such luck it is difficult to retell this without speaking in terms of a miracle. For it turned out that at the time he received our call, the ambassador was in a meeting with the ambassador of Sudan to Ethiopia. He, in turn, directed his immigration officials to allow us entry into Sudan, regardless of what was stated on our visas.

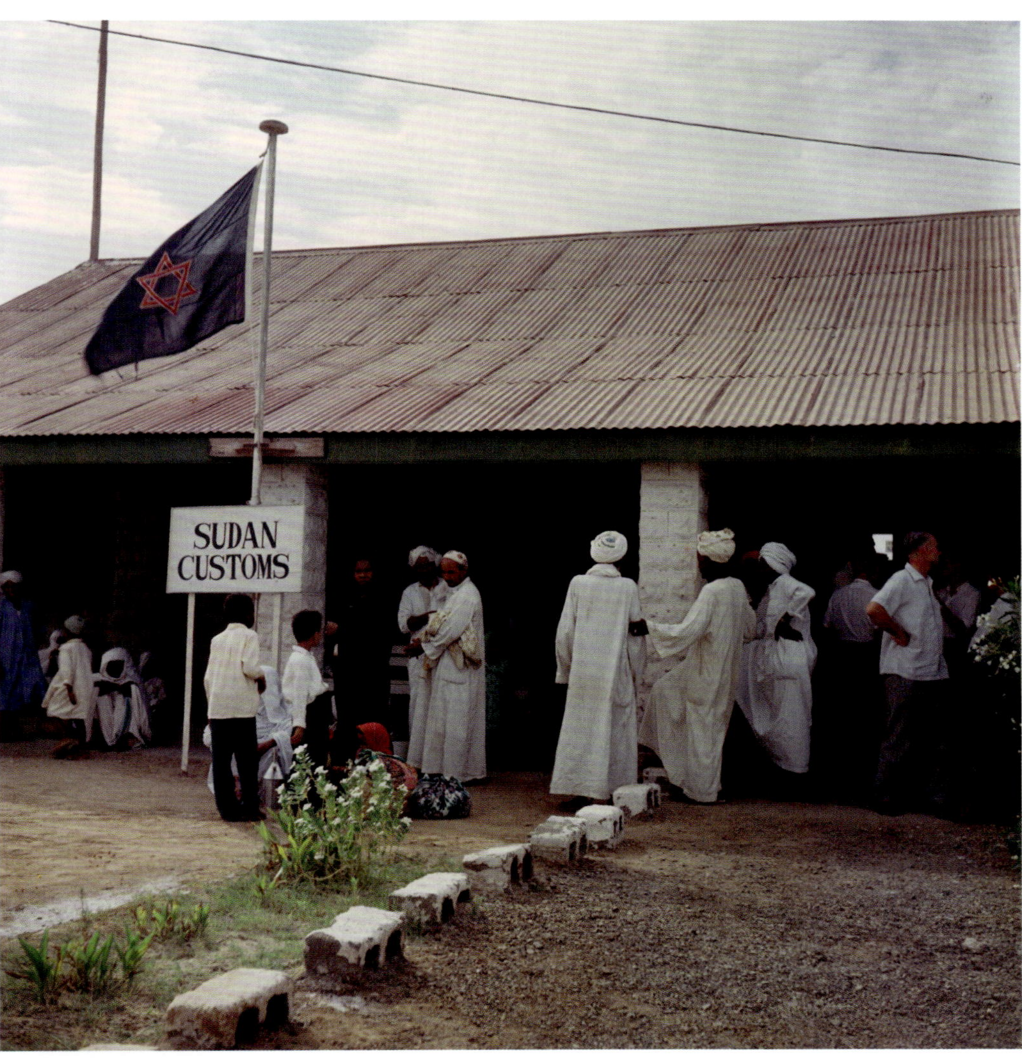

Todd Webb, *Untitled* (44UN-7955-585), Sudan, 1958
Sudan Customs building, Kassala.

BOYHOOD

There are five boys in all, none of us older than eight. One turns to his fellow, straightening his finger into the barrel of a gun, his thumb a trigger. The other raises his hand in surrender, his mouth curved into an "argh." Police and Thief, everyone knows that game. Another set of boys stand as a duo of famous musicians would. One clutches an invisible microphone. The other strums a rock guitar, entertaining a sea of clamoring fans. The Police and Thief boys and the singing duo do not glance at their viewer. Lost in the exuberance of their alternate selves.

Now think of him standing in the middle of his peers, his arms folded, peering at you. What did he want to become, this boy refusing to stand like us?

Imagine him pictured alone, and from the side. The photograph is unfocused. He is lanky in the way boys that age can be. Seen from the side, in an unfocused photograph, he is still the boy with a severe look. As if all he wanted in his life was to be left alone.

I'll tell you the story of that second photograph. Late one afternoon when we were about twelve, I asked him to accompany me to see the photographer, my uncle. I saw he was worried about something. "What is it?" I asked. He wouldn't say. When we got to the entrance to the studio, my uncle had just finished with some clients, including a man whose shirt opened to reveal a cowrie-stringed necklace.

"Boy, you can talk to me," my uncle said.

But he shook his head and began to cry. "Ah, look, a boy as big as you are is crying like a baby," the photographer said. "If you don't stop crying, I won't take a photo of you." He wiped his eyes then.

What you see in the photograph is a boy who has just stopped crying, trying hard to show some bravado. And when you know a man as a boy, you know all there is to know about him.

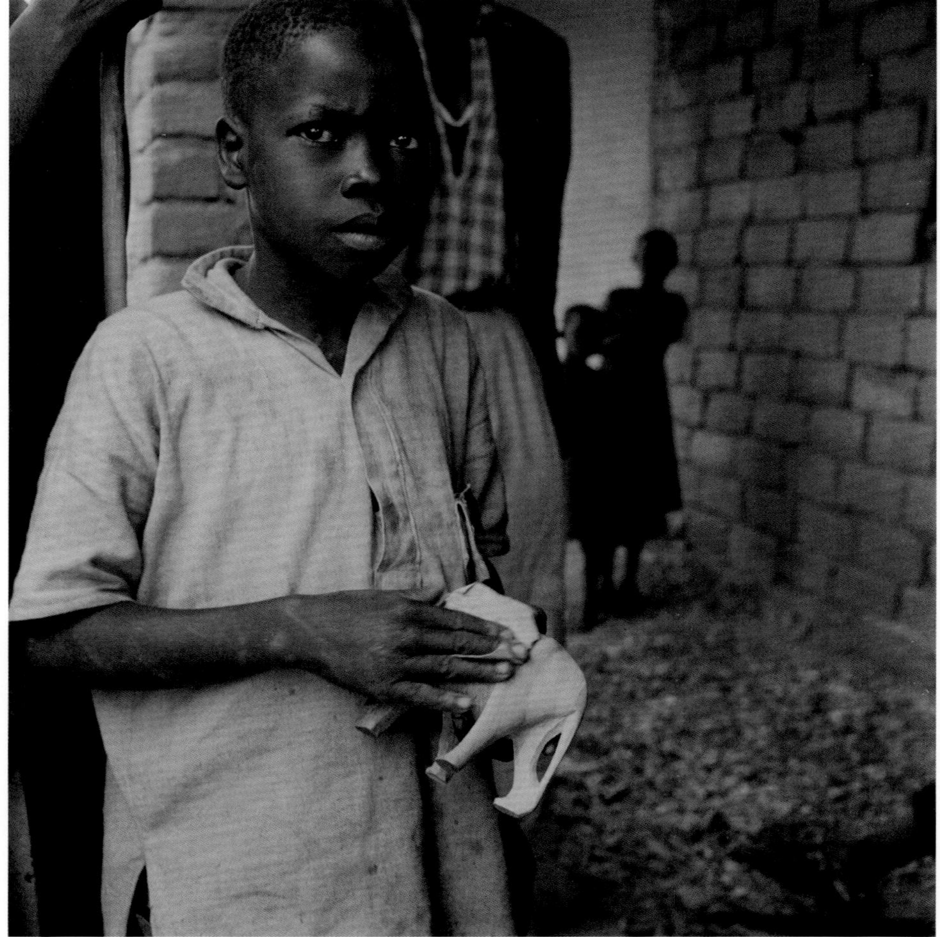

Todd Webb, *Untitled* (44UN-7721-696), Kenya, 1958
Boy working as part of a woodcarving cooperative, Machakos.

OUT OF WATER

She pulls him out of water.

Only at this time, earlier than the earliest fisherman, can she think of what weight she bears of life. Morning by morning she arrives to consider the river, to see what its endless eddies can teach her. The sound of one wave licking another makes her shudder in anticipation.

There is a stretch of moored canoes. She turns attention to one closest to her, also closest to the edge of the river, as though abandoned in haste. She approaches it, curious but unhopeful. First, she sees the outline of a moving bulge. Then when she reaches it, knows that bulge as human. Suppose she walked to the river as if the slant of her body were the valley inching to meet a hill, or a vine curling to encircle a wide trunk, slow but steady, guided by a premonitory hand. Her body sways with uncertainty. Hers is a body weighted not merely by age but by the accumulation of regrets. Yet now she stares at a son. There is a moment so total it halves your life, no matter if you're sixty-five.

She seeks his face in the approaching light, and wonders. What is this son the river has brought? She kneels by the bank, holding the canoe for support.

She holds his face against the light of dawn, but it is not bright enough for her to see. She brings his face to hers and pours breath on his chin. Then he sneezes, what sounds like a purr. For her it is then he comes alive. She pours breath on his chin and he comes alive.

She wonders.

Just when it becomes brighter, he lets out a cry. Darkness might have quieted him. Dawn had tricked her. This light, she might have thought, will expose what the river has brought to me. Not a theft, a reclamation. When she presses him to herself and covers him in her scarf, his cry recedes. It is enough for her to think the words without irony: my child. A name sufficient to turn her home.

This story survives without a witness. How she manages to walk the distance of a quarter-hour unchallenged, how she is seen with a bulge on her chest, but in the hurry of her movement the child appears formless, how because of her hurry she lacked the shamed gait of a thief.

Not theft but reclamation. The river swirls and spits out a child. What makes a mother is the moment of first grasp, an embrace without antecedent. This is how it is with her. She wouldn't, from this morning on, refer to the child as anything but hers.

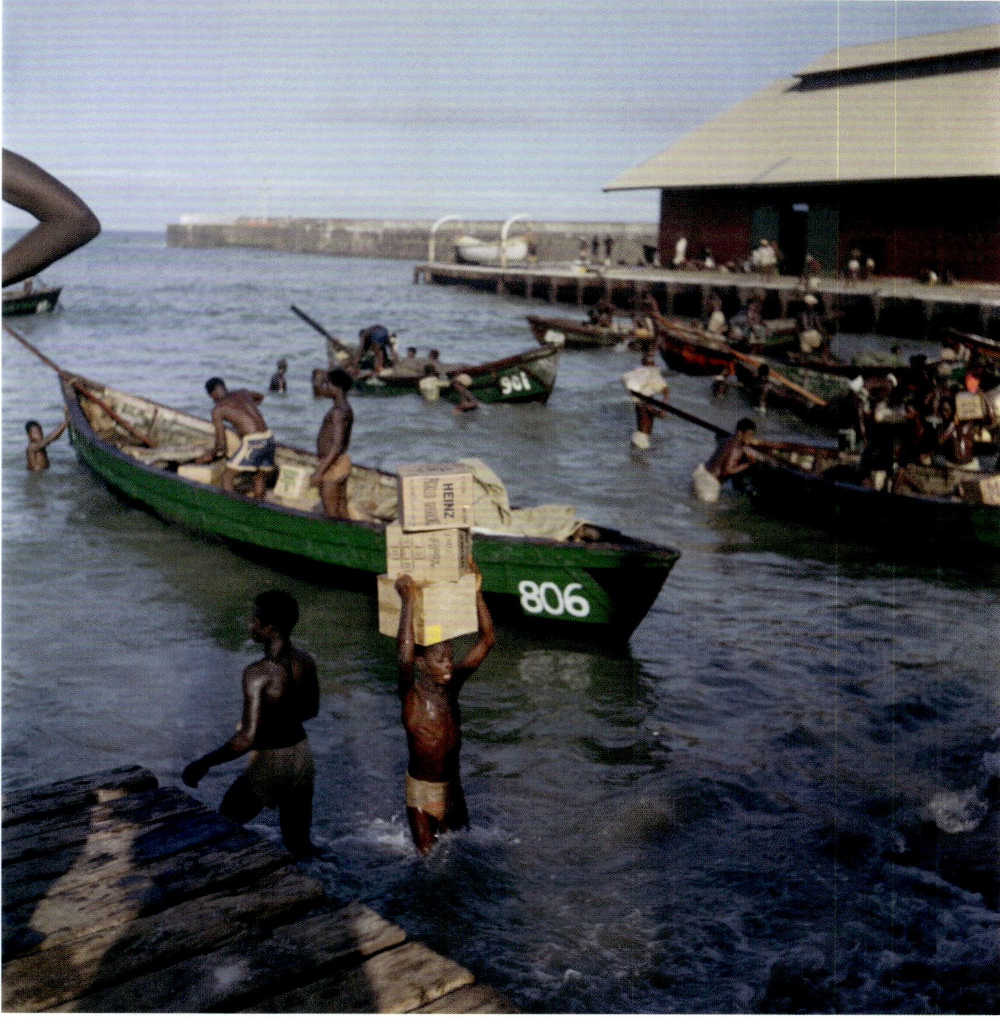

Todd Webb, *Untitled* (44UN-7913-191), Ghana, 1958
Unloading cargo from the boats, Accra harbor.

ENDNOTES

Writers of fiction are quick to point out that stories evolve in the process of being written, that characters turn complex, sometimes even intransigent, or at the very least begin to act in ways that stray from their original intention. To proceed with fiction, I needed to give up photographic certitude. Hence, the order in which I have written about Todd Webb's photographs is a conceit, as is much of what I narrate. I take account of realities that connect across self and space and time.

If documentary photographs, when they depict unnamed subjects, require particularized responses, my goal was to speculate on the identities of individuals in Webb's photographs, by allotting stories and meditations to them.

To look at these photographs is to consider the outset of modernity in several colonial and postcolonial African countries. Webb was there to photograph the moment of promise, and now I am looking at the remains of those who have passed into history.

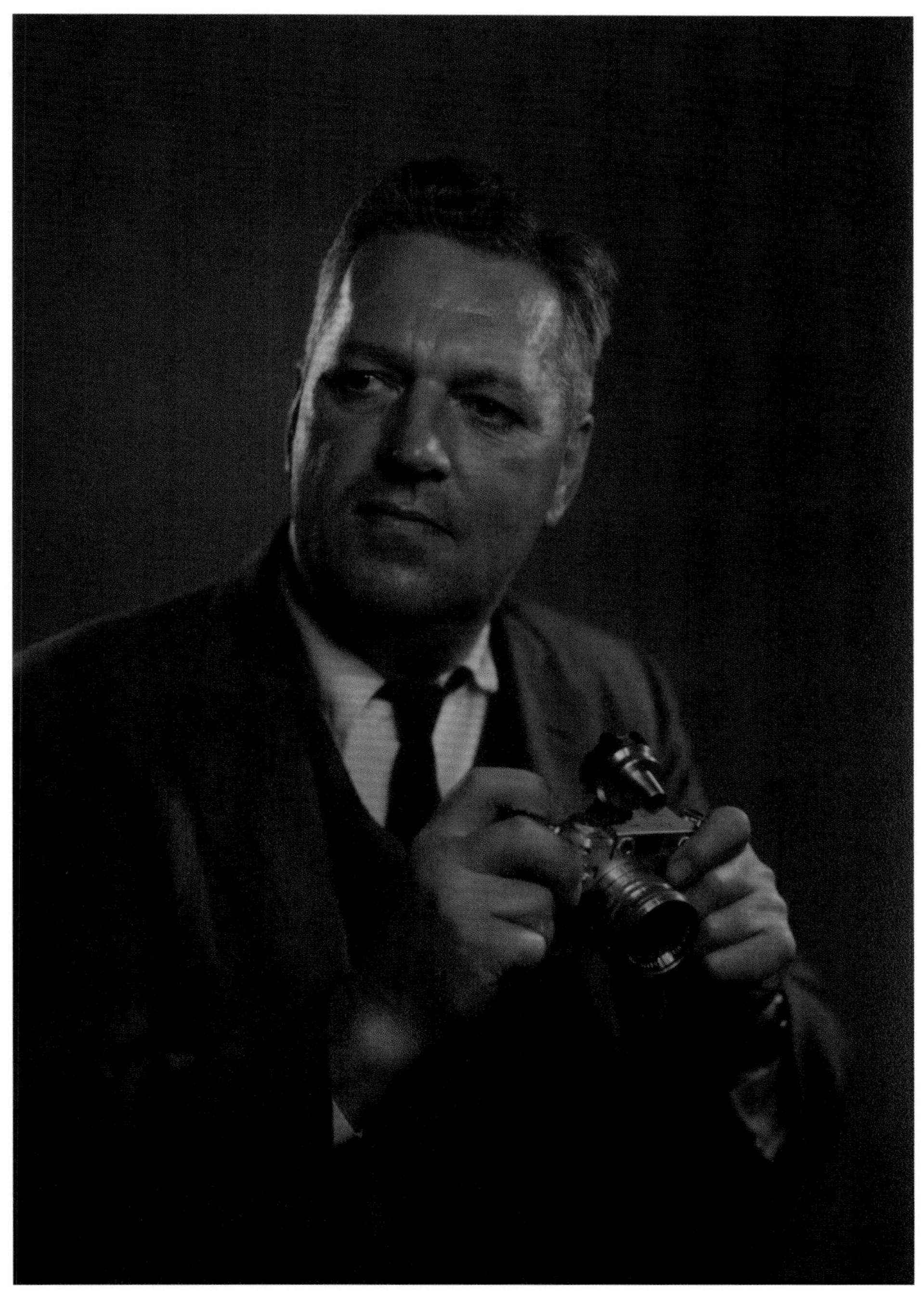

Unknown photographer (Fernandes Photographic Studio), portrait of Todd Webb,
Salisbury, Southern Rhodesia (Zimbabwe), 1958
Todd Webb had his portrait taken holding his own camera in the Fernandes Photographic Studio.
Stamped on the back is "Exclusive Portrait by Fernandes, Salisbury, Southern Rhodesia, P.O. Box 359."

United Nations Images

Published here with their original United Nations captions and descriptions.

These descriptions provide insight into the UN's political views and their impetus for photographing the extractive industries, commerce, technology, and independence movements in the different countries, as documented by Todd Webb in this book.

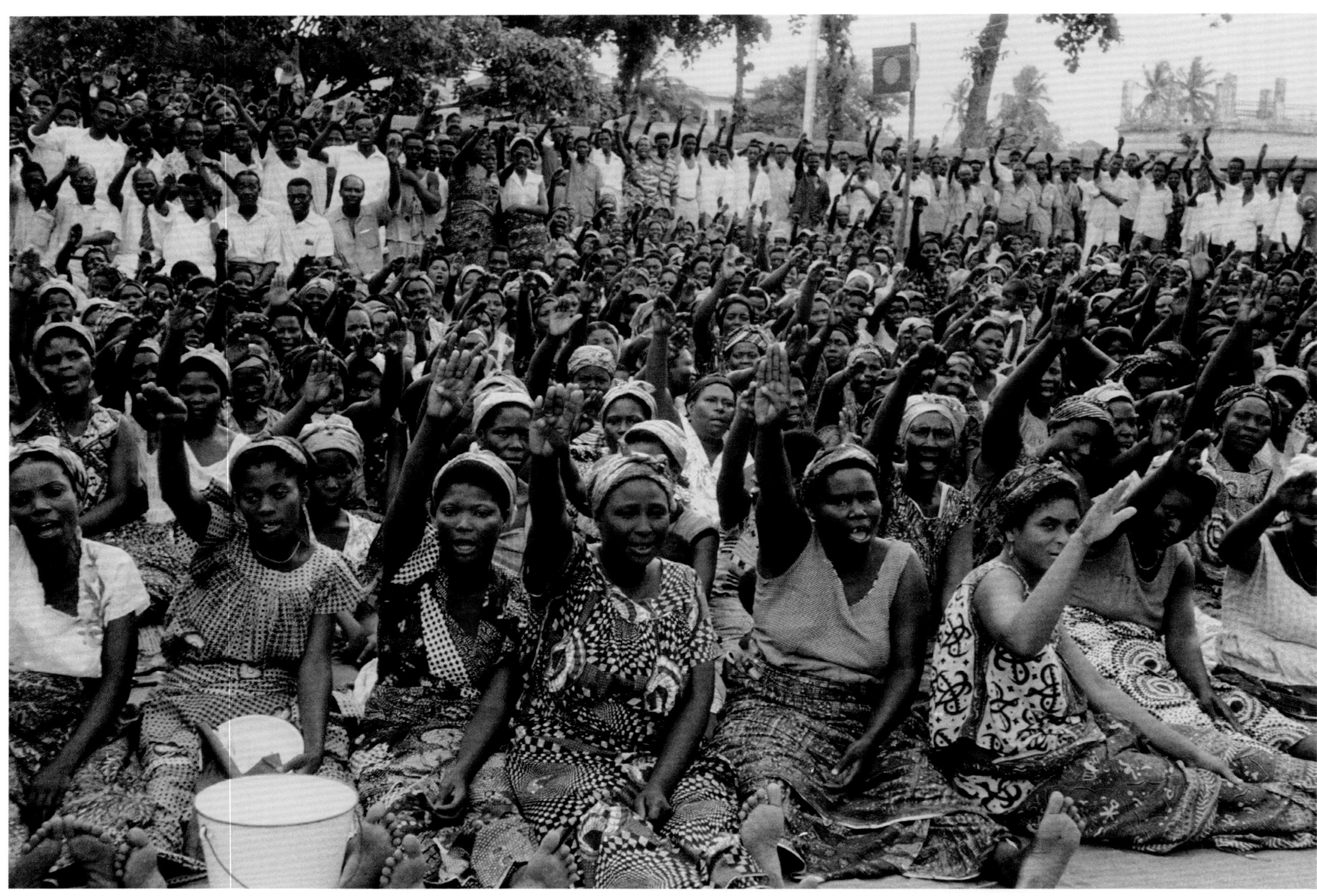

Lomé, Togoland
"Elections in Togoland"
On 27 April 1958, the men and women of the UN Trust Territory of Togoland under French Administration have elected a new Chamber of Deputies to replace the former Legislative Assembly. An international staff, serving under a United Nations Commissioner, has been on hand since early March to observe the elections and the preparation for them. The Comité de l'unité [T]ogolaise, the main opposition party, won a decisive victory. Crowd singing the party song at the rally of the Juvento party on election eve in Lomé. The Mouvement de la Jeunesse Togolaise (JUVENTO) considers itself a political party but is not recognized as such by the government.
UN Photo: Todd Webb

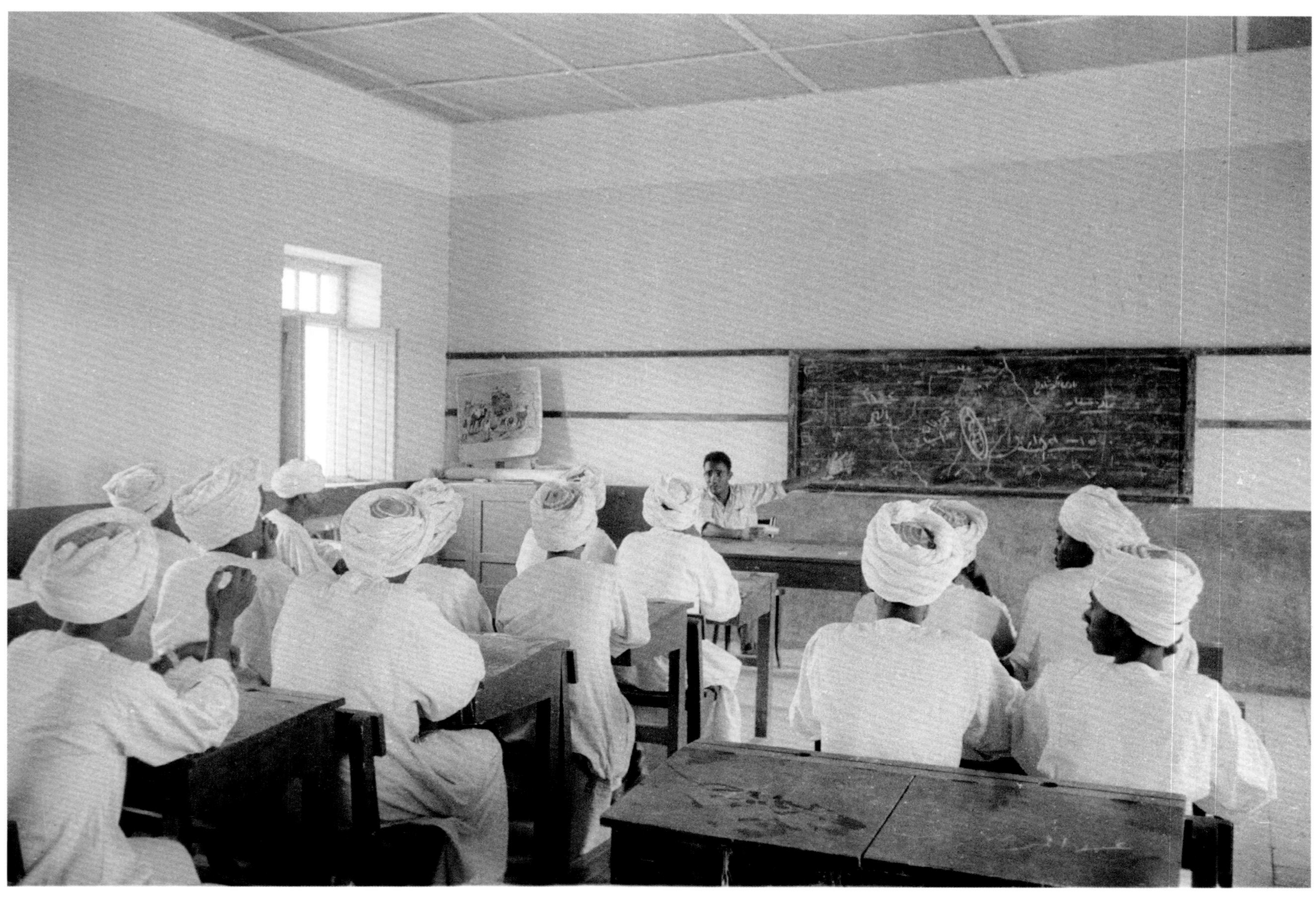

Barkat, Sudan
"Progress in the Sudan"
The remarkable progress achieved during the last fifty years in the social and economic transformation of the Sudan is evidence of the enormous changes taking place throughout Africa today. This photograph shows an adult education class in session at Barkat. The class, which is for the benefit of adult farmers who were unable to obtain education in their youth, is sponsored by the Sudan Government. Among other things, they are instructed in the history of the Sudan and of Africa.
UN Photo: Todd Webb

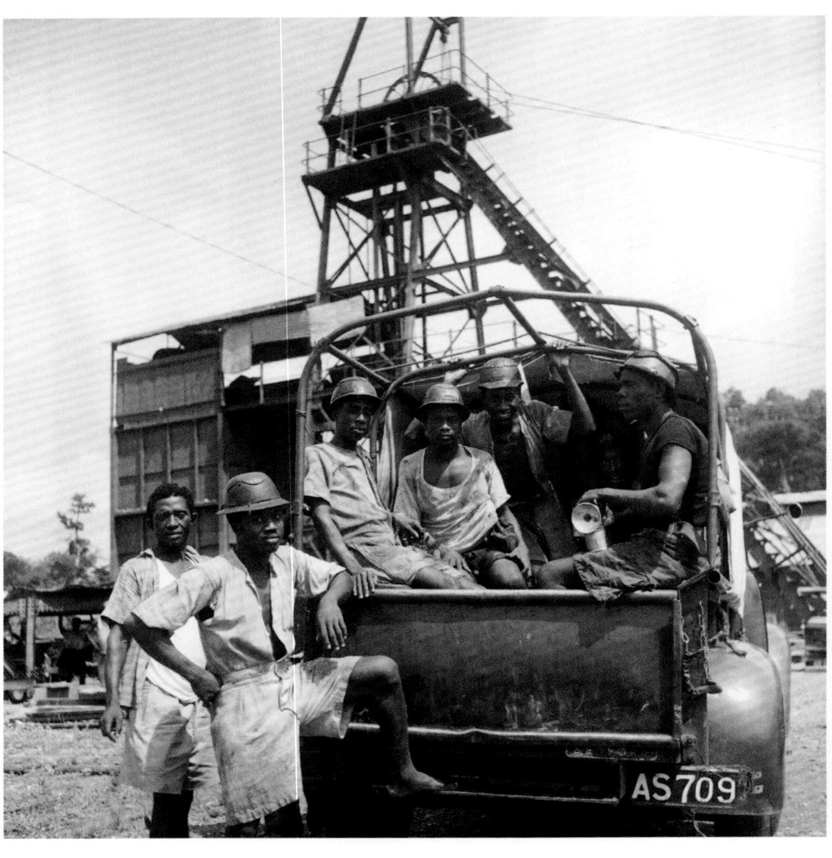

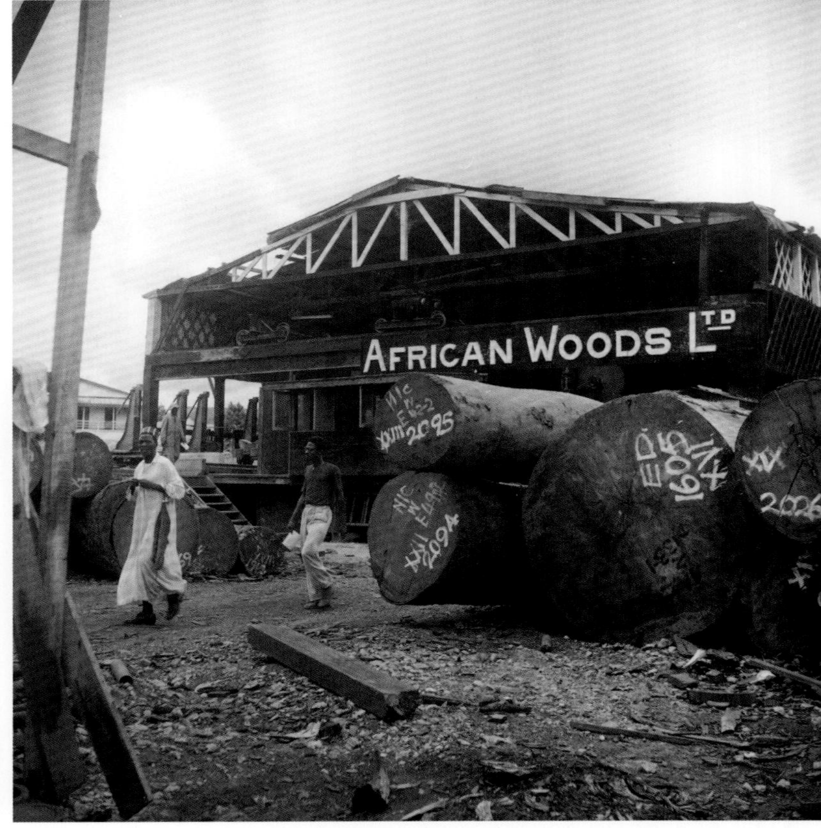

Konongo, Ghana
"Economic Development in Ghana"
In addition to being the world's largest producer of cocoa, Ghana has substantial wealth in timber, gold, and diamonds. Members of the maintenance crew at the Konongo gold mine, which is temporarily closed for repair.
UN Photo: Todd Webb

Kumasi, Ghana
"Economic Development in Ghana"
In addition to being the world's largest producer of cocoa, Ghana has substantial wealth in timber, gold, and diamonds. At the African Woods Ltd in Kumasi timber is sorted and graded before being shipped by rail to Takoradi for export.
UN Photo: Todd Webb

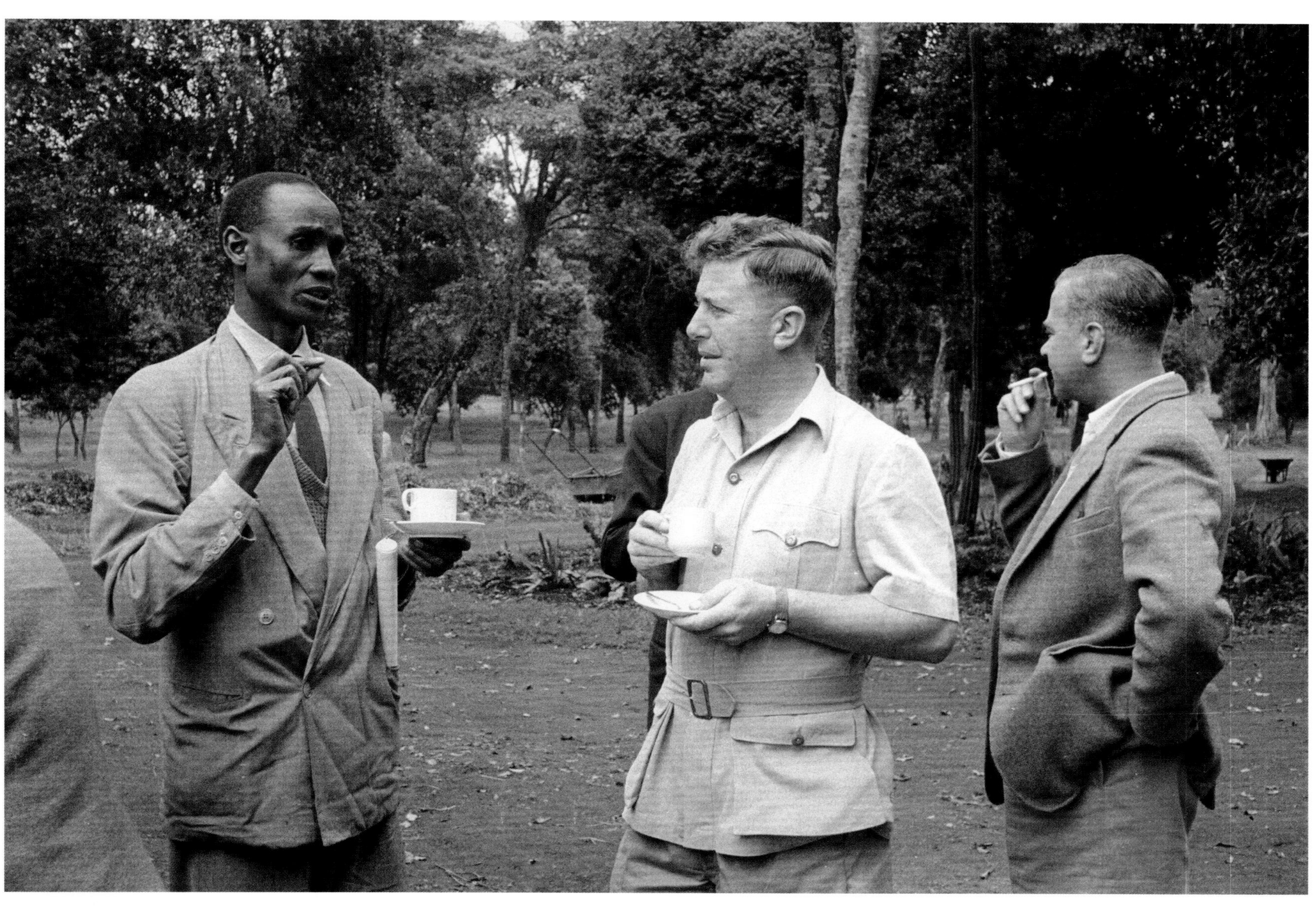

Nairobi, Kenya
"Kenya"
In order to provide them with a better insight into the operation of a small European farm, some thirty African farmers were recently invited to visit the James Moore Farm near Nairobi. Here, one of the visiting farmers (l.) enjoys a cup of tea while discussing farming problems.
UN Photo: Todd Webb

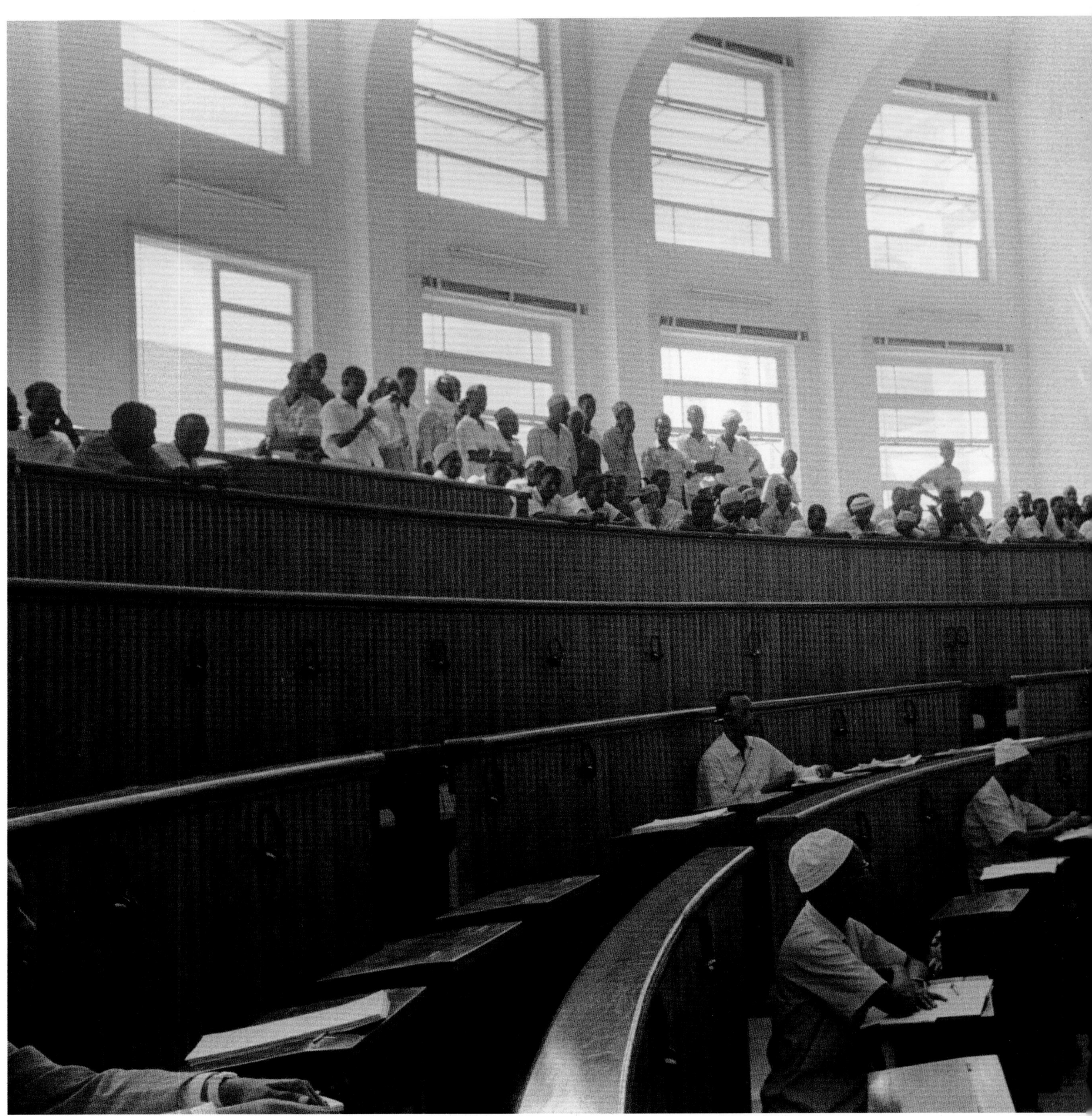

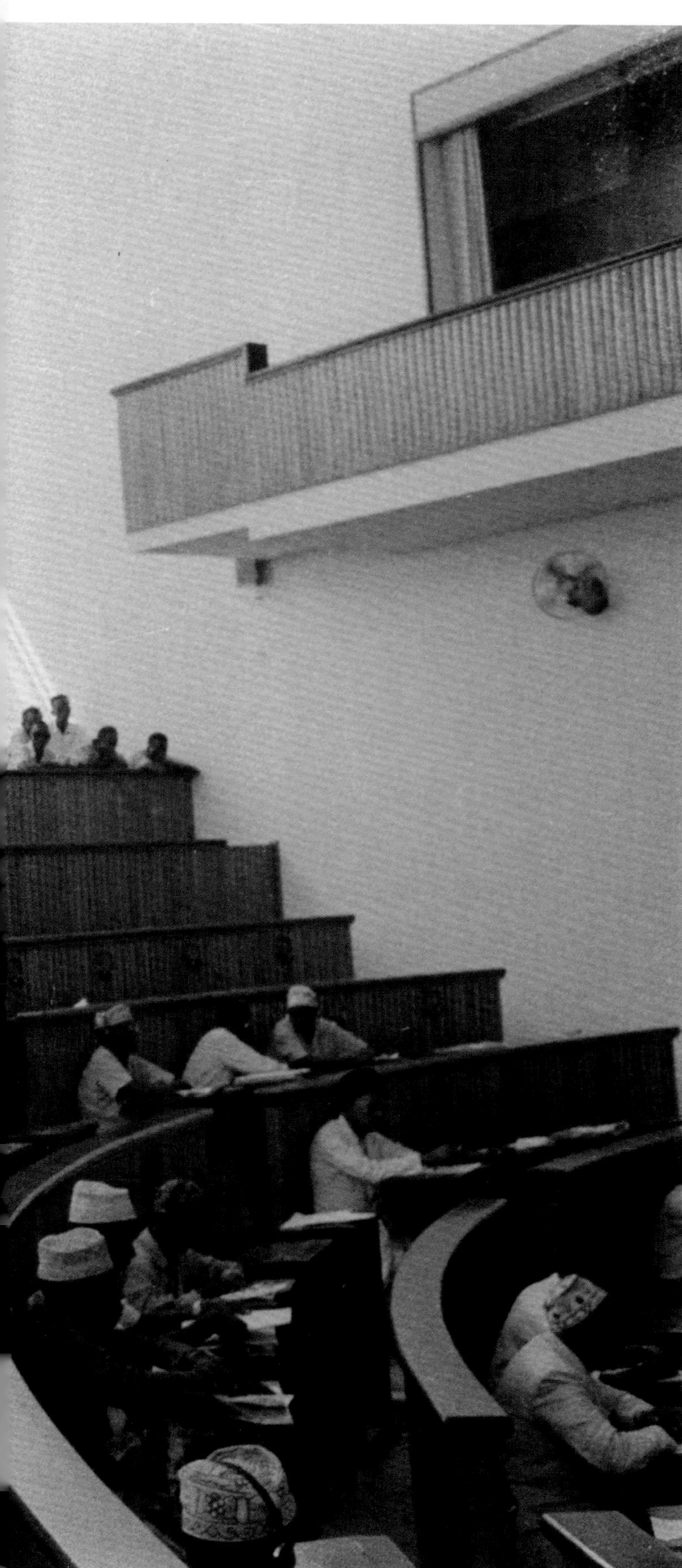

Magadiscio [sic], Somalia
"A Continent Awakes"
Although the overwhelming majority of the 210 million people in Africa make their living on the land, enormous changes are taking place. New nations are being formed, there is an interesting worldwide demand for the continent's minerals and raw materials, power sources are being developed, communications opened up by rail, road, and sea, and local industries are springing up. Through the new United Nations Economic Commission for Africa the governments are also working together to promote the economy of the continent and to raise living standards. The Trust Territory of Somaliland, under Italian Administration, will become an independent state in 1960 and important steps toward self-rule have already been taken. In this photograph the elected Legislative Assembly is seen in session.
UN Photo: Todd Webb

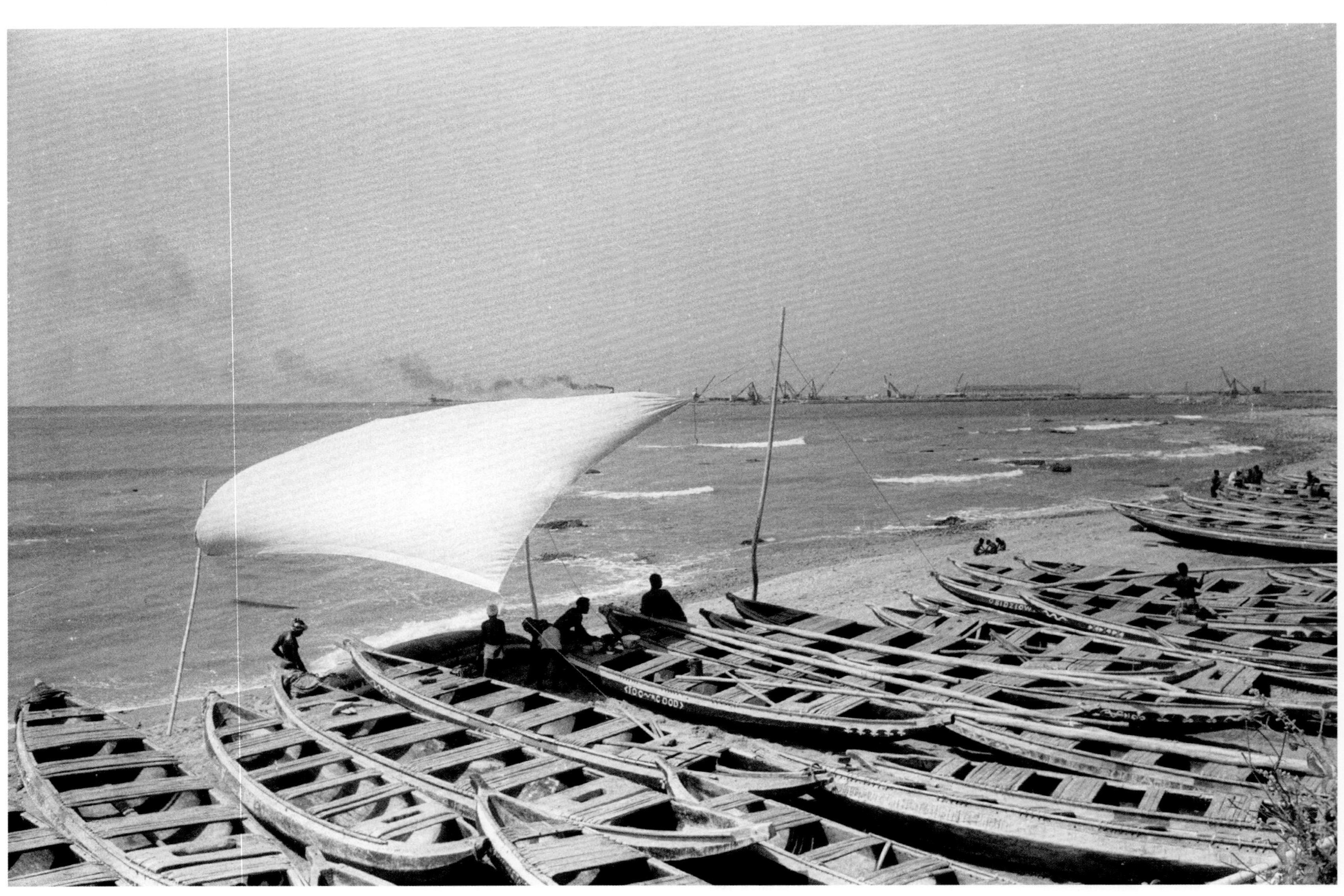

Accra, Ghana
"Trade and Harbour Development in Ghana"
At the present time Takoradi is Ghana's only modern, deep-water harbor. While some 30,000 tons of cargo are landed monthly by surf boats at Accra, the operation is both difficult and costly and a new harbor is under construction at Tema, some 16 miles from the capital. View of Tema harbor under construction, with a fleet of fishing canoes in the foreground.
UN Photo: Todd Webb

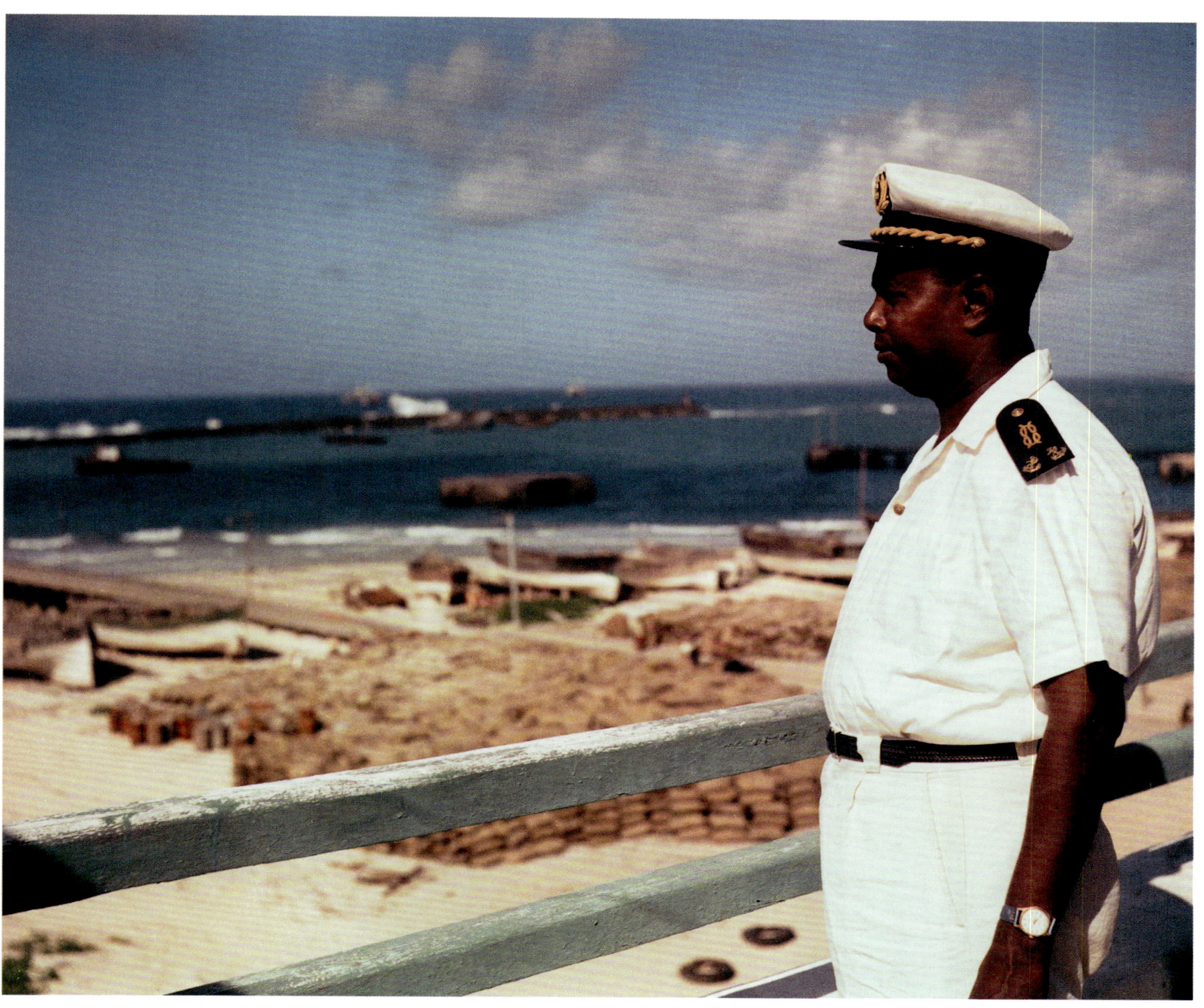

Magadiscio [sic], Somaliland
"A Continent Awakes"
Although the overwhelming majority of the 210 million people in Africa make their living on the land, enormous changes are taking place. New nations are being formed, there is an interesting worldwide demand for the continent's minerals and raw materials, power sources are being developed, communications opened up by rail, road, and sea, and local industries are springing up. Through the new United Nations Economic Commission for Africa the governments are also working together to promote the economy of the continent and to raise living standards. The harbormaster of Magadiscio [sic]. Cargo and people must be taken to and from ships by lighters.
UN Photo: Todd Webb

United Nations Brochure

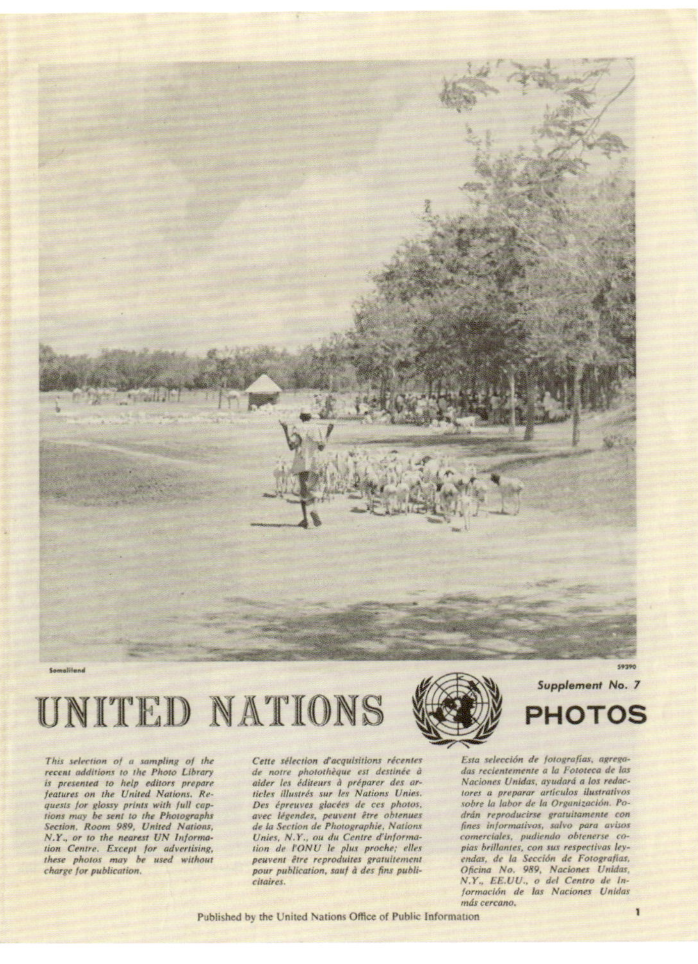

Somaliland 59390

UNITED NATIONS PHOTOS

Supplement No. 7

This selection of a sampling of the recent additions to the Photo Library is presented to help editors prepare features on the United Nations. Requests for glossy prints with full captions may be sent to the Photographs Section, Room 989, United Nations, N.Y., or to the nearest UN Information Centre. Except for advertising, these photos may be used without charge for publication.

Cette sélection d'acquisitions récentes de notre photothèque est destinée à aider les éditeurs à préparer des articles illustrés sur les Nations Unies. Des épreuves glacées de ces photos, avec légendes, peuvent être obtenues de la Section de Photographie, Nations Unies, N.Y., ou du Centre d'information de l'ONU le plus proche; elles peuvent être reproduites gratuitement pour publication, sauf à des fins publicitaires.

Esta selección de fotografías, agregadas recientemente a la Fototeca de las Naciones Unidas, ayudará a los redactores a preparar artículos ilustrativos sobre la labor de la Organización. Podrán reproducirse gratuitamente con fines informativos, salvo para avisos comerciales, pudiendo obtenerse copias brillantes, con sus respectivas leyendas, de la Sección de Fotografías, Oficina No. 989, Naciones Unidas, N.Y., EE.UU., o del Centro de Información de las Naciones Unidas más cercano.

Published by the United Nations Office of Public Information

1

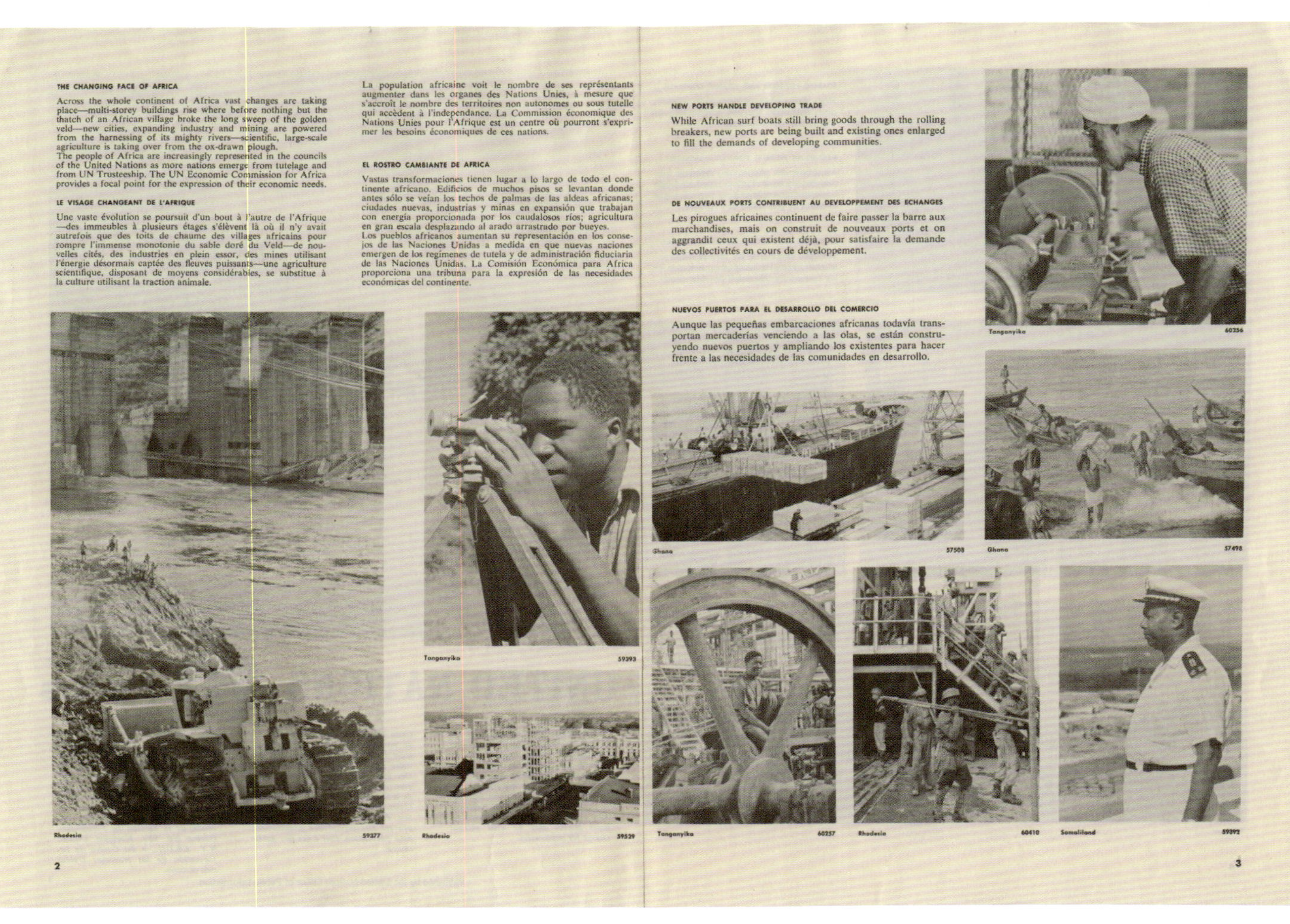

THE CHANGING FACE OF AFRICA

Across the whole continent of Africa vast changes are taking place—multi-storey buildings rise where before nothing but the thatch of an African village broke the long sweep of the golden veld—new cities, expanding industry and mining are powered from the harnessing of its mighty rivers—scientific, large-scale agriculture is taking over from the ox-drawn plough.

The people of Africa are increasingly represented in the councils of the United Nations as more nations emerge from tutelage and from UN Trusteeship. The UN Economic Commission for Africa provides a focal point for the expression of their economic needs.

LE VISAGE CHANGEANT DE L'AFRIQUE

Une vaste évolution se poursuit d'un bout à l'autre de l'Afrique—des immeubles à plusieurs étages s'élèvent là où il n'y avait autrefois que des toits de chaume des villages africains pour rompre l'immense monotonie du sable doré du Veld—de nouvelles cités, des industries en plein essor, des mines utilisant l'énergie désormais captée des fleuves puissants—une agriculture scientifique, disposant de moyens considérables, se substitue à la culture utilisant la traction animale.

La population africaine voit le nombre de ses représentants augmenter dans les organes des Nations Unies, à mesure que s'accroît le nombre des territoires non autonomes ou sous tutelle qui accèdent à l'independance. La Commission économique des Nations Unies pour l'Afrique est un centre où pourront s'exprimer les besoins économiques de ces nations.

EL ROSTRO CAMBIANTE DE AFRICA

Vastas transformaciones tienen lugar a lo largo de todo el continente africano. Edificios de muchos pisos se levantan donde antes sólo se veían los techos de palmas de las aldeas africanas; ciudades nuevas, industrias y minas en expansión que trabajan con energía proporcionada por los caudalosos ríos; agricultura en gran escala desplazando al arado arrastrado por bueyes.

Los pueblos africanos aumentan su representación en los consejos de las Naciones Unidas a medida en que nuevas naciones emergen de los regímenes de tutela y de administración fiduciaria de las Naciones Unidas. La Comisión Económica para Africa proporciona una tribuna para la expresión de las necesidades económicas del continente.

Rhodesia 59377

Tanganyika 59393

Rhodesia 59529

2

NEW PORTS HANDLE DEVELOPING TRADE

While African surf boats still bring goods through the rolling breakers, new ports are being built and existing ones enlarged to fill the demands of developing communities.

DE NOUVEAUX PORTS CONTRIBUENT AU DEVELOPPEMENT DES ECHANGES

Les pirogues africaines continuent de faire passer la barre aux marchandises, mais on construit de nouveaux ports et on aggrandit ceux qui existent déjà, pour satisfaire la demande des collectivités en cours de développement.

NUEVOS PUERTOS PARA EL DESARROLLO DEL COMERCIO

Aunque las pequeñas embarcaciones africanas todavía transportan mercaderías venciendo a las olas, se están construyendo nuevos puertos y ampliando los existentes para hacer frente a las necesidades de las comunidades en desarrollo.

Tanganyika 60256

Ghana 57508

Ghana 57498

Tanganyika 60257

Rhodesia 60410

Somaliland 59392

3

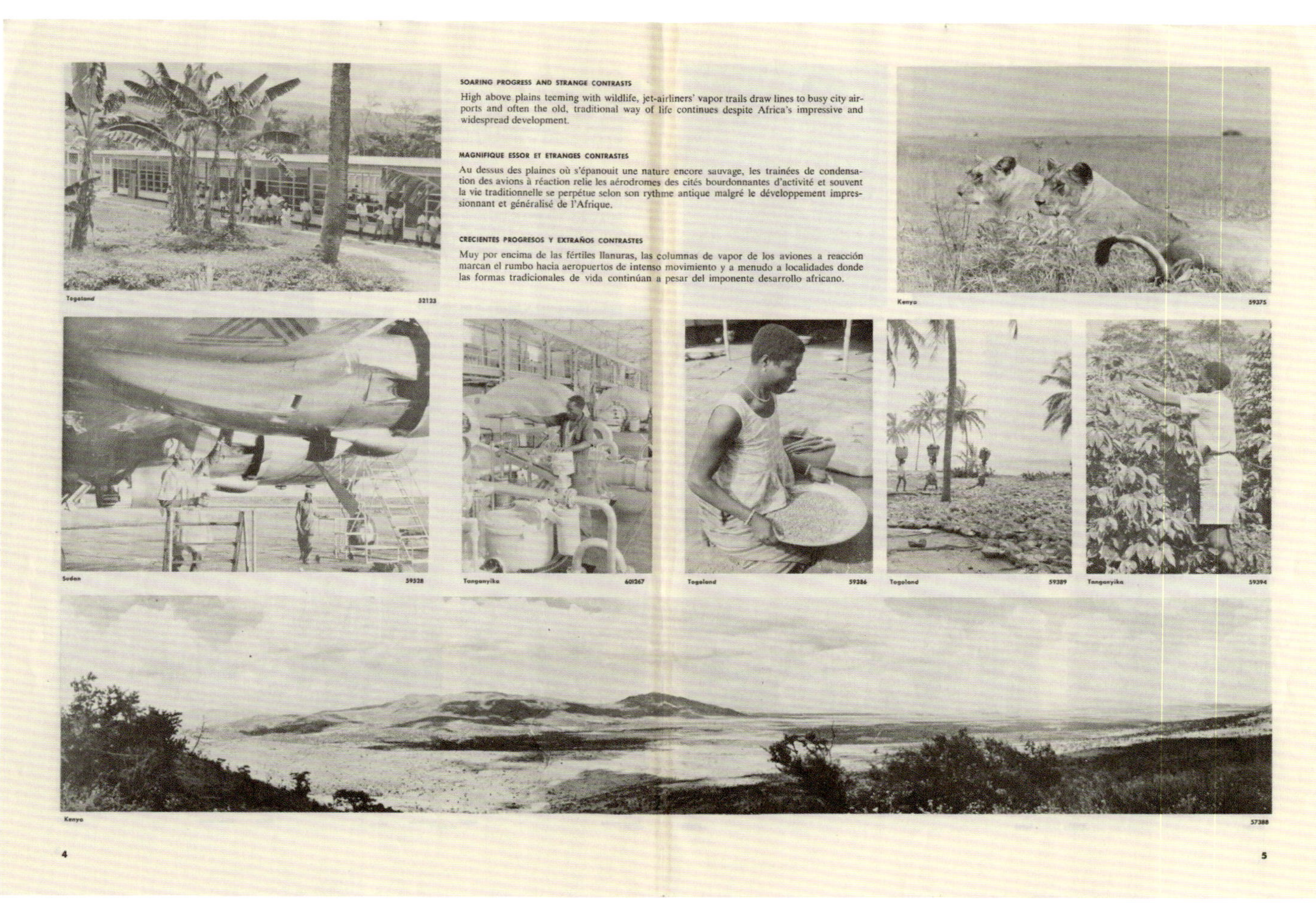

SOARING PROGRESS AND STRANGE CONTRASTS

High above plains teeming with wildlife, jet-airliners' vapor trails draw lines to busy city airports and often the old, traditional way of life continues despite Africa's impressive and widespread development.

MAGNIFIQUE ESSOR ET ETRANGES CONTRASTES

Au dessus des plaines où s'épanouit une nature encore sauvage, les trainées de condensation des avions à réaction relie les aérodromes des cités bourdonnantes d'activité et souvent la vie traditionnelle se perpétue selon son rythme antique malgré le développement impressionnant et généralisé de l'Afrique.

CRECIENTES PROGRESOS Y EXTRAÑOS CONTRASTES

Muy por encima de las fértiles llanuras, las columnas de vapor de los aviones a reacción marcan el rumbo hacia aeropuertos de intenso movimiento y a menudo a localidades donde las formas tradicionales de vida continúan a pesar del imponente desarrollo africano.

Togoland 52123

Kenya 59375

Sudan 59528

Tanganyika 601267

Togoland 59286

Togoland 59289

Tanganyika 59394

Kenya 57389

4

5

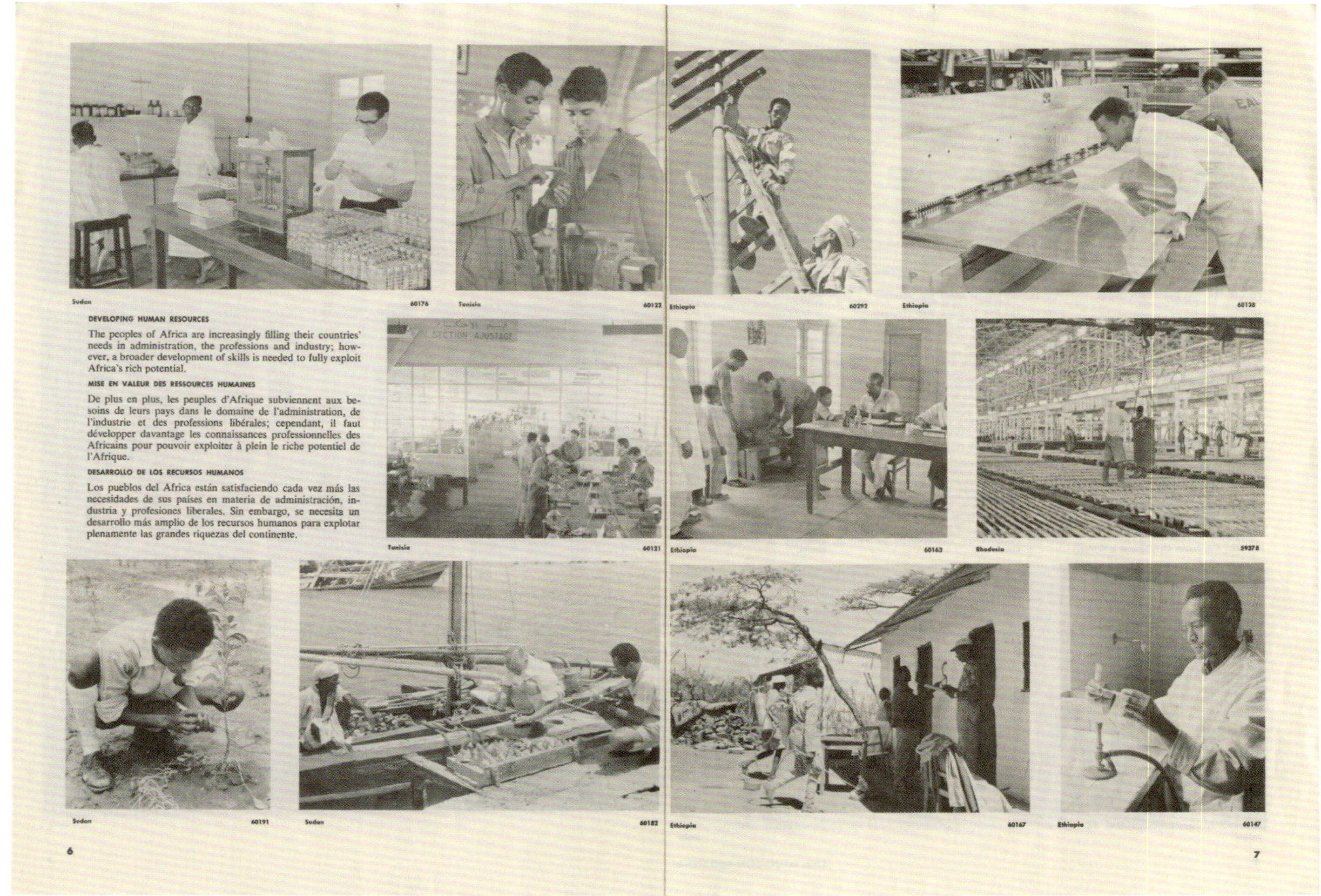

Sudan 60176

Tunisia 60122

Ethiopia 60292

Ethiopia 60138

DEVELOPING HUMAN RESOURCES

The peoples of Africa are increasingly filling their countries' needs in administration, the professions and industry; however, a broader development of skills is needed to fully exploit Africa's rich potential.

MISE EN VALEUR DES RESSOURCES HUMAINES

De plus en plus, les peuples d'Afrique subviennent aux besoins de leurs pays dans le domaine de l'administration, de l'industrie et des professions libérales; cependant, il faut développer davantage les connaissances professionnelles des Africains pour pouvoir exploiter à plein le riche potentiel de l'Afrique.

DESARROLLO DE LOS RECURSOS HUMANOS

Los pueblos del Africa están satisfaciendo cada vez más las necesidades de sus países en materia de administración, industria y profesiones liberales. Sin embargo, se necesita un desarrollo más amplio de los recursos humanos para explotar plenamente las grandes riquezas del continente.

Tunisia 60121

Ethiopia 60163

Rhodesia 59378

Sudan 60191

Sudan 60182

Ethiopia 60167

Ethiopia 60147

6

7

NOTES

Introduction
Aimée Bessire and Erin Hyde Nolan

[1] Throughout this book, we use the names of the countries at the time of Webb's commission in 1958 with the contemporary name in parentheses at their first mention in each essay. The number of countries is based on 1958 maps of Africa, when Northern and Southern Rhodesia were listed as territories in the Federation of Rhodesia and Nyasaland. The territories had their own administrations, which complicates their distinction as part of a larger country or countries of their own. Webb refers to visiting "Northern Rhodesia" and also talks about his visit to the Federation of Rhodesia and Nyasaland.

[2] Our notion of the multi-authored photograph has been shaped by many different texts. See, for example, Geoffrey Batchen, "Photography and Authorship", October 7, 2012<https://www.fotomuseum.ch/en/explore/still-searching/articles/26932_photography_and_authorship>; Ahmet Ersoy, "Ottomans and the Kodak Galaxy: Archiving Everyday Life and Historical Space in Ottoman Illustrated Journals ", *History of Photography*, 40/3 (2016), 330–357; Catherine A. Lutz and Jane L. Collins, *Reading National Geographic* (Chicago: University of Chicago Press, 1993); Mary Roberts, *Istanbul Exchanges: Ottomans, Orientalists, and Nineteenth-Century Visual Culture* (Oakland, California: University of California Press, 2015); Ariella Azoulay, *Potential History: Unlearning Imperialism* (London: Verso Books, 2019).

[3] Todd Webb, Africa Journal, 1958, 1.

[4] The images do not present the same focus on ethnicity and culture as photographs from *National Geographic* or other publications from the same era, as seen in *National Geographic* 2, 4, and 5 (1958).

[5] The 1,978 negatives and additional ephemera have yet to be exhibited or published.

[6] Todd Webb, Journal, March 14, 1946, 7.

[7] Todd Webb, John Simon Guggenheim Memorial Foundation Fellowship Application, October 27, 1954.

[8] Todd Webb, Journal, January 29, 1958, 415.

[9] *Ibid.*

[10] Todd Webb, Journal, March 14, 1958, 421.

[11] Todd Webb, Letter to Lucille Webb, Salisbury, South Rhodesia, June 23, 1958.

[12] Todd Webb, Africa Journal, 1958, 1.

[13] *Ibid.*, 1–2.

[14] Todd Webb, Journal, April 4, 1960.

[15] "I have just about broken even with my per diem and expenses. But I do want to get some presents and I have just enough to make it home. Just like the State Fair when I was a kid." Todd Webb, Letter to Lucille Webb, Norfolk Hotel, Nairobi, July 26, 1958.

[16] Todd Webb, Letter to Lucille Webb, Salisbury, Southern Rhodesia, June 23, 1958.

[17] Todd Webb, Journal, April 18, 1947.

[18] Gordon Parks, "The Restraints: Open and Hidden," *LIFE* magazine, September 1956.

[19] Todd Webb, Africa Journal, 7.

[20] Jolene Rickard, "Visualizing Sovereignty in the Time of Biometric Sensors," *South Atlantic Quarterly* 110, 2 (2011), 465–486.

The United Nations Itinerary for Todd Webb, 1958

[1] See International Journal of Middle Eastern studies system of transliteration <https://www.cambridge.org/core/journals/international-journal-of-middle-east-studies/information/author-resources/ijmes-translation-and-transliteration-guide>.

A Snapshot of the Togoland (Togo) Election, 1958
Aimée Bessire

[1] Brian Kenneth Digre, "The United Nations, France, and African Independence: A Case Study of Togo," *French Colonial History* 5 (2004), 196.

[2] Todd Webb, Africa Journal, 4.

[3] West African Correspondent, "Olympio On Top: The Togo Elections," *Africa Today* 5/4 (July–August 1958), 6–12.

[4] Todd Webb, Journal, April 28 1958.

The Myth of Africa
Aimée Bessire

[1] Okwui Enwezor, "Part One: The Uses of Afro-Pessimism," *Snap Judgments: New Positions in Contemporary African Photography*, ed. Okwui Enwezor (New York: International Center of Photography; and Göttingen: Steidl, 2006), 11.

[2] Todd Webb, Africa Journal, 1.

[3] At least the UN's definitions of order, development and civilization.

[4] V. Y. Mudimbe, *The Idea of Africa* (Bloomington, Indiana: Indiana University Press, 1994), xi.

[5] *Ibid.*, xi–xii.

[6] Todd Webb, Africa Journal, 1.

[7] *Ibid.*, 21.

[8] *Ibid.*

[9] Todd Webb, Letter to Lucille Webb, Tanga, Tanganyika, July 17, 1958.

[10] Todd Webb, Letter to Lucille Webb, Salisbury, South Rhodesia, June 22, 1958.

[11] Okwui Enwezor and Octavio Zaya, "Colonial Imaginary: Tropes of Disruption: History, Culture and Representation in the Works of African Photographers," in *In/Sight: African Photographers, 1940 to the Present*, ed. Clare Bell, Okwui Enwezor, Danielle Tilkin, and Octavio Zaya (New York: The Guggenheim Museum, 1996), 20.

[12] A great deal has been written about the history and usage of photography during the colonial era. See for example, Melissa Banta and Curtis Hinsley, *From Site to Sight: Anthropology, Photography and the Power of Imagery* (Cambridge, MA: Peabody Museum of Harvard University and Harvard University Press, 1986); Enwezor and Zaya, "Colonial Imaginary," in *In/Sight: African Photographers, 1940 to the Present*; Christraud M. Geary, *In and Out of Focus: Images from Central Africa 1885–1960* (Washington, D.C: Smithsonian Institution Press, 2002); Erin Haney, *Photography and Africa* (London: Reaktion Books, 2010); Christraud M. Geary, "Missionary Photography: Private and Public Readings," *African Arts* 24/4 (1991); Paul Landau, "Empires of the Visual: Photography and Colonial Administration in Africa," in *Images and Empires: Visuality in Colonial and Postcolonial Africa*, ed. Paul S. Landau and Deborah D. Kaspin (Berkeley: University of California Press, 2002), 141–71.

[13] Enwezor, *Snap Judgments*, 12.

[14] Todd Webb, Journal, April 21, 1958, 424.

[15] "The United Nations and Decolonization," United Nations <https://www.un.org/dppa/decolonization/en/history/international-trusteeship-system-and-trust-territories>.

[16] In April 1958, the Conference of Independent African States took place in Accra, Ghana, and declared the importance of the UN and established a UN African group in New York. See Catherine Hoskyns, "The African States and the United Nations 1958–1964," *International Affairs (Royal Institute of African Affairs)* 40/3 (July 1964), 466.

[17] D.I. Ajaegbo, "First Development Decade, 1960–1970: The United Nations and Economic Development of Africa," *Transafrican Journal of History* 15 (1986), 2.

[18] Todd Webb, Letter to Lucille Webb, Tanga, Tanganyika, July 18, 1958

[19] Looking at travel brochures and even websites for safari experiences in Tanzania, one still sees the marketing of the "cultural experience" alongside the viewing of animals in the Ngorongoro Crater or Serengeti. Many safaris offer for tourists to visit a Maasai boma, or traditional homestead. Maasai individuals even market their own culture, by standing on the road near the Crater and other popular sites, charging tourists to take their photographs.

[20] "United Nations Photos, Supplement No. 7," United Nations Office of Public Information, 2

[21] African photographers were active on the continent as early as 1839 with the earliest surviving vintage prints from 1840. See Erin Haney, *Photography and Africa* (London: Reaktion Books, 2010), 13.

[22] "Sleet, Moneta J. Jr.," *Encyclopedia.com* <https://www.encyclopedia.com/history/encyclopedias-almanacs-transcripts-and-maps/sleet-moneta-j-jr>.

[23] Haney, *Photography and Africa*, 27–28.

[24] See Christraud M. Geary's essay, "Eye Witnesses to History: African Professional Photographers in Togo and Ghana (1880–1960)," and "James Barnor on Photography in Ghana in the 1950s," in this book.

[25] We see similar qualities in the portrait photography of Seydou Keïta from Bamako, Mali, and many other photographers across the continent. See André Magnin (ed.), *Seydou Keïta* (Göttingen: Steidl, 1997).

[26] While the first three issues of an earlier manifestation of the magazine, *The African Drum*, failed in 1951, when they targeted images of "tribal life" to a savvy urban, Black South African population, the restructured *Drum*, with its photographs and stories of contemporary life was a success. See Okwui Enwezor, "A Critical Presence: *Drum* Magazine in Context," in *In/Sight*, 182.

[27] *Ibid.*, 181.

[28] *Ibid.*, 184–85.

[29] Todd Webb, Africa Journal.

[30] Todd Webb, Journal, April 4, 1960, 476.

Eyewitnesses to History: African Professional Photographers in Togo and Ghana, 1880–1960
Christraud M. Geary

[1] The post appeared ninety-three years later, on the occasion of another such visit by His Royal Highness, The Prince of Wales, Prince Charles and his wife Camilla, the Duchess of Cornwall. "1925: Maiden Visit of a Prince of Wales," *Modern Ghana*, November 5 2018 <https://www.modernghana.com/news/895376/1925-maiden-visit-of-a-prince-of-wales.html>.

[2] Among by now many publications are such classics as Tobias Wendl and Heike Behrend (eds), *Snap Me One: Studiofotografen in Afrika* (Munich: Prestel, 1998); Pascal Martin Saint Léon and N'Goné Fall (eds) with Frédérique Chapuis et al, *Anthology of African & Indian Ocean Photography* (Paris: Editions Revue Noire, 1999). Later overviews include Erin Haney, *Photography and Africa* (London: Reaktion Books, 2010); Charles Gore (ed.), "African Photography," *African Arts* special issue 48/3 (2015); Christraud M. Geary, "The Image of the Black in Early African Photography," in *The Image of the Black in African and Asian Art*, ed. David Bindman, Suzanne Preston Blier, and Henry Louis Gates, Jr (Cambridge, MA: Harvard University Press, 2017), 141–66; and Michael Graham-Stewart and Francis McWhannell, *Broad Sunlight: Early West African Photography* (London: Michael Graham-Stewart, 2020), which contains an extensive register of all foreign and local photographers active in the region before 1920, as well as 130 of their photographs. On picture postcards, see Christraud M. Geary, *Postcards from Africa: Photographers of the Colonial Era* (Boston: MFA Publications, 2018)

[3] Odumase was the seat of a Swiss Basel Mission station established in 1857, where missionary photographers first introduced photography and were later joined by African professional image-makers. See Veit Arlt and Nii O. Quarcoopome, "Photography, European Emblems and Statecraft in Manya Krobo (Ghana), about 1860–1939," in *Through African Eyes: The European in African Art, 1500 to Present*, ed. Nii O. Quarcoopome (Detroit: Detroit Institute of Arts, 2010), 59–72.

[4] Christraud M. Geary, "Through the Lenses of African Photographers: Depicting Foreigners and New Ways of Life, 1870–1950," in *Through African Eyes*, 86–99 (96).

[5] See "James Barnor on Photography in Ghana in the 1950s" in this book, 82–93). The literature also reflects this emphasis on people; many books, catalogues, and essays have been published about Africans and portraiture, for instance John Peffer and Elisabeth Lynn Cameron (eds), *Portraiture & Photography in Africa* (Bloomington: Indiana University Press, 2013).

[6] Besides F. F. Olympio, the Aguiar Brothers, also of Afro-Brazilian origin, were active. See Philippe David, "Photographer-Publishers in Togo," in *Anthology of African & Indian Ocean Photography*, 42–47; and Philippe David, *Le Togo: Cartes Postales, 1888–1914* (Saint-Maur-des-Fossés: Editions Sépia, 2007).

[7] Erin Haney, "Lutterodt Family Studios and the Changing Face of Early Portrait Photographs from the Gold Coast," in *Portraiture & Photography in Africa*, 67–101.

[8] For a detailed life history of Acolatse see Philippe David, *Alex A. Acolatse 1880–1957: Hommage á l'un des premiers photographes togolais* (Lomé: Editions Halo, Goethe Institut, 1992).

[9] Christraud M. Geary, "African Photographer Frederick Grant and Registering Copyright in 1884," in *The Power of Gold: Asante Royal Regalia from Ghana*, ed. Roslyn A. Walker (Dallas: Dallas Museum of Art; New Haven and London: Yale University Press, 2018), 57–69.

[10] Erin Haney, "'If these Walls could Talk!' Photographs, Photographers, and Their Patrons in Accra and Cape Coast, Ghana, 1840–1940," PhD thesis, School of Oriental and African Studies, University of London, 2004.

[11] Haney, "Lutterodt Family Studios," 78, 83.

[12] Vera Viditz-Ward, "Studio Photography in Freetown," in *Anthology of African & Indian Ocean Photography*, 32–41.

[13] Geary, *Postcards from Africa*, 22, 95–97, 101.

[14] Terence Dickinson, *Gold Coast Picture Postcards (1898–1975)* (Dronfield, UK: West Africa Study Circle, 2003).

[15] "Ashanti Goldfields Corporation," Wikipedia<https://en.wikipedia.org/wiki/Ashanti_Goldfields_Corporation>.

[16] Geary, *Postcards from Africa*, 49–50, 72; Graham-Stewart and McWhannell, *Broad Sunlight*, 18; Andrea Franc, *Wie die Schweiz zur Schokolade kam: Der Kakaohandel der Basler Handelsgesellschaft mit der Kolonie Goldküste (1893-1960)* (Basel: Schwabe, Basler Beiträge zur Geschichtswissenschaft, 2008), 132.

[17] According to his granddaughter, Kate Tamakloe, James K. Bruce-Vanderpuije changed the original spelling of the family name from Vanderpuye to Vanderpuije, and asked all of his family members to do the same. While some texts on the photographer use the original spelling, this essay honors the late Mr. Bruce-Vanderpuije's chosen name (Kate Tamakloe, email communication with Aimée Bessire, April 23, 2020).

[18] This summary is based on Tobias Wendl's essay "James K. Bruce-Vanderpuye" in Wendl and Behrend, *Snap Me One*, 64–73; and "Isaac H. Bruce-Vanderpuije recalls–, What photography is not, and why it needs appreciation," *FOTOTAA*, September 13, 2018 <https://fotota.hypotheses.org/5415>; see also "Accra a Century Ago: Life in Ghana before independence – in pictures," *The Guardian*, March 7, 2017 <https://www.theguardian.com/cities/gallery/2017/mar/07/accra-a-century-ago-ghana-before-independence-in-pictures>.

[19] See "Isaac H. Bruce-Vanderpuije recalls," *FOTOTAA*.

[20] Wendl made this observation in "James K. Bruce-Vanderpuye," 64.

[21] See Renée Mussai (ed.), *James Barnor: Ever Young* (Paris: Les Editions Clémentine de la Féronnière; London: Autograph, 2015). Among the many online resources are a Wikipedia entry about Barnor<https://en.wikipedia.org/wiki/James_Barnor#cite_note-NewsAfrica-18>; "James Barnor," *Autograph ABP*<http://autographabp-iadl.co.uk/artists/james-barnor/>; "James Barnor, Ever Young: An interview with Renée Mussai," *Africa is a Country*, July 11, 2019 <https://africasacountry.com/2019/11/james-barnor-ever-young>. See also Conversation between James Barnor and Aimeé Bessire, 2019, pp. 82–93.

[22] James Barnor, interview with Aimeé Bessire, November 1, 2019.

[23] See W. J. Varley, "The Castles and Forts of the Gold Coast," *Transactions of the Gold Coast & Togoland Historical Society* 1/1 (1952), 1–17. Julius Aikins may have accompanied Varley and his wife on a trip to several forts, and while most of the photographs were taken by Mary Varley, two images by Aikins are included: Ill. 2. *Elmina. Round Tower*; Ill. 10. Kormantin. *M.W. Bastion and Tower.*

[24] For more on Barnor's association with *Drum* while in Ghana, see James Barnor, interview with Aimeé Bessire, November 1, 2019.

[25] Lauri Firstenberg, "Postcoloniality, Performance, and Photographic Portraiture," in *The Short Century: Independence and Liberation Movements in Africa 1945–1994*, ed. Okwui Enwezor (Munich: Prestel, 2001), 175–179. A selection of *Drum* photographers' images follows on pages 180–217, with Barnor's photograph Fig. 7, p. 191.

Various film clips of this moment can be found online, for example "Ghana's Independence 1957 | Today in History | 6 March," *YouTube* <https://www.youtube.com/watch?v=UwfQvvYvrBE>.

[26] Todd Webb, Journal, July 8, 1958.

Seeing in Color: Todd Webb's Color Photography and the United Nations Commission

Aimée Bessire

[1] James Barnor, interview with Aimée Bessire, November 1, 2019.

[2] Many scholars have written about the racial biases of color film. See, for example, Sarah Lewis and Michael Famighetti, *Vision & Justice*, special issue of *Aperture* 223 (2016); Lorna Roth, "Looking at Shirley, the Ultimate Norm: Colour Balance, Image, Technologies, and Cognitive Equity," *Canadian Journal of Communication* 34/1 (2009), 111–136; Syreeta MacFadden, "Teaching the Camera to See My Skin: Navigating Photography's Inherited Bias Against Dark Skin," *Buzzfeed*, April 2, 2014 <https://www.buzzfeednews.com/article/syreetamcfadden/teaching-the-camera-to-see-my-skin>. Many have also written about the painful ways in which photography has been used to distort racial difference from its inception in the nineteenth century to today. See, for example, Molly Rogers, *Delia's Tears: Race, Science, and Photography in Nineteenth-Century America* (New Haven, CT: Yale University Press, 2010); Tanya Sheehan, *Study in Black and White: Photography, Race, Humor* (University Park, PA: Penn State University Press, 2020); Deborah Willis, *Picturing Us: African American Identity in Photography* (New York: New Press, 1997), to name but a few.

[3] Michel Frizot, "A Natural Strangeness: The Hypothesis of Color," in *The New History of Photography*, ed. Michel Frizot (Köln: Könemann Verlagsgesellschaft, 1998), 422.

[4] Scholars have theorized the subjectivities of how the human eye perceives colors. For example, the Young-Helmholtz theory, or tri-chromatic theory (based on theories of Thomas Young and Hermann von Helmholtz) suggests that the eye has three separate cone cells, each distinguishing a unique color: violet, green, or red. (See Thomas Young, "The Bakerian Lecture: On the Theory of Light and Colours," *Philosophical Transactions*, Royal Society, London, 1802.) Ewald Hering proposed the opponent process theory, which posited that colors are perceived in oppositions with three pairs of opponent colors: red/green, yellow/blue, and white/black (See Ewald Hering, *The Theory of Binocular Vision: Ewald Hering (1868)*, ed. Bruce Bridgeman and Lawrence Stark; trans. Bruce Bridgeman (New York: Plenum Press, 1977)).

[5] Webb talked about the distinction in "seeing" in 1947: "As soon as I get a good day, I want to start shooting up my Kodachrome. When I do that I almost have to stop shooting black and white because the seeing is so different." Todd Webb, Journal, October 6, 1947.

[6] Katherine A. Bussard, "Full Spectrum: Expanding the History of American Color Photography," in *Color Rush: American Color Photography from Stieglitz to Sherman*, ed. Katherine A. Bussard and Lisa Hostetler (New York: Aperture; and Milwaukee: Milwaukee Art Museum, 2013), 4.

[7] *Color Rush*, 20.

[8] French filmmaker Jean-Luc Godard famously refused to use the Kodak film available in 1978 for a Mozambican government commission, deeming it "inherently racist" because of its inability to record the realities of Black skin. See "Jean-Luc Godard," *Wikipedia*, July 5, 2020 <https://en.wikipedia.org/wiki/Jean-Luc_Godard>

[9] See Roth, 119–120. In the 1980s, Kodak developed Gold Max film specifically to capture a range of skin colors. Before that time, Fuji film was preferred for its slightly better representation of the subtleties of dark skin tones.

[10] Lisa Hostetler, "Real Color," in *Color Rush*, 17.

[11] *Color Rush*, 21.

[12] For more background on the connections between documentary, the FSA, and black and white photography, see: Walker Evans, *American Photographs* (New York: The Museum of Modern Art, 1938); James Agee and Walker Evans, *Let Us Now Praise Famous Men: The American Classic, In Words and Photographs, of Three Tenant Families in the Deep South* (East Hampton, NY: Harper's Books, 1941); Sarah Hermanson Meister (ed.) *Dorothea Lange: Words and Pictures* (New York: Museum of Modern Art Publications, 2020).

[13] Todd Webb, Journal, August 19, 1946.

[14] Todd Webb, Journal, August 10, 1947.

[15] On August 19, 1946, Webb wrote in his journal that he was going to "invest" in a Harrison Color Corrector set to enhance his color work, and, although it would be expensive, he says: "…if I am going to do a little color work I would like to do it right."

[16] *Ibid.*

[17] Todd Webb, Journal, February 6, 1954.

[18] Todd Webb, Journal, December 13, 1957.

[19] Todd Webb, Journal, January 20, 1958, 413.

[20] Todd Webb, Journal, June 25, 1948.

[21] For more on the images that may have impacted Webb's perceptions of Africa, see Aimée Bessire, "Myth of Africa," in this volume, 44–49.

[22] As early as 1937, the *Milwaukee Journal* published a candid color photograph, which was followed later that year by color images of the Hindenburg explosion in the *New York Sunday Mirror*. See *Color Rush*, 4

[23] *National Geographic* began hand-coloring black and white photographs as early as 1910 ,and published their first color image, an autochrome, in the July 1914 issue. It was also one of the first magazines to print images from 35 mm color Kodachrome images, which they endorsed in 1937. See *Color Rush*, 38.

[24] *Ibid.*

[25] There is no information in Todd Webb's journals or letters that fully explains why *LIFE* magazine paid for the film for his walk across the United States with the intention of publishing the images, yet never included them in the magazine.

[26] Gordon Parks, "The Restraints: Open and Hidden," *LIFE* magazine, September 24, 1956, 98–109.

[27] "Segregation in the South, 1956," Gordon Parks Foundation <http://www.gordonparksfoundation.org/gordon-parks/photography-archive/segregation-in-the-south-1956>.

[28] Todd Webb, Africa Journal, 18.

[29] *Ibid.*, 13.

[30] "Kassala," Wikipedia <https://en.wikipedia.org/wiki/Kassala>.

[31] See Ali Jimale Ahmed, "Todd Webb's Excursions into Somalia (or, Todd Webb in Somalia)," in this book, 154–61.

[32] Ali Jimale Ahmed, email communication with Aimée Bessire, March 22, 2020.

[33] Webb described photographing the scene in a letter to his wife Lucille: "They were having an outdoor class…and they were so delighted to be photographed. It was so lovely, I can hardly believe it…. It made my day…. What it has to do with the UN, I don't know?" Todd Webb, Letter to Lucille Webb, July 17, 1958, Tanga, Tanganyika.

[34] While today boys and girls both wear school uniforms, this privileging of the education of sons over daughters is still dominant in many parts of rural Tanzania, despite the Ministry of Education's attempt to create gendered equality in access to education.

[35] Todd Webb, Africa Journal, 20.

[36] It is interesting to note that Webb also printed his color negatives in black and white, because he did not know how to process color film.

Landscaping: Todd Webb's Representations of a Changing African Topography

Erin Hyde Nolan

[1] Susan Sontag, *On Photography* (London: Allen Lane: Penguin Books Ltd., 1978), 5.

[2] Liz Wells, *Land Matters: Landscape Photography, Culture and Identity* (London: I.B. Tauris, 2011), 2.

[3] On the history of sisal production in Tanganyika (Tanzania), see Hanan Sabea, "Reviving the Dead: Entangled Histories in the Privatisation of the Tanzanian Sisal Industry," *Africa: Journal of the International African Institute* 71/2 (2001), 286–313.

[4] Todd Webb, Journal, July 19, 1958, 433.

[5] *The Yearbook of the United Nations*, 1960 Part 1: The United Nations. Section 1: Political and security questions. Chapter 5: Declaration on granting independence to colonial countries and peoples, 44 <https://unyearbook.un.org/>.

[6] Aleksandr Gelfand, United Nations Archives and Records, conversation with Erin Hyde Nolan, February 5, 2020. By 1960, of the seventeen newly added states to the United Nations, sixteen were from the African continent.

[7] Deborah Bright, "Photographing Nature, Seeing Ourselves," in *America in View: Landscape Photography* 1865 to *Now*, ed. Douglas R. Nickel, Deborah Bright, and Jan Howard (Rhode Island School of Design Museum of Art, East Greenwich, RI: Meridian Printing, 2012), 1.

[8] Nicholas Natanson, *The Black Image in the New Deal: The Politics of FSA Photography* (Knoxville: University of Tennessee Press, 1992), 7.

[9] W. J. T. Mitchell, "Introduction," in *Landscape and Power*, ed. W. J. T. Mitchell (Chicago, Ill: Univ. of Chicago Press, 2009), 5.

[10] Cyliro Kinesa, Bird specialist in Serengeti, in communication with Jefta Kishosha, March 6, 2020.

[11] Wells, *Land Matters*, 12.

[12] Mitchell in *Landscape and Power*, 12–13.

[13] Four years later in 1964, Northern Rhodesia attained independence as The Republic of Zambia, and Nyasaland became the independent nation state of Malawi. Southern Rhodesia would be ratified as Rhodesia in 1965 but would not gain independence as Zimbabwe until 1980. Catherine Hoskyns, "The African States and the United Nations 1958–1964," *International Affairs (Royal Institute of International Affairs)* 40/3 (1964), 466, 472–473.

[14] As Webb noted, "I was even more surprised to hear that [Africans] were paid one tenth as much as a white man doing the same work," Todd Webb, Africa Journal, 23.

[15] The notion that landscape is not a noun, but instead a verb comes from W. J. T. Mitchell. See *Landscape and Power*, 1.

[16] Webb, Africa Journal, 22–23.

[17] Joel Snyder, "Territorial Photography," in *Landscape and Power*, 183.

[18] Gary van Wyk, "'Yesterday, Today, Tomorrow' Bush– Shooting in the Federation," in this volume, 182–91.

[19] Webb details the size of Kariba Lake: "175 miles long and in some places 20 miles wide, " Webb, Africa Journal, 22. It was not only people, but also wildlife, rising waters, and river ecology that were dramatically changed by the dam project. Chris Malcolm, "The Environment as Photographic Surface," in *Survey Practices and Landscape Photography Across the Globe*, ed. Erin Hyde Nolan and Sophie Junge (London: Routledge, 2022).

[20] Wells, *Land Matters*, 6; Eleanor Hight and Gary Sampson, "Introduction," in *Colonial Photography: Imag(in)ing Race and Place* (London: Routledge, 2002), 2–5.

[21] Chris Malcolm, "The Environment as Photographic Surface," in *Survey Practices and Landscape Photography Across the Globe*, ed. Erin Hyde Nolan and Sophie Junge (London: Routledge, 2022)

[22] Todd Webb, Letter to Lucille Webb, July 3, 1958.

[23] Rebecca Solnit, "Reclaiming History: Richard Misrach and the Politics of Landscape Photography," *Aperture* 120 (1990), 35.

[24] Mitchell, in *Landscape and Power*, 12.

[25] Wells, *Land Matters*, 6.

[26] See Jan-Lodewijk Grootaers, "Historical Synopsis of the African Countries Visited by Todd Webb in 1958," in this volume, 20–21.

Todd Webb's Excursions into Somalia

Ali Jimale Ahmed

[1] John Berger, "Appearances," in *Another Way of Telling*, John Berger, Jean Mohr, and Nicolas Philibert (New York: Pantheon, 1982), 83.

[2] Samuel Taylor Coleridge, *Biographia Literaria or Biographical Sketches of my Literary Life and Opinions* (London: R. Fenner, 1817), 153.

[3] Berger, 112.

[4] The author has included both the Somali transliteration, Arbaca Rukun, and the Arabic transliteration following the International Journal of Middle East Studies standards, Arba' Rukun. The mosque name means four (Arba') columns (Rukun).

Yesterday Today Tomorrow Bush – Shooting in the Federation

Gary van Wyk

[1] R. S. Garfield Todd, *Africa Today Pamphlets: 4, The Federation of Rhodesia and Nyasaland* (New York: The American Committee on Africa, Inc., 1959), 32.

[2] *Ibid.*, 33.

[3] "Rhodesia – The Years Between," Rhodesian Heritage, June 26, 2010 <https://rhodesianheritage.blogspot.com/2010/06/rhodesia-years-between-1923-1973.html>.

[4] Todd Webb, Letter to Lucille Webb, July 3, 1958.

[5] Jeffrey Cavanaugh, "FOREX Africa: The CFA Franc aka The African Euro," *The Moguldom Nation*, February 12, 2014 <http://afkinsider.com/41946/forex-africa-african-euro/#sthash.bAiuUVxB.dpuf>.

[6] Todd Webb, Africa Journal, 1958, 23.

[7] Todd Webb, letter to Lucille Webb, June 22, 1958: "Ranger is 8 years older than Arthur but like him in so many little ways."

[8] Arthur Tyrrell's precise position at the UN during 1958 is specified in a list of UN personnel interviewed that is included as an annex in a UN report of September 20, 1958, entitled "Report of the Expert Commission on United Nations Public Information." See A/3928 English Annex II Page 1, accessible online at <https://search.archives.un.org/uploads/r/united-nations-archives/1/f/6/1f68058d684e9c58f367e133355c63f-9f123a69bcd9c756e672acc1359f82b62/S-0846-0004-02-00001.pdf>.

[9] Lucille Webb, Letter to Todd Webb, July 14, 1958, "Al and Mary are having a picnic this Saturday and Mary said she would invite the [Arthur] Tyrrels [sic] but I have not heard whether they can come or not. I know you are not keen for another trip but Arthur is thinking about next year and wanted to know if I would let you got to the Pacific. I assured him that I would not deprive you of such an opportunity. They have spent this year's budget on you but of course they will have a new one next year and by the time it rolls around, you may be ready to go somewhere… Arthur told me you said Rhodesia was like Omaho [sic]. I did laugh because it sounds like my saying that Rome is like Chicago. Wasn't it nice of the [Ranger] Tyrrells to send me a present?"

[10] Todd Webb, Letter to Lucille Webb, July 3, 1958, "I suppose Arthur sang his 'South African song' at a dinner that Lucille attended"; in the same letter Todd Webb describes Ranger [Tyrrell] as "like Arthur but not quite as lively." See also Note 9 above for other evidence of the Webbs' social relationship with Arthur Tyrrell.

[11] Todd Webb, Letter to Lucille Webb, June 23, 1958.

[12] This explains the importance of Northern Rhodesia to the Federation, and for Imperial Great Britain, these copper fields, combined with new Canadian mines, returned "British copper" to the dominant position it last held during the 1800s. However, the American recession of 1957–58 and Russian dumping of copper reduced 1959 earnings to £69m from £114m.

[13] "Operation Noah Memorial" <http://zimfieldguide.com/mashonaland-west/operation-noah-memorial>.

[14] Todd Webb, Letter to Lucille Webb, Salisbury, Rhodesia, June 22, 1958.

[15] Michelle Alexander makes this point in *The New Jim Crow: Mass Incarceration in the Age of Colorblindness* (New York: The New Press, 2012).

[16] South African novelist Stuart Cloete makes this claim in his study on Rhodes, *Against These Three*, a biography of Rhodes, Lobenghula, and Transvaal president Paul Kruger, begun in the 1930s but published in 1946. Cloete, shaped by the experiences of the Second World War, felt that fascism could be said to have begun with Rhodes. See Paul Maylam, "Rhodes & Hitler: The Naked Truth," *The Journalist*, May 6, 2015 <https://www.thejournalist.org.za/spotlight/rhodes-hitler-the-naked-truth>.

[17] Wikipedia provides a good summary of these events: "Rudd Concession," Wikipedia <https://en.wikipedia.org/wiki/Rudd_Concession>.

18 This cultural group is not to be confused with the South African Ndebele, renowned for their mural art and beadwork.

19 The text of the Royal Charter of the BSAC is accessible online at "BSAC Charter 1889: Charter of the British South African Company" <https://www.rhodesia.me.uk/charter/>.

20 The Palace Hotel went through several changes over the years, including the tower block that was added in the 1950s. See "Bulawayo Memories" <http://www.bulawayomemories.com/aroundtown/hotels.html>.

21 Statistical evidence suggests that in 1961, 612,573 Africans were employed in Southern Rhodesia, of which forty-five percent were immigrants, mainly from Nyasaland. See discussion on "Alternate history" <https://www.alternatehistory.com/forum/threads.rhodesia-has-white-majority.312321/page-2>.

22 This reference is to Henri Cartier-Bresson's philosophy of the photograph as capturing a "decisive moment," which was also the title of a book of his photography, *The Decisive Moment: The Photography of Henri Cartier-Bresson* (New York: Simon and Schuster, 1952).

23 Self-government was selected via referendum; 14,856 votes were cast out of a possible 18,810, with 8,774 for self-government and 5,989 for Union with South Africa. See W. D. Gale, M.B.E., "The Years Between 1923–1973: Half a Century of Responsible Government in Rhodesia," Our Rhodesian Heritage <https://rhodesianheritage.blogspot.com/2010/06/rhodesia-years-between-1923-1973.html>.

24 Carlos Lopes, *Balancing Rocks: Environment and Development in Zimbabwe* (Harare: SAPES Books, 1996).

25 Njabulo Ncube, "2008 Assessment: Reporter's Notebook: Zimbabwe," Global Integrity Report. Archived from the original on July 15, 2012 <https://archive.is/20120715142551/http:/report.globalintegrity.org/Zimbabwe/2008/notebook>.

26 David Lan, *Guns and Rain: Guerillas and Spirit Mediums in Zimbabwe* (Oakland: University of California Press, 1985), 228.

27 "White People in Zimbabwe," Wikipedia <https://en.wikipedia.org/wiki/White_people_in_Zimbabwe#cite_ref-57>.

Of Color: Todd Webb's Images of Africa in the American Civil Rights Era
Casey Riley

1 Martin Luther King, Jr, "Loving Your Enemies," sermon delivered at Dexter Avenue Baptist Church, Montgomery, Alabama, November 17, 1957.

2 Todd Webb, Journal, April 26, 1947.

Listening to Todd Webb's Images of Tanganyika and Zanzibar
Rehema Chachage

1 Tanganyika and Zanzibar now constitute the United Republic of Tanzania. Independent Tanganyika, which existed from 1961 to 1964, was only the mainland part of present-day Tanzania. The Articles of Union (April 22, 1964) and Act of Union (April 25, 1964) formalized the union of the People's Republic of Zanzibar and Pemba with Tanganyika to form the United Republic of Tanganyika and Zanzibar, which officially changed its name to the United Republic of Tanzania the following year. See "Tanganyika," Wikipedia <https://en.wikipedia.org/wiki/Tanganyika>; "Articles of Union," Wikipedia <https://en.wikipedia.org/wiki/Articles_of_Union>.

2 Tina Campt, *Listening to Images* (Durham, NC: Duke University Press, 2017).

3 The territory was seized from the Germans at the end of the First World War. The United Nations thereafter gave the British colonial government mandate over the territory; having them play a "big brother" role of "guiding" the country–for a limited, though not specified amount of time after which the country would become independent. See, among many other references on this, Godfrey Mwakikagile, *Life in Tanganyika in the Fifties: My Reflections and Narratives from the White Settler Community and Others* (Grand Rapids, Michigan: Pan African Books Continental Press, 2006).

4 "Seeing Africa: 1958," Todd Webb Archive <http://www.toddwebbarchive.com/about>.

5 Webb also captures some of the white colonial officials who were in the country at the time.

6 To do away with one we have to do away with the other, since it is the relation between them which makes one a "settler" and the other "native." See Mahmood Mamdani, "When does a settler become a native? Reflection of the Colonial Roots of Citizenship in Equatorial and South Africa," Inaugural Lecture, University of Cape Town, South Africa, May 13, 1998.

7 Todd Webb, Letter to Lucille Webb, Dar es Salaam, July 8, 1958.

8 Todd Webb, Letter to Lucille Webb, Dar es Salaam, July 18, 1958.

9 Mwakikagile, *Life in Tanganyika*, 155–409.

10 Todd Webb, Letter to Lucille Webb, Dar es Salaam, July 18, 1958.

11 Here, the word tense is used in reference to Campt's concept, which is also an extension of Darieck Scott's concept of "*muscular tension*." Campt illuminates the ways in which tension, such as clenched jaws or pursed lips, can be understood–not as portrayals of people frozen in time by the camera, but rather as "an active, tense, and expressive practice of both restraint and constraint," Campt, 50–57.

12 *Ibid.*, 5–6.

13 *Ibid.*, 5.

14 *Ibid.*, 51.

15 *Ibid.*, 57–58. In her text, Campt theorizes the concept of "stasis" as the invisible vibrations of a body which is otherwise appearing to be still.

16 bell hooks argues for the photograph as living-proof of those who were and those who are; as that which has the ability to reveal and enable us to remember (and re-member) severed and fragmented histories; and as that which has the ability to call us back to the past, to connect ourselves to a recuperative, redemptive memory that enables us to construct radical identities that transcend the limits of the colonizing eye. See bell hooks, "In Our Glory: Photography and Black Life," in *Art of My Mind: Visual Politics* (New York: The New Press, 1995), 54–64.

17 Here I am specifically referring to the historical canon and archives connected to Africa and more specifically, Tanzania. As a reference, see Michel-Rolph Trouillot, *Silencing the Past: Power and the Production of History* (Boston, MA: Beacon Press, 1995), 26. Here, Trouillot describes the mechanisms behind silences entering the process of historical production. Questioning the things that make some narratives powerful enough to pass as history while others remain silenced, he writes (in summary, as quoted from Basu and de Jong in "Utopian archives, decolonial affordances: Introduction to special issue," *Social Anthropology* 24/1 (2016) 5–19 (7–8): "silences enter the process of historical production at four crucial moments: the moments of fact creation (the making of sources); the moment of fact assembly (the making of archives); the moment of fact retrieval (the making of narratives); and the moment of retrospective significance (the making of history in the final instance) leading us to question history itself."

18 Bibi is a Swahili term used in reference to a woman or grandmother. In this case, it is used to mean grandmother.

19 Other than from my sister.

20 Babu is a Swahili term used for grandfather, and ancestor, or an old man, a patriarch, a progenitor. In this case, it is used to mean grandfather.

21 My sister, for example, uses baking as a coping mechanism. Growing up, I used to enjoy pushing her to a point of agitation, because I knew that as a result, only good things would come (out of the oven).

BIBLIOGRAPHY

Ajaegbo, D. I., "First Development Decade, 1960–1970: The United Nations and Economic Development of Africa," *Transafrican Journal of History* 15 (1986), 1–17

Amkpa, Awam, and Tamar Garb, *African Photography from the Walther Collection: Distance and Desire: Encounters with the African Archive* (Göttingen: Steidl; New York: The Walther Collection, 2013)

Arlt, Veit and Nii O. Quarcoopome, "Photography, European Emblems and Statecraft in Manya Krobo (Ghana), about 1860–1939," in *Through African Eyes: The European in African Art, 1500 to Present*, ed. Nii O. Quarcoopome (Detroit: Detroit Institute of Arts, 2010), 59–72

Banjo, Adewale, "The Politics of Succession Crisis in West Africa: The Case of Togo," *International Journal on World Peace* XXV, 2 (2008), 33–55

Banta, Melissa and Curtis Hinsley, "19th Century Visions of the Exotic," in *From Site to Sight: Anthropology, Photography and the Power of Imagery* (Cambridge, MA: Peabody Museum of Harvard University and Harvard University Press, 1986), 39–47

Bell, Clare, Okwui Enwezor, Olu Oguibe, and Octavio Zaya, *In/sight: African Photographers, 1940 to the Present* (New York: Guggenheim Museum Publications, 1996)

Bright, Deborah, "Photographing Nature, Seeing Ourselves," in *America in View: Landscape Photography 1865 to Now*, ed. Douglas R. Nickel, Deborah Bright, and Jan Howard (Rhode Island School of Design Museum of Art, East Greenwich, RI: Meridian Printing, 2012), 31–51

Campt, Tina, *Listening to Images* (Durham, NC: Duke University Press, 2017)

Chagas, Edson, Daniela Baumann, Joshua Chuang, and Oluremi C. Onabanjo, *Recent Histories: Contemporary African Photography and Video Art* (Göttingen: Steidl, 2017)

Chapuis, Frédérique, "The pioneers of St. Louis," in *Anthology of African and Indian Ocean Photography* (Paris: Revue Noire Publications, 1999), 49–60

Coombes, Annie, *Reinventing Africa: Museums, Material Culture and Popular Imagination in Late Victorian and Edwardian England* (New Haven and London: Yale University Press, 1994)

Coote, Jeremy and Elizabeth Edwards, "Images of Benin at the Pitt Rivers Museum," *African Arts* 30, 4 (1997), 26–35, 93

David, Philippe, *Alex A. Acolatse 1880–1957: Hommage à l'un des Premiers Photographes Togolais* (Lomé: Editions Halo, Goethe Institut, 1992)

____, "Photographer-Publishers in Togo," in *Anthology of African & Indian Ocean Photography*, ed. Pascal Martin Saint Léon and N'Goné Fall, with Frédérique Chapuis et al (Paris: Editions Revue Noire, 1999), 42–47

____, Le Togo. *Cartes Postales, 1888–1914* (Saint-Maur-des-Fossés: Editions Sépia, 2007)

Dickinson, Terence, *Gold Coast Picture Postcards* (1898–1975) (Dronfield, UK: West Africa Study Circle, 2003)

Digre, Brian Kenneth, "The United Nations, France, and African Independence: A Case Study of Togo," *French Colonial History* 5 (2004), 193–205

Enwezor, Okwui, "A Critical Presence: Drum Magazine in Context," in *In/sight: African Photographers, 1940 to the Present*, 179–91

Evans Hunt, Betsy, Sean Corcoran, and Daniel Okrent, *I See a City: Todd Webb's New York* (New York: Thames & Hudson, 2017)

Franc, Andrea, *Wie die Schweiz zur Schokolade kam. Der Kakaohandel der Basler Handelsgesellschaft mit der Kolonie Goldküste (1893–1960)* (Basler Beiträge zur Geschichtswissenschaft; Basel: Schwabe, 2008)

Firstenberg, Lauri, "Postcoloniality, Performance, and Photographic Portraiture," in *The Short Century. Independence and Liberation Movements in Africa 1945–1994*, ed. Okwui Enwezor (Munich: Prestel, 2001), 175–79

Geary, Christraud M., "Impressions of the African Past: Interpreting Ethnographic Photographs from Cameroon" *Visual Anthropology* 3/2–3 (1990), 289–315

____, "Old Pictures, New Approaches: Researching Historical Photographs," *African Arts* 24/4 (1991), 36–98

____, and Virginia Lee Webb (ed.), "Different Visions? Postcards from Africa by European and African Photographers and Sponsors," in *Delivering Views: Distant Cultures in Early Postcards* (Washington, D.C.: Smithsonian Institution Press, 1998)

____, "Early African Photographers," in In and *Out of Focus: Images from Central Africa, 1885–1960* (Washington, D.C.: Smithsonian Institution Press, 2002), 103–10

____, *In and Out of Focus: Images from Central Africa, 1885–1960* (Washington, D.C.: Smithsonian Institution Press, 2002)

____, "Through the Lenses of African Photographers: Depicting Foreigners and New Ways of Life, 1870–1950," in *Through African Eyes: The European in African Art, 1500 to Present*, ed. Nii Quarcoopome (Detroit: Detroit Institute of Arts, 2010), 86–99

____, "The Image of the Black in Early African Photography," in *The Image of the Black in African and Asian Art*, ed. David Bindman, Suzanne Preston Blier, and Henry Louis Gates, Jr (Cambridge, MA: Harvard University Press, 2017), 141–66

____, "African Photographer Frederick Grant and Registering Copyright in 1884," in *The Power of Gold: Asante Royal Regalia from Ghana*, ed. Roslyn A. Walker (Dallas: Dallas Museum of Art; New Haven and London: Yale University Press, 2018), 57–69

____, *Postcards from Africa. Photographers of the Colonial Era* (Boston: MFA Publications, 2018)

Franziska, Jenni, "Through the Lens: In Bamako, a Group of Young Photographers Engage a Changing City," *Aperture* 227 (2017), 34–37

Gore, Charles (ed.), "African Photography," *African Arts* 48/3 (2015), 1–5

Graham-Stewart, Michael, and Francis McWhannell, *Broad Sunlight: Early West African Photography* (London: Michael Graham-Stewart, 2020)

Granqvist, Raoul, *Photography and American Coloniality: Eliot Elisofon in Africa, 1942–1972* (East Lansing: Michigan State University Press, 2017)

Hahn, Hans Peter, "On the Circulation of Colonial Pictures," in *Global Photographies: Memory – History- Archives*, ed. Sissy Helff and Stefanie Michels (Bielefeld: Transcript Verlag, 2018), 89–108, esp. 94

Haney, Erin, "'If these Walls could Talk!' Photographs, Photographers, and Their Patrons in Accra and Cape Coast, Ghana, 1840–1940," PhD thesis, School of Oriental and African Studies, University of London, 2004

____, *Exposures: Photography and Africa* (London: Reaktion Books, 2010)

____, "Lutterodt Family Studios and the Changing Face of Early Portrait Photographs from the Gold Coast," in *Portraiture & Photography in Africa*, ed. John Peffer and Elisabeth Lynn Cameron (Bloomington: Indiana University Press, 2013), 67–101

Hight, Eleanor and Gary Sampson, "Introduction," in *Colonial Photography: Imag(in)ing Race and Place*, ed. Eleanor Hight and Gary Sampson (London: Routledge, 2002), 1–19

Hoskyns, Catherine, "The African States and the United Nations 1958–1964," *International Affairs (Royal Institute of African Affairs)* 40/3 (July 1964), 466–80

Keïta, Seydou, "Seydou's Story," in *Flash Afrique: Photography from West Africa*, ed. Gerald Matt and Thomas Mießgang (Vienna: KUNSTHALLE Wien, 2001), 66–69

Kratz, Corinne A., *The Ones That Are Wanted: Communication and the Politics of Representation in a Photographic Exhibition* (Berkeley: University of California Press, 2002)

Landau, Paul, "Empires of the Visual: Photography and Colonial Administration in Africa," in *Images and Empires: Visuality in Colonial and Postcolonial Africa*, ed. Paul S. Landau and Deborah D. Kaspin (Berkeley: University of California Press, 2002), 141–71

Lewis, Sarah and Michael Famighetti, *Vision & Justice*, special issue of *Aperture* 223 (2016)

Lutz, Catherine A., and Jane L. Collins, *Reading National Geographic* (Chicago: University of Chicago Press, 1993)

Malcolm, Chris, "The Environment as Photographic Surface," in *Survey Practices and Landscape Photography Across the Globe*, ed. Sophie Junge and Erin Hyde Nolan (London: Routledge, 2022)

McFadden, Syreeta, "Teaching the Camera to See My Skin: Navigating Photography's Inherited Bias Against Dark Skin," *Buzzfeed*, April 2, 2014 <https://www.buzzfeednews.com/article/syreetamcfadden/teaching-the-camera-to-see-my-skin>

Mitchell, W.J.T., *Landscape and Power* (Chicago, IL: University of Chicago Press, 2009)

Mofokeng, Santu, "The Black Photo Album," in *Anthology of African and Indian Ocean Photography* (Paris: Revue Noire Publications, 1999), 69–74

____, "Trajectory of a Street Photographer," in *Anthology of African and Indian Ocean Photography* (Paris: Revue Noire Publications, 1999), 265–70

Monenembo, Tierno, "Portrait of my Grandfather," in *Anthology of African and Indian Ocean Photography* (Paris: Revue Noire Publications, 1999), 206–7

Mussai, Renée (ed.), *James Barnor: Ever Young* (Paris: Les Editions Clémentine de la Féronnière; London: Autograph, 2015)

Mustafa, Hudita Nura, "Portraits of Modernity: Fashioning Selves in Dakarois Popular Photography," in *Images and Empires: Visuality in Colonial and Postcolonial Africa*, ed. Paul S. Landau and Deborah D. Kaspin (Berkeley: University of California Press, 2002)

Natanson, Nicholas, *The Black Image in the New Deal: The Politics of FSA Photography* (Knoxville: University of Tennessee Press, 1992)

Nimis, Erika, "The golden age of black and white in Mali," in *Anthology of African and Indian Ocean Photography* (Paris: Revue Noire Publications, 1999), 105–8

____, "Yoruba Studio Photographers in Francophone West Africa," in *Portraiture and Photography in Africa*, 102–40.

Oguibe, Olu, "Photography and the Substance of the Image," in *In/sight: African Photographers, 1940 to the Present* (New York: Guggenheim Museum Publications, 1996), 231–50

Peffer, John and Elisabeth L. Cameron, *Portraiture and Photography in Africa* (Bloomington: Indiana University Press, 2013)

Plattner, Steven W, Roy E. Stryker, Cornell Capa, Esther Bubley, John Vachon, Sol Libsohn, Harold Corsini, Todd Webb, Charlotte Brooks, Russell Lee, Martha M. M. Roberts, Charles E. Rotkin, Gordon Parks, Edwin Rosskam, and Louise Rosskam, *Roy Stryker, U.S.A., 1943–1950: The Standard Oil (New Jersey) Photography Project* (Austin: University of Texas Press, 1983)

Rakotoson, Michèl, "My Uncle, My Memory," in *Anthology of African and Indian Ocean Photography* (Paris: Revue Noire Publications, 1999), 218

Rogers, Molly, *Delia's Tears: Race, Science, and Photography in Nineteenth-Century America* (New Haven, CT: Yale University Press, 2010)

Roth, Lorna, "Looking at Shirley, the Ultimate Norm: Colour Balance, Image Technologies, and Cognitive Equity," *Canadian Journal of Communication* 34/1 (2009), 111–136

Sabea, Hanan, "Reviving the Dead: Entangled Histories in the Privatisation of the Tanzanian Sisal Industry," *Africa: Journal of the International African Institute* 71/2 (2001), 286–313

Saint Léon, Pascal Martin and N'Goné Fall (eds), with Frédérique Chapuis et al, *Anthology of African & Indian Ocean Photography* (Paris: Editions Revue Noire, 1999)

Salvesen, Britt, and Diana Tuite, *After Atget: Todd Webb Photographs New York and Paris* (Brunswick, Maine: Bowdoin College, Museum of Art, 2011)

Sekula, Allan, "The Body and the Archive," *October* 39 (1986), 3–64

Schildkrout, Enid, "The Spectacle of Africa through the Lens of Herbert Lang: Belgian Congo Photographs 1909–1915," *African Arts* 24/4 (1991), 70–85, 100

Schildkrout, Enid, "Revisiting Emil Torday's Congo: 'Images of Africa' at the British Museum," *African Arts* 25/1 (1992), 60–69, 99–100

Sheehan, Tanya, *Study in Black and White: Photography, Race, Humor* (University Park, PA: Penn State University Press, 2020)

Stewart, Susan, "The Souvenir," *On Longing* (Durham: Duke University Press, 1993), 132–50

Smith, David, "'Racism' of Early Color Photography Explored in Art Exhibition," *The Guardian*, January 25, 2013 <https://www.theguardian.com/artanddesign/2013/jan/25/racism-colour-photography-exhibition>

Snyder, Joel, "Territorial Photography," in *Landscape and Power*, ed. W. J. T. Mitchell (Chicago: University of Chicago Press, 1994), 175–201

Solnit, Rebecca, "Reclaiming History: Richard Misrach and the Politics of Landscape Photography," *Aperture* 120 (1990), 30–35

Sontag, Susan, "Fascinating Fascism," in *Under the Sign of Saturn* (New York: Farrar, Straus & Giroux, 1980), 73–105

____, *On Photography* (London: Allen Lane Penguin Books Ltd, 1978)

The United Nations Report, 1960

Varley, W. J., "The Castles and Forts of the Gold Coast," *Transactions of the Gold Coast & Togoland Historical Society*, 1/1 (1952), 1–17

Viditz-Ward, Vera, "Studio Photography in Freetown," in *Anthology of African & Indian Ocean Photography*, ed. Pascal Martin Saint Léon and N'Goné Fall, with Frédérique Chapuis et al (Paris: Editions Revue Noire, 1999), 34–41

Webb, Todd, Africa Journal 1958, Todd Webb Archive

____, Journal: Part 1, Todd Webb Archive

____, *Todd Webb* (Chicago: The Institute, 1956)

____, *The Gold Rush Trail and the Road to Oregon* (Garden City, NY: Doubleday, 1963)

____, *Todd Webb, Photographs: Early Western Trails and Some Ghost Towns* (Fort Worth, TX: Amon Carter Museum, 1979)

____, and Drury B. Alexander, *Texas Homes of the Nineteenth Century* (Austin: University of Texas Press, 1984)

____, *Looking Back: Memoirs and Photographs* (Albuquerque: University of New Mexico Press, 1991)

____, and Michael Alpert, *Todd Webb: A Photographer's Welcome Home* (Orono: University of Maine Press, 2008)

Wells, Liz, *Land Matters: Landscape Photography, Culture and Identity* (London: IB Tauris, 2011)

Wendl, Tobias and Heike Behrend (eds), *Snap Me One: Studiofotografen in Afrika* (Munich: Prestel, 1998)

Wendl, Tobias, "James K. Bruce-Vanderpuye," in *Snap Me One: Studiofotografen in Afrika*, ed. Tobias Wendl and Heike Behrend (Munich: Prestel, 1998), 64–73

Willis, Deborah, *Picturing Us: African American Identity in Photography* (New York: New Press, 1997)

AUTHOR BIOGRAPHIES

Ali Jimale Ahmed
Ali Jimale Ahmed holds an MA in African Area Studies and a PhD in Comparative Literature from the University of California, Los Angeles (UCLA). Poet, cultural critic, short-story writer, and scholar, Ahmed is Professor and former chair of Comparative Literature at Queens College of the City University of New York, where he also teaches for the Africana Studies Program and the Department of Classical, Middle Eastern, and Asian Languages and Cultures; he is also on the Comparative Literature faculty at the CUNY Graduate center. His books include *The Invention of Somalia* (1995), *Daybreak Is Near: Literature, Clans, and the Nation-State in Somalia* (1996), *Fear Is a Cow* (2002), *Diaspora Blues* (2005), *The Road Less Traveled: Reflections on the Literatures of the Horn of Africa* (2008, coedited with the late Taddesse Adera), *When Donkeys Give Birth to Calves: Totems, Wars, Horizons, Diasporas* (2012) and *Gaso, Ganuun iyo Gasiin* (a novel) (2018; roughly translated as "Kraal, Milk, Sustenance"). His poetry and short stories have been translated into several languages, including Japanese, Danish, Bosnian, Portuguese, and Turkish.

James Barnor
Born in 1929 in Ghana, James Barnor experienced first-hand his country's independence as well as the formation of the diaspora to London in the 1960s. In the early 1950s, he opened his famous Ever Young Photographic Studio in Accra, where he immortalized a nation craving modernity and independence in an ambiance that was animated by conversation and highlife music. He was the first photo-journalist to collaborate with the *Daily Graphic*, a newspaper published in Ghana by the London Daily Mirror Group. Close to *Drum*, an important lifestyle magazine founded in South Africa in 1951 and symbol of the anti-apartheid movement, he did several assignments for them in a climate of euphoria and celebration. In 1959, two years after Ghana's Independence, James Barnor left for London, a city in the throes of becoming a multicultural capital, to further his photographic knowledge. He discovered color processing at the Colour Processing Laboratories Ltd, Edenbridge, the leading color laboratory in Britain, and also attended the Medway College of Art, Rochester, Kent. His photos were published on the front cover of *Drum*. He eloquently caught the zeitgeist of Swinging London and the experiences of the African diaspora in the capital. Toward the end of the 1960s he was recruited by Agfa-Gevaert and returned to Ghana to set up the country's first color laboratory. There he stayed for the next twenty years, working in his new X23 studio as an independent photographer and for a handful of State agencies in Accra. Today James Barnor lives in the UK devoting most of his time to his work, in a spirit of transmission.

Aimée Bessire
Aimée Bessire teaches courses in African art and culture, African photography, contemporary art, and history of photography at Bates College. She received her PhD and MA specializing in African Art from Harvard University and has a MA in Ancient Near Eastern and 20th-century art from NYU's Institute of Fine Arts. Bessire was a Helena Rubinstein Fellow in Critical Theory and Curatorial Studies at the Whitney Museum Independent Study Program. She has published on contemporary African art and photography and Sukuma culture in Tanzania. She is currently working on a manuscript on Sukuma power objects.

Rehema Chachage
Rehema Chachage is a visual artist whose practice can be viewed as a performative archive which untraditionally collects stories, rituals, and other oral traditions in different media (performance, photography, video, text as well as physical installations); which traces hi/stories directly tied to women in the Swahili region; and, which employs written texts, oral and aural stories, melodies, and relics from several re-enacted/performed rituals as source of research. She has a BA in Fine Art (2009) from Michaelis School of Fine Art, University of Cape Town; and an MA Contemporary Art Theory (2018) from Goldsmiths, University of London. Currently she is doing her PhD in practice with the Academy of Fine Art in Vienna with her research focusing on the archive and its methodologies, specifically observing ways of doing the archive differently through one's practice as an artist. www.rehemachachage.com

Betsy Evans Hunt
Betsy Evans Hunt is the Executive Director of the Todd Webb Archive in Portland, Maine. She first met Todd and Lucille Webb when they visited her gallery in 1989. A wonderful friendship and partnership ensued. They had similar sensibilities artistically and socially, both interested more in the integrity of Todd's work and its presentation than in commercial opportunity. As fate would have it, they did pretty well and enjoyed themselves thoroughly along the way. Evans Hunt inherited the responsibility for the Todd Webb Estate in 2008 and since then has pursued her goal to educate the public about Webb and his oeuvre. She shepherded and edited the book on Webb's New York photographs, *I See a City* (Thames & Hudson, 2017) and is currently working on several other related projects. Before moving to Maine in 1988, she was director of a photography gallery in San Francisco (1978–81), managed Robert Mapplethorpe's Studio in New York (1981–83), catalogued the collection at the Addison Gallery of American Art, Andover, MA (1984–86), and completed Sotheby's American Art Course in 1987.

Christraud Geary
Christraud M. Geary is an independent scholar and Teel Senior Curator Emerita of African and Oceanic Art at the Museum of Fine Arts, Boston, after holding this position from 2003 to 2014. A cultural anthropologist with a doctorate from the Goethe University, Frankfurt am Main, Germany, she conducted long-term research on the history and the arts of the Cameroon Grassfields, a highland region in the western part of the country. Her findings have appeared in several books and numerous essays. Geary soon focused on early colonial photography in Cameroon and other parts of the African continent, and joined a cohort of scholars, who began pioneering research on the history of photography and Africa in the 1970s. From 1990 to 2003, she served as Curator of the Eliot Elisofon Photographic Archives, National Museum of African Art, Smithsonian Institution in Washington D.C., where she built and oversaw a postcard collection of over 10,000 cards of Africa. She has organized photographic exhibitions and published catalogs and books. Among her publications are *Delivering Views: Distant Cultures in Early Postcards* co-edited with Virginia-Lee Webb (1998) and *In and Out of Focus: Images from Central Africa, 1885–1960* (2002). She is the author of many essays, most recently of "The Image of the Black in Early African Photography" in: Bindman, Blier, and Gates, Jr. (eds) *The Image of the Black in Africa and Asia* (2017); and "Early Photographers and the Afterlife of Their Images, 1860–1930" in: Anderson and Aronson (eds.) *African Photographer J. A. Green: Reimagining the Indigenous and the Colonial* (2017). Her most recent book is *Postcards from Africa. Photographers of the Colonial Era* (2018).

Jan-Lodewijk Grootaers
Jan-Lodewijk Grootaers is Curator of African Art and Head of the Arts of Africa and the Americas at the Minneapolis Institute of Art. Trained in cultural anthropology at The University of Chicago, he publishes regularly about the arts of Africa. He specializes in the history and cultures of the Ubangi region in Central Africa.

Emmanuel Iduma
Emmanuel Iduma is the author of *A Stranger's Pose*, a book of travel stories, which was longlisted for the 2019 Ondaatje Prize, and *The Sound of Things to Come*, a novel. His stories and essays have been published widely, including in *The Millions*, *LitHub*, *Aperture*, *British Journal of Photography*, *Art in America*, *Guernica*, and *The New York Review of Books*. He was awarded an arts writing grant from the Creative Capital/Andy Warhol Foundation for his essays on Nigerian artists. He teaches at the School of Visual Arts, New York, and divides his time between Lagos and New York.

Erin Hyde Nolan
Erin Hyde Nolan is a Visiting Assistant Professor at Maine College of Art. As an art historian, she examines the photographic history and visual culture of the Islamic world, particularly in Europe, the Mediterranean and Central Asia. Between the many intersections of these fields, Hyde Nolan investigates the cross-cultural circulation of people, objects, and ideas, considering how modes of artistic exchange open alternate frameworks of meaning and reception. Her current book manuscript, *Portrait Atlas: The Circulation of Portrait Photographs Between the Ottoman and Euro-American Worlds*, is in progress. From 2010 to 2016, she managed the Todd Webb Archive. She received her PhD from Boston University in 2017 and her research has been supported by the Kunsthistorisches Institut-Florenz, Museum of Fine Arts, Houston, and Getty Research Institute, among others. Before attending graduate school, Hyde Nolan worked at the Peggy Guggenheim Collection, the Harvard Art Museums, and the Morgan Library & Museum.

Casey Riley
Casey Riley is Curator and Head of Photography and New Media at the Minneapolis Institute of Art (Mia), where she oversees the research, exhibition, and preservation of nearly 14,000 works of art. A specialist in the history of photography as well as American visual and material culture, she is the author or co-author of several publications concerning photographic archives, women's history, and the history of collecting. Prior to her appointment at Mia, she served as Assistant Curator at the Boston Athenaeum and a consulting curator for the Isabella Stewart Gardner Museum in Boston, Massachusetts. She holds a BA in the History of Art from Yale University, an MA in English from Middlebury College, an MAT from Brown University, and a PhD in American Studies from Boston University.

Gary van Wyk
Born in Zimbabwe in 1960, Gary van Wyk completed graduate degrees in law, fine arts, and art history in South Africa. Active in the anti-apartheid Resistance Art Movement, he was exiled to Zimbabwe in 1986. He completed his PhD in Art History at Columbia University as a Fulbright Scholar and received a Rockefeller award for research in South Africa and Lesotho, which contributed toward *African Painted Houses*, a *NY Times Book Review* top architectural book for 1998. *Apartheid: Calibrations of Color*, which received a Notable Book Award from the African Studies Association, is among more than fifty books on African topics that he edited for young adults. In 1997, he co-founded Axis Gallery, which "made New York history by inserting African art into the Chelsea art scene" (Holland Cotter, *New York Times*). He curates exhibitions for Axis Gallery, the art foundation Alma On Dobbin, and independently. His recent publications and exhibitions include *Our Anthropocene: Eco Crises*, on artist's books and environmental crises, *Shangaa: Art of Tanzania*, and *József Jakovits: Surrealist, Primitivist, Kabalist.* He also wrote the volume on Pop Art for Prestel's series "50 works of art you should know."

PICTURE CREDITS

All photographs by Todd Webb unless otherwise stated © 2021 Todd Webb Archive

p. 18 United States Central Intelligence Agency. *Africa, Administrative Divisions*. [Washington, D.C.: Central Intelligence Agency, 1958] Map. Retrieved from the Library of Congress, <www.loc.gov/item/97687636/> Courtesy Library of Congress, Geography and Map Division

p. 51 Postcards from the collection of Christraud M. Geary

p. 52 Photograph by Christraud M. Geary, 2005

p. 53 Postcards from the collection of Christraud M. Geary

p. 56 Postcards from the collection of Christraud M. Geary

p. 57, top and center Postcard and print published with the permission of the Basel Mission Archives.

p. 57, bottom Postcard from the collection of Christraud M. Geary

p. 58, top and center rows Postcards from the collection of Christraud M. Geary

p. 59 Published with the permission of Kate Tamakloe, James K. Bruce-Vanderpuije Archives

p. 61 Published with the permission of Kate Tamakloe, James K. Bruce-Vanderpuije Archives

pp. 62–63 Published with the permission of James Barnor and Galerie Clémentine de la Féronnière

p. 83 Published with the permission of James Barnor and Galerie Clémentine de la Féronnière

p. 84 Published with the permission of James Barnor and Galerie Clémentine de la Féronnière

pp. 88–89 Published with the permission of James Barnor and Galerie Clémentine de la Féronnière

pp. 92–93 Published with the permission of James Barnor and Galerie Clémentine de la Féronnière

p. 191 Zimbabwean banknote from the collection of Gary van Wyk

ACKNOWLEDGMENTS

We want to acknowledge that this book was written in 2020 during the protests against systemic racism and police brutality in the United States and across the world. As two white women, we stand in solidarity with the Black individuals who have suffered as victims of violence and all those who have taken to the streets to end these injustices. This book is dedicated to them.

This project would not have been possible without the photography of Todd Webb and our friends at the Todd Webb Archive. We are deeply thankful to Betsy Evans Hunt, the Archive's Executive Director, for phoning us when she discovered the treasure trove of negatives from Todd Webb's 1958 trip to the African continent. Betsy showed us the incredible images and sparked our three years of focused research. Her support and unwavering excitement helped us manifest this project. Thank you for everything, Bets!

We are also profoundly grateful for Sam Walker, the Todd Webb Archive's Associate Director, who spent countless hours working on the images for this book. Sam's patience with us and hard work scanning and mastering hundreds of photographs have made the visuals of this book as lush and beautiful as Todd Webb would have wanted. We are thankful for Sam's skills and the aesthetic eye he brings to all of his work. We also have to acknowledge the magical six degrees of separation from Sam Walker and the synchronous connections he helped us make over the past three years. Without Sam's introduction to Bill Ewing, we might not have met the team at Thames & Hudson. Deep gratitude, Sam!

Our heartfelt thanks go to all of the book's authors, Ali Jimale Ahmed, James Barnor, Rehema Chachage, Betsy Evans Hunt, Christraud M. Geary, Jan-Lodewijk Grootaers, Emmanuel Iduma, Casey Riley, and Gary van Wyk. Their essays make this book shine and bring thoughtful perspective to Todd Webb's photographs from 1958. We have been impressed and humbled by the amount of time and energy each of the authors put into their contributions. Thank you all!

We want to express our deepest gratitude and respect for all of the people who are present in the pages of this book, whose work and daily lives are imaged through Todd Webb's lens. Even though we do not know all of your names, your professions, your families, or your histories, we offer our sincere thanks for all you have taught us about a time period, the challenges of the colonial era, and the importance of agency. Your images have encouraged us to reflect on our own status and positionality, and how identity—yours or ours—reflects both cultural context and personal choice.

This project would not have been possible without the insight and support of Casey Riley, our co-curator of the accompanying exhibition, "Todd Webb in Africa: Outside the Frame," and Curator and Head, Department of Photography and New Media, Minneapolis Institute of Art. It has been a pleasure to work with Casey on the project and we are deeply thankful to her and to Joseph Doherty and Jennifer Komar Olivarez for their work and the Minneapolis Institute of Art for hosting the exhibition.

We are so grateful for the entire editorial team at Thames & Hudson, London. Thank you, Bill Ewing, for introducing the project to Andrew Sanigar. And thank you Andrew, for believing in it and for your kind support and astute guidance through all steps of the process. We are also deeply grateful to Kate Edwards, whose clear and thoughtful editorial suggestions polished all of our words and made the book even better. We know there are many people behind the scenes at T&H who also deserve a shout out, including the editorial and production teams and designers. To all of you—thank you for making this book all that it is, even while working from home during Covid-19 quarantines.

We would also like to thank Martin Andersen for his beautiful book design. Martin, it was clear from the start that you really understood Todd Webb's work. Your thoughtful designs help make the visual connections in the book. Thank you for everything!

We are very grateful for the assistance and support of Clémentine de la Féronnière and Camilla Cardia at Galerie Clémentine de la Féronnière. Thank you both for connecting us with James Barnor, setting up the video interview, providing copyright permissions, and high-resolution images to publish in this book, and for all of your kindness and professionalism.

We also wish to thank Kate Tamakloe at the James K. Bruce-Vanderpuije Archives (and Mr. Bruce-Vanderpuije's granddaughter) for her assistance and for providing permissions to publish her grandfather's photographs. We are also grateful to the Basel Mission Archives.

Many thanks, too, to John C. McIlwaine and Alexandr Gelfand and all of the staff at the United Nations Audiovisual Library and Photo Archive for their research support, and Leslie Squyres, Archivist at the Center for Creative Photography, for providing the Todd Webb Archive with photocopies of the letters Todd and Lucille Webb sent to each other during Todd's five months of African travel.

We benefited from the interrogation of ideas and creative analysis provided by Colby College students in Erin's Contemporary Global Photographies class (January 2020). Their active collaboration and fresh perspectives enhanced our own reading of the photographic images presented on these pages.

And, we cannot forget our loved ones! Thank you Mark, Blakey, and Clay, and James, Mom and Dad for your love and encouragement. Thank you Chris, Elise, and Clara, and Mom, Dad, Kathryn and Alex for your unending support. Words cannot express our gratitude for your patience while we had hours of in person and phone meetings (especially during Covid-19 shelter in place orders) over the past three years.

INDEX

Page numbers in *italics* refer to illustrations

On p. 2: Todd Webb, *Untitled* (44UN-7960-596), Sudan, 1958
Man riding his bike through the center of Kassala.

First published in the United Kingdom in 2021 by Thames & Hudson Ltd,
181A High Holborn, London WC1V 7QX

First published in the United States of America in 2021 by Thames & Hudson Inc.,
500 Fifth Avenue, New York, New York 10110

Reprinted 2021

Photographs mastered by Sam B. Walker
Designed by Martin Andersen / Andersen M Studio

British Library Cataloguing-in-Publication Data
A catalogue record for this book is available from the British Library

Library of Congress Control Number 2020940837

ISBN 978-0-500-54539-3

Printed and bound in China by C & C Offset Printing Co. Ltd

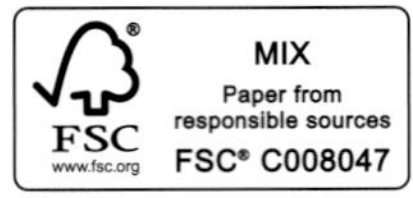